RECONSTRUCTION

RECONSTRUCTION

ARCHITECTURE, SOCIETY AND THE AFTERMATH OF THE FIRST WORLD WAR

Edited by

Neal Shasore and Jessica Kelly

BLOOMSBURY VISUAL ARTS
LONDON • NEW YORK • OXFORD • NEW DELHI • SYDNEY

BLOOMSBURY VISUAL ARTS
Bloomsbury Publishing Plc
50 Bedford Square, London, WC1B 3DP, UK
1385 Broadway, New York, NY 10018, USA
29 Earlsfort Terrace, Dublin 2, Ireland

BLOOMSBURY, BLOOMSBURY VISUAL ARTS and the Diana logo are
trademarks of Bloomsbury Publishing Plc

First published in Great Britain 2023
Paperback edition published 2024

Cover design: Eleanor Rose

A catalogue record for this book is available from the British Library.

A catalog record for this book is available from the Library of Congress.

ISBN: HB: 978-1-3501-5294-6
        PB: 978-1-3502-8392-3
        ePDF: 978-1-3501-5295-3
        eBook: 978-1-3501-5296-0

Typeset by Integra Software Services Pvt. Ltd.
Printed and bound in Great Britain

To find out more about our authors and books visit www.bloomsbury.com
and sign up for our newsletters.

CONTENTS

Contents

FIGURES

Figures

CONTRIBUTORS

Harriet Richardson Blakeman is a doctoral student at Edinburgh College of Art, University of Edinburgh, researching Scottish hospital architecture of the first fifty years of the National Health Service. She was part of the *Survey of London* team from 1991 to 2018, contributing to a number of their volumes, and has published on the architectural history of hospitals. She is the creator and author of an online architectural gazetteer, Historic Hospitals (https://historic-hospitals.com).

Eileen Chanin is an award-winning historian at the Australian National University, Canberra. Her latest book, written as Visiting Fellow of King's College London, is *Capital Designs: Australia House and Visions of an Imperial London* (2018).

Jonathan Clarke is a freelance architectural and construction historian. His research interests focus on nineteenth- and early-twentieth-century buildings and structures, especially those serving commerce or industry, or involving pioneering techniques or technology. He has published widely in these areas, including *Early Structural Steel in London Buildings: A Discreet Revolution* (2014), peer-reviewed articles, and chapters and biographical entries in edited collections. He has recently completed a PhD at the University of Cambridge on the development of speculative offices in interwar England, funded through the AHRC Collaborative Doctoral Partnership scheme.

Elizabeth Darling is Reader in Architectural History in the School of History, Philosophy and Culture, Oxford Brookes University. Her research focuses on inter-war modernism, the environments of social welfare reform, and gender, and very often the intersections among all these things. Her publications include *Re-forming Britain: Narratives of Modernity before Reconstruction* (Routledge, 2007), *Women and the Making of Built Space in England, 1870–1950* (Ashgate, 2007, co-edited with Lesley Whitworth), *Wells Coates* (RIBA Publications, 2012) and *Suffragette City, Women, Politics, and the Built Environment* (Routledge, 2020; co-edited with Nathaniel Walker) as well as numerous articles for journals including the *Journal of British Studies* and *Gender and History*. Between 2014–2017 she collaborated with Dr Lynne Walker on AA XX 100, a project to commemorate the centenary of women's admission to the Architectural Association School of Architecture, which resulted in an exhibition, international symposium and the book *AA Women in Architecture 1917–2017*. Her current work focuses on the material and spatial cultures of broadcasting in the 1930s.

Barry Doyle is Professor of Health History at the University of Huddersfield. He has worked extensively on the history of hospitals in England, France and Central Europe, including a book on urban hospitals in northern England and a University of

Huddersfield–funded project on the economics and politics of hospitals in interwar Poland, Czechoslovakia and Hungary. His current work focuses on a history of First Aid in Britain and France with Rosemary Cresswell and a project on hospital care in Britain's sub-Saharan colonies between the wars.

Alistair Fair is Reader in Architectural History at the University of Edinburgh and a historian of twentieth-century architecture in Britain. His recent publications include *Modern Playhouses: An Architectural History of Britain's New Theatres, 1945–1985* (2018), while his current work is exploring topics including 'community' and architecture, the history of the Scottish new towns, and architecture in post-war Edinburgh.

Julian Holder is Senior Associate Tutor in Architectural History, University of Oxford, a Visiting Fellow at Kellogg College, and deputy editor of *Architectural History*. He has held a number of posts in academia and conservation and was a former inspector of historic buildings with English Heritage, Casework Officer of the Twentieth Century Society, and Director of the Scottish Centre for Conservation Studies, Edinburgh College of Art. Widely published, his recent publications include *'Beauty's Awakening': Arts and Crafts Architecture* (2021) and (with Elizabeth McKellar) *Neo-Georgian Architecture 1870–1970: A Reappraisal* (2016).

H. Horatio Joyce is Director of Public Programs and Education at the Garden Conservancy, New York. He was formerly the Andrew W. Mellon Curatorial Fellow in the Department of Drawings and Prints at the Metropolitan Museum of Art in New York. From 2015 to 2018 he was a PhD scholar of the SAHGB (Society of Architectural Historians of Great Britain) while working on his doctorate at Oxford University. His most recent publications include 'Introduction: Rethinking the American Renaissance' in the special collection that he guest-edited for the SAHGB's journal *Architectural History*, 'The New History of the American Renaissance'; and 'Disharmony in the Clubhouse: McKim, Mead & White and the Making of the Harmonie Club of New York' (*Journal of the Society of Architectural Historians*, December 2019).

Jessica Kelly is Senior Lecturer in Contextual and Theoretical Studies and Research Degrees Leader at University for the Creative Arts. Her research explores the mediation of architecture in the twentieth century. Her book, titled *No More Giants: J.M. Richards, modernism and The Architectural Review*, will be published by Manchester University Press in 2022.

David Frazer Lewis is Associate Professor of Architectural History and the Historic Built Environment at the University of Oxford. His research interests include the architecture of modern Britain and the United States, the design of sacred architecture, and the Gothic Revival. His most recent book is *A. W.N. Pugin* (2021).

Kieran Mahon is Senior Lecturer in Interior and Spatial Design at Camberwell College of Arts, University of the Arts London, UK. His research interests include the architecture of twentieth-century progressive education and collaborative curriculum design. His recently completed PhD, 'Transactive Environments' (2021), offers a layered microhistory of Dartington Hall School, Devon (1926–1987), an independent, co-educational progressive boarding school. The research was generously supported by a scholarship from the SAHGB.

Elizabeth McKellar is Professor Emerita in Architectural History at the Open University and the President of the SAHGB. Her publications include *The Birth of Modern London 1660–1720* (1999, 2021); *Articulating British Classicism: New Approaches in Eighteenth-Century Architecture* (2004); *Neo-Georgian Architecture 1880–1970* (2016); and *Landscapes of London 1660–1840* (2013). The latter book was the winner of the Society of Architectural Historians (US) Elisabeth Blair Macdougall Award 2017. She is currently writing a biography of John Summerson supported by a Paul Mellon Senior Fellowship in 2018–2019 and a Leverhulme Emeritus Fellowship for 2021–2023.

Rebecca Preston is a historian with the English Heritage London blue plaques scheme. Her recent publications include, with Fiona Fisher, 'Light, Airy and Open: The Design and Use of the Suburban Public-House Garden in England Between the Wars', *Studies in the History of Gardens and Designed Landscapes*, 39 no.1 (2019) and, with Lesley Hoskins, 'Behind the Scenes: The Development of London's Interwar Suburban Shopping Parades', *Architecture and Culture*, 6 no.1 (2018).

Clare Price is Head of Casework for the Twentieth Century Society and is currently researching Church of England churches built between the wars for a DPhil in Architectural History at the University of Oxford. A qualified Chartered Surveyor, Clare holds an MA in Geography from the University of Cambridge and an MSc in Conservation of the Historic Environment. Clare has worked in commercial property and conservation for over 20 years. Recent publications include co-editing *100 Churches, 100 Years* (2019) and the chapter on chancel screens in the twentieth century in Mark Kirby (ed.), *Chancel Screens since the Reformation* (2020).

Robert Proctor is Senior Lecturer in Architectural History & Theory at the University of Bath. He studied Architectural History at the Universities of Edinburgh and Cambridge, completing a PhD at the latter in 2002. From 2002 to 2014 he lectured at the Glasgow School of Art, developing a research interest in mid-twentieth-century British architecture. His book *Building the Modern Church* was published in 2014. He is now completing a book on the architectural practice of Sir Percy Thomas.

Neal Shasore is Chief Executive and Head of School at the London School of Architecture. An architectural historian, his work has focused on British architectural culture between the wars. He was previously Leverhulme Early Career Fellow at Liverpool School of Architecture. His first book is *Designs on Democracy: Architecture and the Public in Interwar London* (2022), and he is currently preparing a new history of the RIBA's headquarters at 66 Portland Place.

Joanna Smith is Senior Architectural Investigator at Historic England, primarily covering London and the South East. She has published on London town halls, West End theatres and the furniture trade in South Shoreditch and contributed to *Greenwich: An*

Architectural History of the Royal Hospital for Seamen and the Queen's House (2000) and the *Survey of London volume 48: Woolwich* (2012). She is currently working, with Matthew Whitfield, on a book on suburbs and suburban development in England between 1830 and 2020.

Geoffrey Tyack, FSA, FRHistS, is an Emeritus Fellow of Kellogg College in the University of Oxford, President of the Oxfordshire Architectural and Historical Society, and Editor of the *Georgian Group Journal*. He has published extensively on the architectural history of Oxford, including that of Rhodes House, and recently completed a book on the history of the urban landscape in Britain for Oxford University Press (2022).

ACKNOWLEDGEMENTS

The proposal for this volume grew out of the Society of Architectural Historians of Great Britain's (SAHGB) Annual Symposium in 2018, supported by the Twentieth Century (C20) Society and the 20s30s Network. Held at Charles Holden's Senate House in the University of London, the conference brought together scholars across two days to discuss reconstruction and democratization and the aftermath of the First World War. The symposium sought to mark the centenary of the cessation of hostilities and to highlight the wealth of new research in and approaches to British architectural history of the first decades of the twentieth century. Our thanks go to all speakers and participants in the symposium and to executive committee of the SAHGB for its support.

We are immensely grateful to the various archives and collections that have supplied images for this volume, including the RIBA, the National Archives, National Monuments Record of Wales, London Metropolitan Archives, and Bodleian Libraries. We would also like to offer special thanks to Hannah Towler for her patience and dedication in redrawing many of the architectural plans included in this volume. Elizabeth Darling has been hugely supportive of our work and this project in particular, and we offer our thanks and appreciation for her generous and insightful foreword to this volume.

Neal Shasore is especially grateful to the Leverhulme Trust who funded an Early Career Fellowship at Liverpool School of Architecture (2017–2020). This project – Civic Centre: Architecture and the Municipal Project in Britain, 1919–1979 (ECF-2017-514) – was the driver behind the symposium call for papers and the completion of this edited volume. The project was enriched by the work and discussions collated here.

Jessica Kelly would like to thank the Museum of Domestic Design and Architecture (MoDA) for generously supporting her work and supplying images. She is grateful to her colleagues at the University for the Creative Arts and the internal funding support that has facilitated much of her work for this project.

As co-editors we would like to thank Alexander Highfield and James Thompson at Bloomsbury Academic for their support and patience as we brought this volume to fruition. Our anonymous peer reviewers provided helpful feedback and encouragement on our initial proposal for the volume. We are indebted to our contributors to this volume for their scholarship and their spirit of collaboration.

FOREWORD: TOWARDS NARRATIVES OF MODERNITY *AFTER* RECONSTRUCTION

Elizabeth Darling

In the early 2000s, I began to write a study of architectural modernism in interwar Britain, a project intended as 'a non-modernist history of [architectural] modernism' (to slightly adjust the art historian of modern Britain Lisa Tickner's helpful phrase). It was to be a history which sought, as she continued, '[to] be adequate to, but larger than, the passionate investments of its various protagonists' and which, at the same time, also resisted the 'compulsion to sort the academic sheep from the avant-garde goats'.[1]

Tickner's book, *Modern Life and Modern Subjects* (2000), formed part of an ongoing reframing of the study of twentieth-century British art. Ultimately informed by the emergence of the Social History of Art in the early 1970s, and more immediately by the New Art History of the 1980s, this, as the quotations suggest, was concerned to look again at how histories of modernism in Britain (especially in the period from the 1900s to the 1930s) had been written and could be rewritten. Emphasis moved from primarily formal analysis against a continental European standard, in which British artists were always to be found wanting, to a concern to understand the painters' and sculptors' work in terms of the specifics of a British modernity.[2] At the beginning of my career, when I felt the same dissatisfaction at the way, in my case, histories of British architectural modernism were conceptualized, it was to these historians' work that I turned. Architectural histories of this period had not yet made the same epistemological moves that would facilitate my rethinking of how I approached my subject. That influence, combined with the work of feminist art and architectural historians, was what I drew on for what became the book called *Re-forming Britain: Narratives of Modernity before Reconstruction*: an opening gambit in my goal to complicate the established canon of what (and who) mattered in twentieth-century British architectural history.[3] In so doing, the concern was to establish

---

[1]Lisa Tickner, *Modern Life and Modern Subjects. British Art in the Early Twentieth Century* (New Haven & London: Yale University Press, 2000): 189.

[2]See, for example, A. L. Rees and Frances Borzello (eds.), *The New Art History* (London: Camden Press, 1986); Jane Beckett and Deborah Cherry (eds.), *The Edwardian Era* (Oxford: Phaidon Press, 1987); David Peters Corbett, *The Modernity of English Art 1914–1930* (Manchester: Manchester University Press, 1997).

[3]The transformative effect of feminist art and architectural histories remains under-acknowledged in the emergence of new approaches. Germinal texts include Linda Nochlin's 1971 essay 'Why Have There Been No Great Women Artists?' reproduced in her *Women, Art, and Power* (New York: Harper and Row, 1988): 136–44; Gwendolyn Wright, 'On the Fringe of the Profession: Women in American Architecture', in Spiro Kostoff (ed.), *The Architect: Chapters in the History of a Profession* (Oxford: Oxford University Press, 1977): 280–308; Roszika Parker and Griselda Pollock, *Old Mistresses: Women, Art and Ideology* (London: Pandora, 1981); Matrix (ed.),

a 'larger' way of writing about architectural history, one which could convey the multiple processes and people which, the historical evidence showed me, went into the making (and the remaking) of the built environment.[4]

At that time, I was content to focus on modernism because so much of the writing on its interwar manifestations seemed unable to go beyond its practitioners' concerns and prejudices and was tied, knowingly or not, to the advocacy of a particular position within a wider architectural culture. There were few deviations from a historiography that was established almost as soon as a modernist architecture began to be practised and which seemed to eschew rigorous historical analysis rooted in the archive.

In that historiography, a recognizable origin 'story' of British modernism had been constructed. In this, the idea of importation and redemption was dominant. Typically, it contrasted the vibrant development of modernism in continental Europe in the late 1910s and 1920s with a Britain that remained content with the historicism into which the pre-war Arts and Crafts movement was presented as having evolved. It argued that since none of the preconditions which had generated modernism elsewhere existed – Cubism, progressive clients, pure talent, for example – modernism could not be generated from within and therefore had to be imported.[5] This importation took various forms. The reporting of European work in the pages of the architectural press and the translation into English in 1927 of Le Corbusier's *Vers une Architecture* were often cited as important turning points in awakening those receptive enough to realize its potential. Modernism's arrival was, however, most often attributed 'to the work of outsiders'.[6] First came the colonial sons, uninhibited by native prejudices, such as Amyas Connell and Basil Ward (both New Zealanders), Raymond McGrath (an Australian) or Wells Coates (a Canadian born in Japan). This group 'started' (although it is rarely specified how) a movement in the late 1920s, which was then shown how to do modernism properly by the émigré architects who arrived from Nazi Germany from around 1933. This narrative gave the sense that modernism, like a cold virus, was something 'out there', waiting to be caught, and stemmed in part from a desire to construct it as the international and inevitable style of the age.

To conceptualize modernism in this way, however, had two significant historiographical implications. In focusing on modernism's supposed internationalism it led to an impulse to generalize and to overlook work that apparently disrupted a common story and definition of that modernism (an approach ratified, of course, by Hitchcock and Johnson's exhibition and book of 1932).[7] So rather than understanding modernism as

---

Making Space. Women and the Manmade Environment (London: Pluto, 1984); Alice Friedman, *Women and the Making of the Modern House* (New York: Harry Abrams, 1997). My research was published as *Re-forming Britain: Narratives of Modernity before Reconstruction* (Abingdon: Routledge, 2007).

[4]By modernism I mean, for the purposes of this discussion, a determinedly new language of architecture formed as a response to new subjectivities, new materials, technologies and media.

[5]William Curtis, *Modern Architecture since 1900* (London: Phaidon, 1990): 221.

[6]Kenneth Frampton, *Modern Architecture: A Critical History* (London: Thames & Hudson, 1987): 252.

[7]Henry-Russell Hitchcock and Philip Johnson, *The International Style, Architecture since 1922* (New York: W.W.Norton & Co., 1995 [1932]).

a transnational impulse shaped by place, it uncoupled a profound cultural shift from its context and established a persistently ahistorical way of accounting for the forms that architectural culture took.

Such an interpretation can be traced to Nikolaus Pevsner's assertion in 1936 that 'England's activity in the preparation of the Modern Movement came to an end during less than ten years after Morris's death'.[8] Deploying the trope of importation for the first time, he argued that it was only in the late 1920s that the 'forms of the Modern Movement began to penetrate into England, the forms which, between 1910 and 1925, had been developed by German, French and American architects'.[9] A similar narrative can be found in John Summerson's writing. As far as he was concerned, everything important in the generation of a modernist architectural culture (indeed architectural culture as a whole) in Britain happened because of the translation of *Vers une Architecture*, and consequent to that. It took, however, several years of 'talk and travel' before anything 'substantial in the new spirit' could be built; a moment he dates to 1933.[10]

As Summerson's characterization signals, in most accounts, the history of British architectural modernism was therefore primarily a phenomenon of the 1930s, a chronology which could be conveniently bookended by the house 'High and Over', designed by Connell for Professor Bernard Ashmole and built at Amersham in 1929–1930 (the 'first' modernist building in Britain) and finishing, a decade later, with the Finsbury Health Centre by Tecton (1938), and Ernö Goldfinger's terrace of three houses at Willow Road, Hampstead (1939). This story was then interspersed with other 'pioneer' moments such as the founding of the Modern Architectural Research (MARS) Group in 1933, the British chapter of CIAM, publications such as FRS Yorke's *The Modern House* (1934) and other buildings such as Tecton's Penguin Pool (1934), Coates' Lawn Road Flats (1934) or Elizabeth Denby and Maxwell Fry's Kensal House (1937). Stylistic analysis usually centred on observations about the clear European influence on the forms of British modernism.[11]

It is a narrative that has proved surprisingly tenacious. Indeed, it has recently undergone something of a resurgence in the wake of the frenzy around the 2019 centenary

---

[8]Nikolaus Pevsner, *Pioneers of the Modern Movement, from William Morris to Walter Gropius* (London: Faber and Faber, 1936): 29.

[9]Ibid.: 69.

[10]John Summerson, 'Introduction' in Trevor Dannatt (ed.), *Modern Architecture in Britain* (London: Batsford, 1959): 12.

[11]For this story see, inter alia, Curtis, *Modern Architecture since 1900*; David Watkin, *A History of Western Architecture* (London: Laurence King, 1992): 559; Jules Lubbock, *The Tyranny of Taste, The Politics of Architecture and Design in Britain, 1550-1900* (London & New Haven: Yale University Press, 1995): Part VI 'Good Modern Design'; Charlotte Benton, *A Different World, Emigré Architects in Britain, 1928-58* (London: RIBA Heinz Gallery, 1995). Notwithstanding my comment above, honourable exceptions include Summerson's essay in *'45-55, Ten Years of British Architecture* and his subsequent essay in Trevor Dannatt, *Modern Architecture in Britain* (London: Batsford, 1959); and Andrew Jackson, *The Politics of Architecture* (London: Architectural Press, 1970), both of which look back to the 1920s with a serious appraising eye, although both are reluctant to accord 'talk, travel and illustration' the same value as buildings, as this author does. For a more holistic view of the 1930s, see David Dean, *Architecture of the 1930s, Recalling the Architectural Scene* (New York: Rizzoli, 1983).

of the Bauhaus and the fact that Walter Gropius and several other of its leading members settled, albeit briefly, in London.[12] And while the narrative, as I wrote in *Re-forming Britain*, was 'not entirely without foundation', it contained and contains slippages and elisions that leave some rather important questions unanswered.[13] Why, for example, did John Rodker think it was worthwhile publishing a translation of Le Corbusier's writing in 1927? What audience was in place that would have assured him of a market for that book? Why did Berthold Lubetkin come to London when he could have stayed in Paris, and after him, all those other émigrés? While on the matter of the bigger, and one might say, key problematic of quite how pre-war pioneering gave way to post-war hegemony, there was a strange and lingering silence.

It was such sticky and unasked questions that I sought to address in *Re-forming Britain*. In order to do so the first step was to move beyond the methods and assumptions that underpinned modernist histories of modernism and which only produced ahistories. These assumptions were (and are) several and pertain not simply to histories of modernism but to architectural history more broadly. They rely on a mode of architectural history which sees it as comprised solely as a series of 'actual monuments', and hence to analyse monuments primarily with reference to others, rather than relating them to the broader contexts within which architecture is embedded.[14] This is paralleled by the tendency to therefore see architecture as something produced solely by architects and to focus on them as protagonists of change. Likewise, a preoccupation with architecture as a primarily formal discipline has closed off a wealth of rich avenues which might have a great deal to tell us about its evolution. The significance of the building types in which British modernism was expressed, for example, reveals its interweaving with wider debates about community and the social reordering of British society after 1918 and hence to architecture's role, spatially, formally, materially and socially, with the modernization of the nation as whole.

The non-modernist history of modernism that I wrote was one which still considered canonical buildings, such as the Finsbury Health Centre, but it did so deliberately in order to present and understand such actual monuments (and indeed projects that went unbuilt) as a part of a wider process: as a set of practices. Only in this way could the emergence of something we call modernism be understood and located historically. Decentring the architect and the building and placing them within a nexus of activities that included the client, the builder, the reformers whose campaigning created new ideas about housing (for example), proposals and prototypes, the users of buildings, the reporting and dissemination of projects and ideas, was a way to show how my

---

[12]For a rather tiresome reprise of the refrain, see Oliver Wainwright, 'Auf Wiedersehn Walter, Why Britain booted out the Bauhaus': 'https://www.theguardian.com/artanddesign/2019/oct/01/beyond-bauhaus-britain-riba-walter-gropius#comments (accessed 7 June 2021). This was a review of the 2019 exhibition, 'Beyond Bauhaus: Modernism in Britain 1933–1966', held at the RIBA Architecture Gallery. For a critique and review of the exhibition, see Elizabeth Darling, Alistair Fair, Jessica Kelly, 'Beyond Bauhaus: Modernism in Britain 1933–1966, *Journal of the Society of Architectural Historians*, vol. 80, no. 4, (Dec 2021): 496–7.

[13]Darling, *Re-forming Britain*: 2.

[14]Hitchcock & Johnson, *The International Style*: 37.

subjects were embedded in a specific space and time. To call this a 'historical turn', one which formed part of a small wave of scholarship from the later 1990s to the mid-2000s might seem odd.[15] In contrast to the methodologies that underpinned the writing of architectural history of previous centuries, however, which have very happily been written in terms of building type or patronage and are embedded in archival research, this is really what it was.

The implications of the historical turn for the discipline of twentieth-century British architectural history were various and relate directly to the concerns of the present volume. An expanded view of who and what constitutes architecture has meant that those who had hitherto been 'othered' by modernist (and indeed other periods) histories can take their place in our understanding of how architectural culture shifts and changes. It is now clear how significant women were in shaping modernism in Britain, as thinkers, writers, reformers, campaigners, clients and designers (if not as professionally trained ones). The case of the housing consultant Elizabeth Denby (1894–1965) was key here. The origin point for my work on British modernism because of her association with one of its most canonical buildings, Kensal House (almost ur-canonical because it was both modernist *and* social housing), tracing her career as a polymathic expert who worked in health, housing, design (to name just a few of her areas of concern), her background in the voluntary sector and collaboration with assorted pressure groups, showed how what became a British modernism was embedded within wider processes of modernization in this country and deeply informed by wider discourses of reform.[16] Moreover, her decision not to leave a personal archive forced me to the archives of, for example, the organizations for and with whom she worked; her imbrication in their papers simulated the way her voice and, more importantly, other voices too were woven into the making of a particular project. To chart this fabric of voices and other factors, legislation, finance, changing religious and community principles, was to read the changing context of British modernity through changing architecture and vice versa.

Denby, in her collaborations with the more familiar figures of British modernism, such as the architect Edwin Maxwell (Max) Fry, with whom she co-designed both R.E.Sassoon House (south London, 1934) and Kensal House (west London, 1936), highlighted the deeply gendered nature of modernist histories and showed how it refused to see anyone but a white, male, heterosexual as protagonist. Although credited at the

---

[15]See John Gold, *The Experience of Modernism, Modern Architects and the Future City, 1928-1953* (London: E & F Spon, 1997); Nicholas Bullock, *Building the Post-war World, Modern Architecture and Reconstruction* (London: Routledge, 2002); Cheryl Buckley, *Designing Modern Britain* (London: Reaktion, 2007); Alan Powers, *Britain. Modern Architectures in History* (London: Reaktion, 2007). On a more general methodological note the work of Sarah Williams Goldhagen, 'Something to Talk about: Modernism, Discourse, Style,' *Journal of the Society of Architectural Historians* 64, no. 2 (June 2005): 144–67 and Hilde Heynen was also significant; Hilde Heynen, *Architecture and Modernity, a Critique* (Cambridge, Mass. and London: MIT Press, 1999).

[16]See my *Elizabeth Denby, Housing Consultant, Social Reform and Cultural Politics in the Inter-war Period* (unpublished PhD thesis, University College London, 2000); Elizabeth Darling, '"A Star in the Profession She Created for Herself": A Brief Biography of Elizabeth Denby', *Planning Perspectives* 20 no. 3 (July 2005): 271–300 and idem, 'Introduction' to Elizabeth Denby, *Europe Rehoused* (London: Routledge International Planning History series, 2015) [1938].

time (with some notable exceptions) for these schemes, it was noticeable how Denby's name gradually disappeared from credit lines as histories were written.[17] An ostensible reason for this would be that she was not professionally trained yet Serge Chermayeff, one of the most feted of interwar modernists, had no formal training as an architect either, but his 'qualifications' (which included a stint as a professional ballroom dancer) have never been challenged.

Seeing Denby more clearly, however, as an example of a woman thoroughly shaped by the century: highly educated, independent, sexually liberated, an agent of her own destiny, and typical of the many women who shaped the built forms of the twentieth century, opened the way to understanding how much the forms – spatial and material – of modernist architecture owed to new ideas about subjectivity and identity more broadly. Denby sought to enable working-class women to develop the modernity she had already achieved and this shaped how she co-designed the schemes in south and west London. Her vision of a re-formed domestic sphere was one that enabled women in particular to be free to be agents of their own leisure and to focus on becoming modern citizens. At the same time, the revised way of seeing allows us to see that such intentions were not unproblematic, as many of the essays in this volume show. Beneath such emancipatory visions often lay an uneasy tension between an envisaging of a certain type of working-class modernity and citizenship that overrode the economic realities of class differences and which was profoundly heteronormative.

The hetereonormativity of modernist histories of modernism is also challenged by the non-modernist stance. Ideas of the modernist architect as hero become quaint (and also tainted with the clichés of imperial 'adventuring'). Instead, he (pronoun used deliberately) is displaced – decentred – into a narrative in which clients who were often gay or bisexual or otherwise resistant to the norms of heterosexual relationships demanded new forms of space to enable them to perform the lives they wished to live in modernity. The decidedly queer coupling of the actors Elsa Lanchester and Charles Laughton, for example, who were important early clients of Wells Coates, enabled the rethinking of space that was key to the development of his particular type of modernism. Similarly the Cambridge don, Mansfield Forbes's homosexuality led him to create, with his protégé Raymond McGrath, the very particular environment of his home-cum-salon Finella (1928–1929), in which other 'outsiders' could gather to discuss new forms of cultural expression.

The expanded and inclusive historiography of modernism which brings in figures like Denby, Lanchester or Forbes, simulates the way that the built environment is created out of conversations, campaigns, friendship networks, political connections, the practicalities of the building site and the availability of materials, inter alia and pushes the researcher to reconstruct the moments from which that environment emerges. It also widens the possible sources on which to draw: not just the architectural archive (centred, inevitably,

---

[17]Elizabeth Darling 'Elizabeth Denby or Maxwell Fry? A Matter of Attribution' in Brenda Martin and Penny Sparke (eds.), *Women's Places: Architecture and Design 1860–1960* (London: Routledge, 2003): 149–70 and for further developments on this theme, idem, 'The Significance of Errors', *The Modernist* 32 (2019): 62–7.

around the architect's personality and, often, the drawing) but also the papers of clients, institutions, the architectural and other media. Thus, modernism can be seen not as something 'out there' but something that emerged from a specific set of circumstances and demand and was contiguous with broader experiences of modernity. It was an integral part of an existing and ongoing conversation about how Britain might be after 1918 and its post-war ascendancy was founded on its rootedness in these conversations about the place and role of architecture in a country experiencing profound change. *Re-forming Britain* was, therefore, devoted to an analysis of how modernist architects worked to dominate those conversations and push them in a particular direction.

Despite the acknowledgement of those wider conversations, the book remained, as noted above, a study of modernist architecture. It may have seen and understood that modernist architecture in a different and larger way, but it very much conformed to modernist tropes in its focus on projects whose makers sought (formally and spatially at least) to 'make it new'. I did not quite succeed in resisting the compulsion to cast out the academic (or, in architectural terms, historicist) sheep. Yet it was clear, not least because of the energy that modernists like Coates and Chermayeff spent delineating themselves from such contemporaries, that the other conversations about what architecture might be in the 1920s and 1930s had an equal potential to influence its direction. In the early 2000s, however, the modernist hold was as yet so strong that the literature on the milieux, architectural and otherwise, where those discussions were taking place was relatively limited. That which existed tended to emerge from a rightist anti-modernist perspective and to focus primarily on stylistic discussion.[18] It was certainly not sufficient to enable a comparative account to be made.

Gradually, however, the modernist stronghold has weakened, and historians have started to see and write historically about those 'academic sheep' who articulated alternative visions of the modern in interwar Britain: that audience which Rodker envisaged would buy *Vers une Architecture* in English, for example. A further process of decentring is, then, underway in which modernism is realigned into a spectrum of modern architectures. The scholars whose work is included in *Reconstruction* have formed part of this evolving way of seeing and collectively the essays in this volume make some very significant contributions to the historiography of interwar architecture.

Methodologically, as readers will soon see, each chapter takes as a given that architecture is a complex process formed out of a messy intersection of competing demands and interests, not just the work of the architect alone. Equally importantly, and this is perhaps the most significant development in non-modernist histories of the interwar, alongside considerations of gender, sexuality and class, an understanding that empire and colonialism have to be considered as integral to architectural (in this context) thinking in this period is core to much of the writing in *Reconstruction*. In the early 2000s, such concerns were not absent from historical analysis but they had not

---

[18]See David Watkin, *The Rise of Architectural History* (London: Architectural Press, 1980); several of the essays in the *Architectural Design* profile, no. 24, *Britain in the Thirties* (1979); Lubbock, *The Tyranny of Taste: The Politics of Architecture and Design in Britain 1550–1960* (New Haven and London: Yale University Press, 1995).

yet become a core mode of enquiry into understandings of the form that architecture and space could take. Many of the chapters in this book show how architecture was shaped by the evolving relationships between Britain and the recently established White Dominions and with colonies that were ever more resistant to the imperial yoke.

Concomitant with this is a challenge to periodization. This begins with the book's title. In their framing of the volume, Jessica Kelly and Neal Shasore argued that this was chosen because it challenged received notions of what this term usually connoted in the historiography of British twentieth-century architecture. Reconstruction with its correlates of action, energy, progression, has habitually been applied to the period after the Second World War, not before. By implication, therefore, the period before this lacked all these qualities and was profoundly moribund. This is a familiar narrative and was why my book sought to document and account for the vibrancy of modernist architectural culture before 1945 and to locate this much further back than usual into the 1920s. Nevertheless, my research was not yet at a stage to make the conceptual leap taken in this volume which is to overturn that cliché and link reconstruction to the period *after* 1918 and present a resounding counterpoint to such characterizations. Thus, with their contributors, Kelly and Shasore work towards a vivid recasting of our understanding of architectural debates and practices in the 1920s and 1930s and, indeed, the twentieth century as a whole. It is a shift which feels particularly timely given our current historical present, which is negotiating a similar terrain of resurgent nationalism and global tensions rooted in the imperial legacy and it promises an epistemological shift that will create a discipline fit to record a diverse future.

Reconstruction therefore presents the reader with an account of a British architecture which was actively engaging with the modern throughout the 1920s and 1930s, and which posits, in particular, the years around 1918 and the later 1920s as crucial moments of architecture's rethinking. Manifested in new forms of office building, land speculation, rural reform, practice organization, reformed public houses, temples to peace and new forms of architectural writing, to name but a few, a vibrant architectural culture sought to work out the form a modern and modernizing nation should take.

INTRODUCTION
RECONSTRUCTION: ARCHITECTURE, SOCIETY AND THE AFTERMATH OF THE FIRST WORLD WAR

Neal Shasore and Jessica Kelly

Reconstruction in relation to architecture and society is both an act and a metaphor. It is a material process of remaking – of faithful restoration – but also of more imaginatively reconstituting, of reassembling component parts of the old into the new. An apt architectural analogy, it relates to construction, to the physicality of building in bricks and mortar. As a historical metaphor, it expresses a layering, in which the present is built on the past; it can serve as a re-enactment which tells us much about attitudes to the past in a present. As an historicist metaphor 'reconstruction' can be seen as a manifestation of the same nostalgic impulse as 'revival', a mediated reimagining of the past. And moreover, reconstruction can be read as a methodological procedure, insofar as it obliges the historian to look for longer trajectories, refractions and diversions in addressing social questions and their rhetoric, in the re-presentation of a 'context' and set of attendant 'texts' in historical writing.

The word 'reconstruction' was one frequently deployed in social and political discourse in the aftermath of the global conflagration of the First World War. In the 1920s, in the wake of a worldwide conflict of unprecedented scale, reconstruction meant surveying what was left of the past and shaping it for the present and future. It was an expression seemingly borrowed from American Civil War political discourse, and one which related fundamentally to ideals of suffrage (in the American context coloured by racial politics). This nuance cannot have been lost among the intellectual – often self-consciously politically progressive – advocates of reconstruction ideas in twentieth-century Imperial Britain, which often related to discussion about the implications of mass democracy and universal suffrage. It was perhaps for this reason that in the American journal, *Historical Outlook*, the progressive National Board for Historical Service lauded Britain for having 'made the most elaborate reconstruction plans'.[1] This praise was in reference to both the government's Ministry of Reconstruction and the sixty committees it oversaw, and to the wealth of wider public discussion about reconstruction.

---

[1]'Some British Reconstruction Views', *Historical Outlook* 10 (February 1919): 95. See Paul Barton Johnson, *Land Fit for Heroes: The Planning of British Reconstruction, 1916–1919* (London: University of Chicago Press, 1968), for a more nuanced historical analysis.

Reconstruction

In twentieth-century architectural history the phrase 'reconstruction' is conventionally associated with the period after the Second World War.[2] It carries with it an implicit optimism, normally in contrast to the 'failure' of similarly motivated projects after 1918. Those studies that do explore post-1918 reconstruction have tended to focus on government policies relating to housing, especially in the wake of the Addison Act of 1919.[3] Though a significant proportion of building activity was devoted to housing, there were other aspects of reconstruction which influenced architectural discourse and practice, and to which design gave some spatial and material expression. The wider programme of government and privately financed reconstruction projects remain under-researched and under-developed in architectural histories of the period. Furthermore, the spirit of reform and regeneration that characterized plans for reconstruction has been over-shadowed. The historiographical focus on the post-1945 Welfare State has obscured the vitality and complexity of reconstruction efforts after 1918. In this context, local and national government, as well as private organizations and charities, initiated projects aimed at rebuilding and reforming society after the war. We explore reconstruction beyond formal policy, treating it as an idea and an impulse which gained momentum into the 1930s. Moreover we have sought to move away from the truncated chronologies of 'inter-war' or 'post-war' and explore how reconstruction debates had longer trajectories, stretching back into the late nineteenth century and pushing forward into the 1940s and 1950s.

The metaphor of 'reconstruction', as we note above, invokes a material re-building, yet this energetic public discourse has been rarely considered in terms of architecture and the built environment. Britain had no major battlefront during the First World War; reconstruction, as we note above, was therefore as much metaphorical as physical, and this has driven our approach.[4] The contributions in the volume comprise a broad historiographical intervention, reassessing the ways in which architecture of this period has been presented in both architectural history and in histories more broadly. We have explored architecture beyond stylistic paradigms and highlighted ways that architecture and the built environment can offer lenses through which to view politics, culture and society.

Writing reconstruction

There was a rich sub-genre of reconstruction writing produced during and immediately after the war that was often politically progressive and which promoted reconstruction in a broader, social, cultural, political and even spiritual sense. A strand of this

---

[2]See Nicholas Bullock, *Building the Post-War World: Modern Architecture and Reconstruction in Britain* (London: Routledge, 2002). Revisionist accounts include John R Pendlebury, Erdem Erten, P. J. Larkham (eds.), *Alternative Visions of Post-War Reconstruction: Creating the Modern Townscape* (London: Routledge, 2015).

[3]See, for example, Mark Swenarton, *Homes Fit for Heroes: The Politics and Architecture of Early State Housing in Britain* (London: Heienemann Educational Books, 1981) and David Jeremiah, *Architecture and Design for the Family in Britain, 1900–1970* (Manchester University Press, 2000).

[4]The physical legacies of the war are discussed in Wayne Cocroft and Paul Stamper (eds.), *Legacies of the First World War: Building for Total War 1914–18* (Swindon: Historic England, 2018).

reconstruction literature can be described as architectural, both in the sense that it was produced by architects and/or planners, and because it discussed design and/or included some kind of spatial proposition. 'Reconstruction' is a phrase littered through the first decade of the *Town Planning Review* under the planner Patrick Abercrombie's editorship, and the prospect either of catalysed pre-war reform or of a new order runs through the records of professional debate at the Royal Institute of British Architects (RIBA) and elsewhere in the architectural press.

In this atmosphere of debate, some of the profession's most articulate voices presented their particular visions of the world remade. In 1917, the architect-craftsman and socialist, C. R. Ashbee, published *Where the Great City Stands: A Study in the New Civics*. The book's first illustration was a '[d]iagrammatic representation showing within each city the qualitative standard should be reintroduced to life by the transformation of Art Schools and Galleries into Creative Guilds' in the form of a circular plan. Ashbee outlined key moments in the history of art, architecture and civilization which he felt would be helpful to those charged with rebuilding society after the conflict. The opening and fundamental question for Ashbee was 'How much of the constructive effort of the last fifty years shall we save from the wreck of the War?'[5] The architect, as an artist, had special responsibilities to bear; as 'an interpreter' of 'the life that goes on around him', the architect's aim was to realize the 'practical poetry of life'.[6] Architecture was understood not just as a product, as a building, but more ambitiously as a force of civilization. It was, therefore, closely entangled with the task of rebuilding society, both physically, culturally and spiritually, after the war. Elaborating a theme so prevalent in William Morris's writings, Ashbee insisted that 'we cannot have the Arts unless we are worthy of them', and good architecture would arise out of a good civilization, an educated and fairer civilization.[7]

The intertwining of the ethical with the aesthetic during this period was evident in the architect-planner and critic Trystan Edwards's book, *The Things Which Are Seen*.[8] Although it was published in 1921, the book was largely written during wartime (the first part was submitted to publishers to gauge interest as early as 1915).[9] Ostensibly an aesthetic treatise, in which Edwards set out a new grammar of design and a new hierarchy of the visual arts, it was intended as a designer's 'roadmap' for the new world. Edwards laid out a new hierarchy of visual arts which was dictated by the needs and wants of the 'average man' (often ventriloquized in Edwards's writing by war veterans) who represented the enfranchisement of a democratic polity. This new order placed

---

[5]C. R. Ashbee, *Where the Great City Stands* (London: The Essex House Press and BT Batsford, 1917): v.
[6]Ibid.: 20.
[7]Ibid.: 55.
[8]A. Trystan Edwards, *The Things Which Are Seen: A Reevaluation of the Visual Arts* (London: P. Allan & Co, 1921). For context see Neal Shasore, 'A Stammering Bundle of Welsh Idealism': Arthur Trystan Edwards and Principles of Civic Design in Interwar Britain', *Architectural History* 61 (2018): 175–203.
[9]He did not have much success even as late as 1918. See Museum of English Rural Life, University of Reading, Special Collections, Reader's Report by Frank Swinnerton for 'The Things Which Are Seen', CW RR/6/265.

the cultivation of human beauty, dress and manners above architecture, painting and sculpture. The world that Edwards was trying to imagine in *The Things Which Were Seen* was one remade in the wake of conflict and one in which social relations were so transformed that the needs and wants of average men would in turn remake the world profoundly. Edwards was so committed to fulfilling the promise of post-war reconstruction that he was still using the expression in the early 1930s to describe his nation-wide programme of low-rise high-density housing through his Hundred New Towns Association, a campaign – as he put it – of national reconstruction.[10]

The little-known architect Sir Ambrose Poynter, who reviewed the *Things Which Are Seen* for the journal *Architecture*, saw the book very much in these terms.[11] He related it to his own book of 1916, *The Coming War*, which advocated for fundamental and urgent reform of industrialized society to enfranchise the working classes to stave off violent revolution.[12] This rear-guard action would preserve Britain's imperial supremacy once Germany had reindustrialized and offer some resistance in the face of America's growing economic interest in South America. Poynter had also recently designed the Torre de Los Ingleses in Buenos Aires as part of the centennial commemorations of the May Revolution, completed in 1916. Argentina was at this time a locus of informal British Imperial control. This building, which would otherwise be overlooked in architectural history, can be read as a material manifestation of Poynter's aspirations for post-war socio-economic reconstruction in the Empire.

Debate about reconstruction was transnational; it was an aspect of a burgeoning discourse of international cooperation.[13] Hendrik Christian Andersen, the Norwegian-American artist, for instance, edited a monumental two-volume work, *Creation of a World Center of Communication*, the first of which was published in 1913, followed by the second in 1918.[14] Inspired by monumental Beaux-Arts planning (plans and designs were produced by Ernest Hébrard), Andersen adumbrated theoretical, economic and legal arguments for a world-centre metropolis, which would transcend nation states and build a society on principles of brotherhood and shared cultural values. This, Andersen argued, would finally put an end to what he described as the 'war problem', securing 'future world harmony'. Andersen's writing captured the anxiety and determination of

---

[10]A. Trystan Edwards, *A Hundred New Towns for Britain* (London: Simpkins & Marshall, 1933). For a more detailed account of the campaign see Neal Shasore, *Designs on Democracy: Architecture and the Public in Interwar London* (Oxford: Oxford University Press, 2022), ch5: 263–326.

[11]Ambrose Poynter, 'Reviews. The Things Which Are Seen', *Architecture. Journal of the Society of Architects* 15 no. 9 (July 1922): 232–8.

[12]Ambrose Poynter, *The Coming War [of International Commercial Competition]* (London: John Murray, 1916): 6.

[13]Luc Verpoest, Leen Engelen, Rajesh Heynickx, Jan Schmidt, Pieter Uyttenhove, Pieter Verstraete (eds.), *Revival After the Great War: Rebuild, Remember, Repair, Reform* (Leuven: Leuven University Press, 2020).

[14]Hendrik Christian Andersen (ed.), *Creation of a World Center of Communication* (Rome, Paris: 1918). For context, see Matthew Mullane, 'Hendrik Christian Andersen's World Conscience', *AA Files* 73 (2016): 40–7. A sceptical but clearly curious Trystan Edwards reviewed the book at the length in 1914, describing it as a 'landmark in civic design'. See A. Trystan Edwards, 'A World Centre of Communication', *Town Planning Review* 5 no. 1 (April 1914): 14–30.

the immediate post-war period; he articulated the feeling that after the unprecedented slaughter and carnage of this war, there must be a tectonic change.

These texts demonstrate the live and vital debates about how to reconstruct cities and society after the war, debates which were often rooted in principles and values established before the war had broken out. There are common socio-political influences on this form of writing: the influence of the Beaux-Arts, American Progressivism and the ideal of City Beautiful is palpable in Ashbee's, Edwards's and Andersen's texts. These common influences point to a cosmopolitan internationalism beyond the parochialism normally associated with English (and Anglophone) discourse of the time, particularly in architecture, while maintaining an inherent (Imperial) Eurocentrism. It also highlights the persistence of many nineteenth-century ideas and concepts during this period. This genre of writing shows that 'reconstruction', though formalized and reified in policy terms in Britain through the Ministry of Reconstruction, was part of a wider reformist impulse. The texts are characterized by their political progressivism, the breadth of their subject matters, their attempt to deal with fundamentals, their attempt to resolve the ethical and aesthetic, their interest in civic life and social questions: in sum, they evidence a deep engagement of architecture with society, often through a progressive lens.

Reconstruction writing also reveals something about how practitioners saw themselves and how they positioned themselves in relation to major social questions. This was a period in which the profession of architecture was changing and architects' claims to professional status were increasingly predicated on a direct appeal to wider society. In the texts above, for instance, architecture was embedded in discussion of broader political, economic and cultural issues, implicitly as a method of thinking, discourse and action. This volume too is predicated on such an understanding of architecture and the built environment as a means of understanding society and culture. Through five sections, we trace how architecture was touched by the broader debates of reconstruction from land reform, town planning and development, to education, industrial relations, licensing and victualling, food production and healthcare. One of our core ambitions in this volume was to help the occasional visitor to the world of architectural history locate themselves and to encourage other kinds of historians to think with and through space, architecture and the built environment.

Architecture in history

In architectural history, the relationship between the building and the context in which it sits has long been a subject of methodological discussion, in particular, under the influence of the New Art History since the 1980s. However, despite the material turns in cultural and social history of recent decades, architecture and the built environment still often play only a cursory role in the wider historical discipline. Moreover, when architecture is discussed, it is normally as an artefact, rather than in terms of the various socio-cultural, political and economic processes which bring built environments into being and which influence their use and occupation. Though the disciplines of architecture and architectural history incorporate methods which recognize architecture as constituting a whole set of practices and concerns beyond just the building, these are rarely deployed in the wider historical discipline.

Methods used in architectural history, however, have more to contribute to other forms of historical writing. We contend that historians, of whatever bent, can and should be equipped with the tools to think through the built environment, space and the material more ambitiously. This can be achieved through having some rudimentary conception of how intentional design is undertaken, perhaps by someone who called themselves an architect. Several chapters in this volume explore the lives and influences of named architects as important factors in shaping the design of the buildings. But our conception of architecture and the built environment is one more rooted in the praxes of a number of agents in a wider cultural field. In this definition architecture consists of intersecting activities including production, mediation and consumption. Architecture defined as this broad field incorporates a whole raft of competing concerns and thereby constitutes a particularly rich kind of historical evidence.

Architecture can stimulate fresh perspectives on well-established historical narratives. For instance, the democratization of society after the war can be told through legislative sources such as the passing of the Representation of the People Act (1918), which widened suffrage by abolishing almost all property restrictions on male voters and extending the vote to property-owning women over 30. But democratization can also be seen through changing models of patronage in architecture. Growing public funding of architectural projects created public spaces and amenities for use by the growing population of citizens. Many of the contributions to the volume trace how public buildings articulated changing definitions of citizenship and the shifting role of the state in people's everyday lives.

The British state sat at the centre of an Imperial polity; coloniality is, therefore, inherent in the definition of citizenship and national identity during this period. Architecture throughout the Empire, and significantly in England, Scotland, Wales and Ireland, communicated the conception of Britain as an Imperial nation, its cities, streets and buildings were expressions of coloniality and Imperial ideology and power. Architectural projects also evidenced the religiosity of post-war culture, often overlooked in narratives of growing secularization. The rise of Liberal Anglicanism is central to several chapters, and though most explicit in evolving methods of church design, it is also present in the shifting role of congregations and communities in organization and funding of church activities.

Architectural history of this period is often focused on questions of style – in the first decades of the twentieth century this involves unpicking historicist strands and schools and separating out the 'International Style' of 'pioneers' from reactionaries and traditionalists.[15] A preoccupation with discernibly modernist buildings and heritage

---

[15]This is despite the fact that modernism was not a style per se, as Sarah Williams-Goldhagen has convincingly argued. Sarah Williams Goldhagen, 'Something to Talk about: Modernism, Discourse, Style', *Journal of the Society of Architectural Historians* 64 no. 2 (2005): 144–67.

has meant that more inclusive histories of British architecture of this era have not yet been told; there has been a perception that as a nation, Britain, and in particular England, was somehow anti-modern (and thereby conservative) and that therefore the mainstream of architectural production contains very little worthy of serious study.[16] In this volume we have taken a different view and formulated a different approach. We look beyond narrow definitions of the experience of modernity. We are less concerned, in this context, with a history of what constituted good design or of particular styles, although formal analysis is deployed as a primary method by almost all of our contributors.

Twentieth-century architecture beyond style

It is possible to argue that there are essentially two architectural histories, in particular when it comes to the study of architecture of the twentieth century. One is an architectural history largely written by and/or for architects, in which the central disciplinary goal is to understand design, through the study of precedent, typology and method and to relate this to a set of techniques and technologies notionally or actually deployed to build. The other is an architectural history more connected to the discipline of art history and indeed the wider discipline of history, in particular urban, cultural and social histories. In this latter case, the architecture as artefact – the design or spatial intervention – can play second fiddle to an analysis of a broader set of processes involved in what we might call the *practice* of architecture and indeed a wider *praxis* of bringing buildings and man-made environments into being: of discourse, mediation and representation, regulation, construction, use and inhabitation. There are overlaps and interlacings, and there are those who have quite deliberately and innovatively sought to blur those boundaries.[17] Indeed, often architectural history is able to nuance and sensitively historically locate certain assumptions about processes and methods of design and construction. But there is some value in stating this distinction – these 'two cultures' of architectural history – baldly. Approaches in this volume generally lead towards the latter, if only to open up space for the former.

In another version of the 'two cultures' binary we have just described, approaches to architecture of the first half of the twentieth century could be divided into those which privilege 'style', a connoisseurial unpicking of motives and forms, and those which are more interested in a robust and dispassionate analysis of 'design'. The distinction is not just semantic. The development of 'design history' in the late 1970s was in part out of frustration with the discipline of 'architectural history', felt to be too dilettantish for

---

[16]Exceptions to this include Julian Holder and Elizabeth McKellar, *Neo-Georgian Architecture 1880–1970: A Reappraisal* (Swindon: Historic England, 2016).

[17]For example: Elizabeth Darling, *Reforming Britain: Narratives of Modernity before Reconstruction* (London: Routledge, 2007); Mark Swenarton, *Cook's Camden: The Making of Modern Housing* (London: Lund Humphries, 2017).

a more robust, often Marxist-inflected, analysis of design and material culture.[18] The recurrent 'style wars' of the 1970s, which were often projected back onto readings of the debates of the 1930s, were perhaps felt to be symptomatic of this disciplinary divide. The more politically and socially engaged investigations into environmental design sit at the other end of the spectrum. Art history, meanwhile, as Crinson and Williams have recently discussed, had largely fallen out of love with architecture, despite it having been a central concern to Germanophone *Kunstwissenschaft* in the nineteenth and early twentieth centuries.[19] These disciplinary distinctions and historiographical trajectories frame our own interventions into the field.

In 2013, for example, Neal Shasore co-convened 'Stylistic Dead Ends? Fresh Perspectives on British Architecture between the World Wars' with David Lewis, a contributor to the present volume. The aim of the conference was to question not only the historicist argument that there had been a proliferation of so-called traditional styles in reaction or opposition to architectural modernism, but more profoundly to 'challenge the lapse into style discourse, and look for formal and theoretical commonalities that transcended stylistic concerns during the period'. Tim Benton provided historiographical reflections on the late 1970s and in particular 'The Cultural Moment of 1979' which spawned the 'Thirties: British Art and Design before the War' exhibition at The Hayward Gallery in collaboration with the Victoria and Albert Museum.[20] It was in response to this exhibition, and to complicate the narrative of interwar modernism, that Gavin Stamp edited a special issue of *AD* in the same year on 'The Thirties',[21] and which led in part to the establishment of the Thirties Society (now the Twentieth Century Society) to seek to protect a more diverse range of built heritage of the period. The Lutyens Exhibition of 1981 also at the Hayward, accompanied by Roderick Gradidge's monograph on Lutyens in the same year,[22] had similar aims of complicating the narrative of twentieth-century British architecture and challenging the dominance of 'modernism'. Describing the 1970s as a 'bad-tempered decade' in which these debates played out, Benton noted how much of the heat had gone out the argument by the 2010s.

The conference opened up a range of approaches to architecture and the built environment of the period, many of which were highly methodologically innovative and which showed exciting directions in the field; these included the influence of science fiction writing on architectural discourse; the mediation of architecture through radio broadcast and the printed press; at that time overlooked geographies of modernity in Britain and the Empire, namely in the suburbs, in the regions and nations of the United

---

[18]For more on the relationship between architectural history and design history, see Jessica Kelly and Claire Jamieson, 'Practice, Discourse and Experience: The Relationship between Design History and Architectural History', *Journal of Design History* 33 no. 1 (2019): 1–15.

[19]Mark Crinson, and Richard J. Williams, *The Architecture of Art History: A Historiography* (London: Bloomsbury Publishing, 2018).

[20]*Thirties: British Art and Design before the War – An Exhibition Organised by the Arts Council of Great Britain in collaboration with the Victoria and Albert Museum, Hayward Gallery* (London: The Arts Council, 1979).

[21]Gavin Stamp (ed.), *AD Profiles: Britain in the Thirties* 49.10-11 (1979).

[22]Roderick Gradidge, *Edwin Lutyens: Architect Laureate* (London: Allen & Unwin, 1981).

Kingdom (in particular Scotland), and in British India, South Africa and the Middle East; and work which deployed archaeological and contemporary sociological readings of interwar housing states on the Isle of Dogs and in Haggerston, respectively. A sound and video installation by the artists Ewen Forster and Christopher Heighes explored the relationship between architecture and classical music through the work of Giles Gilbert Scott. Despite this, however, there remained a bulk of work on the proliferation of various styles used by non-modernist architects of the period; the 'stylistic straitjacket', as Shasore described it, was an apt metaphor for an inability within the discipline to shake off the language of style as its primary analytical mode.

The event which led to this book was in many senses a follow-up to 'Stylistic Dead Ends?'; it involved a number of the same participants and showed a maturing of much of the work discussed half a decade before. But the framing of the 2018 symposium, 'Architecture, the Built Environment and the Aftermath of the First World War', sought to jettison style more directly. Papers were selected that discussed architecture and the built environment explicitly in relation to the twin impulses of democratization and reconstruction and sought to provide an opportunity for architectural historians to demonstrate how methodologically the built environment, broadly conceived, can be placed in, and contribute to, wider urban, cultural, social and political histories of the period. Though it solicited histories of design, it laid emphasis on typological studies, analyses of educational systems and regulation, and the ways in which these generated form, rather than stylistic analysis per se.

This emphasis did not go unnoticed, and in the immediate aftermath of the event, discussion on social media among prominent participants in the symposium turned specifically to this issue. Alan Powers tweeted: 'But can't we look at style again one day? Is it such a threat? I feel it has been shunned to the point where nobody knows what to say any more, but with all this contextual knowledge we should be able to do it better than before.' In response, Alistair Fair argued for the relevance of style primarily 'in cases where it mattered to contemporaries' but laid greater emphasis on 'textual sources' as indexes of 'what the buildings were meant to do/be/mean'. Elizabeth Darling asserted that '[i]n the best historical work, style has not been disappeared as a category of analysis but it has rightly been decentered in favour of an approach which considers architecture as a set of practices & processes of which "formal significance" (as [Wells] Coates put it) is but one part'. Whether social media lends itself to the nuance of methodological and historiographical analysis is debatable, but the exchange in a public forum translates how actors in the field deploy methods and approaches with refreshing directness. It captures the methodological intervention posed by this volume.

Powers has subsequently elaborated his conception of 'style' as more about 'stylishness', about 'rightness' and an appreciation for compositional technique, rather than 'style' in terms of a *Kunstwollen*.[23] He is particularly concerned with studies of style in the education of designers, whose historical studies can fail to arm them with any tools to enrich their

---

[23] Alan Powers, 'We Need to Talk about Style', *Architecture Foundation: 100 Day Studio*, https://www.youtube.com/watch?v=kef7s0hNsVI (accessed 23 April 2022).

9

own approach to design consciously. But an idea of 'rightness' as a universal value, rather than fundamentally subjective and determined through cultural hegemony, remains problematic. As educators based in an art school and architecture school respectively, these questions, insofar as they relate to praxis and teaching, resonate with us; the disciplines of history, and specifically architectural history, have perhaps failed to address them in recent years. We are interested in how style can be read in its social, cultural and political context as well as how style relates to ideologies and systems of value.

We do not want, however, visitors to the sometimes strange cosmos of architectural history either to be put off by any mention of style or to indulge its language simplistically. In the case of the 1920s and 1930s, as Darling's foreword points out, there is still much basic work to do in revising and expanding our conception of architectural culture. This volume focuses primarily on the social and cultural histories of architecture and the built environment and seeks to relate these to certain formal strategies of planning and design. We selected work that could serve as a model for how the wider discipline of history could use architecture and the built environment as a particular and often instructive form of historical evidence in particular in writing histories of the 1920s and 1930s. Architecture – design, commissioning, development and use – serves not just as a backdrop but plays a constitutive role in a given context. Architecture is not just about design but sets off a whole set of social, intellectual, economic and other processes which can, if analysed carefully, provide a useful constellation of agents, ideas and actions which tell the historian much about a society.

Terminology

In much of the architectural-historical literature on the interwar years, the 1920s is often subsumed into the 1930s. In this volume we have jettisoned the phrase 'interwar' or 'inter-war' outside of this introduction. We have done so for a number of reasons: firstly the label 'inter-war' is essentially anachronistic. It belongs, by definition, to a context in which another war had begun. Contemporaries might have anticipated this in some instances, but it was not predetermined. Fittingly architectural, the *OED*'s first use of 'interwar' is ascribed to Osbert Lancaster in *Homes Sweet Homes* (1939). Secondly the prefix 'inter' suggests a mere betweenness. It encourages a low acuity, even a myopia, drawing the shortest path between points. Such a tight periodization is particularly unhelpful in the disciplines of art and architectural history, disciplines which historically have been susceptible to using such delineation to exclude particular buildings and their designers from their purview.

We also want to blur the edges around 1918 and 1939, rather than seeing the 'interwar' years as an ellipsis between the long nineteenth century and the second half of the twentieth. As such the years immediately after the war were charged with attempts to reconcile the ideas and principles from before the war, with the new contexts and conditions after it. This generative energy of the years following the war is often overlooked in histories that focus on the betweenness of the 1920s and 1930s.

We have tried to limit references to the 'First World War' for similar reasons; it presupposes a second, and we are trying to recapture contemporaneity, without the looming spectre of another global conflict. Instead, we often refer to the 'war' and to the post-war period. For the avoidance of doubt, when contributors are discussing the 1939–45 conflict, they use the 'Second World War', and the 'post-WW2' period. It is in the same spirit that all the images in the book are contemporaneous to our period. The only exceptions are the plans, which have been redrawn. Though contemporary architectural drawings serve as a form of evidence themselves, technical drawings sourced for reproduction can be difficult to read for non-specialists. We felt that a clear and uniform visual language for plans would help readers quite literally orient themselves in buildings, supported by photographic and other graphic forms of contemporaneous representation.

Structure

The volume is divided into five sections, each title led by a present participle, that indicates a particular ideal or set of activities which characterized the period. They are designed to evoke contemporaneity through the use of the continuous present. We want to emphasize the proactive or dynamic character of this period in contrast to what is often portrayed as an era of stasis.

The focus of the volume is on architecture's intersection with the social. How architecture relates to communities, but also social organization through formal governance – the parish, the diocese, the local authority – and through informal and commercial social units – the association or voluntary body, but also the architectural practice. Our contributors have approached buildings and the built environment in an expanded field, exploring how we can understand architecture in the context of broader sociopolitical contexts and, importantly, what architecture can reveal about this period. Each section looks at architecture's place with the broad social, political and cultural shifts of the decade after the war.

The first section, 'Promoting the business of architecture', considers the commercial and financial aspects of the architectural profession and building. Architecture was evolving as a profession and a business during this period, in the context of growing commercialism in Britain. Jessica Kelly's chapter looks at the promotional activities of The Architectural Press publishing house, in particular their two magazines *The Architects' Journal* and *The Architectural Review*. The chapter traces how the magazine's editors responded to the commercial demands facing the architectural profession by evolving a particular form of architectural 'criticism', which sought to promote the services of architects to the market of the 'architectural public'. Kelly explores how architecture navigated the changing commercial landscape of the post-war reconstruction market. Staying with the architectural profession, Horatio Joyce looks at how British architects were influenced by the large-scale, corporate architectural firms in America. Focused on the relationship between American and British architectural practice during this period, Joyce emphasizes the sense of 'Anglo Saxon union' growing between the two countries, which was tempered by the rather different approaches to corporations in Britain compared to America. Shifting from the profession to commercial development, Jonathan Clarke's chapter on speculative office buildings in London highlights the importance of privately financed building in the city, which has been dismissed or overlooked in existing histories. Clarke also maps the interactions and overlaps of public and private finance in the construction and occupation of these buildings, which set important precedents for state relations with the private sector throughout the twentieth century. Clarke focuses on government legislation (such as the 1909 Steel Frame Act) and its impact on architecture and building in London. Eileen Chanin considers the architecture of the 'New London', a reconstructed Imperial Metropolis. Chanin traces the stories of a quartet of buildings in the Aldwych/Kingsway in London: Kodak House, Australia House, Bush House and India House. Chanin explores both the global political ambition, the local and regulatory role of the London County Council and the impact of commercial and colonial agendas in the design of these four buildings, exposing the intricate web of interests and conditions that constitute architectural production.

The focus on legislation is picked up in the second section titled 'Designing community infrastructure', in which the authors ask how architecture responded to and communicated changing ideas about the role of the state and the church in post-war England, Wales and Scotland. Definitions of citizenship and public life were shifting in the post-war context. The chapters in this section consider case studies of how different institutions of the state and religion experimented with different forms of architecture and how the stories of particular buildings reveal narratives of experimentation in the organs and structures of public life. Looking at different typologies from housing estates to churches, these chapters each consider how architecture signalled the shifting relationships between religious or state-led institutions and their publics. Alistair Fair analyses housing estates in Scotland and how the provision of community centres and social spaces gave spatial form to conceptions of community, citizenship and leisure during the period. This includes reflections on how political theories of citizenship, expanding leisure time and changing recreational activities were captured and expressed architecturally. The design of community centres articulated a top-down ideal of society and illustrated the concerns and preoccupations of local government and voluntary-sector reformers after the war. Similarly top-down or patrician standards of morality, productive leisure and temperance were articulated through the design of improved public houses during this period. Julian Holder's chapter on the Carlisle Experiment argues that the changed design and management of public houses was an expression of anxieties about the physical and moral values of British society, particularly among demobilized soldiers and the working class.

Turning from state to church, Clare Price discusses ecclesiastical patronage in England as a barometer for democratization inside and outside of the Anglican Church. Price considers the role of local congregations in the design of local churches in the 1920s. As the Church of England sought to engage parishioners in the liturgy, so to the process of church design and building became one of collaboration and interaction between communities, architects and church officials. Price details the machinations of decision-making in local church design and the evolving place of the architect in communities. The stories of these buildings reveal the visions and struggles of post-war democracy.

Section three – 'Building a rural citizenry' – looks at rural and countryside communities through the lens of post-war conceptions of community and citizenship. This offers an important counterweight to the typical focus of architectural discourse on cities. Elizabeth McKellar's chapter on the work of Annabel Dott explores Dott's involvement in the design of rural communities for disabled ex-servicemen. McKellar weaves together this overlooked area of reconstruction architecture, with the study of a career of an 'amateur' women architect. Dott's use of media to promote her own work and to position herself as an architect reveals new perspectives on the practices of architects during this period. Annabel Dott designed housing as part of the Land Settlement Programme. This government programme for resettling soldiers on small holdings is the subject of Rebecca Preston and Joanna Smith's chapter. The authors trace how the programme was shaped by pre-war ideals of pre-industrial community and the post-war rural revival movement. Kieran Mahon's chapter is about education in a rural context and how the village colleges built in Cambridgeshire between were shaped by Henry Morris's (Chief Education Officer for the county) ideas about education, community and rural reconstruction. The story of village colleges usually focuses on Impington College, designed by Walter Gropius and Maxwell Fry. Mahon's chapter by contrast contextualizes Impington as part of a longer narrative of the architectural and conceptual evolution of the village collages. Focusing on Morris's writing, as much as the formal and spatial design of the colleges, Mahon's chapter, like McKellar's, looks at the range of people and activities that constituted architectural practice, beyond the work of trained architects.

The fourth section, 'Binding subjects through statecraft', turns attention to architecture in Imperial towns and cities in England, Wales and South Africa after the war. Architecture was employed in efforts to bind the empire together and to promote England's imperial power and history. Geoffrey Tyack considers the work of Herbert Baker in the context of Rhodes House in Oxford, Cecil Rhodes and the British Empire in South Africa. Tyack explores the symbolism in Baker's design of Rhodes house and its relationship with other memorializing architecture during the period, particularly Baker's work for the Imperial War Graves Commission. Tyack's chapter emphasizes the dual function of promoting and memorializing the British Empire that was inherent to Baker's designs. Robert Proctor takes the civic buildings designed by the architect Percy Thomas and interprets them as examples of an optimistic vision of social democracy rooted in ideals of social welfare and citizenship, anticipating the mature Welfare State of the 1940s and beyond. Thomas's designs show how notions of democracy and citizenship were both shaping and shaped by architecture. David Lewis's chapter also considers democratization but in the context of Egypt, which declared independence from the British protectorate in 1922. British troops and ex-pats remained stationed in the country throughout this period, creating a complex political context. Lewis's chapter tells the story of the design of the Anglican Cathedral in Cairo and how the changing political context of the British Empire after the war was recorded in changing architectural form. The evolution of the design of the

Cathedral revealed changing colonial politics but also an emphasis on technology and modernity within the Anglican church during this period.

These chapters explore how imperialism was inherent to architecture in Britain, not just a characteristic of architecture in colonized countries of the British Empire. A number of authors note the language of the colony in relation to housing schemes and social reconstruction: in smallholdings, in small rural housing schemes, in the shaping of the community centre. There is more work to be done to address race and coloniality in relation to architecture. We have also not included substantial work on housing or on memorialization, although these topics are touched on in several chapters. As explained above, these topics tend to dominate studies of architecture after the First World War, and we wanted to broaden the field of analysis to include other areas of architectural activity during the period.

The volume's final section serves as an epilogue and was developed in response to the context of the COVID-19 pandemic. The questions of how to reconstruct after a crisis took on a new significance for us as editors during 2020 and 2021, as we finalized this volume together with our collaborators. As we are faced with the need of devising a progressive programme of economic and social reconstruction of our own, the fundamental theme of the book has taken on an even greater urgency than we could have anticipated. The COVID-19 pandemic has displaced H1N1 – the Spanish Influenza – in our collective imagination. The lockdowns, high death tolls and the complete disruption of public and private life that ensued forced us to look back at the post-1918 period with different perspectives.

The influenza pandemic from 1918 to 1920 has been revisited by historians and the media as a model for the impact and responses to a global pandemic. What is striking is how silent historical records are on the impact of the influenza on discourses of design, planning and habitation. Our concluding section therefore takes the form of an epilogue offering two perspectives on the architecture and space of healthcare. Harriet Richardson's and Barry Doyle's chapters both explore how the changing design of hospitals after the war revealed evolving ideas about health and well-being as well as understanding of disease and transmission. Furthermore, the changing provision of medical care through new and different types of hospital and new models of public funding demonstrated the shifts towards democratization that are explored throughout the volume. Both chapters show how the architecture of health and medicine and the infrastructure of medical provision was changing in the decades before the National Health Service was established in 1948. Again, this volume shifts attention back to post-war reconstruction in an effort to understand the period through its architecture, as well as understanding architecture in its particular historical context.

The contributions that make up this volume demonstrate a vital discourse and practice in architecture and the built environment. Contributors demonstrate convincingly how much architecture – the processes of bringing built environments into being as much as the artefacts – help us to access social histories of the period. They set out a terrain of active research and enquiry, and we hope they will stimulate further interventions into this maturing field.

SECTION I
PROMOTING THE BUSINESS OF ARCHITECTURE

On New Year's Day, 1920, the 'Estate Market' column in *The Times* turned its attention to the question of 'higher buildings with higher values' in the London property market. There had been an 'immense volume of business' in London freeholds and leaseholds over the course of 1919 as business and commerce recovered from the effects of war: 'Just as judicious advertising in the Press is now recognised as indispensable to business success, so the importance of being in the most prominent thoroughfares is seen to be essential for the same purpose ... The main thing is to be in the public eye.'[1] There was a growing pressure for business accommodation in central London which was leading inevitably to higher site values, but also ever taller buildings. 'The release from Government occupation of a great many hotels and other premises has not done much to relieve the pressure,' the article continued, and it anticipated that demand may prove to be so great that 'in time a new type of building may be sanctioned in London – new to London, and probably peculiar to it – something intermediate between the larger structures, such as those in Kingsway, and the "skyscraper."'[2] The development of the Aldwych Site, and in particular the Bush Terminal Building (though unnamed in the article), would set a precedent for a new form of higher building in London – 'if accommodation must be found and lateral extension is impossible the alternative of going higher may have to be faced.'[3]

The 'Estate Market' analysis aroused comment from one of the leading commercial architects of his day, Delissa Joseph.[4] He drew attention to the restrictive nature of the London Building Act (1894) – 'The Prescription Act, otherwise known as the law of light and air', as he called it – which limited London building heights to 80 ft (plus two additional storeys of uninhabitable additional roof height, the 80+2 rule).[5] It had been brought in to restrict the tendency of the Queen Anne Mansion blocks then in vogue to push to ever greater heights.[6] The act was, in Joseph's analysis, 'defective in so far as it is inelastic', and he called for reform: a new limit of 200 ft should be instituted

---

[1]'The Estate Market', *The Times* (1 January 1920): 7.
[2]Ibid.
[3]Ibid.
[4]A prominent Jewish architect, Delissa Joseph was also married to Lily Joseph of the famous Solomon artistic dynasty.
[5]Delissa Joseph, 'Higher Buildings for London', *The Times* (10 January 1920): 6.
[6]See Simon Pepper and Peter Richmond, 'Upward or Outward? Politics Planning and Council Flats, 1919–1939', *Journal of Architecture* 13 no. 1 (2008): 53–90. The article includes a discussion of Joseph's advocacy for taller buildings in relation to developments in social housing design.

(especially for sites facing parks, open spaces and the riverside), with control over elevations secured either by the London County Council or a 'Ministry of Fine Arts' (another cause of Joseph's and the architecture profession which eventually manifested itself in the creation of the Royal Fine Arts Commission in 1924). Such measures would prevent the Manhattan craze for 'skyscrapers' and allow for 'democratic' control over the appearance of buildings in the city.

In response to a growing number of letters on the subject in the pages of *The Times*, the RIBA convened a special committee, 'The London Building Act Committee', including a number of leading commercial practitioners and prominent architects of department stores, among them Delissa Joseph, Austen Hall and Sir Henry Tanner, the former architect in the Office of Works who had set up a successful city-based practice with his sons. The Tanners had been involved with the rebuilding of Regent Street, and their client list included the Peter Robinson Department Store on Oxford Street which Hall later extended.[7]

The committee developed a series of lobbying points around Joseph's proposed reforms to the act (including tempering his ambition of buildings 200 ft high down to 150 ft), and deputations were dispatched to a number of bodies including the City of London Corporation and the London County Council in March 1921. At the latter meeting, the Chairman of the LCC Buildings Act Committee framed the discussion: 'you will not find us, as I am afraid you have been led to believe, old crusted Tories [the Council was Conservative-led at this time]; quite the contrary. You will find that we have very democratic and receptive minds [...] We want to hear your up-to-date ideas'.[8] In response the deputation was careful to note that the origin of their agitation 'was obviously traceable to the fact that, after the Armistice, it was found that central London was much congested'.[9] They explained that empty buildings were quickly filled up, that rents were high and heavy premiums were paid for leases; growth was rapacious in the capital and no space could be spared. In response, greater elasticity within the regulatory framework for the heights of buildings was needed, and a commensurate relaxation of the regulations for the cubical contents of commercial buildings, such as department stores.[10]

The debate around higher buildings for London, explicitly connected to post-war commercial recovery, encapsulates the themes that link the chapters in this opening section. It draws attention to the power of the print media in architectural agitation in the post-war years. This was a discussion carried out not only in the architectural and trade press (discussed in Jessica Kelly's piece) but also in the pages of *The Times* where powerful 'public opinion' could be fashioned.[11] It related to regulation,

---

[7]See *The Survey of London: Oxford Street*, https://www.ucl.ac.uk/bartlett/architecture/sites/bartlett/files/sol_oxfordst_chapter12.pdf (accessed 13 November 2021).

[8]RIBA Drawings and Archives Collection, London Building Acts Committee Minutes 1 (20 January 1921 – 8 December 1930), Minutes (3 March 1921), fo.15 [see inset memorandum of deputation].

[9]Ibid.

[10]Ibid.

[11]See James Thompson, *British Political Culture and the Idea of 'Public Opinion', 1867–1914* (Cambridge: Cambridge University Press, 2013).

specifically the power of the London County Council in determining the regulation which would ultimately give the city its built form, as Eileen Chanin discusses. It also draws attention to specific forms of architectural practice, namely commercial practice, as undertaken by firms like Tanner, Joseph and myriad others, advocating for their client base. And in turn it opens up the question of what kinds of services these architects provided for their clients, one explored by Horatio Joyce in relation to the influence of American practice and professionalism. Finally, this all related to commercial development – in this case retail, residential and office development – and the susceptibility of the dense urban landscape in the City of London – discussed by Jonathan Clarke in his chapter – to the detrimental effects of 'cliff-like' tall buildings, producing the feeling of cavernous, wind-swept depths for the pedestrian. Clarke dissects the role of speculative property developers in shaping the post-war city and challenges architectural history to look again at the entanglement of public and private enterprise.

The development of the Aldwych site which framed the discussion of higher buildings in London was the culmination of the Kingsway scheme, much vaunted as an early success of the LCC, as Eileen Chanin discusses in her chapter. The tall buildings debate also framed discussion around a parallel but distinct development at Regent Street, though connections between the two have been surprisingly little explored. Regent Street, originally developed by John Nash, was built on Crown land, and as the 99-year leases began to fall in, development picked up pace. In answering 'why can't we keep old Regent Street?', Henry Tanner responded that '[t]he value of property has so tremendously increased that it is essential that higher buildings should be erected in place of the old low ones in order that more room should be available in the same place of letting offices'.[12] Commercial architecture in the post-war years has been little considered,[13] but it was a lively area of practice even if the architecture was often found wanting. Joseph's obituary noted that in his professional work, he 'found little scope for originality, being obliged to make the commercial purpose of the building his chief concern'.[14] Commercial practice, nevertheless, was a taboo subject – it brought the architect's professionalism into perilously close contact with the operations of the market. Jessica Kelly picks up on this theme in her discussion of The Architectural Press's cultivation of a 'public' through promoting the services of architects to a growing market of potential consumers. We should see Delissa Joseph's endorsement of the 'popularizing' of architecture (as he put it) in this context too.[15] Discussion of tall buildings in public *fora* like The Times, and outside the sometimes narrow confines of the trade press, is a clear demonstration of this.

---

[12]'The New Regent Street', *The Architects' Journal* (12 September 1923). The article was an extract from a longer piece by Tanner in *The Weekly Dispatch*.

[13]See Elain Harwood and Alan Powers (eds.), *Twentieth Century Architecture 14: Building for Business* (London, 2020).

[14]'Mr Delissa Joseph', *The Times* (11 January 1927): 16.

[15]Delissa Joseph, 'The Popularizing of Architecture', *The Times* (9 June 1908): 8.

Commercial practice, as the higher-buildings episode demonstrates, was also linked to concerns about 'Americanisation' after the war. This ranged from the types of client, the forms of architecture and tenor of regulation, as well as the operations of architects themselves. Horatio Joyce's essay on 'Professionalism' examines how the ideas and practices of large American architectural firms impacted on the business of architecture in Britain, both in private practice and also in large 'official' architecture departments. A figure like Henry Tanner is typical of how these apparently opposite forms of practice could be bridged: a public servant for much of his career, Tanner led a commercial practice in partnership with his sons in retirement, designing for large development schemes, including hotels and commercial units, in the West End. Arguably his experience in the public sector made him more alert to commercial opportunities: as the prevalence of his interventions on Regent Street, led by the quasi-public administration of Crown Lands, shows. We might think also of figures such as Alfred Bossom, a British-born architect who made a fortune designing Manhattan skyscrapers. Bossom, who returned to Britain in old age and became a long-serving Conservative MP, advocated persistently for reorganization and modernization of the construction industry derived from American practices, though he was adamantly against skyscrapers in London.[16]

Each of the chapters in this section explores the commercial imperatives and motivations of the architectural profession after the war. The business of architecture and development is therefore considered from a range of perspectives outside of design. Methodologically these contributions show a range of forces operating on built form: changing forms of practice and office organization; the pressures of the need to mediate architecture and development to wider, 'public' audiences; increasingly complex forms of regulation, arbitrated by relatively modern forms of democratic urban governance; and the compromises and partnerships an increasingly large state apparatus made with private speculative development. What readers will observe is a linked story about the reconstruction of the market, of business and commerce, and how this was translated in terms of the social and public.

---

[16]Alfred C. Bossom, *Building to the Skies: The Romance of the Skyscraper* (London: The Studio, 1934). He repeatedly disavowed tall buildings as 'totally inappropriate for England', e.g. in Alfred C. Bossom, 'American Architecture', *Journal of the Royal Society of Arts* (8 June 1928): 761–84.

CHAPTER 1
CRITICISM: THE ARCHITECTURAL PRESS AND THE PUBLIC
Jessica Kelly

The market for architectural services changed in the aftermath of the war. Legislation such as the Housing and Town Planning Act (1919) had transformed national and local government into patrons of architecture on a scale much larger than before. Private businesses and public utility societies were now starting to build again following the hiatus of building during the war. In this new market, architects were competing with speculative builders for the attention of these new patrons. Architects had to promote their expertise and specialist skills by new and more effective means. This meant exploring the potentials of public relations and advertising, which were developing as industries in their own right in the burgeoning consumer culture of the 1920s.

The media landscape in Britain was also changing rapidly; the British Broadcasting Company expanded the potential audience for discussions of all types of culture, including architecture. This commercialization of architecture and changing media was coupled with the changing civic and democratic culture of Britain; citizenship had been redefined following the extension of the Representation of the People Act in 1918 and new government departments like the Ministry of Health were changing the relationship between the government and the people. The new patrons, new competitors, new media outlets and new conceptions of who constituted an 'architectural public' meant that architecture as a profession and as a discipline had to present itself to a new audience. The 'architectural public' comprised the people involved in making decisions about architecture and construction, namely government officials and municipal authorities involved in public works as well as private business patrons and speculative developers. This fundamental shift in architectural practice and professionalism was evident in the design of new homes, civic centres and commercial offices, but it was also present in the changing form and content of architectural magazines.

The challenge facing the profession was how to speak to this new audience about architecture; how to make architecture relevant, even interesting; how to make it intelligible; how to change people's perspectives and ideas about architecture and thereby about architects? Editors, journalists and critics helped to both frame and answer these questions.[1] By the 1920s there were numerous professional publications relating to

---

[1] The nineteenth-century origin of architectural journals and publications is the subject of Mari Hvattum and Anne Hultzsch, *The Printed and the Built: Architecture, Print Culture and Public Debate in the Nineteenth Century* (London: Bloomsbury, 2018).

architecture and building. In Hugh Casson's account of architectural journalism, written in 1948, he named *The Builder*, *The RIBA Journal*, *The AA Journal*, *Architect and Building News*, *The Architect's Journal* (*AJ*) and *The Architectural Review* (*AR*) as just a selection from hundreds of competing titles.[2] Casson argued that *Architect and Building News* had been the most important periodical of the period between the world wars.[3] However, this chapter is concerned with the *AJ* (weekly) and the *AR* (monthly), both titles produced by The Architectural Press publishing house. Building on their origins in the nineteenth-century Arts and Crafts and wider design reform movement, this pair of magazines pursued a particular agenda during the 1920s, which reveals the evolving function of architectural publishing after the war.

The Architectural Press publishing house had a long association with advertising and promotion, which meant that it was particularly well positioned to respond to the new demands facing the architectural profession after the war. The company was owned jointly by Percy Hastings and Maurice Regan. Percy Hastings had worked in advertising for Talbot Newspaper and Co, the original owners of the *AR*. When Talbot and Co went bust in 1900, Hastings was part of a syndicate that formed to buy up the publishing portfolio. The new company, called Technical Journals and Co, employed William Regan (Maurice Regan's father) as a consultant to help with advertising and in 1907 he also became a shareholder in the company.[4] By 1925 Technical Journals and Co had become The Architectural Press and that year Percy Hastings brought out one of the other shareholders to become joint owner with Maurice Regan. In 1926 Percy Hastings retired and passed the joint-chairmanship to his son, Hubert De Cronin Hastings. In the same year, De Cronin Hastings began editing the Supplement section in the *AR*. By 1927 he was editor of the entire magazine. In the *AJ* and the *AR* after the war, the editors and owners were developing a form of architectural criticism that aimed to interpret and promote architecture for a lay public reader.

Existing histories of the *AR* are largely focused on the period after 1927 when De Cronin Hastings was editor and the magazine became known for its innovative layouts and photography and its overt promotion of modern architecture.[5] This periodization is typical of the broader historiography of modern architecture in Britain, which posits 1927 as a 'turning point'.[6] However, in the years prior the magazine was changing in

---

[2] Hugh Casson, 'One Hundred Years of Type-Set Architecture', *The AA Journal* LXIV, no. 723 (1948): 6.

[3] Ibid.: 12.

[4] This history is recorded in a card index compiled by Brian Hanson, which is held in the private papers of Lady Susan Lasdun, who was kind enough to let me photograph it.

[5] See for example: Richard Hollis, 'Building a Graphic Language', *Eye* no. 7 (1998): 40–6 and Richard Williams, 'Representing Architecture: The British Architectural Press in the 1960s', *Journal of Design History* 9, no. 4 (1996): 285–96. Jessica Kelly, '"To Fan the Ardour of the Layman": The Architectural Review, The MARS Group and the Cultivation of Middle Class Audiences for Modernism in Britain, 1933–1940', *Journal of Design History* 29, no. 4 (2016): 350–65.

[6] See William Whyte, 'The Englishness of English Architecture: Modernism and the Making of a National International Style, 1927–57', *Journal of British Studies* 48, no. 2 (2009): 441–65 for a deconstruction of this myth of 1927 in the history of modern architecture in Britain.

ways that reveal the shifting relationship between the press and the profession.[7] The *AR* in the 1920s was experimenting with not only what architectural criticism could be but perhaps more profoundly to whom it should be addressed.

Starting with a series of adverts produced by Dawnay and Sons (an engineering firm) and evolving into editorials and experiments in styles of writing about architecture, the *AR* was exploring ways in which the profession could engage with the architectural public and persuade them of their expertise. Even if these magazines continued to be read predominantly by architects, their editors and critics were increasingly preoccupied with how to write about architecture for lay readers.[8] The magazines' editors were asking not only who should judge architecture but also what methods of judgement should be employed and indeed to what ends.

The magazine was joined in this endeavour by other organizations concerned with engaging public audiences in architecture and culture more broadly, namely the BBC and The Architecture Club. Tracing the evolution of architectural criticism on the pages of the *AR* and *AJ* throughout the 1920s, the chapter reveals the shifting priorities of editors, writers, designers and manufacturers, bringing to the fore the increasing role of promotion and advertising in architectural culture and practice.[9] Between 1920 and 1927 the *AR* explored the function of architectural criticism as a means of promoting architecture to public audiences. This chapter will explore how architectural criticism evolved during this period as a means of both promoting the expertise of architects and as a tool to cultivate engaged public audiences who could understand and appreciate the work of architects.

The history of *The Architectural Review* and public engagement with architecture

In April 1920, the news and comment page of the *AR* reproduced extracts of an article by architect and educator, William Richard Lethaby, one of the more prominent advocates for the Arts and Crafts Movement in the early twentieth century, under the heading 'Pedantry and Punditry'.[10] Lethaby was at this time heavily involved in the Design and Industries Association (DIA) and concerned with promoting 'decency, cleanliness,

---

[7]For more on the origins of modernism and modernity in British Architecture see Elizabeth Darling, *Reforming Britain: Narratives of Modernity before Reconstruction* (London: Routledge, 2006) and Elizabeth Darling, 'Institutionalizing English Modernism 1924–33; From the Vers Group to MARS', *Architectural History* 55 (2012): 299–320.

[8]I have written elsewhere about the *AR*'s attention to the lay reader in the 1930s but this chapter traces this preoccupation from 1920 onwards. See Kelly, 'To Fan the Ardour of the Layman'.

[9]This is discussed in more detail in Neal Shasore, *Designs on Democracy: Architecture and the Public in Interwar London* (Oxford: Oxford University Press, 2022).

[10]Lethaby was a member of the Arts and Crafts Movement; he was one of the founders of the Art Workers' Guild and founder of the Central School of Arts and Crafts in 1896. 'Chronicle and Comment. Salient Features of the Months Architectural News: Architecture, Pedantry and Punditry', *The Architectural Review* (May 1920): 71.

order' and 'fitness' in design and architecture.[11] Lethaby's original article (which had been a talk given at the launch of the DIA) had been published the previous month in the *London Mercury*, which was a monthly publication concerned with the arts, edited by J. C. Squire. Through Squire, the *London Mercury* had a growing link with architecture; in 1922 he founded the Architecture Club, discussed in more detail later in this chapter. The *London Mercury* was part of the growing media culture that was presenting architecture to the middle classes in Britain. The *AR*'s coverage of Lethaby's article from the *London Mercury* signalled the links between the two publications and marked the beginning of the *AR*'s attention to writing about architecture for lay readers.

Lethaby's article was a call for the public to judge architecture more actively. He implored his reader to 'take notice of what he sees in the streets'.[12] He argued that architecture had been mystified and isolated from the interest and understanding of ordinary people; it had been rarefied into realms of expertise and become a subject of 'pedantry and punditry'.[13] Without ordinary people who were interested in and had an intelligent appreciation of architecture, British civilization would stagnate; so Lethaby demanded, for the sake of civilization, that his readers 'do not pass by in a contemplative dream, or suppose that it is an architectural mystery, but look and judge'.[14] He implored the public to ask questions about the buildings around them, to ask, '[I]s it tidy, is it civilized, are these fit works for a proud nation?'[15] This was a call for architectural criticism in the form of the public critically engaging with buildings. This issue of the public's engagement with architecture and design had its roots in nineteenth-century design reform campaigns but were being reimagined in the post-war context of civic reconstruction, growing consumer culture and economic turmoil.

The Arts and Crafts movement, proselytized by William Morris and his followers, was based on the idea that design originated in the values and practices of society. From this perspective, Arts and Crafts proponents argued that industrialization and mass production had eroded the values of honesty and unity and with it the standards of design and architecture. Morris and others, developing the tenets of Augustus Pugin and John Ruskin, looked to pre-industrial models of production as the basis of their utopian ideals for design. Through organizations such as the Art Workers' Guild and the Arts and Craft Exhibition Society (both founded in the 1880s) artists, architects, designers, craftsmen and writers worked together to promote values such as the importance of function, truth to materials and unity between the arts. In 1896, a new title – *The Architectural Review* – was published for the first time, intended as a magazine for the broad family of creatives and professionals involved in the 'art of

---

[11]W. R. Lethaby, 'Architecture as Form in Civilisation', *The London Mercury* (March 1920), Julian Holder, '"Design in Everyday Things": Promoting Modernism in Britain, 1912–1944', in Paul Greenhalgh (ed.), *Modernism in Design* (London: Reakton Books, 1990): 129.

[12]W. R. Lethaby, 'Architecture as Form in Civilisation', in *The London Mercury* (March 1920), *Form in Civilisation; Collected Papers on Art and Labour* (London: Oxford University Press, 1922): 15.

[13]Ibid.

[14]Ibid.

[15]Ibid.

architecture'. As the front page of the new magazine declared, it was for the 'artist, archaeologist, designer and craftsman'.[16]

Henry Wilson, the first editor of the *AR*, was a member of the Art Workers Guild (AWG) and he used the magazine as a vehicle to explore and promote the ideas and values of the Arts and Crafts. This link continued into the twentieth century as the magazine's editorial board and then individual editors were all drawn from the founders of the AWG.[17] In 1905 Mervyn McCartney was appointed editor and remained in post until 1921. McCartney was known for his neo-Georgian architecture and was described by his successor W. G. Newton as 'looking upon architecture more as an art than a profession'.[18] McCartney was replaced by Ernest Newton, who was joined by his son W. G. Newton.

Since its founding, the content and form of the *AR* had followed the changing discourses and agendas of design reform. After the war, the role of the press in architecture was shifting as the persuasive and promotional potential of publishing was embraced by the architectural profession. The *AR* had always been a site for debating and disseminating the ideas of its editors and contributors. In the 1920s it increasingly became a tool with which to engage the broader public in issues of design and architecture and to promote the architectural profession.

In 1915 the DIA was set up by a group of artists, architects and businessmen, with the agenda of applying the principles of the Art and Crafts movement to industrialized mass production.[19] In doing so they planned to bolster the standards of Britain design and architecture.[20] The working committee of the DIA met in the same building as the AWG, 6 Queen Square in London, setting them firmly in the context of the Arts and Crafts, but with the new aim of embracing mass production and imbuing it with the values of good design. This meant that the DIA turned their attention to the retailers and consumers of design, as well as its manufacturers and producers.

In a speech to the DIA in 1915, Lethaby explained that the problem with previous attempts to improve design standards had been that they kept the designer, the manufacturers and the 'purchasing public' in 'separate compartments'.[21] Instead the DIA proposed much closer contact between the 'several branches of production and distribution'.[22] The press were tasked with explaining the DIA 'aims and ideals' to the

---

[16]John E. Newberry, 'The Architectural Review: A Magazine for the Artist, Archaeologist, Designer and Craftsman'. *The Architectural Review*. London (November 1896).

[17]In 1901 the editorial committee members were John Belcher, Reginald Blomfield, Frank Baggallay, Gerald Horsley, W. Millard, Mervyn McCartney, E. J. May, Ernest Newton, E. S. Prior, Halsey Ricardo, Leonard Stokes, Norman Shaw. Reginald Blomfield, *Memoirs of an Architect* (1932): 103.

[18]Brian Hanson, Card Index, p. 22. See also Julian Holder and Elizabeth McKellar, *Neo-Georgian Architecture 1880–1970: A Reappraisal* (London: Historic England, 2016): 7.

[19]Michael T. Saler, *The Avant-Garde in Interwar England: Medieval Modernism and the London Underground* (Oxford: Oxford University Press, 1999): 62.

[20]Julian Holder, '"Design in Everyday Things": Promoting Modernism in Britain, 1912–1944', in Paul Greenhalgh (ed.), *Modernism in Design* (London: Reaktion Books, 1997): 123–43.

[21]W. R. Lethaby, 'Design and Industry' (1915), *Form in Civilisation; Collected Papers on Art and Labour* (London: Oxford University Press, 1922): 46.

[22]Ibid.

public.[23] Criticism, Lethaby explained, should be less concerned with the individual tastes of critics and more focused on the betterment of British industry.[24] The DIA immediately established a programme of public promotion and education of consumers.[25]

Neither Mervyn McCartney nor the Newtons were members of the DIA. However, throughout the 1920s the *AR* increasingly adopted what Michael Saler calls the DIA point of view.[26] This meant that the editors of the magazine increasingly embraced their role of promoting the architectural profession for both commercial and civic interests. Other journalists such as Noel Carrington, John Gloag and Christopher Hussey were also involved in this promotional work.[27]

The architectural criticism that evolved on the pages of the *AR* in the 1920s ingeniously aligned the commercial interests of architects with lofty civic ideals. This overlap between advertising, publicity work and civic education was characteristic of British culture in the 1920s as public relations became an increasing part of the work of national and local government.[28] Civil servants were preoccupied by the need to create a 'well informed public opinion' in the years after the war and they increasingly drew on the expertise of advertising and public relations professionals.[29] In the *AR*, this overlap was revealed in the advertorials of Dawnay and Sons Ltd.

Dawnay and Sons 'Advertorials'

Ten months after publishing the extracts from Lethaby's *London Mercury* article, the *AR* published an advert from the constructional engineering company Dawnay and Sons (**Figure 1.1**). In this ad, the company signalled its intention to run a 'series of announcements' which would be 'framed to interest the public in the architect' and promote architect's 'professional services'.[30] The series would 'show clearly why it is as essential in building to have the services of the architect as in legal matters it is necessary to employ a lawyer'.[31] The strategy behind Dawnay and Sons' campaign differentiated their adverts from others featured in the *AR* at this time. The conventional mode of

---

[23]Ibid.

[24]Ibid.: 48.

[25]The first exhibition was at The Whitechapel Gallery in London in October 1915 called *Design and Workmanship in Print*.

[26]Saler, *The Avant-Garde in Interwar England*: 73.

[27]Hussey who wrote for *Country Life* magazine set up the Vers Group in 1923–24. See Darling, 'Institutionalizing English Modernism 1924–33': 302. See also Glenn Hooper, 'English Modern: John Gloag and the Challenge of Design', *Journal of Design History* 28, no. 4 (2015): 368–84.

[28]T. S. Simey, 'A Public Relations Policy for Local Authorities', *Public Administration* 13 (1923): 243, Jacquie L'Etang, *Public Relations in Britain: A History of Professional Practice in the 20th Century* (London: Lawrence Erlbaum, 2004): 24.

[29]L'Etang, *Public Relations in Britain,* 20. See also Shasore, *Designs on Democracy* (2022) forthcoming.

[30]Dawnay and Sons Announcement, 'Public Appreciation of Architects', *The Architectural Review* (March 1921): x.

[31]Ibid.

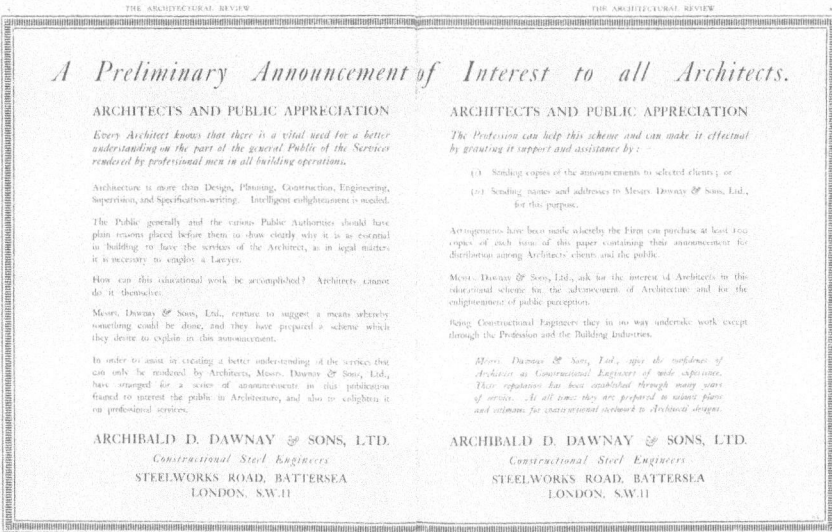

Figure 1.1 Dawnay and Sons Ltd, Announcement 'Public Appreciation of Architects', *The Architectural Review* (March 1921): x–xi, courtesy of the Museum of Domestic Design and Architecture

communication was a direct advertisement to architect-readers by manufacturers, construction companies and office suppliers. The Dawnay and Sons announcements also appealed directly to architects, but they positioned the company as the 'champions' of the architectural profession.

In the first advert Dawnay and Sons explained that they understood how important it was to promote architect's expertise to the public but that architects, constrained by professional etiquette, may wish to avoid actively promoting themselves. This sentiment was echoed by Herbert Read in 1933.[32] Writing about the formation of the group Unit One, Read described how artists and architects had to be 'propagandists' for their work but that it was 'generally considered questionable taste for an artist to employ a publicity agent and openly advertise himself'.[33] Over a decade earlier, sensible to these constraints, Dawnay and Sons had stepped in to advertise on behalf of architects.

Dawnay and Sons specialized in steelwork, a venerable business with a reputation for structural engineering.[34] Before the war they had worked with Adams, Pearson

[32]Herbert Read, *Unit One: The Modern Movement in English Architecture, Painting and Sculpture* (Cassell, 1934): 11–12.
[33]Ibid.
[34]The Air League of the British Empire, *Industrial Britain: Britain's Message to the Empire from the Air*, vol. 1: Engineering, Motor and Aircraft Industries (London: The Albion Publishing Co. Ltd, 1930), https://www.gracesguide.co.uk/File:Im1930IB-CC.jpg

and Holden, providing the steel work for Evelyn House Oxford Street; they were also well known for their work in aircraft and factory construction, particularly during the war. They were responsible for some of the finest aircraft buildings in the country as well as providing steelwork for some of the largest buildings in England including the Stock Exchange and the School of Hygiene in Bloomsbury, as well as many cinemas and theatres.[35] The company – or perhaps more accurately, their advertising agents – recognized that Dawnay and Sons' commercial interests were closely tied to the interests of architects: the more architects were commissioned, the more business potentially available to Dawnay and Sons.

The innovative advertising strategies suggest that Dawnay and Sons were working with an advertising agency, which were becoming ubiquitous in both commercial and non-commercial fields during this period.[36] There are no records of which agency the company worked with; it may have been a firm such as Godbolds Advertising Agency, who were advertising in aviation publications during this period (**Figure 1.2** and **Figure 1.3**).[37] Surviving examples of Dawnay and Sons adverts in *Flight* magazine between 1917 and 1918 show that the company were experimenting with their advertising techniques during the war (**Figure 1.4** and **Figure 1.5**). Between February 1917 and November 1918, the company ran a series of adverts each featuring a keyword such as 'Service' or 'Specialisation', which described the company's brand values. Although the adverts did mention the products that the company produced (standardized steel components

Figure 1.2 Godbolds Advertising Agency Advertisement, *Aeroplane* (3 October 1917), courtesy of aviationancestry.co.uk and FlightGlobal

---

[35]Ibid.

[36]Aeron Davis explains that after the war most commercial advertising in the United States in particular was handled by advertising agencies. The establishment of Advertising Associations in both the UK and the United States during the 1920s suggests that the advertising industry in Britain was similar to that in the United States. Aeron Davis, *Promotional Culture: The Rise and Spread of Advertising, Public Relations, Marketing and Branding* (Cambridge: Polity Press, 2013): 16.

[37]The firm's director, E. H. Godbold, was listed in 1934 as a member of the council of the Institute of Practitioners in Advertising, in *Who's Who in the Motor Trade*, https://gracesguide.co.uk/1934_Who's_Who_in_the_Motor_Trade:_Name_G

Figure 1.3 Godbolds Advertising Agency Advertisement, *Aeroplane* (24 July 1918), courtesy of aviationancestry.co.uk and FlightGlobal

Figure 1.4 Dawnay and Sons Ltd, 'Service' Advert, *Flight* (1 February 1917), courtesy of aviationancestry.co.uk and FlightGlobal

for aircraft factory construction), their primary purpose was to promote the brand and position Dawnay and Sons as a source of expertise and authority.

In January 1920 a new advert appeared in a similar style (**Figure 1.6**), but this time Dawnay and Sons sought to engage their consumers directly, announcing, 'our object is to ask you to write to us'. This was the same technique used in the announcements in the *AR* the following year (**Figure 1.1**), in which the text explained that the architect could aid in Dawnay and Son's endeavour to engage the public with architecture and the services of architects, by cutting out the announcement and sending it to their clients. Alternatively, architects could send the names and addresses of their clients directly to Dawnay and Sons (whose address dominated the bottom third of each announcement)

Figure 1.5 Dawnay and Sons Ltd, 'Specialisation' Advert, *Flight* (8 November 1917), courtesy of aviationancestry.co.uk and FlightGlobal

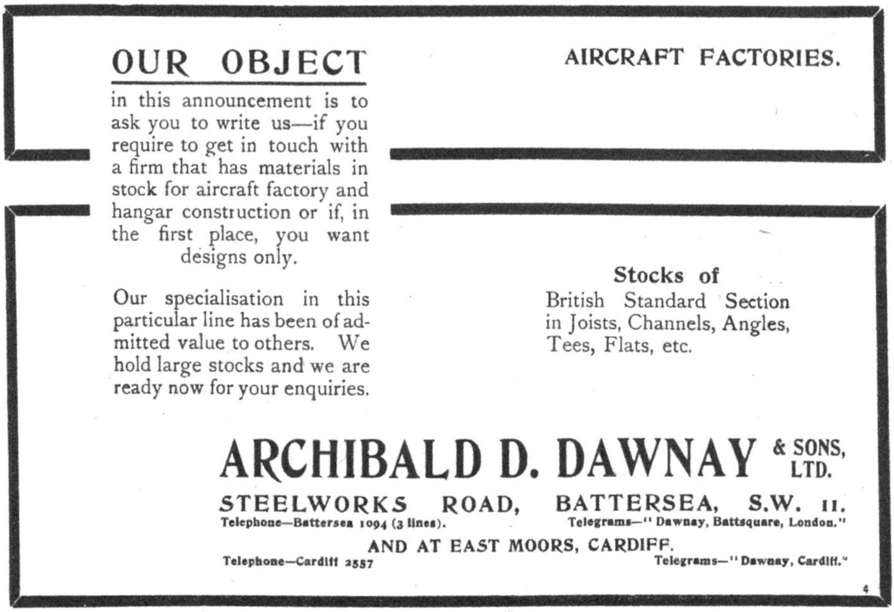

Figure 1.6 Dawnay and Sons Ltd, 'Our Object' Advert, *Flight* (18 January 1918), courtesy of aviationancestry.co.uk and FlightGlobal

and they would send a copy of the magazine out to the client. This was of course also advertising for the *AR* itself, who described the announcements as 'an enterprising and public spirited scheme'.[38]

The ads referred to themselves as 'announcements', which reinforced the educational dimension of their content. However, they were more akin to what we would today refer to as an 'advertorial', being a combination of an advert and an editorial. In the series of fifteen, monthly advertorials (between March 1921 and January 1923) Dawnay and Sons directly addressed the architectural public of officials and others who could potentially commission an architect's services. This was the public that the *AR* would discuss and experiment with writing for, over the coming years.

The advertorials offered the reader a basic introduction to the history of architecture in Britain. In the top corners of the double-page spreads were rectangular sections entitled 'What to Look For', which contained illustrations of different historic architectural styles from Norman to Gothic and Renaissance. In the left-hand corner was an illustration of a building, sometimes with the name of the building and details of the architect below; underneath were the dates periodizing the style. On the right-hand side were drawings of particular details characteristic of that style, such as scalloped capitals for Norman architecture and vaulting for Gothic architecture. These sections were giving the public the basic tools with which to look at and understand buildings and the language to describe them.

The advertorials were also promoting architects as cultural and civic decision-makers and architecture as an object of national significance. The first three advertorials focused on the practical understanding of what architects did and what they contributed. In the second, titled 'To Build Is Every Man's Ambition', the text explained that when a client first visited an architect, the client would quickly come to understand why the realization of their ideals relied upon 'the expert knowledge and trained vision of the architect'.[39] It detailed the various technical and legal procedures that architects undertook in the process of designing and constructing a building but above all emphasized that the architect turned a building 'into something of worth, a thing of beauty'.[40] The following month's advertorial expanded this claim, stating that a 'fine building is a national asset' and concluding that

[a]s the public find increasing pleasure and inspiration in fine Architecture, so will the debt of the community to architects be ever more highly appreciated.[41]

The fourth advertorial emphasized the public contribution of architects. Entitled 'The Architect and Public Health', the text explained that before the establishment of

---

[38]'Chronicle and Comment. Salient Features of the Months Architectural News: Educational Propaganda', *The Architectural Review* (March 1921): 70.
[39]Dawnay and Sons Announcement, 'To Build Is Everyman's Ambition', *The Architectural Review* (May 1921): xi.
[40]Ibid.
[41]Dawnay and Sons Announcement, 'The Influence of Fine Architecture', *The Architectural Review* (June 1921): xi.

the Ministry of Health in 1919, architects had long been concerned with the issue of public health.[42] The architect was a health specialist and was responsible for progress in issues pertaining to public health such as sanitation, ventilation, lighting, damp courses, size and proportions of dwellings.[43] By comparing the work of architects to the newly established Ministry of Health, Dawnay and Sons were aligning architects with the concerns and priorities of the post-war society.

They were also pointing to the fact that architects (and Dawnay and Sons themselves) were increasingly involved in the work of government departments; most prominent among them was Raymond Unwin who had been appointed chief architect of the Ministry of Health's Housing Division.[44] Dawnay and Sons had municipal connections; before his death in 1919 the company founder Archibald Davis Dawnay was Major of Wandsworth (1908–1919) and throughout the 1920s the company secured contracts with the government's Office of Works, most notably the Wood Street telephone exchange completed in 1929.

The language of the advertorials cast architects and architecture in the light of national identity, citizenship and civic responsibility. In 'The Architect and History', architecture was described as a measure of the debt nations owe to one another and that without architecture, civilization and culture 'would have been lower'.[45] The language of nations allied together and of citizens serving the nation ran through all fifteen announcements and borrowed from the language of the League of Nations, which was founded in January 1920. In the eighth advertorial, for instance, titled 'Architecture and Citizenship', architecture was described as a civic possession that created civic pride. Dawnay and Sons explained that the public recognition of architects and interest in architecture was in the national and global interest. In the final advertorial, they labelled the architect a public servant, whose important contribution should be recognized as such.

The Dawnay and Sons advertorials conflated the business interests of the construction company, the business interests of architects and civic importance of the 'education' of the public. Dawnay and Sons were blurring of the line between commercial and civic imperatives for public engagement with architecture. The advertorials were defining a way of writing about architecture that was based on interpreting, and thus promoting, the work of architects for a public readership. This type of architectural criticism had the dual task of promoting architects and educating the public. In the vein of the DIA and its antecedents in nineteenth-century design reform, the Dawnay and Sons advertorials approached the aesthetic and architectural education of the public in commercial terms, as an endeavour to produce more and better consumers for architecture.

The advertorials were an exploration of ways in which to present the work and expertise of architects to the public. The approach quickly began to move from the

---

[42]Dawnay and Sons Announcement, 'The Architect and Public Health', *The Architectural Review* (July 1921): xi.
[43]Ibid.
[44]For more see Mark Swenarton, *Homes Fit for Heroes: The Politics and Architecture of Early State Housing in Britain* (Heinemann Educational Books, 1981).
[45]Dawnay and Sons Announcement, 'The Architect and History', *The Architectural Review* (October 1921): xi.

advertising pages of the *AR* onto its editorial pages as the magazine became increasingly concerned with setting the tone and content of writing about architecture for a public readership.

W. G. Newton, as editor of the *AR*, took up Lethaby's call for the public to look at and judge the architecture surrounding them but Newton asked, what were the criteria for this judgement and how should it be arbitrated? Through these questions, Newton manoeuvred the *AR* into the position of mediator between the architectural profession and the public.

Who is to judge? The responsibility of criticism

The June 1922 issue of the *AR* opened with an editorial titled 'Taste in Architecture' by W. G. Newton.[46] It was 'rare indeed', Newton stated, to find 'architectural taste among cultivated people'.[47] These otherwise 'cultivated people' were not 'without interests or opinions' and were forthcoming with their opinions on literature, music or drama but they were hesitant and diffident in their thoughts about architecture. The problem was that people judged architecture according to their 'individual preferences'; they did not use 'principles of judgement'.[48] This gulf of knowledge, language and perspective between architects and laymen – their different means and methods of judging architecture – resulted in a situation in which

> [w]hat the architect admires the layman dislikes. What the layman thinks wonderful, mysterious, the architect criticises as being not architecture but a masquerade of art.[49]

Newton's editorial puzzled over who was at fault in perpetuating this situation – whose judgement should be trusted, public or professional? He asked whether 'the architect' was 'really speaking with authority or … expounding an esoteric and hardly intelligible tradition? Who is going to judge?'

The answer was the critic. Critics were needed to bridge the divide between architects and the cultivated laymen concerned with architecture. Newton condemned existing architectural criticism in architectural papers, which relied only on the expert criteria and was unintelligible to the layman, and he criticized the broader media for not discussing architecture at all. He wrote:

> It is time that serious papers and reviews opened their pages to real architectural criticism, a criticism of plan and treatment with a full and sympathetic

---

[46]Ernest Newton died in January 1922 and his son W. G. Newton continued as sole editor of the *AR*.
[47]W. G. Newton, 'Taste in Architecture', *The Architectural Review* (June 1922): 135.
[48]Ibid.
[49]Ibid.: 137.

understanding of the problem to be solved. They have their critics of play and novel, poem and symphony, picture and statue; and the result is that people can talk and think intelligently about these subjects. Until there is some such machinery for the fusion and interplay of ideas and opinions on what has been called the Mistress Art, there must be in an exaggerated form this question of the diverse standpoint of layman and specialist, and architecture must remain, to its own undoing, what it seems to be now, a cult of almost Egyptian mystery.[50]

Newton was demanding a type of criticism that could explain and interpret architecture for the layman and could educate them in how to look at and how to judge architecture – a form of criticism that would equip the public to properly judge architecture. Newton was casting criticism as a means of explaining the work of architects, making it accessible and undoing a tyranny of taste that had limited the layman's understanding and appreciation of architecture. In the same way as the Dawnay and Sons advertorials, Newton was aligning the commercial interests of architects promoting their expertise with the civic interests of educating the public for the cultural good of the nation. Newton explained that architecture was more than individual houses – that the building of public buildings is a public concern and the public currently did not feel enfranchised to discuss architecture. Just as the DIA had tasked the media with guiding the public in issues of design and architecture, Newton was arguing that critics should intervene to educate the public in how to judge architecture.

The *AR* was not alone in this call for enfranchising and engaging architectural criticism. In the same year as Newton's editorial on taste and judgement in architecture, J. C. Squire, editor of the *London Mercury*, established The Architecture Club, with the express aim 'to enlarge the public appreciation of good architecture and the allied arts'.[51] The idea for the group was said to have originated from a conversation between Squire and the architect Oswald P. Milne who argued that 'if architecture was to take its right place of importance in the modern world [architects] must tell people what they were doing and thinking both in the press and elsewhere'.[52] The group was made up of 'architects, writers and laymen', people generally concerned with raising the cultural standards of Britain and of creating opportunities to promote 'the best work of to-day'.[53]

In August 1922 the *AJ* featured a two-page article about the new club. The *AJ* started by describing the current problem facing architecture, with details that echoed Newton's editorial in the *AR* two months before – namely that the public lacked interest in or understanding of architecture. This lack of engagement was dangerous, the *AJ* explained, because 'we get the kind of building that we as a community demand and deserve … it is only as the general public demands fine buildings, that we shall get dignified and worthy

---

[50]Ibid.: 138.
[51]Editorial, 'Architecture, the Public and the Architecture Club', *The Architect's Journal* (2 August 1922): 141.
[52]Ibid. Oswald P. Milne was part of a later Arts and Crafts tradition, a generation younger than the founders of the Art Workers Guild, though he still subscribed to their fundamental architectural principles.
[53]Ibid.

towns'.[54] The poor condition of Britain's architecture at the time, the *AJ* insisted, was not due to a lack of skill or willingness among architects but because of a lack of knowledge and engagement among the public. The solution was to 'educate the public or the private owners or public bodies who control and commission building to have the strong desire for the knowledge of how to judge the best thing'.[55] The *AJ*, like the *AR* and the Dawnay and Sons advertorials before it, were arguing that the press should be striving to cultivate a public that was capable of judging architecture. The tool with which to cultivate this public judgement was architectural criticism.

This was where The Architecture Club was going to intervene. They aimed to create 'a public opinion about architecture – an architectural atmosphere – by promoting the description and criticism of architecture in the press and by holding exhibitions of modern work'.[56] The club was said to be based on the Architecture League in New York and the circumstances of architecture in that city were what Squire and his colleagues were aiming to achieve in Britain, a situation in which

> [e]very intelligent citizen knows the names of the architects and what buildings they have designed. Architecture is a common topic of conversation and the commercial magnates have realized that fine architecture is a commercial asset.[57]

The Architecture Club was founded in the same year that the British Broadcasting Company was set up; initially a government-imposed obligation on a group of wireless manufacturers, in 1926 it would become the semi-public institution of the British Broadcasting Corporation (BBC).[58] The organization embodied the combination of commercial concern and civic interests and the company pursued the dual aim of educating and entertaining its audiences. BBC programming discussed architecture from the beginning. The promotional and educational potential of mass broadcasting was increasingly recognized and businessmen and professionals, such as architects, were eager to experiment with these potentials. The activities of The Architecture Club and the beginnings of the BBC, as well as the writing in the architectural press, signalled a new type of culture in which critics and journalists mediated expertise and culture to a broader audience.[59]

In 1924, W. G. Newton returned to the issue of architectural criticism. He wrote a series of articles in the *AR* entitled 'The Bases of Criticism'. The series opened with Newton decrying the current tone and content of discussions of architecture in the popular press. He noted a recent article in the *Times Literary Supplement* in which the author accused modern architecture of becoming 'subject to vanity'.[60] Newton condemned this

[54]Ibid.
[55]Ibid.
[56]Ibid.: 142.
[57]Ibid.
[58]For full history see Asa Briggs, *The BBC: The First Fifty Years* (Oxford: Oxford University Press, 1985).
[59]I have discussed this in more detail elsewhere: Kelly, '"To Fan the Ardour of the Layman"', 350–65.
[60]W. G. Newton, 'The Bases of Criticism', *The Architectural Review* (February 1924): 174.

type of coverage, which did not engage with the complexity of architectural practice. Criticism should, he said:

> [d]ay after day, or month after month, say a little good about good things, and make each reader feel a little indignant, and also a little personally responsible for obviously bad things, then we shall feel that things are on the right lines.[61]

The job of architectural criticism in this sense was not to critique the work of architects based on the taste of the critic but to engage the public's judgement or 'conscience'. Newton described how the press should be after:

> The conscience of the citizen at large, so that he will at the lowest be intolerant of such planning muddles as the approach to Victoria Station … and that he may perhaps be so moved to open his eyes that he will help us, whose business it is to make new things about the country, to a better understanding of what we do.[62]

Newton was describing the press, which Lethaby had also described in his speech for the DIA, as a tool to promote the work and expertise of architects and to cultivate a public that were engaged with architecture. In this context, the architectural profession had to provide a clear language for architectural criticism that would clarify the terms of criticism for other journalists and critics. Newton's Bases of Criticism articles covered 'expression of plan', 'expression of structure', 'style', 'paint and stucco', 'wealth of nations', 'golden treasures' and aimed to clarify the terms of architectural criteria on which architecture could be judged.

The fifth article in the Bases of Criticism series returned to the question of taste. Newton warned against architects' complacency even with the growing attention paid to architecture. He warned that while it might feel like the 'propaganda is doing its work' and the public's taste was changing – 'more and more they like the things we like' – there was still a long way to go until the public's criteria for judging architecture aligned sufficiently with the expectations of architects.[63] Newton argued that the vast majority of people still wanted 'prettiness', which meant decoration and ornament. The problem was that people were still focused on details – as he had argued in the 1922 article. The aim of criticism therefore should be to persuade people that architecture is not prettiness but a broader 'handling of a material problem' in a manner that satisfied the practical and emotional side of man.[64]

Newton was still concerned by the disjuncture between architects and laymen and their judgement of architecture, he lamented, 'why do we think good and right what our fellow citizen cannot sympathize with? Why does our gorge rise at the prettiness which

---

[61]Ibid.
[62]W. G. Newton, 'The Bases of Criticism – V', *The Architectural Review* (July 1924): 40.
[63]Ibid.
[64]Ibid.

they aim at and love?'[65] In his caution over the effectiveness of its work so far, Newton still saw criticism as the means of bridging this gulf of 'us' and 'them', between architects and the public. Having started as the overt advertising and commercial branding in the Dawnay and Sons advertorials, Newton's writings signalled that the promotion of architects' expertise was now firmly the task of journalists and critics.

The *AJ* Survey of Criticism and the *AR* Supplement

Although by 1922 the *AR* were articulating a clear position on what criticism was and what it should do, there was by no means a consensus among the profession; the topic of the form and function of criticism was hotly debated. In 1926, the range of opinions on the subject was captured in a survey conducted by the *AJ*. The magazine sent out 300 questionnaires to members of the architectural profession. The responses were reported in two articles in May 1926 by the *AJ*'s editor, Christian Barman. Barman had joined the *AJ* in 1925; he had previously edited the journal of the Society of Architects and moved in circles with DIA members such as Jack Pritchard. Together with Hubert De Cronin Hastings, Christian Barman's time at The Architectural Press was pivotal in the shift towards architectural criticism for an architectural public.

The main question in the *AJ*'s 1926 criticism survey was whether architects should criticize each other's work (anonymously or under their own names) in either the technical or the public press. Two hundred and twenty-one respondents were in favour of this type of criticism in the technical press, and 187 in favour of it in the public press.[66] Importantly, among those against criticism in any form was Mervyn McCartney, former editor of the *AR*, which explained the magazine's shift towards criticism from 1921 onwards, after McCartney retired. In response to follow-up questions asking whether that criticism should be praise or censure, 214 saw no distinction and 220 voted against limiting criticism to eulogizing buildings (and avoiding critiquing their faults). While the survey returned an overwhelming majority in favour of architect's critiquing each other's work in public, the detail of the responses, which Barman explored in his two extended articles, revealed a more nuanced picture of varying definitions of architectural criticism and its purpose. Those who objected to architectural criticism in any form (47 respondents) were concerned for the solidarity and dignity of the profession. Barman acknowledged that 'the public can have no confidence in experts who are continually wrangling amongst themselves'.[67]

Other objections included the impossibility of perfection and an 'unfriendly feeling' among the profession. Even among those who supported architectural criticism there were questions over whether criticism should be paid and the professional etiquette that

---

[65]Ibid.

[66]By the editor, 'Our Criticism Inquiry: Part One of the Editor's Report', *The Architects' Journal* (28 April 1926): 647.

[67]Ibid.

would govern it. There was a feeling that critics should be guided by their duty to the profession. Barman contended that the dignity and welfare of the profession would be served by criticism that aimed to 'raise the profession in the public esteem'.[68]

The questionnaire demonstrated a swell of support for the sort of criticism that acted as 'interpreter' for the public, which aimed to bolster public knowledge and engagement with architecture. In his second article reflecting on the responses to the criticism questionnaire, Berman noted that 'this theory of criticism, in which the critic is regarded as an appreciative interpreter has gained many adherents of late'.[69] Support for this 'interpretative' criticism rested on what Barman called the 'national aspect', which referred to the public esteem and knowledge of both the profession and of architecture. Cowles Voysey summed up this perspective in his list, the uses of criticism:

a. It helps to form a unified and generally accepted standard of judgement.

b. It stimulates public interest in architecture.

c. It gives architect and layman a sound knowledge of the principles of art.[70]

Oswald P. Milne echoed these points in his opinion that an important function of criticism should be 'to get the public to realize the value of employing a competent architect rather than no architect at all'.[71] Howard Robertson wrote that 'in my opinion writing by architects on their subject is one of the best methods of interesting the public and eventually improving public taste'.[72] This was the sort of criticism that W. G. Newton had been calling for in his editorials in the *AR*.

Sir Edwin Lutyens argued that 'laymen possessed of the necessary architectural knowledge' would produce 'better, more impartial and more salutary criticism' than architects themselves.[73] Newton favoured critics like C. H. Reilly, whom he praised for writing in a manner that 'will chime with the outlook of the ordinary citizen'.[74] Reilly, who was a trained architect and head of the Liverpool School of Architecture, but no longer particularly active in practice, was, for Newton, the ideal critic. He was knowledgeable but not in competition with fellow architects; he was an expert with a perspective and a language that could pique the interest of the public while maintaining the integrity of the subject. Whether it was delivered by architect-critics or knowledgeable laymen, the

---

[68]Ibid.

[69]By the editor, 'Our Criticism Inquiry: Conclusion of the Editor's Report', *The Architects' Journal* (19 May 1926): 684.

[70]'Our Criticism Inquiry: Part One of the Editor's Report' *The Architects' Journal* (28 April 1926): 650.

[71]Ibid.

[72]'Our Criticism Inquiry: Conclusion of the Editor's Report' (19 May 1926): 685.

[73]Ibid.

[74]W. G. Newton, 'Architectural Criticism. Book Review of *Some Architecture Problems of To-day* and *Some Manchester Streets and Their Buildings* by C. H. Reilly, Liverpool University Press, 1924', *The Architectural Review* (February 1925): 89. As well as an educator, Reilly was an architectural journalist, producing pioneering articles for the *Manchester Evening News* and other titles; see Peter Richmond, *Marketing Modernism: The Architecture and Influence of Charles Reilly* (Liverpool University Press, 2001): 124.

purpose of criticism was to interpret the work of architects and cultivate a public capable and willing to judge architecture.

This returned to the theme of judgement, which had been central to W. G. Newton's writing in the *AR*. Berman quoted Eric Hayman who wrote that 'criticism is neither praise nor censure but judgment'.[75] This somewhat opaque statement was further explained by Mr H. V. Lanchester who said that criticism 'need not involve the distinction of praise or censure, for it may be based on the interpretation of needs and the attitude of mind towards architectural developments'.[76] Judgement in this sense meant an understanding of architecture, an appreciation of the reason for something rather than a designation of it being good or bad.

The *AR* was not adverse to publicly criticizing architecture, but more often they favoured this form of interpretive criticism. In May 1926, the same month that Berman's final report on the criticism inquiry was in the *AJ*, W. G. Newton was joined as editor of the *AR* by Hubert De Cronin Hastings. Son of Percy Hastings, De Cronin Hastings also became joint-chairman of The Architectural Press. Hastings had inherited his father's concern for the commercial as well as the artistic agenda of the magazine. He was responsible for the *AR* Supplement, which was at the back of the magazine and contained the sections 'Craftsmanship', which showcased recent examples of designed objects and crafts, 'Views and Reviews', the reviews section and 'A London Diary' a news and comment section.

Under Hasting's editorship the Supplement became the experimental space in the *AR*, exploring new styles of photography, graphics and layout and new types of writing. The first issue of Hasting's supplement opened with a series titled 'The Modern Movement in Continental Decoration', in the Craftsmanship section.[77] It was written by Phillip Morton Shand under the pseudonym 'Silhouette'. Shand was not an architect; he was a journalist and author who had published widely on food and wine in the early 1920s. Influenced by the Architecture Club, he had become interested in writing about architecture and had published articles in *Architecture* and in the *AJ* before working at the *AR*. He was the epitome of the knowledgeable layman whom Lutyens had earlier described.

The first article of Shand's series in the Supplement was called 'The Evolution of the Ensemblier' and it explored the influence of the 1925 Paris Exposition Internationale Arts Decoratifs et Industriels Moderne on interior design. In particular, Shand explored the role of the 'Ensemblier' who was a sort of design consultant that mediated between the client and craftsperson or designer. Shand's article set the tone for the Supplement with its focus on how modernism had developed different forms of expertise and was shifting the relationships between professionals and their public clients.

The experiments with writing in the Supplement continued with Arthur Trystan Edwards's series, 'What the Building Said'. This series had first appeared in 1925 in

---

[75]'Our Criticism Inquiry: Conclusion of the Editor's Report' (19 May 1926): 685.
[76]Ibid.
[77]Silhouette, The Modern Movement in Continental Decoration: 1. The Evolution of the Ensemblier', *The Architectural Review* Supplement (May 1926): 248.

Architecture, the journal of the Society of Architects edited by Berman. Hastings took it up for the *AR* and began publishing it in his second issue of the Supplement in June 1926. Trystan Edwards, a protégé of Reilly's at Liverpool, had made early forays into journalism and criticism followed by service in the Housing Division of the Ministry of Health under Raymond Unwin. By the early 1920s he was an established voice in architecture and 'civic design'. His 1924 book *Good and Bad Manners in Architecture* had established his particular form of criticism that conflated the art of manners' and the 'art of architecture'.[78]

Neal Shasore has explored how in *Good and Bad Manners* Trystan Edwards presented the language of good manners and of architectural politeness as the appropriate language of architectural criticism.[79] It was this type of writing that he used for 'What the Building Said' in the *AR*. The articles were narrated conversations between buildings in London's West End. For instance, the first instalment in the *AR* was called 'Overheard in Regent Street'.[80] This article had the Swan and Edgars Shop (described as an example of Regency Architecture) talking to the New Criterion building, the Piccadilly hotel and Vigo House. Trystan Edwards was condemning these new buildings, which were replacing Nash's original Regent Street designs, for their lack of architectural manners and this was expressed in the impolite tone and argumentative language of the exchanges that he narrated, for instance, this exchange between Vigo house, the Carrington and the new Quadrant:

> At the moment of my arrival Vigo House was indulging in the pastime of explaining to its neighbours who it was and who they were, making rather odious comparisons.
>
> 'Please understand' said the new double domed structure, 'that I am the only really modern building in Regent Street. I represent the last word in architectural design. Just look at my domes. Who has ever seen domes like that before? That is what I call originality. Whereas my predecessor only had one dome to form the focal point of the vista looking down the Quadrant, I have been generous and have provided two domes.'
>
> 'Are there two vistas now then?' piped Carrington's the little Regency building opposite, 'or are you thinking more of your own symmetry than of the composition of the street?' 'Vista indeed' said the new Quadrant, 'I with my little turret am the chief point of interest here'.[81]

These imaginary conversations between buildings were a way of presenting Trystan Edwards's arguments about urbanity and architectural politeness in a manner that was

---

[78]Neal Shasore, '"A Stammering Bundle of Welsh Idealism": Arthur Trystan Edwards and Principles of Civic Design in Interwar Britain', *Architectural History* 61 (2018): 182.

[79]Shasore, '"A Stammering Bundle of Welsh Idealism"': 184.

[80]Arthur Trystan Edwards, 'What the Buildings Said. I – Overheard in Regent Street', *The Architectural Review* (June 1926): 294.

[81]Ibid.

engaging and intelligible to a lay readership. The 'layman' was also employed as a figure in criticism to ventriloquize the opinions of the critic. This series in the *AR* was serving two functions – one as an experiment in how to engage public readers with the issues of urban design and architectural manners and secondly, as a model for new, engaging and accessible ways that architects and critics could write about architectural topics for lay readers.

Both Morton Shand's and Trystan Edwards's series continued for several months as Hastings continued to shape the *AR* Supplement into a pioneering space for modern architecture and interpretive criticism in the magazine. In 1927 Hastings took over editorship of the AR from W. G. Newton, after which the style and tone of the Supplement began to spread into the rest of the magazine. Through their editorship of the *AR* and the *AJ*, Hastings and Berman answered W. G. Newton's question of 'who was to judge' architecture: it would be the critics and journalists they commissioned to fill the columns of their magazines. The promotional agenda of the Dawnay and Sons announcements had evolved into the editorial agenda of the magazine; promoting the architectural profession was now a key function of the *AR*.

The Architectural Press, with owners who were attuned to the concerns of advertising (Hasting and Regan families), its historical links to the reforming agendas of the Arts and Crafts movement and the DIA, and its editors who were keen to embrace the new functions of journalism and criticism (W. G. Newton, Christian Berman and Hubert De Cronin Hastings), was particularly well equipped to adapt to the new context of architecture after the war. As such, the *AR* and the *AJ* evolved into sites for the promotion of the architectural profession. The particular form of 'interpretive criticism' that they pioneered in the 1920s became a defining characteristic of architectural journalism by the 1930s. This meant more broadly that these architectural magazines and other media organizations including the BBC and the work of The Architecture Club were now bridging the gap between the profession and its publics.

In 1948, Hugh Casson, who was by that time one of the editors of the *AR*, described the three functions of the architectural magazine as being:

> To record contemporary buildings as they are built and to provide the raw material of architectural history.
>
> To provide technical information for the use of practising architects – thus acting as a loose-leaf reference book which is constantly brought up to date.
>
> To provide space for the literary discussion of architecture and the allied arts.[82]

However, the fourth function that Casson does not mention was to publicize and promote the work and expertise of architects to the broader architectural public. This interpretive criticism continued as editorial policy for the next two decades. Although Casson did not acknowledge it, the other editors were aware of the magazine's role in

---

[82]Casson, 'One Hundred Years of Type-Set Architecture': 6.

engaging the public in issues of architecture. In 1947 they articulated the *AR*'s place alongside the BBC and Penguin publishers as a media outlet explaining architecture and culture to the broader public audience:

> The Review has been alone in supplying undiluted 'Third Programme' for half a century, without asking for or without getting a single round of applause (like that given to BBC after just 13 weeks).[83]

Architectural criticism as a means of defining, interpreting and promoting architect's skills and cultivating a market from their services was now an integral function of the magazine.

Select bibliography

Primary

The Air League of the British Empire. *Industrial Britain: Britain's Message to the Empire from the Air*, vol. 1: Engineering, Motor and Aircraft Industries (London: The Albion Publishing Co. Ltd, 1930), https://www.gracesguide.co.uk/File:Im1930IB-CC.jpg
The Architect's Journal (1920–8).
The Architectural Review (1920–32).
Brian Hanson Card Index of History of The Architectural Press in the private collection of Susan Lasdun, photographed by author.
Casson, Hugh. 'One Hundred Years of Type-Set Architecture'. *The AA Journal* LXIV, no. 723 (1948).
Lethaby, W. R. 'Design and Industry'. (1915), *Form in Civilisation; Collected Papers on Art and Labour*. London: Oxford University Press, 1922.
Lethaby, W. R. 'Architecture as Form in Civilisation'. In *The London Mercury*, March 1920, *Form in Civilisation; Collected Papers on Art and Labour*. London: Oxford University Press, 1922.
Who's Who in the Motor Trade. https://gracesguide.co.uk/1934_Who's_Who_in_the_Motor_Trade:_Name_

Secondary

Darling, Elizabeth. 'Institutionalizing English Modernism 1924–33; From the Vers Group to MARS'. *Architectural History* 55 (2012): 299–320.
Davis, Aeron. *Promotional Culture: The Rise and Spread of Advertising, Public Relations, Marketing and Branding*. Cambridge: Polity Press, 2013.
Holder, Julian. '"Design in Everyday Things": Promoting Modernism in Britain, 1912–1944'. In *Modernism in Design*, edited by Paul Greenhalgh, 123–43. London: Reakton Books, 1990.
Holder, Julian and Elizabeth McKellar. *Neo-Georgian Architecture 1880–1970: A Reappraisal*. London: Historic England, 2016.
Hollis, Richard. 'Building a Graphic Language'. *Eye*, no, 7 (Summer 1998): 40–6.

---

[83]The Third Programme was a cultural magazine radio programme launched by the BBC in 1947. Editors, 'The Next Half Century', *The Architectural Review* (January 1947): 21.

Hvattum, Mari and Anne Hultzsch. *The Printed and the Built: Architecture, Print Culture and Public Debate in the Nineteenth Century*. London: Bloomsbury, 2018.

Kelly, Jessica. 'To Fan the Ardour of the Layman: The Architectural Review, The MARS Group and the Cultivation of Middle Class Audiences for Modernism in Britain, 1933–1940'. *Journal of Design History* 29, no. 4 (2016): 350–65.

L'Etang, Jacquie. *Public Relations in Britain: A History of Professional Practice in the 20th Century* (London: Lawrence Erlbaum, 2004).

MacCarthy, Fiona. *A History of British Design, 1830–1970*. London: George Allen &Unwin, 1979.

Saler, Michael T. *The Avant-Garde in Interwar England: Medieval Modernism and the London Underground*. Oxford: Oxford University Press, 1999.

Shasore, Neal. 'A Stammering Bundle of Welsh Idealism: Arthur Trystan Edwards and Principles of Civic Design in Interwar Britain'. *Architectural History* 61 (2018).

Shasore, Neal. *Designs on Democracy: Architecture and the Public in Interwar London*. Oxford: Oxford University Press, 2022.

Suga, Yasuko. 'Modernism, Commercialism and Display Design in Britain: the Reimann School and Studios of Industrial and Commercial Art'. *The Journal of Design History* 19, no. 2 (Summer 2006).

Swenarton, Mark. *Homes Fit For Heroes: The Politics and Architecture of Early State Housing in Britain*. Heinemann Educational Books, 1981.

Whyte, William. 'The Englishness of English Architecture: Modernism and the Making of a National International Style, 1027–157'. *Journal of British Studies* 48, no. 2 (2009): 441–65.

Williams, Richard. 'Representing Architecture: The British Architectural Press in the 1960s'. *Journal of Design History* 94 (1996): 285–96.

CHAPTER 2
PROFESSIONALISM: THE AMERICAN INFLUENCE ON BRITISH ARCHITECTURAL PRACTICE
H. Horatio Joyce

In 1942, in the middle of the Second World War, John Summerson was feeling optimistic about the future of British architecture. In an article for *Horizon* magazine, he predicted that after the war architecture would be rendered '*effective* in English life' and 'the relation of the architect to the public' changed and clarified.[1] What did he think would bring about this important development? Large architectural offices, especially those attached to local and national authorities, like the 'intelligent and imaginative office of L. H. Keay, the Liverpool Housing Director', the pioneering work of R. A. H. Livett as Leed's Housing Director, and 'the architectural department of the Miners' Welfare Commission, admirably run by J. H. Forshaw' (**Figure 2.1**).[2] Official architectural departments such as these would move to the centre of the profession and their welfarist projects would redefine prestigious architecture.

Until recently Summerson's prediction seemed prescient. Reconstruction after the Second World War was understood in nostalgic terms: a time when architecture really was brought into service for community in contrast to the profit-driven culture of architecture today. In the last five years however a new body of scholarship has painted a more nuanced picture of that period, showing no shortage of private interests and at times even corruption.[3] Large offices too it turns out were more complicated than has been allowed. As this chapter shows, there was nothing inherently political or welfarist about them. Rather it shows that large architectural offices first took shape as private practices in the United States, which grew and evolved in response to the emergence of big business around the turn of the twentieth century. Maximization of profit and the preservation of the status of the professional architect were the twin engines driving them. Large offices came to Britain through a set of crises emanating from the war, which spurred the government to adopt the precept of industrial concentration based on the American model of big business.

---

[1] John Summerson, 'Bread & Butter and Architecture', *Horizon* (October 1942): 234, 235.
[2] Summerson, 'Bread & Butter and Architecture': 235.
[3] Alistair Kefford, 'Actually Existing Managerialism: Planning, Politics and Property Development in Post-1945 Britain', *Urban Studies* (September 2020): 1–15; Guy Ortolano, *Thatcher's Progress: From Social Democracy to Market Liberalism through an English New Town* (Cambridge: Cambridge University Press, 2019); Catherine Flinn, *Rebuilding Britain's Blitzed Cities: Hopeful Dreams, Stark Realities* (London: Bloomsbury Publishing, 2018); Ewan Harrison, '"Money Spinners": R. Seifert & Partners, Sir Frank Price and Public-Sector Speculative Development in the 1970s', *Architectural History*, 61 (2018): 259–80; Reinier de Graaf, *Four Walls and a Roof: The Complex Nature of a Simple Profession* (Cambridge, MA: Harvard University Press, 2017), ch16.

Figure 2.1 Betteshanger Colliery, Northbourne, Kent, *c.* 1934, supervised by J. H. Forshaw of the Miners' Welfare Committee, photograph by Henry Felton. Source: Historic England Archive, CC47/00555

The origins of large offices in America

For most of the nineteenth century American architects practised in much the same way as architects in Britain, or for that matter, most other parts of the world: alone or in small partnerships with a handful of employees if any at all.[4] Like they did elsewhere American architects tended to regard themselves as artists as well as gentlemen. But around the turn of the twentieth century a new kind of architectural practice began to emerge in the

---

[4]There were exceptions. In England, for example, George Gilbert Scott, whose Spring Gardens are noted below.

United States. These were often partnerships with large staffs that openly embraced the business aspects of practice.

The firm of McKim, Mead & White was a catalyst in this development – in large part because of the willingness of the partners to evolve in response to the novel economic conditions of the period, even as this meant turning away from things like teamwork and collaboration that had once been central to their conception of architectural practice. The major economic change affecting architecture in these years was the mushrooming size of businesses, as firms merged in an effort to capture a share of newly integrated national markets after the end of the Civil War (1861–65) and rein in overhead costs in response to a sustained depression in prices.[5] These new corporations, which began with railroads but soon moved into almost every industry, generated larger and more complex building projects that in turn required larger architectural offices with more diverse expertise to handle them.

Providing this service meant reconceptualizing architectural practice. Two partners, Charles F. McKim (1847–1909) and Stanford White (1854–1906), had both begun their careers in the office of Henry Hobson Richardson (1838–1886), at a time when Richardson was working increasingly under the influence of the English arts and crafts movement. Indeed, by the mid-1870s, Richardson had relocated from New York City, the centre of the new corporate economy, to Brookline, Massachusetts, where he set about integrating work and family under one roof in a rural environment removed from the economic freneticism of city life (**Figure 2.2**). His dozen or so assistant-pupils worked in individual curtained-off alcoves, when not taking breaks, as Richardson encouraged them to do, to browse his extensive collection of books, models, and drawings, or to play tennis on the lawn outside or walk in the nearby woods.[6]

After joining into partnership with William R. Mead (1846–1928) in 1879, the new firm of McKim, Mead & White moved ever further from Richardson's ideal of practice.[7] Within a few years they'd relocated from the small town of Newport, Rhode Island, to New York City and went from being mostly suburban and country house architects to the favourite architects of the new corporate elite, like the financiers J. P. Morgan and

---

[5]The classic study on the rise of the modern corporation is Alfred D. Chandler Jr., *The Visible Hand the Managerial Revolution in American Business* (Cambridge, MA: Belknap Press, 1977). For more recent scholarship, see Naomi R. Lamoreaux and William J. Novak (eds.), *Corporations and American Democracy* (Cambridge, MA: Harvard University Press, 2017). The impact of corporations on the development of architectural practice in this period has yet to be studied as it has for professions such as engineering by David F. Noble, *America by Design: Science, Technology, and the Rise of Corporate Capitalism* (New York: Alfred A. Knopf, 1977).

[6]"Studio and Office of Mr. H. H. Richardson, Architect, Brookline, Mass." *The American Architect and Building News* XVI, no. 470 (27 December 1884): 304.

[7]On McKim, Mead & White's office, see Michael Osman, *Modernism's Visible Hand: Architecture and Regulation in America* (Minneapolis and London: University of Minnesota Press, 2018): 165–84; Bernard Michael Boyle, 'Architectural Practice in America, 1865–1965-Ideal and Reality', in Spiro Kostof (ed.), *The Architect: Chapters in the History of a Profession* (1977; Berkeley and Los Angeles: University of California Press, 2000): 313–37; Mary N. Woods, *From Craft to Profession: The Practice of Architecture in Nineteenth-Century America* (Berkeley: University of California Press, 1999): 119–37; Paul R. Baker, *Stanny: The Gilded Life of Stanford White* (New York, 1989): 199–210; and Leland M. Roth, *McKim, Mead & White, Architects* (New York: Harper & Row, 1983): 57–66, 115–16.

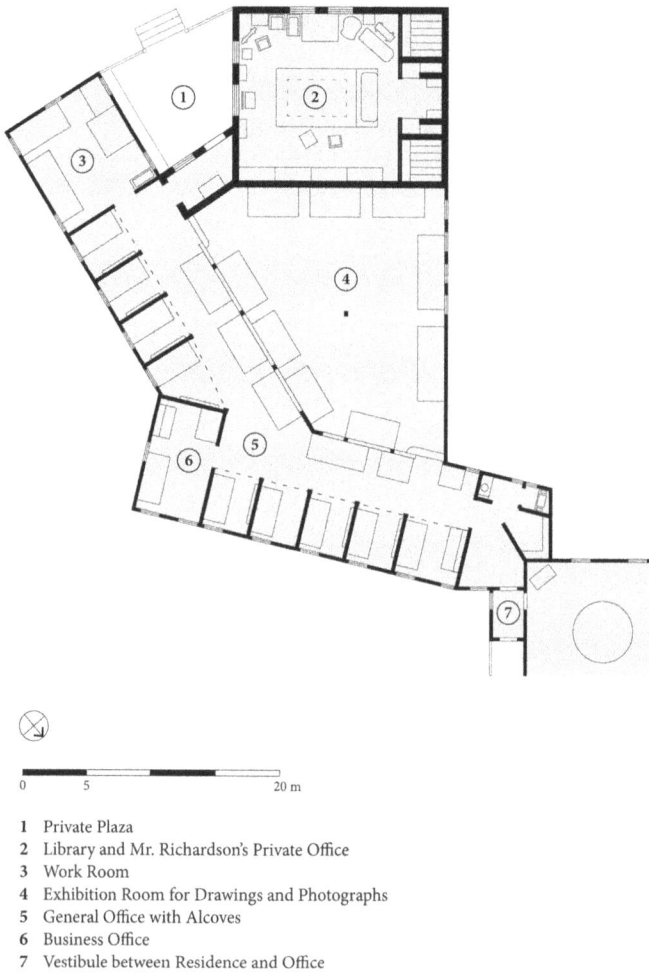

1 Private Plaza
2 Library and Mr. Richardson's Private Office
3 Work Room
4 Exhibition Room for Drawings and Photographs
5 General Office with Alcoves
6 Business Office
7 Vestibule between Residence and Office

Figure 2.2 Plan of H. H. Richardson's office, Brookline, Mass., *c.* 1884 (American Architect and Building News 16 (27 December 1884): 304

Henry Villard, serving at times as company architects (as they did for Villard when he was president of the Northern Pacific Railroad) as well as building their non-profit institutions and urban palaces. This increased activity required an expanded staff, which rose to more than 100 employees in the early 1890s, making them the largest office in the United States and likely the world.[8] It also pushed the partners to adopt new technologies

---

[8]By comparison, the largest British office up until that point had probably been George Gilbert Scott in London at mid-century, which was reported to have close to thirty in all, 'counting pupils, salaried assistants, and clerks'. William Whyte, 'Scott's Office and its Influence', in Geoffrey Tyack and William Whyte (eds.), *Sir George Gilbert Scott 1811–1878* (Donington: Paul Watkins Publishing, 2014): 213–29. See also Sam McKinstry and Ying Yong Ding, 'Business Success and the Architectural Practice of Sir George Gilbert Scott, *c.*1845–1878: A Study in Hard Work, Sound Management and Networks of Trust', *Business History* 59, no. 6: 928–50.

that might be advantageous like the telephone, standardized forms and time-and-progress schedules borrowed from industrial settings.[9] McKim, Mead & White's transformation into a corporate office was cemented in 1894 when it acquired the lease for a full floor of 160 Fifth Avenue (**Figure 2.3**). This larger space facilitated the division of responsibilities between the partners (who had earlier celebrated their collaboration) and the specialization of their office staff: beginning draftsmen, tracers, specification writers, constructionists ('who devised the heating and plumbing and determined what

FIFTH AVENUE

1   Reception Rooms
2   Draughting Room
3   Waiting Room
4   General Office, including Contractors
5   Perspectives and Sketches
6   Vestibule
7   Book keeping and Accounts
8   Specifications
9   Individual Offices for Firm Members

Figure 2.3 Plan of the offices of McKim, Mead & White at 1 West 20th Street, New York, *Engineering and Building Record* (11 January 1890)

[9]For an example of an early time and progress schedule see large chart, 5 April 1892, box 244, fo. McKim, Mead & White – Contractors, McKim, Mead & White Architectural Records Collection (PR 042), New-York Historical Society.

masonry and steel were needed for a building'), secretaries, and stenographers, who occupied small cubbyhole-like offices attached to those of each partner.[10]

McKim, Mead & White's previously unpublished office rules from the same year they moved to 160 Fifth Avenue, offer clues about what life was like inside the office (**Figure 2.4**).[11] Of all the rules – fifteen in total – only number four, governing who could

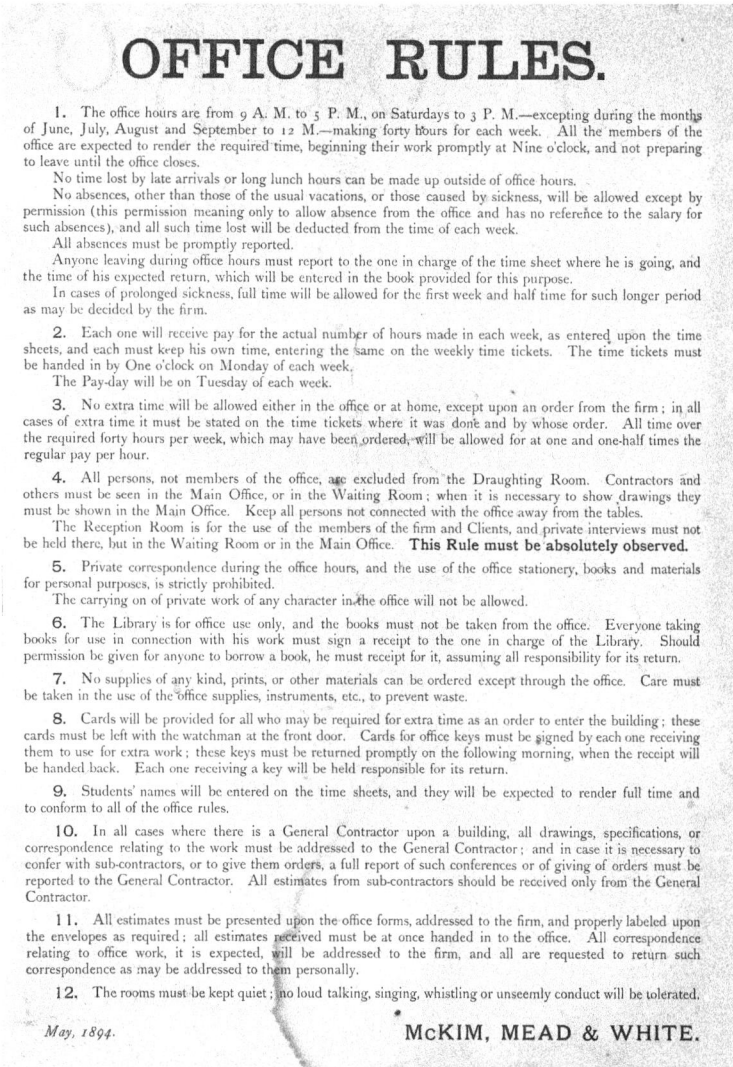

OFFICE RULES.

1. The office hours are from 9 A. M. to 5 P. M., on Saturdays to 3 P. M.—excepting during the months of June, July, August and September to 12 M.—making forty hours for each week. All the members of the office are expected to render the required time, beginning their work promptly at Nine o'clock, and not preparing to leave until the office closes.

No time lost by late arrivals or long lunch hours can be made up outside of office hours.

No absences, other than those of the usual vacations, or those caused by sickness, will be allowed except by permission (this permission meaning only to allow absence from the office and has no reference to the salary for such absences), and all such time lost will be deducted from the time of each week.

All absences must be promptly reported.

Anyone leaving during office hours must report to the one in charge of the time sheet where he is going, and the time of his expected return, which will be entered in the book provided for this purpose.

In cases of prolonged sickness, full time will be allowed for the first week and half time for such longer period as may be decided by the firm.

2. Each one will receive pay for the actual number of hours made in each week, as entered upon the time sheets, and each must keep his own time, entering the same on the weekly time tickets. The time tickets must be handed in by One o'clock on Monday of each week.

The Pay-day will be on Tuesday of each week.

3. No extra time will be allowed either in the office or at home, except upon an order from the firm ; in all cases of extra time it must be stated on the time tickets where it was done and by whose order. All time over the required forty hours per week, which may have been ordered, will be allowed for at one and one-half times the regular pay per hour.

4. All persons, not members of the office, are excluded from the Draughting Room. Contractors and others must be seen in the Main Office, or in the Waiting Room ; when it is necessary to show drawings they must be shown in the Main Office. Keep all persons not connected with the office away from the tables.

The Reception Room is for the use of the members of the firm and Clients, and private interviews must not be held there, but in the Waiting Room or in the Main Office. **This Rule must be absolutely observed.**

5. Private correspondence during the office hours, and the use of the office stationery, books and materials for personal purposes, is strictly prohibited.

The carrying on of private work of any character in the office will not be allowed.

6. The Library is for office use only, and the books must not be taken from the office. Everyone taking books for use in connection with his work must sign a receipt to the one in charge of the Library. Should permission be given for anyone to borrow a book, he must receipt for it, assuming all responsibility for its return.

7. No supplies of any kind, prints, or other materials can be ordered except through the office. Care must be taken in the use of the office supplies, instruments, etc., to prevent waste.

8. Cards will be provided for all who may be required for extra time as an order to enter the building ; these cards must be left with the watchman at the front door. Cards for office keys must be signed by each one receiving them to use for extra work ; these keys must be returned promptly on the following morning, when the receipt will be handed back. Each one receiving a key will be held responsible for its return.

9. Students' names will be entered on the time sheets, and they will be expected to render full time and to conform to all of the office rules.

10. In all cases where there is a General Contractor upon a building, all drawings, specifications, or correspondence relating to the work must be addressed to the General Contractor ; and in case it is necessary to confer with sub-contractors, or to give them orders, a full report of such conferences or of giving of orders must be reported to the General Contractor. All estimates from sub-contractors should be received only from the General Contractor.

11. All estimates must be presented upon the office forms, addressed to the firm, and properly labeled upon the envelopes as required ; all estimates received must be at once handed in to the office. All correspondence relating to office work, it is expected, will be addressed to the firm, and all are requested to return such correspondence as may be addressed to them personally.

12. The rooms must be kept quiet ; no loud talking, singing, whistling or unseemly conduct will be tolerated.

May, 1894.   McKIM, MEAD & WHITE.

Figure 2.4 Office Rules, May 1894, McKim, Mead & White Architectural Records Collection, POR 042, New-York Historical Society, 83078d

---

[10]Baker, *Stanny*: 206.

[11]The office rules were printed on a large placard and presumably hung in the drafting room, where the largest number of employees worked. Office Rules, May 1894, McKim, Mead & White Architectural Records Collection (PR 042), New-York Historical Society.

go where, was given special emphasis: '*This rule must be followed absolutely.*' Clients were restricted to the reception rooms, near the front of the office, and were out of bounds to all but the partners, while contractors were to be seen either in the main office or waiting room. Other rules stated what time employees were expected to show up for work (promptly at 9 a.m.), leave (not before 5 p.m.) and submit their time tickets (by 1 p.m. Monday) for payday (on Tuesdays). Loud talking, singing and whistling were prohibited. These procedures and the overall system of the office organization were adapted from tendencies then developing in large corporations, and they were passed down through McKim, Mead & White's young assistants, more than 500 in all, a number of whom such as Henry Bacon, Thomas Hastings, and Cass Gilbert went on to lead the next generation of large American offices.[12]

It was these types of employees that most interested a British visitor to McKim, Mead & White in 1909. Charles H. Reilly, the head of the Liverpool School of Architecture, visited the firm as well as Carrere & Hastings, 'the second most prominent firm' in the United States, expressly to study their systems of large office organization.[13] His tour was financed by the industrialist William Hesketh Lever (later Viscount Leverhulme), founder of the eponymous soap business and a rare supporter of industrial concentration in Britain before the war.[14] In an article published on his return in the *Journal of the Royal Institute of British Architects*, Reilly wrote that, contrary to what one might expect in a large office like McKim, Mead & White, assistants were treated like artists rather than 'mere draughtsmen, tracing, copying, or enlarging the exact details of their master'.[15] The names of the most senior draftsmen appeared on the front door together with those of the partners and their renumeration was generous – '£500 to £600 a year', 'more than double what we can afford to pay' in England.[16]

Underlying the success of McKim, Mead & White's office organization, Reilly further observed, was the recent proliferation of American architecture schools, based on the system of the Ecole des Beaux Arts in Paris. The assistants had all attended either the Ecole itself or one of the new American schools.[17] Not only did this provide McKim, Mead & White with highly trained assistants, but it also relieved the office of the responsibility of training, as Richardson had set up his office to do and McKim, Mead & White had also done for a time. Notably, the partners dropped this component by the time they'd moved to 160 Fifth Avenue in 1894, the same year McKim founded the American Academy in Rome to bolster the education of architecture students enrolled in American schools. McKim, his partners and like-minded colleagues such as Daniel H.

---

[12]See 'Office Roll of McKim, Mead & White', Charles Moore, *The Life and Times of Charles F. McKim* (Boston and New York: Houghton Mifflin Company, 1929): 327–37.

[13]Charles H. Reilly, 'The Modern Renaissance in American Architecture', *Journal of the Royal Institute of British Architects* 3, no. 17 (June 1910): 634.

[14]Leslie Hannah, *The Rise of the Corporate Economy* (Methuen and Johns Hopkins University Press, 1976): 45–6.

[15]Reilly, 'Modern Renaissance': 632.

[16]Ibid.: 632, 634.

[17]Ibid.: 634.

(who led a large office in Chicago) also supported those schools, often with substantial financial backing from the corporate elites they worked for.[18]

The development of large offices in Britain

When Charles Reilly returned home, he set about transforming the Liverpool School of Architecture into a version of the schools he had seen in the United States. With financial backing from William Lever, Reilly designed a new school building based on the architecture school at Harvard by McKim, Mead & White, hung American prize drawings on the walls and sent out an American-style prospectus.[19] He created a study abroad programme that gave the best students first-hand experience in large offices in the United States, and he worked to link Liverpool and other British architecture schools more closely with the British School in Rome on the model of the American Academy in Rome.[20]

But despite Reilly's best efforts to support large architectural offices in Britain through a ready supply of highly trained assistants, such offices did not yet exist and would not for several more years. This was because most building projects did not require large and expertly staffed offices like those in the United States, since Britain did not have vast transcontinental railroad companies and other types of large corporations. The reason, according to business historian Alfred D. Chandler, was that British industrialists regarded 'their companies as family estates to be nurtured and passed down to their heirs rather than mere money-making machines'.[21]

British architects regarded their firms in similar terms. Indeed, a gentlemanly ethos appears to have grown stronger in the profession around the turn of the twentieth century in reaction to developments in the United States. In 1892, with the British press filled with mostly positive reports about the alliance of businessmen and architects behind the construction of the World's Columbian Exposition in Chicago – to celebrate the 400th anniversary of Christopher Columbus's arrival in the Western Hemisphere – the so-called Memorialists, led by Thomas Graham Jackson and Richard Norman Shaw,

---

[18]For example, the nearly 100 incorporators of the American Academy in Rome in 1905 were a mix of prominent architects, artists, and businessmen, among them financiers J. P. Morgan (its principal benefactor) and Henry L. Higginson; corporate lawyer Elihu Root; industrialist Henry C. Frick; and railroad presidents Charles Francis Adams and William K. Vanderbilt. *The American Academy in Rome: Officers, Acts of Incorporation, by Laws* (New York: J. J. O'Brien & Son, 1905): 7–8.

[19]Joseph Sharples, 'Catalogue of Exhibits', in Joseph Sharples (ed.), *Charles Reilly & The Liverpool School of Architecture, 1904–1933* (Liverpool: Liverpool University Press): 88.

[20]Reilly, 'Modern Renaissance': 632; Louise Campbell, 'A Call to Order: The Rome Prize and Early Twentieth Century British Architecture', *Architectural History* 32 (1989): 131–51; Peter Richmond, *Marketing Modernisms: The Architecture and Influence of Charles Reilly* (Liverpool: Liverpool University Press, 2001): 46–50. On the American Academy in Rome see Fikret K. Yegül, *Gentlemen of Instinct and Breeding: Architecture at the American Academy in Rome, 1894–1940* (Oxford: Oxford University Press, 1991).

[21]Alfred D. Chandler Jr., 'The Emergence of Managerial Capitalism', *The Business History Review* 58, no. 4 (Winter 1984): 497.

published a manifesto, *Architecture—a profession or an art.*[22] However, seen against the backdrop of changes in the organization of architects' offices in the United States, it seems fair to wonder whether the real question being asked was not *Should architecture be considered a business, as it is in America?*

So entrenched was the idea of the gentleman that it took a war and direct government intervention to overcome British resistance to large organizations in business as well as in architecture.[23] Beginning with the massacre of British troops at the battle of Somme in the war because of poor munitions, manufacturers and trade unionists were recruited into government.[24] Alfred Mond, the owner of the chemical company Brunner-Mond and a vocal proponent of industrial concentration, was appointed First Commissioner of Works with responsibility for munitions factories and nearly all other government buildings.[25] After the war, as Minister of Health, Mond oversaw a vast public housing scheme for returning servicemen initiated by his predecessor, Michael Addison. Publicly sold as 'homes fit for heroes' by the government, the 600,000 new houses were in fact an insurance policy against Bolshevism and Revolution: to placate combat-trained working-class men returning to slums and disillusioned by war.[26] In any event, it was a building boom that called for an entirely new approach to architectural practice and is as close to a formal beginning for the large architectural office in Britain as any.

In order to handle the building campaign a new administrative superstructure was developed, controlled by the government in London through the Ministry of Health's new Housing Department which bore a striking resemblance to central organizational methods of American corporations.[27] Interestingly, the Housing Department strongly encouraged local authorities to hire 'competent architects' rather than engineers or surveyors as they'd always done in the past for municipal projects. In the larger cities

---

[22]Thomas Graham Jackson and Richard Norman Shaw (eds.), *Architecture – a Profession or an Art: Thirteen Short Essays on the Qualifications of and Training of Architects* (London: John Murray, 1892). See also William Whyte, Oxford Jackson, *Architecture, Education, Status, and Style 1835-1924* (Oxford: Oxford University Press, 2006).

[23]Still as Andrew Saint has shown, the idea of the gentlemen architect remained powerful into the 1920s and 1930s. Andrew Saint, *The Image of the Architect* (New Haven and London: Yale University Press, 1983), ch5. My analysis draws on Leslie Hannah's research on the corporate turn in British business, including 'Visible and Invisible Hands in Great Britain', in Alfred D. Chandler, Jr., and Herman Daems (eds.), *Managerial Hierarchies: Comparative Perspectives on the Rise of the Modern Industrial Enterprise* (Cambridge, MA: Harvard University Press, 1980): 41–76; *Rise of the Corporate Economy*; and 'Managerial Innovation and the Rise of the Large-Scale Company in Interwar Britain', *Economic History Review* 27, no. 2 (1974): 252–70.

[24]My understanding of this subject has benefited enormously from corresponding with Dennis Wardleworth and reading his 'Building the Modern Corporation: Corporate Art Patronage in Interwar Britain' (PhD thesis, Nottingham Trent University, 2002), Chapter 3. See also Alfred J. Chandler Jr., *Scale and Scope* (Cambridge, MA: Harvard University Press, 1990): 295–7; Hannah, *Rise of the Corporate Economy*: 29–31.

[25]In 1926 Mond spearheaded the creation of the Imperial Chemical Industries, 'the largest merger in British manufacturing industry in terms of its capitalization'. Hannah, *Rise of the Corporate Economy*, 90–1.

[26]Mark Swenarton, *Homes Fit for Heroes* (London: Heinemann Educational Books, 1981): 79; Daniel T. Rodgers, *Atlantic Crossings: Social Politics in a Progressive Age* (Cambridge, MA: Harvard University Press, 1998), ch9.

[27]Swenarton, *Homes*: 136–7.

such as London, Manchester and Sheffield this led to the creation of new salaried positions for architects.[28]

The war also opened the door to large architectural offices in private practice. The United States' decisive role in the war effort undercut some of the cultural resistance to American organizational methods, helping to bring about a merger movement in British industry and an increased presence by US corporations in the country.[29] This created bigger, more complex building projects that required larger architectural offices. This was sometimes satisfied by US architects themselves, as in the case of Devonshire House in London, an office building completed in 1926 by Thomas Hastings (a former McKim, Mead & White assistant) with Reilly serving as consultant.[30] But more often it was British architects touting American work experience who won the commissions. The architect Alfred Bossom (1881–1965) capitalized on his knowledge of time-and-progress schedules from two decades spent in the US designing skyscrapers before returning in 1923.[31] Thomas S. Tait of the firm of John Burnet Tait & Partners drew on his American expertise from time in the New York office of Donn Barber to complete Unilever House in 1933, the American Beaux-Arts-inspired London headquarters of the Lever Brothers.

In 1926 Francis Lorne, another Burnet and Tait partner, parlayed a decade of experience in the American firms of Cross & Cross and Bertram Grosvenor into a manual for British architects interested in embracing the business aspects of private practice.[32]

> Within the last few years there has been a decided tendency toward more modern methods and a greater efficiency in business, and as Architecture, of all the Arts and Professions is more closely allied to business than any other, it has been affected by this movement. To become more efficient is a healthy tendency in any endeavour, and the methods whereby we may become so are therefore of great moment to the Architect as to all other professional and business men.[33]

Lorne's book was heavily illustrated with ready-to-use charts and forms in all five sections, covering 'responsibilities', 'administration', 'record keeping' and 'financial accounting'. The very first illustration highlighted the advantages of partnerships with a division of responsibilities, with one partner overseeing 'business administration' and another 'designing and drawings' (**Figure 2.5**). One of the most important responsibilities falling

---

[28]Ibid.: 139–40.

[29]Rodgers, *Atlantic Crossings*: 367–91.

[30]Andrew Saint, 'Americans in London: Raymond Hood and the National Radiator Building', *AA Files*, no. 7 (1984): 30–43; Mira Wilkins, 'An American Enterprise Abroad: American Radiator Company in Europe, 1895–1914', *Business History Review* 43 (Fall 1969): 326–46; and Jonathan Clarke, 'American-Trained Structural Engineers and Contractors in London, 1895–1910', in *Proceedings of the Fifth International Congress on Construction History* 1 (2015): 463–72.

[31]'Obituary-Lord Bossom of Maidstone', *The Builder* (10 September 1965), 545; 'M.P. Retired after 28 Years: Sir Alfred Bossom Looks Back', *Kentish Express* (October 1959): 92B.

[32]'Francis Lorne', Dictionary of Scottish Architects, http://www.scottisharchitects.org.uk/architect_full.php?id=203488 (accessed 27 July 2020).

[33]Francis Lorne, *Architectural Office Administration* (London: Technical Journals LTD, 1921), preface.

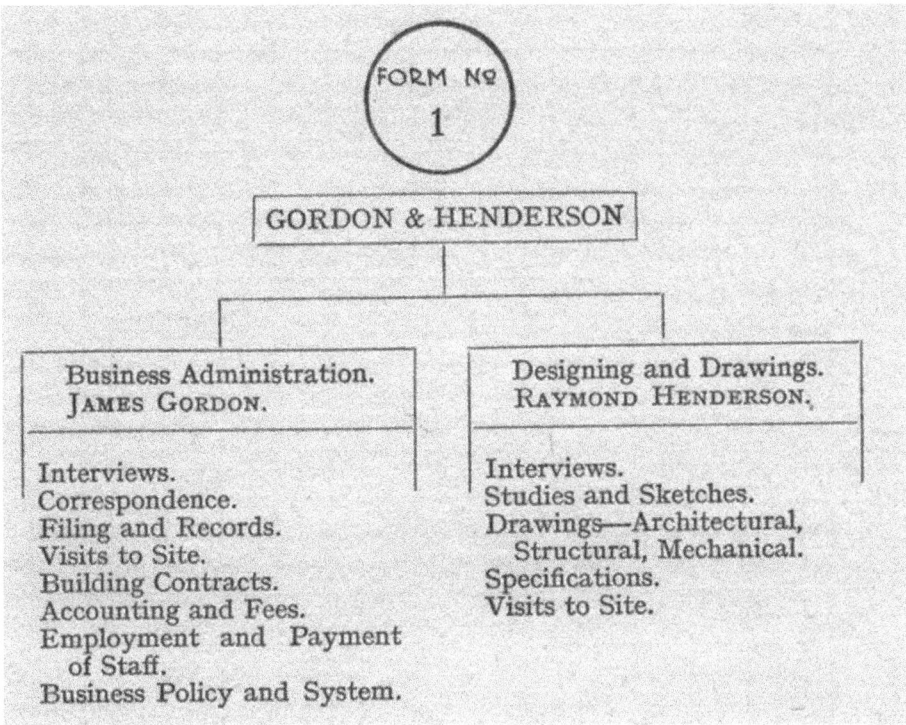

Figure 2.5 'A typical chart of duties' for the imaginary firm of Gordon & Henderson, as illustrated in Francis Lorne's Architectural Office Administration (1920)

under business administration was record keeping, Lorne argued, 'a subject of no less importance than drawings'. He advised that all outgoing letters should 'be dictated to a secretary … and typed' because it saved 'an enormous amount of time' – something also practised by Mckim, Mead & White, whose partners each had a small stenographers' office adjoining their own.[34] Lorne later turned his manual into *The Information Book of Sir John Burnet, Tait & Lorne* (1933).[35]

The Slump in the late 1920s and 1930s began a downward march for large private offices however as big commercial projects became less frequent. The state meanwhile generated a growing number of substantial jobs through the nationalization of certain industries and proto-welfare state initiatives. These were done in-house by greatly expanded existing architecture departments and a slate of new ones for local and national authorities and trusts.[36] It was here, unexpectedly, in large public offices that Reilly's

---

[34]Lorne, *Architectural Office Administration*: 20.

[35]Francis Lorne, *Architectural Office Administration* (London, 1920); Francis Lorne, *The Information Book of Sir John Burnet, Tait & Lorne* (Westminster: Architectural Press, 1934).

[36]Julian Holder, 'A State of Approval: Neo-Georgian Architecture and His Majesty's Office of Works, 1914–1939', in Julian Holder and Elizabeth McKellar (eds.), *Neo-Georgian Architecture 1880–1970: A Reappraisal* (Swindon: Historic England, 2016): 124, 126–7, 133.

students became leaders: G. Noel Hill as City Architect to the Corporation of Manchester; J. Blankett, Deputy Borough Architect, Newport, Monmouthshire; and N. Dunby, Town Planning Assistant to the Tynemouth and North Shields Corporation (reportedly the first woman to be appointed to such a position in England), among others.[37]

In response to the growing number of large official architecture departments *The Architects' Journal* invited architect R. D. Manning to consider the conditions and opportunities they presented for young architects in a series published in 1938.[38] Though Manning was on the whole supportive of the departments he was concerned about their effect on the professional status of the architects who worked in them. He reported that the Air Ministry and an unnamed borough engineers' office, for instance, had teams of architects working like clerks under the supervision of engineers. The situation was only nominally better in the Office of Works. Manning wondered whether the reluctance in that venerable office to promote younger architects was not motivated by a pernicious desire to extinguish individuality. "'The longer the service, the better the servant'".[39]

He was reassured however by conditions in the Miners' Welfare Committee – 'a babe amongst official architects' departments'.[40] Led by John Henry Forshaw, a graduate of the Liverpool School of Architecture, the committee was responsible for designing pithead baths for coalfields throughout the country. Forshaw's experience as a student studying abroad in the office of Flagg & Chambers in New York City may have served as a model for the small project-based teams he organized at the Miners' Welfare Committee, which Manning believed was crucial for the artistic integrity enjoyed by the architects.[41] Each team contained three to seven men and worked like 'a small architectural unit, complete in itself, led by a man who ranks officially as an Architect'.[42] These architects were separated from (but worked in close co-operation with) the administration and their names appeared under any illustrations of work in the press.[43] As for their assistants, 'it is evident that … [they] are allowed a freedom and exercise of initiative beyond anything I have heard of in other departments'.[44] There was an 'obvious connection', Manning believed, 'between the procedure followed and the atmosphere prevailing in this office and the fact that the quality of the architecture produced is so good'.[45]

---

[37]Lionel B. Budden (ed.), *The Book of the Liverpool School of Architecture* (Liverpool: University Press; London: Hodder and Stoughton, 1932): 44.

[38]R. D. Manning, 'Official Departments I. The L.C.C.', *The Architects' Journal* (2 June 1938): 933–5.'Official Departments II. H. M. Office of Works', *The Architects' Journal* (9 June 1938): 975–7; 'Official Departments III. The Air Ministry', *The Architects' Journal* (16 June 1938): 1015–7; 'Official Departments IV. Two Typical Offices', *The Architects' Journal* (30 June 1938): 1101–2; 'Official Departments V. Miners' Welfare Committee: Architects' Department', *The Architects' Journal* (14 July 1938): 63–4.

[39]Manning 'H. M. Office of Works': 976.

[40]Manning, 'Miners' Welfare Committee': 63.

[41]Joseph Sharples, 'Reilly and his Students, on Merseyside and Beyond', in Joseph Sharples (ed.), *Charles Reilly & The Liverpool School of Architecture, 1904–1933* (Liverpool: Liverpool University Press, 1996): 29.

[42]Manning, 'Miners' Welfare Committee': 63.

[43]Ibid.

[44]Ibid.

[45]Ibid.

The committee's system was not perfect, however. Manning reported that there were too few architects for the volume of work, the result being that they often had to sign off on projects they were not completely satisfied with. And the department's practice of restricting site visits to all but the most senior architects meant that junior and intermediate grades never got to see a job, 'either in progress or completed'.[46] Even so, for Manning, the committee remained an exemplar of what large public offices could achieve for the public, the profession and architecture. 'To those of who believe in the function of architects as servants of the community, and in the possibilities of the official department as a vehicle of good architecture, the Miners' Welfare Committee Architects' Department, with all its defects, represents a confirmation of your beliefs and a reason for hope in the future development of our work.'[47]

Conclusion

Five years after Manning's report on 'the babe of architectural departments', John Summerson highlighted Forshaw's department in his *Horizon* magazine article. Summerson like Manning was impressed by the unique organization of the office. He predicted that offices such as these would not only reconstruct Britain after the end of the Second World War but also reconceive the role of the architect in relation to society. What Summerson overlooked was that offices like Forshaw's had only been created because of the war and related crises that threated the status quo, that they had originally developed as private practices in the United States in response to the evolution of big business on the one hand and a desire on the other to maintain the social and artistic status of the architects who worked in them. The architect as a servant to the community was never part of the original equation.

But for a short period in the late 1940s and 1950s it seemed as though Summerson might have been right. There were dire predictions about the future of private practice in Britain, that it was nearing extinction owing to the dominance of official architectural departments.[48] In the end, however, the government offered a lifeline, a change of policy that forced local authorities to partner with a new breed of private developer such as Ravenseft and Freedman and Maynard.[49] Thus began a new chapter of large architectural offices in Britain, which more closely resembled their origins in the United States in the service of profit rather than community.

---

[46]Ibid.: 64.

[47]Ibid.

[48]'The Architect's Dilemma', *The Economist* (25 July 1953); John Swarbrick, letter to the editor ('Architects in Private Practice. Their Extinction or Survival'), 25 October 1947, ScGG/271/3, Series 6: Personal correspondence file, 1936–1951: Personal Correspondence, L-Z, 1946–1949, Sir Giles Gilbert Scott Papers, Royal Institute of British Architects, London.

[49]Flinn, *Rebuilding Britain's Blitzed Cities*, ch6; Kefford, 'Actually Existing Managerialism'.

Select bibliography

Primary

Archival sources

John Swarbrick, letter to the editor ('Architects in Private Practice. Their Extinction or Survival'), 25 October 1947, ScGG/271/3, Series 6: Personal correspondence file, 1936–1951: Personal Correspondence, L-Z, 1946–1949, Sir Giles Gilbert Scott Papers, Royal Institute of British Architects, London.

Large chart, 5 April 1892, box 244, fo. McKim, Mead & White – Contractors, McKim, Mead & White Architectural Records Collection (PR 042), New-York Historical Society.

Office Rules, May 1894, McKim, Mead & White Architectural Records Collection (PR 042), New-York Historical Society.

Grey literature

The American Academy in Rome: Officers, Acts of Incorporation, by Laws. New York: J. J. O'Brien & Son, 1905.

Jackson, Thomas Graham and Richard Norman Shaw (eds.). *Architecture – a Profession or an Art: Thirteen Short Essays on the Qualifications of and Training of Architects.* London: John Murray, 1892.

Lorne, Francis. *Architectural Office Administration.* London: Technical Journals LTD, 1921.

Lorne, Francis. *The Information Book of Sir John Burnet, Tait & Lorne.* Westminster: Architectural Press, 1934.

Sharples, Joseph (ed.). *Charles Reilly & The Liverpool School of Architecture, 1904–1933.* Liverpool: Liverpool University Press, 1996.

Newspapers and periodicals

The American Architect and Building News
The Architects' Journal
The Builder
The Economist
Horizon
Journal of the Royal Institute of British Architects
Kentish Express

Secondary

Articles

Clarke, Jonathan. 'American-Trained Structural Engineers and Contractors in London, 1895–1910'. *Proceedings of the Fifth International Congress on Construction History* 1 (2015): 463–72.

Ewan Harrison. '"Money Spinners": R. Seifert & Partners, Sir Frank Price and Public-Sector Speculative Development in the 1970s'. *Architectural History* 61 (2018): 259–80.

Kefford, Alistair. 'Actually Existing Managerialism: Planning, Politics and Property Development in Post-1945 Britain'. *Urban Studies.* September 2020: 1–15.

Saint, Andrew. 'Americans in London: Raymond Hood and the National Radiator Building'. *AA Files*, no. 7 (1984): 30–43.

Chapters (in edited volumes/collections)

Boyle, Bernard Michael. 'Architectural Practice in America, 1865–1965-Ideal and Reality'. In *The Architect: Chapters in the History of a Profession*, edited by Spiro Kostof, 313–37. 1977; Berkeley and Los Angeles: University of California Press, 2000.

Holder, Julian. 'A State of Approval: Neo-Georgian Architecture and His Majesty's Office of Works, 1914–1939'. In *Neo-Georgian Architecture 1880–1970: A Reappraisal*, edited by Julian Holder and Elizabeth McKellar, 122–35. Swindon: Historic England, 2016.

Whyte, William. 'Scott's Office and Its Influence'. In *Sir George Gilbert Scott 1811–1878*, edited by Geoffrey Tyack and William Whyte, 213–29. Donington: Paul Watkins Publishing, 2014.

PhDs/unpublished research

Dennis, Wardleworth. 'Building the Modern Corporation: Corporate Art Patronage in Interwar Britain'. PhD thesis, Nottingham Trent University, 2002.

Books

Chandler Jr., Alfred D. *The Visible Hand the Managerial Revolution in American Business*. Cambridge, MA: Belknap Press, 1977.

de Graaf, Reinier. *Four Walls and a Roof: The Complex Nature of a Simple Profession*. Cambridge, MA: Harvard University Press, 2017.

Flinn, Catherine. *Rebuilding Britain's Blitzed Cities: Hopeful Dreams, Stark Realities*. London: Bloomsbury Publishing, 2018.

Hannah, Leslie. *The Rise of the Corporate Economy*. Methuen and Johns Hopkins University Press, 1976.

Noble, David F. *America by Design: Science, Technology, and the Rise of Corporate Capitalism*. Oxford: Oxford University Press, 1979.

Ortolano, Guy. *Thatcher's Progress: From Social Democracy to Market Liberalism Through an English New Town*. Cambridge: Cambridge University Press, 2019.

Osman, Michael. *Modernism's Visible Hand: Architecture and Regulation in America*. Minneapolis: University of Minnesota Press, 2018.

Rodgers, Daniel T. *Atlantic Crossings: Social Politics in a Progressive Age*. Cambridge, MA: Harvard University Press, 1998.

Roth, Leland M. *McKim, Mead & White, Architects*. New York: Harper & Row, 1983.

Saint, Andrew. *The Image of the Architect*. New Haven and London: Yale University Press, 1983.

Swenarton, Mark. *Homes Fit for Heroes*. London: Heinemann Educational Books, 1981.

Whyte, William. *Oxford Jackson: Architecture, Education, Status, and Style 1835–1924*. Oxford: Oxford University Press, 2006.

Woods, Mary N. *From Craft to Profession: The Practice of Architecture in Nineteenth-Century America*. Berkeley: University of California Press, 1999.

CHAPTER 3
REGULATION: THE 'NEW LONDON'
Eileen Chanin

In the Victory parades of 1919, servicemen marched past three acres of wasteland on the eastern stretch of the Strand. Temporary YMCA huts housed dormitories and canteens for allied troops on this sizeable swathe of undeveloped ground in the heart of London. Long a public eyesore, it had been the focus for change in the years before the war when municipal reformers embarked on reshaping London for the modern world, with visions of a more harmonious environment built for the future, styled as 'New London'.[1]

The need to reconstruct central London existed on both sides of 1914. Architecture in London has always been part of the city's ongoing history of regeneration in response to social, cultural, political and economic changes. London's urban character at the turn of the century reflected Victorian laissez-faire individualism; municipal reformers wished to redress the lack of robust planning regulation in nineteenth-century urban development. By war's end, it was evident that pre-war calls to improve central London were essential. The war upset all aspects of life including the need for urban renewal; this need was keenly felt in the war's aftermath.

Histories of London's architecture of the early twentieth century give little account of this necessity and how it was met on the Strand.[2] Comparatively little attention has recently been given to London's architecture of this period. Standard accounts remain those from Alastair Service (1975, 1977), Colin Cunningham (1981), A. Stuart Gray (1988) and Richard Fellows (1995, 2000).[3] In general, the focus on architects and style in these overviews of the period now appears limited. Cunningham (for example), who

---

[1]T. Raffles Davison, 'New London', *British Architect* 66 (December 1906): 431–9, in a supplement to this issue of the journal.

[2]Contemporary observations on Kingsway's development come from Harold P. Clunn, *London Rebuilt, 1897–1927: An Attempt to Depict the Principal Changes Which Have Taken Place, with Some Suggestions for the Further Improvement of the Metropolis* (London: J. Murray, 1927). For a critique James H. Winter, *London's Teeming Streets* (London: Routledge, 1993): 207–16. For a recent round-up see Dirk Schubert and Anthony Sutcliffe, 'The "Haussmannization" of London?: The Planning and Construction of Kings way-Aldwych, 1889–1935', *Planning Perspectives* 11 no. 2 (1996): 115–44.

[3]Alastair Service, *Edwardian Architecture and Its Origins* (London: The Architectural Press, 1975); Alastair Service, *Edwardian Architecture: A Handbook of Building Design in England, 1890–1914* (London: Thames and Hudson, 1977); Colin Cunningham, *Victorian and Edwardian Town Halls* (London: Routledge & Kegan Paul, 1981); A. Stuart Gray, Jean Breach, and Nicholas Breach, *Edwardian Architecture: A Biographical Dictionary* (Ware, Herts.: Wordsworth Editions, 1988); Richard Fellows, *Edwardian Architecture: Style and Technology* (London: Lund Humphries, 1995); Richard Fellows, *Edwardian Civic Buildings and Their Details* (Boston: Architectural Press, 2000). More recently, Alan Powers has called for review of architecture of this period in *The Architectural Review*: 'British Architecture before the Great War', Part One: 11 November 2014; Part Two: 30 December 2014.

was the first to study twentieth-century town halls in detail, said little about the influence of civic emulation on their architectural form. Additionally, few studies have considered how architecture is influenced by city government.[4]

Consideration of the effects of this influence is called for because of the way that regulatory instruments and financial aspects of public governance shape the built environment.[5] Accounts of the ties between building regulations, finance and the built form remain marginal in histories of the period, which are typically narrated in terms of architectural style with emphasis on individual architects. These generally overlook how a building's construction results from negotiating plans for its intended purpose with managing safety and other statutory regulations, and how meeting these requirements determines a building's design and function. This is surprising given the architectural activity that occurred when, in the competitive environment of the New Imperialism (from the 1870s to 1914), building capitals was linked to forging national identity and cities worldwide were being reshaped into 'grand capitals'.[6]

Responding to these changes at the close of the long nineteenth century, plans were developed to reconstruct London as a capital worthy of Britain's Empire. With Britain then the world's leading creditor nation, its leading trading nation and the producer of a third of the world's manufactured exports, an entwined vision was held for London to assert its primacy as the centre of the world's commerce, as well as to become a capital worthy of the Empire.[7]

Achieving this 'New London' depended on regenerating the Strand and its adjacent precinct towards Holborn, under a mile to the north. Nowhere was the problem of London's need for improvement greater than in this nucleus of the city. Vital connections were made across London via this pivotal zone, but congested conditions on the Strand and its adjacent narrow laneways, particularly at its eastern end, restricted movement across the city especially from north to south. Opening up London's centre to meet traffic

---

[4]For a history of public building in London over the long nineteenth century (and growing popular awareness of London's status as the metropolitan centre of a world empire) see M. H. Port, *Imperial London: Civil Government Building in London 1850-1915* (New Haven: Published for the Paul Mellon Centre for Studies in British Art by Yale University Press, 1995).

[5]Bookending this period are the building regulations introduced in the London Building Act (1894) and the London Building Act 1930. For their details: Banister Fletcher, *The London Building Acts, 1894-1909*, 5th edn. (London: Batsford, 1914); Bernard Dicksee (ed.), *The London Building Act 1930*, 6th edn. (London: Stanford, 1931).

[6]To give example, once Italy unified in 1871, Rome was declared a national capital with parts of the city undergoing modernization. Cultural geographers have led in studies of this history. For example, Michiel Wagenaar, 'Townscapes of Power', *GeoJournal* (May 2000): 3–13; Felix Driver and David Gilbert (eds.), *Imperial Cities: Landscape, Display and Identity* (Manchester: Manchester University Press, 2003).

[7]Contemporary attempts to rethink London as a city of the twentieth century variously envisaged and described it as 'New' and 'Imperial': London Society, *London of the Future, Under the Editorship of Sir Aston Webb* (London: T. Fisher Unwin, 1921); David Gilbert, 'London of the Future: The Metropolis Reimagined after the Great War', *Journal of British Studies* 43, no. 1 (January 2004): 91–119. On Britain's trading prowess (and demise through the first half of the twentieth century): Barry Eichengreen, 'The British Economy between the Wars', in Roderick Floud (ed.), *The Cambridge Economic History of Modern Britain 2, Economic Maturity: 1860-1937* (Cambridge: Cambridge University Press, 2004): 314.

needs was long overdue. For nearly a century, nothing had come of earlier proposals to remove constrictions in the area, despite some dozen Parliamentary Select Committees appointed to consider plans to improve metropolitan London. Improvements never happened while the question of who would meet the costs of them remained unresolved.[8]

In 1889, the London County Council (LCC) replaced the Metropolitan Board of Works (in existence for thirty-three years). The LCC's formation sprang from an ongoing movement to reform the government of London (that was fostered by the London Municipal Reform League, many of whose protagonists subsequently became members of the first London County Council and influenced its early policy).[9] Swayed by reformers like social investigator Charles Booth, citizens and politicians felt the urgency of betterment. Technological advances and growing democratic engagement encouraged change. Social, cultural and political ideas fostered new ideas about city space and architecture. Parliament entrusted the LCC with powers to make London healthier to live in, more beautiful to look at, and more inspiring to inhabit.

Empowered with regulations aimed at ensuring better and safer building, the LCC seized the opportunity to remove disorderliness from Central London's 'miserable streets' (that Booth's poverty maps charted so clearly) and to raze Dickensian slums from the Strand's eastern end. The London County Council (Improvements) Act (1899) gave the Council parliamentary authority to widen the Strand opposite St Clement Danes and to link it to Holborn through a newly constructed thoroughfare that would be a great artery of London. The LCC swept away from the area tenements (some which were little changed from the seventeenth century), as well as the notoriously insanitary area of Clare Market (chiefly a meat market) with its network of narrow courts. It cleared about twenty-eight acres, of which twelve and a quarter were taken for new streets and fifteen and three-quarters left for building purposes.[10] This gave the LCC a large area called the Holborn to Strand Improvement, where the new crescent of Aldwych and artery of Kingsway would link Holborn directly to the Strand. Over time, the LCC, in connecting Aldwych and Kingsway to the Strand and reconstructing adjacent areas, entirely changed the character of the neighbourhood.

Kingsway was 100 feet wide, unlike the narrow streets that made up the greater part of London at the time.[11] The LCC envisaged a consistently harmonious architectural

---

[8]Percy J. Edwards and London County Council, *History of London Street Improvements 1855–1897* (London: Printed for the London County Council by Truscott and Son, 1898): 10. Edwards was Clerk of the Council's Improvements Committee.

[9]Background and details are outlined in John Davis, *Reforming London, the London Government Problem, 1855–1900* (Oxford: Oxford University Press, 1988); Andrew Saint (ed.), *Politics and the People of London, The London County Council 1889–1965* (London: Hambledon Press, 1989); Susan D. Pennybacker, *A Vision for London, 1889–1914: Labour, Everyday Life and the LCC Experiment* (London: Routledge, 1995).

[10]Sir Gwilym Gibbon and Reginald W. Bell, *History of the London County Council 1889–1939* (London: Macmillan and Co, 1939): 452.

[11]Kingsway narrowed to 80 feet for a short distance at its northern end in Southampton Row. The average width of street in London was 60 feet and 28 feet in the City of London. Edwards, *Street Improvements*: 11; 'London's Lessons from America', *Builder* (29 May 1925): 819.

treatment for the new straight street, just over three-quarters of a mile long. It had more formal French models in mind than the irregular architectural compositions found in London.[12] Buildings would rise on Kingsway that would be more healthful and better serve twentieth-century needs and therefore would express London's modernity.[13] Aspirations for Kingsway to be London's finest business thoroughfare were conveyed to King Edward Vll when he opened the street in October 1905. Improvement, and by association modernity, was the essence of the extensive Holborn to Strand scheme.

It was the most important and spectacular scheme of urban improvement that had ever been placed before Parliament – with an estimated capital outlay of £6m gross or deducting recoupment, about £1.75 million net (roughly equivalent to £192.5 million today).[14] The recoupment principle enabled an authority to buy more land than was actually required to form a new road or other improvement, so that by the profit made on reselling the surplus it would recoup a substantial part of the cost of the improvement. Kingsway's width reflected the control that the LCC exercised over streets and their frontages. It became 10 feet wider than originally intended when the Council estimated that a net saving of £18,400 (over £2 million today) would be gained by making Kingsway 100 feet wide, enhancing the value of adjoining surplus land which would be sold after its improvement.[15]

To the dismay of those who followed its progress, Kingsway and the Aldwych crescent leading to it developed more slowly than anticipated. London developers resisted the increasing regulatory control over development in areas assigned to the LCC including the Council's requirements to ensure the structural safety of buildings and to 'style' this central hub with expensive Portland stone fronts. Consequently, sites facing the much-heralded 'boulevarde' developed slowly and erratically. Moreover, the three acres of council land between Aldwych and the Strand remained undeveloped. This posed

---

[12]As were seen in designs sought by the Council and in responses from architects: London County Council. Improvements Committee, *Holborn to the Strand Improvement: Designs Submitted by Selected Architects for the Strand and Crescent Frontages, October 1900* (London: The Council, 1900). 'From Holborn to Strand: An Ideal Street. Suggestions for plans by R. Norman Shaw, Reginald Blomfield and Halsey Ricardo, 'Mervyn McCartney', *Architectural Review* 7 (1900): 118–26.

[13]On how London was seen as diseased, with street reform likened to medical intervention see Winter, *Teeming Streets*, xi. David Rooney, 'Visualization, Decentralization and Metropolitan Improvement: "Light-and-Air" and London County Council Photographs, 1899–1908', *Urban History* 40, no. 3 (2013): 462–82.

[14]Sir Harry Haward, *The London County Council from Within, Forty Years' Official Recollections* (London: Chapman & Hall Ltd, 1932): 254. Haward was among the chief officers of the Council, serving as its financial comptroller (1889–1919). American political economist Henry George's promotion of the 'single tax' on land inspired Britain's taking world lead in discussing the tie between planning regulations and property values and capturing the 'unearned increment' in land value. Rachelle Alterman, 'Land Use Regulations and Property Values: The "Windfalls Capture" Idea Revisited' in Nancy Brooks, Kieran Donaghy, Gerrit-Jan Knaap, *The Oxford Handbook of Urban Economics and Planning* (Oxford: Oxford University Press, 2012): 755–86, 760. On the cross fertilization of ideas among municipal activists: Shelton Stromquist, 'Thinking Globally, Acting Locally': Municipal Labour and Socialist Activism in Comparative Perspective, 1890–1920', *Labour History Review* 74, no. 3 (December 2009): 233–56. In 2018, the relative value of £1 from 1899, in simple purchasing power, is roughly £110.60, measuringworth.com

[15]Edwards, *Street Improvements*: 256.

a problem to the LCC which relied on its own financial resources for works of road improvement and because slum clearance was a rate-borne service.[16]

Four buildings within a stone's throw of this focal point – Kodak House (1911), Australia House (1918), Bush House Central Block (1925) and India House (1930) – helped achieve the LCC's ambitions for 'New London'. This chapter draws on archival research into records pertinent to these buildings to look at how some of the governing principles and regulatory controls of the LCC influenced how each building was conceived and constructed.[17]

Architecture, like government, is a collaborative process of many parts and involves regulatory authorities. To read building case files, building plans, and various reports associated with these key buildings allows us to follow how they took shape and to appreciate how the LCC, along with other geopolitical influences, decided aspects of their final form. The archives offer contemporary perspectives on the built form of central London. They show how a complex dance between new approaches taken to buildings and their function, and enmeshed imperial, national, and local aims and requirements, influenced the development of this focal zone of Strand-Aldwych-Kingsway and gave the precinct its character. They reflect the extent to which architects and developers were bound by rules that regulatory authorities stipulated and that a building was 'constructed' as much by regulatory observation as by design aspiration. 'Style' is not the defining lens of analysis, although it is discussed necessarily, as it altered in the time under discussion in response to the changing uses demanded from buildings. However, far from being a parade of styles for which this era is sometimes decried, it is a critical time of building and architectural improvement that went hand in hand with desires for 'betterment' to redress the wrongs of nineteenth-century London and to shape it into an imperial metropolis. Progress made in the years before 1914 influenced directions taken in the years after 1918.

As Jessica Kelly puts it, architecture is a complex field of activity of hidden or invisible processes and collaborations occurring among invisible, anonymous and overlooked people, and processes, that produce a building.[18] The case files for these buildings show the discussion, disagreement, compromise and solutions arrived at 'behind the scenes' that produced the finished building. They make clear that architecture is more than the work of individual architects, that there are many 'authors' behind a building, collaborating in these many activities, and that regulations shaped buildings more than has generally been discussed in architectural history. Moreover, as this chapter discusses, each building highlights the differences and continuities in building in inner London before and after the war. Herein lies the value of looking at these four significant

---

[16]No external funding went to the Council for road construction and improvement. From 1919, the Ministry of Transport could provide government funding for road works. Gibbon and Bell, *History*: 442.

[17]See Eileen Chanin, *Capital Designs, Australia House and Visions of an Imperial London* (Melbourne: Australian Scholarly Publishing, 2018).

[18]Jessica Kelly, 'Anonymity and Hidden Mechanisms in Design and Architecture', *Architecture and Culture* 6, no. 1 (2018): 5.

buildings that were cornerstones to the vision then held for an imperial metropolis. Their conception, construction and contribution to ambitions for the 'New London' that Aldwych-Kingsway represented are outlined.

Kodak House

The Eastman Kodak Company's success in producing photographic products, like its Box Brownie camera (1900) which enabled everyone to take snapshots, meant that the company had outgrown its Clerkenwell headquarters. George Eastman, Kodak's managing director, was a champion of change, a great industrialist of the era.[19] He invented roll film, and by bringing it into the mainstream he revolutionized photography. By 1896 Eastman Kodak, the company that he incorporated in 1892 was the leading supplier of film stock internationally and it dominated in the plate, film, camera and motion picture industries. Eastman, who personified American entrepreneurialism, and was symptomatic of increasing investment in Britain from across the Atlantic, sought larger premises in central London that would give the company a more extensive showroom, offices, storehouse and a distribution centre (particularly for its European branches).[20]

Eastman was a decisive man and accustomed to closely directing any company activity. It appears that he foresaw likely resistance from the LCC, which presented him with several hurdles. The council advertised its Kingsway-Strand development at the 1908 Franco-British Exhibition, displaying the few buildings erected on the surplus land of the development by way of wooden models.[21] Exclusively, its block at 65 Kingsway, on the street's western side, where Kodak Ltd. proposed to build, showed a paper model, suggesting that negotiations for this site were then underway. The company proposed to purchase this block subject to being able to build a building that suited its business requirements. The company warned the LCC that if it did not obtain the Council's consent for this, it saw no reason to go to the expense of erecting a new building.[22] The LCC hoped that Kodak's occupation of the site would flag Kingsway's importance but refused to grant freehold on the site. The company signed a lease for a period of ninety-nine years (the standard in London in this period).

At the cutting edge of technological innovation in its operations, Kodak appreciated the possibilities afforded by new technologies but that changes they introduced could also challenge safety concerns and regulations. Most of the mechanical equipment

---

[19]Elizabeth Brayer, *George Eastman, A Biography* (Rochester, NY: University of Rochester Press, 2006): 112.

[20]Eastman Photographic Materials Company (later Kodak Ltd.) was then headquartered (as it is presently) at Rochester, in western New York State. Its head office for London in Clerkenwell Road was designed by Arts and Crafts architect George Walton (1898), as were the Eastman Company Exhibition (1897) and Kodak shops and showrooms in London and in Europe up to 1904.

[21]Franco British Exhibition Architectural model of Kingsway and Aldwych 1908, Photograph, LCC Photograph Library Collection, London Metropolitan Archives, Collage Record no. 248258.

[22]GLC/AR/BR/17/034636/03, Burnet to Riley, 18 March 1910. W. Edward Riley was architect to the London County Council (1899–1920).

coming into use in building construction was non-existent in 1890, and while building regulations increased under the LCC's oversight to coincide with the escalating advances made in material science and building technology, regulatory measures generally lagged behind such progress.[23] Eastman knew this only too well from the buildings and factory complexes that he had already built. He appreciated that building and safety codes in London had not yet taken account of or been adjusted for advances in construction methods and materials (as with methods of steel frame and reinforced-concrete construction being used in America at the time). Furthermore, Eastman was acutely aware of the explosive and hazardous nature of nitrate film and the nervousness about it held by municipal authorities.[24] Meeting their safety requirements would be essential to Kodak's planned use and storage of film in the proposed building.

Determined to gain building permission, Eastman engaged the architect John Burnet. The Council could only have been happy with this choice. The architect du jour in London, Burnet was then extending the British Museum (for which he was knighted when it was completed in 1914). Burnet was one of the small number of British architects with French training, having studied at the École des Beaux-Arts in Paris. His friendship with Charles Follen McKim and other leading American Beaux Arts exponents took him to the United States twice, in 1896 and 1908. Inspired by ideas developed from his American observations, Burnet built distinctive early elevator office buildings in Glasgow (Atlantic Chambers and Waterloo Chambers, both 1899). Moreover, with a flourishing office in London from 1904, Burnet received council approval for the General Accident Assurance Building in Aldwych (built in 1909–1911).

Eastman, who perfected the techniques of mass production long before Henry Ford, brought them into the automobile industry, registered a shift towards greater efficiency in buildings. Eastman's credo was that a practical and workable plan was a basis for all things in connection with a good building; he expected architects to go along with what he wanted and sketched his ideas for Burnet.[25] He gave his sketches to his architects in America who drew just what he wanted and these plans were sent to Burnet for adaptation.[26] To get building approval, Eastman needed assistance from Burnet, and his principal draughtsman Thomas Tait, in Kodak's negotiations with the LCC over regulations and restrictions affecting buildings and building sites. These arose either indirectly from legislative enactments or from rights and easements which determined the extent and nature of structures that could be erected.[27] Applications for development

---

[23]'Supervision of Modern Building', *Builder* (3 April 1925): 540.

[24]In 1908, Kodak began producing the world's first commercially practical safety film using cellulose acetate base instead of unstable combustible nitrate base, which continued to be used in cinematography into the 1950s. Plans for the Kingsway building included a cinematograph theatre, which was required to comply with the strict building code specified by the Cinematograph Act 1909 (the first to regulate cinema).

[25]Brayer, *George Eastman*: 299, 303.

[26]Ibid.: 299.

[27]The Tribunal of Appeal under the London Building Act at the Surveyors' Institution heard examples of cases arising from determinations on boundaries, some of which went to the High Court. 'Tribunal of Appeal under the London Building Act', *Builder* (14 June 1912): 693–4.

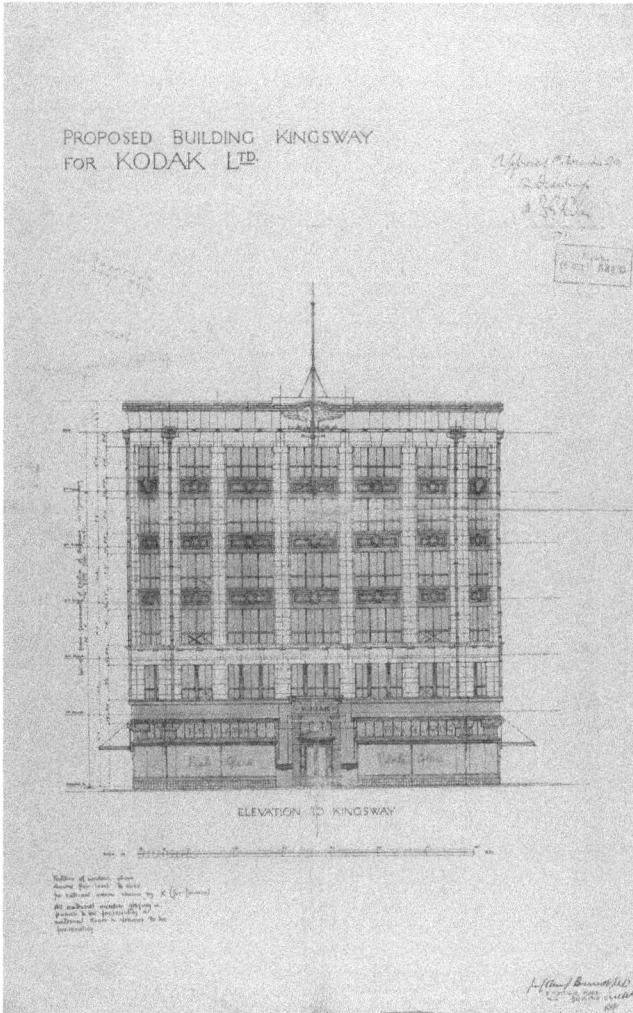

Figure 3.1 J. J. Burnet, Elevation to Kingsway, Proposed Building for Kodak Ltd., 1910, London Metropolitan Archives, from Kodak House, Building Act case file, 65 Kingsway, GLC/ AR/BR/17/034636/03

proposals were subject to the London Building Acts (from 1894). Key sections of the acts requiring particular observation were those regarding improvements (to meet height restrictions and controls of frontages on improved streets) and escape (to meet fire regulations).[28] LCC Committees responsible for these sections scrutinized drawings for a proposed building before consenting to its construction (**Figure 3.1**).[29]

---

[28]The London Building (Amendment) Act 1905 required new buildings to be equipped with means of escape from fire.

[29]Drawings were submitted to the Improvements Section of the LCC before they proceeded to the Building Act Section, from which the case would be passed to the Escape Section and then return to the Building Act Section.

Building height was limited to 80 feet to the cornice from the pavement level, plus two storeys in the roof, to a total of 100 feet unless the Council agreed to any greater height. Consent was subject to objections to the increased height from all surrounding parties within a distance of 100 yards. The site on Kingsway's west side occupied a long rearward block (with returns to Keeley Street to the south and Wyld Court to the north). It was bounded by a school playground belonging to the LCC at its rear; rooms belonging to the Grand Lodge of Freemasons and the Wesleyan Society on Wyld Court; and ground belonging to the LCC on Keeley Street. Structural safety and concerns over fire hazards and fire safety were paramount in London.[30] Hence observing fire regulations and respecting concerns over fire hazards became fundamental to the building's design. The inflammability of celluloid (with the increasing use of inflammable film) caused great concern – likewise the number of fires that occurred in premises using and housing film (as Kodak wished to do in its building).[31]

Significantly, the company wanted a functional steel-framed open-plan building, effectively a warehouse providing unobstructed floor space on each floor. However, the Council limited cubical extent (defined as the space within the external surfaces of a building's walls and roof and the upper surface of the floor of its lowest storey). Unobstructed floor space and free cubic space added greatly to the risk of fierce fire conflagrations. The LCC regulated steel-framed buildings through the (General Powers) Act 1909 (known as the 'Steel Frame Act'). Steel framework construction also permitted large windows. Burnet wanted clear plate glass in the windows of the facade to Kingsway and the building's two splayed corners on each side (with steel casements as were detailed for all the windows of the building).[32] The Council required that all the windows of Kodak's building should be of fire-resisting material in fire-resisting frames and allow access in the event of fire. Burnet and Tait modified their plans, installing leaded panes to meet the Council's approval. Other than the two shopfronts flanking the building's entrance, it permitted external windows in panes of 1 foot 5 inches wide by 4 feet 8 inches high and in squares not exceeding 16 square inches. Burnet's application for a shelter over the entrance doorway was not permitted, as the Council did not allow shelters to be erected at premises used for trade purposes.[33] Burnet and Tait adjusted their design to suit regulations regarding fire hazard, fire safety, and access required by the fire brigade.[34] Council requirements for Kingsway

---

[30]London had never forgotten the lessons of the Great Fire and thereafter remained acutely concerned about fire. The First International Fire Prevention Congress, convened in London in 1903, focused on fire suppression and fire prevention.

[31]By way of example from contemporary literature: 'The Safety of the Public – Prevention of Fires', *The British Journal of Photography* 55, no. 2536 (1908): 945. In 1915 the LCC received special powers from Parliament to vet all premises storing celluloid; it regularly cautioned shopkeepers of the dangers of celluloid and celluloid products.

[32]GLC/AR/BR/17/034636/03, Burnet to Riley, 11 April 1910. The company's office building in Rochester featured large windows.

[33]GLC/AR/BR/17/034636/03, Superintending Architects Department, 20 December 1910.

[34]As under the LCC (General Powers Act), 1908, configuring elevators and stairwells: Fletcher, *Building Acts*: 493–6.

frontages resulted in a building with Classical echoes; a main feature of the building was a central stairwell from the ground to the first floor. Classical echoes were, however, pared-down.

Kodak's building flagged that the 'New' was possible on Kingsway if even through a Council-directed Beaux-Arts prism. Pilasters on its upper floors, enclosing steel-framed glazing with cast-iron spandrel panels with bronzed electroplating, reflected the building's steel-framed structure. Kodak House was among the earliest buildings to benefit from the Steel Frame Act. The building's structural frame (that the act allowed) also enabled the building to appear with a facade that evolved from 'the construction within'. By echoing its structural frame, it honestly expressed its frame structure and the building's function. Burnet and Tait invested a utilitarian building with grace by honestly expressing its warehouse nature. This was so radically different to the elevations of many of London's office buildings that were detailed with ornate stonework or sculpture to resemble palaces. Architectural historian W. R. Lethaby and others writing to the *Times* lambasted such buildings of stale Victorian historicism and criticized them for being 'dead' architecture.[35]

Blending Classical balance (including an axial plan) with unornamented functionalism, Burnet and Tait met LCC requirements and Kodak's needs. Theirs was a modern solution offering greater light and freer-flowing space that suited growing desires for functionality in commercial buildings. Architectural critic Trystan Edwards rightly noted, 'This is a warehouse and expresses the fact unequivocally. Moreover, it has the distinction of being one of the first buildings erected in England which carried the scale of the large ground floor window opening to the storeys above.'[36] Kodak's Box Brownie was an innovative milestone: its hallmark being simplicity and functionality, it established a new mass market for photography. Likewise, Kodak's building, straightforward in design and functional, introduced a fresh note to central London. Effectively a warehouse faced in Portland stone, Kodak's building was a signpost for the future: its simplicity and functionality became the prototype for later buildings. The unornamented, streamlined facade and verticality of its pilastered and windowed front became a signature of later designs by Burnet and Tait (including Vigo House (1920–1925) and Adelaide House (1919–1925), both in London), and of Deco style in general.[37]

---

[35]*The Times* supported critics such as C. F. A. Voysey and H. V. Lanchester: 'Further Strand Improvement', *Times* (29 October 1910): 16.

[36]A. Trystan Edwards, *The Architectural Work of Sir John Burnet and Partners* (Geneva: Masters of Architecture, 1930): xiii. Edwards approved of the Kodak building's honesty, which he described as demonstrating the lofty ideal of 'Truthfulness' which he applauded. On Edwards see Neal Shasore, 'A Stammering Bundle of Welsh Idealism': Arthur Trystan Edwards and Principles of Civic Design in Interwar Britain', *Architectural History* 61 (2018): 175–203.

[37]As the prototype of countless commercial buildings of the 1920s and 1930s: David Walker, '(Sir) John James Burnet', *Dictionary of Scottish Architects*, online at scottisharchitects.org.uk.

Australia House

Key to the LCC's ambition for developing Aldwych-Kingsway were desires by the newly federated Commonwealth of Australia (1901) to build its first diplomatic mission there, on a block at the Strand's eastern end facing St Clement Danes Church.[38] From 1904, the Australian Commonwealth appreciated the attraction of this strategic Strand-Aldwych-Kingsway location, equidistant between the Bank of England and Westminster, at the junction where the boundaries of Westminster and the City met. The Commonwealth made freehold title a condition of its development of the Strand-Aldwych site; negotiations over it were protracted.[39] By 1907 more than regulatory control was concerning the LCC which faced financial problems due to its reliance on the recoupment principle. The Council concentrated on the burden of the rates calculated upon the *net capital* cost of the improvement scheme. By looking to when the surplus lands of the various improvements could be income-producing it did not consider the additional temporary charges on the rates incurred during the development period or the temporary loss of rateable value during that time. The self-reliant Council believed that civic benefits came from its retaining freehold sites because once new buildings were developed on them their rateable value increased. Only in the most exceptional circumstances would it consider parting with its freeholds on surplus lands arising from executing street improvements. Improved rateable value was estimated to be nearly four times as much as the rateable value before the improvement or an increase of over 280 per cent.[40] Yet resistance to the LCC's insistence on a higher quality of building erected in the Strand-Aldwych precinct slowed development there and what the LCC could recoup from their opening it up. This prolonged loss of rateable value strained the Council's debt charge. Moreover, this rising cost, and with it rising rate charges, burdened ratepayers who followed the progress of the Holborn to Strand scheme with the keenest interest as press reports attest. Furthermore, large outlays on street improvements and tramways over fourteen years culminated in 1906–1907 in the largest capital expenditure by the Council in any one year up to 1920, thereby increasing its net debt by 160 per cent to over £48 million (over £5 billion today).[41] As the Council itself foresaw, '[t]he great importance of Street Improvements in London is perhaps exceeded only by the difficulties attending their inception and execution'.[42] Strip cartoons by W. K. Haselden which the *Daily Mirror* featured from 1904 attacked the Council for being improvident with managing costs. Haselden's trenchant portrayal, throughout 1906, of LCC officers as the 'Bandits of Bumbledown' and as rapacious thieves grown fat at the expense of London ratepayers,

---

[38]From 1906 onwards Britain's self-governing Dominions (former colonies) assumed greater responsibility and independence over their own affairs.
[39]Chanin, *Capital Designs*: 49–50, 128, 161ff.
[40]Haward, *County Council*: 256.
[41]Ibid.: 185.
[42]Edwards, *Street Improvements*: 2.

hit home. The Strand's easternmost block that the Australians eyed earned the greatest ire from Haselden because, despite its prominent position, it lay unimproved and vacant since 1900 when improvement of the Strand began.

The LCC was directly elected by the people of London and the County Council elections of March 1907 were fought over Council finances. The Council's rapidly growing capital expenditure and commitment to costly schemes, such as for electricity and tramways, cost the Progressive Party their seats (which they had held from 1889), and overwhelmingly swept into Council the more conservative Municipal Reform Party. Intent upon keeping rate-borne expenditure down, they held power into 1934. But in 1908, Aldwych (as one observer put it) was 'a vast solitude and Kingsway a mere track for racing motor cars'.[43] Ultimately it became clear that Australia's desire to build on the LCC's prized Strand-Aldwych site matched the Council's need to balance its financial position. In 1907, the Commonwealth of Australia's State of Victoria had leased part of the LCC's wedge-shaped horn of land that the Commonwealth wanted at the Strand's eastern end. The Government of Victoria built a steel-framed elevator building facing the Strand at the corner of what came to be called Melbourne Place. Opened in 1909, Victoria House stood on a narrow template but the six-storey building was equipped with the latest facilities to serve as Victoria's display and information centre.[44] To be a hub for Victoria's interests it was also to be the southwest corner of a larger Commonwealth building intended to extend opposite St Clement Danes. In 1912, Sir George Reid, Australia's first High Commissioner to London (1910–1915), engaging the rhetoric of the day that called for making London the City of Empire, persuaded the Council to relinquish the freehold on the easternmost point of the Strand with his argument that Australia would erect a Grand Hall of Empire in the proposed Commonwealth building if it was built there.[45]

Given the delayed development on Aldwych and associated rising debt charges, the LCC relinquished its freehold on the block in 1912, anticipating that the Australian building would expedite development of other unoccupied sites in the neighbourhood. It was in any case under statutory obligation to sell improved surplus lands by October 1929 to repay part of the debt arising from their improvement. In loans raised for these improvements, the value of surplus lands was set off as an asset against the gross debt incurred. A municipal loan, for whatever purpose, should be repaid usually in not more than sixty years.[46] Improved property was expected to pay part of the debt arising from the improvement, to avoid burdening the ratepayer. Concern in London regarding LCC

---

[43]Hanslip Fletcher, *London Passed and Passing, a Pictorial Record of Destroyed and Threatened* Buildings (London: Sir Isaac Pitman & Sons, 1909): 195.

[44]Chanin, *Capital Designs*: 124; on the building generally: 117–27.

[45]Changes of government in Australia delayed Commonwealth Government action to build in London until a Federal Labor Government gained a majority in April 1910. It steered through Federal Parliament the High Commissioners Act, enabling the Commonwealth to proceed with its building plans in London.

[46]Northumberland Avenue (1873–1876) was the only important scheme of street improvement which showed a net profit to ratepayers (of just under £120,000). Haward, *County Council*: 159. Edwards, *Street Improvements*: 58.

debt and its costs partly explains why Australia House was so heartily welcomed upon its completion, when its addition to Aldwych offered the LCC the ability to recover some of its costs from regenerating the precinct. Construction on Australia House began in 1913 and progressed slowly through the war. In 1918, Australia House opened (and absorbed Victoria House). Once built, its scale and grandeur signalled the centrality of its Aldwych precinct (near Fleet Street and the Law Courts). Australia House, by so defining the still largely vacant Aldwych zone, anchored the area's subsequent development (**Figure 3.2**).

Considerations of civic manners dictated that anything built on the Commonwealth's block should be in the Classical style by virtue of its proximity to Somerset House, an unsurpassed example of classic architecture in London. Treatment harmonious with it was a Council condition for developing the easternmost Strand-Aldwych corner.[47] Planning law, including height restrictions, was one thing; respect for past structures was another.[48] The literature of the day abounds with concern about this 'etiquette' of

Figure 3.2 Australia House, Victory March (3 May 1919), J. Beagles & Co. London, National Library of Australia, PIC Box PIC/7963 #PIC/7963/5

---

[47]Chanin, *Capital Designs*: 174. The LCC insisted that buildings erected on the north side of the Strand should be faced in Portland stone, in a style that was Palladian or classical, in keeping with the Italianate Somerset House. Pressure to observe this was directed to the Council in the press. Examples include 'Aldwych and the Strand', Letters to the Editor, *Times* (28 December 1905): 9; 'Strand Improvement', *Builder* (21 January 1905): 56.

[48]Andrea Zemgulys, 'Building the Vanished City: Conservationism in Turn-of-the-Century London', *Nineteenth-Century Prose* 35, no. 1 (Spring 1999): 35–54. Growing interest taken in conserving historical monuments and spaces was an aspect of renovating old city areas that emerged at the turn of the century and into the early twentieth century in all large centres.

street urbanity that architectural critic Trystan Edwards insisted was essential. Edwards propagated in his critical texts, including his best-known work, *Good and Bad Manners in Architecture* (1924), that buildings should 'mind their manners' and be respectful of each other and of their own place on the street.[49] To maintain good manners, buildings must show courtesy and deference to one another; principal public buildings require formal pre-eminence.

This suited the Commonwealth's desire to build impressively. Its international competition for the new capital city of Canberra (1911–1912) demonstrated its robust approach to urban design.[50] As did cities such as Melbourne and Sydney, which grew rapidly and underwent urban renewal at the turn of the century. Principal Commonwealth government buildings in Australia were erected in classical style. Like the new Navy which it was building at the time, the Commonwealth wanted its free-standing building to express the promise of Australia.[51] Aspiring to create a fitting symbol of its nationhood, the Commonwealth insisted on building as it wished (while being prepared to accommodate LCC regulations). It engaged Scottish Architects A. Marshall Mackenzie & Son whose experience amply qualified them for the task in London.[52] The Commonwealth Government architect John Smith Murdoch oversaw the Mackenzies' plans; he shared their classical disposition having trained under Mackenzie before migrating to Australia. Their collaboration exemplifies the interrelationships that connected the British world as part of its entwined history, let alone the 'invisible factors' (such as trust and respect) that were underlying in professional networks.[53] Styled in majestic Beaux Arts manner with a beaux-arts axial plan, the building's Francophile character was dressed with Roman-Doric columns and sculptural flourishes that typified prestigious Edwardian buildings. Its Classicism bordered the Strand's eastern end fittingly (for the LCC's purposes). It balanced counterparts erected at the island's western end: the reconstructed Gaiety Theatre complex, which the LCC had reconstructed fifteen years earlier (1903) as the 'gateway' to their Strand-Holborn regeneration; and the French-derived *Morning Post* Building (1907) facing it.

In other respects, Australia House was a modern structure. It was also among the earliest of the steel-framed buildings designed in accordance with the LCC's

---

[49]Neal Shasore, 'Conversations with Buildings', *Architectural Review* 235 (April 2014): 4, 120–1.

[50]The international competition was awarded to Walter Burley Griffin, who trained under Frank Lloyd Wright.

[51]The naval forces of the six Australian colonies were amalgamated upon their federation. The Australian government decided to establish a Commonwealth naval force for local defence that would also be capable of forming a fleet unit within the imperial naval forces. The Royal Australian Navy was formed in July 1911.

[52]Mackenzie built Aldwych's Waldorf Hotel (1908) in Grand Manner. His son, Alexander Mackenzie, had worked in Paris with the internationally successful Beaux Arts exponent René Sergent who designed for the financial elite of the Progressive Era on both sides of the Atlantic.

[53]G. A. Bremner, 'The Expansion of England? Rethinking Scotland's Place in the Architectural History of the Wider British World', *Journal of Art Historiography* 18 (2018): 1–18. Julie Willis, 'Architectural Movements: Journeys of an Inter-Colonial Profession', *Fabrications: Networks and Flows* 26, no. 2 (2016): 158–79. On how shared architectural expertise made the British world legible and bound the empire together: Daniel Maudlin, 'Beginnings: Early Colonial Architecture', in G. A. Bremner (ed.), *Architecture and Urbanism in the British Empire* (Oxford: Oxford University Press, 2015): 22. Kelly, *Anonymity*: 6.

Steel Frame Act (1909). Large steel spans tapered its eastern frontage and enabled its grand hall space.[54] Its services, offering the latest functional features (lifts, heating, communication networks, mechanical and electrical equipment), contrasted with the deficiencies of government offices in Whitehall.[55] Its central atrium and staircase of white Australian Angaston marble offered the building an airiness that matched Australian sense of 'limitless' space in the nation's vast continent. From its opening, the building was an 'open house' serving Australians in London; its open access reflected the egalitarian nature of Australia's society. Australian servicemen met their king (George V) at its opening, were served by their government's Commonwealth Bank in a branch of the bank that was installed in the building to meet their needs and manned the exhibition of war relics displayed in the Hall in 1918. Into the 1920s, the building's basement theatre regularly served as a popular public dance hall. Shops related to Australian interests were part of its ground-level frontage on the Strand. If styled with a majesty befitting a chancery, this democratization of space (so unlike government buildings elsewhere in London that did not offer such commercial or cultural services) signalled a multipurpose use of buildings that at the time was already being more commonly experienced across the Atlantic.[56] Australia's wealth of resources made it a vital Imperial partner. In demonstrating this abundance, the building's monumentality and rich furnishing made it an unparalleled standing advertisement for Australia. Its marble-clad 'Hall of Empire' served commercial purposes; it stemmed from trade displays that up to then were generally presented at World Exhibitions, like the Franco-British Exhibition where London's own 'White City' rose at Shepherd's Bush (emulating that of the Chicago World's Fair of 1893). In 1909, Victoria House was the first government building to exhibit such displays in central London, and Australia House displayed Australian products in its grand exhibition hall, thus bringing Empire products to the Strand.

As London's first purpose-built Dominion building, it contributed significantly to pre-war visions of a reconstructed New (and Imperial) London. For in ensuing years, other Dominions followed Australia's example in opening this new kind of building (the Dominion House) nearby. And, just as Sir Laurence Gomme read Australia House, the landmark High Commission buildings came to signify that London could at last claim that it was 'the Empire City'.[57]

---

[54]On structural and design decisions in the building: Chanin, *Capital Designs*: 209–10.

[55]Michael Port spells out these deficiencies: *Imperial London*: 42–51.

[56]When Australia House opened it was comparable to Cass Gilbert's Woolworth Building (1913), with shops and services for its occupants and the richness of materials used in its detailing (such as veined marbles). Gail Fenske, *The Skyscraper and the City The Woolworth Building and the Making of Modern New York* (Chicago: The University of Chicago Press, 2008).

[57]Laurence Gomme, 'Australia and the Island Site, Aldwych', *Builder* (29 December 1911): 357. Gomme was Clerk to the London County Council (1900–1914). In the order of their opening in London, following Australian example, were the High Commission buildings for Canada (1925), India (1930), and South Africa (1933). The government of New Zealand leased smaller premises on the Strand from 1916; in 1963, it built New Zealand House, a tower block at Haymarket.

Bush House, Central Block

Much had been learned during the war about improving supply lines in order to support the war effort. The lessons learned could lead to greater efficiencies in methods of distribution to meet post-war needs including shortages.[58] American transportation magnate Irving T. Bush was acutely aware of improving distribution channels. As the Executive Officer of the Port of New York (1917–1919), Bush oversaw the despatch of American troops and supplies across the Atlantic. At war's end Bush predicted an era of prosperity ahead. 'We all know that there were many conditions before the war which were sadly in need of reform,' he said in 1919. 'Out of it all progress is being made every day. It is difficult to recognise it day by day, but as we look back it will loom large.'[59] Bush eyed the start of a new era in world trade.[60] Expecting commercial recovery more rapidly than generally anticipated, and to take advantage of pent-up consumption demands as the British economy returned to a peacetime footing, Bush looked to expand in London. He sought to amplify export opportunity for the near 800 companies engaged in the cooperative sales idea that he recently established in Bush Terminal Sales Building, New York (also known as Bush Terminal Tower) (1918). This was an early skyscraper of thirty storeys erected at 130 West 42nd Street, a few steps east of Broadway. The soaring Trade Centre, billed as an 'International Buyers Club', dominated its West Forty-second street district.[61] Bush Terminal City (1892–1925) was his Company's shipping and warehousing service at Brooklyn. A vast warehousing and distribution facility, covering 200 acres at its peak, the ambition of its operations was captured in the title Irving Bush gave to his book, *Working with the World* (1928). Both gave examples of American capacity for technological superiority and organizational capabilities which American investors like Bush brought to Europe post-war.[62]

Bush, as president of the Bush Terminal Buildings Company of New York, leased the Council's valuable Aldwych site for ninety-nine years at a ground rent of £55,000 a year (£2.58 million today, then believed to be the largest ground rent for any property in London).[63] There he built a prominent eponymous complex of distinct buildings. First to be built was the Central Block, eight storeys high, which opened in 1925. Two contiguous buildings, extending east and west, were subsequently constructed in stages over several years (**Figure 3.3**). Detailed drawings for the design for the western wing were prepared in 1927 and for the east wing in 1930. Both were built in sections, with their northern

---

[58]Charles F. G. Masterman, *England after War, a Study* (London: Hodder & Stoughton, 1922): 24–5. Masterman considered one of the greatest benefits of the war was the interaction made by Britons of the British Isles with those from Greater Britain, as from Australia and India.

[59]'I. T. Bush predicts era of prosperity', *New York Times* (20 July 1919): 23.

[60]*Bush Terminal Sales Building* [Prospectus] (New York: William Green, 1918): 2.

[62]Tom Nicholas, 'Enterprise and Management' in Floud, *Cambridge Economic* History: 239.

[61]Ibid., 12. It also housed the offices of its New York architects Helme & Corbett.

[63]'Our London Correspondent, a Government Wing in Bush House', *Manchester Guardian* (7 September 1934): 8; Haward, *County Council*: 256.

74

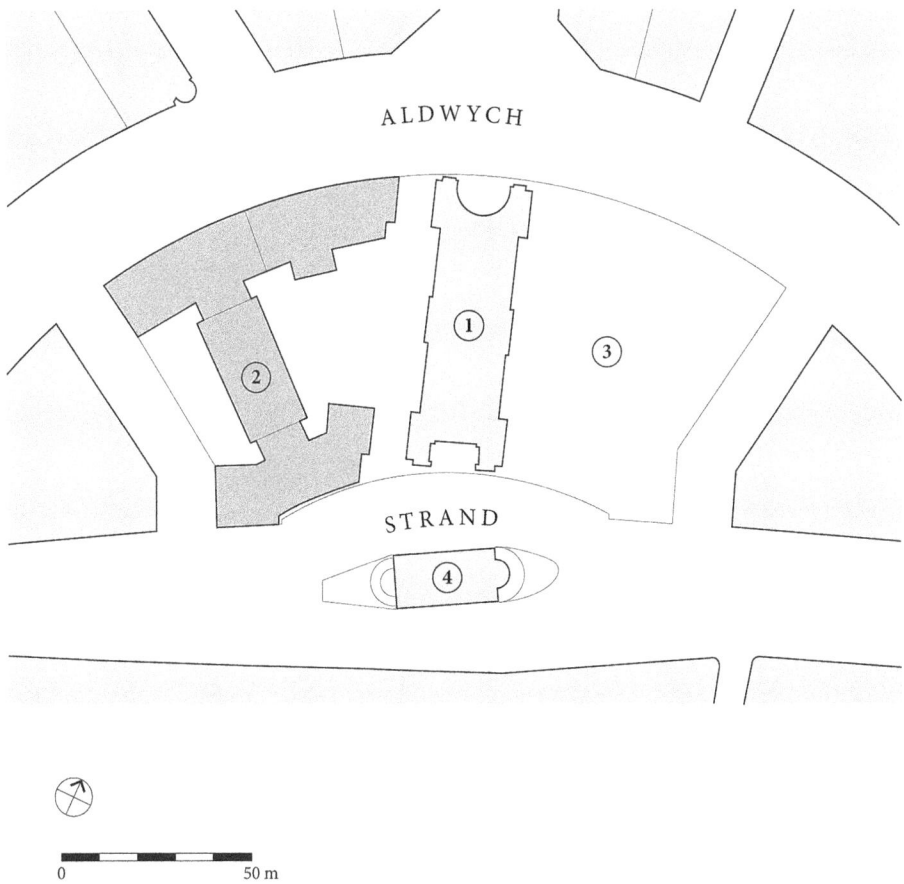

1 Bush House Central Block
2 Bush House Proposed Western Development
3 Bush House Future Eastern Development
4 St Mary-Le-Strand

Figure 3.3 Site plan of the Aldwych including Bush House, drawn by Hannah Towler

sections (facing Aldwych) erected ahead of their southern sections (facing the Strand). The entire complex occupied 500,000 square feet (the size of eight football fields or five times as big as a Manhattan city block) when completed in 1935. Not only did the Bush Company's motto 'Efficiency and Economy through Cooperation' attract the cost-conscious Council, but Bush House's Central Block (known as the Bush Sales Building and modelled on New York's Bush Terminal Tower) was purposely designed to extend the distribution of manufactured products. Its construction on Aldwych-Strand suited the LCC's aspiration that central London's streetscape reflected the city's standing as the commercial centre of the Empire. Moreover, growing concerns were held in Britain before the war over its declining productivity relative to competitors like Germany and

America.[64] The influential weekly *The Builder* featured articles on building in America following the appointment of its new editor Herbert Wills (1913). Wills had worked in New York with McKim, Mead, & White and appreciated the relative importance of American contemporary constructional advances. In 1925, the LCC sent their chief architect, G. Topham Forrest (1919–1935), known for his interest in skyscrapers, to the United States to investigate and report on the construction and regulatory control of buildings in the metropolitan centres of the Eastern States.[65]

For Bush, the LCC's site offered a unique real estate opportunity during the chaos of immediate post-war Reconstruction, a time of uncertainty and hesitation as Britain's war-time controls relaxed spasmodically. Bush was intent on building rapidly due to the costly site, soaring prices and high wages. Between December 1919 and April 1920, New York architects Helmle and Corbett submitted blueprint plans to the LCC for the first building – a single eight-storeyed building of approximately 110,000 square feet facing the centre line of Kingsway and the Strand. In July, Harvey Corbett, the influential skyscraper designer responsible for New York's vertically expressive Bush Terminal Tower, was in London to negotiate construction for Bush's building. Excavation began in 1921, the new building's steel frame reached its fourth floor level that July. The LCC was criticized for its failure to impose harmony on Kingsway. On Aldwych it required that the Classicism of adjacent Australia House be respected. Corbett trained at the École des Beaux-Arts, but he searched for a modern manner free of historical allusion, championed modern requirements for air, light and utility, and studied and imagined the future city. Bush's company wanted its building to operate as a hub: a meeting place for merchants; an information and educational centre for buyers; and a distribution centre for London. It served as a sophisticated sales and trading building by presenting selected merchandise in a physical 'network' of specially displayed showrooms. The complex's scale heralded the ascendancy of the business centre in the city landscape and anticipated the future in which specialized salespeople and service industries grow the city.

Bush House Central Block was erected amidst debate over increased building height in London; letters to the *Times* argued that height limits and zoning needed review. In response, a County Hall spokesman viewed skyscrapers as inappropriate for London owing to the respect held for London's historical buildings and the traditions surrounding them. As Bush House went up he stated, 'We hope to erect in London a building which will not only be useful, but from the viewpoint of architectural beauty and sympathy with the surroundings, will be a credit both to London and to our enterprise.'[66] Corbett agreed. In his opinion as a qualified engineer, building on London's clay bed made it structurally impossible to build beyond up to 150 feet; besides, streets darkened by higher

---

[64]Literature of this period is replete with concerns about Britain's competitive complacency. Today the story of the long interwar period (including after the Second World War) is regarded as the story of Britain's loss of economic pre-eminence, and historians study how this transformation came about.

[65]G. Topham Forrest, *Report by G. Topham Forrest, the Architect to the Council, on the Construction and Control of Buildings and the Development of Urban Areas in the United States of America* (London: London County Council, 1925).

[66]'Higher Buildings for London', *Times* (14 January 1920): 8.

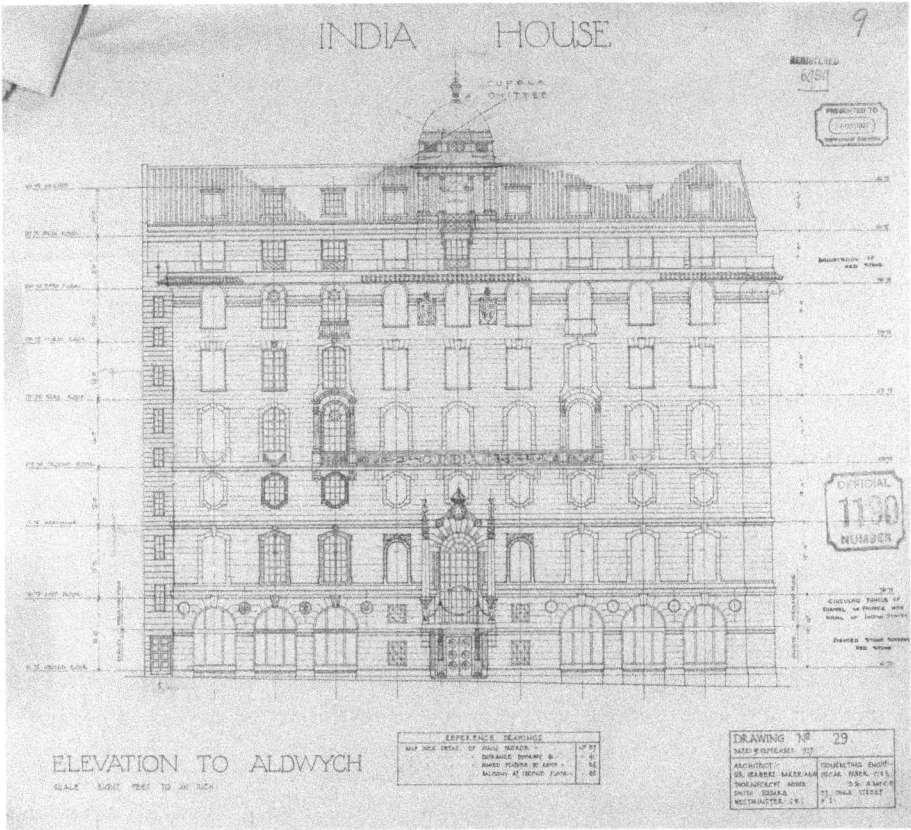

Figure 3.4 Sir Herbert Baker, Elevation to Aldwych, India House, 1927, London Metropolitan Archives, with permission from the Baker Family, LCC/VA/DD/R/633

elevations would rob London of its quaint old-fashioned atmosphere.[67] Strand-side proximity to the street's early eighteenth-century church St Mary-le-Strand and Fire Brigade limitations dictated Bush House's height: the final graduated setback of its roof line rose no more than 120 feet high at its centre (**Figure 3.4**).

Working with local architect H. Rogers Houchin, Corbett aimed to make Bush House an architectural success, worthy of becoming the keystone to Kingsway and centre point of Aldwych's south side (such as the LCC had long envisaged). The building gave a grand aspect looking south from Kingsway by virtue of its Classical references. Two 12-feet-high Classical male figures, cut from Indiana limestone by sculptor Malvina Hoffmann, stand above its entrance, in the centre of a recessed arch supported by Corinthian columns in its portico. One representing the United States, the other Great Britain, they clasp the torch of progress and pledge friendship over an altar. The pair represent an

---

[67]"Higher Buildings for London. Mr Harvey Corbett's Views', *The Journal of the Society of Architects* 15, no. 6 (April 1922): 162.

English-speaking Union which optimists like Irving Bush hoped, in the euphoria of post-war reconstruction, 'may be a vital force in the world for its good'.[68] Longitudinal section drawings for the building detail neoclassical decorative elements for its interiors. Fluted columns figured with Corinthian tops belie the industrial progressiveness of Bush's operations but also indicate the continuity of the classical tradition in terms of design features that would linger in British architecture through the 1930s. The building's interior was styled with elements like classical urns and timber panelling, as might be expected in a gentleman's club. Such familiar period features undoubtedly reassured customers in the discomforting post-war years, when Britain's economy was slow to recover. Bush Sales Building, by its self-assured neoclassical emphasis, combined tradition in its design and novelty in its purpose; doing so, it linked pre- and post-war directions in London's built form with self-assured aplomb.

India House

Britain emerged from the war with greatly extended imperial possessions. In hindsight, 1918 is the high noon of the empire; although this was less clear to many British associations at the time. They relied heavily on the security of the empire through the 1920s and 1930s, clinging to continuities while Britain's empire was unravelling against the backdrop of world events in an irrevocably changed world. Old-style imperialists were confident of the Second British Empire's future, as more than 2.5 million men from the empire fought for Britain. Hence, they wanted to invest central London with Imperial character (overlooking reforms that fundamentally restructured the empire). They favoured the European classical tradition of architecture as the 'order of the day', to impart continuities. Yet how valid was European Classicism, projecting Imperial power and permanence, during transformation from empire to Commonwealth? Giving symbolic meaning to architecture that served political purpose became problematic as audiences developed different readings of Empire in a dysfunctional Imperial system during post-war decolonization. Constructing London premises for the Indian High Commission – founded in 1919, as part of initial steps towards Indian independence – highlighted this dilemma. The task of constructing India House was given to Sir Herbert Baker, the foremost architect of empire. Schooled under Cecil Rhodes and Alfred, Lord Milner, Baker designed Pretoria's Government House (1906) and Union buildings (1913); Government House, Nairobi (1925); and the Secretariat blocks, New Delhi (1913–1927), which were modelled in part on Wren's design for the Royal Naval College at Greenwich.

Baker adhered to the European classical tradition and also believed that architecture should have symbolic purpose. He aimed 'to give architectural expression to a common dignity and distinction in the instrument of government as a united whole'.[69] For him,

---

[68]'Balfour Unveils Bush House Statue', *New York Times* (5 July 1925): 5.
[69]Herbert Baker, 'The New Delhi: Eastern and Western Architecture: A Problem of Style', *Times* (3 October 1912): 7–8.

architectural Classicism represented law, order and government, and thus the principles of classical architecture embodied the ideals of the British Empire.[70] The tradition of Palladian style for civic buildings, by expressing the qualities of law, order and government, symbolized the reach and authority of the British Empire, and allowed the spirit of British sovereignty to be stamped in stone and bronze.

India House stands on Aldwych on the north-western corner of Bush House's west wing (1928). The case for India House passed to the Improvements Section of the LCC at the end of December 1926.[71] Case files and drawings dating from late 1926 to 1929 allow us to follow the progress made in the building's development and design. They show, for example, how resolution was reached over the difficult crescent site. The building's outline reflects its awkward location with the curve of Aldwych on its north side, lower levels on its south Strand side, the throughway of Montreal Place to its west, and the north-west wing (1928) of Bush House at its eastern abutment. Its frontage of about 130 feet faces the Aldwych. It has a return frontage of about 100 feet on Montreal Place, and its depth to the back of the building towards the Strand is 236 feet. It covers about 12,400 square feet.

In South Africa and India, Baker projected Imperial power by making his neoclassical buildings interact theatrically with the dramatic South African landscape and sweeping scale of New Delhi. By comparison, Aldwych was a cramped site without the scale or drama of South African and Indian settings. Baker worked with Alexander Thomson Scott, Baker's chief assistant from 1922, and consulting structural engineer Oscar Faber. A leading British authority on cement, Faber, co-founded the Concrete Institute (1908), a body devoted to construction in reinforced concrete and a forerunner of the Institution of Structural Engineers.[72] Faber's expertise reflected the technical knowledge which architects were now required to draw on.[73] Baker sought approval for plans for a building on twelve floors. These initial plans evoked Baker's Secretariat Buildings in New Delhi: overall Baker's Aldwych design was a smaller variant of this.[74] Initially, progress was relatively swift. The Building Acts Committee approved twenty drawings.[75]

However, constraining issues included those of height, load-bearing and access (fire) regulations. Height restrictions influenced the building's Aldwych elevation. Planned to be 84 feet high, the LCC insisted on a maximum height of 80 feet above the pavement level to make the building's cornice level with that of Bush House. Consequently, the line of the building's facade, following the curve of Aldwych, is of the same height

---

[70]Ibid.

[71]GLC/AR/BR/06/058956, 31 December 1926.

[72]A champion of reinforced concrete, Faber disseminated technical knowledge for collective advantage in the bimonthly journal *Concrete & Constructional Engineering* (published from 1906) and co-edited the *Concrete Yearbook* from its start in 1924.

[73]Baker and Faber worked together on the Barclays Bank Building, Cape Town (1927–34).

[74]Thomas Metcalf, 'Architecture and Empire (Sir Herbert Baker's Work as Contrasted with That of Edwin Lutyens)', *History Today* 30, no. 12 (1980): 7.

[75]With a facade punctuated by a series of differently shaped windows, a cupola rather than a dome, and a much smaller front doorway: GLC/AR/BR/06/058956, 8 November 1927.

as the adjacent wing of Bush House. Further constraint came from by-laws for the regulation of lamps, signs or other structures overhanging the Public Way, which also reflected the Council's desire for uniformity in elevations. Here, public opinion too bore upon the Council's rule book, with which Baker would have to contend. Large advertising hoardings surrounding the LCC's Strand island site provoked the ire of the public. Citizens urged that outdoor advertising be regulated in order to check visual offence. Following on from the Regulation of Advertisements Act, 1907, public outcry mounted in the 1920s over flagrant outdoor advertising that continued to disfigure the city environment. Support grew for the Advertisement Regulation Bill with its second reading in the House of Lords in March 1925; public opinion was increasingly more clamorous about minimizing representation on street frontages.[76]

Baker sought to express the Indian vernacular on the building's elevation: initial plans drew a cupola at the building's top (to conceal its lift gear room 9 feet above the roof level). The cupola was minimized and then omitted from subsequent drawings submitted to the LCC (**Figure 3.4**).[77] And, in mid-1928, when applying for permission to erect balconies to overhang the public footway, Scott was required to revise the dimensions figured on earlier drawings. Orientalist motifs that Baker proposed for India House's facade ultimately became more discreet than he planned because public distaste for representation on buildings restrained Baker from achieving a more elaborately figured exterior for the building. Council consented to four shallow balconies on the building's facade and a central projection over its main entrance.[78] It is flanked by a pair of slender granite columns, surmounted by seated lions sculpted in stone with elephants' heads for plinths, under an emblematic shield bearing the Star of India crested with a crown. A frieze bearing Hindustani characters carved in bold relief above the entrance named the building. Open work balustrading and ornamental carving about the windows further ornament the facade. Coloured stone medallions representing the arms of Indian Provinces appear in the spandrels of the arched openings of the basement story.

With plans approved, the Secretary of State for India in Council took up the lease on the site. *The Times* published notice of construction on 7 January 1928 (a Council requirement).[79] As was standard practice, work on the building was required to commence within six months and to be completed within eighteen months. Copies of the approved plans were deposited with the district surveyor to ensure that construction conformed

---

[76]'Lord Newton's Bill', *Builder* (13 March 1925): 409. The contemporary press featured frequent complaints about the damage being done to the urban environment by advertising. Billposters were regarded as visual pollution. Over 300 London architects petitioned the LCC to address the grievances of many with respect to advertising disfigurement: Richardson Evans, 'Advertising Disfigurement', *Westminster Review* 151, no. 3 (1899): 244–58. See the journal of the Scapa Society for the Prevention of Disfigurement in Town and Country: Society Checking the Abuses in Public Advertising, *A Beautiful World. The Journal of the Society for Checking the Abuses of Public Advertising* (London: Society for Checking the Abuses of Public Advertising, 1893–1922).
[77]GLC/AR/BR/06/058956, Drawing 29, 19 September 1927.
[78]GLC/AR/BR/06/058956, Superintending Architect's Report, September 1928.
[79]'Shipping', *Times* (7 January 1928): 2.

to regulations. Building operations could then begin immediately. This was thought to be essential; relations between Britain and India were increasingly strained, with India fast moving towards home rule.[80] India House opened in July 1930, in the presence of His Majesty the King-Emperor. Press reports described this 'Empire House', the second Dominion House on Aldwych, as putting the finishing touch to the LCC's Aldwych Project. Today, it is recognized as a 'London House' in that it was built in keeping with the London Building Act under the aegis of the LCC and their improvement plans for Aldwych-Kingsway.[81]

Conclusion

Visions held of a revived central London, before the war and following it, hinged on the empty spaces of Strand-Aldwych-Kingsway which the London County Council had levelled to develop. Buildings to go up there were seen as a means of improving the urban environment and also celebrating the city's unrivalled political and economic status. The war arrested development there, which was resumed in war's aftermath. Ambitions held by its progressive founders at the Council's formation imparted a high tone to the Council's administration that never left it; this in turn stamped the buildings which it consented to being built in Strand-Aldwych-Kingsway.[82] The LCC reimagined the area with buildings that would reflect London's importance in global trade and capital finance and that would convey civic dignity and Imperial dynamism. Architects' ambitions feature less prominently throughout the reconstruction of this central precinct when Council rule books determined what could be built. As seen with each of the four prominent buildings erected there, the agenda of the client, the idea of the architect (or several of them, besides engineers and other consultants) and the requirements of regulatory authorities (including the LCC and London Fire Brigade) interacted to shape a design. So too did geopolitical influences that inspired how these buildings were conceived and constructed, used and seen.

While at first London seemed relatively unscathed in 1918, it became clear through the years following it that the world and architecture were irrevocably changed. Before the war, Kodak House set the architectural standard for Aldwych-Kingsway. It met the LCC's desire for buildings that expressed Beaux Arts Classicism yet its simplified facade also introduced a fresh note of modernity to the neighbourhood. Its multipurpose use (as a distribution warehouse, marketing office, film processing laboratory, shop, cinema) set a pattern; overall, it flagged how commercial buildings could be functional while rational, spacious and elegant. Australia House took this development further, and

---

[80]The Simon Commission (1928) culminated in the Government of India Act of 1935.

[81]Simon Bradley and Nikolaus Pevsner, *London 6 Westminster* (New Haven, CT: Yale University Press, 2003), 330.

[82]Haward, *County Council*: 421.

its scale and detailing injected a grandeur to the eastern Strand that set the tone for the precinct. Australia's High Commission building asserted Australia's pride in its nationhood, while the Council read Australia House as signifying that London was the imperial capital. The opening of the winged extensions to the Bush Sales Building completed the Council's scheme for improving central London in 1935. The commercial practicality of Bush House heralded future building use. Press reports saw its winged extensions as the capstone to Kingsway, representing London's latest accomplishment in modern street design, 'expressive of the finest modern ideals'.[83] LCC officers then could satisfy themselves that the buildings erected under the Council's watch by the government of Australia and for the Indian High Commission, and American companies Eastman Kodak and Bush Terminals Buildings Company achieved the Council's urban ideal. Each building offers a snapshot of some of the issues and interactions that were at play, including how inextricable were the local and the global influences that shaped them, during the years surrounding the war. None more so than India House. By the time it was erected as a visible representation of the imperial idea, the empire was unravelling with Britain on the path to the decolonization that evolved over the ensuing decades. Still, although London lost its pre-eminence as global hub, these four landmark buildings, if only a part of London's ongoing rebuilding, were emblematic of the New London that was constructed at the time. Together these buildings and the Strand-Aldwych-Kingsway where they stand, and which they modernized, read as a document in the history of a time of great change.

Bibliography

Primary

Archival Sources
London Metropolitan Archives

Grey Literature
Bush Terminal Sales Building [Prospectus], New York, William Green, 1918.

Newspapers and Periodicals
The Builder (London)
The Financial Times
Manchester Guardian
The New York Times (1857–1922)
SCAPA (London) (1893–1922)
The Times

---

[83]'Rebuilding London', *Financial Times* (4 July 1927): 5.

Secondary

Websites

Powers, Alan. 'Part One: British Architecture before the Great War'. *The Architectural Review* (11 November 2014) online at architectural-review.com/places/united-kingdom/part-one-british-architecture-before-the-great-war (accessed 8 February 2019).

Powers, Alan. 'Part Two: British Architecture before the Great War'. *The Architectural Review* (30 December 2014) online at architectural-review.com/today/part-tw0-british-architecture-after-the-great-war (accessed 8 February 2019).

Walker, David. '(Sir) John James Burnet'. Dictionary of Scottish architects 1660–1980 (DSA), online at scottisharchitects.org.uk/architect_full.php?id+200088 (accessed 18 February 2020).

Articles

Bremner, G. A. 'The Expansion of England? Rethinking Scotland's Place in the Architectural History of the Wider British World'. *Journal of Art Historiography* 18 (2018): 1–18.

Gilbert, David. 'London of the Future: The Metropolis Reimagined after the Great War'. *Journal of British Studies* 43, no. 1 (January 2004): 91–119.

Kelly, Jessica. 'Anonymity and Hidden Mechanisms in Design and Architecture'. *Architecture and Culture* 6, no. 1 (2018): 5–15.

Metcalf, Thomas. 'Architecture and Empire (Sir Herbert Baker's Work as Contrasted with That of Edwin Lutyens)'. *History Today* 30, no. 12 (1980): 7.

Rooney, David. 'Visualization, Decentralization and Metropolitan Improvement: "Light-and-Air" and London County Council Photographs, 1899–1908'. *Urban History* 40, no. 3 (2013): 462–82.

Schubert, Dirk and Anthony Sutcliffe. 'The "Haussmannization" of London?: The Planning and Construction of Kings way-Aldwych, 1889–1935'. *Planning Perspectives* 11, no. 2 (1996): 115–44.

Shasore, N. E. "A Stammering Bundle of Welsh Idealism': Arthur Trystan Edwards and Principles of Civic Design in Interwar Britain'. *Architectural History* 61 (2018): 175–203.

Stromquist, Shelton. 'Thinking Globally, Acting Locally': Municipal Labour and Socialist Activism in Comparative Perspective, 1890–1920'. *Labour History Review* 74, no. 3 (2009): 233–56.

Wagenaar, Michiel. 'Townscapes of Power'. *GeoJournal* (May 2000): 3–13.

Willis, Julie. 'Architectural Movements: Journeys of an Inter-Colonial Profession'. *Fabrications: Networks and Flows* 26, no. 2 (2016): 158–79.

Zemgulys, Andrea. 'Building the Vanished City: Conservationism in Turn-of-the-Century London'. *Nineteenth-Century Prose* 35, no. 1 (1999): 35–54.

Chapters in Edited Volumes

Alterman, Rachelle. 'Land Use Regulations and Property Values: The "Windfalls Capture" Idea Revisited'. In *The Oxford Handbook of Urban Economics and Planning*, edited by NancyBrooks, Kieran Donaghy, Gerrit-Jan Knaap, 755–86. Oxford: Oxford University Press.

Baines, Dudley, and Robert Woods. 'Population and Regional Development'. In *The Cambridge Economic History of Modern Britain. Volume 2: Economic Maturity 1860–1939*, edited by Roderick Floud and Paul Johnson, 25–55. Cambridge: Cambridge University Press.

Eichengreen, Barry. 'The British Economy between the Wars'. In *The Cambridge Economic History of Modern Britain. Volume 2: Economic maturity 1860–1939*, edited by Roderick Floud and Paul Johnson, 314–43. Cambridge: Cambridge University Press.

Goebel, Stefan. 'Cities'. In *The Cambridge History of the First World War, vol. 2 The State*, edited by Jay Winter, 358–81. Cambridge: Cambridge University Press.

Maudlin, Daniel. 'Beginnings: Early Colonial Architecture'. In *Architecture and Urbanism in the British Empire*, edited by G. A. Bremner, 19–50. Oxford: Oxford University Press.

Nicholas, Tom. 'Enterprise and Management'. In *The Cambridge Economic History of Modern Britain. Volume 2: Economic Maturity 1860-1939* edited by Roderick Floud and Paul Johnson, 227–52. Cambridge: Cambridge University Press.

Books

Brayer, Elizabeth. *George Eastman, A Biography*. Rochester, NY: University of Rochester Press, 2006.

Bush, Irving T. *Working with the World*. New York: Doubleday, Doran & Co., 1928.

Chanin, Eileen. *Capital Designs, Australia House and Visions of an Imperial London*. Melbourne: Australian Scholarly Publishing, 2018.

Clunn, Harold P. *London Rebuilt, 1897-1927: An Attempt to Depict the Principal Changes Which Have Taken Place, with Some Suggestions for the Further Improvement of the Metropolis*. London: J. Murray, 1927.

Cunningham, Colin. *Victorian and Edwardian Town Halls*. London: Routledge & Kegan Paul, 1981.

Davis, John. *Reforming London, the London Government Problem, 1855-1900*. Oxford: Oxford University Press, 1988.

Dicksee, Bernard (ed.). *The London Building Act, 1930*, 6th edn. London: Stanford, 1931.

Driver, Felix and David Gilbert (eds.). *Imperial Cities: Landscape, Display and Identity*. Manchester: Manchester University Press, 2003.

Edwards, A. Trystan. *The Architectural Work of Sir John Burnet and Partners*. Geneva: Masters of Architecture, 1930.

Edwards, A. Trystan. *Good and Bad Manners in Architecture*. London: P. Allen & Co., 1924.

Fellows, Richard A. *Edwardian Architecture: Style and Technology*. London: Lund Humphries, 1995.

Fellows, Richard A. *Edwardian Civic Buildings and Their Details*. Oxford: Architectural Press, 2000.

Fenske, Gail. *The Skyscraper and the City: The Woolworth Building and the Making of Modern New York*. Chicago: The University of Chicago Press, 2008.

Fletcher, Banister. *The London Building Acts, 1894-1909*. 5th edn. London: Batsford, 1914.

Fletcher, Hanslip. *London Passed and Passing, a Pictorial Record of Destroyed and Threatened Buildings*. London: Sir Isaac Pitman & Sons, 1909.

Forrest, G. Topham. *Report by G. Topham Forrest, the Architect to the Council, on the Construction and Control of Buildings and the Development of Urban Areas in the United States of America*. London: London County Council, 1925.

Gibbon, Sir Gwilym and Reginald W. Bell. *History of the London County Council 1889-1939*. London: Macmillan and Co, 1939.

Gray, A. Stuart, Jean Breach, and Nicholas Breach. *Edwardian Architecture: A Biographical Dictionary*. Ware, Herts: Wordsworth Editions, 1988.

Haward, Sir Harr. *The London County Council from Within, Forty Years' Official Recollections*. London: Chapman & Hall Ltd, 1932.

The London Society. *London of the Future, by the London Society, under the Editorship of Sir Aston Webb*. London: R. Fisher Unwin, 1921.

Masterman, C. F. G. *England after the War*. London: Hodder & Stoughton, 1922.

Pennbybacker, Susan D. *A Vision for London, 1889-1914: Labour, Everyday Life and the LCC Experiment*. London: Routledge, 1995.

Port, M. H. *Imperial London: Civil Government Building in London 1850–1915*. New Haven, CT: Published for the Paul Mellon Centre for Studies in British Art by Yale University Press, 1995.

Saint, Andrew (ed.). *Politics and the People of London, The London County Council 1889–1965*. London: Hambledon Press, 1989.

Service, Alastair. *Edwardian Architecture and Its Origins*. London: The Architectural Press, 1975.

Service, Alastair. *Edwardian Architecture: A Handbook to Building Design in Britain 1890–1914*. London: Thames and Hudson, 1977.

Winter, James. *London's Teeming Streets, 1830–1914*. London: Routledge, 1993.

CHAPTER 4
DEVELOPMENT: SPECULATIVE OFFICE DEVELOPMENT AND PUBLIC SECTOR TENANTS
Jonathan Clarke

Writing in 1933, a correspondent for the *Times* noted how Londoners could 'scarcely fail to notice' the 'mushroom growth of outer suburbs' but would likely not appreciate 'the phenomenal pace of post-War rebuilding in the central areas of City and West End'. 'Only those few who are architecturally sensitive', the journalist ventured 'will pay much heed to the growing bulk and new faces of shops and offices and blocks of flats'.[1] By the same token, while the historiography of the period has paid heed to the scale, style and dynamics of much commercial development, city centre and suburban, it has remained curiously insensitive to one key constituent of the urban built environment: speculative offices. In part this stems from an understandable focus on the earlier origins of the building type, and its extraordinary, often controversial, proliferation in the second half of the twentieth century: intermediate developmental stages seldom garner proportionate attention.[2] This is owing partially to the destruction of many of these buildings during the Second World War: of the estimated 20 million square feet of lost London office space, a not insignificant proportion was from this period.[3] But mostly, it was the later twentieth-century pronouncements of financial journalists and property industry insiders, based on personal or interviewee recollections, which set the tenor of characterizations of the era and subsequent historical overviews. Oliver Marriott believed that 'in relative terms

---

[1]'A New Plan for London', *Times* (14 June 1933): 15. The author was probably Charles Marriott (1869–1957), the *Times*' art and architecture critic, 1924–40.
[2]Robert Thorne, 'Post-war Listing: Informative Report on Office Buildings in London 1945–60' (unpublished English Heritage Historians' Report, 1987); Nicholas Bullock, *Building the Post-war World: Modern Architecture and Reconstruction in Britain* (London: Routledge, 2002); Elain Harwood, *Space, Hope, and Brutalism English Architecture, 1945–1975* (New Haven and London: Yale University Press, 2015).
[3]Dan Cruickshank, 'Origins of Offices', *Architectural Review* 174 (November 1983): 81–4; Robert Thorne, 'Office Building in the City of London 1830–1880' (unpublished paper presented at an Urban History Group Colloquium, London, September 1984); Richard MacCormac, 'The Dignity of Office', *Architectural Review* 190 (May 1992): 76–8; Maurice W. Beresford and Rachael Unsworth, 'Locating the Early Service Sector of Leeds: The Origins of an Office District', *Northern History* 44, no. 1 (March 2007): 75–109; Ralph Turvey, 'Office Rents in the City of London 1867–1910', *The London Journal* 23, no. 2 (1998): 53–67; Joseph Sharples '"The Visible Embodiment of Modern Commerce": Speculative Office Buildings in Liverpool, *c*.1780–1870', *Architectural History* 61 (2018): 131–73. Lionel Brett, 'The Developers', *Architectural Review* 72 (September 1965): 165–7. In 1935 one-quarter of the City's buildings were under thirty years old, with office accommodation accounting for the largest share of floor space. See John H. Dunning and E. Victor Morgan (eds.), *An Economic Study of the City of London* (London: Allen and Unwin, 1971): 31.

there was little speculative building', presupposing that the 'voluminous legacy of offices' left by the Victorians, and the 'troubled economic conditions of the twenties and thirties' produced 'only a weak and highly unpredictable demand for new space'.[4] Jack Rose thought that 'office blocks were generally owner-occupied, although there were some developed for letting by a few investment companies, mainly in the City of London'.[5] And more recently, scholars and academics have reinforced an overarching narrative of withered speculative office development between the wars. Peter Scott, for example, noted 'the few really substantial speculative office blocks which were built during the era, such as London's first "skyscraper", Bush House' often proved 'slow to let'.[6]

Yet commercial property developers, whether specializing in, or including, speculative offices within mixed-use portfolios, were significant shapers of urban form and function between the wars. Often their largest and most costly investments, speculative offices both embodied the growth in commercial, professional or bureaucratic work and capitalized on the rising land and rental values its urban concentration produced. Unlike owner-occupied buildings which were built under contract for specific clients, speculative offices were designed for unknown tenants or buyers, with no formal commitment from these end users of the completed building. They were first and foremost financial investments, designed to reap profits from the sale or letting of the building on the anticipation that a demand would exist or would form when put on the market. Like American skyscrapers, they were typically the most suitable machine to make inner-urban land pay, and the bigger (assuming strong demand), and more efficient, the machine, the greater the likely profits. In this period legislation mostly prevented the habitable portion of buildings from rising above 100 feet, yet through framed construction technologies, and more skilful planning, speculative office blocks between the wars typically harnessed far bigger sites, and extracted considerably more net, or lettable, space than their pre-war equivalents. Lettable space was often in the high tens or even hundreds of thousands of square feet, floor space indexes (a building's total floor area to the size of its 'footprint') grew to mid-single digits, and floor plan efficiencies (the proportion of the rentable area, discounting lifts, toilets, communal areas and other gross space) climbed to 60, even 70 per cent.[7] London, the financial centre of Europe and nexus of the British Empire, saw the construction of scores of speculative office buildings on the grandest of mid-rise scales. Among these were Adelaide House, Bush House, and Thames House, the latter the largest 1930s office block outside North America. Legislative leniency in Liverpool and Manchester saw a small handful of speculative offices rise well above metropolitan strictures. Manchester's Sunlight House, for instance, rose '200 feet from the red rock

---

[4]Oliver Marriott, *The Property Boom* (London: Hamish Hamilton, 1967): 18–19.
[5]Jack Rose, *The Dynamics of Urban Property Development* (London: E. & F. N. Spon, 1985): 145.
[6]Peter Scott, *The Property Masters: A History of the British Commercial Property Sector* (London: E. & F.N. Spon, 1996): 81 and Peter Scott, 'The Evolution of Britain's Urban Built Environment', in Martin Daunton (ed.), *The Cambridge Urban History of Britain vol.3. 1840–1950* (Cambridge: Cambridge University Press, 2001): 512. Scott's source for this was Marriott, *Property Boom*: 20–1.
[7]This information, and much else not specifically referenced, is drawn from the author's PhD thesis, 'The Development of the Speculative Office in Inter-war England' (University of Cambridge, 2020).

foundations to its roof ridge',[8] housing fourteen storeys of offices above the basement and ground floor restaurants and shops.

This chapter reassesses the established accounts of speculative office development, such as they exist. But it is more concerned with the complex, untold and at times surprising engagement and interpenetrations of the private and public sectors as mediated through speculative offices. Taking the war as a starting point, and the socio-economic changes unleashed in its immediate aftermath, it looks initially at an exodus of businesses out of the primal City cradle of the speculative office. Property developers responded to this migratory demand, financing enormous new buildings on the City's periphery and deep within the modern-day City of Westminster. This slow, centrifugal dispersal saw enormous offices arise within the West End, along the Thames Embankment and, by the late 1930s, on the southern Albert Embankment. Comparable, but lesser, patterns of post-war demand, and municipal improvement, saw huge, new speculative office blocks appear also in Liverpool, Manchester and especially Birmingham.

The second part of this chapter looks at state impingement and intervention in the commercial property sector. It shows how David Lloyd George's wartime coalition government impacted on the construction and occupancy of offices. Partly this related to building materials and cessation of activity, but more consequential was the requisition of offices and other premises by ministerial departments and other state bodies and agencies. Reliance on, and support of, the speculative office sector grew between the wars, and the increasingly intertwined nature of state-as-lessee/private sector-as-lessor relationship prefigured the controversial 'Lessor Scheme' office programme after the Second World War. Roundly condemned for their architectural mediocrity, this initiative also affirmed in the eyes of some critics, the government's engagement with the so-called powers of darkness, in this context, commercial developers.[9] Indeed, this chapter closes with a broader historiographical observation that a cultural bias against speculative commercial development driven, in part by an increasingly shrill and self-righteous preservation movement, has blinkered architectural historians to the richness of commercial architecture and its place within the political economy of this period. These lines of enquiry offer fresh insight into the overlapping spheres of government and commerce and its built expression.

The war and its aftermath

In London at least, the war and its aftermath profoundly influenced the pattern and dynamics of speculative office development through the 1920s. Bomb damage, however, was negligible. An isolated incidence occurred on the night of 13–14 October 1915, when

---

[8]'Sunlight House', *Manchester Guardian* (12 May 1931): 6.
[9]Peter Mandler, 'Rethinking the "Powers of Darkness": An Anti-history of the Preservation Movement in Britain', in Melanie Hall (ed.), *Towards World Heritage: International Origins of the Preservation Movement 1870–1930* (London and New York: Routledge, 2011): 221–39.

two Zeppelin bombs landed beside the new Moorgate Hall, Finsbury Pavement, then nearing completion.[10] These scarcely dented the steel frame or proprietary filler-joist concrete floors of Richardson and Gill's building.[11] By 1917, this 220-foot-long flagship building for one of the City's older developers, the Wool Exchange, Ltd (established 1884), was fully tenanted by 'various important trading companies'.[12]

The immediate effects of the war were however more keenly felt with the imposition of restrictions on steel construction and an embargo, from 1916, on new commercial building. Construction faltered perhaps designed under the 1909 'Steel Frame Act', and redesigned in reinforced concrete under the LCC's regulations of 1915, but then halted until the cessation of hostilities. Such stop-start development bedevilled the realization of many large offices, such as Nos 37–41 Gracechurch Street (1915–1920; FR Gould Wills, architect).[13] Such interferences caused acute frustration to developers and builders. Edward Scarlett Trehearne (1876–1948), a director of City and Kingsway Estates Limited and brother of the architect Alfred Frederick Trehearne (1874–1962), railed against the 'tyrannical behaviour' of the government, citing the halting of one building which, nonetheless, was accompanied by a demand for increased land tax.[14] More egregious still to many developers, and the displaced tenants of their properties, was the compulsory requisition of a broad range of buildings, both newly completed and longer-standing 'in the interests of the State'.[15] Imperial House, Tothill Street (1913–1915) and Victory House, Cockspur Street (1914–1915), both by Metcalf and Greig, were immediately requisitioned, the former by the War Office's Contracts Department, the latter by HM Board of Admiralty, Board of Invention and Research.[16] Others were commandeered in Kingsway and other great 'office streets',[17] augmenting the scores of residential, institutional, educational and entertainment properties that were also pressed into the war effort.[18]

Within the City of London, muted wartime business conditions rubbed off on the rental market. Many firms lost much of their male clerical and managerial workforce to the war effort. Although replaced by 'their fathers and grandfathers, to manage these businesses',[19] and female auxiliaries (necessitating 'lavatory accommodation for ladies … at considerable cost and loss of letting space')[20] demand for office space reduced to

---

[10]Photograph showing bomb damage to Moorgate Hall following the Zeppelin raid on the night of 13–14 October 1915. Imperial War Museum catalogue number LC 34. Available online: https://www.iwm.org.uk/collections/item/object/205214747 (accessed 23 March 2020).

[11]'Current Architecture. Moorgate Hall, London, E.C', Architectural Review, 39 (June 1916): 140.

[12]'Illustrations. Moorgate Hall, Finsbury Pavement, E.C', Builder (2 March 1917): 150.

[13]'37–41, Gracechurch-Street, E.C', Builder, 25 August 1916, 112; 'The Commercial Bank Building', Builder (12 November 1920): 545; 'The City's First Ferro-Concrete Bank', British Builder 106 (June 1920): 108.

[14]'Currente Calamo', Building News (22 May 1918): 376.

[15]'Commandeered London', Times (9 October 1919): 11.

[16]Building News, 17 November 1915, 558; Architects' Journal (31 December 1919), 842; Builder (24 June 1921), 798; Historic England Archives, BL 22946.

[17]Peter Cowan et al., The Office: A Facet of Urban Growth (London: Heinemann Educational, 1969): 30, 34.

[18]'Commandeered London', Times, 9 October 1919: 11.

[19]Business Premises. Report from the Select Committee on Business Premises together with the Proceedings of the Committee, Minutes of Evidence and Appendices, 1920 (HC Papers vol. 6 no. 237): 28, Q. 767.

[20]Ibid.: 77, Q. 2198.

below pre-war levels.[21] This changed the dynamics of the landlord-tenant relationship, with many firms, large and small, demanding hefty reductions in rent or refusing to renew leases.[22] Government intervention stirred matters. The compulsory closure of the Stock Exchange directly impacted on offices within the neighbouring Drapers' Garden Estate. Its owner, The County Land and Building Company, saw rentals almost halve.[23] Elsewhere, the largest office developer of all, the City of London Real Property Company (CLRP) saw profits from net rentals fall from 5.12 per cent in 1915 to 4.06 per cent in 1917.[24] When its architect, Leo Sylvester Sullivan, returned from the Western Front, it was to a period of renewed building activity for the firm, amid a drastically changed economic milieu.

Immediately after the war the tables turned. A surge of inflation sent demand for City accommodation rocketing to unprecedented levels, with consequences that rippled out far beyond the Square Mile. As Turvey summarized, '[p]rovincial and foreign firms sought to establish themselves in London; turnover in the markets of the City rose rapidly so that firms had to expand to at least their pre-war size, and men returned from the services were returning to their old jobs or setting up on their own'.[25] The reduction in building during the war and continued occupancy of properties by government departments exacerbated the shortage, which became particularly acute in the winter of 1919–1920. Tenants, who exercised their wartime leverage to obtain short tenancies, faced demands for the renewal of contracts at enormously inflated figures, sometimes at five or six times the original sum.[26] Amid rising discontent and accusations of excessive profiteering, the City Tenants Defence Association (formed in 1920 to fight enormous increases in rents being demanded by freeholders) found it 'absolutely necessary to force the hand of the Government'.[27] In 1920 a Select Committee of the House of Commons duly considered the matter but felt that 'sufficient additional accommodation will, in course of time, become available by the erection of new buildings on sites not now fully utilized, and by the tendency of some classes of businesses to seek accommodation in less central areas where premises can be obtained at lower rentals'.[28]

Both eventualities came to pass. The City saw a flurry of speculative office building in the years following armistice, including Richardson and Gill's Nos 43–53 and 56–60; Moorgate Street (1919–1920 and 1921–1922); L. S. Sullivan's No. 85 Gracechurch Street (1920); Henry Tanner's Nos 6–10; Moorgate Street (1920–1921); W. T. Hanman's Gresham House, Old Broad Street (1920–1923); and Gordon & Gunton's Finsbury Circus House (1921–1924). Many of these were for the Wool Exchange, Ltd and CLRP, the managing

[21]Ralph Turvey, *The Economics of Real Property. An Analysis of Property Values and Patterns of Use* (London: G. Allen & Unwin Ltd, 1957): 33.

[22]*Report from the Select Committee on Business Premises*: 28, Q. 767.

[23]Ibid.: 83, Q. 2447.

[24]Ibid.: 83, Q. 2428.

[25]Turvey, *Economics of Real Property*: 35.

[26]'Dearer City Offices', *Times* (11 May 1920): 13; 'City Notes', *Times* (16 July 1920): 19.

[27]'Dearer City Offices': 13.

[28]'City Rents Ramp', *Financial Times* (8 April 1921): 2.

director of the latter proclaiming in 1920 that 'what we are building now will not meet the demand; nothing like'.[29] By 1923, the ground area of CLRP's buildings had reached some thirteen acres, a 65 per cent increase compared to 1914.[30] However, the biggest buildings were supplied by opportunistic new companies, formed with the purpose of developing specific sites. Largest of all in the 1920s was Adelaide House on the City's Thameside edge – London's tallest commercial building when completed in 1924, and probably the first English speculative office to achieve a three-figure net floor area. Sir John Burnet & Tait's structurally expressive eye-catcher provided 160,000 square feet on eleven deep, open floors, each capable of housing different firms, large and small alike. Shipping and insurance companies were encouraged to relocate here from their traditional stronghold around Lloyd's Register by virtue of 'facilities for the erection of aerials if desired', the height and open position of the building making it 'peculiarly suitable for receiving and transmitting wireless messages'.[31] A rooftop eighteen-hole golf green, the brainchild of building's owner, Australian-born financier and industrialist Richard Tilden Smith (1865–1929), was doubtless intended to appeal to tenanting firms' upper managerial echelons. An adjacent roof garden harbouring seventy fruit trees and a rockery, a lofty haven '170 feet above the roar of the traffic, the river with its chugging tugs and the bellowing of Billingsgate porters' acknowledged the increasing feminization of clerical work.[32] In 1921, when construction of Adelaide House began, women already made up 46 per cent of Britain's clerks.[33]

The City's increased supply of modern office space was not enough to avert a westerly drift of those businesses that did not have to cluster around its specialized exchanges, markets and salesrooms. This process had, to some extent, begun in the Victorian era, with municipal street improvements triggering the construction of shops, flats and lettable office 'chambers' along new thoroughfares such as Victoria Street and Shaftesbury Avenue. But it was the realization of the LCC's grandly imperial Kingsway-Aldwych project before the war that opened a bold new axis of speculative office development beyond the City. Besides company headquarters, such as Kodak House (see Chanin chapter in this volume), most of the grandiloquent, 100-foot-high, stone-faced buildings were by Trehearne and Norman, mainly for City and Kingsway Estates Limited. Others were developed by longer-established property companies seeking to capitalize on the growing demand for extra City office space. The Law Land Company, Ltd which began in 1884 with a focus on residential and shop property noticed Kingsway's 'phenomenal' growth as a 'great new business centre' and consequently sought a stake in London's greatest commercial boulevard.[34] By 1917, thanks to its Kingsway properties, gross rentals

---

[29]*Report from the Select Committee on Business Premises*: 81, Q. 2352

[30]In 1914 the company had some 8½ acres (five of which was freehold); in 1923 this had risen to 13 acres (eight freehold). *The City of London Real Property Company Limited, 1864–1964* (London, CLRP): 21; *The Economist* (8 December 1923), 1020.

[31]'The Estate Market', *Times* (30 January 1925): 10.

[32]'Flourishing Roof Garden in the Heart of London', *Dundee Evening Telegraph* (18 August 1927): 2.

[33]Gregory Anderson (ed.), *The White-Blouse Revolution: Female Office Workers since 1870* (Manchester: Manchester University Press, 1980): 2.

[34]'Law Land Company (Limited)', *Times* (5 March 1914): 16.

from its offices more than doubled that of its flats.[35] But it was the buildings resumed and completed soon after the end of hostilities, or those produced wholly between the wars, that were best positioned to house the overspill of City firms. Most impressive of all was Bush House, built within the Aldwych crescent in five phases spanning 1920 to 1935 for the wealthy American businessman Irving Tar Bush (1869–1948) and managed from 1923 by a British subsidiary, Bush House, Ltd. Closing the axial view along Kingsway, the original, central block was early on prevented from reaching anything like the height of his thirty-storey Bush Tower in Manhattan (1917–1918), causing one American journal to denounce the LCC, and those owners of neighbouring properties opposed to it as 'enemies of the skyscraper in London'.[36] This was perhaps just as well, since upon completion in 1923 to designs by New York architects Helme and Corbett, its 110,000 square feet of rentable space proved over-capacious. It was not until 1925 when only the ground-floor suite and one-half of the seventh floor (totalling 17,000 square feet)[37] remained unlet that 'the demand for office accommodation was … sufficient to make the proposed extension of the Bush House a paying proposition'.[38] Thereafter, the success of the venture, comprising flanking east and west blocks (**Figure 4.1**), and embodying new, transatlantic approaches in office planning, fenestration, services and building management (including ruthlessly efficient advertising and rental campaigns), was remarkable. By 1935, when the south-west wing was completed, nothing within

Figure 4.1 A 1940s aerial view of Bush House, with Kingsway – and offices including Adastral House – in the upper left of the image, Harold P. Clunn, *London Marches On* (Caen Press, 1947), author's collection

---

[35]'Law Land Company', *Times* (23 March 1917):13.

[36]*Buildings and Building Management* (13 December 1920): 55.

[37]'Bush House', *Times* (12 May 1925): 8.

[38]Harold Clunn, *London rebuilt, 1897–1927* (London: John Murray, 1927): 52–3.

the 500,000 square feet of overall floor space remained untaken – this final component having been pre-let to the Office of Works.[39]

With a modicum of justification, Bush House, Ltd claimed that London's 'most distinguished and best serviced office building' was partly responsible for 'the exodus from the older quarters of the City to the new "Square Mile" round Kingsway-Aldwych'.[40] But other, looser and more diaphanous West End subdistricts also saw the construction of increasingly large and efficient speculative blocks through the 1920s and 1930s: Wellington House, Strand (1924–1925), Brettenham House, Lancaster Place (1931–1923); Golden Cross House, Charing Cross Road (1932–1923) and even (in its original semblance) Broadcasting House, Portland Place (1930–1921) to name but four.[41] Such buildings formed part of a more functionally and architecturally diverse built environment. And in terms of range and extent of office provision, the City still had no equal. Nevertheless, one of the most remarkable transformations of inner London between the wars was the creation of new office locales on urban land where land ownership was less fragmented, permitting larger units of development. In these more peripheral places, developers were not so much animated by the flight of businesses out of the Square Mile than the general rise of the professional service sector. Between 1920 and 1940 the number of limited companies increased by 93 per cent, two-thirds of which were formed in the service sector; by 1939 half the labour force was employed in the service sector.[42] Commercial clerks alone increased from 478,000 in 1911 to 1.278 million in 1931.[43] Yet a sizeable proportion of this was in public administration: until the war the state accounted for 12–13 per cent of Gross National Product; by 1929 this had risen to 24 per cent, and by 1938, 29 per cent.[44] All this translated to a sustained demand for office space to house the burgeoning numbers of private and public sector white-collar workers. As a *Times* correspondent noted, the 'vast pent-up force of reconstruction' was only temporarily lulled by the great depression: it 'has only reduced the pace; it has not stopped rebuilding'.[45]

Resplendent among the metropolis's new office districts was Millbank, a 'low, marshy locality' running back from the Thames between the Palace of Westminster and Vauxhall Bridge.[46] A disastrous Thames flood of 1928 had seen governmental, institutional and

[39]'Bush House', *Times* (28 September 1934): 9; TNA WORK 50/11.

[40]*Yorkshire Post and Leeds Intelligencer*, 27 September 1928, 5 and 'Bush House', *Times* (20 November 1924): 11.

[41]'Few people perhaps realize that Broadcasting House was an early developer's building'. Edward Jamilly 'Patrons, Clients, Designers and Developers: The Jewish Contribution to Secular Building in England', *Jewish Historical Studies* 38 (2002): 92.

[42]Derek Matthews, *The Priesthood of Industry: The Rise of the Professional Accountant in Business Management* (Oxford: Oxford University Press, 1998): 142. Mark Thomas, 'The Service Sector', in Roderick Floud and Paul Johnson (eds.), *The Cambridge Economic History of Modern Britain. Vol. 2: Economic Maturity, 1860–1939* (Cambridge: Cambridge University Press, 2004): 99.

[43]Ibid.: Table 5.1: 100.

[44]David J. Jeremy, *A Business History of Britain, 1900–1990's* (Oxford: Oxford University Press, 1998): 107.

[45]'A New Plan for London', *Times* (14 June 1933): 15.

[46]Arthur Griffiths, *Memorials of Millbank, and Chapters in Prison History*, vol. 1 (London: Henry S. King & Co., 1875): 29.

residential buildings submerged under feet of water, and loss of life, but the London County Council's Millbank Improvement Scheme which included a widened Horseferry Road linked to the new Lambeth Bridge (completed in 1932, and providing the most direct route to the City) augured well for commercial development 'an ideal area for office accommodation'.[47] In 1929 the second Duke of Westminster, Hugh Richard Arthur Grosvenor, began selling parts of his Millbank estate to mitigate huge projected liabilities for estate duty.[48] Associated London Properties, Limited (ALP), one of London's newest, and fastest-growing property developers, was poised as a major purchaser. In 1930, at the behest of its chairman and managing director, Walter Henderson-Cleland, a 'forceful personality' who considered the district 'ripe for development', this company purchased eight acres of freehold land from the Duke that ran westwards behind Thames House (see below).[49]

ALP went on to acquire further neighbouring land (spending £900,000 by 1934), simultaneously disposing of cleared sites as freeholds or on building leases, as well as erecting speculative offices for its own revenue.[50] In what was described as 'the largest property development in London for many years', involving 'the removal and re-housing of approximately 600 families', the years leading up to the war saw ALP build two residential blocks and some of the largest, most efficiently planned office blocks in the country: Horseferry House (block 2), Great Westminster House; Stanley House; Cleland House; Neville House; and Abell House (**Figure 4.2**).[51] All were islanded or near-islanded, permitting superior levels of daylight, and all were framed in reinforced concrete, a form of construction that became more competitive for office buildings in the late 1930s thanks to more permissive design regulations.[52] Apart from Horseferry House's extension (by E. Howard & Partners), all were designed by flourishing commercial firm T. P. Bennett and Son, whose principal Sir Thomas Penberthy Bennett (1887–1980) had (in common with other leading commercial architects) served in the Office of Works and could, by 1935, be described by Henderson-Cleland as 'our architect … whose eminence in the architectural world needs no elaboration from me'.[53] The largest of all, Great Westminster House, housed four acres (174,000 square feet) of office space above shops and garages, despite its relatively low, sub-regulatory height (**Figure 4.3**). The cluster of ALP buildings was fringed or abutted by those procured or purchased by other property

---

[47]J. L. Fisher, 'Architecture To-Day', *Financial Times* (29 July 1930): 12.

[48]F. H. W. Sheppard, Gen. (ed.), *Survey of London, vol. 39, The Grosvenor Estate in Mayfair, Part 1 General History* (London: Athlone Press, for the London County Council, 1977): 78.

[49]'Obituary', *Times* (10 August 1945): 7. 'Associated London Properties', *Financial Times* (28 July 1930): 7.

[50]F. H. W. Sheppard, Gen. ed., *Survey of London, vol. 39*, ch4, fn6.

[51]'Obituary', *Times* (10 August 1945): 7; *London Gazette* (22 May 1934): 3313. 'Associated London Properties', *Times* (10 July 1935): 22.

[52]See Jonathan Clarke, 'The Exception, Not the Norm: Pre-1940 Concrete-Framed Commercial Offices in England', in James W. P. Campbell et al. (eds.), *Further Studies in the History of Construction: The Proceedings of the Third Conference of the Construction History Society*, Queens' College, Cambridge, 8–10 April 2016 (Cambridge: Construction History Society, 2016): 357–70.

[53]Notably Sir Henry Tanner (1849–1935), Sir Frank Baines FRIBA (1877–1933), Harry Bulkeley Creswell (1869–1960) and Leo S. Sullivan (1878–1964). 'Associated London Properties', *Times* (10 July 1935): 22.

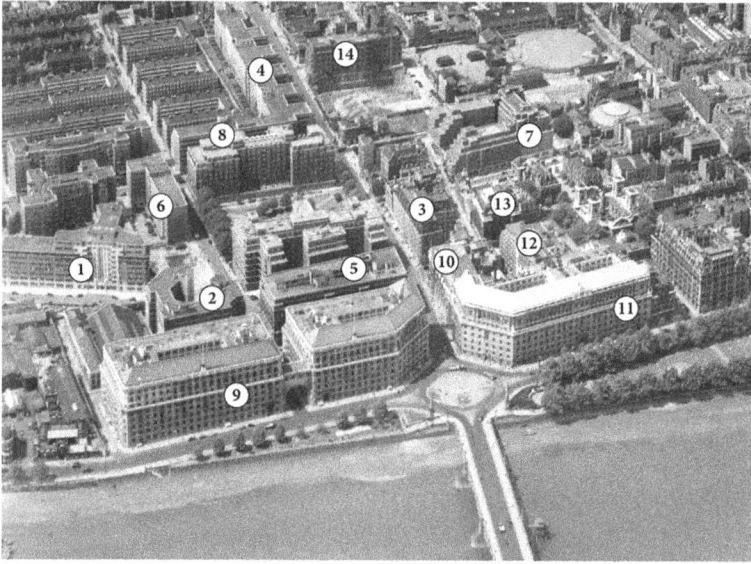

Speculative Offices

1 Abell House *(1939-40)*
2 Cleland House *(1938-9)*
3 Dean Bradley House *(1938)*
4 Great Westminster House *(1936-7)*
5 Horseferry House *(1932-3; 1934-5)*
6 Neville House *(1937-8)*
7 Romney House *(1930-2; 1937-8)*
8 Stanley House *(1937-8)*
9 Thames House *(1929-31)*

Owner-occupied Offices

10 Ergon House *(1927-8)*
11 Imperial Chemical House *(1927-9)*
12 Transport House *(1926-7)*
13 Thorneycroft House *(1922-3)*
14 'The Steel Frame Building' *(1940-1)*
    (Govt. offices; later The Citadel)

Figure 4.2 Offices completed in the 1930s on the brownfield former Millbank estate, © Historic England Archive. Aerofilms Collection, EAW001430

companies: Romney House (1931–1939, in three phases; Michael Rosenauer and E. Frazer Tomlins for Holloway Properties Ltd), Horseferry House, block 1 (1932–1933; EGW Souster for Marlborough Investment Trust) and Dean Bradley House (1937–1938; Wimperis, Simpson and Guthrie, for Benson Greenall, Esq).[54]

---

[54]John Faber, *Oscar Faber: His Work, His Firm and Afterwards* (London: Quiller Press, 1989): 44. James 'Benson' Greenall (b. 1890), formerly an architect in 'Greenall & Cole' and a Planning Inspector in the Ministry of Health, sold the building to the Pall Mall Trust, Ltd in 1938, which immediately leased it to the Office of Works on a term of 21¼ years. 'Dean Bradley House, Horseferry Road, S.W.1'. Available online: https://thenewwiperstimes.com/2019/05/28/deanbradleyhouse/ (accessed 24 March 2020); TNA WORK 50/11.

Figure 4.3 T. P. Bennett's Great Westminster House, erected in 1936–1937 for Associated London Properties. Its light-grabbing 'comb' plan-form was enabled by the generous Millbank site. Source: Historic England Archive, CC47_01373

Fronting all this was Sir Frank Baines's grimly monumental Imperial Chemical House and Thames House, truly 'office buildings on the grand scale'.[55] The former was emblematic of the 1920s merger wave and the giant multidivisional firm, but Thames House announced the commercial property sector's growing significance. Erected in 1929–1931 when 'the demand for office accommodation in London far exceed[ed] the supply'.[56] It was a hugely ambitious yet astute venture by Anglo-Properties, Limited, a firm that registered in 1928 (becoming a public company under the name Thames House Estate, Ltd, in 1931) and described as 'Lord Melchett's finance corporation'.[57] Its director was Henry Ludwig Mond, 2nd Baron Melchett (1898–1949), the only son of Sir Alfred Mond, Ist Baron Melchett (1868–1930), founder and first chairman of ICI. With big corporate backing, Henry Mond financed the biggest interwar office building outside the United States, with 772,000 square feet of floor space spread over eleven floors and

---

[55]J. L. Fisher, 'Architecture To-Day', *Financial Times* (21 March 1934): 10.
[56]Ibid.: (29 July 1930): 12.
[57]*Skinner's Property Share Annual* 1950–1: 264; *The Stock Exchange Official Yearbook* 1965, 1297. 'Building Schemes and Steel', *Yorkshire Post and Leeds Intelligencer* (18 May 1929): 13.

housed within twin riverside blocks.[58] In planning terms it was regressive, internal light courts had already been supplanted by 'external lightwells' (as exemplified by Bush House), but in building services and management terms, if not capacity, it approached transatlantic norms. As a pioneer multi-tenant building in a nascent business locale, it had to provide for the varied needs of its estimated tenant population of 5,000 workers. It gave room to restaurants, private dining rooms, board rooms and committee rooms (available by the hour, half day, or day), tobacco kiosks, confectionary stalls, hairdressing saloons, travel bureaus, squash racquet courts, and swimming pools.[59] Like mid-sized skyscrapers, which housed comparable net floor areas, it was conceived as a self-contained business enclave.

After the Second World War, Harold Clunn thought 'the new Millbank quarter is unlike any other district of London', its former slums 'swept away and great new blocks of offices, shops, flats and artisan dwellings erected in their place'.[60] Certainly no other could match its sweeping, tabula rasa renewal for intensity, pace or variegation. Nevertheless, throughout the 1930s ambitious office developments sprouted along major thoroughfares and alongside historic squares, displacing residents and disrupting the historic urban grain. Buildings such as the New Adelphi (1936–1938; Stanley Hamp), Berkeley Square House (1937–1938; Gordon Jeeves and Hector O. Hamilton) and Russell Square House (1939–1941) constituted bulky, often ungraceful additions to distinguished or leafy locales. The advance of rentable office space was not confined to Westminster. City Gate House, Finsbury Square (1930–1931) and Ibex House, Minories (1935–1937) made full use of more generous sites in the City's outer precincts. And south of the Thames, Howard and Souster's Waterloo Bridge House (1937–1938) and Lambeth Bridge House (1939–1940) both capitalized on the enhanced connectivity afforded by their respective rebuilt river crossings, much like their north-bank counterparts, Brettenham House and Thames House.

For all the new shoots of commercial redevelopment in London, it was England's second largest city, Birmingham, that exemplified concentrated speculative office development during this period.[61] By the late 1930s 'vast municipal estates ringed the city periphery'.[62] Thanks to municipal improvement schemes involving the widening of arterial roads and street junctions, its central business district vaunted large, efficiently planned offices and shops loosely zoned around a proposed Civic Centre.[63] Local developers, including the young Jack Cotton (1903–1964) availed themselves

---

[58]'Thames House', *Financial Times* (7 April 1930): 4; 'Europe's Largest Office Building', *Estates Gazette* (3 May 1930): 1; 'Thames House, Grosvenor Road, London', *Architectural Review* 70 (November 1931): 167.

[59]'Modern Offices: No. II. Thames House', *Office Equipment* 1 (April 1933): 181.

[60]Clunn, *London Marches On*, 4. A British shipping agent, Harold Philip Clunn (1879–1956) was best known for his *Face of …* series of topographical books – and his pragmatic attitude to London's growth and redevelopment.

[61]Anthony Sutcliffe, 'The "Midland Metropolis": Birmingham, 1890–1980', in George Gordon (ed.), *Regional Cities in the UK, 1890–1980* (London: Harper & Row, 1986): 25.

[62]Gordon E. Cherry, *Birmingham: A Study in Geography, History and Planning* (Chichester: J. Wiley, 1994): 144.

[63]See Supplement to *Estates Gazette* (July 1934): 1–3.

of the generous new building sites, commissioning Birmingham's leading commercial architects, Essex & Goodman, Crouch, Butler & Savage, S. N. Cooke, Herbert O. Ellis and Clarke, W. Norman Twist, to make the best use of them. One locus of activity was the intersection of Great Charles Street and Newhall Street, with York, Lancaster, Richmond and Lombard Houses offering tenanting firms the type of spacious, well-lit and serviced office space customary in London as well as heralding a bulky new scale to Birmingham's business buildings (**Figure 4.4**). Other cities saw earlier, lesser flourishes, or individual buildings on grander scales. Liverpool, which had seen an 'office boom' in the mid-nineteenth century, experienced a short-lived 'building

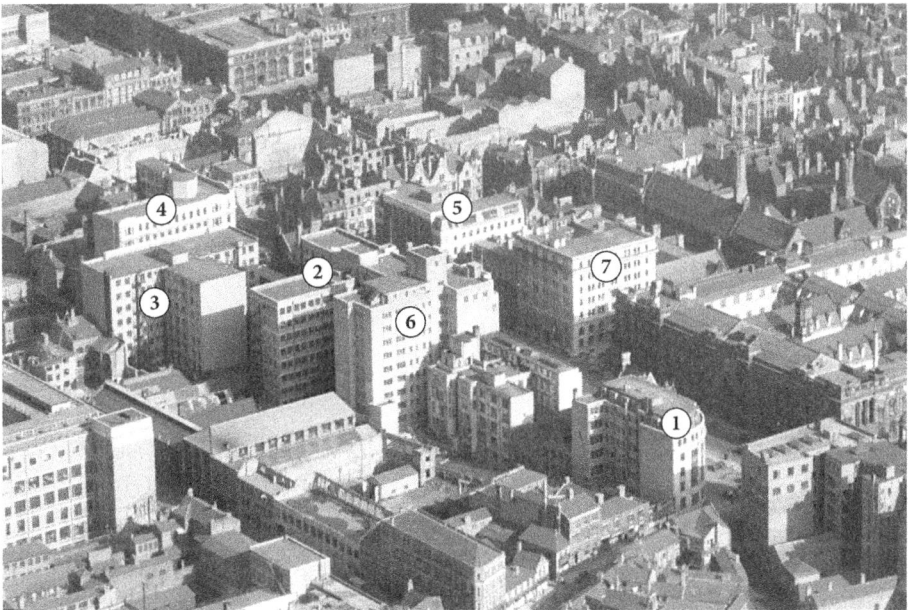

Speculative Offices

1   Civic House *(1931-2)*
2   Lancaster House *(1932-3)*
3   Lombard House *(1933-4)*
4   Richmond House *(1931-2)*
5   York House *(1930)*

Owner-occupied Offices

6   Colonial Mutual Life offices *(1939)*
7   Stock Exchange Buildings *(1928)*

Figure 4.4 A 1948 aerial view of one of Birmingham's new business districts – Great Charles Street and Newhall Street, Historic England Archive © Historic England Archive. Aerofilms Collection, EAW013563

boom'[64] in the mid-1920s that included Wellington Buildings, The Strand (1923–1924 by Colin S. Brothers) and Dominion Buildings, Brunswick Street (*c.* 1923 by Holt & Glover), both close to each other within the waterfront office district. Manchester's Sunlight House (1926–1932), designed by the Russian-born Jewish architect-developer Joseph Sunlight (né Schimschlavitch) (1889–1978), housed fourteen storeys of offices above the basement swimming pool and ground-floor restaurants and shops, many in the giant mansard roof and towers. Described by *The New Yorker Magazine* as 'Manchester's nearest approach to a skyscraper', much of the 150,000 square feet of office space was let within months of the building's opening, some to petroleum and engineering firms, but most significantly, to government departments.[65] Indeed, scale, multifunctionality, clustering and the emergence of new office districts all constituted major changes within the speculative office sector, but perhaps the most compelling development was their tenants, the 'official lessees'.

Commandeers to 'official lessees': government occupancy of commercial offices

The practice of government departments and agencies leasing office space from the commercial sector began in earnest during the war and continued after in a state of near-constant dependency. Over the course of five wartime years, dozens of new ministries and departments, interim and permanent, were created, resulting in a mammoth expansion of the staffs of these 'large and complicated administrative machines'.[66] It was estimated that the clerical staff employed in the civil departments rose almost threefold, from a total of 53,500 at the start of the war to 148,000 in February 1918.[67] This placed an enormous burden on the Office of Works, the department responsible for providing accommodation, whether by building, leasing or commandeering. Greatest priority was given to staff engaged in the most urgent war work, with departments such as the Ministry of Munitions housed as close as possible to Whitehall. By 1916 'every available vacant building of any size … had been hired for Government purposes, and the Office of Works had no alternative but to commandeer premises in private occupation to meet the continuous and increasing demand'.[68] To relieve the congestion in Whitehall, and interfere least with private and commercial interests, the policy adopted by the Office of Works was to acquire clubs, hotels, flats, institutional and public buildings across a wide area. Hundreds of buildings, including London's most notable landmarks,

---

[64]'Building Boom at Liverpool', *Builder* (25 May 1923): 866.
[65]A. J. Liebling, 'The Lancashire Way', *New Yorker*, 22 November 1941, 50. An advertisement in the *Manchester Guardian* (23 July 1932): 3, claimed 'Eight Top Floors Already Let to Inland Revenue, Ministry of Labour, to Shell Mex & B.P. Ld., and Babcock & Wilcox Ld.'
[66]'Staffs of Government Offices', *The Times* (20 March 1919): 6.
[67]Ibid.
[68]'Housing of Public Departments', *The Times* (13 January 1917): 3.

were 'commandeer[ed] in the interests of the State'[69] – much to the irritation of some occupants and owners. Members of the National Liberal Club, for example, regarded 'their building as a triumph of domestic architecture, and quite unsuitable ... for the purpose of offices'.[70]

Inevitably, given the scale of the demand, commercial and institutional offices were drawn into the mix. Few City offices seem to have been seized, H. P. Berlage's Holland House, Bury Street (1914–1916) being one, but in Kingsway, Windsor House, Queen's House, Lincoln's Inn House, Imperial House, Pen Corner, and the General Electric Company's building were all requisitioned, as were offices closer to Whitehall.[71] For example, W. D. Caröe's lavishly dressed Millbank House, erected in 1903–1906 for the Ecclesiastical Commissioners, was 'commandeered by the Office of Works for the accommodation of the staff of the Ministry of Pensions'.[72] But the Office of Works' preferred procurement strategy was to erect, convert or lease buildings for other departments, thereby minimizing the 'great expense [...] in regard to compensation for interference with business, loss of goodwill, & c'.[73] Thus, the offices it erected in 1912–1915 in Kingsway for the Public Trustee, a highly successful and remunerative department that opened in 1908 with a staff of five, provided extremely timely. Its staff, which by 1912 had already swelled to 230, numbered 724 in 1917 (594 or 82 per cent of which was female).[74] The building was hailed as a paragon of efficiency 'on account of its essentially commercial treatment in design, construction and general plan'.[75] The more usual procedure, however, was taking commercial office floor space on long leases, ideally secured before the buildings' completion. Early in the war it seemingly brokered leases of York House, Kingsway (1914–1915; Trehearne & Norman), Imperial House, Tothill Street (1914–1915; Metcalfe and Greig), and Victory House, Cockspur Street (1914–1916; Metcalf and Greig), the latter occupied by HM Board of Admiralty, Board of Invention and Research but becoming Norway House following Armistice and alterations by FTW Goldsmith, of London, and Johs. Th. Westbye, of Stavanger.[76]

The relinquishment and vacating of properties dragged out long after the cessation of hostilities, extending in many cases beyond the final ratification of peace on 10 January 1920. The delay was a source of frequent complaint and grievance; the Kingsway Tenants' Association, for instance, demanded the immediate return of their workplaces. Sir Alfred Mond, then First Commissioner of Works (from 1916 to 1921), was compelled to set out,

---

[69]'Commandeered London', *The Times* (9 October 1919): 11.

[70]'Clubs as Government Offices', *The Times* (7 September 1916): 3.

[71]'Commandeered London', *The Times* (9 October 1919): 11.

[72]'News', *Financial Times* (5 October 1918): 2.

[73]'Housing of Public Departments', *The Times* (13 January 1917): 3.

[74]'New Offices for the Public Trustee, Kingsway, W.C.', *Building News* (2 August 1912): 149. According to this source Sir Henry Tanner and H. A. Collins were the principal architects, although later accounts name A. J. Pilcher. Report by Sir Leonard Powell and Charles T. Ruthen on the Public Trustee Building, Kingsway, dated 16 July 1917, 1 in TNA PT 1/31.

[75]Ibid.: 4.

[76]Ibid.: '"Norway House," Cockspur-street', *Builder* (24 June 1921): 798.

in parliament and the press, a schedule for the releasing of museums, galleries, hotels and other public buildings.[77] Part of the problem was that the work of administering demobilization itself entailed a level of staffing that offset the shrinkage and disbanding of temporary, wartime departments. But the more intractable and longer-term issue was the large number of new, permanent State Departments. As Mond pithily put it:

> Great establishments like the new Ministry of Supplies, the Pensions Ministry, the Ministry of Food, the Ministries of Health Reconstruction, and the National Service, and last, but certainly not least, the great Ministry of Transport, all mean more staff and more accommodation.[78]

The reorganization and relocation of departments and office space was overseen by the Cabinet Committee on Accommodation, drawn from the War Cabinet and the Office of Works, and drawing on the interim reports of the committee appointed to inquire into the organization and staffing of government offices.[79] Decentralization from Whitehall, and even Westminster, was encouraged and by early 1919 sanction was given to 'the erection of Government offices for some 12,000 Department staffs and clerks some miles from Central London'.[80] One outcome of this was the enormous Ministry of Pensions headquarters, in Acton (1919–1922; James G. West) which housed over 5,000 employees and was applauded by *The Builder* as 'architecture reduced to its simplest terms … expressive, dignified and straightforward'.[81] Nevertheless, despite the economies and efficiencies of such buildings, it was to the private sector, rather than its own architects, that the Office of Works mostly turned to in meeting the office-space needs of the burgeoning civil service. Building anew incurred large and immediate capital expenditure, whereas renting and reconditioning existing properties reduced annual outlays and gave the flexibility required by the ever-enlarging machinery of government.

The formative pattern set through wartime expediency, of leasing buildings as they neared completion, continued unabated, as did, initially at least, a requisition mindset. Kingsway, where government departments had been slow and reluctant to vacate, remained a prized location and showed a range of procurement strategies some of which grew in the succeeding decades. The commandeering approach was exemplified by the Air Ministry, which, obliged to leave the Hotel Cecil in 1919, moved to Empire House on the corner of Kingsway and Aldwych. By 1921 it had expanded to the adjoining India House and Canada House (also erected by Trehearne and Norman in 1913–1915), the three buildings renamed Adastral House after the department's motto *Per Ardua*

---

[77]'House of Commons', *Times* (16 November 1918): 10; 'The Clearing of the Museums', *The Times* (25 March 1919): 14; 'Commandeered Buildings', *The Times* (2 April 1919): 9.
[78]'The Clearing of the Museums', *The Times* (25 March 1919): 14.
[79]Sir Alfred Mond chaired both the War Cabinet Committee on Accommodation and the Office of Works Committee on Accommodation.
[80]'The Clearing of the Museums', *The Times* (25 March 1919): 14.
[81]'The New Pensions Office, Acton', *Builder* (1 September 1922): 312.

Ad Astra.[82] Directories show the Meteorological Office and HMSO were also resident, although not the scores of electrical engineering firms that tenanted the buildings in 1915. These had been driven out later in the war by the Board of Trade.[83] Such imperious behaviour by the State did eventually abate, only to reappear at the eve of the Second World War.

More typical was York House, which continued to be occupied by the Inland Revenue Department following the taking of a 21 years' lease in 1915, when the building neared completion.[84] Victory House (1919–1920) and Prince's House (1919–1921) however signalled a new direction in procuring official office space. Both were designed by Trehearne & Norman, but the former was commissioned, and the latter shaped by the Office of Works. Victory House, 'believed to be the first large commercial building begun and finished in London since the war put a stop to all civil building operations', was authorized on a contract price of £7,465 yet came in £600 under budget, thanks to the architects' adoption of a fixed price contract, a 'rather novel system' at the time.[85] Prince's House, on the other hand, seems to have been redesigned with the government as known lessee, and the Office of Works acting more as a facilitator than as a client. Appropriation accounts of the sums granted by parliament show that £4,574 was spent on the 'adaptation' of the building, a large sum that probably encompassed revisions by Trehearne & Norman.[86] Responsible for most of Kingsway's pre-1930 buildings, this firm could be depended on to maximize floorspace and minimize costs. Indeed, Princess House's net floor area of 54,000 feet, extracted from a 7,800-foot footprint, gave a floor space index of 6.92 – a figure that placed it among the most efficient of all interwar offices.[87] From the Office of Work's perspective, such buildings reproduced, if not surpassed, the spatial efficiencies and architectural sensibilities embodied in its own foray into Kingsway-style commercial architecture, the Public Trustee Building. This provided 57,000 square feet of well-lit, usable floor space and was ranked 'amongst the best in London' by an investigation into the wartime utilization of office accommodation.[88] Because 'architectural effect has not been allowed to interfere with the commercial utility of the premises', it did 'not compare in nobility and monumental character of design with the great permanent office buildings of H.M. Government'.[89] Nonetheless, it was deemed

---

[82]Francis R. Banks, *The New Penguin Guide to London* (Harmondsworth: Penguin, 1986): 236.
[83]1915 and 1921 POD; *Return Showing … Premises Hired or Requisitioned by or on Behalf of H.M. Office of Works, etc., 1917–18* (Cmd. 1689): 5.
[84]TNA 1/12398/45003.
[85]'Current Architecture: Victory House, Kingsway', *Architectural Review* 48 (December 1920): 144, 147.
[86]Civil Appropriation Accounts, 1921–1922 (HC-1923 vol.17 no. 7): 90. Certainly, in terms of externally commissioned buildings, the Office of Work's 'chief technical advisors' were 'in close and constant touch with practising architects … though the relationship is such that in all matters of architectural design the responsibility rests entirely with the practising architect'. 'The Architectural Organisation of His Majesty's Office of Works', *Official Architect* (January 1938): 135.
[87]'Princess House, Kingsway', *Architects' Journal* (18 May 1921): 613.
[88]TNA PT 1/31. Report by Sir Leonard Powell and Charles T. Ruthen on the Public Trustee Building, Kingsway, dated 16 July 1917: 3.
[89]Ibid.: 3 and 4.

'an extremely well-managed and commercial structure which from the broad business-like point of view, if not from the narrow and cramped Civil Service outlook, reaches a lofty eminence upon the pedestal of perfection'.[90]

The Civil Service's size, complexity and spending increased enormously between the wars. Between 1913 and 1939 expenditure surged from 6.8 per cent to 25.4 per cent of GNP 'reflecting a major, permanent increase in the role of the state' and staffing doubled, from 73,511 to 152,117, excluding the Post Office.[91] In accommodation terms, this placed increasing reliance on the private sector. By 1922, the Office of Works administered almost 5,300 properties throughout the United Kingdom, exclusive of Royal, Diplomatic, Consular and other residences and historic monuments. The great majority of these, 77 per cent, were hired, and the largest category, 'accommodation of administrative staff, &c.', was procured almost exclusively from the private sector (91 per cent of over 3,000 buildings) (**Figure 4.5**).[92] Furthermore, the rental costs of this category alone came to £840,000, more than 73 per cent of the total, and some 5½ times that spent on hired

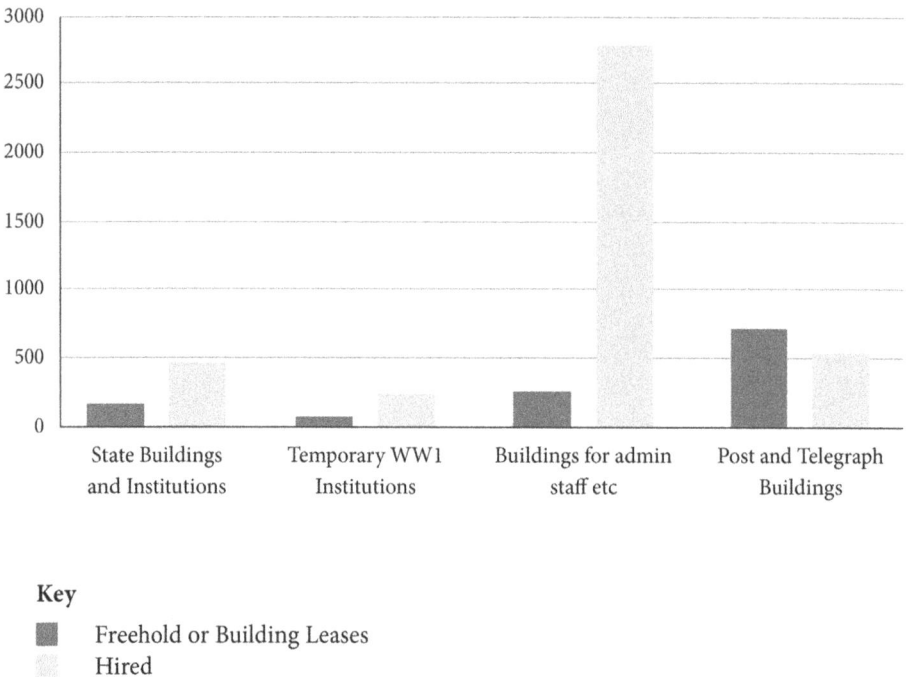

Key

■ Freehold or Building Leases

▢ Hired

Figure 4.5 By 1922 the number of hired buildings for general office use far exceeded those of other functions. Data source: *Interim and Final Reports of the Committee on Crown and Government Lands* (1922) (Cmd. 1689)

---

[90]Ibid.: 9.

[91]Rodney Lowe, 'Bureaucracy Triumphant or Denied? The Expansion of the British Civil Service, 1919–1939', *Public Administration*, 62 (Autumn 1984): 291.

[92]Interim and final reports of the Committee on Crown and Government Lands, 1922 (cmd. 1689): 25.

Post and Telegraph Buildings, the second largest category.[93] No published comparable figures exist for the later years, but it might reasonably be supposed that the number of buildings in this inordinate category increased, and the proportion rented remained at similar or even higher levels.[94]

The Office of Works did, of course, design buildings that fell within this disparate grouping, Labour and Employment Exchanges being the most common. But for housing Civil Service departments, centrally and regionally, it mostly turned to large, modern commercial offices. Taking the Inland Revenue as one example, the Office of Works only erected a small handful of dedicated Inland Revenue Offices (namely at Hounslow, Darlington, and Macclesfield) where private sector provision was wanting.[95] For the most part, they found multiple floors in such buildings as Manchester's Sunlight House, Birmingham's Richmond House, London's Colquhoun House, Broadwick Street (1936–1937; Bertie Crewe & Kay) and Clifton House, Euston Road (1935–1936; Richardson & Gill). And, as previously noted, the final wing of Bush House was acquired by the Office of Works, 'to relieve the very severe congestion of the Inland Revenue Department at Somerset House'.[96] Other state departments were similarly housed, with, unsurprisingly, those in the vicinity of Whitehall proving especially popular. Horseferry House was occupied by the Board of Education,[97] Great Westminster, Dean Bradley, and Stanley House by the Office of Works,[98] and on the eve of the war, Cleland House by the Home Office (Aliens Department) and Air Raid Precautions Department.[99] Surprisingly, the grandest (in scale, if not grandiloquence) of all post-war speculative offices, Thames House, did not give room to government departments, despite its connection with Sir Alfred Mond. Like scores of other offices, however, it did house a new class of tenant characteristic of the period: state-controlled or state-sanctioned public corporations and boards. Following such legislations as the Agricultural Marketing Act, 1933, and the Unemployment Act, 1934, Thames House saw an influx of new bodies including the Milk Marketing Board and the Unemployed Assistance Board take their place among the more established commercial tenants (**Figure 4.6**).

The Second World War occasioned the widespread requisitioning of properties once more, and in another echo of the Great War and its aftermath, the late 1940s saw an acute shortage of office space. Governmental response, implemented by the Ministry of Works, showed new directions but also revealed older continuities. The Ministry erected over 200 Inland Revenue Offices before 1950.[100] It also built large offices for the Ministry of Labour and National Service, and the Ministry of National Service,

[93]Ibid.

[94]In 1949 the Ministry of Works was responsible for some 23,500 buildings – a more than fourfold increase from the 1922 figure. 'Official Building in 1949', *Builder* (18 August 1949): 227.

[95]1949–50 Civil Estimates (HC 1948–49 v26 no. 77-x), 43; 1950–1 Civil Estimates (HC 1950 vol. 1 no. 7), 46; No. 77-x), 43.

[96]HC Deb (25 February 1936): 309 col. 355.

[97]Civil Appropriation Accounts, 1936 (HC 1937–38 vol. 20 No. 16, 669).

[98]Ibid.: 429; Civil Appropriation Accounts, 1937 (HC 1938–9 vol. 20 No. 18, 403).

[99]Civil Appropriation Accounts, 1938 (HC 1939–40 v9 No. 6, 428).

[100]Annual report of the Ministry of Works, 1949 (cmd. 8538): 11.

Figure 4.6 A corner of the Milk Marketing Board's marketing department in Thames House, as captured on 26 July 1934, Douglas Miller/Hulton Archive via Getty Images, 3402980

among other departments.[101] But it was its controversial 'Lessor Scheme' that marked a logical progression from the procurement strategies of the 1920s and 1930s. Under this programme, private developers were able to circumvent building restrictions by erecting offices in London and provincial centres on condition they were leased to departments at a fixed rate of interest, typically 8 per cent.[102] From 1947, when construction began, to the early 1950s, when the last of some thirty lessor blocks were completed, millions of square feet of office space were procured from the private sector for exclusive government use: 'Thus central government's most direct patronage in the 1940s supported the private sector.'[103] The main source of controversy was the lowly calibre of architecture concomitant with a Ministry 'committed to saving public expenditure rather than securing good architecture.'[104] The context for this post-war policy had emerged in the previous decades, and its most direct progenitor was probably Richmond

---

[101] Ibid.

[102] Bullock, *Building the Post-war World*: 254.

[103] Harwood, *Space, Hope and Brutalism*: 387. For details of the London buildings, which alone provided 1.32 million square feet of floorspace, see J. M. Richards, 'New London Office Buildings: The Lessor Scheme Critically Examined', *Architects' Journal* (30 March 1950): 394–8.

[104] Bullock, *Building the Post-war World*: 254

Figure 4.7 Richmond House, Newhall Street, Birmingham, photographed in 1932 by Sydney Newbery (1894–1985). Architectural Press Archive/RIBA, RIBA73020

House, Newhall Street, Birmingham (**Figure 4.7**). Erected in 1931–1932 to designs by Herbert O. Ellis and Clarke for a private development company ('Richmond House (Birmingham) Limited'), it was immediately, and wholly, 'occupied by the whole of the staff engaged in the Inland Revenue administration of Birmingham',[105] on a 42-year lease. From a practical perspective, it was outstanding, but its dreary, stripped Classicism augured a more prosaic post-war aesthetic response typified by the lessor scheme blocks.

---

[105]TNA WORK 50/5. 'Richmond House, Birmingham', *Architects' Journal* (31 August 1932): 251.

State skewing of the property market?

The foregoing discussion has shown how the war acted as a catalyst to the commercial property sector, with a soaring need for office space in its immediate aftermath spurring the construction of a new generation of office blocks, mostly beyond the City of London. This demand was enough to warrant 'Office buildings on the grand scale', some clustered in new districts such as Kingsway and Millbank, others peppered throughout the West End and central London.[106] Beyond London, speculative office developments, principally, but not exclusively in those cities that had seen the emergence of identifiable office districts in the previous century, also spoke of buoyant demand, and robust, evolving urban economies. Especially in the industrial cities, which contained a shifting mix of declining manufacturing and expanding service-orientated industries, the growth of office buildings challenges the stereotypical views of economic stagnation and slump following the war. Nevertheless, the scale of demand and response should not be overstated. The demand for rentable office space after the war was uneven, geographically and temporally, and was not always met by speculatively built premises. The mainstay in most towns and smaller cities was rooms above shops, adapted premises or lettable floors in owner-occupied buildings.[107]

An important and heretofore missing part of the story, state involvement in the commercial property sector, raises questions about whether this skewed, or even buoyed, the market between the wars. The war catalysed the lessee/lessor relationship between the state and the private sector, which deepened and expanded between the wars as the civil service swelled. Even if counterfactual, it is tempting to wonder whether, for instance, Manchester's Sunlight House would have let so readily or fully, or Birmingham's Richmond House would even have been built, had the Ministry of Works not brokered government occupancy, or given indication, or firm commitment, of such. The near-certainty that 'official lessees' would be forthcoming in a district such as Millbank possibly encouraged developers to build on grander scales than they might otherwise have done. What seems more certain is that official lessees were coveted and that their presence subtly altered rental market dynamics, even disrupting the incipient zoning of core districts. Mayfair's Berkeley Square was one such locus, particularly Lansdowne House (1933–1935), Benson Greenall's earlier speculation, also designed by Wimperis Simpson & Guthrie.[108] In 1937 this block of luxury flats was 'disembowelled … to make the building suitable for [government] offices', thus contravening the wishes of the LCC's Town Planning Committee which 'approved it for residential purposes only'.[109] One Labour MP, George Buchanan, referring to local government experience, noted

---

[106]J. L. Fisher, 'Architecture To-Day', *Financial Times* (21 March 1934): 10.

[107]The *Estate Gazette*'s annual property market reviews, based on the received opinions and experiences of estate agents and other landed professions, provide an unparalleled insight into local and regional patterns.

[108]Dean Bradley House, Horseferry Road, S.W.1' Available online: https://thenewwiperstimes.com/2019/05/28/deanbradleyhouse/ (accessed 24 March 2020).

[109]HC Deb (1936–37): 320 col. 327, 335.

that 'the moment it was known that the Corporation were after any land or buildings up went the price'.[110] The next nearby building to be occupied by a government department was a purpose-built speculative office block, Berkeley Square House, that was somewhat disingenuously featured in *Official Architect* as 'the new Air Ministry building'.[111] The presence of such dependable (presumably) high-rent-paying tenants likely elevated the average rental values in Berkeley Square and elsewhere. Besides the state's direct patronage of the speculative office sector as official lessor, therefore, it may have exerted a more subtle, pervasive effect by raising the rental values and hence the viability of speculative developments in emergent business districts. For all the many and varied instances and effects of state intervention in the commercial property sector in the first half of the twentieth century, however, its intention as far as available records disclose, was securing accommodation, not financial gain. Thereafter, the lines blurred. Indeed, one of the more significant aspects of the 1960s property boom was the increasingly complex and murky relationships between private developers and nationalized bodies, corporations and local authorities, where profit was the shared, primary motive behind hundreds of city-centre speculative offices.[112]

Conclusion

Beyond the dynamics of the commercial property sector, state intervention, protagonists' motivations and other objects of enquiry, this chapter exposes the limitations of architectural historiography, which has remained largely insensitive, hostile even, to commercial property speculation, particularly office buildings. In part this reflects a broader professional disdain for commercial architecture and those involved with it. As Alan Powers noted, 'From the nineteenth century onwards, a class distinction operated between "commercial architects", specialising in office and warehouse buildings, and others with a more general and supposedly more altruistic type of practice'.[113] Also responsible is the pejorative lens through which the building type is usually glimpsed. Richard MaCormac, in explaining the remarkable 'misfit between what interests architectural historians, and what actually happened', deftly encapsulated this common perception of drab utilitarianism: 'it says something about the values of our society, that it is unable to apportion significance to the office as architecture because perhaps it conjures no feelings of faith, community, pleasure or awe, and it is a revealing insight into our ideas about cities, about work and private interest writ large'.[114]

---

[110]Ibid.: col. 345.

[111]'Berkeley Square House', *Official Architect*, 2 (December 1938): 241.

[112]See Ewan Harrison, 'Money Spinners': R. Seifert & Partners, Sir Frank Price and Public-Sector Speculative Development in the 1970s', *Architectural History* 61 (2018): 259–80.

[113]Alan Powers, *Britain. Modern Architectures in History* (London: Reaktion Books, 2007): 22.

[114]MaCormac, 'The Dignity of Office': 76.

Such architectural historiographic disregard is clearly geoculturally specific: the reverence and awe accorded to skyscraping transatlantic offices was, and is, phenomenal. Had the advocates of taller English buildings in the 1920s won the day, then our historiography might have been different – although probably not. Many 'higher buildings' protagonists were drawn from 'the powers of darkness', which was 'identified vaguely and inconsistently as property owners, developers, capitalist interests, or the unappreciative masses'.[115] In preservationist historiography, which whiggishly pitted its righteous cause in opposition to the activities of rapacious developers, commercial development, tall and short, was darkness writ large. Even though, as Peter Mandler has shown, these two movements, for development and for preservation, were not always in binary opposition, preservationist thinking and rhetoric has undoubtedly inflected architectural historiography.

The net effect of all this was for a partial, fleeting gaze that alighted primarily on prestigious headquarters buildings by eminent architects or those bearing the hallmarks of proto or full-blown modernism, thus overlooking swathes of more stylistically traditional speculatively built offices. This historiographic bias has not only been to the detriment of understanding the office building type, but to fuller appreciations of the built environment in the early decades of the twentieth century, specifically that embracing or embodying the interactions and overlaps of the public and private sectors. Even if the state 'was still in the grip of Victorian individualism, reluctant to trespass on the sacred rights of private property', as this chapter has shown, it was also an eager and assertive collaborator, a guiding hand even.[116] In fact, the appropriation and procurement of private space, with speculative offices repurposed as instruments for the realization of governmental administration, could be seen as the state extending its reach, geographically and bureaucratically, and by extension, the frontiers of liberal governmentality. As such, this chapter ostensibly helps counter 'the commonly held belief that pre-1945 Britain was lightly governed'.[117] But for all the insights that this facet of the urban built environment gives into the nature of liberal governance in the 1920s and 1930s, the power and influence of the central state should not be overstated, nor the agency of urban capitalist-developers in shaping the fabric of the city be underplayed. Rather, it was, and continues to be, the dialectical tensions between the state and business, preservation and development, lessors and lessees, and the optics of darkness and light that constituted the generating and transformative mechanism of the commercial urban built environment: 'we will not make full sense of the one without the other'.[118]

---

[115]Ethan Carr, review of *Towards World Heritage* by Melanie Hall, ed., in *Heritage & Society* 8 no. 2 (November 2015): 191.

[116]Mandler, 'Rethinking the "Powers of Darkness"': 226.

[117]James Epstein, review of Patrick Joyce, *The State of Freedom: A Social History of the British State since 1800* in *American Historical Review* 119, no. 3 (June 2014): 982.

[118]Mandler, 'Rethinking the "Powers of Darkness"': 238.

Select bibliography

Primary

Archival sources
Command Papers; Debates (House of Commons); Select Committee Reports etc. (available at
https://parlipapers.proquest.com/parlipapers).
The National Archives (WORK 50; TNA PT 1).

Newspapers and periodicals
*Architects' Journal, Architectural Review, Builder, Buildings and Building Management, British
Builder, Building News, The Economist, Estates Gazette, Financial Times, Manchester Guardian,
Office Equipment, Official Architect, Times, London Gazette, New Yorker, Yorkshire Post and
Leeds Intelligencer.*

Secondary

Websites/digital resources/databases
https://www.iwm.org.uk/collections/item/object/205214747
https://thenewwiperstimes.com/2019/05/28/deanbradleyhouse/

Articles

Beresford, M. W. and R. Unsworth. 'Locating the Early Service Sector of Leeds: The Origins of an
Office District'. *Northern History* 44, no. 1: 75–109.
Cruickshank, D. 'Origins of Offices'. *Architectural Review* 174, no. 1041 (1983): 81–4.
Jamilly, E. 'Patrons, Clients, Designers and Developers: The Jewish Contribution to Secular
Building in England'. *Jewish Historical Studies* 38 (2002): 75–103.
Lowe, R. 'Bureaucracy Triumphant or Denied? The Expansion of the British Civil Service,
1919–1939'. *Public Administration* 62, no. 3 (1984): 291–310.
MacCormac, R. 'The Dignity of Office'. *Architectural Review* 190, no. 1143 (1992): 76–8.
Richards, J. M. 'New London Office Buildings: The Lessor Scheme Critically Examined'.
Architects' Journal 111 (1950): 394–8.
Sharples, J. '"The Visible Embodiment of Modern Commerce": Speculative Office Buildings in
Liverpool, *c.* 1780–1870'. *Architectural History* 61 (2018): 131–73.
Turvey, R. 'Office Rents in the City of London 1867–1910'. *The London Journal* 23, no. 2 (1998): 53–67.

Chapters (in edited volumes/collections)

Mandler, P. 'Rethinking the "Powers of Darkness": An Anti-History of the Preservation
Movement in Britain'. In *Towards World Heritage: International Origins of the Preservation
Movement 1870–1930*, edited by M. Hall, 221–39. London and New York: Routledge, 2011.
Scott, P. 'The Evolution of Britain's Urban Built Environment'. In *The Cambridge Urban History
of Britain, vol. 3, 1840–1950*, edited by M. Daunton, 495–523. Cambridge: Cambridge
University Press, 2001.
Sutcliffe, A. 'The "Midland Metropolis": Birmingham, 1890–1980'. In *Regional Cities in the U.K.
1890–1980*, edited by G. Gordon, 25–40. London: Harper & Row, 1986.
Thomas, M. 'The Service Sector'. In *The Cambridge Economic History of Modern Britain, vol. 3,
1860–1939*, edited by R. Floud and P. Johnson, 99–132. Cambridge: Cambridge University Press,
2004.

PhDs/unpublished research

Clarke, J. 'The Development of the Speculative Office in Inter-war England' (unpublished PhD thesis, University of Cambridge, 2020).

Thorne, R. 'Office Building in the City of London 1830–1880' (unpublished paper presented at an Urban History Group Colloquium, London, 1984).

Thorne, R. 'Post-war listing: Informative Report on Office Buildings in London 1945–60' (unpublished English Heritage Historians' Report, 1987).

Books

Anderson, G. (ed.). *The White-Blouse Revolution: Female Office Workers since 1870*. Manchester: Manchester University Press, 1980.

Banks, F. R. *The New Penguin Guide to London*. Harmondsworth: Penguin, 1986.

Bullock, N. *Building the Post-war World: Modern Architecture and Reconstruction in Britain*. London: Routledge, 2002.

Cherry, G. E. *Birmingham: A Study in Geography, History and Planning*. Chichester: J. Wiley, 1994.

Clunn, H. *London Rebuilt, 1897–1927*. London: John Murray, 1927.

Cowan, P. et al. *The Office: A Facet of Urban Growth*. London: Heinemann Educational, 1969.

Dunning, J. H. and E. V. Morgan (eds.). *An Economic Study of the City of London*. London: Allen and Unwin, 1971.

Faber, J. *Oscar Faber: His Work, His Firm and Afterwards*. London: Quiller Press, 1989.

Griffiths, A. *Memorials of Millbank, and Chapters in Prison History*, vol. 1. London: H. S. King & Co, 1875.

Harwood, E. *Space, Hope, and Brutalism English Architecture, 1945–1975*. New Haven and London: Yale University Press, 2015.

Jeremy, D. J. *A Business History of Britain, 1900–1990's*. Oxford: Oxford University Press, 1998

Marriott, O. *The Property Boom*. London: Hamish Hamilton, 1967.

Matthews, D. *The Priesthood of Industry: The Rise of the Professional Accountant in Business Management*. Oxford: Oxford University Press, 1998.

Rose, J. *The Dynamics of Urban Property Development*. London: E. & F. N. Spon, 1985.

Scott, P. *The Property Masters: A History of the British Commercial Property Sector*. London: E. & F. N. Spon, 1996.

Sheppard, F. H. W. (ed.). *Survey of London, vol. 39, The Grosvenor Estate in Mayfair, Part 1*. London: Athlone Press, for the London County Council, 1977.

Skinner's Property Share Annual 1950–1. London: Thomas Skinner, 1951.

The Stock Exchange Official Yearbook. London: Thomas Skinner, 1965.

Turvey, R. *The Economics of Real Property. An Analysis of Property Values and Patterns of Use*. London: G. Allen & Unwin Ltd., 1957.

SECTION II
DESIGNING COMMUNITY INFRASTRUCTURE

In the post-war years the design of public houses was increasingly in the province of the architect, catalysed by the State Management Scheme or 'Carlisle Experiment' developed by the Government's Central Control (Liquor) Board during wartime to curb excessive drunkenness amongst munitions workers. The board employed a team of 'official architects' (i.e. in the employ of the state), led by Harry Redfern, to develop what became known as the 'New Model Inn', which influenced pub design for the next two decades. Design reform was very much at the heart of the Carlisle Experiment; architectural design was deployed to sanitize the iniquitous Edwardian pub. One of the board architects' tactics was to remove brewers' advertising from pub exteriors and in doing so they stimulated a revival in the craft of painted inn signs, a tradition associated with eighteenth-century taverns and pubs.[1]

It was a revival which endured. A corollary of the success of the Carlisle Experiment's New Model Inn prompted major brewers to develop 'Improved Public Houses' to stymie the risk of Prohibition and perpetuate state intervention, as Julian Holder discusses in his essay. In 1930, *Country Life* noted the 'revival that has taken place in the last few years of the sign-painter's craft', in both 'country towns and villages'.[2] It excited collaborations between architects and craftsmen: at Joseph Hill's The Dolphin in Kingston-Upon-Thames, a sign was produced carved in wood and gilded; for Alfred Blomfield's Mitre Pub for Watney, a lead-coated sheet steel lamp was produced by the Morris Singer foundry.

Discussion of the inn-sign revival reached an even larger audience through an exchange of letters in *The Times* in 1932. The architect Basil Oliver, who had worked on the Carlisle Experiment, noted other centres of 'revival' in East Anglia, namely Cambridgeshire, West Suffolk and especially Colchester in Essex: 'There is at least one firm of brewers, trading in East Anglia, who are systematically reforming all their sign-writing with the aid of the large-scale sheets … of lettering designed by Mr Eric Gill', which were available for purchase at the Photograph Stall of the V&A.[3] Gill had produced a number of signs himself in collaboration with the artist Denis Tegetmeieir at the instigation of the museum's director.[4]

The correspondence in *The Times* revealed the misgivings observers had about contemporary signage; pub and inn signs had started to become mere advertisements for breweries, eroding the idiosyncrasies of English village and urban life. This concern was

---

[1]It was felt to be part of, but distinct from, the older tradition of trade signs.
[2]'Illumination in Signs', *Country Life* (22 March 1930): 86.
[3]Basil Oliver, 'Inn Signs', *The Times* (25 August 1932): 6.
[4]Eric Gill, 'Inn Signs', *The Times* (31 August 1932): 6.

a manifestation of the wider rural preservationist movement promoted by figures like the architect Clough Williams-Ellis in his popular polemic *England and the Octopus*, a tract against untrammelled suburban sprawl.[5] The architect Guy Dawber, with Williams-Ellis one of the leading lights of the Campaign for the Preservation of Rural England (CPRE), pleaded with the brewers, 'who are putting up such excellent attractive buildings [to] … initiate a campaign for beautifying them with well-designed and painted subject signs', which would 'be conducive to good business and give employment to many artists who are endeavouring to make the charm and beauty of our countryside compatible with modern developments'.[6] They could do so, correspondents suggested – tongue in cheek – with names and signs that would reflect modern life: 'The Car and Starter', 'The Plug and Throttle' and 'The Gudgeon Pin' were mooted as fitting titles, reflecting the emerging 'carscape' of rural and suburban England.[7]

All this agitation in the columns of the *Times* led in part to an exhibition of Inn Signs held at the Building Centre, New Bond Street, in November 1936, a collaboration between the Brewers' Society and the CPRE. Critically, it was coordinated by architects, including Basil Oliver alongside Guy Dawber, Albert Richardson, who had written about eighteenth-century inns and taverns, and Edwin Lutyens, whose Drum Inn in Cockington, Devon, had provided another model for the Improved Public House. The exhibition included signs for urban pubs and taverns, but it also included many painted for new suburban establishments and countryside inns. An unexpected success, it was visited by 18,000 people over one month, and of the 429 exhibits, a number came from the State Management Scheme as well as from leading brewers.

The exhibition, and indeed the 'Inn Sign Revival' campaign more broadly, draws together a number of cognate themes running through the next two sections. Straightforwardly, it demonstrates how architects conceived of their practice as extending beyond just the production of buildings. Design and design reform touched many other departments of life. It also demonstrates the long reach of reconstruction – in this case from a craft revival initiated during war time which continued to manifest itself into the 1930s and indeed beyond. But foremost, it represents the interpenetration of town and country and attempts to understand and improve the new suburban condition which so typified the 1920s and 1930s.

The essays in the next two sections loosely deal with 'town' and 'country', respectively, but the essays and themes contained within them often reveal their imbrication. David Matless's *Landscape and Englishness* (1998) considered rural reconstruction in considerable depth, but it also showed the rhetorical interdependency and interpenetration of town and country in the writings of figures such as Clough Williams-Ellis and the planner, Thomas Sharp.[8] In the quarter century since the book's publication there has been a considerable body of work on rural modernity in social and cultural

[5]Clough Williams-Ellis, *England and the Octopus* (London: G Bles, 1928).
[6]E Guy Dawber, 'Inn Signs', *The Times* (9 May 1936): 15.
[7]'Inn Signs Old and New', *The Times* (2 March 1936): 15.
[8]David Matless, *Landscape and Englishness* (London: Reaktion Books, 1998).

history. Matless also charted critiques of suburbia, and urban historians such as Michael John Law have increasingly sought to reframe accounts of the experience of suburban modernity more positively.[9] Architectural histories of the 1920s and 1930s have been less interested in the suburban and the rural – aside from stylistic phenomenon such as the Tudoresque[10] – but the essays in these sections show that there is fertile ground for further research deploying methods of social and cultural history, and historical geography, alongside architectural histories.

In the post-war years, architects became advocates for rural preservationism, and for sound suburban development, united against the 'sprawl' of private speculation and the resulting 'villadom', as some contemporary commentators described it. The essays in these two sections explore aspects of suburban modernity and a number of common concerns in the development of town and countryside. They deal, in many cases implicitly, with an ambiguity and uncertainty about the suburban zone, and in others, contributors remind us that the countryside was a place of active development and modernity alongside, or indeed in contrast to, rural nostalgia and economic agricultural decline. The essays also reveal much about the architect's positionality, often serving as the agent of the liberal state as the profession sought to protect its privileges and demonstrate its usefulness to an enfranchised mass democracy, building on the themes of professional service discussed in Section I.

Architects' newly defined obligations to the public frequently coincided with rural preservationism and the defence of principles of good development by the state and industry. One such instance of this is in the reform of pub design, increasingly at the hands of architects as we have seen and as is described in more detail in Julian Holder's essay. Current historiography tends to valorize this ultimately heavy-handed interventionism by the British state, and the biopolitical control it exemplifies (perversely, given the ultimate ends of producing more life-taking munitions for war). Architects were deeply implicated in these forms of liberal governmentality.

Holder's essay makes brief mention of the Arts and Crafts *impresario* Lawrence Weaver, one-time architectural editor of *Country Life* who wrote with excitement about 'The Public House of the Future' for that title in 1916, reflecting not only on the developments by Redfern for the Carlisle Experiment but also the Public House Trust scheme and the People's Refreshment House Association, pro-temperance organizations which had been active in rebuilding pubs.[11] Weaver's interest in this subject was at least twofold: first, Weaver frequently proselytized for the use of architects, and these were architect-designed buildings; second, in describing Gretna, he praised it as a 'veritable club', thus drawing attention to the pub's function as a centre of communal social life.[12]

---

[9]Michael John Law, *The Experience of Suburban Modernity: How Private Transport Changed Interwar London* (Manchester: Manchester University Press, 2014).

[10]See for instance Gavin Stamp, 'Neo-Tudor and Its Enemies', *Architectural History* 49 (2006): 1–33.

[11]See Lawrence Weaver, 'The Public House of the Future', *Country Life* (16 September 1916), 329–30; idem. (23 September 1916): 357–8.

[12]Ibid.: 357.

However, Weaver lamented that pubs had not provided a suitable service 'for the youth of the countryside or for the women of the cottages'.[13]

In the immediate post-war years, Weaver was an advocate for the village club movement, penning a survey of *Village Clubs and Halls* published in 1920 in which he provided numerous examples of architect-designed buildings.[14] The Village Clubs Association had been fostered by the Agricultural Club in 1918 as a means of countering the effects of rural depression and of stimulating political and social life among those communities: 'The young men and women who had been absent from the villages during the war,' it was observed in the *Town Planning Review*, 'found on their return a depressing absence of opportunities for social intercourse, for recreation and intellectual improvement'.[15] The new Village Clubs would be 'social centres, established and managed on broadly democratic lines' to provide 'some of the attractions and amenities and opportunities for educational development which the towns afford'.[16] Weaver and the Village Clubs Association were adamant that these would not be patrician 'top-down' initiatives but would be 'the outcome of the people's own desire'.[17] The Village Club would be 'the centre of communal life and activity, a place where all the members of the community, of whatever degree, can meet on common, and equal ground'.[18] These themes are picked up in Kieran Mahon's essay on the Village College in the next section.

The emphasis on democratic control and empowerment is significant given the top-down development of the community centre that Alistair Fair charts in his essay on this new typology. This is all the more notable given the community centre's origin in American liberal political discourse. Margaret Woodrow Wilson, addressing the American Civic Association in 1916, talked of the concept of a 'social center' and the school house as a 'community center'.[19] She similarly saw the community centre as part of an infrastructure of 'non-partisan, non-exclusive organisation' for direct democracy, as a form of people's assembly. The American Civic Association which had fostered the City Beautiful Movement and promoted the concept of the 'civic centre' may indeed be partly responsible for the coining of 'community centre' as a term.

Lawrence Weaver was also an advocate for disabled ex-serviceman and acted as the client for the Haig Memorial Homes housing association built off the back of a fund launched in 1928. A national scheme, the first development was opened in Morden in 1932 on the periphery of the London County Council's St Helier Estate in south-west London. The Morden estate was designed by George Grey Wornum (Weaver's near neighbour) who designed courtyards of neo-Georgian terraces, with brightly coloured

---

[13]Ibid.

[14]Lawrence Weaver, *Village Clubs and Halls* (London: Country Life, 1920).

[15]Harold Lacey, 'Village Clubs Association', *Town Planning Review* 9, no. 3 (December 1921): 166.

[16]Ibid.

[17]Lawrence Weaver, *Village Clubs and Halls* (London: Country Life, 1920): 1.

[18]See Jeremy Burchardt, 'State and Society in the English Countryside: The Rural Community Movement 1918–39', *Rural History* 23, no. 1 (2012): 81–106.

[19]'The School House as a Community Center, Margaret Woodrow Wilson' (Washington, DC: American Civic Association, 1916).

doors and shutters, designed as a 'model group of community dwellings', and avoiding 'the charity-giving air of so many Victorian examples'.[20] In common with many new estates, there was a concern from the start about the social and communal life of the estate. As Wornum's wife, the artist Miriam Wornum later recalled, 'There was no money for any social service work, but they let us have a cottage in which we could start various activities. … We did quite a lot of things in a communal way and for the children.'[21] After Weaver's premature death in 1931, however, Wornum was responsible for the design of the Lawrence Weaver Institute and Club Rooms on the same site, opened in 1933, essentially an estate community centre, providing a hall with a stage, and club facilities for men and women. It was a fitting tribute to Weaver who had helped to reinvigorate the Village Club movement as part of rural reconstruction after the war, its ideal here imagined in a suburban setting of a cottage estate.

The elision of the community centre and village hall typology and ideal in projects like the Lawrence Weaver Institute is significant. We should see the Village Club movement, though focused on rural communities, as contiguous with the development of community infrastructure in urban and suburban contexts too. The suburban, Garden City-inspired form of the Haig Homes and the 'village club' community centres were an effective bridge to the sorts of initiatives that Fair charts in 1930s Scotland. Fair uses the typology of the 'community centre' as a lens through which to trace evolving ideas of citizenship. In particular, he explores how the design and programme of the centres intersected with debates about productive leisure time and physical recreation, seen in part as a means of mitigating economic deprivation in so-called 'Special Areas' where the effects of depression were felt especially keenly. Looking ahead to Section III, 'Special Areas' are discussed in Smith and Preston's essay on land settlement. Lawrence Weaver makes an appearance here too: as Mark Swenarton has chronicled, he effectively ran the rural branch of the state housing programme in the form of the Land Settlement Scheme which dispensed small-holdings to returning servicemen and often experimented with novel forms of constructional technology, including concrete and rammed earth.[22] Preston and Smith examine the regeneration of rural life after the war, and there is perhaps an irony that the failure of land settlement programmes was attributed to the lack of social and community infrastructure there.

Religion, and especially the established church, was much concerned with devising such an infrastructure, as Matthew Grimley has described in his work on Liberal Anglicanism.[23] It was Liberal Anglicans who had first defined the socio-political aspirations of a welfare state in the wake of the war. Some manifestations of this ideal

---

[20]'The Lawrence Weaver Institute, Morden', *Architect and Building News* (6 January 1933): 10–11.

[21]Miriam Wornum and Grey Wornum, 'Grey Matter' (unpublished memoirs), chapter entitled 'Haig Homes': 3.

[22]The influence of the Land Settlement Scheme is discussed at length by Joanna Thomas and Rebecca Preston in their essay found in Section III. Also see Mark Swenarton, 'Rammed Earth Revival: Technological Innovation and Government Policy in Britain, 1905–1925', *Construction History* 19 (2003): 107–26.

[23]Matthew Grimley, *Citizenship, Community, and the Church of England: Liberal Anglican Theories of the State between the Wars* (Oxford: Oxford University Press, 2004).

are discussed in the final essay in this section on the 'Parish' and parochial church design. Religion remained a dominant force in society, politics and culture after the war. Architectural historians of this period need to 'think religiously'; organized religion remained a major shaping factor in the built environment, though its forms of patronage were shifting. Not only, as Clare Price's essay shows, were there new forms of democratic participation in the commissioning of parish churches, but religion inflected debates about housing, in particular in the voluntary sector and through Ecclesiastical Commissioners, who managed the Church's significant land holdings. Clare Price's chapter on the 'Parish' considers how the design of local parish churches revealed the changing relationship between church authorities and local communities. The changing role of the architect in these church-building projects also speaks of the growth of community representation in building projects and the professional reluctance with which it was often met. Price's piece focuses on the ordinary parishioner's role in the Parochial Church Councils which were able to exert considerable influence on church design. It is notable that these mechanisms were inherently chauvinistic, undoing the strong female philanthropic influence on church design which had become such an important tradition in the nineteenth century and first decade of the twentieth. Price's piece helps us to understand the shift in the prestige of church design in light of democratization, without recourse to simplistic assumptions about secularization.

The essays that comprise the following two sections share a number of common themes of community and social infrastructure, rural reconstruction and suburban morphology. Readers will find that some of the ideas introduced here apply equally to Section III. In this section, however, we look specifically at how a new community infrastructure was created to underpin societal reconstruction. We examine a number of component parts of that infrastructure and their architectural manifestations: the reification of the community, and the need for it to have a physical 'centre'; the 'New Model Inn' as an ideal public house for the working class; and the formation of new or more populated parishes and the making of their spiritual centre. These were instruments of social control and methods of social organization; they were tools of liberal governmentality. The architect – certainly the mainstream liberal incarnation of the architect – was a convenient, if sometimes unwitting, co-conspirator in this, imagining and giving form to these systems of control.

CHAPTER 5
COMMUNITY CENTRE: NEW HOUSING ESTATES IN SCOTLAND
Alistair Fair

In January 1939, the *Scotsman* discussed the recent appearance of community centres in Scotland, concluding that they represented 'a social revolution that has come to stay'.[1] These centres were the 'product of housing changes during the last fifteen years', namely suburban house-building by local authorities (for rent) and speculative builders (predominantly for sale) which had followed the end of the war:

> Thousands of families have been moved from overcrowded, unhealthy areas in cities and towns to new colonies outside. Thousands more are laying their foundations in the new housing estates. Colonists they are, in all truth. Old friends, old habits of living, old haunts and associations have been left behind. New friendships, new habits, new haunts have to be found if healthy social living is to go on. Community ties must be created, outlets obtained for community effort.[2]

In these circumstances, the *Scotsman* ascribed a redemptive role to the community centre. These buildings offered 'social and recreational salvation' to 'hapless colonists'.[3] They would create new communities and would allow individuals to expand their horizons through participation in leisure and educational activities.

In 1939, it was reported that there were nine community centres in Scotland, with one more being under construction and a further thirty planned.[4] Others were projected across the UK; the model of a centre designed by Maxwell Fry was shown at the New York World's Fair that year.[5] Spatially, and often also in terms of the activities they housed, these buildings had well-established institutional forebears, including village halls, working men's clubs, and miners' institutes, as well as the communal buildings erected by the likes of the Cadburys, the Rowntrees, and William Lever on the

---

[1]'Scotland and the Community Centre: A Social Revolution That Has Come to Stay', *Scotsman* (18 January 1939). An early version of part of this essay was presented at the Institute of Historical Research's 'Homes Fit for Heroes' centenary conference in 2019. My thanks to the organizers: Matthew Bristow, Elizabeth Darling, Mark Swenarton and Matthew Whitfield. For their help and advice as I expanded and revised the material I would like to thank Tom Hulme, Jessica Kelly, Barbara Neilson (Glasgow City Archives), Simon Pepper, Robert Proctor, Lou Rosenburg, Neal Shasore, and David Weir (Renfrewshire Archives).
[2]Ibid.
[3]Ibid.
[4]Ibid.
[5]'Community Centre', *Focus* 4 (1939): 25–30.

influential estates which these philanthropic employers created. Pioneering work done in community building had also been initiated by the Dunfermline-born philanthropist Andrew Carnegie, whose interventions in the town's Pittencrieff Park after 1903 were intended to create a new civic focus. University settlements were a further influence, as were nineteenth-century liberal ideas about civic engagement.[6] But whereas the idea (and sometimes also the architecture) of a 'hall' evoked the medieval (or its Arts and Crafts reformulation), the term 'community centre' was new in the 1930s, reflecting the repackaging of these ideas by reformers and policymakers in response to contemporary concerns about citizenship, the city and leisure. The subject could be contested. In 1939, one Edinburgh councillor deemed 'this community business' to be 'a lot of tommy rot'.[7]

This chapter interrogates the terms in which early community centres were discussed and explores the forms that some of these projects took. It augments the literature on the ways in which conceptions of community were recast in the aftermath of the war, amid parallel discussions of citizenship and leisure, by considering how these ideas found spatial form. In so doing, it focuses on Scotland, partly to balance existing writing on the idea of 'community' on new housing estates in England and partly to complement studies of post-1919 Scottish housing.[8] The chapter begins by considering Cameron House, a social centre serving a new estate on Edinburgh's south side. It then looks west, examining a largely unexecuted municipal community centre in late 1930s Glasgow. Finally, a similarly unbuilt project in Johnstone shows the way in which, by 1935, the Scottish Office sought to encourage a new, improved kind of housing scheme in which community ideals would be foregrounded. To some extent, the involvement of the state here might seem to pre-figure the later 'Welfare State', and certainly post-1945 developments nationally built on the ways in which leisure had been drawn into the framework of social policy during the 1920s and 1930s.[9] Nonetheless, the project at Johnstone, like the others discussed in this chapter, also gave tangible form to concerns and strategies which illustrate the specific context of the aftermath of the war.

The emergence of the community centre

The idea that the community was both a rhetorical and literal unit of organization and identity was well established by 1918 and developed further during the next two decades, not least as it could be linked by contemporaries to wider ideas of collective citizenship. As Tom Hulme has argued, citizenship was defined and practised during

---

[6]Andrzej Olechnowicz, *Working-Class Housing in Britain between the Wars: The Becontree Estate* (Oxford: Clarendon Press, 1997): 141–2.
[7]'Community Centre: An Edinburgh Scheme Criticised', *Scotsman* (29 March 1939).
[8]E.g. Olechnowicz, *Working-Class Housing*. Lou Rosenburg, *Scotland's Homes Fit for Heroes: Garden City Influences on the Development of Scottish Working Class Housing, 1900 to 1939* (Edinburgh: The Word Bank, 2016).
[9]Robert Snape, 'The New Leisure, Voluntarism, and Social Reconstruction in Inter-war Britain', *Contemporary British History* 29, no. 4 (2015): 51–83.

the 1920s and 1930s at both national and local levels.[10] New 'national' conceptions and indeed legal definitions of citizenship were made manifest by wartime service and the expanded franchise, but they did not displace more local ideas of citizenship, which, building on Victorian traditions of localism, took such forms as civics education, engagement with local government or participation in festivals and pageants. Increasing emphasis was also placed on the healthy body as a mark of citizenship. The roles of the individual and the state were further subjects of debate. Some nineteenth-century thinkers had come to advocate collective, state-encouraged approaches to the working class and the formation of urban community in preference to individualism and laissez-faire attitudes.[11] This change had its roots in liberal thought, at some remove from the conventional representation of Gladstonian liberalism's emphasis on individual rights. In fact, John Stuart Mill had proposed that civic duty and collective political engagement would secure personal liberties, while in 1861, Thomas Hill Green suggested that civic engagement was the necessary consequence of liberty, arguing that the role of the state was to maintain the conditions in which liberty might flourish.[12] Citizenship could thus be understood as both a status and an activity.[13] It offered local and national identities; it could be actively practised, whether by means of exercise or pageantry; it supplied a basis for interventions in (and engagement with) the built environment. For reformers, citizenship was active, communal and engaged, concerned with the common good as much as the individual's rights. The debate gained particular significance during the 1930s in view of the rise of totalitarianism in continental Europe, which some contemporaries saw as the consequence of a passive population.[14]

Questions of citizenship came to be associated with the broader subject of leisure. Leisure assumed greater prominence in workers' lives after 1918, prompted by the growth of new forms of mass culture (not least cinema) and reductions in the length of the working week; women, in particular, were increasingly cast as 'consumers' of leisure.[15] However, as Robert Snape has argued, leisure was 'simultaneously emancipatory and problematic'.[16] The pre-1914 thinking of Green and others suggested a view of leisure as a social good from which a new post-war society might grow, but only if the 'correct' activities were encouraged. Earlier worries that certain (perhaps commercialized or alcohol-fuelled) activities were incompatible with civic culture were joined by new concerns about such things as the cultural impact of American films.[17]

---

[10]Tom Hulme, *After the Shock City: Urban Culture and the Making of Modern Citizenship* (London: Royal Historical Society, 2019), 22–3.

[11]Ibid.: 23.

[12]Ibid.

[13]Richard Weight and Abigail Beach, 'Introduction', in Richard Weight and Abigail Beach (ed.), *The Right to Belong: Citizenship and National Identity in Britain, 1930–1960* (London: IB Tauris, 1998): 1–18, 2.

[14]Frederic J. Osborn, *Overture to Planning* (London: Faber and Faber, 1941): 27.

[15]Snape, 'New Leisure': 55–6.

[16]Ibid.: 55.

[17]Ibid.: 53.

One arena in which these ideas were debated after 1918 was the voluntary sector. The key group was the National Council of Social Service (NCSS). Founded in 1919, it coordinated the work of local organizations and, on paper if not always in practice, took a radical, reforming stance.[18] Inspired by the liberal tradition of Green and others, several strands of thought informed its activities, including the notion that community engagement was the bedrock of democratic society, the idea that the working class should be encouraged to offer civic leadership, a wish to promote the productive use of leisure time, and a sense that urban areas lacked the community spirit felt to exist in villages.[19] Citizenship was defined by the NCSS in broad, participatory terms, encompassing work, home, and family life. It favoured forms of recreation which were 'improving', often communal, and typically not commercialized.

The NCSS's interests in citizenship and leisure led to the formation of its New Estates Community Committee (NECC) in 1928. The creation of this committee recognized the significant way in which the urban environment had been reshaped since the end of the war in 1918 and the extent to which this development had become contested. The 1919 and subsequent housing acts led to a substantial programme of council house construction across Britain which lasted until 1939, while significant numbers of suburban houses were also built for private sale and rent. Output varied from year to year, and from place to place, making generalizations difficult, but overall, in England and Wales, 28 per cent of new housing during the 1920s and 1930s was built by local authorities.[20] In Scotland, however, the figure was 68 per cent, and in some places such as Glasgow, it was higher still.[21] Across Britain, the influence of garden city ideals meant that suburban housing for the working and middle classes was built at lower densities than hitherto, but the contrast was especially distinctive in Scotland (**Figure 5.1**). Low-density four-in-a-block flats and semi-detached or terraced houses with gardens were very different from the high-density older tenements of inner Glasgow and Edinburgh. Some commentators questioned the effect of such low-density layouts on residents. We have already noted the *Scotsman*'s discussion in 1939 of the apparent lack of community among 'hapless colonists'. That same year, the paper also quoted a talk given to the Edinburgh City Business Club, in which it was claimed that the quiet that middle-class residents valued in the suburbs could be disorientating for the transplanted working classes.[22] It was reported that children were getting into mischief, men were 'moody', and that there was 'a good deal of neurasthenia' among women.[23] In these circumstances, the NECC saw an opportunity. The absence, as yet, of commercialized leisure activities

---

[18]Ibid.: 62.

[19]Olechnowicz, *Working-Class Housing*: 8–10, 137–55.

[20]Annette O'Carroll, 'Social Homes, Private Homes', in Miles Glendinning and Diane Watters (ed.), *Home Builders: Mactaggart and Mickel and the Scottish Housebuilding Industry* (Edinburgh: RCAHMS, 2015): 283–95, 286.

[21]Ibid. The distinctiveness of the Scottish experience reflected vigorous use of slum-clearance powers, especially in the 1930s, plus lower levels of owner occupation.

[22]'Community Centre: An Edinburgh Success', *Scotsman* (25 January 1939).

[23]Ibid.

Figure 5.1 Housing at Pinkie Road, Musselburgh, East Lothian © East Lothian Museums Service

on the new estates and the lack of inherited local traditions left the way clear for the encouragement of new social networks.[24] Ernest Barker, the NECC's chairman and a prominent figure in these debates, thus argued in 1937 that residents should

> create a social and cultural life [...] instead of relying solely on the wares of the commercial conveyor of amusements. This widening of the circle of creative interests constituted a new chapter in the history of English culture – it was developing a new organ of democracy.[25]

There were several assumptions in all these arguments: a preference for non-commercial forms of leisure, a tendency for middle-class commentators to see the working class as a homogenous group, a degree of anti-suburban prejudice, and an idealized view of the pre-industrial English village (and Scottish burgh).[26]

As an organization, the NCSS was not unique in suggesting that community spirit should be encouraged.[27] For example, the Gas Light and Coke Company's showpiece housing scheme, Kensal House in west London (1937), included not only sixty-eight

---

[24]Snape, 'New Leisure': 67.
[25]'Social Interests on New Estates', *The Times* (10 April 1937): 9.
[26]James Greenhalgh, 'Consuming Communities: The Neighbourhood Unit and the Role of Retail Spaces on British Housing Estates, 1944–1958', *Urban History* 43, no. 1 (2016): 158–74.
[27]Olechnowicz, *Working-Class Housing*: 137–80.

flats but also a children's nursery as well as rooms for adult recreation, in which gendered activities such as clothes-making and furniture construction could take place.[28] Residents formed a committee to manage the buildings and grounds. The aims were to develop individuals' skills, to encourage productive forms of recreation, to reinforce the family and, by giving residents the possibility of self-management, to strengthen the democratic ideal. The project was in part the product of commercial imperatives, being a 'modern' showcase for gas products in the face of competition from electricity, but its conception also reflected the firm's progressive stance and links to the design reform movement. In particular, Kensal House embodied the ideas of the reforming housing consultant Elizabeth Denby, who collaborated with the architect Maxwell Fry on the building's design.

Kensal House can also be understood in terms of contemporary official recommendations about the kinds of facilities that should be provided alongside working-class housing. In this respect, the state, too, was increasingly concerned with leisure and community. The Tudor Walters report in 1918 called for housing to be accompanied by the construction of communal institutions. Raymond Unwin was a member of the Tudor Walters committee and had previously included a club house in the layout for Hampstead Garden Suburb, co-designed with Barry Parker. A 1935 report by the Juvenile Organisations Committee of the Board of Education similarly discussed 'the need for youth community centres on new housing estates'.[29] In order to render life 'enjoyable, co-operative and progressive', it proposed centres with a hall and gymnasium, plus recreation rooms, a workshop, crafts room and library.[30] In 1935, the Department of Health for Scotland (DHS) oversaw a study tour of continental housing projects, reporting that 'community' seemed to be planned for in these schemes through the provision of reading rooms, workshops for crafts, gymnasia and restaurants, and that similar facilities 'might help to woo the Scot from his rather grim community outlook and strengthen those gregarious and sociable instincts which at present his surroundings do little to encourage'.[31] The report concluded by recommending 'the provision, in close proximity to the houses, of improved facilities for rest, recreation, and social intercourse'.[32] A 1936 joint memorandum by the DHS and the Scottish Education Department (SED) on the subject of 'community life in new housing schemes' took up this idea, again proposing the construction of communal facilities.[33]

By this date, the nomenclature applied to this sort of building was changing. In 1937, the NECC was renamed the Community Centres and Associations Committee. This term 'community centre' had emerged in recent years, as the architects Flora and Gordon Stephenson noted in the 1942 report of a project looking at this building type, supported

---

[28]Elizabeth Darling, *Re-forming Britain: Narratives of Modernity before Reconstruction* (Abingdon: Routledge, 2007): 157–67.

[29]Olechnowicz, *Working-Class Housing*: 174; Board of Education, 'Juvenile Organisations Committee: Report on the Need for Youth Community Centres on New Housing Estates' (London: HMSO, 1935): 3.

[30]Board of Education, 'Juvenile Organisations Committee': 4 and 6.

[31]DHS, 'Working-Class Housing on the Continent' (Edinburgh: HMSO, 1935): 10.

[32]Ibid.: 25.

[33]DHS and SED, 'Community Life in New Housing Schemes' (Edinburgh: HMSO, 1936): 3.

by the Leverhulme Trust, the NCSS, the Royal Institute of British Architects, and the Housing Centre.[34] Although, as we have seen, halls, institutes and settlements were well-established building types, the repackaging of these precedents as the 'community centre' suggested modernity. The key word is 'centre'. The 1930s and 1940s saw the creation of a growing number of specialist, reforming 'centres' which were concerned with aspects of contemporary life and citizenship, including organizations such as the aforementioned Housing Centre as well as new architectural types such as the health centre.[35] The term 'centre' itself promised efficiency. For example, the so-called civic centres built in Britain during the 1920s and 1930s were, at a time of administrative expansion, intended to centralize local-government departments within a single, often monumental headquarters complex. Civic centres' often traditional architectural styles thus belied their progressive conception and relationship with contemporary ideas of local government.[36] 'Centre' also suggested expertise: a centre would accommodate specialist knowledge and skills and, potentially, would be the place in which that expertise was communicated to others.

Housing and education legislation made municipally sponsored community centres possible, while circumscribing what they might offer. Section 86 of the Education Act 1921 reflected established concerns about the bodily health of the population in the wake of the war by enabling support for centres and equipment intended for physical training, as well as playing fields.[37] Section 90 of the Housing (Scotland) Act 1925 permitted housing authorities to support the provision of 'buildings or land which in the opinion of the Board will serve a beneficial purpose in connection with the requirements of the persons for whom the housing accommodation is provided'.[38] Section 107 of the equivalent Act in England was similar. This legislation was the work of the reformist Conservative government elected in October 1924, which encouraged slum clearance and promoted the use of innovative construction methods in council housing, leaving traditional techniques to underpin a revival of private-sector housebuilding.[39]

In 1937, the Physical Training and Recreation Act provided the means for local authorities and voluntary bodies in England and Scotland routinely to create and

---

[34]Flora and Gordon Stephenson, *Community Centres – a Survey by Flora and Gordon Stephenson for the Community Centres Joint Research Committee* (London: Percy Lund, 1942): iii.

[35]Elizabeth Darling and Alistair Fair, '"The Core": the Centre as a Concept in Twentieth-century British Planning and Architecture. Part One: the Emergence of the Idea', *Planning Perspectives*, early online publication 2022.

[36]Johanna Roethe, '"A Pretty Toy" or "Purely Functional"? Town, City and County Halls in the Interwar Period', in Elain Harwood and Alan Powers (ed.), *The Architecture of Public Service: Twentieth Century Architecture 13* (London: C20 Society, 2017): 25–41, 26; Neal Shasore, 'Southampton Civic Centre: Patronage and Place in the Interwar Architecture of Public Service', in Elain Harwood and Alan Powers (ed.), *The Architecture of Public Service: Twentieth Century Architecture 13* (London: C20 Society, 2017): 41–61, 41. See also Robert Proctor's chapter on the work of Percy Thomas in the present volume.

[37]Board of Education, 'Juvenile Organisations Committee': 9.31% of the First World War recruits had been unfit for service (Hulme, *Shock City*: 141).

[38]Board of Education, 'Juvenile Organisations Committee': 8. The 1936 Housing Act made similar provisions.

[39]Mark Swenarton, 'Houses of Paper and Brown Cardboard: Neville Chamberlain and the Establishment of the Building Research Station at Garston in 1925', *Planning Perspectives* 22, no. 3 (2007): 257–81.

manage centres for physical activity and social purposes. Such centres were no longer restricted to the estates built by housing authorities, as had previously been the case. The primary goal of the legislation was to increase levels of fitness. During the parliamentary debate, the president of the Board of Trade, Oliver Stanley, hoped that 'keep fit' might flourish; in his view, good health was a duty, although he suggested that the timing of the legislation – at a time of rearmament – was coincidental.[40] At the same time, it was recognized that these centres could have a wider role. Introducing the legislation, Stanley reported that the shorter working hours of recent years had created more time for leisure.[41] This development, he suggested, 'will demand some more active occupation than just sitting about and resting. Are we to occupy it by going to more football matches and more cinemas?' In terms which echoed the wider programmes of cultural reform being pursued by the likes of the BBC, Penguin Books and the architectural press, he went on: 'the real use of leisure will call for the development of interest, of taste, of knowledge'.[42]

Alongside the wish to promote physical fitness, there are three further contexts for the 1937 legislation. First, we have already noted the growing number of official reports which proposed the construction of centres for communal activities on new estates. Although a generalized community spirit was one ambition, some of these reports also touched – like Oliver Stanley – on the specific question of leisure, rendering it increasingly an area of interest for government. For example, the DHS and SED had in 1936 referred to the 'urgent need' to provide for the 'useful and healthy occupation of leisure time', and in particular the 'development of character, mind and body' among the young.[43] A second 'official' context for the 1937 legislation, particularly in Scotland, is found in the targeted interventions made by government in response to the Depression of the early 1930s. A community centre in Dumbarton, for example, was set up by the commissioner for Special Areas using the provisions of the Special Areas (Development and Improvement) Act 1934 and formed part of an emerging system of social services targeted at the unemployed.[44] The actions of several pioneering local authorities form a third context. For example, the London County Council (LCC) – spurred on by such members as Ruth Dalton and Lewis Silkin – was increasingly not only supporting centres but also seeking to initiate them.[45]

The 1937 legislation stressed the value of partnerships between the 'statutory and voluntary bodies', along with a degree of self-management.[46] Similarly important was the idea that centres should avoid sectional interests; they were to have cross-community appeal. By this date, a centre very much on these lines was already in operation in Edinburgh, and it is to that which we now turn.

---

[40]*Hansard*, HC Deb (7 April 1937), vol. 321: col.201.
[41]Ibid.: cols.205–6.
[42]Ibid.
[43]DHS and SED, 'Community Life': 3.
[44]National Records of Scotland [hereafter 'NRS'], ED27/328, Dumbarton Community Centre, 13 May 1969.
[45]London Metropolitan Archives ['LMA'], LCC/CL/HSG/01/046 REQ, Ruth Dalton to Herbert Morrison, 28 December 1936.
[46]NRS, ED39/2, 'A Brief Account of the Work of the National Council of Social Service' [1937]: 8.

Edinburgh: A new settlement

In 1919, Edinburgh Corporation sought to acquire land on what was then the southern edge of the city at Prestonfield in order to build housing for residents transferred from the Pleasance and Causewayside slum areas.[47] In 1927, the city architect, Ebenezer MacRae, reported on his plans. Five hundred and ninety-six dwellings were projected, at sixteen houses per acre, being a mixture of 'three apartment' (i.e. two bedroom) four-in-a-block flats, and 'four apartment' flats in three-storey blocks.[48] Within the estate was a property originally built in 1770, Cameron House. It was handed over by Edinburgh Corporation in 1930 to the Edinburgh University Settlement to be run as a 'Social and Educational Centre'.[49] A donation of £500 was also made.

The Settlement had been founded in 1905. The idea was that students would live in the Settlement Building, situated in High School Yards in the Old Town, and would lead community activities. The initiative was typical of university settlements elsewhere and co-existed with other reformist activities within Edinburgh's Old Town.[50] The Settlement was reportedly encouraged to expand its work to Prestonfield by the residents themselves, some of whom had engaged with its activities at High School Yards. As the 1930 Annual Report put it:

> The people from the crowded slum areas of the Pleasance and Causewayside migrated out to Prestonfield, and at first felt, like other prospectors, very isolated and cut off from their old associations. The Corporation has provided excellent houses for the slum dwellers, but this alone is not enough; the people must create for themselves a new communal life such as they have never known before.[51]

The person who facilitated this shift of focus was the Settlement's warden, Grace Drysdale. As at High School Yards, activities at Cameron House were presented in 'improving' terms. They included such things as debating clubs. In some cases a long game was perhaps being played: it was reported that 'a kazoo band [...] though hardly coming under the head of music [...] will some day [...] develop into the orchestra for the community'.[52] Particular attention was given to children's activities, the aim being to 'prevent the return of the children to their old slum haunts' and also to encourage leadership.[53] The annual reports are inevitably celebratory but suggest successes.

---

[47]Edinburgh City Archives [hereafter 'ECA'], 0228/01, Prestonfield file.
[48]ECA, SL2/1/4, Housing and Town Planning Committee, 24 January 1927.
[49]University of Edinburgh Centre for Research Collections ['CRC'], GD20/8, Annual Report, 1930: 6.
[50]E.g. Elizabeth Darling, 'Womanliness in the Slums: A Free Kindergarten in Early-Twentieth-Century Edinburgh', *Gender and History* 29, no. 2 (2017): 359–86.
[51]CRC, GD20/8, Annual Report, 1930, 7.
[52]Ibid.
[53]Ibid.: 8.

Toddlers in the play club, for example, were reported to be of 'better physique' and to have 'greater self-control' and 'energy'.[54] All this took place within a building which was calculatedly domestic: 'an atmosphere of home' – understood in terms of an idealized, reforming middle-class domesticity – was the intention (**Figure 5.2**).[55] Cameron House was thus conceived as a site of 'reform' in a way that complemented the new flats on the estate more generally.

By 1934, the Settlement was considering if it should also take an interest in the adjoining Niddrie Mains estate, which was being developed by the Corporation to relieve the St Leonards slum area.[56] Here the tenants were perceived to be different from those at Prestonfield. The Settlement suggested that while some Niddrie residents came from what was termed 'a good class', others were from lodging houses.[57] Space was left in the layout for public buildings, and the city authorities actively 'feued' these sites

Figure 5.2 Dinner in the Playroom at Cameron House © British Association for Early Childhood Education

---

[54]CRC, GD20/8, Annual Report, 1933: 31–2.
[55]CRC, GD20/8, Annual Report, 1930: 7. For further discussion on the extent to which new suburbs were intended to encourage middle-class values, see e.g. Alison Ravetz, *Council Housing and Culture: The History of a Social Experiment* (London: Routledge, 2001): 83–5, 100, 118, 161–2.
[56]CRC, GD 20/7/1, Settlement Executive Committee, 10 October 1934.
[57]Ibid.

(i.e., allocated and sold them).[58] A college was created, a joint venture of the Settlement and the city authorities, and in 1937 it was reported that women's favourite classes were sewing and cooking, while men enjoyed gymnastics and boxing.[59] Meanwhile a residents' welfare association came into being, with the aim 'to improve the moral, intellectual, and social well-being of the community'.[60] There was also a committee of residents, interested parties and members of the city council, while a tenants' association created a social centre within a hut supplied by the city council.[61]

Given the wider context in which housing estates, homes and community centres were intended to be sites of reform, it is not surprising to read Grace Drysdale complaining in 1933 that 'undesirable characters from Edinburgh are coming down' to Prestonfield.[62] Of course, as Andrzej Olechnowicz and others have pointed out, the faith that model institutions and planning alone would encourage change was surely misplaced, not least as the home (and elective models of community relationships) assumed ever-greater significance in residents' lives.[63] Nonetheless, inspectors at Niddrie reported that residents were prospering in their new surroundings and that what were termed 'rough and difficult' tenants were doing well.[64] (The subsequent history of the estates was, however, mixed: much of Niddrie Mains has been demolished, whereas Prestonfield is largely intact.)

Here, therefore, was an important re-fashioning of the reformist project, with the Settlement, previously an inner-city concern, transferring its attentions to the emerging suburbs. While Edinburgh Corporation's role was fairly minimal, namely the provision of the building and a small grant, it was not entirely absent, with the local authority working collaboratively within the terms laid down by the legislation. To the west, however, a more interventionist approach was being taken by the authorities in Glasgow, as the next section of this chapter discusses.

Glasgow: Civic initiative

In September 1936, Glasgow Corporation's Sub-committee on Sites and Buildings agreed that 'the Director [of Housing] should be instructed to prepare a plan showing a civic centre which would be suitable for a large housing development scheme'.[65] The 'scheme' in question was Knightswood, a large municipal estate to the north-west of the city centre, begun in the 1920s; the site was on Alderman Road. In this context, the term 'civic centre' had a specific meaning. While it could be used to describe a grand

---

[58]ECA, Edinburgh Corporation, 2 May 1929.
[59]CRC, GD20/8, Annual Report, 1937: 33.
[60]ECA, 0255/20, Niddrie box.
[61]ECA, SL39/2/17, Properties Subcommittee, 23 June 1931.
[62]ECA, H228/12, Grace Drysdale to Town Clerk, 12 October 1933.
[63]Olechnowicz, *Working-Class Housing*: 8, 214.
[64]ECA, 0255/019, Report of Housing Inspector visit, 8 June 1936.
[65]Glasgow City Archives ['GCA'], Glasgow Corporation, Sub-committee on Sites and Buildings, 4 September 1936.

municipal headquarters (of the kind noted above), it could also refer to a more modest complex of buildings provided as part of a new housing estate, intended partly to foster social life.[66] At Knightswood, the centre was to include a public library and swimming baths, as well as several halls. As with (administrative) civic centres elsewhere, efficiency was an important aim, with the minutes of a meeting in 1938 noting that 'it was to avoid scattered unrelated provision of public services being made that ex-Convener McKinlay had proposed and finally received corporation approval to the community centre scheme'.[67] Other sites had previously been identified for the baths and library, but they were now reallocated.[68] The centre was to be funded according to the provisions of the 1925 Housing (Scotland) Act. Work began in 1939 but was interrupted by the Second World War, and only part of the scheme was eventually completed.

The provision of the centre reflected, on the one hand, growing interest on the part of (Labour) city councillors and officials in this sort of facility. In 1937, the *Herald* reflected on the recent growth of community centres in Glasgow:

Glasgow was the pioneer authority in providing community centres at housing schemes. The first was established at Hamiltonhill in 1925. The success of this centre has induced the Department of Health to write to other local authorities urging them to establish community centres for new areas. The Glasgow Labour administration intends to provide a chain of community centres for the new suburbs, some of which were built without any consideration for social activities.[69]

At Hamiltonhill, just north of the city centre, the city authorities had in 1919 received a donation to be put towards housing provision, but in the event the money was diverted to the construction of a social centre.[70] Amid the estate's sash-windowed, neo-Georgian housing, the arts and crafts inflections of this building stood out. A colonnaded entrance led into a foyer flanked by rooms for reading and games; the main hall seated 200.[71] The centre accommodated physical training classes, sewing and cookery demonstrations, lectures, and gardening and football clubs.[72] Evidently it was a success: by 1936, there were requests to enlarge it.[73]

Glasgow's plans for Knightswood were encouraged by central government reports. In February 1936, the city's Medical Officer of Health, A. H. Macgregor, suggested that the Knightswood site 'be considered in connection with the possible development of what are now coming to be known as "community centres"', citing the 1935 report on youth

---

[66]'Town Planning in Thames Valley', *Times* (25 September 1925): 4; Roethe, 'A Pretty Toy': 25.
[67]NRS, DD6/340, Minutes of meeting between Secretary of the DHS and the Convener and Sub-Convener of Glasgow Housing Committee, 26 January 1938.
[68]Ibid.; GCA, D-TC 8/20/39, Memo for David Stewart, 30 April 1936.
[69]'Community Centre for City Housing Site', *Herald* (19 February 1937).
[70]GCA, Glasgow Corporation, Housing Committee, 4 August 1926.
[71]Corporation of Glasgow Housing Department, 'Review of Operations' [1927]: n.p.
[72]*Hansard*, HC Deb 15 February 1938 vol. 331 c. 1681.
[73]GCA, Glasgow Corporation, Sites and Buildings Sub-committee, 20 March 1936.

community centres issued by the Board of Education (discussed above); the 1936 DHS/ SED report on community life was subsequently also referred to.[74] Whereas the social centre at Cameron House in Edinburgh was created within an existing building and was primarily intended for classes, lectures, discussion groups and children's activities, the Knightswood project was not only all-new but, in the spirit of the 1935 Board of Education report, was dedicated to physical health as well as other forms of recreation. In November 1936, the DHS Chief Architect, John Wilson, outlined the scheme:

> Mr McNab [Glasgow's Director of Housing, 1932–1941] called on me this morning to discuss a proposal to place a civic centre on a large piece of open ground on the south side of the [Knightswood] scheme. [...] It is proposed to erect a large hall with a small hall attached with all the necessary offices, and, at the back of this building, a large swimming bath with a flat roof over part of the building for sun bathing.
>
> To the north of this large building there are two buildings with some ornamental water and gardens between them. The one is a small public library, and the other a community centre with gymnasium and rooms for clubs, i.e. boy scouts, girl guides, etc.[75]

The Deputy Town Clerk elaborated on this brief a couple of months later, noting that the centre would provide accommodation for youth organizations, tenants' groups, Mothercraft and specialist medical instruction.[76] Here, then, was a building dedicated to physical health and 'improving' recreational pursuits: classes, meetings, reading, dramatic performances and musical concerts. These ideas remained, although their physical arrangement was altered during the course of design. A later scheme placed the pool at the heart of the main building, alongside the hall and the library; a separate building to the south was planned for welfare and medical provision (**Figure 5.3**).

The proposed mixture of facilities was not unusual. It echoed on a smaller scale the large civic centres of the period; it also reflected the legislation by means of which community centres were funded, as well as the typical contemporary definition of citizenship in terms of physical health as well as civic engagement. Contemporaneous community centres often accommodated both bodily and mental recreation and, by extension, bodily reform. As the NCSS's Ernest Barker put it:

> given proper encouragement, men and women, and boys and girls, may discover for themselves the joys and values of self-created pleasures. Music, drama,

---

[74]GCA, D-TC 8/20/39, A. M. MacGregor to Town Clerk, 21 February 1936. GCA, Glasgow Corporation, Sub-committee on Sites and Buildings, 2 April 1937; NRS, DD6/340, W. Gordon to DHS Secretary, 25 February 1937.
[75]NRS, DD6/340, J. Wilson memorandum, 17 November 1936.
[76]NRS, DD6/340, W. Gordon to DHS Secretary, 25 February 1937.

'Keep-fit' activities, cycling, rambling, hobbies, and the like, have all their place in the constructive use of leisure time, and are enjoyed most when they are done actively rather than heard or seen passively.[77]

The result would be 'sturdy and healthy bodies'. Gymnasia were common; so too were swimming pools, as in Alan Reiach's competition winning design of 1938 for Ilkeston (which also included a fire station).[78] Norris Green, in Liverpool, had a communal canteen.[79] Slough's large Social Centre of 1937 was provided by the local landowner, Slough Estates, and featured space for sunbathing and winter sun-ray treatment.[80]

Medical provision, too, was not unusual and similarly reflected the wider emphasis on good health as an element of citizenship. Nonetheless, the Medical Officer of Health's description of the Knightswood community centre as a 'positive health centre' brings to mind a particular model, namely the Pioneer Health Centre, Peckham.[81] This scheme had been inaugurated in 1926 by two local doctors and was, in effect, a social centre incorporating a medical practice; members would not simply come when they were ill. By 1935, the 'Peckham Experiment' was housed in a new building, designed by Owen Williams and opened with much publicity, suggesting that it may well have been known in Glasgow.[82] As was intended at Knightswood, it provided facilities for communal

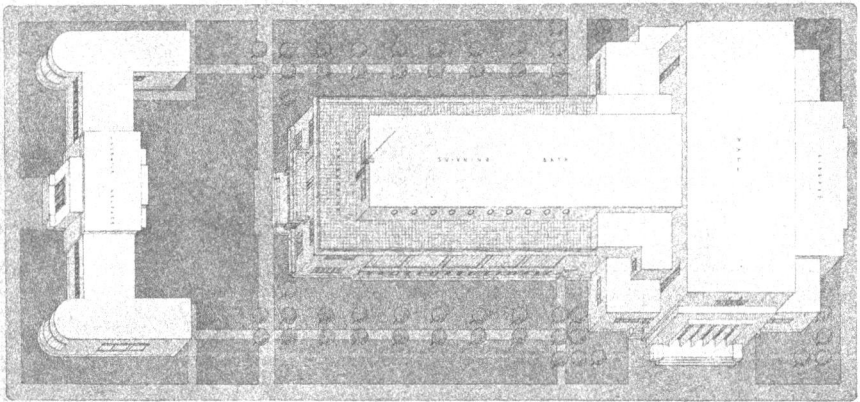

Figure 5.3 Proposed Knightswood Community Centre, *c.* 1937, from 'Housing Department Review of Operations, 1919 to 1937', courtesy Glasgow City Archives, D-TC7/12/2

---

[77]Ernest Barker, 'Community Life', offprint from *Community* (January 1938).
[78]'Community Centre at Wythenshawe', *Guardian*, 15 September 1936; 'Competition for Community Centre and Fire Station, Ilkeston', *Architects' Journal*, 88/211 (15 December 1938): 995.
[79]'Community Centre', *Guardian* (30 December 1938).
[80]'Slough Social Centre', *Times* (29 September 1937): 9.
[81]GCA, D-TC 8/20/39, A. M. MacGregor to Town Clerk, 21 February 1936. For Peckham, see Darling, *Re-forming Britain*: 54–72.
[82]E.g. 'Peckham Experiment', *Scotsman* (28 March 1935).

recreation and physical exercise, including a pool. Self-reliance and participation were encouraged. The social club was intended to revive the sense of community which the centre's founders felt had been destroyed by urbanization. The building's large windows and glazed internal partitions offered views of activities taking place within the centre, the aim being to encourage individuals to choose to take part and thus to take responsibility for themselves. A self-service canteen was similarly conceived. Fundamentally, it was hoped that a sense of participatory citizenship would develop.

The close relationship between the improving aims of the 'Peckham Experiment' and the design of its building demonstrates the extent to which community centre architecture was thought to be able to foster change. Ernest Barker, for example, called for buildings with 'dignity and purpose' which would be 'a credit and an inspiration'.[83] In the case of the proposed Knightswood centre, John Wilson of the DHS noted approvingly in late 1936 that 'the small scale sketch designs on modern lines promise very well and shew [sic] a level of design we have not obtained from Glasgow hitherto'.[84] It was reported that account had been taken of 'the natural simplicity of the surrounding houses', and so 'no attempt has been made to design a building with elaborate ornamentation, but rather to gain effect by a treatment on modern broad and simple lines'.[85] The design's visual modernity – not least its curved Crittall windows and flat roof – nonetheless contrasted with the neo-Georgian styling of the nearby houses, as did its unrendered brickwork. If the housing represented one contemporary view of good design, in which Georgian Classicism was often understood as something neighbourly, 'civic', rational and even 'modern' in its proportional, standardized basis, then the Knightswood community centre might also be understood as an example of a 'good' modern architecture.[86] In 1942, Flora and Gordon Stephenson hoped that community centres would serve as a good example in this regard:

> In one or two cases, the Community Centre in its attempt to develop individuality has abandoned dignity. The buildings, particularly on the interior, look like flashy, modernistic cinemas. Although such cheap and tawdry effects may have momentary appeal, they do not wear well. Above all, they do nothing to raise the standards of architectural appreciation among those who use the buildings.[87]

Their choice of words presented the ideal centre as a place whose design was distinct from contemporary commercialized leisure architecture, being instead intended to shape the taste of its users in ways that paralleled the improving nature of the activities

---

[83]Barker, 'Community Life'.
[84]NRS, DD6/340, J. Wilson memorandum, 17 November 1936.
[85]NRS, DD6/340, 'Report by the Director of Housing on a Proposed Civic or Community Centre Suitable for a Large Housing Scheme'.
[86]Louise Campbell, 'Foreword', in Julian Holder and Elizabeth McKellar (eds.), *Neo-Georgian Architecture, 1880–1970: A Reappraisal* (Swindon: Historic England, 2016): x–xvi.
[87]Stephenson and Stephenson, *Community Centres*: 57. These arguments echo J. M. Richards, *An Introduction to Modern Architecture* (Harmondsworth: Penguin, 1940), e.g.: 86–7.

it contained. The centre at Knightswood – clearly modern, but not flashily so – can be understood in these terms.

In March 1937, the DHS approved the plans for Knightswood, agreeing that the capital cost of the centre could be charged against the Housing Revenue Account.[88] Tenders were invited, and building work began. The proposals were exhibited at the 1937 Housing and Health Exhibition and then reached a wider audience through their inclusion in the North Scottish Pavilion at the 1938 Empire Exhibition in Glasgow: 'one of the exhibits is to be a large panel on which will be portrayed, by means of photographs, etc., a number of municipal services and, *inter alia*, it has been agreed to illustrate the best existing Community Centre scheme'.[89] The city authorities now planned further community centres. Although a proposed centre at King's Park was rejected because the housing had not been built by the Corporation, centres were planned for other areas: Blackhill, Balornock and Robroyston, Carntyne, Penilee, Pollok and Hillington.[90] The outbreak of war halted these plans, although some of the identified sites (for example, Pollok) came to house later community centres. At Knightswood, the part-built centre was placed on a 'care and maintenance basis' in autumn 1940.[91] The shell of the Welfare building was by then largely finished, but the larger pool/hall/library structure had only reached first-floor level. While the Welfare block was fitted out after 1945 and remains in use, the part-completed larger building was later demolished.

Johnstone: Community planning

As we have seen, one factor promoting the construction of community centres was the argument, by the middle of the 1930s, that recent housing estates were failing to foster a sense of community and citizenship. By this date, there was also a growing reaction to the design of these estates. In 1935, Sir John Stirling Maxwell, an early member of the Royal Fine Art Commission for Scotland, and a founding member of the National Trust for Scotland, hoped that private architects would be involved by Glasgow Corporation in developing the land at Pollok which the city had recently acquired from him.[92] While the city's Housing Committee rejected this suggestion, they nonetheless agreed that a move away from 'dull monotony' was desirable.[93] The DHS was making similar arguments. The *Paisley and Renfrewshire Gazette* referred in 1935 to 'the Department's campaign

---

[88]GCA, D-TC 8/20/39, letter from W. Murrie, 8 March 1937.

[89]GCA, Glasgow Corporation, Housing Committee, 21 April 1937; D-TC 8/20/39, Henry Ellis to Town Clerk, 12 February 1938.

[90]GCA, Glasgow Corporation, Sub-committee on Sites and Buildings, 21 January 1938. 16 September 1938 and 3 February 1939; Stanley Gale, *Modern Housing Estates* (London: Batsford, 1949): plates IX and X.

[91]GCA, Glasgow Corporation, Sub-committee on Sites and Buildings, 6 December 1940.

[92]'Pollok Estate Scheme', *Herald*, 5 January 1935.

[93]Ibid.

for improved architectural treatment in housing schemes', noting that the Howwood Road scheme in the small town of Johnstone would represent the 'first fruits' of this campaign.[94]

The Howwood Road scheme formed part of Johnstone Town Council's efforts to deal with substandard housing. In 1935, 200 properties were deemed uninhabitable.[95] One thousand new houses were planned for Howwood Road, plus churches, schools and open space.[96] Several potential layouts were drawn up in-house, and a meeting was arranged with the DHS.[97] At this meeting, it was suggested that the scale of the proposals demanded a considered approach:

> The suggestion [...] was that the first part should be laid out with a view to the development of the whole; that some provision should be made in the scheme for a hall or picture-house, and particularly a children's playground. They realised this was altogether a new venture. It was now a common complaint that all over Scotland to-day they were having too much of a stereotyped layout and building in the new housing schemes. Now they were going to get a little latitude from the Board of Health in the improvement of design and lay-out. They were not belittling the work or energy of Mr Mitchell by agreeing to give him a consultant.[98]

The DHS's new-found interest in design reflected the enthusiasms of the Secretary of State for Scotland, Godfrey Collins, who told Parliament in 1935 that 'drab and mean' estates would never produce people with a 'bright and healthy outlook'.[99] In October 1934, he appointed an Architectural Advisory Committee to consider 'the incorporation of architectural quality and amenity in the lay-out, planning and external treatment of houses for the working classes'.[100] The committee included James Barr (an engineer), Grace Drysdale (of Cameron House) and the architects John Begg, Frank Mears, James Miller, Thomas Tait, plus the DHS's John Wilson. Its creation came amid wider debates about architects' status and the nature of practice. Legislation in 1931 restricted the use of the title 'registered architect' to those who met certain criteria, cementing the idea of the architect as a qualified professional.[101] At the same time, some younger designers increasingly conceived their work in 'social' terms, encouraged by new approaches to

---

[94]'Howwood Road Scheme: Interest of Health Department', *Paisley and Renfrewshire Gazette* (23 November 1935).

[95]Paisley, Renfrewshire Archives [hereafter 'RA'], Johnstone Town Council, Housing Committee, 22 April 1935.

[96]'Howwood Road Scheme: Interest of Health Department', *Paisley and Renfrewshire Gazette*, 23 November 1935.

[97]RA, Johnstone Town Council, Housing Committee, 27 May 1935.

[98]'New Town at Howwood', *Paisley and Renfrewshire Gazette* (29 June 1935).

[99]*Hansard*, HC Deb 21 February 1935 vol. 298 c. 561.

[100]DHS, 'Report of the Scottish Architectural Advisory Committee on the Incorporation of Architectural Quality and Amenity in the Lay-out, Planning and External Appearance of Houses for the Working Classes' (Edinburgh: HMSO, 1935): 3.

[101]Mark Crinson and Jules Lubbock, *Architecture: Art or Profession? Three Hundred Years of Architectural Education in Britain* (Manchester: Manchester University Press, 1994): 85–6.

architectural education which emphasized the collaborative nature of practice and the potential for design to be an agent of social reform.[102] In this context, it is not a surprise that the DHS study of continental housing estates concluded that new Scottish housing schemes should be designed by architects, rather than being seen as 'hack-work'.[103] Stirling Maxwell's hopes for Pollok could be understood similarly.

Collins's committee concerned itself not only with the physical appearance of buildings, but also the integrated planning of housing estates. Thinking perhaps of Manchester's ongoing development at Wythenshawe, and using terms which firmly embedded planning within the civic project, they noted:

> We have been much impressed, in the case of one or two large authorities in England, with the statesmanlike manner in which the lay-out of large housing estates has been conceived and extended, and with the civic and financial benefits that have accrued to the authorities concerned by taking the long view. These estates include ample space for recreation, adequate shopping and welfare centres, libraries, halls, churches, cinemas and in some cases new and important industries, all conceived and designed from a town planning viewing, to form dignified and orderly setting for the social life of new communities.[104]

They concluded that 'houses should be primarily regarded not as independent units of accommodation but as the component parts of some carefully envisaged and scientifically designed entity of community life'.[105] Their recommendations accorded with other contemporaneous DHS reports, including the 1935 study of continental European housing and the 1936 joint DHS and SED memorandum on community life (both discussed above), and confirmed the interest of Edinburgh policymakers in this area. Howwood Road would thus become a demonstration of the DHS's interest in architectural quality and community planning.

In these circumstances, it is unsurprising that the department encouraged Johnstone Town Council to appoint an architect for the project. By September 1935, Thomas Tait had been selected.[106] Tait had impeccable local connections, having been born in nearby Paisley, where the Hawkhead Infections Diseases Hospital was completed to his office's designs in 1936.[107] He was a partner in the architectural firm of Burnet Tait and Lorne, which was the continuation of Sir John James Burnet's London practice. Although there was also a Glasgow practice bearing Burnet's name, Burnet Tait and Lorne increasingly sought work north of the border, and in 1934 it was selected to design the new building

---

[102]John R. Gold, *The Experience of Modernism: Modern Architects and the Future City* (London: Spon, 1997): 142–4.

[103]DHS, 'Architectural Quality': 17.

[104]Ibid.: 8.

[105]Ibid.: 9.

[106]RA, Johnstone Town Council, Housing Committee, 23 September 1935.

[107]Historic Hospitals, online at https://historic-hospitals.com/gazetteer/renfrewshire/ (accessed 20 May 2021).

in Edinburgh for the Scottish Office, subsequently named St Andrew's House.[108] In addition, by the end of 1936, Tait was working on the 1938 Empire Exhibition in Glasgow.[109] In view of his firm's involvement at St Andrew's House, one wonders if the DHS recommended Tait to Johnstone. The archives are silent on the matter, but Tait was, as we have noted, a member of their Architectural Advisory Panel on housing design, and his practice had particular knowledge of the design of workers' housing, having completed a number of houses on the planned estate built for Crittall Windows workers at Silver End, Essex, in 1928.[110]

Tait's layout for the Howwood Road estate was developed through the winter of 1935–1936 (**Figure 5.4**).[111] Its axial symmetries anticipate the Beaux-Arts planning of the Empire Exhibition site. Low-rise blocks of flats with smooth rendering, low-rise roofs and curved balconies were to be arranged on streets flanking a grand central avenue, and there were to be communal buildings containing clubrooms, a library, and dental and maternity clinics.[112] Who called for their inclusion? The archives seem not to say: perhaps the Town Council, the DHS or even Collins himself. Maybe Tait was

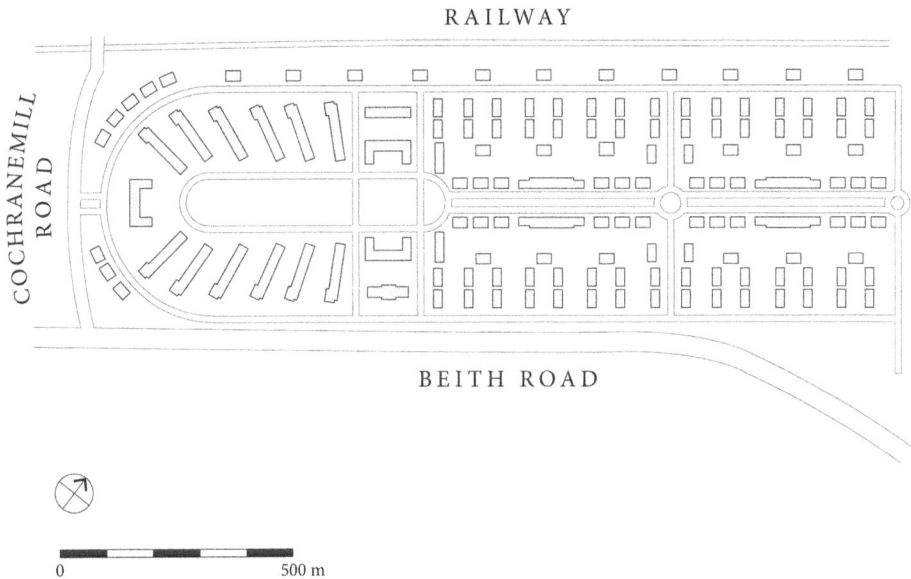

RAILWAY

COCHRANEMILL ROAD

BEITH ROAD

0   500 m

Figure 5.4 Howwood Road scheme, Johnstone. Plan showing the proposals as of *c.* 1936, with flats and communal buildings around a grand central avenue, drawn by Hannah Towler based on a photograph of the model in RIBA Collections

[108]David M. Walker, *St Andrew's House: An Edinburgh Controversy, 1912–1939* (Edinburgh: Scottish Development Department, 1989): 28.

[109]'Empire Exhibition in Glasgow in 1938', *Scotsman* (6 October 1936).

[110]Graham Thurgood, 'Silver End Garden Village, 1926–1932', *Thirties Society Journal* 3 (1983): 36–42.

[111]E.g. RA, Johnstone Town Council, Special Meeting, 6 January 1936.

[112]'New Scottish Housing Scheme Development: Attractive Layout', *Scotsman* (28 February 1936).

inspired by the community buildings (designed by others) at Silver End? Whoever had the idea, Collins was delighted:

> I am writing to offer you my heartiest congratulations on the very high standard of architectural quality which [the plans] reveal. The variety of treatment in the lay-out, with its many interesting features, the simple yet attractive elevations of the houses, the pleasing way in which the communal centre fits naturally into place, and the broad, ample conception of the whole scheme all lend character and distinction to a fine piece of work.[113]

Collins suggested that the results demonstrated 'the wisdom of employing the best professional skill in housing work'. He concluded:

> Your magnificent effort clearly shows how much can be done to secure greatly improved modern amenities with first-class architecture in our housing schemes, and I trust that your example will be widely followed by other authorities throughout the country.[114]

Work soon began on the housing.[115] The communal buildings, however, seem never to have been built, derailed like Knightswood by the outbreak of war in 1939. Indeed, there seem to be no surviving designs for them.[116]

Nonetheless, the Johnstone scheme is significant, for several reasons. First, it demonstrates the extent to which 'community' thinking had permeated central government by the mid-1930s. It also shows how the terms of the debate had shifted. No longer would good housing alone lead to reform, nor, indeed, was it sufficient to graft multifunctional community facilities onto a scheme already begun, whether by voluntary action or state initiative. Now, the estate was planned as an integrated whole, with the *Scotsman* referring to 'modern ideas of planning, not only of the individual houses but of a whole estate for community life'.[117] In 1936, Howwood Road was described as 'a new garden city';[118] the local newspaper called it a 'new town'.[119] It was, in fact, much smaller than the new towns which would be begun after 1945, but there are hints of another planning form which started to be discussed during the 1930s, namely the neighbourhood unit.[120] Motivated by practical and idealistic concerns, neighbourhood

---

[113]RA, Johnstone Town Council, Special Meeting, 10 February 1936.
[114]Ibid.
[115]RA, Johnstone Town Council, Housing Committee, 15 November 1937.
[116]London, RIBA Archives, PA858/6, comprises a sheet of drawings only of the houses, dated 1936.
[117]'New Scottish Housing Scheme Development: Attractive Layout', *Scotsman* (28 February 1936).
[118]'Provost and Housing', *Paisley and Renfrewshire Gazette* (9 May 1936).
[119]'New Town at Howwood', *Paisley and Renfrewshire Gazette* (29 June 1935).
[120]E.g. Gold, *Experience of Modernism*: 146–8 (on the MARS Group Plan, a string of neighbourhoods linked by transport routes); Patrick Abercrombie and J. H. Forshaw, *County of London Plan* (London: Macmillan, 1943): 25–9. Wythenshawe offers a useful example before 1939.

units were intended through their size, layout and facilities to encourage community spirit and local identity. Although the Howwood Road scheme was never fully realized, the fact that it was conceived in these terms links it to ideas which would become orthodox after 1945.

Conclusions

After 1919, community centres were to be simultaneously agents of change and representations of the communal ideal. In essence, these centres were a 'modern' response to the challenges of the present: urbanization, poverty, illness, perceived social breakdown. At the same time as they were rooted in the present, they also embodied the promise of a different future. By encouraging what seemed to be productive forms of recreation as well as physical health, the aim was a transformed population. Architecturally, their facilities varied, but the term 'community centre' was sufficiently well understood for the BBC to present a series of talks on the subject in 1937, and for the *Scotsman* in 1939 to declare it had 'come to stay'.[121] The state had by then come to play an increasingly significant role in financing these centres, but the voluntary sector's contribution remained important, while community centres also demonstrate clearly the persistence of 'local' interpretations of citizenship and the agency of local authorities.

Leisure, culture and citizenship remained important topics of debate after 1945.[122] Lewis Silkin, involved in the LCC's discussions of community centres in the 1930s, was by 1946 Minister of Town and Country Planning.[123] That year, with reference to the new towns programme, he argued that 'a new series of Becontrees [the LCC's largest estate] would be fatal';[124] such estates, it was suggested, lacked 'civic sense' and 'community life'.[125]

Similarly, when the plans for East Kilbride new town were being drawn up in 1947, the DHS criticized recent Glasgow suburbs, calling them 'an unco-ordinated mass [...], with no civic identity, practically no independent social facilities.'[126] Community centres, the SED noted that same year, were 'training grounds for democratic citizenship'.[127] We might also draw a connecting line between the broadly conceived 1930s community centre and the multifunctional leisure centres of later decades, which combined spaces for the arts, sports and social gatherings.[128] At the same time, there were changes after 1945,

---

[121]Olechnowicz, *Working-Class Housing*: 174; 'Scotland and the Community' (n. 1 above).

[122]For more on this, see Alistair Fair, *Modern Playhouses: An Architectural History of Britain's New Theatres, 1945–1985* (Oxford: Oxford University Press, 2018): 9–44.

[123]LMA, LCC/CL/IISG/01/046 REQ, notes of meeting on 25 February 1938.

[124]*Hansard*, HC Deb 8 May 1946 vol. 422 cc. 1072–1184 (*c*. 1088).

[125]Ibid., *c*. 1076.

[126]DHS, 'New Town at East Kilbride' (Edinburgh: HMSO, 1947), 2. See also Alistair Fair, 'Citizenship, Community and the New Towns in Post-War Scotland', in Clarisse Godard-Desmerest (ed.), *The New Town of Edinburgh: An Architectural Celebration* (Edinburgh: Birlinn, 2019): 193–216.

[127]SED, 'Planning for Community Centres, Village Halls and Playing Fields' (Edinburgh: HMSO, 1947): 20.

[128]For leisure centres generally: Otto Saumarez Smith, 'The Lost World of the British Leisure Centre', *History Workshop Journal* 88 (Autumn 2019): 180–203. For Billingham Forum: Fair, *Modern Playhouses*: 104–6.

not least typological specialization and a diminished role for the voluntary sector. New architectural types such as the arts centre, the civic theatre and the subsidized Repertory theatre emerged. Like 1930s community centres, these buildings were dedicated to an 'improving' form of leisure but had a particular emphasis on performance.[129] Meanwhile, post-war health centres emulated the medicalized, statist model of the Finsbury Health Centre (1938) rather than the pluralism of the Pioneer Health Centre.[130] In parallel, citizenship was increasingly understood in 'legal' terms.[131] The debates of the 1920s and 1930s are thus distinctive, and of significance in their own right, not simply as the precursor to subsequent attempts to plan for community life in post-1945 Britain.

Select bibliography

Primary

Archives
Edinburgh City Archives
0228/01: Prestonfield file
0255/20: Niddrie box
H228/12: Town Clerk's files
Edinburgh Corporation Minutes
Glasgow City Archives
Glasgow Corporation minutes
Town Clerk's files
Hansard
London Metropolitan Archives
LCC/CL/HSG/01/046: Community Centres on Housing Estates
National Records of Scotland
DD6/340: Housing (Scotland) Act 1935, Glasgow
ED27/328: Community Facilities
ED39/2: National Council of Social Service
Renfrewshire Archives, Paisley
Johnstone Town Council minutes
RIBA Archives, London
PA858/6: T.S. Tait archive
University of Edinburgh Centre for Research Collections
GD20/7 and 20/8: Edinburgh University Settlement
Periodicals
Architects' Journal
Focus
Herald
Paisley and Renfrewshire Gazette
Scotsman
Times

---

[129]Fair, *Modern Playhouses*: 52–9.
[130]Darling, *Re-forming Britain*: 80.
[131]Hulme, *Shock City*: 214.

Grey literature

Board of Education. *Juvenile Organisations Committee: Report on the Need for Youth Community Centres on New Housing Estates*. London: HMSO, 1935.

Department of Health for Scotland. *Report of the Scottish Architectural Advisory Committee on the Incorporation of Architectural Quality and Amenity in the Lay-out, Planning and External Appearance of Houses for the Working Classes*. Edinburgh: HMSO, 1935.

Department of Health for Scotland. *Working-Class Housing on the Continent*. Edinburgh: HMSO, 1935.

Department of Health for Scotland. *New Town at East Kilbride*. Edinburgh: HMSO, 1947.

Department of Health for Scotland and Scottish Education Department. *Community Life in New Housing Schemes*. Edinburgh: HMSO, 1936.

Scottish Education Department. *Planning for Community Centres, Village Halls and Playing Fields*. Edinburgh: HMSO, 1947.

Stephenson, Flora, and Gordon Stephenson. *Community Centres – a Survey by Flora and Gordon Stephenson for the Community Centres Joint Research Committee*. London: Percy Lund, 1942.

Books

Gale, Stanley. *Modern Housing Estates*. London: Batsford, 1949.

Osborn, Frederic. *Overture to Planning*. London: Faber and Faber, 1941.

Richards, J. M. *An Introduction to Modern Architecture*. Harmondsworth: Penguin, 1940.

Secondary

Campbell, Louise. 'Foreword'. In *Neo-Georgian Architecture, 1880–1970: A Reappraisal*, edited by Julian Holder and Elizabeth McKellar, x–xvi. Swindon: Historic England, 2016.

Crinson, Mark, and Jules Lubbock. *Architecture: Art or Profession? Three Hundred Years of Architectural Education in Britain*. Manchester: Manchester University Press, 1994.

Darling, Elizabeth. *Re-forming Britain: Narratives of Modernity before Reconstruction*. Abingdon: Routledge, 2007.

Darling, Elizabeth. 'Womanliness in the Slums: A Free Kindergarten in early-twentieth-Century Edinburgh'. *Gender and History* 29, no. 2 (2017): 359–86.

Darling, Elizabeth, and Alistair Fair. '"The Core": the Centre as a Concept in Twentieth-century British Planning and Architecture. Part One: the Emergence of the Idea.' *Planning Perspectives*, early online publication 2022.

Fair, Alistair. *Modern Playhouses: An Architectural History of Britain's New Theatres, 1945–1985*. Oxford: Oxford University Press, 2018.

Fair, Alistair. 'Citizenship, Community and the New Towns in Post-War Scotland'. In *The New Town of Edinburgh: An Architectural Celebration*, edited by Clarisse Godard-Desmerest, 193–216. Edinburgh: Birlinn, 2019.

Gold, John R. *The Experience of Modernism: Modern Architects and the Future City*. London: Spon, 1997.

Greenhalgh, James. 'Consuming Communities: The Neighbourhood Unit and thc Rolc of Rctail Spaces on British Housing Estates, 1944–1958'. *Urban History* 43, no. 1 (2016): 158–74.

Historic Hospitals, online at https://historic-hospitals.com/gazetteer/renfrewshire/ (accessed 20 May 2021).

Hulme, Tom. *After the Shock City: Urban Culture and the Making of Modern Citizenship*. London: Royal Historical Society, 2019.

O'Carroll, Annette. 'Social Homes, Private Homes'. In *Home Builders: Mactaggart and Mickel and the Scottish Housebuilding Industry*, edited by Miles Glendinning and Diane Watters, 283–95. Edinburgh: RCAHMS, 2015.

Olechnowicz, Andrzej. *Working-Class Housing in Britain between the Wars: The Becontree Estate*. Oxford: Clarendon Press, 1997.

Ravetz, Alison. *Council Housing and Culture: The History of a Social Experiment*. London: Routledge, 2001.

Roethe, Johanna. '"A Pretty Toy" or "Purely Functional"? Town, City and County Halls in the Interwar Period'. In *The Architecture of Public Service: Twentieth Century Architecture 13*, edited by Elain Harwood and Alan Powers, 25–41. London: C20 Society, 2017.

Rosenburg, Lou. *Scotland's Homes Fit for Heroes: Garden City Influences on the Development of Scottish Working Class Housing, 1900 to 1939*. Edinburgh: The Word Bank, 2016.

Saumarez Smith, Otto. 'The Lost World of the British Leisure Centre'. *History Workshop Journal* 88 (Autumn 2019): 180–203.

Shasore, Neal. 'Southampton Civic Centre: Patronage and Place in the Interwar Architecture of Public Service'. In *The Architecture of Public Service: Twentieth Century Architecture 13*, edited by Elain Harwood and Alan Powers, 41–61. London: C20 Society, 2017.

Snape, Robert. 'The New Leisure, Voluntarism, and Social Reconstruction in Inter-War Britain'. *Contemporary British History* 29, no. 4 (2015): 51–83.

Swenarton, Mark. 'Houses of Paper and Brown Cardboard: Neville Chamberlain and the Establishment of the Building Research Station at Garston in 1925'. *Planning Perspectives* 22, no. 3 (2007): 257–81.

Weight, Richard, and Abigail Beach. 'Introduction'. In *The Right to Belong: Citizenship and National Identity in Britain, 1930–1960*, edited by Richard Weight and Abigail Beach, 1–18. London: IB Tauris, 1998.

CHAPTER 6
PUBLIC HOUSE: THE CARLISLE EXPERIMENT AND THE IMPROVED PUBLIC HOUSE
Julian Holder

'HURRY UP PLEASE ITS TIME': in T. S. Eliot's 'The Waste Land', published in 1922, the poem's narrative is regularly fragmented by the familiar cry of the pub landlord at closing time. Across forty lines of free verse this call increasingly interrupts a conversation between two women discussing the reunion of a husband and wife at the end of the First World War. Usually interpreted as a disruptive modernist device this sudden introduction of vernacular speech has formal affinities with other modernist works such as the inclusion of tram tickets, cane seating, and other material of everyday life in early Cubist collages by Picasso and Braque, or the conducting of Russian factory sirens by Avraamov in his 'Symphony of Sirens', also of 1922. However, considered historically this section of Eliot's seminal modernist poem can also be seen to represent much of the drive for respectability and sobriety that characterized what was increasingly called the Improved Public House.

Viewed in this light the poem alludes not only to the introduction of closing times ('Hurry up please its time'), but troop demobilization ('When Lil's husband got demobbed'), the use of re-settlement payments ('He'll want to know what you done with that money he gave you'), the poor state of the national diet ('You have them all out, Lil, and get a nice set he said'), the scarcity of men of a marriageable age ('others can pick and choose if you can't'), illegal abortions ('It's them pills I took, to bring it off, she said'), and the pressing issue of birth control ('She's had five already, and nearly died of young George'). In its lines we witness not only the appearance of the new 'professional' landlord, the increased visibility of women in pubs, but also just how many more aspects of pub life were catalysed by the war. Ultimately the threat of the nationalization of the brewing industry, or indeed the total abolition of alcohol argued for by sections of the powerful Temperance Movement, cemented most of these changes during the period of reconstruction to become the Improved Public House. After all, in the United States prohibition was introduced in 1920, so why not in the UK?

Eliot's words unwittingly or otherwise illustrate the immediate post-bellum context that led to enormous changes in both the design and management of the public house. That context included the social problems associated with demobilization (going 'demob happy'), the poor national diet (the result of diverting animal fats to armament production), and increasing calls for better methods of birth control from women (as the post-war birth rate expanded to an all-time peak).

Reduced opening hours had originally been introduced to curb the drunkenness that affected the efficiency of the 'war-machine'. Other legislative measures brought in under the Defence of the Realm Acts which began in 1914 included lowering the strength of beer to 2 per cent (earning it the nickname 'near beer'), banning the sale of spirits (as grain was needed primarily to feed the nation) and removing the overt advertising of alcohol. The landlord was now most likely a manager, quasi-civil servant even,[1] whose livelihood was not tied to being open all hours on demand, and tied to only selling alcohol, but increasingly relied on running an orderly pub for both sexes and not a disorderly drinking den seen as the preserve of men only.

This essay looks at the government's decisive intervention into the brewing industry during the war – generally known as the Carlisle Experiment – and the new type of public house architecture it created. It takes as its time frame the creation of the government's Central Control Board (Liquor Traffic) in 1915 and what was to all extents an assessment of its long-term effectiveness by the report of the Royal Commission on Licensing published in 1932. Often overlooked as a historical source, the verbatim reporting of the commission echoes not only Eliot's use of language but that recorded by an equally useful documentary source: the reports compiled over four years by Mass-Observation in its Worktown study of Bolton began in 1937.[2] By 1932 the argument for total prohibition on a national scale had abated and the major brewers had grown into modern businesses capable of diversifying into new markets. These markets embraced the notion of a pub as a form of social, or recreation, centre with an emphasis on the family and drinking in moderation. It has been estimated that from the end of hostilities up until 1939 between 5,000 and 6,000 building projects were undertaken by brewers, many designed along 'Improved' lines and replacing the earlier types of pub.[3] The Royal Commission's findings effectively validated the Carlisle Experiment seventeen years on. Following the publication of its report the brewing industry responded by adopting the lessons (or veiled government threats?) of the Carlisle Experiment on an even larger and more ambitious scale, and from 1935 the number of new premises increased considerably with 526 in the peak year of 1938.[4] Additionally, as David Gutzke and Michael Law have shown, by 1932 the 'road-house' as a distinctive extension of the lessons of the Carlisle Experiment was starting to become significant as patterns of leisure changed during the 1930s.[5]

---

[1]An interesting claim by Olive Seabury, *The Carlisle State Management Scheme* (Carlisle: Bookcase, 2008): 41.

[2]Mass-Observation, *The Pub and the People; a Worktown Study* (London: Century Hutchinson, 1987) (originally published 1943). It is also interesting to compare Worktown reports with those compiled by observers for the State Management scheme in Carlisle which can be found in TNA HO 190.

[3]Estimating figures for public houses is not straight forward and estimates vary due to factors such as treating license applications as evidence of a pub being built. These figures are the most reliable and come from David W. Gutzke and Michael John Law, *The Roadhouse Comes to Britain; Drinking, Driving and Dancing, 1925–1955* (London: Bloomsbury, 2017): 14.

[4]David W. Gutzke, *Pubs and Progressives: Reinventing the Public House in England, 1896–1960* (DeKalb: Northwestern University Press, 2006): 209.

[5]Gutzke, *The Roadhouse*. The creation of this new building type is a subtly different story to that told in this essay.

One of the most unexpected consequences of the war then was the transformation of the drinking culture of Edwardian England.[6] This witnessed the introduction not only of those legislative changes mentioned above but the increased sale of food and non-alcoholic drinks, the eradication of gambling by the introduction of games for pleasure, and, as a corollary, the growth in the number, class, gender and age of customers.[7] As a result of the war, public houses, and their gardens, became respectable establishments run by a system of 'disinterested management'.[8] Such a change to the architectural character of the public house between 1915 and 1932 was realized through the agency of design – to effectively 'design out' drunkenness. The designers in question were a cadre of socially motivated architects, led by Harry Redfern (1861–1950), and who were employed directly by the government on a salaried basis to design the new type of pub and create new standards of behaviour. Until this time brewers had commissioned private architects and contractors to design pubs merely as an instrument for increasing their profits from the sale of alcohol. These were the creators of the large opulent 'gin-palaces' of the type that typified late Victorian and Edwardian Britain.[9]

In many respects the new types of public house were hard to recognize as pubs compared to their forebears. More stylistically restrained as a result of being professionally designed they were often found in, or more usually on the edge of, the new suburban estates built by the state or private enterprise or set back from the kerbs of the equally new system of arterial roads and bypasses necessitated by increased car ownership. Fuelled by this suburban expansion their impact was significant. As one commentator noted 'the new public house is revolutionizing the drinking habits of the nation'.[10] To achieve this the public house effectively sobered up to become a 'home away from home', even if only round the corner.

---

[6]This essay is based on unpublished research commissioned from the author by English Heritage and conducted between 1993 and 1995. I should like to record again my thanks to CAMRA (Dave Gamston and Peter Barnes) for their assistance. Despite the passage of time the findings are substantially the same but are now greatly informed by the work of David W. Gutzke, only some of which are cited below. The successor body, Historic England, has now resumed research in this area with the publication of Emily Cole's three-volume research report *The Urban and Suburban Public House in Inter-war England* (Research Report Series, 004-2015) and a series of associated projects. It is a pleasure to now also acknowledge her help.

[7]David W. Gutzke, 'Gender, Class and Public Drinking in Britain during the First World War', *Histoire Sociale/Social History* 27, no. 54 (1994): 367–91.

[8]Disinterested management was a heavily contested concept trying to balance social responsibility and profit in the licensed trade, its definition eventually being settled by the Southborough Committee in 1927 as 'the conduct of a public house by a manager with a fixed salary and having no commission on the sale of food and non-intoxicants. They (the Committee) took as types of disinterested management, Public House Trusts and Associations and State Management', see H.M. Government, Southborough Report on the Disinterested Management of Public Houses, 1927 (Cmnd 2862).

[9]Mark Girouard, *Victorian Pubs* (London, Studio Vista, 1975).

[10]Gutzke, *Pubs*: 225. The official records of the Central Control Board and the Carlisle and District State Management Scheme are held at TNA HO 190 – and which also contain some records relating to the Royal Commission on Licensing.

Early reforms – the Trust House movement and the Birmingham Surrender Scheme

Early positive attempts to reduce drunkenness around the turn of the century, as opposed to calls for total prohibition, came from two directions. First were the Public House Trusts established throughout the country by philanthropic supporters of the Temperance Movement in return for modest return on their investments. Such trusts aimed to modify consumption by 'improving' the management of public houses.[11] Usually this involved adapting existing premises, but there were also notable purpose-designed trust houses starting with The Fox & Pelican in Grayshott, Hampshire, opened in 1899. Designed by Read & MacDonald in a loose but learned version of Queen Anne (more Domestic than Dutch), with an inn sign designed by Walter Crane, and a salaried (so financially disinterested) landlord, facilities included not only traditional bars for alcohol ('for the working man'), a coffee room ('for the passing cyclist or traveller'), four bedrooms ('for all classes'), a small library (books donated by local resident George Bernard Shaw), a stable, bicycle shed and a garden.[12] Better known is The Drum, Cockington, Devon (1934–1936), designed by Sir Edwin Lutyens, and which was to become the public face of the improved public house.

A second attempt to curb drunkenness emerged in Birmingham where, also informed by the then powerful Temperance lobby, the Licensing Magistrates were trying to encourage the design of a 'better-class' of public house in the suburbs. In 1897 Birmingham's Bishop Gore was reported to have said that 'public houses of that day were all wrong; that they ought to be on the lines of a German beer-garden, where there was no reflection on a man or his wife and children if they were seen going in or going out'.[13] Such continental models (generally modelled on German beer halls before the war, but Gallic cafes and brasseries following it) found favour in the Birmingham of Municipal Socialism. The so-called Birmingham Surrender Scheme established that a licence for a large new suburban pub was granted only in return for the 'surrender' of two, three or more poor-quality city centre pubs of the type campaigners – and progressive brewers – wanted to see closed. However, such pubs were more often 'improved' (or 'reformed' in the language of the nineteenth century) only in terms of the quality of their architecture more than their managerial system.

---

[11]For the background to such Improved Public Houses see Robert Thorne, 'The Movement for Public House Reform 1892–1914', in D. J. Oddy and D. S. Miller (eds.), *Diet and Health in Modern Britain* (London: Croom Helm, 1985): 249–54; Peter Bailey, *Leisure and Class in Victorian England: Rational Recreation and the Contest for Control, 1830–1885* (London: Croom Helm, 1978), and David W. Gutzke, 'Gentrifying the British Public House, 1896–1914', *International Labor and Working-Class History* 45 (1994): 29–43.

[12]Grayshott and district refreshment association limited, *The Fox and Pelican Inn, Grayshott, Hants: Some Account of Its Inception and Aims* (Haslemere, 1899).

[13]Basil Oliver, *The Renaissance of the English Public House* (London: Faber & Faber, 1947): 83.

The control of liquor – 'fighting Germany, Austria and drink'

Despite these attempts to improve the public house on the eve of war, as John Turner has succinctly put it, the national situation was worrying; '*Per capita* drink consumption in the thirty years before the war was the highest ever recorded, drunkenness accounted for almost 30% of criminal proceedings, and drink expenditure consumed a large proportion of working-class budgets'.[14] With the passing of the first Defence of the Realm Act on 8 August 1914, restrictions concerning opening hours came into force within a week. This was to be the first of three restrictions on the sale of alcohol over the course of the war. On 28 February 1915 the Chancellor of the Exchequer, David Lloyd George (an ardent teetotaller) declared that drink was doing more damage to the war effort than 'all the German submarines put together' and that the nation was fighting 'Germany, Austria and Drink; and as far as I can see the greatest of these deadly foes is Drink'.[15]

Initially throughout the country opening hours were reduced to two and a half at midday and to two or three in the evening. Alcohol could not be sold – either in a pub, off-sales, or from the many grocers' shops who held licences to sell alcohol – until 12 p.m. So-called grocers' licences were thought to offer 'special temptations for private and secret drinking, especially among women'.[16] With no sales allowed between 2.30 and 6.00 p.m. this new pattern of opening hours was intended to allow meals to be taken together as a family, and for men to return home with their wages at the end of the week without being tempted to spend them on drinking and gambling in the pub on the way home. This was crucially important from a social point of view. As one commentator, an experienced University Settlement worker noted, 'if he chooses at the weeks end [*sic*] to hand his wife only five or ten shillings she has no remedy'.[17]

The shell crisis, war socialism, and the Central Control Board

A further restriction on sales of alcohol was imposed as a result of the 'shell crisis' of May 1915 when it became clear that, as a headline in *The Times* of 14 May stated, British attacks were reduced due to 'limited supply' of shells.[18] The response of Asquith's new coalition government was to create a Ministry of Munitions in July 1915, with Lloyd George as its first minister – responsible, as he privately recorded, 'for the terrible task of manufacturing engines for human mutilation and slaughter'.[19] One of his first actions

---

[14]John Turner, 'State Purchase of the Liquor Trade in the First World War', *The Historical Journal* 23, no. 3 (1980): 589.

[15]David Lloyd George, *War Memoirs*, 2 (London: Oldhams Press, 1934): 325.

[16]H.M. Government, *An Examination of the Evidence before the Royal Commission on Licensing (England and Wales), 1929–1930* (London: H.M.S.O.,1931): 247.

[17]Anna Martin, 'The Future of the Public House; from the Woman's Point of View', *The Englishwoman* 46 (1 April 1920): 171.

[18]'Need for Shells', *The Times* (14 May 1915): 8.

[19]Lloyd George, *War*: 143.

was to establish the Central Control Board (Liquor Traffic) on 10 June 1915 which effectively nationalized the liquor trade in various defined areas.

Nationalization had been considered in 1914 ('They'll buy my brewery over my dead body', exclaimed one major brewer)[20] but was quickly dismissed as an idea on the grounds of cost. Nonetheless this limited intervention was a bold and decisive impediment into the workings of a capitalist economy – part of the draconian wartime controls which came to be known collectively as 'War Socialism'.[21] The dangers drink posed were not simply to armament production and military efficiency but to the social order of the country itself at a time of international class tension and when fear of revolution was in the air. The coalition government had to tread carefully. As Mike Rose has written, even during the war '[a]ny legislation on the drink question which appeared to contain class bias was likely to increase the chances of unofficial strikes and industrial unrest in militant areas like Clydeside'.[22]

The board was led by the banker and diplomat Lord D'Abernon.[23] Prominent Temperance campaigners, such as Waldorf Astor, were invited to join as were the brewer Sir William Waters Butler, chairman of Mitchells & Butlers of Birmingham,[24] and in 1917 fellow brewer, Sir Sydney Oswald Nevile.[25] Despite their occupation both men were keen advocates of the 'improved public house' and saw that brewers needed to exercise a sense of social responsibility if their businesses were to avert the threat of nationalization. As such they set themselves against the smaller, local brewer who pursued a 'business as usual' approach.

The first Control Orders are issued – Enfield, Cromarty Firth and Gretna

The first area-specific Control Order of any significance was issued on 2 January 1916 and covered Enfield Lock to safeguard armament production at the nearby Royal Small Arms Factory. With only four pubs and one off-licence to serve the newly expanded and well-paid workforce the board sanctioned the state purchase of the Greyhound, the Royal Small Arms Hotel, the Ordnance Arms, and the Swan and Pike to both manage and ultimately extend.[26] The Scottish villages of Invergordon and Cromarty followed in

[20]Sydney O. Nevile, *Seventy Rolling Years* (London: Faber & Faber, 1958): 103. The brewer was William Waters Butler.

[21]On the Control Board see Robert Duncan, *Pubs and Patriots: The Drink Crisis in Britain during World War One* (Liverpool: Liverpool University Press, 2013).

[22]Michael Rose, 'The Success of Social Reform? The Central Control Board (Liquor Traffic) 1915–21', in M. R. D. Foot (ed.), *War and Society: Historical Essays in Honour and Memory of J.R. Western* (London: HarperCollins, 1973): 73.

[23]Robert Duncan, 'Lord D'Abernon's "Model Farm": The Central Control Board's Carlisle Experiment', *The Social History of Alcohol and Drugs* 24, no. 2 (2010).

[24]David W. Gutzke, 'W. Waters Butler and the Making of a Progressive Brewer in Britain, 1890–1922', *Histoire Sociale/Social History* XLVIII, no. 96 (Mai/May 2015): 2–25.

[25]Alistair Much, 'Improving the Public House in Britain, 1920–40: Sir Sydney Nevile and "Social Work"', *Business History* 54, no. 4 (2010): 517–35.

[26]On the Enfield Lock pubs see TNA HO 185/339, and on the factory see Tim Putnam and Dan Weinbren, *A Short History of the Royal Small Arms Factory Enfield by Royal Ordnance* (The Centre for Applied Historical Studies: Middlesex University, *c.* 1992).

April 1916 when the Admiralty applied for the board to close nineteen licensed premises and impose strict controls on the remaining thirty-nine.

Finally, in July 1916, came the order to control the sale of alcohol in Gretna which culminated in the state purchase of not only all 119 public houses in Carlisle and its surrounding area but four breweries. Eventually this area was extended to cover 500 square miles taking in Carlisle and stretched from Ecclefechan in the north to Maryport in the south. Such decisive action was deemed necessary not merely to control drunkenness among munitions workers but also that of the large number of builders working on the construction of the national munitions factory being established at Gretna. This was the largest of the seventy-three new sites begun by the Ministry by the end of 1915 and it straddled the English-Scottish border. In total it covered an area of 9,000 acres, being 9 miles long, 2 miles wide and contained within a fence 17 miles in length.[27] The scale of the undertaking (employing advanced American construction techniques only seen previously in Britain in the creation of Trafford Park industrial estate)[28] was astonishing and produced 1,000 tons of cordite per week – more than all the other explosive factories in the country put together. Little wonder that the novelist Sir Arthur Conan Doyle described it following a visit as 'perhaps the most remarkable place in the world'.[29]

However, if its construction was remarkable the impact of the 20,000 extra residents on the district, of which barely half were munitions workers, was devastating. The largest number were the builders – navvies predominantly from Ireland and Glasgow with a reputation for hard work and hard drinking. Their reputation was well deserved. As a result of this expansion of the population convictions for drunkenness in Carlisle rose alarmingly from 250 in 1914/15 to 953 in 1916 when construction was at its peak. The Reverend G. Bramwell Evens, a local Wesleyan Minister, described the scene vividly when he wrote 'into this quiet city of 50,000 inhabitants ... Men fought like beasts; fierce fights raged round the doors of public houses. The diminished police force was unable to cope with the situation. Almost every alley was littered with prostrate drunken men. The main thoroughfare of Carlisle was Bedlam'.[30]

'Turning public houses into public palaces' – the Carlisle Experiment, 1915–1921

As the Trust House movement had realized, 'what is called the "drink problem" is in its essence a public house problem'.[31] The Central Control Board appointed Henry Redfern – always known as Harry – as its chief architect to address the architectural

---

[27]See Wayne Cocroft, 'The Workshop of the World Goes to War', in Wayne Cocroft and Paul Stamper (eds.), *Legacies of the First World War: Building for Total War, 1914–18* (London: Historic England, 2018). See also H. M. Government, *History of the Ministry of Munitions* (London: H.M.S.O., 1922).

[28]Brian Bowen, 'The Building of the British Westinghouse Electric and Manufacturing Plant, Trafford Park, Manchester, 1901–2: An Early Example of Transatlantic Co-operation in Construction Management, Trafford Park', *Construction History* 25 (2010): 85–100.

[29]*Annandale Observer* (1 December 1916).

[30]Rev G. Bramwell Evens, *The Truth about Direct Control in Carlisle* (York, Bramwell Evens, 1917): 4.

[31]*The Saturday Review* (20 April 1927).

issues.[32] Joining him as his principal assistant was Joseph Seddon (born. 1882), the son of architect J. P. Seddon, and two stalwart Arts and Crafts practitioners, George Walton (1867–1933) and Charles Voysey (1857–1941).[33] Last but not least was Basil Oliver (1882–1948)[34] who became the local architectural assistant. All were members of the Art Workers Guild and so steeped in the ideology of the Arts and Crafts movement, and between them they turned 'many public houses into public palaces'.[35] Only Oliver, the son of a brewer, had any architectural experience of designing public houses. In 1915 he had designed the Stone and Fagot Inn at Little Yealdham in Essex for the family firm, Oliver Bros, one of the many hundreds of small regional brewers that then characterized the brewing industry.[36] Exhibited at the Royal Academy, perhaps it was this that had brought him to Redfern's attention when establishing the office.

One of Redfern's first tasks was the opening up of pub interiors by the demolition of internal walls and partitions, and the reduction in the number of entrances and exits to aid the regular inspections carried out by both the police and the Control Board. Particular animus was retained for 'the snug', a small, practically private room common in northern pubs, where drunkenness, gambling and other 'vices' could be hidden from view. Bar counters also had to be 'improved' by a reduction in their length. This was to end what Lord D'Abernon termed 'Perpendicular drinking', that's to say standing at the bar to drink rather than do so sitting down. Standing to drink at a long bar was seen as a further encouragement towards drunkenness. To counteract this and deny male drinkers standing room, the provision of at-seat service became almost obligatory with the widespread introduction of tables and chairs.

The simple point here is that there was nothing else to do in Carlisle's pubs but drink alcohol while standing in a crush of men struggling to get to the bar and then hurriedly drink more before the new 9.30 closing time. For construction and munitions workers alike the train to Carlisle from Gretna – complete with female police officers – only arrived with five or (if they bribed the driver as they often succeeded in doing) ten minutes before closing time. On arrival each navvy would order several drinks (beer and then whiskey – known as a 'cooler followed by a heater') for himself and others (what was known as 'treating' – or 'a round'), take them into a small unobserved room, or 'snug', or lose themselves in the crowd and drink them rapidly before closing time.

---

[32]'Obituary', *The Builder* 178 no. 669 (19 May 1950). As yet Redfern has received little scholarly attention. His own account of his work is 'Recent Inns in the State Management District', *Journal of the Royal Institute of British Architects* (3 April 1939).

[33]On Walton see Karen Moon, *George Walton: Designer and Architect* (Oxford: White Cockade, 1993). Voysey's work for the Board is all but forgotten in the many studies of his life. He was employed to provide colourful framed prints and posters to take the place of the advertisements that had formerly provided some decoration to the pub interior and designed the Board's logo. Examples are held in the RIBA Archives.

[34]Stephen Oliver, 'Basil Oliver and the End of the Arts and Crafts Movement', *Architectural History* 47 (2004): 329–60.

[35]Quoted in Moon, 162, from a note by Voysey on Walton in the RIBA library.

[36]See *Architects' Journal* (5 November 1919): 573–5. See also Robert Elwall, *Bricks and Beer: English Pub Architecture, 1830–1939* (London: British Architectural Library, 1983).

Bottles of spirits were also bought to take onto the streets after closing time. Little wonder the Reverend Evens called late-night Carlisle Bedlam. Its city centre pubs were typically small, cramped, insanitary beer houses found in back alleys – 'a splendid allay in secrecy and furtiveness' as Evens noted – and usually run by 'pensioners and widows'.[37] Such establishments were simply overwhelmed by the size of the workforce. Young women who were inexperienced drinkers, and away from home, also fell foul of the unusual wartime conditions in Carlisle to the extent that the board established a specific enquiry into female drunkenness given the moral panic it created.[38]

The first state public houses

Initially, and for the duration of the war until the passing of a new Licensing Act in 1921, Redfern's work was the surveying of Carlisle's pubs – many no more than 'poky drinking dens' according to Labour's Ernest Selley.[39] Those deemed unsuitable for conversion – as over 50 of the initial 119 in state ownership were (and especially where over-provision was an issue) – were closed and compensation was paid by the Board to the owners.

Where they could be improved, such as at the Museum Tavern, the Joiners Arms, the Milbourne Inn, the Albion and scores of others, they were reconfigured in favour of improved inspection gained through the creation of a 'light and airy' interior, a central servery (rather than a long bar) allowing uninterrupted views, plenty of seating, the addition of toilets for both sexes, dining rooms, kitchens, separate women's rooms and the removal of all advertising of alcohol. As a specialist barrister later advised brewing companies when applying for a licence, '[i]f you are making alterations, get all the light and air you possibly can into your premises. Drunkenness and misbehaviour are often greatly due to a lack of either, or both'.[40]

As an early example of Control Board work, the Albion Tavern underwent nine months of alterations – which added what was termed a cafe to the first floor and brasserie to the ground. When it reopened on 7 June 1917 a leaflet announced that '[i]ntoxicants will be sold between 12 and 2-30 p.m. and between 6 and 9 p.m. in all parts of the house, but will only be sold with food in the upstairs Café'. Similarly, the Joiners Arms, despite its modest size, was altered to have not only an enlarged public bar with seating but a partitioned-off women's bar between it and the smoking room. Perhaps most tellingly the Board hoped that by removing advertising there will be 'little to suggest that the buildings are public houses except for their names or signs'.[41]

---

[37]Nevile, *Seventy*: 101.

[38]See Duncan, Chapter 6, 'Helping Our Weaker Sisters to Go Straight'. See also David W. Gutzke, *Women Drinking Out in Britain since the Early Twentieth Century* (Manchester: Manchester University Press, 2016).

[39]Ernest Selley, *The English Public House as It Is* (London: Longmans, Green and Co, 1927): 36.

[40]Alexander F. Part, *The Art and Practice of Innkeeping* (London: Heinemann, 1922): 189.

[41]John Hunt, *City under the Influence: The Story of Half a Century of State Pubs* (Carlisle: Bookcase, 1971): 28.

Thus, with the reduction in the alcoholic strength of beer, the banning of spirits, the control of opening hours, the end of 'treating' and the removal of long bars to reduce 'perpendicular' drinking, there were considerable impediments to insobriety and pubs became hard to identify. The building type itself was being transformed together with the culture it shaped.

However, while drunkenness was discouraged to support the war effort the encouragement of female customers became an unwritten policy of the board. As David Gutzke has written, '[t]his was a momentous social transformation'.[42] Necessarily the provision of women's toilets became a major innovation. This is far more significant than it might at first appear and the gendering of the public house – often regarded as a working-class men's club – signals a significant cultural shift that affords the plan and interior decoration particular importance as many later writers confirmed.

The Gretna Tavern – 'the public house of the future'

Such restructuring of existing pubs was but a part of the board's early work but in their first annual report they were also eager to stress 'the constructive side of their work'.[43] This can be seen most clearly in The Gretna Tavern (**Figure 6.1**), the first of the seven large ambitious refreshment taverns created in Carlisle which offered more than the modest improvements carried out on existing pubs. They were called refreshment taverns to reposition the pub as a place where the emphasis was not on alcohol but temperate relaxation. Originally a post office built in 1863, it was enlarged in 1874 by the acquisition of the former Athenaeum next door before being made redundant. Stone-built, classical and imposing, it boasted large, high-ceilinged interiors, including a spacious well-lit sorting office to the rear which became 'an admirable restaurant'. In addition to offering both food and drink (alcoholic and non-alcoholic), newspapers and stationery were also laid out, some postal services maintained, a gramophone and piano installed, and concerts held with musicians playing from a gallery in the rear dining room.

On its official opening on 20 July 1916 it was welcomed by the architectural editor of *Country Life*, then one of the leading promoters of architectural modernity, Lawrence Weaver, as 'the first-fruits of the new idea for the public house of the future'.[44] It was converted quickly by a team of eighty builders in just ten days according to Walton and judged 'no less interesting for being makeshift'.[45] Apart from *Country Life* the tavern

---

[42]Gutzke, *Gender*: 367.

[43]H.M. Government. *First Report of the Central Control Board* (cmd 8117) (London: H.M.S.O. October 1915): 6. The reports, and further administrative records, for 1916–1920 are held in Cumbria Archives.

[44]*Country Life* (23 September 1916): 357. On this important conversion see TNA HO 190/1037. Lawrence Weaver's role as an important architectural critic and proselytiser of Arts and Crafts values has yet to be fully appreciated but see Lawrence Trevelyan Weaver, *Lawrence Weaver 1876-1930; an Annotated Bibliography* (York: Inch's Books, 1989).

[45]*Country Life,* ibid.

Figure 6.1 'The Gretna Tavern', Carlisle, for the Central Control Board (opened 1916), photograph possibly by W. A. Mackinnell, RIBA Collections, RIBA139567

received widespread publicity in both the national and specialist press; *The Quiver* contrasted it favourably with the more typical Victorian gin palace and noted that

> the lure of the first Government public inn is not garish lights glinting upon mirrors and coloured bottles; it is not fast barmaids; it is not even beer. What tempts the patrons and calls them inside is cleanliness, loftiness, brightness, and the knowledge that they will be quickly and comfortably served with good food, with or without beer, just as they may wish. No spirits whatsoever are sold.[46]

Clearly aping the methods employed by the popular network of Edwardian tearooms (the constructive side of the Temperance Movement) such as the ABC chain or more famously Lyons Corner houses,[47] female waitresses seem to have had as strong an impact on male behaviour as their traditional barmaid counterparts had.[48] 'Do our navvy friends … try jesting with these ladies?' asked Weaver. 'Not at all; they are not only well behaved but rather shy.'[49] Not only was the unfamiliar presence of respectable

---

[46]A. C. Marshall, 'The Future of the Public House; a Plea for State Control', *The Quiver* (April 1917): 484.

[47]D. J. Richardson, 'J. Lyons and Co. Ltd.: Caterers and Food Manufacturers, 1894–1939' in Oddy, *Diet*.

[48]See Peter Bailey, 'Parasexuality and Glamour: The Victorian Barmaid as Cultural Prototype', *Gender and History* 2, no. 2 (Summer 1990): 148–72. Note the 1908 licensing bill sought to ban women working in pubs. For the growth of professionalism see also 'A barmaid's day', *Picture Post* (8 April 1939).

[49]*Country Life* (23 September 1916): 357.

female customers found to modify male drinking habits but also female waiting staff, indeed waiting staff generally, had the effect of reducing alcohol consumption through inhibiting their behaviour, even if it led to an early departure. Further 'gentrification' included Redfern's refusal to design spittoons for the bar – a usual requirement of the time.

During the alterations the post office counter became the long 'beer-bar' with barrels stacked on trestles behind. This was a large but shallow space placed to the front of the building and clearly hoping to attract only those customers intending to have 'a quick one'. Elsewhere, to the back and side of the building, were large 'refreshment rooms' with tables and chairs to counteract 'perpendicular drinking'. This was just as well as after two months, 'Already the beer bar has been found uselessly big – customers dislike drinking at it and neglect it for the tables in the refreshment room'.[50]

It may not simply have been the size of the beer bar that customers objected to but its 'battleship grey' interior. Quickly the colour scheme was changed to a warmer 'rosy-pink', floral decorations were brought in and red artificial leather used to re-upholster the seating. Despite this initial setback the tavern was deemed 'a huge success; week by week sales of food go up and the sales of beer decrease', declared Weaver, who joyously concluded: 'We are in a veritable club.' Such an interesting class-based perception is not at all uncommon and was even voiced by King George V when he visited on 18 May 1917 and remarked that '[i]t was a modern clubhouse for the working man'.[51]

Over the next few months Redfern and his team altered the London Tavern, the Albion and the Pheasant in a similar way to become the new type of 'refreshment house' – the Pheasant also supplying take-away lunches for local school children. These all encouraged non-alcoholic drinks, food and various forms of entertainment including bowling, billiards, listening to live music or the gramophone – in short anything that was thought to slow down the rate of alcohol consumption.[52]

Gracie's Banking

If the Gretna Tavern felt like a middle-class club to the King and *Country Life*, Gracie's Banking in nearby Annan was hailed by another publication as 'a real recreation centre'.[53] Made up of an odd agglomeration of existing buildings, it was centred on a temporary new building designed by George Walton 'made of timber, tarred black like an old punt, but livened with white windows and yellow shutters and green shutters'.[54] Intended to ease pressure on the six small local pubs and, ironically, more akin to a German beer

[50]Ibid.
[51]Seabury, *Carlisle*: 66.
[52]Ibid, *Carlisle*: 60.
[53]London Temperance Legislation League, *Constructive Licensing Reform; Public Management of the Liquor Trade in Carlisle and Parts of Scotland* (London, fourth edition, n.d.): 8.
[54]*Country Life* (23 September 1916): 358.

hall (so of course called a 'refreshment room'), it incorporated not only a traditional 300 seat beer hall (with a long counter for waiting staff for the obligatory at-table service) but also a 100-seat restaurant – complete with large inglenook fireplace – adjacent to it. Both these rooms could, during busy times, be opened up to form one large 400-seat space.

In another part, Gracie's boasted two billiard tables, a cinema, sweet shop, tea room, quoits pitch, putting green, post-office services on Fridays and Saturdays, gardens and a bowling green laid out to the edges of a large rose-clad double-sided loggia, or colonnade, to the main building. This colonnade (to allow for spectators of the outdoor games) also acted as a polite transitioning device in its role as an entrance route that might modify rowdiness on arrival and departure. It was deemed another early success of the Board: 'A man may come here with his wife and children', it was reported and '[f]riends may meet here and discuss their affairs over a pot of tea or a mug of beer, certain that they will not be pressed to buy more beer when the mug is empty'.[55]

However, not everyone favoured these new type of refreshment taverns or such heavy state intervention. The relative merits of the Carlisle Experiment were hotly debated in the correspondence pages of the *British Medical Journal*; drinking alcohol was still considered by many to be of medical benefit.[56] One letter, from Dr E. Lloyd Owen, Medical Officer of Health for South Carnarvonshire, argued in December 1917 that it was 'Socialism carried very far' and 'a confession of impotence for the State to become rivals on a huge scale to private caterers as the only plan for discouraging the use of intoxicants'.[57] Like many Owen still saw the state's involvement in even trying to modify consumption as making it complicit in the promotion of alcohol. 'Nationalize railways, sugar, milk, and other beneficial things if you will', he concluded, 'but do not nationalize the drink traffic any more than you would adopt gambling houses, opium dens, or brothels'.[58]

Brewers look to the future – problems of turning sobriety to profit

Towards the end of 1917 the progressive Brewers' Society and the anti-prohibition National Trade Defence Association established a joint committee 'with the object of securing full consideration of the problems of reconstruction'.[59] By February 1918 it had agreed a set of working principles (it seems drawn up chiefly by Nevile) that laid out the approach of 'the trade' to the improved pub for the next decade or more. Seeking to break away from government control and put its own house in order, it argued, 'That improvements which involve an enlargement of premises and provide opportunities for greater social amenities are in the interests of temperance [rather] than a rigid adherence

---

[55]Marshall, *Quiver*: 486.
[56]On the medical debate concerning alcohol see Thora Hands, *Drinking in Victorian and Edwardian Britain – beyond the Spectre of the Drunkard* (London: Palgrave, 2018).
[57]*British Medical Journal* (15 December 1917): 813.
[58]Ibid.
[59]Quoted in Oliver, *Renaissance*: 21.

to existing restrictions on licensed premises.'[60] However sincerely the brewers may have wished to enlarge their premises and provide social amenities – as at the Gretna Tavern and Gracie's Banking – such changes involved the brewer in often lengthy and expensive approvals to be granted by Temperance-friendly magistrates who had been encouraged to 'Make drink stink'. This was one of the rallying cries of that section of the Temperance movement that held that the worse pubs became the easier was the argument in favour of total prohibition. Of course, the brewers' position was in stark contrast to the Control Board who in Carlisle not only held a monopoly but had Crown Exemption from planning restrictions, so faced none of the brewers' difficulties.

With the end of hostilities in 1918 there was an expectation that the Carlisle Experiment would end in 1919 when the board was scheduled to be abolished. Many brewers hoped so, but Temperance campaigners saw it as their best chance to introduce prohibition nationally. The consensus, even among Carlisle's residents, was that the experiment had been a success. 'The majority of us', wrote another doctor, 'would be very sorry to see a return to the old order, the long hours, and the innumerable temptations to drink which beset the path of the working man and woman in every part of the country'.[61]

In many respects the future character of the public house was settled in debates between 1919 and 1921, which is between the end of the Central Control Board and the passing of the new Licensing Act of 1921: it was to be 'Improved'. Despite a final compensation bill of £900,000 the exchequer was seeing a profitable return on the experiment. Although it considered nationalization again – pushed for by the Labour Party – the Treasury was not prepared to countenance the costs which were now four times those of the wartime estimates. The experiment lived on in Carlisle as the Central Control Board was replaced by a new form of state control, the Carlisle and District State Management Board. One bitter critic saw this in military terms and argued, '[T]he Control Board dug itself in, and has continued its occupation, as a Social Experiment, ever since.'[62]

While Harry Redfern stayed on to become the State Management Scheme's new chief architect, with Seddon as his assistant, Walton, Voysey and Oliver soon returned to private practice. Redfern and Seddon, now joined by Ernest A Streatfield to replace Oliver, thus became part of the large body of official architects employed during the war who were kept on after the cessations of hostilities. As has been noted elsewhere the rancour this engendered with architects in private practice was to continue throughout the reconstruction period as the Office of Works took on the widening portfolio of government work.[63]

---

[60]Nevile, *Seventy*: 125.

[61]*British Medical Journal* (26 April 1919): 530.

[62]Ernest E. Williams, The Carlisle Experiment, *The National Review* (October 1928). Williams's article was attacked by *The Observer* as ingenious and subtle propaganda against public ownership according to *The Living Age* who reprinted it in advance of the 1928 US presidential election when the repeal of Prohibition was a major issue.

[63]I discuss this further in '"A State of Approval": Neo-Georgian Architecture and His Majesty's Office of Works, 1914–1939', in Julian Holder and Elizabeth McKellar (eds.), *Neo-Georgian Architecture: A Reappraisal* (Swindon: English Heritage, 2016).

The brewers take the initiative – women and children first

While keeping an eye on the experiment, the brewers – led by board members Sir Waters Butler and Sydney Nevile – wasted no time in seizing the initiative from the government whom it sought to beat at its own game. The crucial innovation for all new pubs was the lounge bar: 'This room', wrote the architect F. W. B. Yorke, 'is of first importance in the larger modern public house … [and where] Perpendicular drinking should be discouraged'.[64] It was also intended as the room to tempt respectable female customers to frequent public houses as the 'lounge is generally furnished with loose furniture which may be arranged to give a sense of privacy to small groups of customers'.[65] While women's rooms died out, it was clear that the lounge had become socially constructed as a female, if not a feminine space, despite being conceived as gender-neutral. Yorke, although writing later, is a perceptive social analyst of the pub writing further that '[f]ormerly, when it was not considered respectable for women to be seen on licensed premises, the smoke room was the superior room, generally reserved for men, and women either shared the public bar or took their quiet and sometimes sly-drink in the out-door department. Until recently the "out-door" was often the only department in which women were allowed'.[66] Middle-class women in particular were entering pubs for the first time as the decreased male population was predisposing many women to 'marry beneath themselves' and so accompany their new husbands to the pub. Yet although women were now, for a variety of reasons, encouraged to use pubs, children were banned or at least kept from being anywhere close to alcohol. Only much later did larger pubs have purpose-designed (and unlicensed) children's rooms where they could be left safely with non-alcoholic drinks while adults went to the bars.

In London it was the brewers Barclay Perkins and Whitbread's (now managed by Sydney Nevile) that in particular embraced the lessons of the Carlisle Experiment. Indeed, Nevile formed a separate development company called the Improved Public House Company and, after considerable opposition, eventually built such pubs as the enormous Welcome Inn, Eltham, the White Hart, Tottenham, and the Robin Hood, Becontree, designed by T. F. Ingram in a variety of styles.[67] The Welcome was well sited to serve the continued expansion of The Royal Arsenal at nearby Woolwich and its associated housing. The local council, in common with others, remained to be convinced of the desirability of having pubs, even improved ones, on their new housing estates. Accordingly many, such as The Welcome, were built as close as possible to the housing but not on council land. The Robin Hood favoured what became known as 'Brewers Tudor' **(Figure 6.2)**, used elsewhere in London, such as at The Rose, Camberwell (a surprising foray into pub design by Simpson & Ayrton) **(Figure 6.3)**, and The

---

[64]F. W. B. Yorke, *The Planning and Equipment of Public Houses* (London: The Architectural Press, 1949): 110.
[65]Yorke: ibid.
[66]Ibid.: 106.
[67]The records are held at the London Metropolitan Archives, GB0074/LMA/4453/N. On The Welcome see *The Architect & Building News* (March 1931): 389–90.

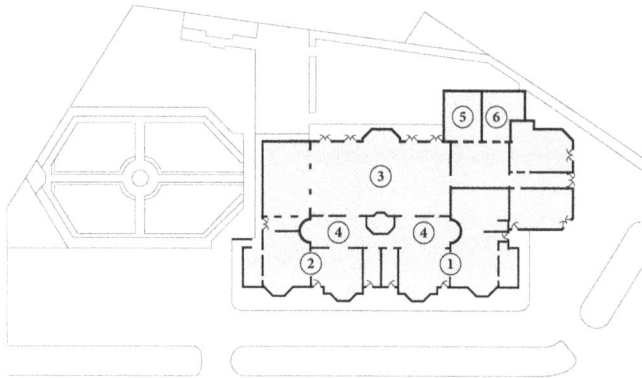

1 Public Bar
2 Saloon Bar
3 Concert Hall
4 Service
5 Women's WC
6 Men's WC

Figure 6.2 'The Robin Hood', Becontree, image from *The Architects' Journal* (June 1935). Plan drawn by Hannah Towler

Figure 6.3 'The Rose', Camberwell, image from W. Bentley Capper, *Licensed Houses and Their Management* (London: Caxton Press, 1925)

Fellowship Inn, Bellingham (1923–1924) (**Figure 6.4**), by its in-house surveyor F. G. Newman assisted by W. H. Fleeming, designed for Barclay Perkins – the latter on an even more prodigious scale to service new London County Council housing estate. The Downham Tavern (1930) – an enormous neo-Georgian box of a building which incorporated an 800-seat concert hall, also by Newman – achieved notice by taking the policy of reducing counter length to its extreme by having none at all, instead providing seated service for over 1,000 customers. Not only did the company need to employ both a pub manager and an entertainment manager; it also supplied over thirty bedrooms for its staff.

'In what style shall we build?'

In 1920 the first of two architectural competitions for public houses took place. Sponsored by the brewer Samuel Allsopp and Sons, it was for a 'Model Public House'. Entrants were informed that although 'a modern building' it should be 'more on the lines of an Eighteenth Century Inn than of a Nineteenth Century Public House'. The following year the Worshipful Company of Brewers (very much encouraged by Sidney Nevile) held a competition and called for the style to be 'a quiet rendering of eighteenth-century English classic'.[68] Increasingly the public house was becoming a respectable new

---

[68]Clive Aslet, 'Beer and Skittles in the Improved Public House', *Thirties Society Journal* 4 (1984): 3.

Figure 6.4 'The Fellowship,' Bellingham. Image from W. Bentley Capper, *Licensed Houses and Their Management* (London: Caxton Press, 1925)

area of design for the developing architectural profession in the reconstruction period. This was confirmed in 1928 when Oliver's Rose & Crown, Newmarket Road, Cambridge (**Figure 6.5**), received the accolade of 'the best building erected' by the Essex, Cambridge and Hertfordshire Society of Architects, and was simultaneously awarded the RIBA's bronze medal for street architecture.[69] Yet again, wrote Randall Philips, its architecture was based on 'the English precedent of Georgian days, yet in an individual way that gives it fresh character'.[70] 'Brewer's Georgian' – perhaps the epitome of the 'architecture of good-manners' and implying the same solidity as 'Banker's Georgian' – was gradually being confirmed as the preferred style of the Improved Public House. But it had its rivals, none more so than in Birmingham and the Black Country.[71]

In Birmingham and its extensive hinterland Mitchell & Butlers pubs became even more exemplary in their adoption (and at times calculated perversion) of the methods instigated in Carlisle – light and airy houses, disinterested management, extensive seating, the availability of food and (increasingly lucrative) non-alcoholic drinks, games

---

[69]*Architects' Journal* (27 November 1929): 831–4.
[70]Randal Phillips, 'The Public House Improved', *Country Life* (2 August 1930): 161.
[71]See Neil Burton, 'Banker's Georgian' in Holder and McKellar, *Neo-Georgian*.

Figure 6.5 'The Rose & Crown,' Newmarket House, Cambridge. Photograph by E. J. Mason (1929), Architectural Press Archive/RIBA Collections, RIBA72110

and entertainment laid on, segregated spaces for women, children's rooms (pioneered in Birmingham) and extensive attractively laid-out grounds.[72]

Brewers now increasingly employed architects of some quality and preferred recognizable architectural styles that conferred some status on their premises and assured the Licensing Magistrates of their good intentions. No longer could pubs be dismissed by the easy slur of 'commercial architecture' when designs such as that of Joseph Hill were being exhibited at the Royal Academy, the RIBA had invited Basil Oliver to address the Institute on the subject of pubs in 1932, and the Rome Prize went to a public house.[73] It also became increasingly clear that when recognizable English architectural styles were employed neo-Georgian was felt most appropriate for the town and Tudor for the countryside. While the more sophisticated urban and city-centre locations demanded neo-Georgian the new generation of suburban 'Wayside' inns, like the Robin Hood, Becontree, tended to be 'mock' Tudor (either half-timbered or stone).[74] Evidence for this is provided by the plan for the rebuilding of the New Talbot, Halifax, designed by the local practice of

---

[72]Fiona Fisher and Rebecca Preston, 'Light, Airy and Open – the Design and Use of the Suburban Public House Garden in Inter-war England', *Studies in the History of Gardens & Designed Landscapes* 39, no. 1 (2019): 5–21.
[73]Basil Oliver, 'English Inns', *Journal of the Royal Institute of British Architects* (14 May 1932): 545–67. See also *The Architects' Journal*, 'English Inns: Lessons from Carlisle' (27 April 1932).
[74]Gavin Stamp, 'Neo-Tudor and Its Enemies', *Architectural History* 49 (2006): 1–33.

161

Jackson & Fox. Two alternatives were suggested – a Georgian treatment ('well suited to a town street') and the 'suggested Tudor treatment' described by the architects as 'interesting but more suitable for a country inn than a town'.[75] If the associative qualities of the Georgian were due to a carefully constructed nostalgia for coaching inns, the mock-Tudor found its authority in greater antiquity and the notion of the yeoman-farmer, and both could be favourably defined against the worst excesses of the glittering Victorian gin palace.

In Birmingham the 'long pull' (a deliberately generous amount of drink – which led to excessive competition according to Butler) had defeated the major brewers' pre-war attempts at reform. Now that such corrupt practices by small brewers and their tenants had been all but eradicated Mitchell & Butler, and others pursued the 'Surrender Scheme' more successfully and were able to instigate the 'fewer and better' policy that created some of the finest pubs of the period.[76] In this new policy a handful of Birmingham architects including G. B. Cox, Holland Hobbiss, James and Lister Lea, and John Surman set the new standard instigated by Charles Bateman. His pre-war example of the Red Lion[77] led to the creation of a wide variety of improved public houses in a virtuoso display of different architectural styles. All were still in the spirit of the Arts and Crafts movement such as – 'in impeccable good taste' – The Antelope by Holland Hobbiss completed in 1922, and the British Oak designed by James and Lister Lea of 1923.[78] The British Oak has all the presence of a later roadhouse but is more urban than suburban given its setting. The large central public bar is balanced at either end by smoke rooms; there is an assembly room for meals and special events, a rear garden with bowling green, and the all-important innovation of a lounge bar. With its expansive plan and curved gables it looks for all the world like a small romantic country house of the seventeenth century engulfed by suburban expansion.

Competing in an expanding leisure market

Of course brewers also now had to outdo the rival refreshment houses – it was no longer simply enough, as *The Lancet* claimed: 'to make the public house a place comparable with a tea-shop or café'.[79] As early as 1906 Alexander Chance, in an attack on the tile work and terracotta of the gin palace, was encouraging Birmingham's architects to 'take advantage of some of the beautiful specimens of oak buildings which they saw scattered about the country in Chester, Hereford, Leominster and other towns'.[80] One of the finest pubs influenced by the Carlisle Experiment (and Chance's observation) and the epitome of what became known as 'the road-house' was The Black Horse, Northfields, Birmingham (**Figure 6.6**). It was designed by Bateman and Bateman's chief architect

---

[75]P. W. Robinson, 'Not Disheartened by Difficulty – a History of the Fountain Head Brewery.' Undated typescript passed to the author in 1994. A copy is held in West Yorkshire Archive Service, Calderdale.
[76]Oliver, *Renaissance*: 80–92.
[77]*Building News*, 86 (1904): 72.
[78]Alan Crawford, Michael Dunn and Robert Thorne, *Birmingham Pubs, 1880–1939* (Gloucester: Alan Sutton, 1986): 81.
[79]*The Lancet* (27 September 1919): 589.
[80]*Building News* (13 July 1906): 66.

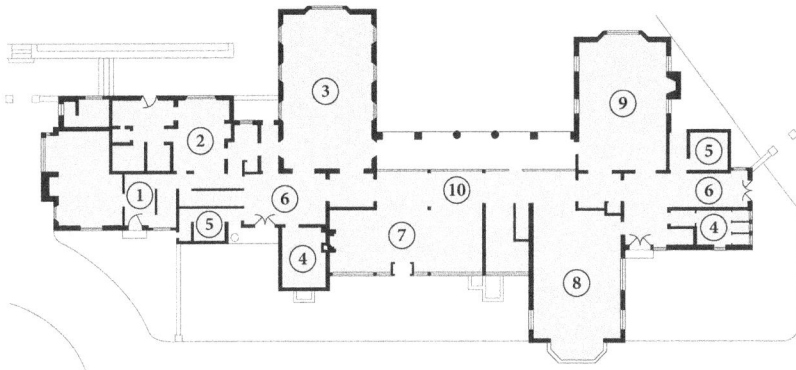

1 Manager's accommodation
2 Kitchen
3 Dining and Assembly Room
4 Women's WC
5 Men's WC
6 Hall
7 Bar
8 Mixed Smoking Room
9 Men's Smoking Room
10 Service

Figure 6.6 'The Black Horse', Northfield, Birmingham (image from author's collection). Plan drawn by Hannah Towler

Francis Goldsbrough in a robust 'Brewers Tudor' and opened in 1929 for Davenport's brewery. Here Chance's ideal was fully realized, Oliver claiming that '[t]his must surely be one of the most sumptuous pubs in the district, if not in England'.[81] Its central public bar led off to smoke rooms and dining rooms contained in the prodigious wings each served by toilets accessed from a spacious hall. Upstairs the large assembly room and committee room look over the extensive grounds including a terrace with loggia, lawned areas, a bowling green, and all capable of being separately served by a large thatched pavilion complete with its own cellarage.

With the general increase in leisure time between the wars, and especially the introduction of standard summer time creating longer daylight hours, charabanc parties (another consequence of the war) were specifically made to such large premises. Their beer gardens and facilities for families were able to accommodate the extra customers but without swamping and alienating the regulars.[82] In the large assembly rooms – which became a feature of many of the larger pubs – live music and dances were held and plays performed by local amateur dramatic societies and others. As *The Morning Post*, the leading trade paper, noted grumpily in 1928 in order '[t]o induce a man to consume half-a-pint of beer today it is necessary to offer him salty tit-bits, give him facilities for playing innocent games of skill and excite his ear with music which plays itself'.[83]

Increasingly the promise held up by The Gretna Tavern and Gracie's Banking of the improved public houses as recreation centres were being realized throughout the country. Other cities and brewers – notably in Liverpool – started to see the financial and political wisdom of pursuing the new market unwittingly created by Carlisle.[84] It was an odd situation whereby an experiment in War Socialism had stimulated the creation of a vibrant new private market.

Back to the state

While the brewers pursued their increasingly costly building campaign the new State Management Scheme carried on altering premises in Carlisle. However in 1928 it became more ambitious and began to design and build new pubs for the first time with the opening of The Apple Tree in Carlisle (**Figure 6.7**). Why the decision was made to start designing and building entirely new pubs rather than simply continue to alter the existing building stock is a major policy change that has yet to be fully explained. It has been suggested that, somewhat ironically given the 'clubby' character in its refreshment taverns, it was a response to the growth of private membership clubs (often associated

---

[81]Oliver, *Renaissance*: 86.

[82]On this see my essay, 'From Chaos to Control: The Development of the Bus and Coach Station in Interwar Britain', in Julian Holder and Steven Parissien (eds.), *The Architecture of British Transport in the Twentieth Century* (London: Yale University Press, 2004).

[83]*The Morning Post* (5 November 1928).

[84]Oliver, *Renaissance*: 107–10. As Oliver notes Harold Davies & Son are the most important practice in Liverpool but others, such as Quiggin & Gee, made significant contributions.

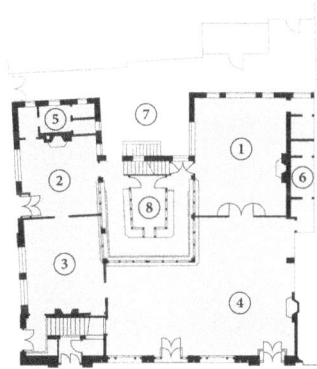

1 Weekend
2 Women 2nd Class
3 Mixed 2nd Class
4 Men 2nd Class
5 Women's WC
6 Men's WC
7 Yard
8 Service

Figure 6.7 'The Apple Tree', Carlisle, image from Basil Oliver, *The Renaissance of the English Public House* (London: Faber & Faber, 1947). Plan drawn by Hannah Towler

with large local employers, political parties or veterans' associations) in Carlisle that were able to 'get round' the Licensing Act as they were private, not public, houses. Between 1921 and 1928 Carlisle opened thirteen such clubs.[85] It may of course also be the success of the major brewers (led by Waters and Nevile) in adopting, and then adapting, the principles of State Management policy that was threatening the Carlisle Experiment so was a reminder that prohibition was still an option however remote.

The plan of the Apple Tree, possibly a first for pub architecture, classifies rooms by gender. According to Oliver the pub is also interesting 'for placing additional bars upstairs, and the adaptability of the rooms for the segregation of the sexes'.[86] This is immediately apparent in looking at the plans which not only classify by gender but also continue classification by class (aping the divisions commonly found in railway companies, swimming pools, etc.). Redfern and his team employed a vaguely seventeenth-century English Renaissance style of architecture in which to clothe the building. On the ground floor the largest space is given over not to what would usually be understood as, and named, 'The Public Bar', but 'Men 2nd Class' and entered directly off the street. Women and men might drink together in the adjacent 'Mixed 2nd Class' bar (also accessible from its own entrance from a side alley, and into the 'Women 2nd Class' off which the 'Ladies Lavatories' were built). The first floor (for 'the better-class of customers') repeated the sexually defined pattern of the ground floor with rooms named as 'Men 1st Class' (off which were the Men's lavatory) and 'Mixed 1st Class' which tellingly provided only a 'Ladies Lavatory'. The second floor was the living accommodation of the manager and his family.

The family pub – securing a licence

Such domestic accommodation was becoming increasingly important as family life became something of a further guarantee of the good character of the landlord when Licensing Magistrates were assessing an application. It was the individual rather than the company that held the license so he needed to be beyond reproach. The restricted opening hours now ensured that a publican (and his family) could enjoy their privacy while managing the business. Added to such domestic traits, training also became a part of the new landlord's working life, or 'calling' as Sydney Nevile would have it. Hence the landlord and his family also became a part of the move towards respectability the brewers needed in order to secure their licences and demonstrate their sense of social responsibility. In the larger pubs of the period landlords might often secure employment on a good salary by a major brewer, and offering a good standard of family accommodation, on the strength of his wife's willingness and ability to manage the restaurant and catering side of the business effectively, and the whole families work in maintaining the gardens. So a public house also had to contain private accommodation

---

[85]Seabury, *Carlisle*: 135.
[86]Oliver, *Renaissance*: 63.

for the landlord, his family and sometimes an often sizeable staff as at the Downham – preferably with its own discreet entrance. 'In the past', Sir Waters Butler argued, licensees were as often as not chosen for 'being centre-forward of a football team, or the ex-eight stone champion, or some other notability'.[87] This growing professionalism could be seen not only in training programmes but the growth of publications aimed at publicans such as W. Bentley Capper's *Licensed Houses and Their Management – a Trade Encyclopaedia* published in 1925 that supported it.

Over the next decade Redfern and his team designed a total of fourteen new pubs along improved lines including the Horse and Farrier (1928) and the Coach and Horses (1929) which tended to follow the vernacular farmhouse typology. The Spinners Arms, completed in 1930, is one of Redfern's most cosily domestic pubs with an unusually small-scale domestic air. It replaced an earlier pub and comprised three bars including the resistantly male zone of the Public Bar, a Mixed Smoking Room, but then also a Men's Smoking Room. As Yorke explained, '[m]odern public houses generally require two smoke rooms or their equivalent, one for men, another termed "general" or "mixed", for both sexes'.[88] Other Redfern pubs included the Crescent (1932) – considered too exotic for Carlisle given its harsh border town character – and the unremittingly *moderne* Earl Grey (1935) designed with art deco–style doors and expressionist brickwork, both of which more fully effected modernity (as did the brewers) after the publication of the Royal Commission's report in 1932. The novelty of the new modernist architecture was in many respects a subversive way of getting around the control of advertising in its popular appeal to attract customers.

The improved public house comes of age; report of the Royal Commission on licensing (1932)

Set up by the new Labour government, the Royal Commission was a logical extension of the party's call for nationalization at the end of the war, which was explored further in the Southborough Committee into the Disinterested Management of Public Houses in 1927 and yet failed to make the argument for it.[89] The commission concluded that 'drunkenness has now been reduced to a point at which it is no longer a social evil'.[90] Why was this? Could it have been the result of the Improved Public House? It seems not. Or not entirely. Time and again those giving evidence to the Royal Commission suggest it is not the Carlisle Experiment that was curbing drunkenness but changing leisure

---

[87] A comment by Butler in the discussion which followed Sydney Nevile, 'The Function of the Brewing Industry in National Reconstruction', *Journal of the Institute of Brewing* 25 (1919): 136.

[88] Yorke, *Planning*: 106.

[89] Stephen G. Jones, 'Labour, Society and the Drink Question in Britain, 1918–1939', *The Historical Journal* 30, no. 1 (1987): 105–22. See also Philip Talbot, 'Disinterested Management; an Early Example of Corporate Social Responsibility', *International Journal of Social Science Studies* 3, no. 5 (2015).

[90] *Royal Commission on Licensing; Summary of the Report Prepared by the National Commercial Temperance League* (London: N.C.T.L., 1932): 14.

habits more generally.[91] This, according to the Chief Constable of Newcastle, 'is really the thing which has produced a much soberer nation than before.'[92] His opposite number in Bradford, and many others who gave evidence over the two years the commission sat, agreed. And overall, they attributed the changed climate of opinion to the 'wider outlook' offered by a 'higher standard of education,' and 'better housing and interest in gardens.'[93]

The attitude and habits of the younger generation in particular gave the commissioners encouragement. It was not simply that since the 1921 Act the cost of alcohol was higher and the opening hours had been relaxed following post-war relaxation but that other forms of American-led entertainment – such as the jazz-inspired dance craze – had risen to offer 'something better than merely sitting in public houses.'[94] A wide variety of alternative attractions to the pub were presented to the commission including outdoor sports and indoor games but also the appeal of the cinema, radio, theatre, dancing, cafes, milk bars, whist drives and evening classes **(Figure 6.8)**. Additionally, in place

Figure 6.8 Male customers listening to a radio concert in the 'Lamb & Flag,' Hoxton, image from W. Bentley Capper, *Licensed Houses and Their Management* (London: Caxton Press, 1925)

[91]On the leisure industry see Stephen G. Jones, 'The Leisure Industry in Britain, 1918–39', *The Service Industries Journal* 5, no. 1 (1985): 90–106, and Robert Snape, Leisure, *Voluntary Action and Social Change in Britain, 1880–1939* (London: Bloomsbury, 2018).

[92]Royal Commission: 78.

[93]Ibid.: 100.

[94]Ibid.: 100. On the Dance Hall see James Nott, *Going to the Palais; a Social and Cultural History of Dancing and Dance Halls in Britain, 1918–1960* (Oxford: Oxford University Press, 2015), and James Nott, 'Dance Halls: Towards an Architectural and Spatial History, c.1918–65', *Architectural History* 61 (2018): 205–33.

of public houses, new suburban estates now boasted outdoor swimming pools or lidos, municipal parks with playgrounds for children, putting courses and tennis courts for adults, boating lakes, refreshment pavilions and tea rooms.

If, as the built evidence suggests, the Licensing Magistrates became more minded to approve new licences for improved houses after 1932, and the commission's findings that the 'social evil' of drunkenness had been successfully curbed, then the brewers were equally keen to try and match the growth of the popular leisure industry to maintain their profits.

While few pubs included cinemas in their new premises, as had been done at Gracie's Banking in 1916, they often sited them close to the new generation of super-cinemas to the mutual benefit of both businesses. Hence Mitchell & Butlers new roadhouse in Birmingham, The Kingstanding, designed by Bateman and Bateman, was on the same major road junction as the Odeon, and the Downham Tavern was close to the Splendid Cinema (**Figure 6.9**).

With such large suburban pubs boasting putting courses, bowling greens and outside bars, it was perfectly possible in the evenings, and especially at weekends, to enjoy the benefits of the pub without taking any alcohol and combine it with a trip to the cinema, dance hall, boating lake or even outdoor swimming pool. In inclement weather and in the evenings, billiards, darts, skittles, indoor games and various entertainments were also available and all encouraged slower consumption due to either participating or spectating.

Figure 6.9 'The Kingstanding', Birmingham, image from *The Architect & Building News* (February 1930)

Conclusion

Based on the evidence presented to the Royal Commission it would be quite wrong to suggest that the Improved Public House was responsible for the reduction in drunkenness that occurred during the period. It is also wrong to suggest that the country was now covered with well-designed pubs masquerading as middle-class country clubs. The social research conducted into the public house in Bolton in 1939 by Mass-Observation gives the lie to both these ideas. However, what it had achieved was probably far more significant in responding to the new world order by creating a market open to a wider section of society than before and a society which was increasingly equitable in terms of gender.[95] In that sense the Suffragist Anna Martin, writing of Carlisle in 1919, was right to announce that '[t]he little grey town in the North has shown the path of salvation'.[96] While allowing for hyperbole the sentiments of *Building* magazine in 1929 were not as ludicrous as may first be thought when one of its reporters claimed, 'If I were asked by an unbeliever to give two proofs of the upwards march of humanity, I would say, "Look at the League of Nations, and look at our new pubs"'.[97] However, perhaps we need to ask if the Improved Public House was merely a great success of private enterprise in its attempts to deflect the threat of nationalization or playing into the hands of the state in its need to improve the health of the nation in the event of any future armed conflicts. Whatever the answer in the immediate post-war waste land viewed with such horror by T. S. Eliot, the improved public house was at least a cause for optimism, an elderly C. R. Ashbee calling it 'one of the greatest achievements of modern democracy'.[98] If so we should recognize that this came about through the agency of architects, led by those employed by the state such as Harry Redfern. Often derided by their colleagues in private practice, it was the work of these 'Official Architects' that brought about the alliance between progressive brewers and reformist governments during the period of reconstruction that led to the improved public house.

Select bibliography

Primary

Archival

Cumbria Archives, SMS 1/6/1/1 (State Management Scheme, General managers reports 1916–20)
London Metropolitan Archives, GB0074/LMA/4453/N (on the Improved Public House Company)

---

[95] Alison Light, *Forever England: Femininity, Literature and Conservatism between the Wars* (London: Routledge, 1991), and John Carey, *The Intellectuals and the Masses* (London: Faber and Faber, 1992).

[96] Anna Martin, *The Future*: 174.

[97] *Building* (4 February 1929): 89.

[98] C. R. Ashbee, *Masters of the Art Workers Guild from the Beginning till AD 1934* [manuscript held at the Art Workers Guild]. Ashbee, who, by removing his workshop from the East End of London to Chipping Camden, was partly removing them from the temptations of the 'unimproved' pub, is here describing the work of past Master Basil Oliver in this extract.

TNA HO 190 (on the Carlisle Experiment)
TNA HO 185/339 (on Enfield Locks)

Grey literature
Emily Cole, *The Urban and Suburban Public House in Inter-war England* (Historic England, Research Report Series, 004-2015)

Newspapers and periodicals
The Architect & Building News
The Architects' Journal
The Brewers Journal
British Medical Journal
The Building News
Country Life
Journal of the Royal Institute of British Architects
The Lancet
The Morning Post

Secondary

Websites
The Brewery History Society at http://www.breweryhistory.com/
The State Management Story at https://thestatemanagementstory.org/

Articles
Aslet, Clive. 'Beer and Skittles in the Improved Public House'. *Thirties Society Journal* 4 (1984): 2–9.
Duncan, Robert, 'Lord D'Abernon's "Model Farm": The Central Control Board's Carlisle Experiment'. *The Social History of Alcohol and Drugs* 24, no. 2 (2010): 119–140.
Fisher, Fiona and Rebecca Preston. 'Light, Airy and Open; the Design and Use of the Suburban Public House Garden in Inter-war England'. *Studies in the History of Gardens & Designed Landscapes* 39, no. 1 (2019): 5–21.
Gutzke, David W. 'W. Waters Butler and the Making of a Progressive Brewer in Britain, 1890–1922'. *Histoire Sociale/Social History* XLVIII, no. 96 (Mai/May 2015): 137–160.
Gutzke, David W. 'Gender, Class and Public Drinking in Britain during the First World War'. *Histoire Sociale/Social History* 27, no. 54 (1994): 367–91.
Gutzke, David W. 'Gentrifying the British Public House, 1896–1914'. *International Labor and Working-Class History* 45 (1994): 29–43.
Jones, Stephen G. 'Labour, Society and the Drink Question in Britain, 1918–1939'. *The Historical Journal* 30, no. 1 (1987): 105–122.
Much, Alistair. 'Improving the Public House in Britain, 1920–40: Sir Sydney Nevile and "Social Work"', *Business History* 54, no. 4 (2010): 517–535.

Chapters
Richardson, D. J. 'J. Lyons and Co. Ltd.: Caterers and Food Manufacturers, 1894–1939'. In *Diet and Health in Modern Britain,* edited by D. J. Oddy and D. S. Miller. London: Croom Helm, 1985: 161–169.
Rose, Michael. 'The Success of Social Reform? The Central Control Board (Liquor Traffic) 1915–21'. In *War and Society: Historical Essays in Honour and Memory of J. R. Western*, edited by M. R. D. Foot. London: HarperCollins, 1973: 242–257.

Books

Duncan, Robert. *Pubs and Patriots: The Drink Crisis in Britain during World War One.* Liverpool: Liverpool University Press, 2013.

Elwall, Robert. *Bricks and Beer: English Pub Architecture, 1830–1939.* London: British Architectural Library, 1983.

Greenaway, John. *Drink and British Politics since 1830: A Study in Policy Making.* Basingstoke, Macmillan, 2003.

Gutzke, David W. *Pubs and Progressives: Reinventing the Public House in England, 1896–1960.* DeKalb: Northwestern University Press, 2006.

Gutzke, David W. *Women Drinking Out in Britain since the Early Twentieth Century.* Manchester: Manchester University Press, 2016.

H.M. Government. *An Examination of the Evidence before the Royal Commission on Licensing (England and Wales), 1929–1930.* London: H.M.S.O., 1931.

Oliver, Basil. *The Renaissance of the English Public House.* London: Faber & Faber, 1947.

Seabury, Olive. *The Carlisle State Management Scheme.* Carlisle: Bookcase, 2008.

Snape, Robert. *Leisure, Voluntary Action and Social Change in Britain, 1880–1939.* London: Bloomsbury, 2018.

CHAPTER 7
PARISH: DEMOCRATIC PARTICIPATION IN SUBURBAN PARISH CHURCHES
Clare Price

In 1917 two books were written from the trenches containing passages that rate as some of the most heartfelt, passionate and poignant to have been produced during the bleakest days of the war. These publications, *The Church in the Furnace* and *Papers from Picardy*, were not written by poets, nor by men later to be feted as literary figures; they were authored by Church of England padres, Chaplains to the British Army.[1] The books include accounts of loss and despair from those who had experienced war first-hand, skilled in their role of providing comfort and spiritual guidance. Much maligned in the writings of those such as Sassoon, Owen and Remarque, more recently the importance of the chaplains has been reassessed. They were not merely effete, ineffective and cigarette-toting; these 'Woodbine Willies' had a profound influence on a revival of Christianity after the war.[2] The chaplains reflected on what the war meant for the future of the Church of England, arguing for a complete change in approach: abandoning pre-war attitudes, entering a period of church reconstruction and looking to the ordinary parishioner for a democratic future. T. W. Pym, writing in *Papers from Picardy*, decried those who 'look to the war to confirm all their pre-war ideas' emphasizing his belief that 'many of those who have given their lives for England gave them, not for the England of 1913 and 1914, but for England as she might be, as one day she shall – please God! – become'.[3] Pym in particular emphasized democratization as the way forward for the post-war reconstruction of the Church of England as a body relevant to all. He was convinced that changes would have to originate at grassroots level, with the ordinary member of the congregation: 'we must let them … have a larger and more rational share in [the Church's] administration'.[4] Without the parishioner on side, Pym predicted, 'he will not help us reset our house in order; he will never even realise that we cannot even attempt to do so without his criticism and his help'.[5]

---

[1] Frederic Brodie Macnutt, *The Church in the Furnace, Essays by 17 Temporary Church of England Chaplains on Active Service in France* (London, 1917); Thomas Wentworth Pym and James Geoffrey Gordon, *Papers from Picardy* (London, 1917).

[2] M. F. Snape, *God and the British Soldier: Religion and the British Army in the First and Second World Wars* (London: Routledge, 2005): ix; Linda Mary Parker, '*Shell-Shocked Prophets: The Influence of Former Anglican Army Chaplains on the Church of England and British Society in the Inter-war Years*' (PhD, University of Birmingham, 2013): 1.

[3] Pym and Gordon, *Papers from Picardy*: 56.

[4] Ibid.: 73.

[5] Ibid.: 73.

These prophetic insights were to become increasingly influential throughout the following century, not only impacting the organizational structure of the Church of England, but also affecting how the church approached the major building projects that it would be compelled to embark upon after both world wars. In particular, exhortations to include ordinary people not only in liturgy but also in ecclesiastical administration resonated with the narrative of democratization after the war. The Emancipation Acts were designed to expand the electorate and the Housing Acts to provide housing for the returning war heroes and their families. The appeal of the chaplains to consider an approach to the ordinary man was therefore a familiar theme. The post-war growth of the suburbs gave the church an ideal opportunity to minister to newly formed neighbourhoods and to build new churches.

The chaplains' focus on the role of the ordinary parishioner can provide us with a new perspective on the architectural history of this period and of these buildings. Exploring this process in the new suburban parishes gives an insight into how the wider culture of democracy manifested itself and how it affected the built form of Anglican churches. This recasts the Anglican Church's architecture as the product of collaboration and interaction, broadening the traditional point of view that attributes the design solely to the single inspiration of an architect constrained by stylistic concerns. Examining these interactions for signs of change provides a route to re-assessing these often eclectic and unresolved structures. This not only reinforces their importance in the development and experience of suburban modernity in the 1920s and 1930s but also casts them in a new light as the precursors to the later Liturgical Reform Movement and therefore part of a continuum in twentieth-century church architecture.

In this chapter, the scene will be set by detailing the new legislation affecting the governance of the Church of England. This provided an impetus for local congregations to get involved in decision-making, and the church's long-held belief in the importance of fostering community activities assisted those willing to take up the challenge. The next section considers the substantial obstacles that had to be overcome by these fledgling communities in making their voices heard and in exerting control over church building projects. The changing landscape of funding will be explored, noting the shift away from benefactors to more diverse sources of funding and the implications for the local projects. Finally, the position of the commissioned architects will be examined, focusing on the obstacles posed by ingrained beliefs and attitudes which threatened the success of these projects. In conclusion, the impact of these struggles on the design of the new churches will be shown to indicate a new direction in church design.

New legislation, new growth

An early stimulus to the arc of change was new legislation. A number of proposed pre-war reforms found expression in the Church of England Assembly (Powers) Act 1919. Commonly referred to as the Enabling Act, it put in place the legal mechanism to formalize the right of ordinary congregations to be involved in decisions relating to church buildings (the compulsory Parochial Church Council or 'PCC') and also a framework to control this involvement (the Diocesan Advisory Committee or 'DAC'). This was vital to the role of the congregations in the building projects after the war, as it gave them a legal prerogative to be involved. Both these bodies therefore had the potential to be vehicles of democratization for the parishes.

The war formed the direct catalyst for the DAC system. Established as early as 1916 as 'War Memorial Committees' their original remit was to deal with the proliferation of memorials and to protect existing churches from a 'terrible disfigurement … spoiling the appearance of some of our most attractive and valuable buildings'.[6] Despite the widening of their powers and their unification of purpose under the 1919 Enabling Act, DACs were neither comprehensive in their coverage of the country, nor legally responsible for new church design, their involvement being at the discretion of the bishop.[7] There was no obligation on the part of the vicar, churchwardens or the PCCs to consult the DACs on their plans either for the design of the new church or for the furnishing of it as, until consecrated, new churches did not fall within the faculty system. Membership of the DAC was specialist, consisting of a mixture of clergy and experts, and as such not a vehicle for expressing the views of the ordinary parishioner. As a result, DAC influence was minimal in terms of expanding the involvement of the local inhabitants; the PCCs were the more important democratizing force and the lay body which was to have the greater impact on the design evolution and architectural form of the new church buildings. Indeed, the Enabling Act could be interpreted as a sign that the chaplains' exhortations for listening to the views of the congregations and a break from the past were indeed being heeded by the Church of England. Certainly, many important changes that originated at grassroots level in the local parishes may well have been stifled had the Enabling Act not formalized the obligatory involvement of the PCC. The PCCs gradually embraced their new role but established attitudes and conventions were difficult to overcome, not only those of the wider church authorities to the laity but particularly the relationship between the PCC and architects.

Pressure on the Church of England to construct more places of worship was initiated by the Housing Act 1919. The growth of the suburbs catalysed by the Housing Acts has been well documented in a number of substantive studies.[8] The parallel construction of churches accompanying this suburban expansion has, by contrast, been largely

---

[6]The Central Council for the Care of Churches, *The Protection of Our English Churches Fourth Report 1928-9* (London: The Central Council for the Care of Churches, 1930): 4.

[7]The Central Council for the Care of Churches, *The Care of Churches: Their Upkeep and Protection Eighth Report 1938-40* (London: The Central Council of Diocesan Advisory Committees for the Care of Churches, 1940): 71.

[8]See for example Alan Arthur Jackson, *Semi-Detached London: Suburban Development, Life and Transport, 1900-39* (London: Allen & Unwin, 1973); Paul Oliver, Ian Davis, and Ian Bentley, *Dunroamin: The Suburban Semi and Its Enemies* (London: Barrie & Jenkins, 1981); Julian Honer, *London Suburbs* (London: Merrell Holberton in association with English Heritage, 1999); Mark Swenarton, *Homes Fit for Heroes: The Politics and Architecture of Early State Housing in Britain* (London: Heinemann Educational Books, 1981).

neglected by scholars.[9] All denominations felt a compulsion to build, but for the Church of England, as the Established Church, it was an obligation rather than a choice to make provision for everyone in England regardless of their individual beliefs.[10] The Church of England was keen to establish communities centred on a new building because it was gravely concerned that without a church presence these new districts would be subsumed by a creeping tide of secularization.[11] However, the rapid development of the suburbs was a phenomenon that the church struggled to accommodate, as addressing the spiritual needs of such an expanding population put a great strain on resources, particularly for the urban dioceses which needed to mobilize to construct new churches in a time of great economic change.

This was not new terrain for the church, having had experience of ministering to new urban areas in the previous century. The mission to the slums in the nineteenth century was a high-profile cause with many dedicated clergy pursuing socialist ideals in wretched circumstances and it attracted philanthropic funding. The association of this movement with the Anglo-Catholic branch of the Church of England and their ideals promoting the provision of beauty in the midst of squalor is well known, as is its impact on the architecture and decoration of churches at the time.[12] But the approach of chaplains after the war was vehemently opposed to the top-down bestowal of condescending largesse from Victorian-minded high church clergy. Instead, they were promoting the rather more down-to-earth concept of considering the opinions of the laity as valid and important. This was not a ministry to the slums. The old attitudes needed to be shed for progress to be made in the democratization of the design process. In the early years after the war, devolving matters to the local church was not an easy path for the urban dioceses accustomed to controlling the process and consulting only with the 'professional' team of clergy, architect and benefactor. Nor, indeed, was it an approach that the architects were familiar with and they were deeply concerned by any threat to the integrity of their designs.

The impact of a changing funding landscape

The majority of new churches in this period were paid for in part from the proceeds of the sale of the sites of redundant churches. However, this resource was insufficient to fund the needs of the growing suburbs. Diocesan fundraising schemes, such as the

---

[9]With the exception of Walford who considers church construction in the specific context of the Diocese of London mission and outreach campaigns: Rex Walford, *The Growth of 'New London' in Suburban Middlesex (1918–1945) and the Response of the Church of England* (Lewiston: Edwin Mellen Press, 2007).

[10]This chapter concentrates on the Church of England, but it should be noted that the situation was similar in Scotland as, despite the Church of Scotland Act of 1921 separating the church from the state, it retained the obligation to provide both parishes and ministry. In Wales the rise in non-conformity had affected the relationship with the Anglican Church and the Church in Wales had concluded the legal process of disestablishment in 1920 after this had been put in train by the Welsh Church Act of 1914.

[11]Callum G. Brown, *The Death of Christian Britain*, 2nd edn (Hoboken: Taylor & Francis, 2009): 87.

[12]John Shelton Reed, '"Ritualism Rampant in East London": Anglo-Catholicism and the Urban Poor', *Victorian Studies* 31 (1988).

London Diocese's *45 Churches Fund*, were aimed largely at contributing sites, manpower and temporary buildings. Other traditional sources of funding were also dwindling. In the early twentieth century, the financial contribution to new church building from independently wealthy incumbents and benefactors reduced considerably. Flew notes in particular the 'loss of the wealthy businessman as a committed supporter' of diocesan fundraising by 1914.[13] Wealthy individuals, local landowners and industry magnates were increasingly finding secular outlets for their philanthropic activities, exacerbated by the church's waning influence in the provision of education and healthcare. It was common for incumbents in the new suburbs to plead with the diocese for assistance owing to the poverty of their populations and the lack of benefactors. Whereas churches built in the previous century frequently benefitted from substantial donations or bequests, and often from women, the funding of new churches in the early-twentieth century continued a late-nineteenth-century drift towards the need for more local fundraising initiatives.[14] Efforts such as door-to door collections, buy-a-brick schemes, bazaars and sales of work were redoubled in attempts to replace gifts. Typically, offerings of sites for new churches continued, especially in conjunction with suburban development, for example, the sites for St Crispin, Withington, and St Nicholas, Burnage, both in Manchester, were donated by Lord Egerton of Tatton.[15] But help with building projects was rare. In turn, the benefactor as an influence on design was also lost and replaced with community input. In the dioceses of Manchester and London during this period only five of the fifty-five new permanent church buildings had a major portion of their cost financed by benefactor funding. Of these it is remarkable that only two, Our Lady of Mercy and St Thomas of Canterbury, Gorton, Manchester and St Anselm, Hayes, London, were funded via a legacy from a female benefactor, both of which were pre-war bequests.[16]

Gorton and Hayes were atypical; overall the diminishing role of women as benefactors was a significant factor in the reduction of women's influence in the design of new churches at this time. Not only was there a diminution of female influence from benefactions, but there is little indication that the newly elected PCCs were open to giving responsibilities to women, despite the mood of emancipation at the time. There are no examples of women holding positions of authority, such as Churchwarden or Treasurer, in the PCCs of the churches in these dioceses. Women were rarely to be found on the Building Committees formed for managing the construction of a new church. This is true even of the relatively enlightened PCCs such as that at St Andrew, Sudbury where there was a commitment to electing a ratio of 50 per cent women to the new committee

---

[13]Sarah Flew, '*Philanthropy and Secularisation: The Funding of Anglican Religious Voluntary Organisations in London, 1856–1914*' (PhD, Open University, 2013): 4.

[14]Flew, 'Philanthropy and Secularisation': 84.

[15]Church of England Record Centre (hereafter, CERC), Ecclesiastical Commissioners' Archives, St Crispin Withington, ECE/7/1/15956; CERC, Ecclesiastical Commissioners' Archives, St Nicholas, Burnage, ECE/7/1/91276.

[16]Greater Manchester County Records Office, Our Lady Gorton Formation of Parish (March 1923), GB127. M422/1/6; CERC, Ecclesiastical Commissioners' Archive, St Anselm Hayes, ECE/7/1/84409.

in 1920.[17] Women's input was inevitably devolved to fundraising efforts via the traditional routes of bazaars, sales of work and catering. There is no doubt that women were vital in these fundraising initiatives and in the community-building function of churches in new suburban areas, both issues that greatly exercised many of the incumbents of these districts.[18] Indeed, the importance of fundraising and community events should not be underestimated as a factor in the provision of new church buildings for these new districts. The most prominent display of this in the churches of the Manchester Diocese was that of the annual Whit Walk. Charlotte Wildman has described this phenomenon with regard to the Roman Catholic Church at the time in some detail, but it is worth noting that the Anglican churches also organized these events and indeed carefully choreographed them so as not to interfere with those of the Catholic churches in their parishes.[19] The preparation for this key event of the year within these communities fell to the ladies of the church.

For the dioceses, local congregations' fundraising was not merely about the amount that was raised, but proof of willing and a firm demonstration of community action. Relocating populations did not have enough disposable income to fund these expensive buildings. Even those who had not been rehoused in slum relocation initiatives were burdened by the cost of mortgages and furnishing their new homes, the latter frequently achieved via the newly respectable medium of the hire-purchase arrangement.[20] As a result, the amounts actually provided, although significant for populations who were far from affluent, in real terms often only provided a small proportion of the necessary amount to erect a permanent church. The proportion of giving from the parish was often small, generally less than 25 per cent of the cost of the final building, but the stake that they did provide gave them a sense of ownership and reinforced their entitlement to be involved in decisions relating to their new church. Local fundraising therefore acted both as a catalyst to allow the dioceses to justify the spending of much needed funds and also to instil a sense of ownership and responsibility for the building by the inhabitants of the district. A substantial building as a symbol to the community was of paramount importance and explains why the effort and cost was expended in erecting a permanent church building when many parishes already had a flexible multipurpose hall and church combined on site.

Funding for provision of new churches was a key issue, not only in facilitating construction, but also as a design influence. The impact of the Enabling Act coupled with a dire crisis in funding was to break the traditional design hegemony held by the

---

[17]London Metropolitan Archives (hereafter LMA), Parochial Church Committee (PCC) Minutes, St Andrew Sudbury (29 December 1919), DRO/124/15.

[18]Callum Brown attributes the decline in church attendance from the 1960s to the loss of the allegiance of women – which makes the restriction of their roles in the parish community and the failure of PCCs to be representative of even greater significance. See Brown, *The Death of Christian Britain*: 10.

[19]Charlotte Wildman, *Urban Redevelopment and Modernity in Liverpool and Manchester, 1918–1939* (London: Bloomsbury Academic, 2016): 148–56.

[20]Michael John Law, *1938: Modern Britain: Social Change and Visions of the Future* (London: Bloomsbury Academic, 2018): 7.

combination of benefactor, architect and incumbent. The benefactor as funder was replaced with a number of more diverse income streams and committees, leaving a void in the dictation of design parameters which local fundraising gradually filled.

Struggles for authority

Most of the churches constructed in the Diocese of London in the 1920s had a congregation that was engaged with the provision of a church building from the very outset and to whom neither the appointment of an architect nor the impetus to build was dictated by the diocese. While the dioceses were deeply involved in the funding of these new buildings and the logistical machinations of providing manpower, matters relating to design were intentionally left to the local parish in the vast majority of cases. In Southwark Diocese, the stated aim of their building programme was that the process of providing the new church should be led at local level.[21] In practice this included design decisions. The local parish committees would often choose their own architects either by local connection, the example of other churches, competition or recommendation. If requested, the dioceses would suggest names of architects to a parish, generally consisting of long-established ecclesiastical architect who advised the diocese in some capacity, often not noted for innovative design. This was hardly a recipe for new and exciting design ideas, nor did it make for a progressive relationship with the PCC. As a result, both the diocese and the architect had effectively to deal with a new, inexperienced and opinionated PCC 'client'.

This caused problems for many of the architects of the period who had been well established before the war, especially in adapting to new budgets and new threats to the design integrity of their church buildings, and as a result, their reputations. Church projects were extremely prestigious in the Victorian and Edwardian era and their elevated status continued after the war.[22] Architects who won cathedral commissions, such as Edward Maufe and Giles Gilbert Scott, were considered 'superstars', and national recognition (such as knighthoods) often followed.[23] Unlike secular projects, church commissions came with an extra responsibility towards a 'higher power' which was taken very seriously. Recognizing the centrality of the church as a vital, influential and integrated part of the cultural basis of everyday life in Britain during this period is essential and emphasizes church architecture as a key facet to the development of suburban areas.[24] The narrative of 'secularisation' and the 'irrelevance of the church' to modern life has blinded many to the fact that to think religiously was part of everyday

[21]Kenneth V. Richardson, *The Twenty-Five Churches of the Southwark Diocese: An Inter-war Campaign of Church-Building* (London: Ecclesiological Society, 2002): 5.

[22]Andrew Saint and Theresa Sladen, *Churches 1870–1914* (London: The Victorian Society, 2011): 11.

[23]David Frazer Lewis, 'Modernising Tradition: The Architectural Thought of Giles Gilbert Scott, 1880–1960' (DPhil, University of Oxford, 2014).

[24]Alister E. McGrath and Darren C. Marks, *The Blackwell Companion to Protestantism* (Malden, MA: Blackwell Pub., 2004): 105.

life in the first half of the century. Britain was until the 1960s 'a highly religious nation'.[25] Even of those who were not regular church-goers the majority believed in God and valued Christianity as a moral code.[26] Cultural innovations had a Christian basis: religious programming filled the early broadcasts of the BBC, so important that a studio dedicated to religious broadcasting was designed for their Portland Place headquarters by Maufe.[27] Remembrance ceremonies to commemorate those lost in the war became an enduring tradition and modern visual art was 'directly associated with Protestantism' as a way of legitimizing it in the public eye and influenced the design of war memorials.[28] Parliament debated church matters routinely, and major church issues, such as the passage of the proposed new Book of Common Prayer through both Houses in 1927–1928, were closely followed by the mainstream media and were considered important national news, the failure of the proposals sending a shockwave through church and state.[29] At the local level, suburban mores favoured churchgoing as an indicator of respectability, and sending children to Sunday School was considered a measure of good parenting. Local newspapers were expected to report in detail on the major events in the local church including the laying of the foundation stone and the consecration of new buildings. Large portions of the sermons from these events were reported too: this was religious coverage, not merely the reporting of a community event.[30]

The building of the local church for the new district was therefore of major significance for the architect and population alike. The pressure to realize a building that would be valued in posterity weighed heavily on the key players and affected their ability to work together. The particular difficulty for architects was that they were designing in an atmosphere that was beginning to champion new styles that they felt were fundamentally secular and incompatible with the loftier ideals of ecclesiastical commissions. This led to an entrenching of positions into the traditions in which they had been trained. Membership of committees of architects advising the dioceses, higher church authorities and grant-giving bodies reinforced their social standing and legitimized their traditional architectural stance.

Being elected to one of these panels was aspirational and considered a great privilege: Charles Spooner, for example, expressed great delight on being selected as a member of the advisory committee for the grant giving body the Incorporated Church Building

---

[25]Brown, *The Death of Christian Britain*: 30.

[26]Stuart Bell, 'The Church of England and the Home Front 1914–1918: Civilians, Soldiers and Religion in Wartime Colchester', *Journal of Beliefs & Values* 37 (2016): 239.

[27]Juliet Dunmur, *Edward Maufe: Architect and Cathedral Builder* (Manchester: Moyhill Publishing, 2019): 233.

[28]Matthew Grimley, 'The Religion of Englishness: Puritanism, Providentialism, and "National Character," 1918–1945', *Journal of British Studies*, 46 (2007): 887; Michael T. Saler, *The Avant-Garde in Interwar England: Medieval Modernism and the London Underground* (Oxford, England: Oxford University Press, 1999): 23; J. M. Winter, *Sites of Memory, Sites of Mourning: The Great War in European Cultural History* (Cambridge: Cambridge University Press, 2014): 97.

[29]John G. Maiden, *National Religion and the Prayer Book Controversy, 1927–1928* (Woodbridge: Boydell Press, 2009): 1.

[30]Numerous examples of this can be found, for example, the report on the consecration of St Gabriel Acton in the *Acton Gazette* (24 July 1931).

Society (ICBS).[31] In the 1920s and 1930s these panels were composed of experienced and distinguished architects who had been in practice for a considerable time before the war, many of whom were of advancing years. Committee members retained their position until they died, the process of replacement being left to their peers who inevitably chose like-minded successors.[32] It is not surprising that they were later disparagingly labelled the 'old boy's network'.[33] Membership overlapped and certain architects belonged to more than one of these panels. Examples include W. D. Caröe who was not only the Ecclesiastical Commissioners' inspecting architect approving buildings for consecration but also a member of the advisory committee for the grant giving body, the Incorporated Church Building Society; Edward Maufe who was on both the ICBS and the London Diocesan Fund's advisory committees; and Charles Nicholson who was a member of Diocesan Advisory Committees for Winchester, Sheffield, Wakefield and Lincoln, the London Diocesan Fund committee and that of the ICBS.[34] As part of their role, these architects also revised and authored the official 'requirements' of such bodies – rules which dictated whether a church was allowed grant funding were approved by the diocese for construction and accepted as worthy of consecration.[35] They imposed their belief in traditional plans, styles and construction materials through these guidelines, justifying the judgements they made on the individual buildings submitted for approval by referring back to what were, effectively, their own rules.[36] Not only did they reject or ask for many (often expensive) modifications to any proposals that did not conform to their ideas of what was 'appropriate' for a church building, they exhibited clear bias for their own panel members. Becoming a member of a committee was clearly a professional advantage in terms of reputation in ecclesiastical circles, but additionally the reports issued by these committees indicate that it was also a passport for approval of designs. New churches designed by architects on these panels were rarely subjected to scrutiny by their committee colleagues. For instance, Charles Nicholson's church of St Lawrence, Eastcote, passed through the committee process without any dissenting comments, despite the fact that the wall thicknesses did not meet the ICBS funding requirements.[37]

The change in the dynamic between parish, architect and funder was particularly problematic for parishes where plans for a new church had been in train since before the war, when the financial situation was very different. Complaints that communities had 'to face the very great increase in the cost of building over pre-war conditions' were

---

[31]Alec Hamilton, *Charles Spooner (1862–1938): Arts & Crafts Architect* (Donnington: Shaun Tyas, 2012): 112.

[32]Gill Hedley, *Free Seats for All: The Boom in Church Building after Waterloo* (London: Umbria Press, 2018): 180.

[33]G. Cope, 'The Sanctuary in the Parish Church', in W. Lockett (ed.), *The Modern Architectural Setting of the Liturgy* (London: SPCK, 1962): 41.

[34]The Central Council for the Care of Churches, *The Protection of Our English Churches Seventh Report 1934–7* (London: The Central Council for the Care of Churches, 1937): 122–8.

[35]Lambeth Palace Library, Incorporated Church Building Society, MB 39 Committee of Architects Minute Book 2 March 1848 to 30 May 1951.

[36]See for example: ICBS, *Architectural Requirements and Suggestions* (London: Incorporated Church Building Society, 1932).

[37]Lambeth Palace Library (hereafter LPL), Consulting Architects' Committee Report for the Incorporated Church Building Society, St Lawrence, Eastcote (3 August 1932), 12108.

common, voiced in this case by the incumbent of Holy Angels, Claremont in the Diocese of Manchester.[38] It seems that architects who had been long-established in practice before the war struggled to adapt their designs to the revised budgets and expectations of the local committees in the post-war period, resulting in a series of poor decisions and unsatisfactory buildings. There was an implied assumption that the project should simply resume where it had left off, perhaps a confirmation of the viewpoint that 'the old men came out again and took from us our victory, and re-made it in the likeness of the former world they knew'.[39]

St Michael and All Angels, Mill Hill, suffered from fundraising difficulties, but the inability of the architect to accommodate the change in the prevailing financial circumstances of the parish was a key influence, leading to the denudation of the architectural integrity of the building. W. D. Caröe designed the new church in 1911, but construction of the first part did not commence until 1921 (**Figure 7.1**). Increases in prices meant that the project was repeatedly reduced in scale and was criticized for the 'abnormal amount of temporary construction' that was necessary to start any building at all on the site.[40] Overambition in both materials and size of the proposals, as well as a failure to adjust the plans to accommodate the financial situation, left the local community with a poorly constructed partial church which was never completed to the original designs. Recognition of the need for economy, and that the pre-war plans were no longer viable, could have led to a much more satisfactory and economical building from the outset. However, this would have entailed Caröe compromising on his strongly held beliefs over the correct design for a church. In common with many of his contemporaries, Caröe approached church design projects with a very different attitude and set of ideals than that of his secular projects, believing that the 'Requirements' of the bodies such as the Ecclesiastical Commissioners for whom he consulted were rigid and could not be varied if ecclesiastical architecture was to be worthy of its sacred purpose.

Despite the redistribution of power in favour of the PCC, it is clear that having an architect open to discussion and negotiation on designs for new churches was essential if a congregation was intent on full engagement. Without these conditions, difficulties arose that were to persist for a surprisingly long time. At St Barnabas, Temple Fortune in London, the finances were an issue but so was the inability of the architects to forge a working relationship with a PCC keen to be involved in design decisions, resulting in a similar catalogue of delays to Mill Hill and to false starts. The involvement of the congregation caused considerable consternation to their first architect, Maurice Webb.[41]

---

[38]LPL, Incorporated Church Building Society, Holy Angels, Claremont, 111660. Holy Angels was a dedication unique in the Anglican church which referenced the appearance of Angels at the Battle of Mons according to Arthur J. Dobb and Derek Ralphs, *Like a Mighty Tortoise: A History of the Diocese of Manchester* (Manchester: The Author [Distributed by Upjohn and Bottomley (Printers) Ltd.], 1978): 229.

[39]T. E. Lawrence and David Garnett, *The Letters of T.E. Lawrence* (London: Cape, 1938): 262.

[40]LPL, Incorporated Church Building Society, St Michael Mill Hill, 11395.

[41]LMA, Correspondence Concerning the New Permanent Church April 1926–August 1939, Letter from Maurice Webb to Revd Turner, London Diocesan Fund, St Barnabas Temple Fortune (28 March 1929), DRO/103/28.

Figure 7.1 St Michael, Mill Hill. Drawing of W. D. Caröe's original design, Consecration Leaflet (1922): 17, Lambeth Palace Library, ICBS_11395 St Michael Mill Hill

Despite having capable and experienced members, the PCC's approach lacked clarity and would have benefitted from a fully interactive relationship with the architect. The Building Committee members were meticulous in their research but were indiscriminate in informing Webb of all their ideas, many before they were properly formed. Webb did not once visit the PCC to discuss the detail with them nor did he appear to grasp the difficult financial situation in the parish or the restrictions under which he was working.[42] This led to no fewer than six complete redesigns from the initial instruction for a church 'on Byzantine lines' through to a final simple Gothic design that failed to win the approval of the London Diocese's Honorary Advisory Committee Architects.[43] This rejection, coupled with the lack of interaction with the parish in order to understand their requirements, led ultimately to his resignation.[44] In contrast to Webb, the parish's chosen replacement architect, Ernest Shearman, attended PCC meetings and gave the impression of considering the proposals put to him by the Building Committee.[45] But it is clear from the frustrated exchanges between the committee and the architect that he was inclined to ignore their input.[46] This constant miscommunication was one of the factors contributing to the building remaining unfinished at the outbreak of the Second World War (**Figure 7.2**).

Some PCCs quickly established the organizational skills and confidence to challenge their architects on design decisions. The early foundation and egalitarian structure of the PCC at St Andrew's Sudbury in the Diocese of London may well have contributed to the strength of their input to the design of their church. Charles Waymouth, the architect, initially designed a barn-like church with an intricate wooden roof and contributed many handcrafted details such as the leaded-light windows and diapered brickwork. The overall design inspiration of the church remained intact through to its completion, leading it to be considered a retrograde design. By referencing the enduring Arts and Crafts tradition, which had been very much in the ascendant in the Edwardian period and continued post-war, Waymouth's design was within the contemporary norms, albeit a 'faint echo' of what had come before.[47] Waymouth's detailed design at St Andrew's did not remain intact however, as the interior was dramatically altered at the insistence of the PCC.[48] The PCC minutes record the robust discussion between the congregation and the architect where some changes were insisted upon, but others roundly defended by the architect and retained.[49] A stone arcade was a major feature that the PCC were adamant should be included, despite the fact that it added almost £2,000 to the construction cost which the parish could ill-afford (**Figure 7.3**). Whether St Andrew's would be considered a more satisfying design without the solidity of a stone arcade is a moot point; the involvement of the congregation in the design is the key factor here, not the success or otherwise of the outcome as judged by later standards. Indeed, it is not possible to understand the built form of St Andrew's without appreciating the design input of the local people as a crucial factor.

In a similar way the PCC at St Mary Cadishead, in the Diocese of Manchester, considered the construction of their church at an early point after election. In 1920

---

[42]LMA, Building Committee Minutes, St Barnabas Temple Fortune (26 February 1929), DRO/103/027.

[43]LMA, Building Committee Minutes, 'Report of the London Diocesan Fund Honorary Advisory Committee of Architects, St Barnabas Temple Fortune' (6 October 1930), DRO/103/27.

[44]LMA, Correspondence Concerning the New Permanent Church April 1926–August 1939, letter from Maurice Webb to Revd Turner, London Diocesan Fund, St Barnabas Temple Fortune (3 February 1931), CDO/103/28.

[45]LMA, Building Committee Minutes, St Barnabas Temple Fortune (30 March 1931), DRO/103/027.

[46]LMA, Building Committee Minutes, St Barnabas Temple Fortune (11 July 1932), DRO/103/027.

[47]Alec Hamilton, *Arts & Crafts Churches* (Lund Humphries, 2020): 121.

[48]Alec Hamilton, 'The Arts and Crafts in Church-Building in Britain 1884–1918' (DPhil, University of Oxford, 2016).

[49]LMA, St Andrew Sudbury, PCC Minutes (10 September 1924), DRO/124/016.

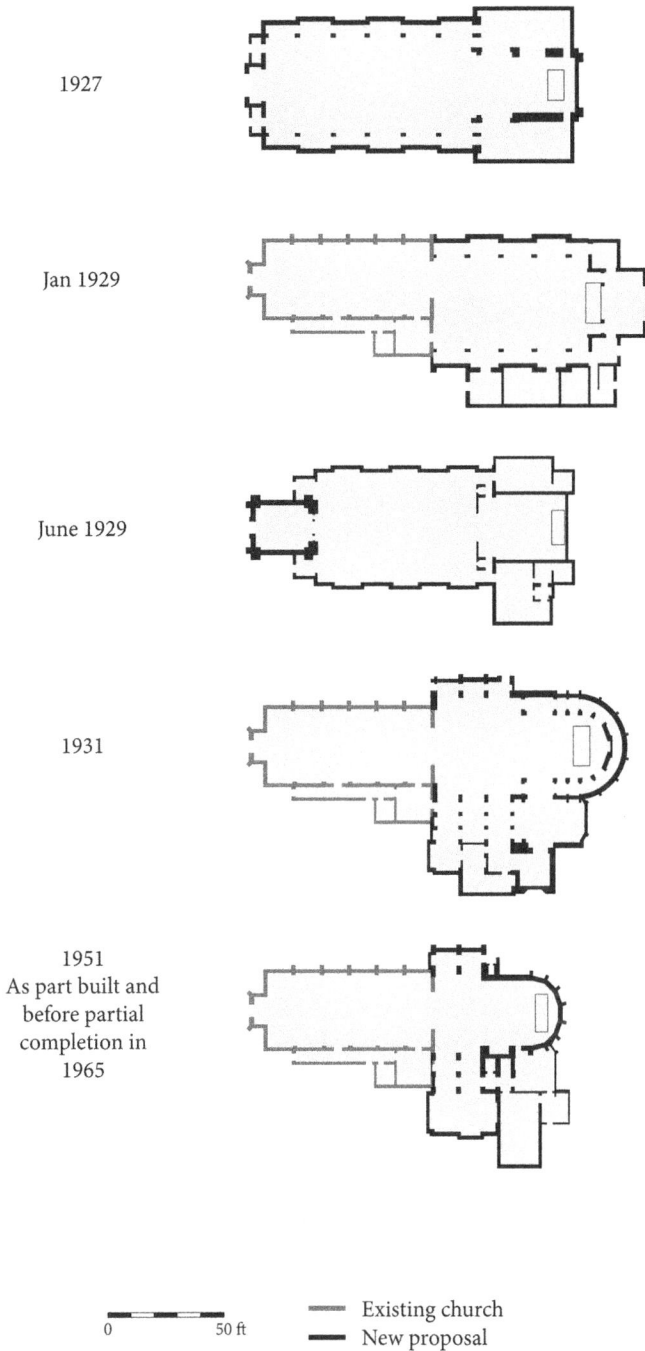

1927

Jan 1929

June 1929

1931

1951
As part built and
before partial
completion in
1965

0   50 ft

Existing church
New proposal

Figure 7.2 Plans for St Barnabas, Temple Fortune showing three of the design iterations of 1927–1929 by Maurice Webb (abandoned) and two by Ernest Shearman of 1931 showing the intended full building, and of 1951 showing the part that had been constructed at the outbreak of the Second World War, drawn by Hannah Towler

Figure 7.3 Interior of St Andrew, Sudbury showing arcade. Lambeth Palace Library, CARE 23/415

enquiries were made by the PCC into the possibility of erecting a concrete church, a remarkably radical suggestion for the date, and it is clear that ongoing discussions were held during the design and construction process as to the type and quality of materials to be used for the building.[50] Although the use of concrete was not pursued, the committee were responsible for major decisions that would change the appearance of the church, such as selecting the option of brick elevations instead of stone and a slated roof instead of tiled – decisions made after they had toured other churches by their architect, Robert Martin (the Diocesan Surveyor), to ascertain the effect of each choice in order to make an informed assessment.[51]

Success at the expense of progress

The economics of the post-war period meant that price rises detrimentally affected some projects, but others were completely stalled both by finances and the inexperience of the newly fledged PCCs. While at the time this was seen as a catastrophic setback, in reality for several parishes it resulted in them gaining the time to explore options, to

---

[50]Greater Manchester County Records Office, PCC Minutes, GB127.L224/3/2/1.
[51]LMA, St Mary Cadishead, PCC Minutes (19 October 1926).

find alternative architects and ultimately to realize a building later in the period that was far more architecturally interesting than their pre-war design. Often the outcome, however successful it is now considered, came at a cost to community involvement. An example of this is the case of St Thomas, Hanwell, in the London Borough of Ealing. The PCC at St Thomas's had been established in 1921, soon after the Enabling Act, and by 1926 had established a Building Sub-Committee from the PCC and begun the process of obtaining funding for a permanent building.[52] This was an actively engaged PCC, which attempted to control the process of designing the new church building by holding a small local competition, which was a relatively unusual way of choosing an architect for ecclesiastical projects. Unfortunately, when the plans of the new church were rejected by the London Diocese Architects' committee, this led to a legal dispute with the chosen local architects over fees.[53] The PCC subsequently appointed Edward Maufe, who had just won the competition to design Guildford Cathedral and represented a safe choice for design approval as one of the members of the architects' committee for the diocese. By appointing Maufe, however, they lost the impetus of achieving a church where the local population had an active role in the design decisions. Maufe's church, constructed in the 1930s, is considered to be 'even more successful' than Guildford Cathedral and is judged one of the most important suburban churches of the time for its artwork and decoration.[54] A small local competition as originally arranged by this parish would certainly not have produced a building of this quality.

However, this success story in architectural terms obscures a failure for democratic control. The major challenge to the PCCs of the time, which has been alluded to in the cases of St Barnabas Temple Fortune and St Michael Mill Hill, was the approach of the architect. At St Thomas's, Maufe stated that his aim was 'to retain authority in the design of this work to its completion'.[55] The PCC requested some input into the choice of furnishings, justifying their plea by noting that they had raised the funds for these specifically: an area that the congregation had some confidence, given the general interest in domestic interior design at the time.[56] However, Maufe derided the church council's suggested furnishings, being convinced that by allowing them input 'it may be impossible to keep any unison in the design, and the church may easily be spoiled thereby' and finally stating that he was 'prepared to design such things for no fee rather than have the Church spoiled'.[57] For the PCC at St Thomas Hanwell the process of realizing a new church included two bruising encounters with architects from the London Diocesan

---

[52]O. Julyan, 'From an Upper Room … Onward' (St Thomas Hanwell Church Collection, 1955): 3.

[53]LMA, St Thomas Hanwell, 1925–50, letter from C. Alan Chilton of Markby Stewart, DL/A/K/01/31/081.

[54]Historic England, 'Church of St Thomas the Apostle, Boston Road W7' (Historic England, 1996).

[55]RIBA Archive, Sir Edward Maufe Papers, 'Church of St Thomas the Apostle, London, Ealing Boston Rd: Erection, Surveys, Redecoration, 1932–1962', letter from Maufe to Secretary Ecclesiastical Commissioners (4 December 1933), MaE/49–53.

[56]Law, 1938: Modern Britain: 7.

[57]RIBA Archive, Sir Edward Maufe Papers, 'Church of St Thomas the Apostle, London, Ealing Boston Rd: Erection, Surveys, Redecoration, 1932–1962', letter from Maufe to Secretary Ecclesiastical Commissioners (4 December 1933), MaE/49-53.

committee and they clearly had little appetite for continuing the fight. Indeed, both Edward and Prudence Maufe donated time and fittings to the church to overcome budgetary constraints.[58] Maufe's reluctance to relinquish any aspect of authorship of this project was typical of his approach to his ecclesiastical commissions as can be seen by a similar attitude to the PCC of All Saints, Weston Green and St George, Goodrington, and can be understood as part of his desire to protect his reputation.[59] This illustrates the difficulties that local congregations faced in exercising their new-found rights, when the response from many of those with the opportunity to guide was to impose.

Conclusion

The increase in collaboration was causing a quiet revolution in church architecture during this period, even if it did not produce what could be identified as a single resolved architectural signature. Attempts towards inclusivity in the process of designing these buildings were to gain momentum during the century, culminating in the Liturgical Reform Movement. Church architecture in the UK in the 1960s and 1970s was transformed under the aegis of this movement, which affected the plan of the buildings and was made possible by the employment of new technology and acceptance of modern building materials. The active involvement of the people in all aspects of church life was one of its underpinning tenets. For the Roman Catholics the changes in architectural form were mandated and accompanied by substantial changes to the liturgy. For the Church of England, the need for reform was less obvious and was not accompanied by liturgical revision. Recognition that the people were part of the process of managing a parish was manifested in their interaction in building projects, which lay the foundations for later physical changes. The birth pangs of this later twentieth-century revolution in architecture can be found in these projects which heralded a new era in the Anglican Church.

The study of the processes and actors involved in the architectural production of these churches places them in context as part of the community and an integral part of suburban development. It reveals a complexity and a significance to these buildings that has long been overlooked, and a key route to their re-evaluation. Looking at the exterior of the churches built in the 1920s, many based on an adapted Gothic or Byzantine style, denuded of their landmark towers by financial expediency and in the thrall of the 'Old Boys' Club' of architects or the diocesan surveyor, it is difficult to see their worth against the more opulent examples of the previous century or indeed the more dramatic designs of the late 1930s and after the Second World War. But the very chaotic and incoherent nature of this architecture is a manifestation of the aspirational struggle that was inherent

---

[58]RIBA Archive, Sir Edward Maufe Papers, 'Church of St Thomas the Apostle, London, Ealing Boston Rd: Erection, Surveys, Redecoration, 1932–1962', letter from St Thomas the Apostle PCC to Maufe (11 October 1934), MaE/49–53.
[59]Dunmur, *Edward Maufe*: 237–8.

in this period. Those architects that considered their reputation threatened, conflicted with their local clients and sought to maintain control of a project by characterizing the clients' opinions as ill-informed and threatening to the transcendent message of the building. The new suburban population, however, were encouraged by an atmosphere which fostered the ordinary person's right to be involved and they agitated for a greater say in constructing a building that was an important part of their lifestyle.

Without the reorganization of the democratic structure that was put in place in the Church of England in the 1920s, later changes to the fabric of the buildings would not have been possible, nor would the eventual acceptance of the need to amend architectural design have begun to emerge. Indeed, the foundations would not have been laid for the post-Second World War Liturgical Reform Movement, which championed input of community as a design fundamental for church buildings. Without the grassroots input of local communities, the gradual modernization of both the architects' and the church's approach to design would not have been achieved. These churches reveal the evolution of the twentieth-century church and, indeed, the story of twentieth-century urban architectural development as a whole.

Select bibliography

Primary

Archival sources

Holy Angels, Claremont, Lambeth Palace Library, London, ICBS File 111660.
Our Lady, Gorton, Greater Manchester County Records Office, GB127.M422/1/6.
St Andrew, Sudbury, London Metropolitan Archives, London, DRO/124/015.
St Anselm Hayes, Church of England Records' Centre, London, ECE/7/1/84409.
St Barnabas, Temple Fortune, London Metropolitan Archives, London, DRO/103/027.
St Crispin Withington, Church of England Records' Centre, London, ECE/7/1/15956.
St Lawrence, Eastcote, Lambeth Palace Library, London, ICBS File 12108.
St Mary, Cadishead, Greater Manchester County Records Office, GB127.L224/3/2/1.
St Michael, Mill Hill, Lambeth Palace Library, London, ICBS File 11395.
St Nicholas, Burnage, Church of England Records' Centre, London, ECE/7/1/91276.
St Thomas the Apostle, Ealing: Erection, Surveys, Redecoration, 1932–1962, British Architectural Library, London, Drawings Collection, MaE/49-53.

Secondary

Articles

Bell, S. 'The Church of England and the Home Front 1914–1918: Civilians, Soldiers and Religion in Wartime Colchester'. *Journal of Beliefs & Values* 37 (2016): 239–40.
Grimley, M. 'The Religion of Englishness: Puritanism, Providentialism, and "National Character," 1918-1945'. *Journal of British Studies* 46, no. 4 (2007): 884–906.
Reed, J. S. '"Ritualism Rampant in East London": Anglo-Catholicism and the Urban Poor'. *Victorian Studies* 31 (1988): 375–403.

Chapters (in edited volumes/collections)

Cope, G. 'The Sanctuary in the Parish Church'. In *The Modern Architectural Setting of the Liturgy*, edited by W. Lockett, 32–41. London: SPCK, 1962.

PhDs/unpublished research

Flew, S. E. J. '*Philanthropy and Secularisation: the Funding of Anglican Religious Voluntary Organisations in London 1856–1914*.' PhD thesis, Open University, 2013.

Lewis, D. F. '*Modernising Tradition: The Architectural Thought of Giles Gilbert Scott, 1880–1960*.' DPhil Thesis, University of Oxford, 2014.

Parker, L. M. '*Shell-Shocked Prophets: The Influence of Former Anglican Army Chaplains on the Church of England and British Society in the Inter-war Years*.' PhD Thesis, Birmingham University, 2013.

Books

Brown, C. G. *The Death of Christian Britain*, 2nd edn. Hoboken: Taylor & Francis, 2009.

Dunmur, J. *Edward Maufe: Architect and Cathedral Builder.* Moyhill Publishing: Manchester, 2019.

Hamilton, A. *Arts & Crafts Churches.* Lund Humphries, 2020.

Hedley, G. *Free Seats for All: The Boom in Church Building after Waterloo.* London: Umbria Press, 2018.

Jackson, A. A. *Semi-detached London: Suburban Development, Life and Transport, 1900–39.* London: Allen & Unwin, 1973.

Law, M. J. *1938: Modern Britain: Social Change and Visions of the Future.* London: Bloomsbury Academic, 2018.

Macnutt, F. B. *The Church in the Furnace, Essays by 17 Temporary Church of England Chaplains on Active Service in France.* London, 1917.

Maiden, J. G. *National Religion and the Prayer Book Controversy, 1927–1928.* Woodbridge: Boydell Press, 2009.

Oliver, P., I. Davis, and I. Bentley. *Dunroamin: The Suburban Semi and Its Enemies.* London: Barrie & Jenkins 1981.

Pym, T. W., and J. G. Gordon. *Papers from Picardy.* London, 1917.

Richardson, K. V. *The Twenty-Five Churches of the Southwark Diocese: An Inter-war Campaign of Church-Building.* London: Ecclesiological Society, 2002.

Saler, M. T. *The Avant-garde in Interwar England: Medieval Modernism and the London Underground.* New York; Oxford: Oxford University Press, 1999.

Snape, M. F. *God and the British Soldier: Religion and the British Army in the First and Second World Wars.* London: Routledge, 2005.

Swenarton, M. *Homes Fit for Heroes: The Politics and Architecture of Early State Housing in Britain.* London: Heinemann Educational Books, 1981.

Walford, R. *The Growth of 'New London' in Suburban Middlesex (1918–1945) and the Response of the Church of England.* Lewiston: Edwin Mellen Press, 2007.

Wildman, C. *Urban Redevelopment and Modernity in Liverpool and Manchester, 1918–1939.* London: Bloomsbury Academic, an imprint of Bloomsbury Publishing Plc, 2016.

Winter, J. M. *Sites of Memory, Sites of Mourning: The Great War in European Cultural History.* Cambridge: Cambridge University Press, 2014.

SECTION III
BUILDING A RURAL CITIZENRY

Section III picks up on themes discussed in the previous section introduction but with a particular focus on rural reconstruction. Visions of post-war reconstruction often looked to rural communities and landscapes as the antidote to unhealthy urban and industrialized environments. This idealization of the rural was coupled with a political and economic motivation to boost the agricultural economy and shore up communities in the countryside, which were threatened by migration to cities. A robust rural economy and society was associated with national identity based on self-sufficiency. The nostalgia for a rural past and an image of 'Englishness' based on village life that permeated the period has been interpreted as the antithesis of modernity and modernism. But this pairing of rural and tradition and the dichotomy of tradition and modernity is over-simplified and ignores the nuance of rural culture and its reconstruction. Alison Light characterized the period after the war as one of 'reaction' but also 'a time when old forms were being recast and traditional attitudes took new form'.[1] The architecture of the rural revival captures something of this form of conservative modernity that Light described as a 'Janus faced modernity' that 'could simultaneously look backward and forwards, it could accommodate the past in the new forms of the present'.[2] As the contributors to this section show, there was a nostalgia for an almost mythical image of rural communities but at the same time, rural life was dynamic and changing. The countryside was not a static site of preservationists: new ideas of rural community, citizenship and economy were driving the reconstruction of built environments, often by architects. Alison Light wanted to explore a history of the 1920s and 1930s that sought to embrace 'disagreements and disturbances rather than homogeneity and unity'.[3] So too the authors in this section trace the ways in which many of the ideas behind rural reconstructed were rooted in the nineteenth century but were reimagined in the new post-war context. To try to complicate ideas of architectural agency, the titles of chapters in this section foreground the ultimate client, the new democratic constituencies of the post-war period, namely the yeoman, the student and the veteran.

In their chapter on the 'Yeoman', Rebecca Preston and Joanna Smith discuss how this reimagined medieval ideal came to represent an image of a modern, productive and respectable member of rural society. Through their analysis of the 1919 Land Settlement

---

[1] Alison Light, *Forever England: Femininity, Literature and Conservatism between the Wars* (London: Routledge, 1991): 10.
[2] Ibid.
[3] Ibid.: 6.

Act and the small holdings schemes established throughout the country, Preston and Smith highlight the government's vision for a rural revival. The potential of rural society to counter the ill effects of industrialization, growing class conflict and inequality was also at the heart of the work of Henry Morris and his vision for the village college. Kieran Mahon's chapter on the 'Student' explores how Morris's ideas for the village college were shaped by pre-war university settlements such as the Toynbee Hall and further forged by his wartime experiences. Although not an architect himself, Morris's writing about the potential of the college buildings to shape the students and the wider community demonstrates the interaction between architecture and wider discourses on education and social reform during the period.

There was also an impetus to improve the lives and prospects of returning soldiers and the next generation, which mapped individual recuperation onto national regeneration. Elizabeth McKellar's chapter on 'Veterans' looks at Annabel Dott's designs for rural homes for soldiers injured and disabled in the war. The need for fresh air and also productive activity on the land shaped the cottages Dott designed and built through her various philanthropic ventures. McKellar's study of Dott's career in architecture shows the importance of the often overlooked middle-class women working in architecture during this period. Dott is a particularly interesting character as she had an aptitude for engaging with modern media to pursue her philanthropy, which was rooted in nineteenth-century practices and ideas. The work of figures such as Lawrence Weaver, Annabel Dott and Henry Morris – none of them practising architects in a conventional sense – was emblematic of the overlaps between government initiatives, commercial interests, rural reconstruction and architecture in the years after the war. Each used architecture to tackle social, cultural and political ills and to reinvigorate Britain's rural communities.

CHAPTER 8
YEOMAN: LAND SETTLEMENT AND COTTAGE SMALLHOLDINGS
Rebecca Preston and Joanna Smith

In 1919 several acts were passed concerned with providing 'homes fit for heroes' as part of the national programme of reform and reconstruction. Most familiar is the Housing, Town Planning &c. (Addison), Act 1919, which required rural and urban local authorities to survey housing needs and draw up plans for state-assisted housing schemes. Its consequences – visible in many urban and suburban estates and in villages across the country – have been extensively investigated by historians.[1] Far less well known is the more disbursed landscape of smallholdings built under the Land Settlement (Facilities) Act, 1919, intended largely for ex-servicemen, and the subsequent state-sponsored schemes for resettling unemployed men on the land in the 1930s.

The Land Settlement (Facilities) Act required county councils and boroughs to acquire land for smallholdings for those who had served in HM Forces or the Land Army. This expanded existing powers for council-provided smallholdings granted by earlier legislation but with a focus on demobilization and the grouping of the smallholdings in 'colonies', provided with the necessary facilities including housing. The results were impressive: by 1924 more than £5,000,000 had been spent on adapting and building new cottages and farm buildings, additional roads and water supply, and local authorities had become 'by far the largest agricultural landowners in England and Wales'.[2] This acquisition represented about 1.5 per cent of British landmass – 'an astonishing amount', as Ian Jack commented recently, 'for a scheme that has left so little trace on the national memory'.[3]

Government land-settlement schemes have been examined in relation to their respective housing policies in Ireland and Scotland, while studies of those in England and Wales have assessed their success in agricultural terms or as communities, and in relation

---

[1]For national surveys, see Mark Swenarton, *Homes Fit for Heroes: The Politics and Architecture of Early State Housing in Britain* (London: Heinemann Educational, 1981); John Boughton, *Municipal Dreams: The Rise and Fall of Council Housing* (London: Verso, 2018) and associated website https://municipaldreams. wordpress.com.

[2]*Land Settlement in England & Wales, Being a Report of Proceedings under the Small Holdings & Allotments Acts 1908 to 1919 for the Period 1919 to 1924* (London: HMSO, 1925): 52, 5–7 (hereafter Land Settlement, 1925).

[3]Ian Jack, Review of *The New Enclosure: The Appropriation of Public Land in Neoliberal Britain* by Brett Christophers, in *London Review of Books* (23 May 2019).

to the revival of certain building technologies.[4] Building on these and related research, this chapter discusses the smallholding schemes created by county and borough councils under the 1919 Act and then the work of the Land Settlement Association and Welsh Land Settlement Society Ltd from 1934 to the Second World War.[5] These are considered in the context of pre-war ideas and are explored as part of longer-established back-to-the-land impulses that continued to exert a strong, cross-political influence in the 1920s and 1930s.[6] Many aspects of land settlement, including food production and the social work entailed in the resettlement of veterans and later, those from industrially depressed areas, were essential to the programme of reconstruction. But these are beyond the scope of the present account which, framed as part of the rural revival movement, outlines the general aims and impact of government-sponsored land settlement, how it was delivered and who it was intended for. In particular, it focuses upon the provision of model accommodation, its planning and design, and its relationship to the larger state-sponsored housing initiative.

Statutory smallholdings and the rural revival

Smallholdings are, as the name suggests, farming units on a modest scale but the term is elastic: in 1918 it covered anything from 1- to 2-acre market gardens to 50-acre dairy holdings. Their size and character varied according to the land and the type of agriculture it supported, with strong regional differences, but they were generally operated by a single family, and sometimes with additional land farmed in common. By the late nineteenth century ideas about 'peasant proprietorship' and settlements of smallholdings were a much-favoured solution for stemming rural depopulation, the moral and physical decline of the urban population and bringing 'new blood' into the farming class to assist in a hoped-for rural revival.[7] Smallholdings featured in Liberal policies relating to land and social reform and state encouragement came in the form of Smallholdings Acts in

---

[4]F. H. A. Aalen, 'Homes for Irish Heroes: Housing under the Irish Land (Provision for Soldiers and Sailors) Act 1919, and the Irish Sailors' and Soldiers' Land Trust', *Town Planning Review* 59, no. 3 (1988): 305–23; Murray Fraser, *John Bull's Other Homes: State Housing and British Policy in Ireland, 1883-1922* (Liverpool: Liverpool University Press, 1996): ch7; Leah Leneman, *Fit for Heroes? Land Settlement in Scotland After World War I* (Aberdeen: Aberdeen University Press, 1989). Carol A. Lockwood, 'From Soldier to Peasant? The Land Settlement Scheme in East Sussex, 1919-1939', *Albion* 30, no. 3 (1998): 439–62; Susanna Wade Martins, 'Smallholdings in Norfolk, 1890-1950: A Social and Farming Experiment', *Agricultural History Review* 54, no. II (2006): 304–30. Mark Swenarton, 'Rammed Earth Revival: Technological Innovation and Government Policy in Britain, 1905–1925', *Construction History* 19 (2003): 107–26.

[5]Peter Clarke, 'The Land Settlement Association 1934-1948: The Evolution of a Social Experiment' (PhD thesis, London School of Economics, 1985); David Jeremiah, *Architecture and Design for the Family in Britain, 1900-70* (Manchester: Manchester University Press, 2000): 57; Joan Thirsk, *Alternative Agriculture: A History* (Oxford: Oxford University Press, 1997): 211.

[6]See Clare V. J. Griffiths, *Labour and the Countryside: The Politics of Rural Britain 1918-1939* (Oxford: Oxford University Press, 2007); Alun Howkins, *Reshaping Rural England: A Social History,* 1850–1925 (Oxford: Routledge, 1992): especially 225–30; Jan Marsh, *Back to the Land: The Pastoral Impulse in England* (London: Quartet, 1982).

[7]Newlin Russell Smith, *Land for the Small Man: English and Welsh Experience with Publicly-Supplied Small Holdings, 1860-1937* (New York: King's Crown Press, 1946): 217–18.

1892, 1907 and 1908 that obliged county councils to purchase land for these purposes. But while this had proved useful for 'country bred' men wanting to obtain land it had done little to encourage 'new cultivators … on newly-equipped holdings'.[8]

Even so, smallholdings continued to be seen as a means of maintaining political stability, improving the health and military fitness of the nation, alleviating urban overcrowding and addressing rural housing conditions. The Board of Agriculture and Fisheries produced advice on the design of smallholding cottages, complete with 'model plans' in 1913 and again in 1914 (hereafter the *BAF Reports* of 1913 and 1914), as part of a wider survey of rural housing.[9] By this time there was growing enthusiasm for taking things further: for grouping smallholdings together, equipping them properly, providing training if necessary and collective marketing of produce. The rhetoric was now of 'land settlement' in 'co-operative colonies', as advocated by campaigners such as the agricultural and social reformer Christopher Turnor.[10]

The use of the term 'colony' in relation to permanent resettlement on the land came to the fore in the nineteenth century. Its currency went beyond Britain, and was used in this sense in Holland, Germany and Belgium, but in an English context it was associated with a range of land experiments: socialist, anarchist and the morally improving. These ran the gamut from utopian to the punitive or disciplinary and were infused with the idea that 'the countryside was *empty*' and that such projects could be 'imposed on an area … like an overseas colony'.[11] As well as repopulating rural districts they were also seen by some as a means of exporting population to the empire.[12] In language and layout, they had a parallel in the 'colony' or 'villa' system of lunatic asylums and other segregated hospitals in Britain, which also emerged from northern Europe at this time.[13] In the context of farming, the colony idea went hand in hand with economic cooperation among, and shared social amenities for, the settlers or colonists.

In the early twentieth century national identity remained, for many, rooted in rural society and the repopulation of the countryside with an independent owner-occupying

---

[8]Christopher Turnor, 'Land Settlement for Ex-servicemen', *Journal of the Royal Society of Arts (JRSA)* (17 December 1915): 99–101.

[9]The board became the Ministry of Agriculture and Fisheries (MAF) in January 1920. The reports were made by committees appointed from 1912 by Walter Runciman, then President of the Board, whose members included Christopher Turnor (as Chairman), Cecil Harmsworth and Raymond Unwin. See Board of Agriculture and Fisheries, *Report of the Departmental Committee on the Equipment of Small Holdings in England And Wales …* (London: HMSO, 1913); *Report of the Committee Appointed by the President of the Board of Agriculture and Fisheries to Consider and Advise the Board on Plans, Models, Specification, and Methods of Construction for Rural Cottages and Outbuildings* (London: HMSO, 1914).

[10]E.g. Turnor, 'Land Settlement', *JSRA* (1915): 100. Christopher Hatton Turnor (d. 1940), a politically maverick Tory Lincolnshire landowner and writer on rural revival, was chairman to the (Conservative) Unionist Social Reform Committee's agriculture sub-committee in 1913 as well as a member of BAF and MAF committees under the Liberal and coalition governments; see notes 11 and 25 and Jane Ridley, 'The Unionist Social Reform Committee, 1911–1914', *Historical Journal* 30, no. 2 (1987): 391–413, 402–5.

[11]Martin J. Wiener, *English Culture and the Decline of the Industrial Spirit, 1850–1980* (Cambridge: Cambridge University Press, 1981): 49; Clarke, 'The Land Settlement Association 1934–1948': 286–7.

[12]Dennis Hardy, *Utopian England: Community Experiments 1900–1945* (London: E. & F. N. Spon, 2000): 25–6.

[13]Gillian Almond, 'Liberty and the Individual: The Colony Asylum in Scotland and England', *History of Psychiatry* 28, no. 1 (2017): 29–43.

peasantry was thought by some a solution to a perceived 'decay of the English race'.[14] The term 'yeoman peasantry' had come into use at the end of the previous century to evoke 'a highly productive and highly secure rural society, a stable foundation for the whole nation'.[15] As a consequence the figure of the yeoman became emblematic of the hardy Englishman and his family. The name Yeoman was also used for a state-funded high-yielding wheat variety, first issued from Cambridge University in 1916.[16] The war had highlighted the dangers of dependence on imports and the desirability of increasing the supply of home-grown food, and in the 1920s and 1930s the 'new yeoman' therefore also came to be associated with the promotion of national self-sufficiency.[17]

During the war, smallholdings and land settlement were drawn into the wider reconstruction agenda, as a reward for those who had fought for the land and a means of rehabilitating disabled servicemen. In 1916 the Small Holdings Colonies Act was passed to allow for the establishment of experimental sites to be studied in relation to demobilization policies. As a consequence of this and further legislation in 1918 some fifteen 'crown colonies' were set up – so called because they were government initiatives, although comparison with the same name for British territory overseas is unavoidable. These were a mixture of profit-sharing farms and smallholdings. Land settlement for ex-servicemen then became a wartime pledge, reiterated during the 1918 general election and, as Mark Swenarton has written, was 'ranked second only to the housing programme in its political importance'.[18]

Planning for land settlement

One important aspect of both the national housing programme and land settlement was housing reform. Social and political concern about the standards of rural and urban dwellings had roots in the pre-war period and by 1914 the two-storey cottage, set in individual garden plots and grouped at the edges of towns or in new self-contained settlements, was the form accepted by most authorities as the ideal working-class housing type for families in England and Wales. Post-war county council smallholdings, like local authority housing schemes, were subject to government approval and followed guidance about planning and design and, although administered by different departments, both kinds of 'homes fit for heroes to live in' shared many of the same minimum standards. Ministry of Agriculture advice on site planning for land settlement was broadly in tune with that of the Local Government Board and then the Ministry of Health and in recommending that rural cottages should be built 'in connection with some existing plan'

---

[14]Alan Howkins, *The Death of Rural England: A Social History of the Countryside* (London: Routledge, 2003): 25; Lockwood, 'Soldier to Peasant': 441.

[15]Clarke, 'The Land Settlement Association 1934–1948': 297–8; Paul Readman, 'Jesse Collings and Land Reform, 1886–1914', *Historical Research* 81, no. 212 (2008): 293–314.

[16]Berris Charnley, 'Rowland Biffen, Little Joss and Yeoman: Looking Back at Two Successes behind the Birth of NIAB in 1919', *Landmark* (NIAB Bulletin) (May 2009): 3–4.

[17]Aalen, 'Homes for Irish Heroes': 306.

[18]Swenarton, 'Rammed Earth Revival': 112.

in order that the new houses would form a 'natural and harmonious development of the village' and not 'isolated and unsociable units'.[19] Rural council housing might be grouped in pairs or blocks of four to six rather than scattered, while for convenience and economy, smallholding colonies could be formed from six to eight homesteads.[20] Aesthetic concerns were generally limited to the 'seemliness' of the cottages' exteriors in relation to their locality, omitting 'calculated irregularities' for plain elevations, and a preference for local materials.[21] The Ministry of Agriculture recognized however that single cottages or pairs were much preferred by labourers, 'and still more by their wives'.[22] Correspondingly, the Women's Housing Sub-Committee, formed in 1917 under Christopher Addison, the Minister for Reconstruction, recommended that country cottages should be built for the most part in pairs and set well back from the road and that, where there was no drainage system, there should be no more than four to the acre.[23] Most smallholdings were not connected to the mains and this arrangement of cottages, dispersed singly and in pairs along existing roads, was the pattern commonly found in the areas studied. Therefore, they tended to differ from the layouts stipulated for local-authority schemes.

Overseeing the building programme was Sir Lawrence Weaver, who had risen during the war to be director general of the Land Department in the Ministry of Agriculture, a post he held until 1922. In the food crisis of 1917–1918 Weaver had been Controller of Supplies at the Board of Agriculture and had founded the National Institute of Agricultural Botany (NIAB) at Cambridge University, largely in response to the success of Yeoman and another variety of wheat.[24] At the Ministry he enlisted a 'little band of ex-soldier architects', including Maxwell Ayrton, John Lee, Oswald Milne, Clough Williams-Ellis and Hugh Maule, to work on the smallholdings.[25] Weaver was architectural editor of *Country Life* from 1910 and in 1913 published the first of three editions of a *Country Life* book on cottage planning and design.[26] Land settlement and cottage smallholdings thus embraced at least three of his particular interests: architecture, agriculture and the land, and provision for ex-servicemen – as captured in a *Country Life* article, 'Homesteads for Heroes', in 1916.[27]

Weaver is not mentioned in the 1913 report but Cecil Harmsworth, MP, places him at the first meeting of the 'Cottage Committee' in December 1912, together with Raymond Unwin and Christopher Turnor.[28] Constance Cochrane, rural district councillor and a respected

---

[19]*BAF Report* (1914): 10; *BAF Report* (1913): 16; Local Government Board, *Manual on the Preparation of State-Aided Housing Schemes* (London: HMSO, 1919) (hereafter *LGB Manual* (1919)): 5; MAF, *Manual for the Guidance of County Council and their Architects in the Equipment of Small Holdings*, 3rd edn revised (London: HMSO, 1920): 6.

[20]Ibid.

[21]*MAF Manual* (1920): 6.

[22]*BAF Report* (1913): 39.

[23]Women's Housing Sub-Committee, *Final Report* (London: HMSO, 1918): 16.

[24]Charnley, 'Rowland Biffen, Little Joss and Yeoman': 3–4.

[25]Rachel Hasted, ed. Paul Stamper, *Domestic Housing for Disabled Veterans, 1900–2014* (Swindon: Historic England, 2016): 11; Swenarton, 'Rammed Earth': 157.

[26]Lawrence Weaver, *The 'Country Life' Book of Cottages, Costing from £150 to £600* (London: Country Life, 1913).

[27]'Homesteads for Heroes', *Country Life* (19 February 1916): 229–32.

[28]The Diaries of Cecil Harmsworth, MP, 1909–1922, *Parliament and Politics in the Age of Asquith and Lloyd George*, ed. Andrew Thorpe and Richard Toye (Cambridge: CUP, 2016): 152.

authority on the improvement of rural dwellings, was appointed as an additional member. Cochrane had been calling for minimum standards since at least 1900, and Harmsworth claimed, '[S]he was worth the lot of us when it came to matters of kitchens, bedrooms, washtubs and the like.'[29] But the second report on the equipment of smallholdings, signed in March 1914, named Charles Varndell from the Office of Woods as advisor on the planning and construction of rural cottages to the committee, which certainly now included Weaver in addition to Turnor, Harmsworth and Unwin.[30] This report, in effect a manual, included plans and elevations of model cottages that had been erected at Letchworth and New Earswick, some from the 1913 report and others newly prepared, and a further ten prize-winning designs from the 1913 *Country Life* National Cottages Competition.

Many of these designs appeared in similar form in three editions of a manual on the planning and construction of smallholding cottages, issued by the Ministry of Agriculture in 1919 and 1920. These included plans for the smallest five-room bungalow cottage (**Figure 8.1**) and variations of the single and semi-detached two-storey five- and six-roomed cottages built on the county council smallholding estates are discussed below. The Ministry's guidance conformed to the recommendations of the Tudor Walters Committee on the standard of cottages, and its architects were said to be 'in complete sympathy with the new attitude towards housing matters in this country.'[31] But escalating costs of labour and materials led, by the 1920 edition of the manual, to minimum requirements becoming the maximum justifiable and the Ministry was obliged to pass many plans that fell below the standard.[32]

The successive reports and manuals from 1913 to 1920 show how attitudes to living space had evolved to the extent that the tenants' almost universal preference for a parlour had been accepted and their provision encouraged where possible. The question of whether or not working-class dwellings should have parlours had exercised reformers well before 1914 but came to the fore in the years leading up to the war. Due to the influence of the Women's Housing Sub-Committee, housing had a focus on 'homes fit for heroines' as well as heroes to live in; this was largely at the behest of those, like Cochrane, who had campaigned for women's suffrage before the war.[33] The Board of Agriculture's investigations of 1912 represented an early engagement with ideal cottage layouts, and the committee's attitude to parlour provision foreshadowed the findings of the Tudor Walters Committee report and Housing Manuals of 1918 and 1919.[34] Consequently, although some continued to regard it as a waste of space, a proportion of both county council smallholding

[29]*Diaries of Cecil Harmsworth*: 152–3.

[30]*BAF Report* (1913): 3; *BAF Report* (1914): iv.

[31]*Land Settlement* (1925): 15.

[32]TNA, Equipment of Smallholdings, c. September 1920, in Land Settlement – Cabinet Land Settlement Committee, 1920, MAF 48/47.

[33]Krista Cowman, '"From the Housewife's Point of View": Female Citizenship and the Gendered Domestic Interior in Post-First World War Britain, 1918–1928', *English Historical Review* 130, no. 543 (2015): 352–83; Barbara MacFarlane, '"Homes Fit for Heroines": Housing in the Twenties', in Matrix, *Making Space: Women and the Man-Made Environment* (London: Pluto Press, 1984); Deborah Sugg Ryan, *Ideal Homes, 1918–39: Domestic Design and Suburban Modernism* (Manchester: Manchester University Press, 2018): 103.

[34]*BAF Report* (1913): 11–12; *BAF Report* (1914): 19–20; Local Government Boards for England and Wales, *Report on the Questions of Building Construction in … the Provision of Dwellings for the Working Classes …* (London: HMSO, 1918): 25; *LGB Manual* (1919): 8–9.

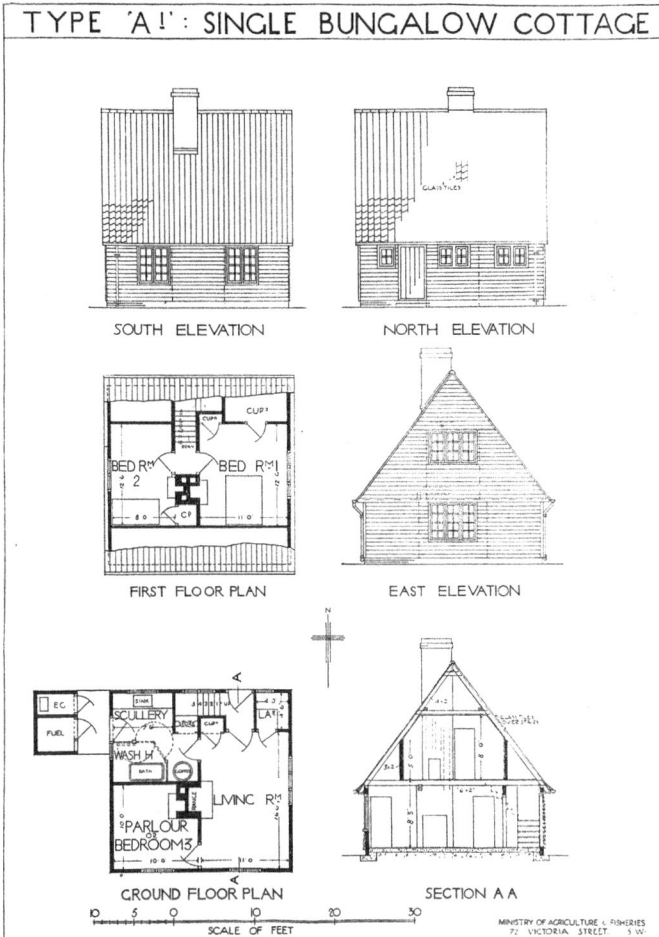

Figure 8.1 Model plan for a single bungalow cottage, Ministry of Agriculture and Fisheries, *Manual for the Guidance of County Councils and Their Architects* (London: HMSO: 1920): 19, The National Archives, MAF 139/40

cottages and local authority council houses were provided with a parlour. But in the case of smallholding cottages there was an understanding that the parlour, 'reception room, study, nursery, sick-room and what not', had a more utilitarian function to those often cited for urban areas.[35] This was as a third or fourth bedroom for the disabled or infirm, for

[35]*MAF Manual* (1920): 14.

seasonal labourers or for smallholders' own families, which were on average 16 per cent larger than those in the rest of the population.[36] Indeed, the parlour-or-bedroom layout was an established arrangement, as had been noted in the 1914 report.[37]

The 'crown colonies' run by the Ministry supported tenanted smallholdings and allowed for experimentation in building methods and types.[38] The latter was particularly the preserve of the colony at Amesbury in Wiltshire, where traditional regional materials and methods such as rammed earth were tested alongside new processes including concrete construction.[39] In Weaver's view, the best examples were those at the Ministry's Sutton Bridge experiment in Lincolnshire, built under its chief architect, Hugh Maule. Weaver reflected that 'it may be claimed that all these cottages, whether of brick or concrete, and whether tiles or thatched, are of seemly aspect and worthy to house the new class of post-war English yeomen'[40] (**Figure 8.2**). Under the 1919 Act the superintending architects of the Ministry provided advice and model designs but the work of planning and building fell upon county councils. They used a mixture of county land agents, county architects, private architects and smallholding specialists. Some authorities set up central farms or horticultural stations, which, as at the London County Council (LCC) and Middlesex County Council (MCC) smallholding estates, provided work and training while individual holdings were established.

Selection of able-bodied prospective smallholders was made on the basis of capital and experience and also favoured those men 'whose wives or other relatives have, as the result of their employment on the land either before or during the War, acquired some knowledge of farm work', and was followed by a one-year probationary period in order that unsatisfactory tenants might be 'weeded out'.[41] Very often, men were settled before accommodation was built, sometimes in army huts, or, as at the largest MCC scheme, in a farmhouse adapted as a hostel.[42]

Not all smallholdings were designed to be entirely self-supporting. A number of part-time or cottage holdings were provided by councils for disabled ex-servicemen, as a means to improve their health and supplement their pensions. These cottages were usually of the smallest bungalow type but were sometimes specially adapted, as, for example, in the cottage provided with an open-air sleeping balcony at Mattingley, Hampshire, designed by A. L. Roberts for tuberculosis sufferers; in Staffordshire, disabled ex-servicemen were provided with five-room bungalows, designed by the County Land Agent, J. M. Hotchkiss.[43] Only around 500 disabled ex-servicemen were settled on these

---

[36]'Agricultural Housing and the Rent of Cottages', *Journal of the Ministry of Agriculture* (March 1920): 1213.
[37]*BAF Report* (1914): 27.
[38]'Settlement and Employment on the Land of Discharged Sailors and Soldiers in England and Wales', extracted from the *International Review of Agricultural Economics* 1921 (October 1920): 11–14.
[39]Swenarton, 'Rammed Earth'.
[40]Lawrence Weaver, *Cottages: Their Planning, Design and Materials* (London: Country Life, 1926): 162–3, 169.
[41]TNA, Board of Agriculture, War Office, etc., *Land Settlement in the Mother Country* (London: HMSO, 1918): 3; Circular, 22 December 1920, in Land Settlement – Probationary period for tenants, 1921–2, MAF 48/42.
[42]LMA, Denham Place Estate: Hostel, 1920–1, MCC/CL/SH/053.
[43]Weaver, *Cottages*: 180–1, figs 211–12.

Figure 8.2a North Side of a Ministry of Agriculture cottage in the 'Crown colony' at Sutton Bridge, Lincolnshire, built under its chief architect, Hugh Maule, Lawrence Weaver, *Cottages: Their Planning, Design and Materials* (London: Country Life, 1926): 165, Authors' collection

Figure 8.2b South Side of a Ministry of Agriculture cottage in the 'Crown colony' at Sutton Bridge, Lincolnshire, built under its chief architect, Hugh Maule, Lawrence Weaver, *Cottages: Their Planning, Design and Materials* (London: Country Life, 1926): 165, Authors' collection

cottage holdings and, despite lengthy training, this aspect of the scheme had a high failure rate due to agricultural inexperience and 'indifferent health', through shell-shock and tuberculosis in particular, or reductions in pensions.[44]

Women who had spent at least six months in full-time Ministry-certified wartime work on the land were also entitled to apply for council smallholdings, and by the end of 1923 a modest number, some 228, had been settled.[45] The Women's Farm and Garden Association established a smallholding colony at Lingfield, Surrey, in 1920 but, although some settlers had served in the Women's National Land Service Corps, this was not part of the main Land Settlement (Facilities) Act scheme and was its only venture.[46] An estate was set apart for dairying for ex-officers and ex-Land Army women on the Ministry's farm settlement at Wantage, Berkshire, where in March 1920 twelve women were on probation; one other woman was settled by the Ministry at Pembrey in South Wales. By April 1923 there were four women tenants of the Ministry's farm settlements, while seventeen county councils had not provided any holdings for women.[47] *Country Life* noted in 1922 that a few holdings had been let to women who had served in the Land Army, including a grower of flowers in Cornwall who had taken a man's place as a shepherd during the war. But as the article – 'The New Yeomen' – stressed, women's contribution was usually essential to the success of a smallholding in the form of unpaid family labour: 'It has even been suggested that before applicants are approved as suitable tenants their wives should be interviewed as well.'[48]

County council smallholding schemes, 1919–1926

In 1925 it was said that in 'no country in the world has so great an effort been made by public authorities to settle discharged sailors and soldiers on the land'.[49] In fact, just under 49,000 ex-servicemen applied for a smallholding in 1919 and 1920 (when the list was closed) in England and Wales. Of the 30,000 considered as realistic applicants, some 22,000 had been settled through the land settlement programme by the end of 1924, which involved the construction of 2,749 new houses by county and borough councils. Not surprisingly the county councils with the greatest numbers of smallholding estates were predominantly rural, the largest being Norfolk which, under successive acts from 1908, owned or leased 35 square miles of smallholdings in the occupation of 2,200 men by 1924.[50] Borough councils also acquired 5,558 acres of land for smallholdings after the

---

[44]TNA, *Report on the Present Position and Future Prospects of Ex-Servicemen Settled on the Land in England and Wales*, 1923, MAF 48/58.

[45]*Land Settlement* (1925): 9.

[46]Anne Meredith, 'From Ideals to Reality: The Women's Smallholding Colony at Lingfield, 1920–39', *Agricultural History Review* 54, no. 1 (2006): 105–21.

[47]'Settlement and Employment on the Land of Discharged Sailors and Soldiers in England and Wales': 13–14. TNA, MAF 48/58.

[48]'The New Yeomen', *Country Life* (11 March 1922): 356.

[49]*Land Settlement* (1925): 5.

[50]Ibid.: 115.

war, some 3,000 of which was taken by the successful Birmingham Corporation scheme at Canwell in Staffordshire, which was provided with sixty new houses.[51] Urban county councils were likewise obliged to provide holdings and these too often had to obtain land outside their boundaries.

The LCC received a large number of applications from ex-servicemen and purchased a 1,325 acre estate with four farms south of the River Thames, at Shorne, near Gravesend in Kent. Here the LCC Architects' Department designed twenty-nine new cottages and thirty-two sets of farm buildings for the forty-seven holdings, which were predominantly for full-time market gardening and poultry farming with ten larger dairy holdings.[52] The cottages were sited along existing roads, scattered or, in the case of those in pairs, placed in more evenly spaced rows, with additional strips of land allocated nearby.[53] Surviving plans indicate that the semi-detached cottages had a living room, scullery and bathroom on the ground floor, and three bedrooms above.[54] Externally they were very similar to some of the model designs in the 1913 and 1914 reports and post-war housing manuals, with a central gable at the front and, at the rear, distinctive eaves sloping to the extensions at each side for the single-storey earth closets, with a yard in the recess between (**Figure 8.3**). Here, as elsewhere, drought and depression in the early 1920s caused many tenants to fail. Ultimately, the LCC struggled to administer the scheme from London and on the Ministry's advice the holdings were taken over in 1924 by Kent County Council.

By 1924, not counting the Shorne estate, the total area of land retained by Kent County Council for its own land settlement scheme was 3,200 acres, organized in over forty-five schemes across the county. The county's diverse geography allowed for a variety of practice, including mixed, fruit and sheep farming and market gardening. The largest property was the 640-acre Skeet Hill Farm estate to the north west of the county in Chelsfield, about seventeen miles from Covent Garden. The twenty-nine holdings were equipped with twenty-five new cottages and seventeen sets of farm buildings, and served mainly for fruit and market gardening.[55] These were designed by the architect to the County Education Committee, Wilfred R. Robinson, who later became county architect. At least four designs of cottage were employed, all apparently detached and facing existing thoroughfares. These exemplified the Ministry's preference for plain elevations, and refusal of 'any attempt to secure elegance at the expense of utility'.[56]

Kent County Council provided a high proportion of equipped holdings and in total, under the 1919 legislation, eighty-five new houses were built across the county.[57] This included a small number of cottage holdings for disabled veterans. After a fifty-two week

---

[51]Ibid.: 37, 136.

[52]Ibid.: 93.

[53]LMA, Shorne Estate: Erection of 23 Cottages, 1922, LCC/CO/CON/03/7250.

[54]Ibid.; LMA, London Picture Archive, Shorne Estate photographs, 1922: 271837–8, 271841–54.

[55]*Land Settlement* (1925): 86–7.

[56]*MAF Report* (1920): 11.

[57]*Land Settlement* (1925): 87.

Figure 8.3 London County Council photograph of the Shorne Estate, Kent, 1922 © London Metropolitan Archives (City of London), 271853

training course at the county training centre or a Ministry-approved farm, men were settled in homesteads on plots of up to three acres. **Figure 8.4** shows the three pairs of roadside cottage holdings built on a six-acre plot for disabled trainees near Hadlow.[58] So the policy of the county councils of both Kent and London was to place its cottages in convenient roadside positions but otherwise to distribute them according to how the land was parcelled up. Little thought seems to have been given to grouping for aesthetic or (with the exception of the Hadlow cottages) social reasons.

Middlesex County Council's approach to smallholding design however conformed more to the government advice on layout and some schemes appeared more akin to the suburban planning of local authority estates. There were already several smallholding estates formed under the earlier legislation within Middlesex and these were augmented after 1919 by the purchase of nearly 1,000 acres on the Denham Place Estate in South Buckinghamshire. This lay to the north of Uxbridge, just outside the county boundary, and by 1923 it was formed into sixty-four holdings, most of which were equipped with cottages, and a horticultural demonstration station.[59]

---

[58]'Kent County Council', *Kent and Sussex Courier* (18 February 1921): 11.
[59]*Land Settlement* (1925): 94–5.

Figure 8.4 Detail of aerial photograph showing three pairs of Kent County Council cottage holdings (to the left of the road) at Sign Post Field, Golden Green, near Hadlow, Kent, built for disabled trainees, 1939; the glass houses in the foreground belonged to a nursery business and the crystalate (shellac) factory at bottom right replaced a Victorian jam factory in the early 1900s © Historic England Archive. Aerofilms Collection, EPW060361

The twelve semi-detached dwellings known as Middlesex Cottages, New Denham, were designed by the County Architect's Department under Henry George Crothall and occupied from 1922. Unusually, they were grouped together into a three-sided square set behind two greens and accessed by a footpath. This kind of layout had been recommended by the 1914 Board of Agriculture Report on rural housing. The smallholders complained that the cottages were ill-drained and that they never received the promised farm buildings. They were sold off in 1926, some to their tenants as was their right after six years, the long strips of detached garden ground fronting the road becoming the plots of speculatively financed suburban housing.[60] The other Denham holdings were dispersed along existing roads through more rural areas of farmland, but these cottages were more regularly grouped than was the practice in Kent. Following the failure of New Denham and also of twenty-two holdings for disabled veterans elsewhere

---

[60]LMA, Denham Place Estate: Middlesex Cottages, 1922–32, MCC/CL/SH/055.

on the estate, the council prioritized experience over ex-servicemen when accepting new tenants. By the late 1920s the Denham holdings were reportedly among the most productive in the country.[61]

Of the 22,000 people settled on smallholdings by county and borough councils in England and Wales between 1918 and the end of 1924 around 10 to 12 per cent quit for financial reasons – a reasonably low failure rate.[62] In regard to the standard of housing provided, Lawrence Weaver concluded that, with few exceptions, smallholder cottages were a credit to their architects and he contrasted councils' work in improving the amenities of the countryside with the 'outrageous rash of shacks' produced by the individual builders of bungalows.[63] Overall the 1919 land settlement programme fared rather better than the equivalent state housing programme, surviving the economic and political turbulence (and drought) of 1920–1921. Thereafter the focus of attention within the Ministry of Agriculture moved elsewhere and the programme for ex-servicemen was wound up in 1925–1926. Subsequent legislation returned the focus of statutory smallholdings provision to supporting small-scale agriculture.

Although the work of the county councils in providing 'statutory smallholdings' was a notable effort it still only represented 11.3 per cent of the total number of smallholdings in England and Wales in 1936.[64] The vast majority were private concerns, often in areas suited to market gardening and so favourable to small-scale production. Some were provided by large landowners, such as Lord Carrington, president of the Board of Agriculture from 1905 to 1911, who by 1914 had created smallholdings or allotments on a quarter of his various estates.[65] But a range of organizations also pursued land settlement in the 1920s and 1930s, including the British Limbless Ex-Servicemen's Association, the Catholic Land Federation and the National Homecroft Association. The latter, the brainchild of John Waugh Scott, promoted 'suburban crofts' on small lots of no more than half an acre for 'wage-earning people' to tend in their spare time.[66] The Surrey Gardens Village Trust was another initiative that aimed to assist 'private dreams of rural resettlement', commencing a smallholdings village at Selsdon Vale near Croydon in 1920.[67] This, like a nearby scheme at Monks Orchard by Percy Harvey Estates Ltd and Munday Dean, near Marlow, by Homesteads Ltd, followed a not uncommon trajectory and evolved into a plotlands settlement.[68]

---

[61]'Denham Small Holdings', *Uxbridge and West Drayton Gazette* (12 July 1929): 19.

[62]*Land Settlement* (1925): 52.

[63]'Some Small Holders' Cottages', *Country Life* (24 October 1925): 645.

[64]Smith, *Land for the Small Man*: 206.

[65]Andrew Adonis, 'Aristocracy, Agriculture and Liberalism: The Politics, Finances and Estates of the Third Lord Carrington', *Historical Journal* 31, no. 4 (1988): 871–97.

[66]Only one scheme at Uckington, near Cheltenham, was ever developed; Jeremiah, *Architecture and Design for the Family*: 57.

[67]Dennis Hardy and Colin Ward, *Arcadia for All: The Legacy of a Makeshift Landscape* (London and New York: Mansell Publishing, 1984): 234.

[68]Ibid.: 179–81; J. D. Bundock, 'Speculative Housebuilding and Some Aspects of the Activities of the Speculative Housebuilder within the Greater London outer Suburban Area, 1919–39' (MPhil thesis, University of Kent, 1974): 422–23.

A second wave of government-sponsored land settlement

In the face of high unemployment and severe economic depression in the early 1930s another aspect of land settlement came to the fore, that of unemployment relief. This embraced both the transformation of industrial workers into bucolic smallholders (**Figure 8.5**) and part-time agricultural activity to supplement family diets and incomes, as well as schemes promoting 'rural-mindedness' to an urban population. Such ideas had surfaced regularly in the nineteenth century and had informed the farm- or land-colony movement, which, as noted above, had sought to redeem the socially undesirable through labour and retrain unemployed men in agriculture, often as a

Figure 8.5 Front cover of a promotional brochure produced by the LSA, n.d., authors' collection

preliminary to emigration.[69] Essex was a favoured location, with colonies at Hadleigh, Laindon, Mayland and Boxted. After the war the lead was taken by the voluntary sector, notably the Society of Friends (or Quakers) who from 1928 developed a 'Seeds Scheme' to assist unemployed industrial workers in the coalfield areas to cultivate allotments and undertook small holdings projects in Wales and the North East.[70] A number of small schemes were operating by the early 1930s, some of a 'self-help' nature initiated by groups of unemployed workers themselves as well as a handful of 'Subsistence Production' projects, which involved both food production and other services, such as boot repairs and tailoring, being undertaken through a system of exchange or barter.[71]

Growing interest within government in pursuing the resettlement of workless men on the land led to a series of meetings in 1933–1934 with voluntary organizations and interested parties. Some of the impetus for state involvement came from the prime minister, J. Ramsay Macdonald, who had previously spoken of colonizing the countryside with a million 'allotment holders'.[72] The preference on all sides was not to use the existing county council smallholding programme, partly because the settlers would be of a different sort to the usual statutory smallholders, who had agricultural backgrounds, whereas the former industrial workers would require special training. Also, Macdonald wanted to keep the government in the background to avoid the scheme becoming 'the subject of party controversy'.[73] What emerged from the discussions was an agreement in principle for an independent and unofficial body to oversee the provision of smallholdings for the unemployed with financial assistance from the government. Meanwhile, attention was directed towards the regions most in need of assistance. As designated by the Special Areas (Development and Improvement) Act 1934, these covered much of Durham and Tyneside, parts of Northumberland and West Cumberland and industrial areas in Wales. Intended to encourage schemes to reduce unemployment, the act also required experiments in land settlement for out-of-work men from the depressed areas with little prospect of re-employment, either in nearby locations or elsewhere in the country. Another element of the government's land settlement proposals was for financial support for the men while they were undergoing training. This came from the Unemployed Assistance Board, established in 1934.

The Land Settlement Association Ltd (hereafter LSA) was formed in 1934 with the help of the Carnegie Trustees, the Society of Friends, the National Council of Social Service and others, with a constitution and rules approved by the government. Its principles, published the following May, set out that it would only establish group settlements, that it would pursue cooperative methods for marketing produce and that, following the

---

[69]Malcolm Chase, 'Out of Radicalism: The Mid-Victorian Freehold Land Movement', *English Historical Review* 106, no. 419 (1991): 319–45; Hardy, *Utopian England*, 2000: 24–5; Clarke, 'The Land Settlement Association 1934–1948': 289–90.

[70]Clarke, 'The Land Settlement Association 1934–1948': 9–10.

[71]The idea was particularly associated with Peter Scott; two schemes were launched, at Brynmawr, Wales, in 1929 and Upholland, near Wigan, Lancashire, in 1934; TNA, Wigan and District Subsistence Production Society: Land Settlement Scheme for the Unemployed at Upholland, 1934–7, MAF 48/281.

[72]Hardy, *Utopian England*: 31.

[73]TNA, Note of a deputation …, 26 October 1933, in Proposed land settlement of the unemployed, 1933–4, MAF 48/273.

'rigid' selection of settlers, it would provide their training and education.[74] The intention was that the LSA would conduct experiments in all types of smallholdings funded by a combination of private charitable donations, Development Commission grants and money from the Special Areas Fund. The proportions from each varied depending on the kind of development and the financial aims and processes of the organization were initially rather ill-defined although the intention was that it would be financially self-sufficient. In early 1935 the LSA became the main agent undertaking land settlement in England for the Special Areas and this came to dominate its activities and funding. As a consequence, what had been conceived as a voluntary body became, in effect, a state-funded agency and never really functioned along business lines.[75]

One of the key players in the discussion was A. C. Richmond, Deputy Secretary of the National Council of Social Service, who went on to become the first chairman of the LSA. Another was the industrialist Percy Malcolm Stewart, chairman of the London Brick Company and Associated Portland Cement Manufacturers Ltd. His contribution was significant; he was an early promoter of the idea to the government and provided the LSA's first settlement but his views were sometimes at odds with those of the association. After his appointment in 1934 as the Commissioner for the Special Areas, Malcolm Stewart favoured a different body, the Homesteads Trust, to work as his agent for land settlement in England and Wales.[76] It was only when the trust failed to materialize that he turned to the LSA. In two of the counties containing Special Areas, Cumberland and Northumberland, responsibility was given to the county councils although their schemes were eventually transferred to the LSA. Durham County Council also pursued its own land settlement programme. A separate society for Wales was established in March 1936, under Geoffrey Crawshay, District Commissioner for Special Areas in Wales.[77] This took a rather different approach, preferring to develop cooperative farms over smallholdings, influenced by different approaches such as those of the Fordson Estate, Boreham, Essex, which had been initiated by the US industrialist Henry Ford.[78]

Land settlement in operation

The ambitious goal set by Malcolm Stewart was for around 2,000 families from special areas to be settled on full-time holdings, revised to 3,000 by Sir George Gillett, his successor as commissioner, in 1937.[79] For England the LSA made an initial agreement to

---

[74]TNA, Land Settlement Association: appointment, constitution and proceedings, 1934, MAF 48/277; Clarke, 'The Land Settlement Association 1934–1948': 49.

[75]Clarke, 'The Land Settlement Association 1934–1948': 55–6, 269.

[76]Ibid.: 45.

[77]'Land Settlement Schemes in Wales', *Journal of the Royal Institute of British* Architects (22 May 1939): 719–24.

[78]See Ford R. Bryan, *Beyond the Model T: The Other Ventures of Henry Ford* (Detroit: Wayne State University Press, 1997), ch2; TNA, Fordson Estate, Boreham, Essex: cooperative land settlement schemes for employees, 1935–46, MAF 48/284.

[79]This and the following paragraph draws on Clarke and William Dampier/Office of the Commissioner for the Special Areas (England and Wales), *Report of the Committee of Enquiry into Land Settlement* (London: HMSO, 1939).

relocate 240 families from the north to the Midlands and the South, quickly increased to 1,440 families and subsequently revised to 2,060. Land for the first settlement was obtained in 1934 and thereafter sites continued to be acquired until 1938. As indicated in **Figure 8.6**, these were located around the country but particularly grouped in and around Bedfordshire, Suffolk and Cambridgeshire, with the single largest estate at Sidlesham in West Sussex, where five farms were divided into 159 smallholdings. Of the twenty-six settlements initiated by the LSA before the Second World War, around two-thirds were long-distance 'transference schemes' with the remainder comprised

Figure 8.6 Map of LSA holdings from a promotional brochure, n.d., authors' collection

of estates leased from the county councils in Northumberland and Cumberland and a handful of settlements for the unemployed outside of the Special Areas, including one at Wyboston in Bedfordshire for London families (**Figure 8.7**). By 1939 some 1,100 holdings were ready for occupation, complete with houses and outbuildings provided by the association. In addition, the LSA undertook other kinds of unemployment relief initiatives, in the form of communal allotments and 'dual-economy' smallholdings known respectively as group holdings and cottage estates. Between 1936 and 1939, the Welsh Land Settlement Society Ltd established four cooperative farms and laid out two estates as smallholdings.

Transforming industrial workers into smallholders took some effort.[80] The LSA required its recruits to undergo a three-month course of 'physical reconditioning'

Figure 8.7 Aerial photograph showing part of the LSA estate at Wyboston, Bedfordshire, spaced out along Rookery Road, Eaton Socon, 1948 © Historic England Archive. Aerofilms Collection, EAW014043

---

[80]Alex Arnall, 'Presenting Rurality: The Land Settlement Association in Interwar England', *Journal of Rural Studies* 83 (April 2021): 177–86.

followed by a period of instruction, normally twelve months, during which time the settler was paid unemployment assistance and a training allowance. Lists of men for consideration were drawn up by the Unemployment Assistance Board, with the Ministry of Labour, and perhaps as many as 20,000 were approached about settlement. Initially men from the same area were settled on the estates, with the villages of Durham supplying many of the Potton settlers, mainly unemployed miners but also general labourers and shipyard workers. But it proved impossible to maintain this approach although the majority of the recruits for the long-distance schemes came from the North East.[81] The intention of the LSA was not to establish self-contained communities and the estates were located near to existing villages although this sometimes represented a significant influx for small rural communities. An estate was said to have made a 'deep and lasting impression on the countryside in which the settlement was located'.[82]

The failure rate was high. Almost half the men gave up while undergoing training; some decided to leave quite quickly, others were unable to persuade their families, who joined them during or after the period of instruction, and a proportion simply failed to make the transition from trainee to tenant. It was a difficult adjustment for men 'accustomed to a regular weekly wage, regular hours of work and holidays' and for families dealing with 'shopping difficulties, the substitution of big open spaces for the animated and crowded streets, the absence of many of the services that are offered by urban local authorities'.[83] Successful settlers received £260 working capital – half a gift, half to be repaid with no interest.

The LSA built any new roads that were required and the houses, with the exception of one estate, as well as glasshouses and other outbuildings such as piggeries and poultry units.[84] There was usually a central farm providing essential services, machinery, feed stuffs and tools as well as plants and livestock for the settlers. This also acted as the marketing depot, collecting, grading and dispatching the produce to market. Each settlement had a warden, later renamed 'estate manager', and staff specializing in horticulture, pigs or poultry. It was the warden who oversaw the road- and house-building activities and the sub-division of the land and, thereafter, the administration of the settlement, albeit under the close control of the head office in London. In devising the layouts of the settlements the primary considerations were agricultural and the need for road access. So a dispersed pattern was preferred, with the holdings scattered along new or existing roads with the cottages, individual, paired or in groups of three, at the front of the plots and out buildings to the side and rear. The back of the holdings were sometimes left unfenced to allow for the land to be ploughed together. By 1937 the LSA's approach to development was reassessed and more effort was put into 'consciously planning' the estates.[85] Thereafter,

---

[81]Clarke, 'The Land Settlement Association 1934–1948': 76.

[82]Dampier/Commission, section 73 para 250.

[83]Dampier/Commission, section 16 para 52, section 88 para 293.

[84]The houses on the Andover estate were provided by the Hurlingham Building Company; Clarke, 'The Land Settlement Association 1934–1948': 74.

[85]'The Housing Work of the Land Settlement Association', *Journal of the Royal Institute of British Architects* (22 November 1937): 76–83.

the subdivision, drainage, house building, fencing etc. were completed before the settlers arrived. The average size of the holdings was 5 acres, rather smaller than the typical county council equivalent, and mainly used for a mixture of market gardening and livestock keeping, although a few specialist holdings were developed.[86]

The initial settlement at Potton, near Biggleswade, had first been acquired for a smallholding scheme in 1934 by Malcolm Stewart, while discussions with the government were still underway. Malcolm Stewart and his agent and surveyor Sir Trustram Eve favoured a layout of cottages grouped into circular blocks around ample greens.[87] But when the site was handed over to the LSA it was planned in a dispersed fashion. The houses were designed by a local architect, Fred Levitt, who was also responsible for Biggleswade Rural District Council's housing. His designs for Potton were used at three other estates but the majority of the LSA houses were the work of Humphrey Pakington, of the practice Pakington and Enthoven, appointed in 1935.[88] As economy was important the designs were variations on a basic theme: that of two or three bedrooms upstairs, sometimes with a bedroom downstairs, that common smallholding plan, often with the eaves taken down to the first-floor level. In this respect they were similar to some of the Ministry's recommended smallholding designs. The buildings materials were 'the cheapest available', often brick and plain tile with boarded gable ends although these varied from location to location, giving each settlement its own character. The most unusual were the flat-roofed cottages with hollow-tile walls rendered in white cement built in Crofton, Cumberland.

In August 1936 the decision was taken to build predominantly detached houses 'for social reasons', an acknowledgement that semi-detached houses were not always ideal for harmonious relations between neighbours working their respective holdings.[89] Each settlement comprised a limited range of house types; at Sidlesham four were used. The holding usually required the labour of all those family members able to work and the cooperation of the settler's wife was considered 'a valuable – perhaps even an indispensable – element in success'.[90] But when the housing stock was reviewed 'from the women settler's point of view' by the housing expert Elizabeth Denby in 1944 she judged them lacking in adequate washing, drying and cooking facilities.[91] The LSA was also rather slow to address the need for communal facilities although it contributed to a new village hall at Fen Drayton, where the estate had doubled the village's population. While at Sidlesham School the West Sussex Education Committee had to address a rapid increase in child numbers by constructing additional classrooms in 1937.[92]

For the group holdings, provided for unemployed workers to keep poultry and grow produce to supplement the family diet and sell the surplus, new dwellings were not

[86]Clarke, 'The Land Settlement Association 1934–1948': 68, 178.
[87]'Potton Land Settlement Scheme', *Biggleswade Chronicle* (2 February 1934): 3.
[88]'The Land Settlement Association', *The Architectural Association Journal* 53 (1937): 181–90.
[89]*JRIBA* (1937): 80.
[90]Dampier/Commission Section 56, para 183.
[91]Clarke, 'The Land Settlement Association 1934–1948': 134.
[92]'Steel Construction for Schools: An Experiment in Flexibility of Design', *The Builder* (2 June 1937): 1217–220.

required as the men simply travelled from their houses to the plots. The LSA inherited some of these from the North East Poultry Scheme which had been run by the Quakers. The cottage homesteads were part-time holdings consisting of a house and half an acre of land grouped in small estates on the outskirts of industrial towns in the Midlands and South of England for unemployed men over fifty. The intention was to provide subsistence and occupation for the men and improve the chances of employment for their adolescent children. Two thousand homesteads were contemplated by the LSA but the agreement with the commissioner was for 250. Between 1937 and 1939 five schemes were started in peripheral locations.[93] Because of the restrictions on ribbon development resulting from government legislation these were planned around access roads with grass verges, retained trees and small greens.[94] The layouts, which had a suburban quality, and the houses were designed by A. G. Sheppard Fidler, who went on to post-war prominence as chief architect of Crawley new town and City Architect of Birmingham.

For their main developments the Welsh Land Settlement Society chose to set out the housing in the form of garden villages, beginning with Boverton, Glamorgan. This approach was intended to allow for social coherence and was thought more appropriate for mining families used to close living in communities with a strong sense of group identity than conventional, more dispersed smallholdings. The housing for the settlements was set out around communal greens, one said to be large enough for a game of football, near to the farms on which the settlers worked.[95] Existing farm buildings were converted to offices, packing sheds or recreational halls for communal use. The architect of the Welsh schemes was Thomas Alwyn Lloyd who had started his career as an assistant to Raymond Unwin at Hampstead Garden Suburb in 1907. He then became consulting architect to the Welsh Town Planning and Housing Trust, responsible for such developments as Wrexham Garden Village and Rhiwbina Garden Village. Durham County Council also opted for the 'suitable grouping' of the houses on their land settlement estates rather than dispersing them around the holdings, which allowed for them to be separately let if the schemes failed.[96] It was in the estates in Durham, Wales and the LSA cottage homesteads programme that the second wave of land settlement came closest to the kind of layouts associated with contemporary urban and rural council housing schemes.

At the outbreak of war official attention moved away from settlement of the unemployed to maximizing food production. So the LSA shifted its focus to agriculturally experienced tenants, something they had first allowed in 1937. Nor did the government regard the creation of smallholdings as 'one of the cornerstones of reconstruction' for the post-war era.[97] The LSA, by now dependent on state funding, had to fall in line

---

[93]The cottage homesteads sites were at Caversham, Long Lawford (near Rugby), Cosby, Dunstable and Elmesthorpe.

[94]*JRIBA* (1937): 83.

[95]*JRIBA* (1939): 719–24.

[96]Dampier/Commission, section 64 para 211.

[97]Clarke, 'The Land Settlement Association 1934–1948': 279.

with a policy towards smallholdings determined by agricultural need rather than social considerations. The part-time holdings were disposed of and a new role was suggested providing 'the first rung on the farming ladder for agricultural men of limited means'.[98] It was agreed that the LSA would continue to manage the estates, ownership of which was transferred to the Minister for Agriculture under the Agriculture Act 1947. The association was finally wound up in 1983.[99]

Conclusion

By 1935 county councils were landlords to 25,000 small farmers, market gardeners and part-time agriculturalists.[100] This was, in no small part, a consequence of the 1919 Act. Despite the many technical and other difficulties involved with the resettlement of veterans at this time, the scheme had, Lord Addison stressed in 1939, a failure rate of no more than 15 per cent.[101] Moreover a survey of 1946 found that these holdings proved to be a reward 'to many of these heroes who finally did get there, especially the equipped holdings with a solid house in a country short of housing, and with sufficient farm buildings',[102] even if the great majority of settlers had come from the ranks of small farmers and smallholders rather than the labouring classes.[103] In the 1930s, by comparison, the state-sponsored land-settlement programme was primarily intended as a relocation scheme for families willing to learn new agricultural and horticultural skills in order to benefit from a healthier life in the countryside. The largest contribution, in terms of numbers resettled, was made by the LSA, who also took the lion's share of the Special Areas Fund made available for land settlement.

The two distinct phases of land settlement scheme in the 1920s and 1930s have been widely studied by agricultural, rural and economic historians but the planning and design associated with these initiatives have received relatively little attention. Meanwhile architectural and design historians have, with notable exceptions, focused predominantly on the urban and suburban, particularly in regard to state-subsidised housing. This chapter has attempted to address this lacuna and to show how the work of settling ex-servicemen and women and, later, unemployed men and their families was intended to contribute to a programme of rural reconstruction. Although the roots of this policy stretched back to the nineteenth century, state-sponsored engagement was hastened by the war, and later the Depression. It was conceived of as a benefit to the welfare of the settlers, and to the nation, through greater food production and in the belief that healthy communities could best be achieved in the countryside.

---

[98]Ibid.: 278.
[99]And legally wound up in 1991. Peter Clarke per comm.
[100]Smith, *Land for the Small Man*: v.
[101]Thirsk, *Alternative Agriculture*: 211.
[102]Smith, *Land for the Small Man*: 220–1.
[103]*Land Settlement* (1925): 8.

When a government Committee of Enquiry into land settlement reported in 1939 it noted the widespread assumption of a deep desire on the part of urban dwellers to get 'back to the land'.[104] But the reality had proved rather different and the committee had not been 'much impressed' by the idea that men 'hanker for the "independence" which a small holding gives'.[105] This aspect of the resettlement vision at least had been called into question. Rural repopulation, when it came to some areas of the country in the late twentieth century, took place in a very different countryside, no longer the place to pursue old dreams of agricultural living or yeoman status.

Select bibliography

Archival material

Circular, 22 December 1920, in Land Settlement – Probationary Period for Tenants (1921–2), TNA, MAF 48/42.
Denham Place Estate: Middlesex Cottages (1922–32), LMA, MCC/CL/SH/055.
Equipment of Smallholdings, c. September 1920, in Land Settlement – Cabinet Land Settlement Committee (1920), TNA, MAF 48/47.
Land Settlement Association: Appointment, Constitution and Proceedings (1934), TNA, MAF 48/277.
Shorne Estate: Erection of 23 Cottages (1922), LMA, LCC/CO/CON/03/7250.

Books

The Diaries of Cecil Harmsworth, MP, 1909–22. *Parliament and Politics in the Age of Asquith and Lloyd George*, ed. Andrew Thorpe and Richard Toye. Cambridge: Cambridge University Press, 2016.
Smith, Newlin Russell. *Land for the Small Man: English and Welsh Experience with Publicly-Supplied Small Holdings, 1860–1937*. New York: King's Crown Press, 1946.
Weaver, Lawrence. *The 'Country Life' Book of Cottages, Costing from £150 to £600*. London: Country Life, 1913.
Weaver, Lawrence. *Cottages: Their Planning, Design and Materials*. London: Country Life, 1926.

Grey literature

Board of Agriculture and Fisheries. *Report of the Departmental Committee on the Equipment of Small Holdings in England And Wales ....* London: HMSO, 1913.
Board of Agriculture and Fisheries. *Report of the Committee appointed by the president of the Board of Agriculture and Fisheries to consider and advise the board on plans, models, specification, and methods of construction for rural cottages and outbuildings*. London: HMSO, 1914.
Dampier, William, Office of the Commissioner for the Special Areas (England and Wales). *Report of the Committee Enquiry into Land Settlement*. London: HMSO, 1939.
Land Settlement in England & Wales, Being a Report of Proceedings under the Small Holdings & Allotments Acts 1908 to 1919 for the Period 1919 to 1924. London: HMSO, 1925.

---

[104]Dampier/Commission, section 79 para 270.
[105]Dampier/Commission, section 111, para 374.

Local Government Board. *Manual on the Preparation of State-Aided Housing Schemes*. London: HMSO, 1919.

MAF. *Manual for the Guidance of County Council and Their Architects in the Equipment of Small Holdings*, 3rd edn revised. London: HMSO, 1920.

MAF. *Report on the Present Position and Future Prospects of Ex-Servicemen Settled on the Land in England and Wales*. London: HMSO, 1923.

Newspapers and periodicals
Country Life
International Review of Agricultural Economics.
Journal of the Ministry of Agriculture.
Journal of the Royal Institute of British Architects.
Journal of the Royal Society of Arts.

Secondary sources

Articles
Arnall, Alex. 'Presenting Rurality: The Land Settlement Association in Interwar England'. *Journal of Rural Studies* 83 (April 2021): 177–86.

Lockwood, Carol A. 'From Soldier to Peasant? The Land Settlement Scheme in East Sussex, 1919–1939'. *Albion* 30, no. 3 (1998): 439–62.

Meredith, Anne. 'From Ideals to Reality: The Women's Smallholding Colony at Lingfield, 1920–39'. *Agricultural History Review* 54, no. 1 (2006): 105–21.

Swenarton, Mark. 'Rammed Earth Revival: Technological Innovation and Government Policy in Britain, 1905–1925'. *Construction History* 19 (2003): 107–26.

Wade Martins, Susanna. 'Smallholdings in Norfolk, 1890–1950: A Social and Farming Experiment'. *Agricultural History Review* 54, no. 2 (2006): 304–30.

Unpublished PhD theses
Clarke, Peter. 'The Land Settlement Association 1934–1948: The Evolution of a Social Experiment'. PhD thesis, London School of Economics, 1985.

Books
Griffiths, Clare V. J. *Labour and the Countryside: The Politics of Rural Britain 1918–1939*. Oxford: Oxford University Press, 2007.

Hardy, Dennis. *Utopian England: Community Experiments 1900–1945*. London: E. & F. N. Spon.

Hasted, Rachel, ed. Paul Stamper. *Domestic Housing for Disabled Veterans, 1900–2014*. Swindon: Historic England, 2016.

Howkins, Alun. *Reshaping Rural England: A Social History, 1850–1925*. Oxford: Routledge, 1992.

Jeremiah, David. *Architecture and Design for the Family in Britain, 1900–70*. Manchester: Manchester University Press, 2000.

Thirsk, Joan. *Alternative Agriculture: A History*. Oxford: Oxford University Press, 1997.

CHAPTER 9
VETERAN: ANNABEL DOTT AND COLONIAL, METROPOLITAN AND RURAL COMMUNITIES
Elizabeth McKellar

Annabel Dott (1868–1937), a philanthropic architect and builder, was a significant and well-known figure in housing and rural reconstruction in the years after the First World War, though she has been largely overlooked in subsequent histories. Discussions of such women benefactors are in danger of becoming caught between, on the one hand, an architectural historiography which celebrates their achievements with Pevsnerian pioneering rhetoric; something ... which is understandable in a discipline in which new female contributors are still being uncovered.[1] On the other hand there has been a strongly entrenched strand in social history which tends to dismiss the efforts of middle- or upper-class women as paternalistic, classist and localized.[2] This gender discrimination further reinforces a prejudice against small-scale, local initiatives in twentieth-century historiography, in favour of national state intervention, which is only now being challenged in recent scholarship. Eve Colpus has powerfully demonstrated how such women – who were born in the nineteenth century but who operated in the early years of the twentieth – might be reconceived in a way which accommodates both their relationship to the traditional moral and social climate in which they grew up and their changing identities in the post-war landscape of new social opportunities.[3] Philanthropy, she writes, was 'part of the reflex and communicative practices individuals used in the inter-war years to make sense of the social, political and cultural changes in the world around them'.[4]

Dott's career presents just such a negotiation between the traditional and the modern. She was firmly part of the Liberal Anglican tradition of communitarianism which opposed both economic competition and class conflict, seeing these as corrosive to national unity, and which sought to ameliorate their effects through civic engagement. This tradition, as Matthew Grimley has shown, continued to exert a strong influence

---

[1]For a more nuanced discussion of women's agency in building in this period see Elizabeth Darling and Lesley Whitworth (ed.), *Women and the Making of Built Space in England, 1870–1950* (Ashgate: Aldershot, 2007), 'Introduction'.

[2]See Alison Creedon, 'A Benevolent Tyrant? The Principles and Practices of Henrietta Barnett (1851–1936), Social Reformer and Founder of Hampstead Garden Suburb', *Women's History Review* 11, no. 2 (2002): 231–52; Eileen Janes Yeo (ed.), *Radical Femininity: Women's Self-Presentation in the Public Sphere* (Manchester: Manchester University Press, 1998).

[3]Eve Colpus, 'Women, Service and Self-actualization in Inter-war Britain', *Past & Present* 238, no. 1 (2018): 197–232.

[4]Eve Colpus, *Female Philanthropy in the Interwar World: Between Self and Other* (London: Bloomsbury, 2018): 2.

from the early twentieth century into the 1930s.[5] Dott's formative influences were rooted in the nineteenth-century East End settlement movement of cultural philanthropy which enabled middle-class women to engage in working-class urban areas as part of a civilizing mission.[6] However, Dott's career stretching from the 1900s to the 1930s also had a global dimension and her impact was certainly more than purely local, largely due to her extensive engagement with the media. After the war she became strongly identified with the reconstruction initiatives following the 1919 Addison Act and the Land Settlement Scheme. Dott's New Liberalism meant that she combined individualism and collectivism, and although she was happiest working on an individual basis she welcomed the new opportunities for action across the private-public divide post-war. Her thinking was firmly grounded in Garden City principles but at the same time she embraced standardization and new technologies. Furthermore, she asserted herself in the public sphere with a string of articles and interviews in the architectural, national and international press. In these she provided a powerful demonstration of a woman actively engaged in shaping the built environment and promoting social reform in relation to a number of contemporary debates regarding gender, domestic space, housing and rural society.

In 1918 Annabel Dott published two articles in the *Architectural Review* (*AR*) in one of which she boldly laid claim to the title of 'The Woman Architect', based on the building of a house for herself in Goathland, Yorkshire, in *c*.1911–1912 (**Figure 9.1**). The other article covered the 'Cottages for Disabled Officers' that she was then in the process of establishing in the same location.[7] Histories of post-war reconstruction have concentrated on the Homes fit for Heroes campaign but the war resulted in other innovative housing schemes for women, including the widowed, and for the disabled which have received far less attention. Some of the best-known of the ex-servicemen's villages include: the Haig Memorial Homes; Westfield War Memorial Village, Lancaster; the Enham Village Settlement near Andover, Hampshire; and the North Memorial Homes in Leicester.[8] This chapter will investigate Dott's philanthropic and architectural activities from the 1910s to the 1930s, including her identity and position as an 'amateur' in the building world as well as her use of the media as a way of articulating and disseminating her ideas.

Foundations: Missions in London and South Africa

It was in the Cape Province, South Africa, that Dott's building activities first began following her marriage on 15 January 1906, at the relatively late age of 37, to the Reverend William Patrick Dott (1867–1938) in St Mary's Anglican Church, Woodstock, where he

---

[5]Matthew Grimley, *Citizenship, Community and the Church of England: Liberal Anglican Theories of the State between the Wars* (Oxford: Oxford University Press, 2004).

[6]Frank Prochaska, *Women and Philanthropy in Nineteenth-Century England* (Oxford: Clarendon Press, 1980).

[7]Annabel Dott, 'The Woman Architect', *Architectural Review* (December 1918): 31–3; Annabel Dott, 'Cottages for Disabled Officers', *Architectural Review* (April 1918): 74–6.

[8]R. Hasted, *Disability in Time and Place*: 35, https://historicengland.org.uk/content/docs/research/disability-in-time-and-place-pdf/ (accessed 25 October 2019).

Figure 9.1 'The Stone House, Goathlands, Yorks' in 'The Woman Architect and Her Work', *Architectural Review* 44 (August 1918): 32

served as Rector. Both Patrick, as he was known, and Annabel came from similar Liberal Anglican backgrounds and were involved in reforming activities in the East End of London. Patrick, after graduating from Oxford, held a position as a curate at All Hallows, Barking, London, while Sarah Frances Annabel (*née* Hall) grew up in Hackney in a middle-class family of moderate means.[9] She stated that 'she had come straight out of school to pass under Mrs. Barnett's guidance' and that her later work was 'directly due to the influence and teaching of … the famous settlement in Whitechapel'.[10] Whitechapel at the time was the centre of a number of radical social and artistic experiments led by Henrietta and Samuel Barnett. Toynbee Hall, founded by them in 1884, exemplified the doctrines of the New Liberalism which had been developed at Oxford by figures such as T. H. Green and Arnold Toynbee. The university settlement was conceived as a means of bridging class divisions, so that it functioned as one commentator wrote 'as a protest against the disastrous cleavage between East and West'.[11] The educational aspect of the Hall's mission was reflected in its buildings which were collegiate in character. They were designed by Elijah Hoole, who had worked with Octavia Hill on model housing, while the architect and socialist C. R. Ashbee was an early resident. He not only decorated the

---

[9]For more see https://northyorkshirehistory.blogspot.com/2019/02/mrs-annabel-dott-goathland-homes-for.html; http://yorkshire255.rssing.com/chan-10297851/latest.php (accessed 3 February 2019).
[10]'Homes of Honour', *The Daily Telegraph* (8 February 1919): 12.
[11]As quoted in Deborah Weiner, 'The Architecture of Victorian Philanthropy: The Settlement House as Manorial Residence', *Art History* 13, no. 2 (1990): 214.

dining hall there with students from the settlement but also opened his School & Guild of Handicraft next door as a workers' cooperative in 1888. Henrietta meanwhile was the promoter of the Whitechapel Art Gallery, also founded that year, in order to provide a national art gallery in the East End. During their time in the metropolis therefore the Dotts were exposed to a model of a two-pronged social and cultural mission, and it is easy to see how this could have been transferred from the 'East' of London to the 'East' of Empire.

The Dotts wedding certificate was signed by Frederick George Green as witness, the architect (with Harry Reid) of Cape Town's Town Hall (1905).[12] Annabel's address was recorded as Green's house 'Hiawatha', showing that she had formed architectural connections from first setting foot in the colony.[13] In her recollections of South Africa she liked to give the impression that her activities as a woman builder in an inhospitable environment were unique. However, this was far from the case as the church where she was married, St Mary's (1859–1864), was designed and built by an even earlier female architect, Sophia Gray (1814–1871). She was the wife of the first Bishop of Cape Town, Robert Gray, who put the construction of Anglican churches at the heart of his campaign to establish a visible presence for British Protestantism in the colony. Following his appointment in 1847 Sophia became both one of the first women deaconesses and 'architect to the diocese'.[14] She was responsible for around forty Gothic Revival churches in the Cape overseeing both their construction and design. Furthermore, these were not the pre-fabricated iron churches that were sent out across the Empire but rather individually produced masonry structures which followed Ecclesiological theories. Gray, as a self-trained architect, utilized the plans and principles set out in the Society's publications and adapted them to local sites and conditions. Indeed, as Alex Bremner writes, 'one of the most remarkable aspects of the spread of Anglican culture throughout the British empire during the Victorian period' was the involvement of non-experts, usually clergymen, in the design and construction of ecclesiastical architecture.[15] Gray's Woodstock church was built of local sandstone laid out in rough-hewn random courses and rendered with lime plaster. The original plan with a simple nave and side aisle was later extended with a chancel. A tower and north transept were added by Herbert Baker in 1897–1898.[16] By the time the Dotts knew it therefore, the structure had the accretive homespun feel of an English parish church, and this organic approach to design was one

---

[12]For more on Green (1850–1927) see https://www.artefacts.co.za/main/Buildings/archframes.php?archid=2010. (accessed 3 March 2020).

[13]With thanks to Lynne Dixon and Dorothy Reed, who are writing a book on Dott, for this observation and much other help.

[14]Desmond Martin, *The Bishop's Churches* (Cape Town: Struik, 2005); Desmond Martin, 'The Churches of Bishop Robert Gray & Mrs Sophia Gray: An Historical and Architectural Review' (Unpublished PhD, University of Cape Town, Cape Town, 2002); Deirdre M. Thackray, '*Sophia Gray (1814–1871): An Architectural Apprenticeship for Home, Church and Empire*' (MA diss., University of York, York, 2017).

[15]G. A. Bremner, *Imperial Gothic: Religious Architecture and High Anglican Culture in the British Empire, c. 1840–1870* (New Haven & London: Yale University Press, 2013): 19–20.

[16]For a sketch of the original church see ibid.: 17.

which was to influence Dott thereafter. Although Dott typically never acknowledged Gray's influence, her predecessor provided an example of one of Bremner's untrained practitioners, creating and producing buildings alongside a busy life as a bishop's wife.

Dott's fullest account of her activities in South Africa was contained in an interview in *The Woman's Leader* – noted as 'the most substantial and vigorous feminist periodical of the 1920s'.[17]

'It began when I was out in South Africa, where my husband, a clergyman, was working,' said Mrs. Dott. 'One of his duties was to be responsible for certain Church property out there. Among these was one of South Africa's few historic buildings – the house where the treaty by which the Dutch ceded Cape Colony to England was signed. It had fallen into considerable disrepair. There were difficulties in the way of getting it put in order, and I had the inspiration of undertaking the job myself … I knew nothing of building, the native men whom I hired almost as little. We had to learn by doing things wrong and then doing them over again. But in the end we saved the house. A little later there was a question of the schools attached to the Church being condemned by the Government inspectors. Emboldened by my previous success I undertook to put them right, and did so.'[18]

She expanded further for the *Daily Mail*: 'I took charge of this work and used to sit in the sun under an umbrella watching the Kaffir workmen and almost telling them where to lay each brick. I used to buy my own materials and plan the day's work for each man.'[19] This disquieting imperialist image highlights an ambiguity which was also to arise in her dealings with her English workmen; Annabel's Ruskinian belief in the dignity of manual labour was on occasion at odds with her high-handed treatment of her workmen. In this she was of course no different from many of her male contemporaries. But it exposes a gap between her rhetoric of cross-class community engagement and her practice which was to become a contentious issue in her next scheme.

'Homes of honour': The Orchards settlement for disabled officers

In 1909 on the Dotts return from South Africa, Patrick became Vicar of St Edward the Confessor, Dringhouses, York. In 1917, impelled by the same sense of patriotic duty which saw Patrick sign up as an army chaplain,[20] the Dotts made available a group of nine cottages specially adapted for 'disabled officers of the public school type and

---

[17]'Women's Print Media in Inter War Britain' website, Wilfrid Laurier University, Ontario: https://interwarfeminism.omeka.net/collections/show/4. (accessed 3 March 2020). Also see 'A Master Woman Builder', *The Vote* (22 April 1921): 442–3.
[18]'The Work of a Woman Builder', *The Woman's Leader* (16 July 1920): 540.
[19]'Gossip Seat: Woman Architect's Idea to Please Maids', *Daily Mail* (21 March 1921): 7.
[20]*The Church Times* (28 March 1919): 298.

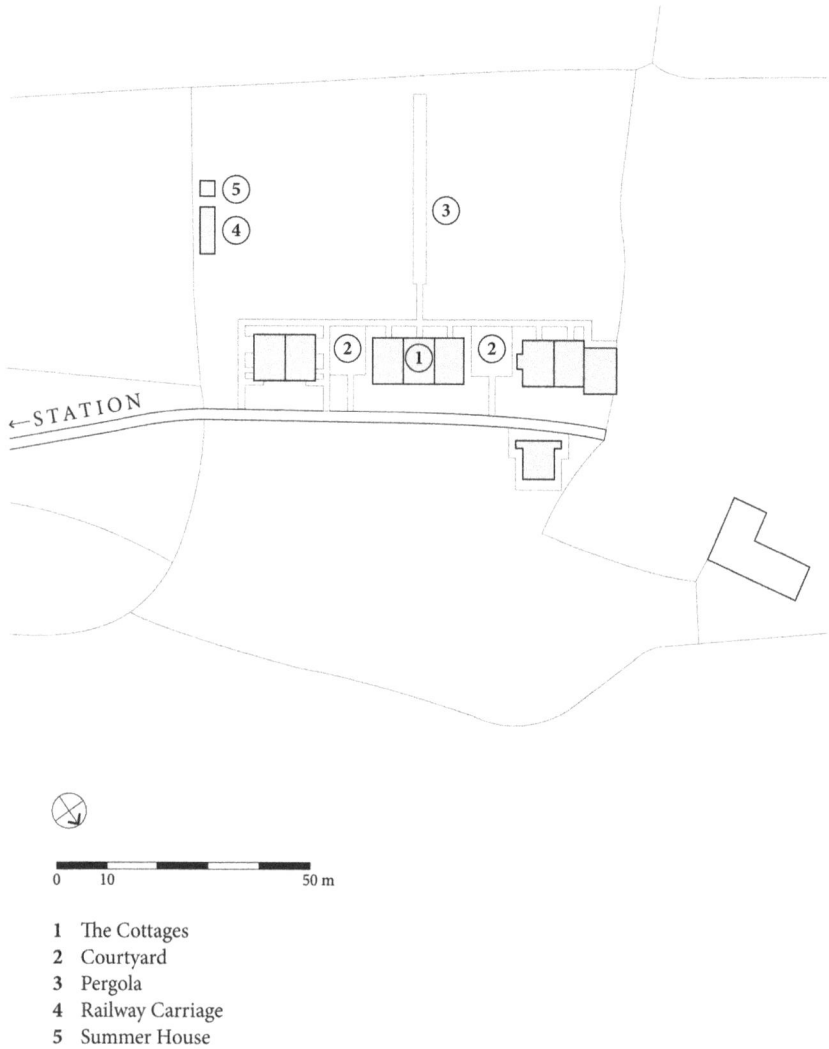

1 The Cottages
2 Courtyard
3 Pergola
4 Railway Carriage
5 Summer House

Figure 9.2 The Orchards, Goathlands, North Yorkshire, site plan as in 1917, drawn by Hannah Towler

their families'[21] **(Figure 9.2)**. There were other similar initiatives founded at the time to establish what the *Daily Telegraph* described as 'Homes of Honour', such as the Housing Association for Officers' Families (1916) or Lady Barrington's settlement at Shrivenham, which was for other ranks.[22] It was Annabel's scheme at Goathland, North Yorkshire, which was to bring her national attention. In her many public pronouncements she

---

[21]Imperial War Museum Archive, as quoted in Caroline Dakers, *The Countryside at War 1914–1918* (Constable: London, 1987), 197.
[22]'Homes of Honour', *The Daily Telegraph* (8 February 1919): 12.

presented it as an individual response to the call to provide charitable housing for special categories, including for disabled ex-servicemen, who were not catered for under the 1919 Addison Act.

Dott outlined the thinking behind the project in two long articles for *The Nineteenth Century and After* in 1918–1919.[23] In selecting this periodical Annabel was following the example of both the Barnetts, who had used it to launch Toynbee Hall with an article in 1884, and Barrington who, in April 1918, just prior to Annabel's own piece, had published on 'The Revival of Village Social Life'.[24] The strategy of using the medium of the press to contribute to and shape the social agenda was one of the ways in which such female reformers could exert influence outside of professional and other male-orientated structures.[25] In her two *Nineteenth Century* contributions Dott laid out in detail a vision for rural settlements which marked a major contribution to the national reconstruction debate. Towards the end of the war a distinction began to be made between those disabled veterans requiring long-term institutional care and those able to work and to live independently.[26] This led to a bifurcation in housing provision between advocates of a segregationist position of separate veterans villages, such as T. H. Mawson, and those who favoured an integrated solution often in more urban locations, for example the Haig Homes (founded 1929).[27] Dott supported a non-isolationist approach but looked to the countryside rather than the town as the ideal environment for creating colonies of family homes for 'shattered men' in 'the peace and healing of the country'.[28] In this she was following the example of the Village Centres Council which established Enham Village in 1919, still running today as Enham Alamein.[29] Her stated aim was to extend the social and economic scope of the Small Holdings Colonies Bill of 1916 which had released 80,000 acres for discharged and disabled soldiers with an agricultural background.[30] Dott's innovation was to include those without previous farming experience, a policy that was later enacted in the Land Settlement (Facilities) Act of 1919. The use of the terms 'settlement' and 'colonies' in the titles of these acts is instructive and much of the approach at the time effectively transferred the thinking behind the missions in

---

[23]Annabel Dott, 'Cottages for Disabled Officers', *The Nineteenth Century and After* 84 (July 1918): 160–70; Annabel Dott, 'The Disabled Officer in Rural Reconstruction', *The Nineteenth Century and After* 85 (February 1919): 359–76.

[24]Charlotte Barrington, 'The Revival of Village Social Life', *The Nineteenth Century and After* 84 (April 1918): 790–809.

[25]Colpus, *Female Philanthropy*: 9; Gillian Darley, 'Octavia Hill: Lessons in Campaigning', in Elizabeth Baigent and Ben Cowell (eds.), *Octavia Hill, Social Activism and the Remaking of British Society* (University of London Press: Institute of Historical Research, 2016): 30.

[26]R. Hasted, *Introductions to Heritage Assets: Domestic Housing for Disabled Veterans, 1900–2014* (Historic England, 2016): 6, https://historicengland.org.uk/images-books/publications/iha-domestic-housing-for-disabled-veterans-1900–2014/ (accessed 28 November 2019).

[27]T. H. Mawson, *An Imperial Obligation: Industrial Villages for Partially Disabled Soldiers and Sailors* (London: G. Richards, 1917).

[28]Dott, 'Cottages for Disabled Officers, *The Nineteenth Century*: 161.

[29]Wayne Cockroft and Paul Stamper (ed.), *Legacies of the First World War: Building for Total War 1914–18* (Swindon: Historic England, 2018): 197.

[30]Dott, 'The Disabled Officer in Rural Reconstruction': 360–1.

the empire and the East End to an English rural context.[31] Preston and Smith and Fair make similar observations about the rhetoric of 'colonisation' in relation to Scottish community centres and land settlements in this volume. At the same time the post-war rural settlements built on the Edwardian 'back to the land movement' movement in trying to rebalance the rural economy, which had suffered badly from depopulation due to depressed wages pre-1914.[32]

Dott's other innovation was to argue that rural colonies, as with their urban counterparts, might be integrated into existing settlements. In a similar way to Henrietta Barnett's vision for her creation at Hampstead Garden Suburb (1906 onwards) Dott hoped to produce a socially cohesive community with educational, social and recreational facilities as well as housing. This was an approach which Lady Barrington also deployed at Shrivenham where she built a Memorial Hall and recreation ground to sit alongside her six cottages. Barrington strongly promoted the role of societies, such as the Women's Institute and the Boy Scouts, plus the employment of a paid female social worker, whom she introduced to initiate and organize educational, work-related and social events.[33] The critical difference was that Barrington was titled, wealthy and socially well connected. But there is a further intriguing parallel with Dott as Barrington too was a proclaimed self-builder. She wrote in her memoirs that she did not approve of the designs sent to her by various architects and 'I therefore determined to design the Institute myself, choosing a style in keeping with the picturesque buildings around.'[34] An architect Romaine Walker was later employed to complete the works, especially the complex internal hammer beam roof and the porch. For Barrington the Village Hall was the essence of Liberal Anglican communitarianism 'as a symbol of the corporate life and manifold interests of the whole village, embodying the ideals and the ambitions of the rural population'.[35] Dott likewise argued that the very presence of the officers' families would increase the social mix of villages so that the settlers could take the lead in local government as well as in social, sporting and educational activities to 'help to dispel the dullness which is the miasma of village life'.[36] Such active and productive models of veteranhood would be preferable to mere survival on inadequate pensions, as Dott argued of the officers: 'Is not their opportunity rural reconstruction? ... As Arnold Toynbee said, the best help a gentleman could give Whitechapel was to live there.'[37] In this way true to Liberal Anglican tenets Dott wished to create a community based not on social or economic strata but on shared communal values and enterprise, which echoed at the local level the wider national moral community.[38]

---

[31]I am grateful to Elizabeth Darling for this suggestion.
[32]Dakers, *Countryside at War*: 131–2.
[33]Barrington, *Revival of Village Social Life*.
[34]Charlotte Barrington, *Through Eighty Years (1855–1935): The Reminiscences of Charlotte, Viscountess Barrington* (London: John Murray, 1936): 236.
[35]Barrington, *Revival of Village Social Life*: 798.
[36]Barrington, *Reminiscences*: 162.
[37]Dott, 'The Disabled Officer in Rural Reconstruction', *Nineteenth Century*: 361.
[38]Grimley, *Citizenship, Community and the Church of England*: 12.

There was some debate as to the most suitable occupations for disabled veterans in rural areas. Commercial trades including bootmaker, sadler and bricklayer formed the basis of the colony at Shrivenham, which was specifically designated for those having 'about 40 per cent of disability'.[39] Others looked to handicrafts as providing suitable employment, such as at the Ashtead Pottery, Surrey, 1923–1935. It was established by Lawrence Weaver, the former architectural editor of *Country Life*, who was director of the Land Settlement Programme at the Ministry of Agriculture after the war.[40] In her articles Dott was dismissive of such isolated initiatives. She wanted to see an integrated economy in which activities that might supplement service pensions embraced both agricultural enterprises, such as poultry farming or bee-keeping, as well as trades: 'organisation, the use of better materials, good transport, and business ability brought to bear on securing the right markets might open a very different future'.[41] Her Goathland colony was called The Orchards, a name which exemplified the small-scale, self-sufficient form of enterprise that she wished to encourage to boost food production and the rural economy. The Orchards were a metaphor for an ecological and social collective through which Dott asserted the value of small cultures in farming, alongside large-scale agriculture, which she admitted would predominate in the future.[42]

The Daily Telegraph noted that The Orchards had been designed by 'a woman architect', however, as Annabel had made clear in her *AR* article on 'The Woman Architect' she was in fact self-trained, although, as she wrote elsewhere, had the opportunity been open to her she would have seized it.[43] The first female architect, Ethel Charles, was only admitted to the RIBA in 1898 and the first women to the Architectural Association in 1917.[44] Statutory registration with the Architects Registration Council (ARCUK) was not compulsory until 1931 and Dott was therefore free to use either term, although in keeping with her Art and Crafts sympathies she favoured 'builder' more often than 'architect'. This choice of terminology allowed her to reinforce her position as an architectural outsider and intimated a more directly Ruskinian connection with the material practices of construction.[45] She 'began a systematic self-training in the theory and practice of the trade' while recuperating on the Yorkshire moors after illness.[46] This was possibly following the stillbirth of a baby daughter on 18 October 1909 in

---

[39] Annual reports 1922 1930, Viscountess Barrington & Welfare Institute for Disabled Ex-service Men at http://www.shrivenhamheritagesociety.co.uk/listing.asp?listID=381. (accessed 28 November 2019).

[40] Hasted, *Domestic Housing for Disabled Veterans*: 10–11; Dakers, *Countryside at War*: 196–200.

[41] Dott, 'The Disabled Officer in Rural Reconstruction': 362.

[42] Ibid.

[43] 'A Master Woman Builder': 442–3.

[44] Jane Darke, 'Women, Architects and Feminism', in Matrix (eds.), *Making Space: Women and the Man-Made Environment* (London: Pluto Press): 19; Elizabeth Darling and Lynne Walker, *AA Women in Architecture 1917–2017* (London: Architectural Association Publications, 2017).

[45] See Mark Swenarton, *Artisans and Architects: The Ruskinian Tradition in Architectural Thought* (Palgrave: Macmillan, 1989).

[46] 'The Work of a Woman Builder': 540.

Scarborough.[47] Dott's subsequent childlessness, as with Henrietta Barnett, must have enabled her to give more time to her own activities than most married women, although remarkably Sophia Gray was a mother to five children. During her convalescence Dott wrote that she studied 'technical books on cottage-building, plumbing, drainage, brick-making and joinery' working towards the Clerk of Works exams, although it is not specified whether she actually sat them.[48] Deirdre Thackray has drawn attention to the fact that Sophia Gray, as a gentleman's daughter, had been educated to draw – a skill which stood her in good stead in her architectural work in South Africa.[49] Dott had no such advantages and therefore she chose the role most suitable for someone of her class and background, that of clerk of works, the position of many self-made, middle-class entrants into the construction industry going back to Nicholas Hawksmoor onwards. Other women both before and after the war were carving out a role for themselves as housing specialists, particularly for interiors and kitchens, and house planning and management began to develop as a fruitful politicized space for female activity, both for its designers and its users.[50] The growth of the expert in this period has been particularly allied to modernism, as with Elizabeth Denby, but as the example of Dott and other philanthropists proves there were alternative networks, particularly media ones, by which a public platform and social impact could be achieved.[51]

Having bought the land at Goathland, Annabel designed the cottages and planned to use a nearby builder but took on the role herself when he refused to use local labour. She then contracted the workmen for the different trades and said that handling the men was the most important skill that she had managed to acquire. She recommended paying 'Trade Union rates (and a little more) … and you ought not to have any difficulties.'[52] Although the *Telegraph* wrote in 1919 that The Orchards were 'coming to completion' the plaque on the houses, commemorating their being 'given by Patrick and Annabel Dott', is dated October 1917. A clue to this apparent inconsistency in their genesis is provided by the *Nineteenth Century* article which stated that 'in some villages it may be possible to secure a group of cottages already built'.[53] For in fact the cottages had originally been erected by the couple in c.1912 as holiday rentals in what was a popular destination in the North York Moors.[54] Dott had proposed that each county should be responsible for creating housing for disabled soldiers guided by a committee consisting of figures such as the Lord Lieutenant, the Colonel of the Territorial Regiment, the County Director

[47]*South Africa* (23 October 1929): 'Births' https://www.eggsa.org/newspapers/index.php/south-african-magazine/332-south-africa-1909-4-october-december.html (accessed 11 September 2019).

[48]'The Work of a Woman Builder': 540.

[49]Thackray, 'Sophia Gray': 88–91.

[50]Krista Cowman, '"From the Housewife's Point of View", Female Citizenship and the Gendered Domestic Interior in Post-First World War Britain, 1918–28', *English Historical Review* 130, no. 543 (2015): 352–83.

[51]Elizabeth Darling, '"The Star in the Profession She Invented for Herself": A Brief Biography of Elizabeth Denby, Housing Consultant', *Planning Perspectives* 20 (2005): 271–300.

[52]'The Work of a Woman Builder': 540.

[53]Dott, 'The Disabled Officer in Rural Reconstruction': 361.

[54]This is confirmed by the Title Deeds to No. 4, with many thanks to the current owner Simon Caunt.

of the Red Cross and local businessmen and donors. Unlike Viscountess Barrington at Shrivenham Annabel failed to obtain a grant from the Red Cross but she did manage to secure the backing of the Middlesborough steel magnate and Lord Lieutenant of the County, Sir Hugh Bell. The Dotts had hoped to grant a lease for the conversion of The Orchards but in the end, despite repeated references to the 'gift' of the cottages, they were in fact paid £1,000 for the freehold in 1917 with funds provided by the Bell family and John Dawnay, later the 9th Viscount Downe of Rushton. Hugh Bell was instrumental in the running of the association, The Goathland Homes for Officers Ltd., to which they were conveyed in 1919.[55]

The Orchards were solid Arts and Crafts–influenced structures whose design, like that of her nearby home The Stone House, echoed the surrounding vernacular. Dott described them as being 'built, like the farmhouses of the district, with grey stone, and the roofs of old red tiles; the mullioned diamond-paned windows and the broad simple outline give them the appearance of … having been there for generations'[56] (**Figure 9.3**). She did not have to look far for precedents for her design as the Rowntree family had built New Earswick by Parker & Unwin just outside York from 1902. In her article on The Stone House, Dott commented that she consulted 'a well-known house-planner' for advice.[57] This was almost certainly Walter Brierley, the so-called Yorkshire Lutyens,

Figure 9.3 The Orchards, Goathlands, North Yorkshire, *c.* 1917, photographer unknown, private collection

---

[55] Annabel Dott, 'A Debt of Honour', *Church Times* (4 April 1919): 322.
[56] Dott, 'Cottages for the Disabled', *Nineteenth Century*: 167.
[57] Dott, 'Woman Architect': 31.

who carried out a great deal of work in Goathland including the church, the parish hall, a hotel, a large house and several cottages between 1892 and 1908.[58] Brierley's home was in Dringhouses, so he was well known to the Dotts, and the plans of The Orchards are almost identical to his Lady Deramore Memorial Almshouses, Heslington, 1903.[59] Furthermore drawings of the scheme in the Borthwick Institute show that Brierley carried out the alterations to the cottages in 1917–1918 which were again paid for by Bell, who was a regular patron of Brierley.[60]

Dott had written that despite their traditional external appearance, '[i]ndoors, however, the modern comfort and arrangement make for the newer life of today. The chief aim in their planning was comfort and labour saving'.[61] It was internally where Dott best deployed the latest thinking in cottage design and planning. The Orchards followed the example, established at New Earswick and later published in Unwin's *Town Planning in Practice* (1909), in adopting a square plan with the offices to the north-facing front and the main living area (without parlour) to the south-facing rear **(Figure 9.4)**.[62] This arrangement allowed for the maximum amount of sunlight and ventilation to penetrate the house; features held to be essential for health and hygiene. Dott recommended the provision of a loggia or 'stoep', the South African term, where the invalid could 'sleep in the open air'; such as the one at the Preston Hall TB colony for veterans.[63] Although she prided herself on the variety of the dwellings, they also had features in common, summarized in her sketch plan. Unlike most small cottages they were of three storeys giving views out over the moors **(Figure 9.3)**. This provided a total of five bedrooms, a living room, scullery and ancillary areas. The service provision was rather modest while the living and sleeping spaces were more generous than was normal, which underlines their original purpose for short-term occupancy, not long-term use, by holiday-makers. The disabled officers formed part of what was defined as the 'New Poor'; that is middle-class families living in reduced circumstances after the war, their small pensions further decreased by recession and inflation. This group were particularly promoted by the *Daily Mail* which was instrumental in creating a new definition of housewifery for those stricken by the 'servant problem', in which labour saving and economy were to the fore.[64] Dott wrote: '[W]e want cottages with labour-saving devices now found only in rich men's houses.'[65] These were what have subsequently been characterized as the 'homes fit for heroines' and in discussing her projects Dott's focus was often more on

---

[58]Patrick Nuttgens, *Brierley in Yorkshire: The Architecture of the Turn of the Century* (York: York Georgian Society, 1984): 17–18.

[59]I am grateful to Edward Waterson for this information as well as the following reference.

[60]William Anelays (builders) were paid £594 12s 6d for these. See Borthwick Institute, University of York – Atkinson-Brierley Archive: Works Book 1908 - c. 1923: f.186.

[61]Dott, 'Cottages for the Disabled', *Nineteenth Century* (1918): 167.

[62]Swenarton, *Homes Fit for Heroes*: 18–23.

[63]Hasted, *Domestic Housing for Disabled Veterans*: 9.

[64]Deborah Sugg Ryan, *Ideal Homes, 1918–39: Domestic Design and Suburban Modernism* (Manchester: Manchester University Press, 2018): 29–30.

[65]Dott, 'Cottages for Disabled Officers' *Architectural Review*: 75.

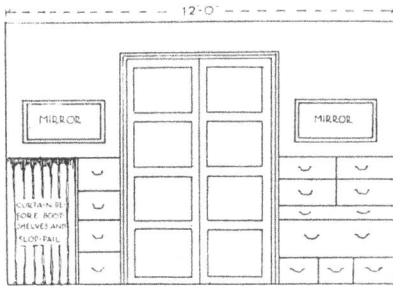

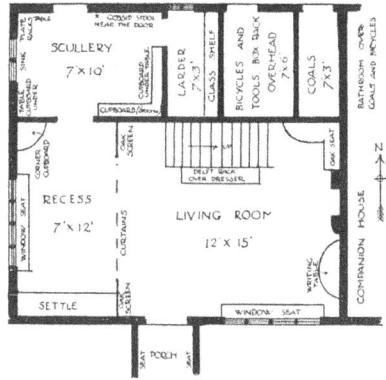

Figure 9.4 Above: The Orchards, internal views of dining area and sitting room. Showing built-in cupboards next to fireplace, settle opposite the window and dining area which could be curtained off and used for invalids to rest in the day or as a children's indoor theatre. Below: The Orchards, plan of typical cottage and sketch of built-in fitment furniture. The plan measures 22 × 22 feet in this sketch. Note the curtain in the bedroom hiding 'boot shelves and slop-pail'.

her female than male occupants.[66] The plan shows the 'Gossip Stool near the door' in the scullery for the maid, a feature which was widely reported in the popular press as evidence of the benefits of having a female designer for the domestic environment.[67] Dott commented that the depletion of men from the war 'offers many opportunities to the woman architect. Her knowledge of domestic science, of cookery, of health, will come into play … a woman accustomed to the daily life of the house can best suggest conveniences and labour-saving appliances'.[68] She recommended the two most essential

[66]Barbara MacFarlane, 'Homes Fit for Heroines: Housing in the Twenties' in Matrix (eds.), *Making Space*: 26–36.
[67]Dott, 'Cottages for Disabled Officers', *Architectural Review*: 76.
[68]Dott, 'Woman Architect': 31.

things as being the provision of hot water up and downstairs and '*space*' which was the result of good planning. An upgraded hot water system and bathrooms were introduced in the modifications made by Brierley in 1918.[69] Such advice was consistent with the recommendations of official housing reports such as those of the Tudor Walters Committee (1918) and the Women's Housing Sub-Committee (1919) which codified Unwin's thinking in official form.[70]

The notion of labour-saving extended to built-in furniture and fittings. In the pre-war period proponents of standardization, such as the Design and Industries Association and writers such as Lethaby and Quennell, had been arguing for a new rational approach to furniture in the home and the amelioration of everyday life, and through it, everyday things.[71] Dott particularly recommended 'fitment furniture' and the living area included features such as integrated window seats and a dresser and corner cupboard, while the bedrooms had built-in wardrobes and combined chests of drawers/washstands (**Figures 9.4**). She wrote of providing these built-in elements that 'the cost is heavy but the saving in labour makes it well worth while … [and] by lessening the size of the

Figure 9.5 Grey Wood, East Sussex, the quadrangle, rear elevation, from 'The Grey Wood in Sussex' brochure (1924), by kind permission of Sussex Archaeological Society

---

[69]Borthwick Institute, University of York – Atkinson-Brierley Archive: The Orchards, Goathland, Plans of Cottages and Improvements, n.d. & 1917.

[70]Swenarton, *Homes Fit for Heroes*: 91–3 and for more on the Women's Sub-Committee see Cowman, "'From the Housewife's Point of View'".

[71]Elizabeth McKellar, 'C. H. B. Quennell (1872–1935): Architecture, History and the Quest for the Modern', *Architectural History* 50 (2007): 222–4; Swenarton, *Homes Fit for Heroes*: 63.

room, a considerable economy is effected in the cost of building'.[72] Another way that costs were reduced was through the use of recycled elements including stone from an abandoned local church and timber from a demolished bridge or sourced from ship-brokers.[73] Given that the Dotts were not rich the issue of how they managed to finance the building of both The Stone House and The Orchards remains a mystery. Despite her later writings, it is also likely that the use of built-in furniture derived from the original use of the cottages as summer holiday lets, where such features would be standard. This would also explain why the Dotts were able to 'donate' the properties free of any tenants or leasehold complications.

The Goathland Settlement, however, was not a great success. A number of veterans and their families did move there and some enterprises were started but the scheme was wound up in 1931 when the charity was terminated. Other more durable settlements secured external funding or relied on large donations and without a grant from the Red Cross or another body it was unlikely to survive long term. By 1931 there were only two disabled officers remaining and the cottages were sold off as private dwellings. Neither did the Dotts retain a strong connection with the project, as in 1919 they moved back down south and in 1920 The Stone House was sold to Joseph Stephenson Rowntree, familiar to Patrick from the family residence in Dringhouses, for £2,000 for use as a hunting lodge.[74]

Pioneering women in the metropolis

The Dotts returned to London from Yorkshire first to St Luke's, Woodside, Croydon (1919–1923) and then to St Mary's, Barnes (1923–1936). In both places Annabel carried out architectural projects: a parish room in Croydon and in Barnes she designed a church hall (1927) with broad eaves and a prominent stoep, inspired by South African architecture.[75] However, outside the church she also became involved in attempts to help ease the crisis in accommodation for single women workers. The war had introduced women into new occupations, including professional ones, and their position was further bolstered by the Sex Disqualification (Removal) Act of 1919. Dott does not appear to have been an active suffragette despite being the subject of a feature article in the Women's Freedom League newspaper, *The Vote*, in 1921. But she was always a strong proponent of women's interests, particularly with regard to education, and she hosted groups of girls at a summer camp every year at her home in Goathland. While in Woodside, Dott had negotiated a payment to sub-let a house in 1920 which she used to rent out rooms to women who needed accommodation. She informed the readers of *The Vote* that she was providing 'self-contained flats' for 'professional women workers' and that 'bona-fide'

---

[72]Dott, 'Cottages for Disabled Officers', *Architectural Review*: 75.
[73]Ibid.:168.
[74]Stone House Schedule of Deeds with thanks to Lesley Mayes.
[75]'The Rector's Wife' *Daily Mail* (2 June 1928): 4.

applicants should contact her for consideration.[76] This initiative became the cause of a subsequent court case which is highly revealing of both Annabel's motivations and her *modus operandi*. The judge noted that Mrs Dott had acted for 'philanthropic reasons, but, through want of business habits on the part of the parties, he thought it would have been almost impossible to arrive at a solution'.[77] It seems therefore that despite her experience in property management in Yorkshire Annabel was still acting in a largely amateur and opportunistic fashion in her own projects. This is in contrast to Sophia Gray who, as the surviving documentation shows, meticulously ran the financing and administration of her building operations, which may have been aided by her exposure to estate management practices during her gentry upbringing.[78]

The model that Dott used in Croydon provided a forerunner on a smaller scale for the Women's Pioneer Housing (WPH) group with whom she was briefly involved from 1920 to 1921.[79] It was one of a number of associations which were created to provide low-rent flats for single professional women in London. The focus of housing reformers to date had been on the working classes but the WPH catered for middle-class employees with a desire for independent living, as opposed to the hostel-type accommodation provided in earlier experiments.[80] Dott was one of the founder members who, in the absence of any government funding, all bought shares in the company which was used to purchase properties suitable for conversion.[81] Other founders included Etheldred Browning and Sydney Bushell, who were both on the Committee of the Women's Section of the Garden Cities & Town Planning Association. Also involved were the journalists and militant suffragettes Helen Archdale, editor of *Time and Tide* magazine, and Dorothy Peel of the *Daily Mail*, author of *The Labour Saving House* (1917) and a member of the Ministry of Reconstruction Women's Advisory Housing Committee. Dott's participation in these leading housing and Garden City planning circles indicates both her status in the field and her engagement with the most up-to-date thinking and practice.

Grey Wood: The communal middle-class rural settlement

Dott's involvement with the Women's Pioneer Housing was only brief and she tendered her resignation in January 1921 'owing to other duties'.[82] This was a reference to her purchase on 30 July 1920 of 50 acres of land at East Hoathly, Sussex, where she intended

---

[76]'A Master Woman Builder': 442–3.

[77]'Action over a House', *Norwood News* (7 April 1922): 7.

[78]Thackray, 'Sophia Gray': 70–1.

[79]She attended four of the first five meetings from August 1920 to January 1921. Women's Pioneer Housing (WPH), Management Committee Minutes, vol. 1 1920–23. With thanks to Bonnie Emmett for this information.

[80]Emily Gee, '"Where Shall She Live?": Housing the New Working Woman in Late Victorian and Edwardian London' in Geoff Brandwood (ed.), *Living, Leisure and Law: Eight Building Types in England 1800–1941* (Reading: Spire, 2010).

[81]WPH website https://www.insidehousing.co.uk/home/home/the-women-who-reinvented-housing-55400 (accessed 29 March 2018).

[82]WPH, Management Committee Minutes, vol. 1, 10 January 1921.

to build her own pioneer housing scheme.[83] This was presumably funded by the receipts from the sales of her properties in Goathland. In this later development, which she planned from the beginning as an ideal community, she was able more fully to realize her vision for new ways of communal, rural living. It was called Grey or Gray Wood and consisted of seventeen dwellings arranged to replicate an Oxbridge college with a central quadrangle flanked by complementary buildings (**Figure 9.5**). Its idiom was a homage to Toynbee Hall, which had also been designed in a neo-Tudor style with a courtyard plan. The use of such revivalist styles in the East End to create 'a quasi-country house aesthetic' has been pejoratively characterized as 'squireachy'.[84] However, Toynbee Hall, as noted previously, was also associated with Ashbee's radical agenda and might equally be interpreted as an architectural symbol of progressive philanthropy. At Hampstead Garden Suburb the same layout was used for Queen's Court, 1927 (Hendry and Schooling for the United Women's Homes Association) and Waterlow Court, 1908–1909 (Baillie Scott for the Improved Industrial Dwellings Company) both set around quadrangles housing single women. The design of the latter extended the medievalizing elements to include a lych gate and a cloister. Annabel was similarly trying to project an image of solidity and longevity for a middle-class audience at Grey Wood, which combined bourgeois values with economical living. She praised it for its 'neighbourliness' combined with its cheapness to build, run and maintain.[85] Here once again she deployed a predominantly Arts and Crafts approach using brick construction with mullioned windows and wood-panelled interiors. This time the ensemble was topped off by a thatched roof, which was the major contributor to a later damaging fire. The cottages were clearly not for labourers having three to four bedrooms, as well as a bathroom and dining and living rooms plus a kitchenette. Prices ranged from £550 for the cottages to £1,450 for some of the large individual houses scattered around the perimeter of the site.[86]

In converting The Orchards, Dott had already begun thinking about ways of achieving more efficient communal services. Like Lady Barrington she advocated the building of a club house which could be used for social activities for children and adults as well as housing a library, common room, billiard room and communal dining room. The latter, she wrote, could work on 'the lines of service flats in London' which would help ease the burden on wives and the number of servants required.[87] She also stressed the importance of physical and educational activities to personal development for both adults and children. The grounds of The Orchards had included a recreation area, tennis court and an old railway carriage for play (**Figure 9.2**). Dott was particularly keen on acting as a therapeutic activity and at Grey Wood there were unrealized plans for an open-air theatre, such as that later built at Dartington Hall, Devon. The Hall was transformed by the fabulously wealthy Leonard and Dorothy Elmhirst from 1925 into a famous educational and artistic centre bolstered by radical innovations in the estate's agricultural

---

[83]I am grateful to Jane Seabrook for this information.
[84]Weiner, 'Architecture of Victorian Philanthropy': 219.
[85]'When Women build', *Daily Telegraph* (19 October 1929): 9.
[86]Sussex Archaeological Society Collections, Grey Wood Brochure (1924).
[87]Dott, 'Cottages for the Disabled', *Nineteenth Century*: 165.

and forestry operations. Dott was also concerned with the issue of wider amenities, such as improved lighting in rural areas. She posited the reuse of some of the electric plant from the decommissioned munition factories and army camps for this purpose.[88] Mawson in his *An Imperial Obligation: Industrial Villages for Partially Disabled Soldiers & Sailors* (1917) had likewise promoted electricity as the means to transform rural life seeing it as the basis for reintroducing a home-working economy, particularly suitable for disabled veterans.[89] At Grey Wood the picturesque site was combined with the latest technology and it was hailed by the *Daily Mail* as the first 'All-Electric Village'.[90] In the following year the 1925 Daily Mail Ideal Home Exhibition featured an 'All-Electric' house, in association with the foundation of the Electrical Association for Women in 1924.[91] There was an electricity station at Grey Wood run by water pumped up from a lake in the extensive grounds. It supplied not only the houses with power and hot water but also a communal laundry, refrigeration plant and bakehouse, and even novelties such as electric irons and kettles **(Figure 9.6)**.[92]

Dott's ideal was a self-contained community, uniting the best of city and country, in a new twist on the Garden Suburb theme, a mode which her mentor Henrietta Barnet had pioneered at Hampstead. Modern conveniences including telephones, guest accommodation and a regular bus service connecting with the railway station were combined with the rustic charm of the buildings set in a sylvan woodland landscape. She saw public transport as essential in helping to lessen social isolation for women in rural areas.[93] Thus while her social vision maintained the norms of Christian reformists she developed a modern technological and economic vision within the cultural continuities of her architectural choices. However, unlike the Garden Suburb ideal the East Hoathly settlement was unusual in not attempting to achieve a social mix, added to which its location within easy reach of London opened it up to weekend commuters as well as permanent residents. There was also a difficult balance to be struck between the ideal of 'neighbourliness' and the need for individual privacy. The 1924 brochure stressed that 'The Quad is not a communal settlement, as at the Varsity, a man can "sport his oak" when he chooses; as in a London block of Flats the Tenants do not necessarily have an intimate acquaintance'.[94] The publication went on to state that they hoped to attract residents from the Services, Civil Servants – particularly colonial ones, 'Varsity and Literary Men' (no mention of women), and lovers of the countryside. However, as at Goathland Annabel severed her connection with the enterprise relatively soon after its completion and put the whole estate up for auction in 1929, only five years after its completion.[95]

---

[88]Dott, 'The Disabled Officer in Rural Reconstruction': 373.
[89]Mawson, *An Imperial Obligation*: 10.
[90]'Woman as Architect', *Daily Mail* (17 June 1924): 7.
[91]Sugg Ryan, *Ideal Homes*: 103–4.
[92]'Woman as Architect', *Daily Mail* (17 June 1924): 4.
[93]Dott, 'The Disabled Officer in Rural Reconstruction': 373.
[94]Sussex Archaeological Society Collections, Grey Wood Brochure (1924), n. p.
[95]This may have been due to ill health as it was reported that she had to be carried to the site on a stretcher during construction. *Daily Mail Atlantic Edition* (9 August 1924): 9.

The Power House and Plant

The Power House has a **45 h.p. Oil Engine** (*Parson's*) and a British Houston generator.
Auxiliary set of 10 h.p. engine and dynamo (not yet erected) in case of emergency.

The Bake House has a huge three-tier oven (*Mabbott's*) ; an electric Washer-up ; an Ice Cream Machine.

The Laundry has an " Ibis " Washing Machine ; a hydro Extractor worked by electricity ; vats, tanks, etc.

The Pumping Shed has an " Amanco " engine.

Another Pumping Shed has a " Petter " engine.

The Water Tower, brick-built, has capacious tanks.

The Boiler House has a boiler which supplies hot water to the Nine Houses of the Quad.

The Circular Saw, in rough shed, is electrically driven.

Fire Appliances.—Canvas hose with copper nozzle, and box on wheels ; " Minimax " fire extinguishers ; fire buckets to every house ; " Merryweather " cistern on wheels, with pump (also suitable for spraying the orchards) ; Water cart with pump.

Chicken Sheds. Bee Barn.

Part of this plant is still to be erected ; it is all on site.

Figure 9.6 Grey Wood, details of power house and electric plant, from 'The Grey Wood in Sussex' Brochure (1924), by kind permission of Sussex Archaeological Society

Conclusion

How then should we assess the contribution of Annabel Dott? On the one hand she can be seen as continuing the individualistic, philanthropic tradition of her forerunners such as Henrietta Barnett and Octavia Hill. Like them she focused on local initiatives but fatally she failed to attract sufficient investment. Without establishing a company, such as that which underpinned Hampstead Garden Suburb or having the financial resources and connections of aristocrats such as Viscountess Barrrington, it was impossible to create a self-contained community with enough land or capital for the long term. However, like Barnett and Gray she was able to circumvent the social constraints imposed on Victorian and Edwardian women and all three of them used the unique position of being a vicar's wife to their advantage – exploiting the physical and social mobility that it conferred with a redefinition of spousal roles within their marriages. Dott constructed an 'assertive public persona', much like Barnett, which helped her negotiate the constraints of her gender and class.[96] Both women were acknowledged as the instigator and implementor

---

[96]Creedon, 'A Benevolent Tyrant?': 234.

of their projects and were able to claim rights of ownership from male partners – something that female architects still struggle with today.[97]

Dott may not have been able to match the creators of entire Garden Cities but her writings and built experiments helped shape a new idea of rural England. Her skilful and highly successful exploitation of the public sphere of print in a newly dynamic and populist way enabled her to expound ideas and promote her schemes to the widest possible audience. She is credited with having provided a model for the modern rural community and as anticipating 'much of Dartington's agenda' in her combination of new technological and commercial enterprises with an interest in architecture and the arts.[98] She saw rural reconstruction as a three-fold process of housing, education of children, and occupation through employment and recreational activities. But her interests extended far beyond simply the rural, and with her experiences of urban, suburban and colonial life we can see her ideas as an attempt to reconcile some of the contemporary tensions between the local, the national and the imperial, between tradition and modernization, as well as between new and old Liberalism. Towards the end of her life she was being identified as a campaigner against suburban 'ugliness' and 'bungalow rash'.[99] Grey Wood in particular, where she hoped to create an enlightened middle-class enclave, might be seen as a shout against suburbanization and the loss of communal identity in the modern city. Dott in combining reconstruction and modernization pioneered a model which combined respect for the character of rural England, through a sensitive use of traditional building materials and styles, with modern social and economic regeneration.

Select bibliography

Archival

Borthwick Institute, University of York – Atkinson-Brierley Archive. 1917. 'The Orchards', Goathland for Mrs Dott: Block Plan of Site [4/19] July 1917; Plans of Suggested Improvements to Caretaker's Cottage, October 1917; Plans of Cottages No.1, 2, 3, 4, 5, 6, 7 and caretaker's, n.d.
Schedule of Deeds. Stone House, Goathland, private collection.
Sussex Archaeological Society Collections. Grey Wood Brochure, 1924.
Title Deeds, No. 4. The Orchards, Goathland, private collection.

Primary and Secondary
Barrington, Charlotte. 'The Revival of Village Social Life'. The Nineteenth Century and After 84 (April 1918): 790–809.

---

[97]Denise Scott Brown, 'Room at the Top? Sexism and the Star System', in Jane Rednell, Barbara Penner and Ian Borden (eds.), Gender, Space, Architecture: An Interdisciplinary Introduction (London: Routledge, 2000): 258–65.
[98]David Jeremiah, 'Dartington Hall: A Landscape of an Exceptional Experiment in Rural Reconstruction', in Paul Brassley, Jeremy Burchley and Lynne Thompson (eds.), The English Countryside between the Wars: Regeneration or Decline (Woodbridge: Boydell Press, 2006): 121.
[99]'When Women Build', Daily Telegraph (19 October 1929): 9.

Barrington, Charlotte. *Through Eighty Years (1855–1935): The Reminiscences of Charlotte, Viscountess Barrington*. London: John Murray, 1936.

Bremner, G. A. *Imperial Gothic: Religious Architecture and High Anglican Culture in the British Empire, c. 1840–1870*. New Haven and London: Yale University Press, 2013.

Cockroft, Wayne and Stamper Paul (ed.). *Legacies of the First World War: Building for Total War 1914–18*. Swindon: Historic England, 2018.

Colpus, Eve. *Female Philanthropy in the Interwar World: Between Self and Other*. London: Bloomsbury, 2018.

Colpus, Eve. 'Women, Service and Self-actualization in Inter-war Britain'. *Past & Present* 238, no. 1 (2018): 197–232.

Cowman, Krista. '"From the Housewife's Point of View", Female Citizenship and the Gendered Domestic Interior in Post-First World War Britain, 1918–28'. *English Historical Review* 130, no. 543 (2015): 352–83.

Creedon, Alison. 'A Benevolent Tyrant? The Principles and Practices of Henrietta Barnett (1851–1936), Social Reformer and Founder of Hampstead Garden Suburb'. *Women's History Review* 11, no. 2 (2002): 231–52.

Dakers, Caroline. *The Countryside at War 1914–1918*. Constable: London, 1987.

Darke, Jane. 'Women, Architects and Feminism'. In *Making Space: Women and the Man-Made Environment*, edited by Matrix, 11–25. London: Pluto Press.

Darley, Gillian. 'Octavia Hill: Lessons in Campaigning'. In *Octavia Hill, Social Activism and the Remaking of British Society*, edited by Elizabeth Baigent and Ben Cowell, 27–44. London: University of London Press: Institute of Historical Research, 2016.

Darling, Elizabeth. '"The Star in the Profession She Invented for Herself": A Brief Biography of Elizabeth Denby, Housing Consultant'. *Planning Perspectives* 20 (2005): 271–300.

Darling, Elizabeth and Lynne Walker. *AA Women in Architecture 1917–2017. Architectural Association Women in Architecture 1917–2017*. London: Architectural Association Publications, 2017.

Darling, Elizabeth and Whitworth Lesley (ed.). *Women and the Making of Built Space in England, 1870–1950*. Ashgate: Aldershot, 2007.

Dott, Annabel. 'Cottages for Disabled Officers'. *Architectural Review* (April 1918): 74–6.

Dott, Annabel. 'Cottages for Disabled Officers'. *The Nineteenth Century and After* 84 (July 1918): 160–70.

Dott, Annabel. 'The Woman Architect'. *Architectural Review* (December 1918): 31–3.

Dott, Annabel. 'The Disabled Officer in Rural Reconstruction'. *The Nineteenth Century and After* 85 (February 1919): 359–76.

Dott, Annabel. 'Homes of Honour'. *The Daily Telegraph* 8 (February 1919): 12.

Dott, Annabel. *The Church Times*. (28 March 1919): 298.

Dott, Annabel. 'A Debt of Honour'. *Church Times* 4 (April 1919): 322.

Dott, Annabel. 'The Work of a Woman Builder'. *The Woman's Leader* 16 (July 1920): 540.

Dott, Annabel. 'Gossip Seat: Woman Architect's Idea to Please Maids'. *Daily Mail* (21 March 1921): 7.

Gee, Emily. '"Where Shall She Live?": Housing the New Working Woman in Late Victorian and Edwardian London'. In *Living, Leisure and Law: Eight Building Types in England 1800–1941*, edited by Geoff Brandwood, 89–109. Reading: Spire, 2010.

Grimley, Matthew. *Citizenship, Community and the Church of England: Liberal Anglican Theories of the State between the Wars*. Oxford: Oxford University Press, 2004.

Jeremiah, D. 'Dartington Hall: A Landscape of an Exceptional Experiment in Rural Reconstruction'. In *The English Countryside between the Wars: Regeneration or Decline*, edited by P. Brassley, J. Burchley and L. Thompson, 116–31. Woodbridge: Boydell Press, 2006.

MacFarlane, B. 'Homes Fit for Heroines: Housing in the Twenties'. In *Making Space*, edited by Matrix, 26–36. London: Pluto Press.

Martin, Desmond. 'The Churches of Bishop Robert Gray & Mrs Sophia Gray: An Historical and Architectural Review' Unpublished PhD, University of Cape Town, Cape Town, 2002.

Martin, Desmond. The Bishop's Churches. Cape Town: Struik, 2005.

Mawson, T. H. An Imperial Obligation: Industrial Villages for Partially Disabled Soldiers and Sailors. London: G. Richards, 1917.

McKellar, Elizabeth. 'C. H. B. Quennell (1872–1935): Architecture, History and the Quest for the Modern'. Architectural History 50 (2007): 211–46.

Nuttgens, Patrick. Brierley in Yorkshire: The Architecture of the Turn of the Century. York: York Georgian Society, 1984.

Prochaska, Frank. Women and Philanthropy in Nineteenth-Century England. Oxford: Clarendon Press, 1980.

Scott Brown, Denise. 'Room at the Top? Sexism and the Star System'. In Gender, Space, Architecture: An Interdisciplinary Introduction, edited by J. Rendell, B. Penner and I. Borden, 258–65. London: Routledge, 2000.

Sugg Ryan, Deborah. Ideal Homes, 1918–39: Domestic Design and Suburban Modernism. Manchester: Manchester University Press, 2018.

Swenarton, Mark. Artisans and Architects: The Ruskinian Tradition in Architectural Thought. Palgrave: Macmillan, 1989.

Thackray, Deirdre M. 'Sophia Gray (1814–1871): An Architectural Apprenticeship for Home, Church and Empire'. MA diss., University of York, York, 2017.

Weiner, Deborah. 'The Architecture of Victorian Philanthropy: The Settlement House as Manorial Residence'. Art History 13, no. 2 (1990): 212–27.

Yeo, Eileen Janes (ed.). Radical Femininity: Women's Self-presentation in the Public Sphere. Manchester: Manchester University Press, 1998.

Websites

On Annabel Dott: https://northyorkshirehistory.blogspot.com/2019/02/mrs-annabel-dott-goathland-homes-for.html; http://yorkshire255.rssing.com/chan-10297851/latest.php (accessed 03 February 2019); https://www.eggsa.org/newspapers/index.php/south-african-magazine/332-south-africa-1909-4-october-december.html (accessed 11 September 2019).

On Frederick Green (1850–1927): https://www.artefacts.co.za/main/Buildings/archframes.php?archid=2010. (accessed 3 March 2020).

R. Hasted, Disability in Time and Place, Historic England: https://historicengland.org.uk/content/docs/research/disability-in-time-and-place-pdf/ (accessed 25 October 2019).

R. Hasted, Introductions to Heritage Assets: Domestic Housing for Disabled Veterans, 1900–2014, Historic England, 2016, 6, https://historicengland.org.uk/images-books/publications/iha-domestic-housing-for-disabled-veterans-1900-2014/ (accessed 28 November 2019).

Viscountess Barrington & Welfare Institute for Disabled Ex-Service Men Annual reports 1922 and 1930 at http://www.shrivenhamheritagesociety.co.uk/listing.asp?listID=381 (accessed 28 November 2019).

Women's Pioneer Housing website: https://www.insidehousing.co.uk/home/home/the-women-who-reinvented-housing-55400 (accessed 29 March 2018).

'Women's Print Media in Inter War Britain' website, Wilfrid Laurier University, Ontario: https://interwarfeminism.omeka.net/collections/show/4. (accessed 3 March 2020).

CHAPTER 10
STUDENT: HENRY MORRIS AND THE FIRST VILLAGE COLLEGES
Kieran Mahon

In 1924, Henry Morris, Chief Education Officer for Cambridgeshire between 1922 and 1954, wrote a short pamphlet with a long title that was to change the course of community education across the country. Initially self-published as *The Village College: Being a Memorandum on the Provision of Educational and Social Facilities for the Countryside with Special Reference to Cambridgeshire*,[1] it set out Morris's vision for the village college. It was a guide on how to merge the educational and ordinary life of the rural population and to create an institution that rivalled those found in towns. The college was to be a multifaceted building for several nearby villages, working as a senior school during the day and adult education and community centre in the evenings and weekends. The new institution would play a significant role in the reconstruction of rural Cambridgeshire, which at the time was the second poorest county in England, despite the affluence of Cambridge.[2]

Completed in 1939, the village college at Impington was the fourth of Morris's institutions to be opened and has long been considered the most architecturally significant. It was one of the few buildings designed in England by Walter Gropius in partnership with Maxwell Fry, revisions overseen by Jack Howe once Gropius had departed for the United States. The building's sleek, tempered modernism combined with its progressive programme charmed the architectural press and critics including Nikolaus Pevsner, whose claim that it was one of 'the best buildings of its date in England, if not the best' has been often repeated.[3] Impington was realized through a progressive network of architects, educators and philanthropists determined to show the public what modernism could do for community education and is an important reminder of how vibrant architectural activity could be before the outbreak of the Second World War.

It was, however, only one part of the story. As this chapter will show, Impington was the culmination of a much longer trajectory of Morris's ideas about community education, architecture and rural reconstruction, ideas forged in the lead up to and aftermath of the war. Impington's influence, and that of its architects, in particular Gropius, has meant that it is often cited as a key turning point for how school design

---

[1]From here on it is referred to as the *Memorandum*; Morris initially self-published the pamphlet in 1924. In 1925 it was republished by Cambridge University Press and again funded by Morris.

[2]Tony Jeffs, *Henry Morris: Village Colleges, Community Education and the Ideal Order* (Nottingham: Educational Heretics Press, 1998): 24.

[3]Nikolaus Pevsner, *Cambridgeshire: The Buildings of England No.10* (London: Penguin, 1970): 412–13.

could be sensitively shaped by modernism, partly paving the way for the Ministry of Education's array of prefabricated building experiments after the Second World War. While recent work has rightly questioned this, it has meant that the specificity of Morris's ideas and the architectural development of the first three village colleges have been somewhat overlooked.[4]

This chapter seeks to redress this through a discussion of the conceptual and architectural designs of the first four village colleges and traces elements of their philosophical origins and contemporary influences. Morris's concept of the village college – a vision that extended beyond Gropius's designs – was shaped by pre-war ideas and wartime experiences. An examination of accepted pedagogical and school-building practices in the 1920s and 1930s shows how far the village colleges departed from educational and architectural convention. The *Memorandum*, shaped by the author's formative years, is an indispensable source for understanding the educator's vision of how the village colleges would work in educational, social and architectural terms. The programme's detailed description reveals distinct spatial relationships which can be read architecturally, showing how the architecture of progressive education was formed, represented and constituted through written documents and networks, as well as through the materiality and images of the buildings themselves. Analysing the design of the first three colleges establishes the basis for a reconsideration of Impington's importance, clarifying the innovations Gropius brought to the project, alongside those Morris had already set in motion.[5]

Morris's formative years: Childhood, Oxford and the war

Understanding Morris's personal, educational and religious experiences contextualizes the village college concept. Born in 1889 in Southport, Lancashire, Henry Morris was the seventh of eight children. He came from a humble background: his mother died when he was young and his father, a plumber, brought up their family in a small

---

[4]See Alan Powers, *Bauhaus Goes West: Modern Art and Design in Britain and America* (London: Thames & Hudson, 2019): 66–70.

[5]Historians of education and former staff members of the village colleges have paid close attention to the educator's life and work. These accounts include M. Dybeck, *The Village College Way* (Cambridge: Cambridgeshire County Council, 1981); D. Farnell, *Henry Morris: An Architect of Education,* MA diss. (Cambridge Institute of Education, 1968); Tony Jeffs, *Henry Morris: Village Colleges, Community Education and the Ideal Order* (Nottingham: Educational Heretics Press, 1998). The most complete biography remains Rée's *Educator Extraordinary* (1973), which draws on Morris's letters and interviews of people who knew him. Architectural historians regularly note Morris's scheme thanks to Gropius's involvement, something which has recently resurfaced following the Bauhaus centenary. See Leyla Daybelge and Magnus Englund, *Isokon and the Bauhaus in Britain* (London: Pavilion Books Group, 2019); Fiona MacCarthy, *Gropius: The Man Who Built the Bauhaus* (Cambridge, MA: Harvard University Press, 2019); Nikolaus Pevsner, *Cambridgeshire: The Buildings of England No.10* (London: Penguin, 1970); Alan Powers, *Bauhaus Goes West: Modern Art and Design in Britain and America* (London: Thames & Hudson, 2019); Andrew Saint, *Towards a Social Architecture: The Role of School-Building in Post-War England* (New Haven and London: Yale University Press, 1987).

semi-detached house. Morris attended the local elementary school until he was fourteen when he secured a job at the local paper, the *Southport Visiter*, and was soon promoted to reporter. His meagre experience of compulsory schooling instilled in him an ambition to shift the focus of learning from childhood to youth and maturity, as well as from didactic discourse to more active ways of learning. Outside work, Morris was involved with the local Anglican Church, organizing events and concerts in the church hall. Rée suggests it was the influence of a local vicar who encouraged him to continue his education at the Harris Institute at Preston which provided a variety of courses for older students.[6] In 1910, he entered full-time university education to read Theology at St David's University College, Lampeter. There he took the first part of an Oxford degree which enabled him to enter Exeter College, Oxford. The influence of religion and the church had a profound effect; he insisted that the architect's obligation was to evoke 'the numinous, that sense of awe'.[7] In later life he spoke about the need of towns to build community centres where people could pass their time in learning and living and wrote: 'I would myself include places for worship, silence and meditation, where the sense of the sacred and eternal could be nourished.'[8]

At Oxford, Morris's tutor was the theologian and historian Hastings Rashdall, author of a three-volume history of the European universities of the Middle Ages, and one of the few individuals that Morris acknowledged as an influence. Rashdall nurtured Morris's intellectual development and faith in the value of education, likely introducing him to the ideas of T. H. Green, a central figure of the British Idealist movement and one of the intellectual progenitors of the New Liberalism, a social and political philosophy with a pervasive influence among progressives in the first decades of the twentieth century.[9] Morris, along with other progressive educators such as John Dewey, Edmond Holmes and Michael Sadler, was very much a product of the Idealist tradition, believing that the transformation of society and the promotion of the 'good life' depended on both citizens' moral attitudes and governmental reform. The village colleges were to later reflect this belief, materially and spatially, enabling active citizens to become their best selves through direct involvement with their community, thus reconciling the twin ideals of communitarianism and individual freedom.[10]

It is also probable that Morris discovered the residential settlement movement through Oxford; settlements, such as Toynbee Hall established by Canon Samuel Barnett, provided a template for the future village colleges. These centres were not just dispensers of charity but research, community and educational hubs where those from privileged and educated backgrounds could live and share their knowledge with poorer neighbours. Although these settlements were mostly urban and did not supply full-time schooling, they influenced other experiments in community education. In 1914, for

---

[6]Rée, *Educator Extraordinary*: 7–11.
[7]Morris cited in Rée, *Educator Extraordinary*: 12.
[8]Ibid.: 12.
[9]Jeffs, *Henry Morris*: 10.
[10]Ibid.: 13.

instance, the Arts and Crafts architect and designer C. R. Ashbee, who had had a long association with Toynbee Hall, wrote *The Hamptonshire Experiment in Education*. The book drew from his experience of Arts and Crafts education and was a blueprint for a new type of school that responded to the needs of rural communities.[11] Settlements, like the village college, were often designed to form a society in microcosm, a social laboratory capable of achieving on a small scale what eventually might be secured on a larger or universal scale. Morris, too, wanted his scheme to become a national network of rural school-based settlements fostering fellowship, association, neighbourliness and a sense of community.[12]

By November 1914 Morris had joined up and was posted to the Inns of Court Officers Training Corps and later commissioned in the Royal Army Service Corps. He served as supply officer to the 41st Division and was a staff officer with the 14th Corps in Italy from 1915 to 1919, reaching the rank of captain and mentioned in despatches. It is difficult to overstate the formative impact the war had on Morris and other young men like him who did not attend the public schools but became officers. The experience that commissions gave them opened doors in the post-war world which would have otherwise remained closed. As an officer he learned about administrative responsibility and leadership and by the time the war was over he had adopted the gestures and voice of a successful public-school product. But the social transformation came at a terrible cost and the war was an episode which Morris rarely spoke about. He had experienced the horrors of the front, losing his friends as well as his faith; during his last days in hospital in 1961, he was heard saying: 'I've seen men hanging on the wire.'[13] Morris was demobilized in 1919 and needed only one more year at Oxford to complete his degree but he could not stay, likely haunted by the memories of better days with lost friends. He also lost the desire to enter the Church – perhaps studying Theology now felt futile – so he transferred to King's College, Cambridge, to read Philosophy. After graduating, he served a brief apprenticeship at the Kent Education Offices. In 1921 he moved back to Cambridge to be assistant secretary for education in the county offices. Following his predecessor's death in 1922, he succeeded as chief education officer at the age of thirty-three.[14]

Accounts of Morris describe him as a complex, mercurial and often contradictory character. Undeterred by his youth or lack of experience, he brought dynamic zeal to his leadership style, which was both inspiring and infuriating to work with. Through his educational experiences, he became attached to the university ideal and developed

---

[11]'C.R. Ashbee', *King's College Cambridge*, https://www.kings.cam.ac.uk/archive-centre/online-resources/online-exhibitions/c-r-ashbee – toc-5 (accessed 24 March 2020). In 1887 Ashbee and his students redecorated Toynbee Hall's Dining Room in line with Ruskin's principles on the dignity of manual work. Through this project, Ashbee had the idea of establishing a new art school, which opened the following year as the Guild and School of Handicraft at Mile End in East London. In 1902, drawn to the rural idyll, Ashbee relocated the Guild to Chipping Camden in the Cotswolds.

[12]Jeffs, *Henry Morris*: 15–18.

[13]Rée, *Educator Extraordinary*: 10.

[14]Ibid.: 10–11.

a social conscience that sought to enrich the quality of compulsory schooling and community education. While his ideas for the reconstruction of education were radical for his time, he endeavoured to maintain their respectability, a tendency which also reached into his personal life as he sublimated his gay identity and was wary of sectional interests and extreme politics.[15] Although he admired Sidney and Beatrice Webb and was sympathetic with the left, he was critical of ideological and minority fanaticism. Instead, he was for the 'scientific commonwealth' – a term he used to describe an absence of irrational anger – and firmly believed in democratic local government, pragmatism, and education as a process where 'the ideal order and the actual order can ultimately be made one'.[16] These beliefs and values, alongside his life experience thus far, went on to shape the *Memorandum* and the eventual formulation of the village college experiment.

Attitudes to pedagogy and school-building

Working in the county offices, Morris would have been aware of educational and architectural developments at state level, some of which shaped his vision of how the village college was to work pedagogically and spatially. In the first half of the twentieth century two themes dominated government responses to state education: the health of the population and access to secondary schools, both of which stemmed from concerns about national performance and international competitiveness. These influenced attitudes to school-building.[17] To offer guidance on these issues, a consultative committee, chaired by Sir William Henry Hadow, was set up and published six reports between 1923 and 1933.[18] Some of its most important recommendations related to the structure of the national school system and curriculum. It advised that the school system be further divided into stages from junior to senior and hoped to encourage new ideas for school design by giving greater autonomy to local county authorities. The 1926 Hadow Report advised that the curriculum should be planned holistically, with subjects taught in relation to each other and practical work provided to stimulate pupils' capacities; it was to promote learners' interests in formal education as well as in their later lives, preparing them for future occupations. In 1931 the committee published an official expression of 'progressive ideas' suggesting that the curriculum was to be thought of in 'terms of activity and experience rather than knowledge to be acquired and facts stored'.[19] With

[15]Ibid.: 15–16, 59.

[16]Morris cited in Rée, *Educator Extraordinary*: 14.

[17]Andrew Saint, *Towards a Social Architecture: The Role of School-Building in Post-War England* (New Haven; London: Yale University Press, 1987): 35–8.

[18]Derek Gillard, 'The Hadow Reports: An Introduction', *Education in England: The History of Our Schools*, http://www.educationengland.org.uk/articles/24hadow.html (accessed 5 January 2020). The six reports were 'Differentiation of the Curriculum for Boys and Girls' (1923), 'Psychological Tests of Educable Capacity' (1924), 'The Education of the Adolescent' (1926), 'Books in Public Elementary Schools' (1928), 'The Primary School' (1931) and 'Infant and Nursery Schools' (1933).

[19]Ibid.

this in mind, Morris's critique of 'pedagogic fallacy' – the tendency teachers have of trying to educate adolescents with exercises and materials suitable only for very mature or gifted young pupils – chimed with the more progressive elements of the government's education policy making.[20]

Such optimism, however, did not correspond with the architectural reality of 1920s and 1930s educational environments. Schools were mainly designed by local-authority architects working to written briefs without consultation from the teaching profession, a practice against which Morris railed.[21] In accordance with the Board of Education's rules and regulations, these briefs detailed the accommodation to be provided, perpetuating conventional teaching practice, which were in turn codified in the school's spaces. Classrooms were set out in lines of pavilions or packed more closely together in blocks, and tended to be grouped together off corridors, lined with rows of rigid locker-desks and orientated towards a blackboard. The semiotics of this spatial arrangement spoke to the authority and expertise of the teacher, dispensing their knowledge to attentive, disciplined children, rather than promoting a more progressive philosophy of student-centred learning.[22]

Historians of this period have shown how school building was shaped by imperatives of economics, science, hygiene and national efficiency that sought to produce a nation of effective, democratically responsible and healthy citizens.[23] Indicative of this tendency was Felix Clay's appointment as architect to the Board of Education between 1902 and 1927, replacing E. R. Robson, which marked the start of a fundamental shift in attitudes to school building that continued well into the 1920s. Clay's appointment saw developments that focused less on conventions of architectural plan and elevation, and more on the management of internal space.[24] Growing recognition of the benefits of through-ventilation, ample sunlight and the value of a hall in which noise did not disturb the surrounding classrooms led to the development of spread-out lines of single-storey buildings, later known as the pavilion plan. While surveillance was never abandoned, it was superseded by an emphasis on a healthy environment for all pupils, a concern that can be traced back to multiple sources, including the work of mid-nineteenth-century public health reformers such as Edwin Chadwick, Margaret McMillan's open-air nursery school in Deptford (opened 1914), and the child-study movement in the United States which

---

[20]Rée, *Educator Extraordinary*: 81.

[21]See UCL Institute of Education Archives/Papers of Harry Alfred Rée, HR19/21. In a talk to the RIBA on 26 April 1945 Morris criticized the practice of only using official county architects as it failed to exploit creative talent across the industry.

[22]Saint, *Towards a Social Architecture*: 37.

[23]See Geraint Franklin, *Inner-London Schools 1918–44: A Thematic Study* (English Heritage, 2009); Elain Harwood, *England's Schools: History, Architecture and Adaptation* (Swindon: English Heritage, 2010); Malcolm Seaborne and Roy Lowe, *The English School: Its Architecture and Organisation, Vol 2 (1870–1970)* (Trowbridge and Esher: Routledge & Kegan Paul Ltd., 1977).

[24]Tom Hulme, '"A Nation Depends on Its Children": School Buildings and Citizenship in England and Wales, 1900–1939', *Journal of British Studies* 54 (2015): 411.

developed new forms of education based on the capabilities and characteristics of children throughout the first half of the twentieth century.

Following the war, social commentators continued to highlight how defects of the body prevented efficient citizenship as well as military advantage. As a result, the physical ideal of the 'good citizen' remained primarily the strong, healthy male body well into the 1920s.[25] To provide for this, schools had to be hygienic and provide for physical needs: classrooms were to be sunny and airy with sufficient lavatories and clean drinking water supplied. When Clay republished the third edition of *Modern School Buildings* in 1929, this change became apparent at the level of central government. Instead of mechanical ventilation, the principle was free cross-ventilation with adequately sized windows on both sides of a room that would provide efficient lighting.[26] In 1936 the Board of Education published its first school-building guidelines since 1926, replacing earlier regulations that had become obsolete in the face of rapid development of elementary education after the war. These gave further attention to the sensory experience of the school; nurseries were advised to use rubber, cork or linoleum instead of floorboards. Similarly, in elementary and secondary schools, architects were encouraged to use wooden blocks instead of floorboards to improve acoustics, as well as coating walls with sound absorbers such as perforated fibre slabs or porous plaster. The opening up of the main block produced a wide range of arrangement and experimentation and throughout the 1920s most elementary schools had incorporated features of the pavilion design with neo-Georgian details remaining popular. One popular variation of this was the quadrangle arrangement that enabled cross-ventilated pavilion-style classrooms with bilateral lighting while retaining a more compact plan. Clay approved of its aesthetic association, both monastic and collegiate, ideals that were also reflected in the first village college.[27]

The *Memorandum*

In the summer of 1924 Morris spent a week in Oxfordshire at the home of J. W. Robertson Scott, founder of *The Countryman*.[28] While there he drafted the twenty-four-page *Memorandum*, which outlined his vision for how the village college scheme would work. The importance of this writing is difficult to overstate; the dissemination of Morris's ideas on educational architecture was a defining aspect of the project and enabled the buildings to be realized. It provided both the programme and a succinct, persuasive

---

[25]Ibid.: 418–19.

[26]Ibid.: 412; Saint, *Towards a Social* Architecture: 38.

[27]Felix Clay, *Modern School Buildings Elementary and Secondary: A Handbook on the Planning, Arrangement, and Fitting of Day and Boarding Schools* (Edinburgh: B.T. Batsford Ltd, 1929): 165.

[28]Launched in 1927 and still in circulation today, the magazine reports on rural issues for people who live and work in the countryside. Robertson Scott, also its first editor, wanted it to challenge overly sentimentalized representations of the countryside. Although his biographers do not say how they met, the relationship presumably equipped Morris with a deeper understanding of contemporary rural issues.

narrative for publicity, which appealed to a range of supporters including educators, policymakers, international financial sponsors and the architectural press.

The pamphlet began with Morris outlining what he termed the 'rural problem', the process of the countryside falling behind the urban centres economically, educationally and culturally, which had a highly detrimental effect on the welfare of rural communities. He argued that the sources of the problem were multiple. Rural de-population, often viewed as a natural by-product of industrialization had, by the 1920s, been a feature of British life for at least eighty years.[29] Rapid population increases in urban centres had attracted the attention and concerns of reformers and politicians more than the quieter countryside and gaps in educational standards between town and country increased. This was compounded by the neo-feudal structure of rural society which contributed to the departure of more able individuals as well as the failings of a weakening school system. The 'squirearchy' and middle classes who controlled local government often did not want to increase rates to pay for better schools and services that might upset the balance of power within their communities. Wider debates around rural renewal and change stemmed from these structural issues, as well as from the physical encroachment of the towns into the countryside, which led to the creation of bodies like the Council for the Preservation of Rural England, set up in 1926.

In particular, Morris observed how the small size and scattered nature of the villages and their schools made their organization and coordination difficult. Teaching staff were underqualified and the more academically able children were often drawn to the better equipped grammar or technical schools nearly always found in the towns. Urban schools were disconnected from the life of the countryside so when leaving school, pupils either stayed there for work or if they did return to the villages, they had little preparation for how to adjust or succeed in the context of rural life.[30] To address these issues, he set out a series of steps which would 'afford the palpable and concrete demonstration of rural reconstruction' in order to reorientate the life of Cambridgeshire through a system of village colleges.[31]

Morris's first recommendation was that the small primary and senior schools across the countryside be consolidated into larger centres, allowing them to be more easily organized as well as benefit from economies of scale and improved accommodation. But simple reorganization of the school system was not enough. A village college was required to unite and coordinate the educational and social agencies which had previously existed in isolation: 'an amalgamation which, while preserving the individuality and function of each, will assemble them into a whole and make possible their expression for the first time in a new institution, single but many-sided, for the countryside.'[32] The aim for the scheme was to establish about ten centres, a system of village colleges to provide for the coordination and development of all forms of education, from primary level to old age,

---

[29]Jeffs, *Henry Morris*: 24.
[30]Morris cited in Jeffs, *Henry Morris*: 25.
[31]Morris, 'The Village College': 157.
[32]Ibid.: 147.

together with social and recreational facilities and the provision of a community centre for the neighbourhood.

By shifting the emphasis to life-long learning, Morris sought to unify the ordinary and educational life of the countryside as well as increase democratic participation through each college's shared management. Active citizenship was more than just the obligation to vote; it required individuals to cultivate their best self, pursue the common good and better themselves through institutions and habits which made the welfare of all the welfare of each.[33] He claimed that the village college could realize this because it was not a foreign institution enforced on the community but instead drew from its pre-existing traditions across a network of villages. It was to be a union of local social services and a composite home for various voluntary bodies of the countryside, thus cementing education into the life of the community.

Of significant importance for the design development of the buildings was Morris's articulation of the project's architectural requirements laid out in the *Memorandum*, which enabled educator and architect to work collaboratively to realize each village college. The scheme was presented in terms of rural reconstruction as well as spatially, as a set of social relationships to be nurtured and synthesized throughout the plan of the new architectural typology. No less than twelve different types of interiors for education, recreation and community use were detailed, along with outdoor spatial requirements such as recreation grounds and school gardens. The multifunctional programming and the relationships between several of these spaces were defined. The hall, for instance, was to be used by the school as an assembly hall, for the midday meal, physical training and plays and concerts during the day, while in the evenings it would serve the community for events such as performances, lectures, dances or other public meetings. Adult evening classrooms were to be shared by different associations or societies and held in the school's practical learning spaces, such as the handicraft workshop or the domestic science room. Used in conjunction with the agriculture education room, a science laboratory was also to be made available and crop demonstrations were to be organized at nearby farms. A library was to house a permanent book collection as well as a reading room for newspapers and periodicals, providing a learning resource which people could 'freely pass to and fro' on their way to classrooms, lecture rooms or demonstration plots.[34] The balance between the senior school, adult activities and community centre was to be carefully maintained so no single group dominated the building's use. Morris illustrated the balance with a simple three-winged diagram that formed two open courts in plan (**Figure 10.1**). One wing represented the school, one was for adult education and recreation, and the central one was for the social and welfare provision for the whole community.

In addition to programme requirements, Morris included a section entitled 'Architecture', discussing the philosophy of design from which the colleges should

---

[33]Jeffs, *Henry* Morris: 13.
[34]Morris, 'The Village College': 148.

Figure 10.1 Morris's illustration in the *Memorandum* showing how the village college might be visualized as two three-sided courts in Henry Morris, *The Village College: Being a Memorandum on the Provision of Educational and Social Facilities for the Countryside, with Special Reference to Cambridgeshire* (Cambridge: Cambridge University Press, 1925)

benefit. He was critical of most rural schools which were 'often bad and seldom beautiful' and equated good architecture with good design, something which was simple and aesthetically pleasing. Morris therefore called for the architect to design:

> A building which will express the spirit of the English countryside which it is intended to grace, something of its humaneness and modesty, something of the age-long and permanent dignity of husbandry; a building that will give the countryside a centre of reference arousing the affection and loyalty of the country child and country people, and conferring significance on their way of life? ... in such a synthesis architecture will find a fresh and widespread means of expression. If the village college is a true and workable conception, the institution will, with various modifications, speed over rural England; and in course of time a new series of worthy public buildings will stand side by side with the parish churches of the countryside.[35]

Again, Morris insisted that the village college would not be a foreign institution enforced on the rural community but instead would draw from local traditions and bring them together into relation, both socially and architecturally, to enhance the existing culture. Its architecture, along with bringing the different aspects of the village college programme together, had capacity for further synthesis. By being locally available and providing for the needs of the whole family, it would abolish the 'duality of education and ordinary life'. It would bring citizens together to become 'a training ground of a rural democracy', finally bringing together good government and self-government. All this was to provide an opportunity for 'creative architecture', a type of noble and public architecture for the English countryside that the state had not yet been able to supply.[36]

---

[35]Ibid.: 153–4.
[36]Ibid.: 155.

On returning to Cambridge, Morris submitted the *Memorandum* to the County Council. They were impressed and agreed in February 1925 to implement the plans on the condition that they were not to entail any further expenditure.[37] In response, Morris demonstrated exceptional independence in both thought and action as Chief Education Officer, a role which was typically managerial and educational, implementing the policies of the Local Education Authority as expressed in Council and Education Committee meetings. To convince these committees of the feasibility of his public plans, he realized he had to raise private money. This set Morris on an energetic programme of fundraising, later being referred to as an 'expert beggar'.[38] By 1927 he had secured several donations to secure the first village college, the largest of which came from the Carnegie Trust for £5,400, who he had directly appealed to in the final pages of the *Memorandum*. Most notably, however, in 1929 Morris borrowed his fare to the United States and secured a grant from the Spelman Fund of New York for £45,000.[39] Faced with such sizeable financial support, the council were practically obliged to enact the scheme; this fundraising strategy established a future pattern for how Morris secured committee support.

The first three village colleges: Sawston, Bottisham and Linton

In 1930, five years after the council approved Morris's plan, the first village college at Sawston was opened by the Prince of Wales. It was designed by county architect H. H. Dunn in consultation with James Shearer, the latter chosen and paid for by the Carnegie Trust.[40] Neo-Georgian in style, it took the form of a symmetrical three-sided open court with the hall placed at its centre, flanked by rooms for manual instruction and domestic science. The south wing featured a low, enclosed arcade that connected the adult education rooms, as well as the library, medical services and the agriculture education room. Across the grass court and fountain stood the north wing composed of five classrooms for the use of the senior school. The yellow bricks, red pantile gables and hipped roofs set in the quadrangle arrangement made it the most formal of all the village colleges. It reflected Morris's desire to recreate the university-like, collegiate atmosphere he had known at Cambridge, fusing the domestic with the civic.

---

[37]Jeffs, *Henry Morris*: 42; Rée, *Educator Extraordinary*: 28. Jeffs points out that the educational authority had no jurisdiction over Cambridge, something which further limited the resources at Morris's disposal.
[38]Rée, *Educator Extraordinary*: 39. The author uses the phrase which came from Leonard Elmhirst who described Morris as one of 'the more expert of beggars'.
[39]Rée, *Educator Extraordinary*: 48.
[40]Ibid. 32 and 43. Herbert Henry Dunn (fl.1882–1925) specialized in school buildings, making additions in 1904–1908 to the De Aston Comprehensive School in Market Rasen, Lincolnshire, and to the County School for Boys in Cambridge. He designed Kesteven and Grantham Girls' School which opened in 1910 and made references to vernacular and Queen Anne styles. Following his work at Sawston, he designed the Shire Hall in Cambridge (1931–1932). See 'Kesteven and Grantham Girls' School', *Historic England*, https://historicengland. org.uk/listing/the-list/list-entry/1412888 (accessed 5 January 2020).

There are other associations at play: Morris's architectural tastes were informed by Geoffrey Scott's *Architecture of Humanism* (1914). Scott related classical principles to human proportions and humane values, arguing that when we look at a building we 'transcribe architecture in terms of ourselves'.[41] For contemporaries, neo-Georgian civic design could be deeply symbolic of social welfare and community needs, offering a way to reintegrate aesthetics with ethics.[42] There was, in other words, serious architectural ambition in Sawston's design, married to developed social and political ideals: it was neither as conventional nor conservative for its time as has been assumed and often unfavourably compared to the later modernist village colleges. Instead, this was a building that embodied a modern understanding of rural life, while tracing a history of human endeavour and achievement in the countryside. It was the first county school of its size to have a separate hall, a wing specially built and suitably furnished for adults and the first to have a library for shared use by the school and by the community. It featured a youth employment office as well as a mechanics workshop, geared towards agricultural engineering, funded by the Elmhirsts of Dartington.[43] There were playing fields for use by both village and school, a medical services room and Warden's house.[44] Many of these features were to become commonplace but in 1930 they were innovative and gave important impetus to the village college scheme.

The economic crisis of the early 1930s slowed progress and the next village college did not open until 1937. In between, however, an important shift took place in Morris's awareness of modernist architecture, art and design, which highlights the collaborative nature of the scheme and the influence of his wider networks. The most significant of these contacts was Morris's friendship with designer and entrepreneur Jack Pritchard, formed while they were both studying at Cambridge. Pritchard, through his later research trips to Europe, had met Gropius and in 1934 helped facilitate the architect's escape from the Nazi regime. On his arrival to London, the German architect moved into the recently finished Lawn Road Flats in Hampstead and Pritchard employed him in his new business venture, the Isokon Furniture Company. Within the first few weeks Pritchard had introduced him to Morris and despite Gropius's basic command of English, Pritchard was impressed how quickly they understood each other. A visit to Cambridge was organized and Morris was soon won over to the cause of modernist design: '[Gropius's] conversation and many months of study of modern architecture

[41]Geoffrey Scott, *Architecture of Humanism: A Study in the History of Taste* (Boston and New York: Houghton Mifflin Company, 1914): 213.
[42]For instance, see Neal Shasore, '"A Stammering Bundle of Welsh Idealism": Arthur Trystan Edwards and Principles of Civic Design in Interwar Britain', *Architectural History* 61 (2018): 179.
[43]In 1925 Dorothy and Leonard Elmhirst bought Dartington Hall in Devon and set up a community with experimental interests in rural reconstruction and progressive education. Dorothy Elmhirst was a millionaire philanthropist who supported charitable causes, many of which aligned with their own project. Morris first wrote to the Elmhirsts in 1928, visited Dartington in the same year, and in 1929, after several requests, they supported Morris's scheme with a grant of £1,000.
[44]Rée, *Educator Extraordinary*: 43. The term 'warden' was Morris's equivalent for headmaster, to further differentiate it from a school, and some details of the position are outlined in the *Memorandum*.

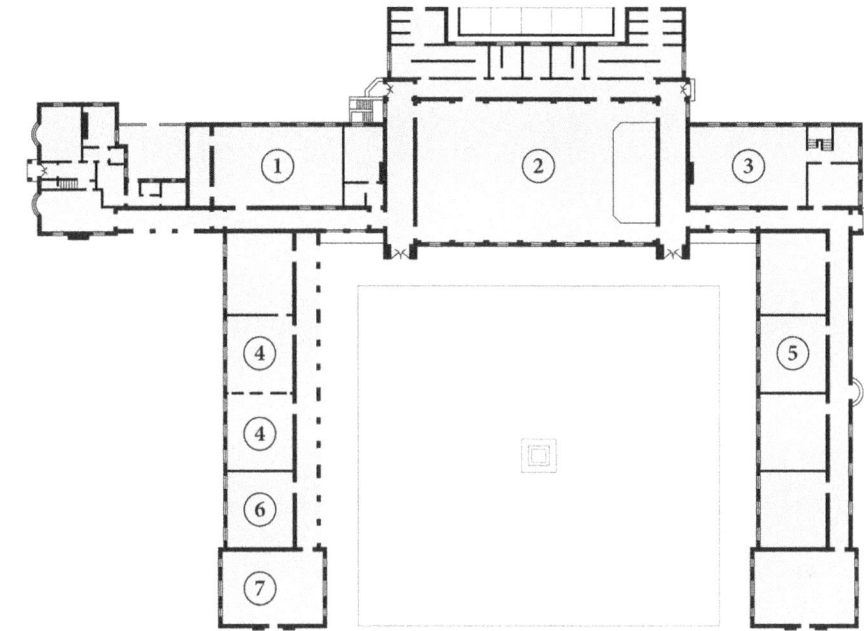

1 Manual Instruction
2 Hall
3 Domestic Science
4 Adult Education
5 Classroom Wing
6 Agriculture
7 Library

Figure 10.2 Ground floor plan, Sawston Village College (1930). Architect: H. H. Dunn. Courtesy UCL Institute of Education/Papers of Harry Alfred Rée (HR27/9), drawn by Gemma Fowlie

techniques confirm me in the necessity of doing all contemporary buildings without regard to traditional style' **(Figure 10.2)**.[45]

In January 1937 the second village college at Bottisham opened, designed by county architect S. E. Urwin **(Figure 10.3)**. Programmatically it remained almost the same as Sawston, drawing some 240 pupils aged between eleven and fifteen, from ten nearby

---

[45]David Elliott, 'Gropius in England', in Charlotte Benton (ed.), *A Different World: Émigré Architects in Britain 1928–1958* (London: RIBA, 1995): 112; Daybelge and Englund, *Isokon and the Bauhaus in Britain,* 86 and 126.

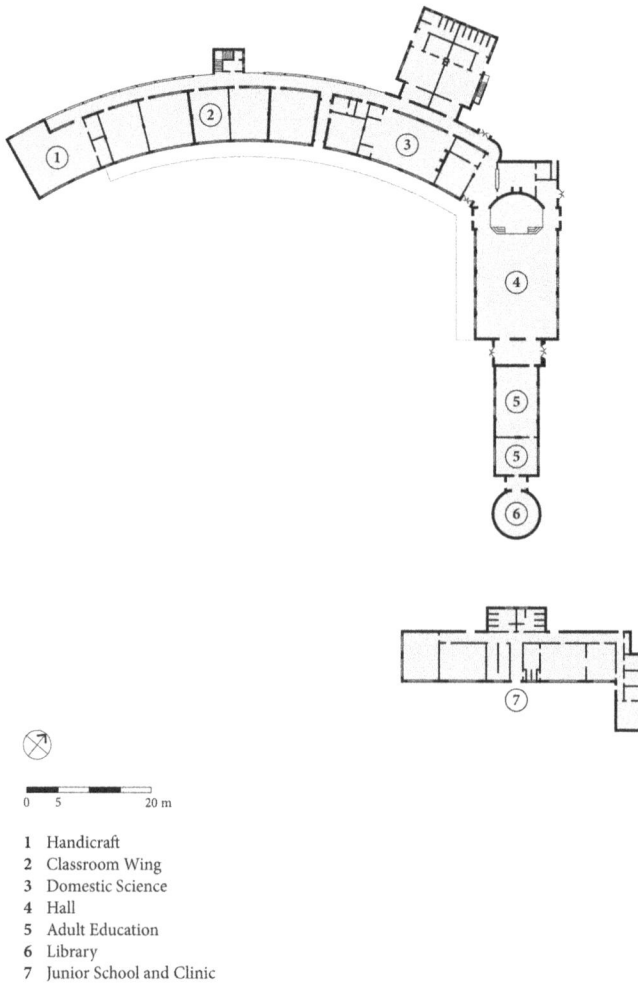

1 Handicraft
2 Classroom Wing
3 Domestic Science
4 Hall
5 Adult Education
6 Library
7 Junior School and Clinic

Figure 10.3 Ground floor plan, Bottisham Village College (1937). Architect: S. E. Urwin. Courtesy *Architects' Journal*, drawn by Gemma Fowlie

villages during the day and used as an adult education and community centre in the evenings and weekends. The important changes were in style and plan. It followed a more restrained, *moderne* idiom and with it a significant increase in glazing. The influence of the open-air school movement can be seen in the large, glazed, folding classroom doors and covered walkways which bring users into more regular contact with fresh air and sunlight. Construction was again in yellow brick, placed on concrete foundations but this time with a steel-framed assembly hall with brick filling, woodblock floors and underfloor heating coils.[46]

---

[46]'Village College, Bottisham', *Architects' Journal* (May 1937): 783–7.

The asymmetrical plan, formed of two separate blocks, was principally single-storey and looser than at Sawston. The main block comprised an entrance, assembly hall and adult wing on a north-south axis. At the north end, a gently curving classroom range – a form which would reappear at Impington – reached out on the east-west axis, suggesting two sides of an open court. Immediately to the south of the main block a small nursery and junior school were built, which included medical rooms, supporting Morris's vision to cater for the welfare of all ages.[47] The *Architects' Journal* reported that the design and equipment within the building was a result of a 'co-operative effort' between the Education Committee, warden and officers of the Board of Education.[48] Close attention was paid to designing tables for the domestic science room, and bright colours were selected throughout. The junior school was treated with primrose, pink, blue, red and orange, while the senior school classrooms were painted with more subdued colours.

Urwin also designed the third village college at Linton, which opened a few months later in March 1937 (**Figure 10.4**). In programme and style it followed his previous work: another low, elegant *moderne* idiom with yellow, handmade bricks. The plan evolved again and, while still asymmetrical, it was closer to Sawston's three-sided court though with a different sequence of spaces. The hall, for instance, was placed off the central axis, in the east wing, next to the main entrance. The classroom wing was straightened but the large sliding doors were retained, facing the south-east to benefit from maximum sunlight. Each classroom's relationship with the exterior was reinforced by steps leading out onto the central grass court. Linton's innovations were subtle but important for what Impington could build on. Although a small entrance hall had been included at Bottisham, a larger crush hall now appeared – a space which evolved significantly at Impington, more successfully uniting the college's various functions.[49] Another innovation was the development of specialized and practical teaching spaces. Even though some of these were included at Sawston, at Linton an art room, practical laboratory, domestic science and needlework room were added. Classroom interiors evolved too with built-in cupboards for storage and pigeon-hole accommodation for each scholar instead of locker desks, the furniture designed by the architect in collaboration with Morris.[50] The colour scheme was chosen by Gropius's Bauhaus colleague László Moholy-Nagy, who

---

[47]Rée, *Educator Extraordinary*: 40; Morris, 'The Village College': 149. Writing to request financial support in 1929, Morris informed Leonard Elmhirst that a nursery school was intended to be included for each college. These were not only for early childhood education but also for the education and training of older girls and parents. Morris wanted to 'realise some of the objectives of the Merrill Palmer School' which he had recently visited in Detroit. Morris outlines the college providing a nursery school room which would also serve as an Infant Welfare Centre as well as a primary school for children aged five to ten.

[48]'Village College, Bottisham', *Architects' Journal* (May 1937): 787.

[49]Samuel E. Urwin, 'Tendencies in School Design: A Paper Read before the British Association', *The Builder* (September 2, 1938): 421. Urwin suggested the crush hall be a space every school should be provided with so scholars could congregate and achieved by increasing the width of a corridor to 15 or 20 feet and located near the entrance and cloak rooms.

[50]'Village College, Linton, Cambs', *Architects' Journal* (October 1937): 573–7.

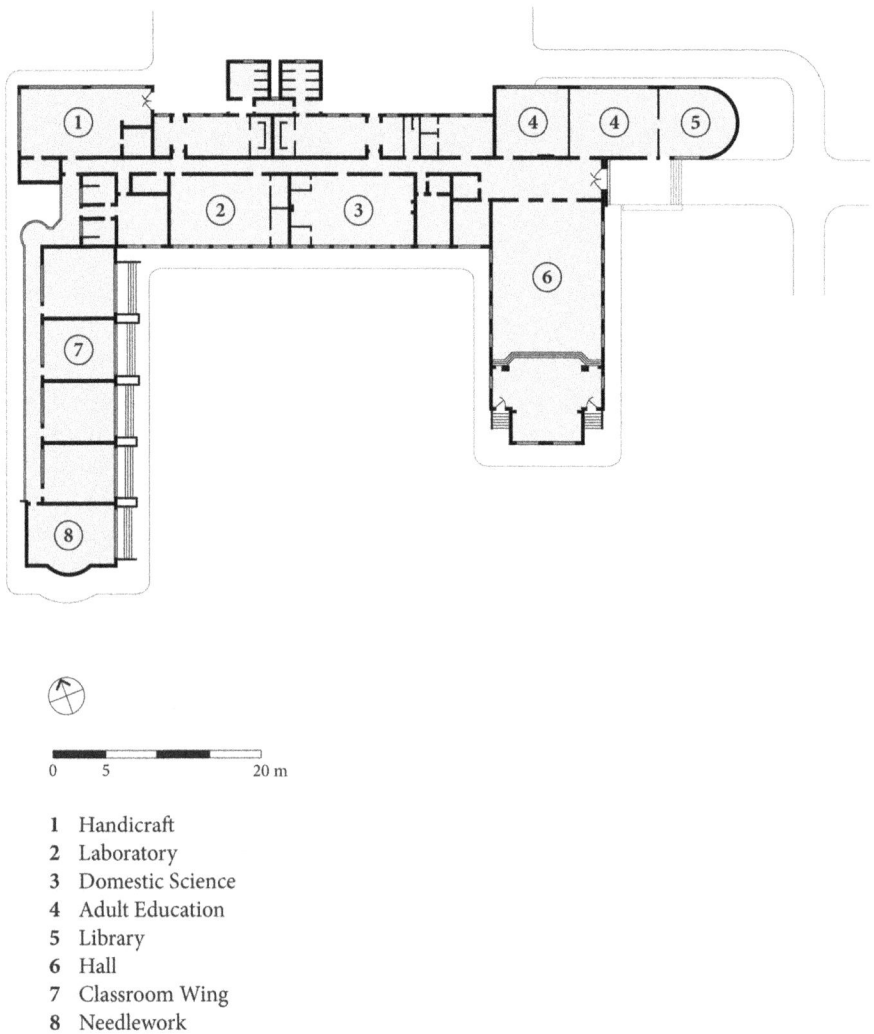

Figure 10.4 Ground floor plan, Linton Village College (1937). Architect: S. E. Urwin. Courtesy *Architects' Journal*, drawn by Gemma Fowlie

1 Handicraft
2 Laboratory
3 Domestic Science
4 Adult Education
5 Library
6 Hall
7 Classroom Wing
8 Needlework

had arrived in London in 1935 and was introduced to Morris possibly during his short stay at the Lawn Road Flats.[51]

The evolving specialization of learning spaces within the first three colleges evidenced the importance Morris placed on aesthetic and practical education, something that for him would dissolve divisions between the vocational and the academic and allow for greater self-expression. Like other Idealists, Morris believed individual self-realization

---

[51]Powers, *Bauhaus Goes West*: 66, 109.

was inseparable from participation in the communal life of society and good citizenship. And although gendered spaces for domestic science and needlework seem conservative by today's standards, recent scholarship has argued that these kinds of activities were defined as a particular feminine conception of citizenship.[52] Understood as a process of self-expression through making, active citizenship was able to be performed through the domestic arts of the home, a site which was now more closely connected to the affairs of the state following the dislocation of the war. At the same time design reformers were seeking to revive interest in craftmanship of all kinds and linked the social and artistic value of handicrafts to the nation asserting that 'the country and country-life must be the basis of national life'.[53] Morris, like his Oxford tutor Hastings Rashdall, wanted vocationally oriented learners to be inducted into the theory underpinning their craft, as well as a general education, as without these they would become mere operatives. The village college in this way was not only to be a place of active learning but also a 'silent teacher' providing an aesthetic education through its high-quality designed environment and original artworks. Each iteration of the village college thus far demonstrated how a modern school might be conceived with a curriculum and community articulated in its architecture. And it was in collaboration with Gropius that this idea was even more clearly expressed.[54]

Impington Village College

Set among trees, Impington (**Figure 10.5**) followed the principally single-storey form of the previous colleges, but its fan-shaped assembly hall with cantilevered canopy and generous glazing announced itself with more assurance. The hall, together with the two-storey block for practical work and the promenade, formed the centre of the plan and represented its community use. The rest of the accommodation was placed in two wings. The first was the gently curving adult education and recreation wing, which included games and meeting rooms as well as a library. The other was the classroom wing for the senior school, planned for some 240 boys and girls aged eleven to fifteen. The classrooms and laboratory were equipped for subject-specific learning, including a stage for English and Drama and map reading tables for geography and history. Like Linton, these were connected by a covered walkway and featured sliding doors that could be fully opened to the landscape. Each wing was accessed from the promenade, which measured some 140 feet long by 20 feet wide, lined with lockers and WCs on one side and staff room and warden's room on the other.

---

[52]See Alice Kirke, 'Education in Interwar Rural England: Community, Schooling, and Voluntarism', PhD diss. (UCL Institute of Education, 2016): 218–27. The author carefully traces this development through the rural activities of the Women's Institute, one of the several organizations that Morris lists in the *Memorandum* to be included in the programme.

[53]William Lethaby cited in Kirke, 'Education in Interwar Rural England': 222.

[54]Saint, *Towards a Social Architecture*: 37.

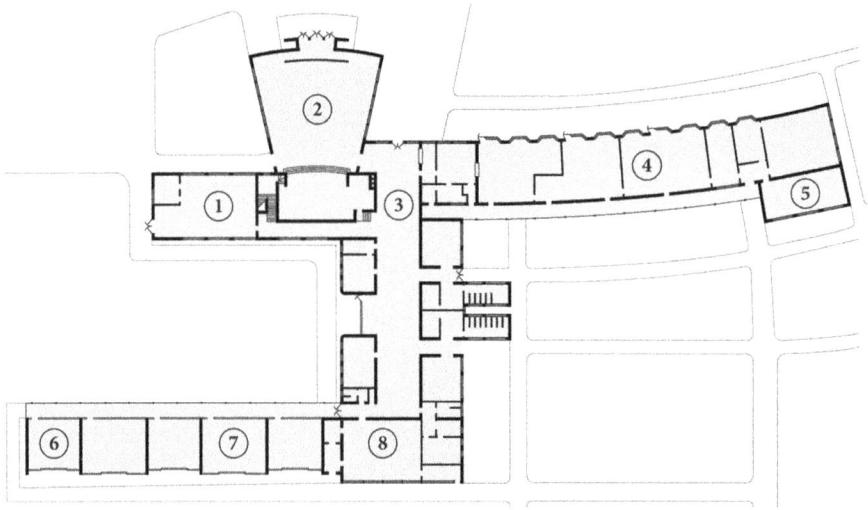

1 Workshop
2 Hall
3 Promenade
4 Adult Education and Recreation Wing
5 Library
6 Classroom Wing
7 Needlework
8 Laboratory

Figure 10.5 Ground floor plan, Impington Village College (1939). Architects: Water Gropius and Maxwell Fry. Courtesy *Architects' Journal,* drawn by Gemma Fowlie

Impington commanded the attention of architects, educationists, artists and critics alike. It featured in Herbert Read's *Education through Art* (1943), held up as a model for how a school building could provide a purposeful aesthetic experience. Pevsner praised it in his *Buildings of England* series and observed:

Can it have been the effect of English picturesque notions on the more rigid intellect of Gropius? As for this loose grouping as such, it must however be said that the village colleges preceding Impington had already used this device, though without the full realisation of its aesthetic possibilities … Perhaps it originated in the mind of Henry Morris, whose idea the Village Colleges had been.[55]

---

[55]Pevsner, *Cambridgeshire*: 412–13.

Though much of Impington's reception and legacy can be justly attributed to Gropius's experience and international reputation, he also had the advantage of drawing on Morris's knowledge and the first three colleges. As Pevsner inferred, Gropius brought a renewed clarity for how the village college architecture responded to its rural context, synthesized its multiple functions and framed new ways of seeing.

Despite Impington's modernist innovations, such as the asymmetrical pin-wheel plan, fan-shaped assembly hall (its roof doubling up as an open-air learning space) and extensive glazing, it clearly contrasted to the dematerialization of Gropius's designs for the Bauhaus Building at Dessau where glass curtain walls dominated the facade and wrapped around structurally significant points. The college was less exposed than the Bauhaus, and the use of familiar yellow gault clay bricks concealed its steel structure and softened the rational plan. Bay windows along the adult recreation wing and ply mahogany panelling of its interiors suggested forms of English domesticity rather than industry or agriculture. And while Gropius's intentions to merge industrial production with craftsmanship at the Bauhaus were crystallized at Dessau, his designs at Impington respected Morris's call for the building to reflect something of the 'humaneness and modesty' of the spirit of the English countryside.[56] It was this aspect of the brief that Gropius followed by developing a 'simpler and more cordial accent', a tempered approach to the machine-age modernism he had developed on the continent and something he had learnt to respect while spending time in the English landscape.[57]

In terms of the plan, the promenade was the pivotal innovation. It synthesized each of the building's components and worked as a place of congregation. Senior school children gathered in the promenade before attending their classes or during inclement weather. With events taking place in the hall, it allowed a freedom of movement for both children and adults to interact or observe exhibited art works. In *Education through Art*, Read conceptually links it to the *peripatos* – the colonnades at Aristotle's Lyceum where he and his students met, talked and speculated – and considered bodily motion, along with aesthetic education, a potent medium for communication and self-expression. Alongside a capacity for ample movement, the promenade worked as a social technology, disseminating knowledge to its users as well as producing knowledge about them. The area demanded daily use: it provided access to lockers, toilets and staff rooms. In observing how students occupied the space, teachers were able to identify behaviours, evaluate and modify them either directly (through the rather non-progressive means of corporal punishment as college logbooks testify) or indirectly, encouraging greater social integration. Morris was particularly proud of the promenade's centrality to the ritual of the midday meal, which he claimed helped students acquire good table manners and sound food habits for life. The school thus provided both for the 'mind and emotions' and for the 'play and exercise of body' which youth required.[58]

---

[56]Morris, 'The Village College': 153.
[57]Powers, *Bauhaus Goes West*: 80.
[58]Morris cited in Jeffs, *Henry Morris*: 56.

Gropius's interpretation allowed further innovations for how the building worked as a viewing apparatus, one which architecturally framed new social and educational relationships, while at the same time employing new technology to disseminate their representation through mass media. The building was intended to look dynamic – numerous components within one composition – that allowed the college to be dramatically represented through photography and that reflected Morris's call for a 'new institution, single but many-sided'.[59] At the back of the hall a cantilevered projection room was situated to play sound films, approved by Morris as local censor. Impington's image itself was employed by a variety of media to convince public audiences that modernism was a logical choice for improving school design, including Abram Games's 'Your Britain. Fight for it Now', commissioned by the Army Bureau of Current Affairs (1942), the documentary film *Children's Charter* (1945) and *The Modern School* by Stillman and Cleary (1949). In these examples it was the strength of Impington's image, rather than the more complex and radical details of its programme, that was used as visual shorthand to educate audiences about architectural and educational progressivism.

Conclusion

For all these reasons, Impington quickly secured its place within a canon of British modernist architecture. Nevertheless, the architectural history of the village college is more extensive, indeed richer, than Gropius's designs alone and Impington's meaning is reliant on its place in a longer trajectory. The first three colleges were not isolated experiments, but rather formative stages in the educational and architectural ideas Morris had been developing for nearly two decades by the time Impington was complete. The impression of Gropius's Impington, developed sui generis as an architecturally 'pure', unmediated modernist response to the village college ideal is fictional. The colleges worked as framing devices, mediating a series of tensions and values: the modern with the traditional, the individual with the social, the executive with the cooperative, in an effort to enhance the educational and democratic life of rural communities. Inevitably, they were not perfect: democratic accountability was not as representative as Morris had hoped and major assumptions were made about student needs that were embedded in tradition. In particular, there was a tension between Morris's desire to see individuals fulfilled and happy, and a sense that the young needed to remain in the area and work on the land like their families had.[60] Critics have also pointed out that the programme depended on the presence of a powerful executive, whether that was a warden or Morris himself, and it is telling that following his retirement the village colleges came to resemble conventional schools rather than maintaining their original programme. Although he saw architecture as a radically civilizing influence on society, there was

---

[59]Morris, 'The Village College': 147.
[60]Caitlin Adams, 'Rural Education and Reform between the Wars', in Paul Brassley et al. (eds.), *The English Countryside between the Wars: Regeneration or Decline?* (Woodbridge: Boydell Press, 2006): 50–1.

undeniable paternalism in his conviction of what was good for a community and in his determination to provide it for them.

The *Memorandum* framed Morris's view of the world, but he rarely acknowledged the sources of his ideas. Dewey had outlined ideas on community education in *School and Society* (1899), 'learning by doing' had been credited to Friedrich Froebel since the nineteenth century and open-air learning had become popular by the 1920s. But it was also this covert eclecticism that spurred him on to synthesize these ideas into practice and to personally secure the financial investment required to give them spatial and material expression. As a gay man and atheist working in local government he was well aware of the risks of being too progressive and did not want his persona or plans to be associated with non-state sanctioned ideas which might have jeopardized his ambitions for rolling the scheme out nationally.

Such criticism should not overshadow the inherent radicalism of the scheme and its continued relevance as a reminder to educators and policymakers alike that schools can take an abundance of different forms. The village college, as originally conceived, offers a laudable alternative to today's highly centralized schools, one which encourages local, cooperative ownership against individual, vested interest and blurs the distinction between life and learning. Morris's legacy also lies in his followers and staff who have continued to develop and implement the concept of community education that he forged. One notable example was Stewart Mason who became chief education officer of Leicestershire in 1949 and set up a string of community colleges including Ashby de la Zouche and Countesthorpe, both of which were run by wardens who had worked at Sawston and Bottisham. Such sites offer further opportunities for investigating the creative connections between educational and architectural ideas, and their possible forms of expression.[61]

Select bibliography

Primary

Architects' Journal
Architectural Review
The Builder
UCL Institute of Education/Papers of Harry Alfred Rée (1914–91)

Secondary

Adams, Caitlin. 'Rural Education and Reform between the Wars'. In *The English Countryside between the Wars: Regeneration or Decline?*, edited by Paul Brassley et al., 36–52. Woodbridge: Boydell Press, 2006.

[61]Rée, *Educator Extraordinary*: 136–7.

'C.R. Ashbee'. *King's College Cambridge*, https://www.kings.cam.ac.uk/archive-centre/online-resources/online-exhibitions/c-r-ashbee - toc-5A (accessed 24 March 2020).

Clay, Felix. *Modern School Buildings Elementary and Secondary: A Handbook on the Planning, Arrangement, and Fitting of Day and Boarding Schools.* Edinburgh: B.T. Batsford Ltd, 1929.

Daybelge, Leyla, and Magnus Englund. *Isokon and the Bauhaus in Britain.* London: Pavilion Books Group, 2019.

Dybeck, M. *The Village College Way.* Cambridge: Cambridgeshire County Council, 1981.

Elliott, David. 'Gropius in England'. In *A Different World: Émigré Architects in Britain 1928–1958,* edited by Charlotte Benton, 107–24. London: RIBA, 1995.

Farnell, D. 'Henry Morris: An Architect of Education', MA diss. Cambridge Institute of Education, 1968.

Franklin, Geraint. *Inner-London Schools 1918–44: A Thematic Study.* English Heritage, 2009.

Giedion, Sigfried. *Walter Gropius: Work and Teamwork.* Dover Publications, 1954.

Gillard, Derek. 'The Hadow Reports: An Introduction'. *Education in England: The History of Our Schools,* http://www.educationengland.org.uk/articles/24hadow.html (accessed 5 January 2020).

Harwood, Elain. *England's Schools: History, Architecture and Adaptation.* Swindon: English Heritage, 2010.

Hulme, Tom. '"A Nation Depends on Its Children": School Buildings and Citizenship in England and Wales, 1900–1939'. *Journal of British Studies* 54 (2015): 406–32.

Jeffs, Tony. *Henry Morris: Village Colleges, Community Education and the Ideal Order.* Nottingham: Educational Heretics Press, 1998.

'Kesteven and Grantham Girls' School'. *Historic England,* https://historicengland.org.uk/listing/the-list/list-entry/1412888 (accessed 5 January 2020).

Kirke, Alice. 'Education in Interwar Rural England: Community, Schooling, and Voluntarism', PhD diss. (UCL Institute of Education, 2016).

MacCarthy, Fiona. *Gropius: The Man Who Built the Bauhaus.* Cambridge, Massachusetts: Harvard University Press, 2019.

Morris, Henry. 'The Village College: Being a Memorandum on the Provision of Educational and Social Facilities for the Countryside, with Special Reference to Cambridgeshire'. In *Educator Extraordinary: The Life and Achievement of Henry Morris,* edited by Harry Rée, 143–57. London: Longman Group Ltd., 1973.

Pevsner, Nikolaus. *Cambridgeshire: The Buildings of England No.10.* London: Penguin, 1970.

Powers, Alan. *Bauhaus Goes West: Modern Art and Design in Britain and America.* London: Thames & Hudson, 2019.

Read, Herbert. *Education through Art.* London: Longman, 1943.

Rée, Harry. *Educator Extraordinary: The Life and Achievement of Henry Morris.* London: Longman Group Ltd., 1973.

Saint, Andrew. *Towards a Social Architecture: The Role of School-Building in Post-War England.* New Haven; London: Yale University Press, 1987.

'Sawston Village College'. *Historic England,* https://historicengland.org.uk/listing/the-list/list-entry/1128038 (accessed 5 January 2020).

Seaborne, Malcolm, and Roy Lowe. *The English School: Its Architecture and Organisation, Vol 2 (1870–1970).* Trowbridge and Esher: Routledge & Kegan Paul Ltd., 1977.

Scott, Geoffrey. *Architecture of Humanism: A Study in the History of Taste.* Boston and New York: Houghton Mifflin Company, 1914.

Shasore, Neal. '"A Stammering Bundle of Welsh Idealism": Arthur Trystan Edwards and Principles of Civic Design in Interwar Britain'. *Architectural History* 61 (2018): 175–203.

'The Village College'. *Historic England,* https://historicengland.org.uk/listing/the-list/list-entry/1127730 (accessed 1 January 2020).

SECTION IV
BINDING SUBJECTS THROUGH STATECRAFT

In the wake of a global conflict, the Imperial nation state and its institutions sought to strengthen ties among its citizens. The binding agent used was a liberal political subjectivity and imaginary. The mainstream of architectural culture in the early twentieth century had a strong liberal inflection, influenced by the idealism of nineteenth-century political philosophy.[1]

The architect Percy Thomas, as Robert Proctor's essay shows, was typical of this tendency – busy 'redrawing the state' for his bureaucratic patrons in a liberal vein. The Welsh National Temple of Peace and Health was one of Thomas's contributions to Cathays Park, Cardiff, celebrated by contemporaries as Britain's first 'civic centre', albeit a piecemeal collection of national and municipal institutions.[2] Thomas's practice became one of the pre-eminent practices (along with Lanchester, Lucas & Lodge, Vincent Harris, Ernest Berry Webber, and Rowland Pierce & Holloway James) designing new municipal complexes of this kind in the first half of the twentieth century.[3] Indeed, Swansea Guildhall – civic centres were often named to evoke historical associations or express political ambition – was the archetypal complex of this kind, bringing together a range of modern, municipal services and places of assembly. Bristol, Swinton and Pendlebury and Tunbridge Wells were all also representative of this new and emerging typology. Proctor notes the liberal political patronage of these projects, and this is no coincidence.

The 'civic centre' was an ideal as much as a typology, growing out of shifting conceptions of liberal political subjectivity. The intellectual and etymological origins of the civic centre continued a debate and practice of the early Progressive Era of the United States in the 1890s. A key ambition of this progressive effort was the creation of the 'City Beautiful', which was an idea derived in fact from Arts and Crafts discourse and a sustained campaign of urban improvement. The phrase 'City Beautiful' was actively propagated by progressives in England, in particular in Lancashire where advocates of the 'New Liberalism' were concentrated.[4] The leading liberal newspaper,

---

[1] For context, see Neal Shasore, *Designs on Democracy: Architecture and the Public in Interwar London* (Oxford: Oxford University Press, 2022).

[2] In the *Town Planning Review*, S. D. Adshead, the first Professor of Civic Design at Liverpool School of Architecture, described Cathays Park, Cardiff, as the first 'British Civic Centre': S. D. Adshead, 'Cathays Park, Cardiff', *Town Planning Review* 1, no. 2 (July 2010): 148–50.

[3] Johanna Roethe, '"A Pretty Toy" or "Purely Functional": Town, City and County Halls in the Interwar Period', in Alan Powers and Elain Harwood (eds.), *Twentieth Century Architecture 13: The Architecture of Public Service* (London: Twentieth Century Society, 2018).

[4] P. F. Clarke, *Lancashire and the New Liberalism* (Cambridge: Cambridge University Press, 1971).

The Manchester Guardian, frequently deployed 'City Beautiful' in headlines relating to urban improvement.[5] The first national conference on 'the City Beautiful' was indeed held in Manchester in 1906[6] and inspired a similar event in Liverpool the following June presided over by the Lord Mayor, John Japp, a Liberal councillor.[7] Philip Rathbone, a scion of a prominent Liverpudlian Liberal merchant family, lectured to the Liverpool Royal Institute on the subject of the City Beautiful in the same year.[8] Both conferences had strong links to the progressive Garden City movement in these cities. The 'City Beautiful' amounted to a burgeoning urban and environmental policy for the 'New Liberalism', a revived social liberal agenda in Britain at the turn of the last century that had grown out of the writings of T. H. Green, Hobhouse and their followers, reacting against laissez-faire economy, rebalancing the rights of the individual with the needs of the community. This was a political philosophy which revivified the intellectual credibility of Liberalism. It was, in its day, socialistic in some of its aspirations and represented a new attitude to public administration and civic participation. This was a period in which architects were negotiating with new cultures of democracy and this is a theme that runs throughout the post-war period.

If the 'City Beautiful' was an overarching ideal, then 'civic art' or civic design was its praxis. In 1909 the head of the Liverpool School of Architecture, the gregarious and influential Charles Herbert Reilly, secured a sizeable endowment from local industrial magnate, Sir William Lever, later Lord Leverhulme, the founder of Sunlight Soap and progenitor of the Port Sunlight model village. Lever, a Congregationalist and Liberal, supported Reilly and the Liverpool School as a conduit for pushing a political ideal. As Reilly, a self-professed Socialist, later described, 'the Whigs and Liberals have turned to education, to the founding and maintaining of the University'.[9]

But Liberal progressivism had other more troubling dimensions. As the historian Duncan Bell has shown, liberalism suffused ideas about not only Imperial development, but also of a transatlantic 'Anglosphere' of Anglo-Saxon racial supremacy. Lord Leverhulme, for example, was implicated in the shadiest forms of commercial colonialism in the Belgian Congo, and his advocacy of Imperial expansion is well known. The progressive exemplar of Port Sunlight on the Wirral had as its negative image Leverville, the centre of Leverhulme's African industrial production, his factory powered by indentured Congolese labour.[10] His interest in American politics and society, though

---

[5]See, for instance, 'Mr Carnegie's "City Beautiful"', *Manchester Guardian* (9 December 1903): 12; 'The City Beautiful: New Islington Hall Address', *Manchester Guardian* (5 February 1906): 5; or 'The City Beautiful', *Manchester Guardian* (30 November 1906): 3.

[6]'The City Beautiful: To Bring Nature into Great Towns', *Manchester Guardian* (26 June 1906): 12.

[7]'The City Beautiful: Housing Reformers at Liverpool', *Manchester Guardian* (28 June 1907): 5.

[8]Peter Richmond, *Marketing Modernisms: The Architecture and Influence of Charles Herbert Reilly* (Liverpool: Liverpool University Press, 2001): 88.

[9]C. H. Reilly, *Scaffolding in the Sky: A Semi-architectural Autobiography* (London: G Routledge & Sons, 1938): 249.

[10]Brian Lewis, *So Clean: Lord Leverhulme, Soap and Civilisation* (Manchester: Manchester University Press, 2008): 154–98.

not explicitly cast in terms of race, certainly places him in the same milieu as Cecil Rhodes, who very much believed in an Anglo-American 'dreamworld of race' as Bell has described it.

Rhodes was an avowed liberal, who aimed 'to keep the English-speaking race together'.[11] Geoffrey Tyack's contribution on Rhodes House shows how Herbert Baker, Rhodes's favourite architect and biographer, sought to give this spatial and material expression. Built a quarter century after Rhodes's death, Rhodes House expressed the values of the Rhodes Trust and its scholarship programme, designed to 'inculcate a deep sense of kinship between elite members of his beloved Anglo-Saxon race', including American citizens.[12] As Tyack shows, Baker used Rhodes House to memorialize not just Cecil Rhodes and the colonial statesman Lord Milner but also those Rhodes scholars who had died during the war. Baker's interest in the monumental and memorial mode had indeed been fostered by Rhodes. In commissioning a memorial to the dead of the Siege of Kimberley (in which he had played such a controversial part during the Boer War), Rhodes had bankrolled Baker's travel round the monuments and temples of the ancient world in Italy, Greece and Egypt in order 'to formulate an adequate commemorative response to those who had fallen'.[13] The resulting memorial, completed in 1904 to the Honoured Dead – a tetrastyle classical temple raised on a tall podium – has been described by Alex Bremner as 'prefiguring in its elemental geometry the memorials to the slaughter of World War One'.[14]

We do not, however, address the design of war memorials in great detail in this volume – there is an extensive body of literature on the subject already. Instead, authors reflect on other forms of commemoration and memorialization often through the establishment of institutions such as Rhodes House. Percy Thomas's Temple of Peace and Health, conceived by another liberal industrialist and politician, serves as a typical example: it was both a centre of the campaign against tuberculosis in Wales and also a focus of international affairs at the headquarters of the Welsh branch of the League of Nations Union. Recent historiography of the development of international relations of course links this new discipline and form of diplomacy to Imperial expansion and especially the Round Table.[15]

The 'Rhodes Colossus' famously conceived of a great line of communication from Cape Town to Cairo, and coincidentally the range of this section spans that same terrain. At Cairo Cathedral, Liberal Anglican ideals were given liturgical form at Adrian Gilbert Scott's new Cathedral. David Lewis traces the changing fortunes of the

---

[11]Duncan Bell, *Dreamworlds of Race: Empire and the Utopian Destiny of Anglo-America* (Princeton: Princeton University Press, 2020): 133.

[12]Ibid.: 141.

[13]G. A. Bremner, 'Stones of Empire: Monuments, Memorials, and Manifest Authority', in G. A. Bremner (ed.), *Architecture and Urbanism in the British Empire* (Oxford: Oxford University Press, 2016): 104.

[14]Ibid.: 105.

[15]A. E. Davis, Vineet Thakur and Peter Vale, *The Imperial Discipline: Race and the Founding of International Relations* (London: Pluto Press, 2020).

Anglican community and its new diocese from wartime through the 1920s and 1930s, discussing the politics of style – from neo-Byzantine to Crusader Gothic – in relation to the Liberal Anglicanism discussed in earlier chapters. Lewis also discusses how the cathedral space – both at Cairo and at Liverpool, designed by the architect's brother, Sir Giles Gilbert Scott – became a place of not only physical congregation but also wireless broadcast, linking disparate parts of Empire and scattered congregants together using new forms of technology.

CHAPTER 11
CITIZENSHIP: WELFARE AND THE DEMOCRATIC STATE IN PERCY THOMAS'S CIVIC ARCHITECTURE
Robert Proctor

The rumblings of a possible new European conflict were already being heard, but at the opening ceremony of Sir Percy Thomas's Welsh National Temple of Peace and Health in Cardiff on 23 November 1938 the earlier war was still prominent in participants' minds, and hopes for a new age of peace and democratic welfare were vividly alive (**Figure 11.1**). In one wing of the building were the offices of the Welsh National Memorial Association, a healthcare organization funded largely by local and national government to treat tuberculosis; and the other wing housed the Welsh League of Nations Union, promoting the cause of peace and international cooperation (**Figure 11.2**). Both had been founded with the patronage of Lord David Davies of Llandinam, the wealthy heir to an industrial empire and former Liberal MP who had been recalled from action on the Western Front to serve as Lloyd George's parliamentary private secretary.[1] Davies had also largely financed the building, and determined its combined themes of peace and health achieved through national and international democratic citizenship, founded on the memory of the fallen in the war, a strong contrast to the militaristic nationalism by then clearly evident in Germany and Italy.[2] Uniting the offices was a large central hall, the 'Hall of Nations', for public assembly, and underneath the vestibule a crypt containing the Book of Remembrance (moved here from the nearby National Museum of Wales), inscribed with the names of all Welsh soldiers who died in the war, a page ceremonially turned every day.[3]

Connections between war, citizenship and welfare were reinforced at the building's opening ceremony, when representative mothers from across Britain and the world took positions on the hall's dais and gave short speeches. Mrs Cederlund of Sweden, for example, hoped the building would remain a 'constant reminder to the people of Wales of their duty to further the cause of progress, freedom, peace, and justice, and of the debt

---

[1] Brian Porter, 'David Davies: A Hunter after Peace', *Review of International Studies* 15 (1989): 27.

[2] E.g. British attitudes to political violence in Europe are touched on in Jon Lawrence, 'Forging a Peaceable Kingdom: War, Violence, and Fear of Brutalization in Post-First World War Britain', *The Journal of Modern History* 75 (2003): 557–89 and Jon Lawrence, 'Fascist Violence and the Politics of Public Order in Inter-war Britain: The Olympia Debate Revisited', *Historical Research* 76 (2003): 238–67.

[3] E. R. Eaton, 'Thoughts in the Crypt and Hall of Justice', *Western Mail & South Wales News* (23 November 1938), Temple of Peace and Health Supplement, 8, in Cardiff University Archives and Special Collections (CUASC), Temple of Peace Box.

Figure 11.1 Ivor Jones & Percy Thomas, Welsh National Temple of Peace and Health, Cardiff, 1931–1938. Photo: Stewart Bale, *c*. 1938; from the Collections of the National Monuments Record of Wales © Percy Thomas

they owe to those who fell in defence of these ideals'. The key to the building was turned by a Welsh mother, Minnie James of Dowlais, who had lost her three sons in the war and who dedicated the building as a war memorial.[4] 'Like the Unknown Warrior', argued Davies, 'they [the mothers] invite us to obliterate distinctions of creed, politics, and class, just as we did in the trenches many years ago, and to dedicate ourselves to a noble and righteous cause'.[5] This chapter argues that the simplified neoclassical architecture of Percy Thomas's Temple of Peace and other civic buildings played a significant role in embodying the political culture that lay behind them, presenting a utopian vision that was not yet a reality of a coordinated democratic state that made large-scale provision for its citizens' welfare, founded on the memory of war.

The two decades after 1918 have often suffered from comparison with the 1945 Labour government's inauguration of the welfare state according to a holistic vision of a reconstructed nation. In contrast, the early twentieth century is viewed as lacking such an unambiguous politics. The welfare state was to some extent coalescing in the

---

[4]'Wales's Tragic Mother Opens the Temple of Peace', *Western Mail & South Wales News* (24 November 1938): 7, CUASC, Temple of Peace Box.

[5]David Davies, 'Temple an Expression of Two Ideals', *Western Mail & South Wales News* (23 November 1938), Temple of Peace and Health Supplement, 2, CUASC, Temple of Peace Box.

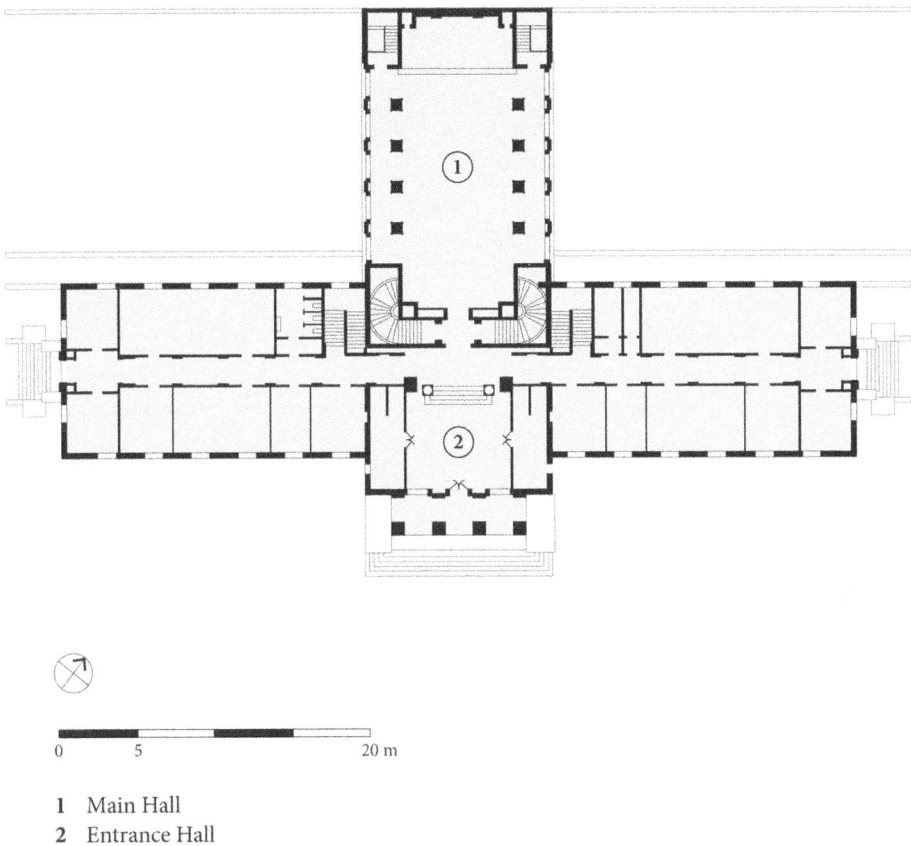

1   Main Hall
2   Entrance Hall

Figure 11.2 Plan of Ivor Jones & Percy Thomas, Welsh National Temple of Peace and Health, Cardiff, 1931–1938, drawn by Hannah Towler

rising state concern with public welfare, already implicated in the National Insurance Act of 1911, and continuing with improvements to education, pensions, medical care and unemployment provision. This new, highly bureaucratic attempt to provide safety nets for those lacking the resources to sustain themselves accompanied the expansion of the franchise to working-class voters and women after the war. Often presented as a reward for the sacrifices of war service, welfare and voting rights were two sides of an increasingly clearly articulated notion of citizenship. Nevertheless a 'mixed economy' of welfare prevailed, characterised by numerous, often dispersed, local government offices, voluntary bodies such as friendly societies and churches, and private companies.[6] The nature and sources of welfare remained fragmented, while the argument for

---

[6]For historical overviews, see e.g. James E. Cronin, *The Politics of State Expansion: War, State and Society in Twentieth-Century Britain* (London: Routledge, 1991); Bernard Harris, *The Origins of the British Welfare State: Society, State and Social Welfare* (Basingstoke: Palgrave Macmillan, 2004); Jose Harris, 'Political Thought and the Welfare State 1870–1940: An Intellectual Framework for British Social Policy', in David Gladstone (ed.), *Before Beveridge: Welfare before the Welfare State* (London: Institute of Economic Affairs, 1999): 43–63.

coherent national schemes of public assistance grew stronger. It was within the power of architecture, however, to embody optimistically such a national, essentially social democratic, vision before it became a reality.

In architectural history, the interest in post-war modernism as an expression of the welfare state and the canonical status of British experiments in modernism in the 1930s have led to an interpretation of modernism as uniquely expressive of this social democratic view of citizenship, although initially not consistently of the state, since many of the pioneering buildings were created by private organizations.[7] The work of Percy Thomas in this period, however, suggests the need for a wider and more complex view, accepting that visions of an egalitarian democratic state in which citizens' welfare was a universal right could be presented in other architectural forms. The neo-Georgian style and the gentle New Empiricist version of post-war modernism that updated it have recently been seen as attempting to create a consistent brand of architecture as a unified image for government-sponsored buildings, especially social housing.[8] Percy Thomas's civic work, from town halls to universities, often assumed the neo-Georgian style and therefore also associated itself with such official architecture, and his more monumental, neoclassical works were also described in such terms. In its elevational, symbolic aspects and in the formal, spatial qualities of architectural composition that relate to it, style may be deliberately intended to evoke resonances and meanings and may (as Thomas's architecture often shows) be intended to promote political interpretations. But equally important are the meanings ascribed to buildings by those who commissioned and argued over them, and the many other ways in which buildings relate to the political frameworks in which they were constructed – not least in the mechanisms of funding that lay behind them.

The histories of Percy Thomas's buildings demonstrate how the welfare state was already being formulated before the Second World War, albeit in multiple and highly contended ways. While there remained a hegemonic political ideal of minimal state interference, the level of involvement of the state in people's lives grew substantially, most notably as increasing responsibilities were demanded of local authorities by central government. Councils became the local manifestations of national policies in action, rephrasing the national in terms of local pride and duty.[9] But there was an overt political debate at local levels, and articulated through building projects, in which local

---

[7]Elizabeth Darling, *Re-forming Britain: Narratives of Modernity before Reconstruction* (London: Routledge, 2007): e.g. 2, 28, 141.

[8]Julian Holder, 'A State of Approval: Neo-Georgian Architecture and His Majesty's Office of Works, 1914–1939', in Julian Holder and Elizabeth McKellar (ed.), *Neo-Georgian Architecture 1880–1970: A Reappraisal* (Swindon: Historic England, 2016): 122–35; Alan Powers, 'Quality in Quality Street: Neo-Georgian and Its Place in Architectural History', in Julian Holder and Elizabeth McKellar (ed.), *Neo-Georgian Architecture 1880–1970: A Reappraisal* (Swindon: Historic England, 2016): 13–24; Alan Powers, 'The Architecture of Public Service' in Elain Harwood and Alan Powers (eds.), *Twentieth Century Architecture 13: The Architecture of Public Service* (2018): 7–23.

[9]N. E. Shasore, 'Southampton Civic Centre: Patronage and Place in the Interwar Architecture of Public Service', in Elain Harwood and Alan Powers (eds.), *Twentieth Century Architecture 13: The Architecture of Public Service* (2018): 41–61.

government willingly framed itself in relation to coherent central, national schemes of economic and social intervention. Meanwhile, often not greatly publicized, there were also more stealthy forms of involvement of central government in civic projects in this period. Much of Percy Thomas's civic architecture of the 1920s and 1930s was crystallized through such interweaving flows of political discourse and public funds. His design work could be argued to represent a newly conceptualized national, state welfare project, while also sometimes attempting to mollify its conservative critics.

The war was the basis for arguments around welfare and state control: the expansion of democracy and citizens' rights after 1918 was both an appreciation of war service and a consequence of wartime social experiences, and arguments for national planning aimed to redirect the state's war effort into peacetime development.[10] Thomas himself served in the war as officer and captain in the Royal Engineers, receiving an OBE for his record, and he later claimed that the war had given him experience 'of dealing with all kinds of men' that became an important factor in his post-war practice.[11] He often evoked this new democratic spirit in his administrative roles at the Royal Institute of British Architects. He supported anonymous architectural competitions, for example, joining the Institute's Competitions Committee, on the grounds that it made architecture 'the most democratic' of all the professions, since 'the architect is appointed on merit alone and not by wirepulling or political influence', giving opportunities to unknown architects of talent.[12] As RIBA President 1935 to 1937, Thomas argued that this professional organization should promote the extension of planning from civic centres to entire cities as a 'National Service'. 'We exist solely to serve the community and we must bend our utmost powers to that end,' he said.[13] Whereas in the past architects had primarily worked for the church and the aristocracy, the predominance in practice of government buildings, hospitals, schools and museums meant that today they served the 'whole community', 'ordinary members of the Great British public'.[14]

Thomas does not seem to have taken an overt party political line, but the town councillors who were his frequent clients often were politically engaged in national debates which they applied to their local situations, and they expected their buildings to express not only a conventional civic dignity but also specific political attitudes. This is especially clear in two of Thomas's buildings, Swinton and Pendlebury Town Hall in Salford and, his greatest achievement, Swansea Guildhall. His civic buildings scheme for Tunbridge Wells, meanwhile, was enmeshed in divisive disagreements over council spending in which party political arguments around national state welfare featured prominently. Even his police and fire stations were conceived of in such terms.

---

[10] Arthur Marwick, *The Deluge: British Society and the First World War* (London: Macmillan, 1973).

[11] Percy Edward Thomas, *Pupil to President: Memoirs of an Architect* (Leigh-on-Sea: F. Lewis, 1963): 28.

[12] Percy E. Thomas and H. V. Lanchester, 'Competitions Past and Present', *Journal of the Royal Institute of British Architects* (13 May 1933): 530, 532.

[13] 'The Inaugural Address by the President, Mr. Percy Thomas, O.B.E., F.R.I.B.A.', *Journal of the Royal Institute of British Architects* (7 November 1936): 9.

[14] Percy E. Thomas, 'The R.I.B.A. Inaugural Address by the President, Mr. Percy E. Thomas', *Architect & Building News* (8 November 1935): 163.

Civic services in local and national democracy: Bristol and Accrington

Police stations, magistrates' courts and fire stations remained under local government control after the war. These institutions were increasingly considered as contributors to welfare, safeguards to democracy and components in the functional interplay of local and national government as embodiments of the state, conceptions that were articulated through architectural design and discourse. Charles Reilly, praising Percy Thomas's approach to planning, explained how in preparing his competition entry for the combined Bristol fire station, police station and courtroom (**Figure 11.3**), Thomas 'interviewed everyone he could think of who could tell him anything about the use of such buildings, from magistrates to firemen and policemen', a statement that chimes with Thomas's claims for his war experiences.[15] After winning the competition in 1924 with his office partner Ivor Jones, his design was praised by the assessors W. Curtis Green and George Oatley for its simple and economical solution to complex planning and site requirements, as well as its refined and expressive elevations; Thomas's report must have convinced the assessors, with great detail on seemingly minor functional

Figure 11.3 Ivor Jones & Percy Thomas, Bristol Police Station, 1924–1930. Photo: *c.* 1951; Bristol Archives, 39864/2/197

---

[15]Charles Reilly, 'Some Younger Architects of Today – Percy Thomas', in *Pupil to President: Memoirs of an Architect*, by Sir Percy Thomas (Leigh-on-Sea: F. Lewis, 1963): 61. The approach was also recommended in A. Calveley Cotton, *Town Halls* (London: Architectural Press, 1936).

points. While some were merely mechanical, such as the fact that uniquely among the competitors, his design allowed each of thirteen fire engines to enter and return without impeding the others, other aspects had social purposes: the firemen's flats had sliding poles into the engine room; a laundry gave onto a flat roof for drying clothes; the police station's charge room gave access to the cells, which were ingeniously linked to the courtroom; and so on.[16] One purpose of the new building was to provide the police with a drill hall for the first time, in which the corporate body of the force could be assembled, inspected and addressed at once. Careful planning of buildings thus organized citizens so that they enacted their chosen roles in relation to and on behalf of each other in a society ordered by the legal and bureaucratic frameworks of the state.

The Bristol building was considered in itself an act of welfare by the city council, partly to enable a central, fast and city-wide fire service involving new communications and engines, but more urgently because the firemen and their families were housed in damp, rat-infested cottages, many unable to live elsewhere because they were expected to be permanently on call. Only senior ranks would have this responsibility in the new building, and they were provided with good-quality housing over the engines in compensation, while lower ranks could live where they chose thanks to a more humane shift system.[17] While the new building was a civic project led by the council's Watch Committee, it was also spurred on by central government: the Home Office complained of the existing police station's lack of facilities, including drill hall, and offered the council half the funding for the police portion of the building provided they went ahead with the comprehensive combined scheme.[18] Thus, a national impetus and funding for modernizing local provision coincided with combined local desires to improve the service for the city's residents; to improve working conditions for its employees; to organize their work into a logical, hierarchical plan in which all actions ran smoothly in relation to each other. And it was equally important to give these institutions an integrated, 'dignified', clearly articulated urban presence, achieved through the use of Thomas's restrained, simplified neoclassicism dominated by a harmonious repetition of neo-Georgian windows in plain Bath stone facades.

Percy Thomas's combined fire station, police station and law courts at Accrington (**Figure 11.4**), won in competition in 1930 and opened five years later, was similar in plan organization and elevations, though adapted to the different site, and similar in its situation between local and national government.[19] Its use of stone facing had been the

---

[16]'Bristol Police and Fire Stations Competition', *Builder* (11 April 1924): 575.

[17]John Swaish, 'Report of the Fire Brigade Sub-Committee', Draft, 9 June 1922, at Bristol Archives (BA), FB/Adm/M/1/2; Draft Report of the Watch Committee [n. d., *c.* April 1923], BA, M/BCC/WAT/2/30; Dennis Hill, *Bristol Fire Brigade 1877–1974: An Illustrated History* (Bristol: Redcliffe Press, 1999): 82.

[18]Draft Report of the Watch Committee, 1923, BA, M/BCC/WAT/2/30; Fire Brigade Sub-Committee, 16 January 1923, BA, FB/Adm/M/1/2.

[19]'New Courts, Police Station and Fire Station, Accrington. Architect: Percy Thomas, P.R.I.B.A.', *Architect & Building News* (28 June 1935): 367–73.

subject of much local argument, many advocating brick as both a local material that could support the town's famous brickworks, and substantially cheaper.[20] The council eventually approved Thomas's preference for stone partly because it would harmonize with the predominant material of most of the town's older buildings and partly because

Figure 11.4 Ivor Jones & Percy Thomas, Accrington Police and Fire Station, 1930–1935. Photo: Stewart Bale, c. 1935; from the Collections of the National Monuments Record of Wales © Percy Thomas

---

[20]E.g. 'New Police and Fire Station. Decision as to Frontage', *Accrington Observer* (7 October 1930): 1; 'Observ(er)ations', *Accrington Observer* (11 October 1930): 8; 'Observ(er)ations', *Accrington Observer* (18 October 1930): 10; 'Bricks v. Stone Question Raised in Town Council', *Accrington Observer* (28 October 1930): 1; 'The New Police and Fire Stations: Conflicting Claims for Bricks and Stone', *Accrington Observer* (17 January 1931): 15–16; all at Accrington Community Library (ACL), file on the building.

stone was considered 'preferable for a public building of this character'.[21] Councillor Richard Constantine argued that '[t]hey wanted something that would suggest the highest in their minds in the town – grandeur, […] and beauty and nobleness', and at a speech at the opening he reaffirmed their decision, praising the building as 'a credit to the citizens of [the] town'.[22] The foundation stone had been laid by the Liberal Home Secretary, Sir Herbert Samuel, whose speech summarized the building as offering 'essential services in the civic life of any community' as well as good conditions and housing for staff, as this project too included firemen's housing. He developed the theme of the relationship between local and national government. National government, he argued, should not intrude on 'the progressive spirit and independence of our municipalities', as '[t]he best government is that which teaches us to govern ourselves'. Though on one hand central government supported the municipality's 'own action', providing half of the police station's funding, the Home Office's threat of withdrawing the offer of a grant had motivated the council to proceed, suggesting a distinctly more complex relationship.[23] At both Bristol and Accrington, the functions of police, justice and fire protection (including also an ambulance service and worker housing) were wrapped in coherent neoclassical stone-faced elevations, raising them to a civic status that also hinted at the larger national framework that demanded and enabled them.

Reimagining a democratic state: Swinton and Pendlebury; Swansea

As the centres of administration of local government and its welfare services, town halls and civic centres (which often also contained police stations, fire stations and law courts) were the most important urban markers of such conceptions of democratic citizenship under local and national government. New town halls were increasingly needed after the war to cope with the growing administrative burden that welfare legislation imposed on councils, including slum clearance and social housing, maternity and child health services, education and the poor law, some aspects allocated to county and county borough councils and others to municipal corporations.[24] Many councils embraced their enhanced duties and expected the buildings they commissioned to accommodate them while demonstrating their importance to citizens of this emerging new society. The purposes of the town hall as vehicle for the proud display of independent local governance and as focal point for a developing 'sense of corporate identity' among citizens remained as important

---

[21]'Observ(er)ations', *Accrington Observer* (11 October 1930): 8, ACL.

[22]'Bricks v. Stone Question Raised in Town Council', *Accrington Observer* (28 October 1930): 1; 'Stately New Home of Police and Fire Brigade', *Accrington Observer* (11 May 1935): 15, ACL.

[23]'New Police and Fire Station. Foundation Stone Laying by Home Secretary', *Accrington Observer* (24 September 1932): 13, 15, ACL.

[24]E.g. see Harris, *The Origins of the British Welfare State*: 175–9, 203–6, 232–52; Percy Thomas, 'The Planning of Municipal Buildings', *Journal of the Royal Institute of British Architects* (23 February 1935): 469–87.

as they had been in the nineteenth century.[25] But the administrative offices of local councils expanded exponentially in the early twentieth century, often the prevailing reason for new buildings and the highest proportion of their accommodation, and the council's work was increasingly concerned with welfare rather than regulation. A more subdued, economical architecture than that of pre-war town halls resulted. And whereas in the nineteenth century the greatest motivation had always been municipal independence, Percy Thomas's civic buildings show how much the national political debate, particularly around reactions to the depression, now formed the framework within which municipal government was conceived.

Percy Thomas and his former colleague Ernest Prestwich won the competition for Swinton and Pendlebury Town Hall (now Salford Civic Centre) (**Figure 11.5**) in 1934, the same year that the Municipal Borough celebrated its promotion from an Urban District Council with the awarding of a charter.[26] The competition thus cemented a new image for this newly elevated council. Once completed in 1938, the combined administrative and ceremonial functions of the building were evident from its serried ranks of neo-Georgian windows (in plain brick walls for economy), its axial arch-windowed entrance and tower marking the monumental staircase and council chamber.[27] The use of brick, the possibility of a tower and the desire for simple but 'dignified' elevations had all been expressed in the competition conditions.[28] The town hall was intended to be part of a larger projected civic centre scheme to include a library and assembly hall, police station and court, and a relocated county school.[29]

Councils should not be regarded as neutral administrators, as their motivations were aligned with party political debates. Swinton and Pendlebury, significantly, was dominated by the Labour Party under whose aegis the post-1945 welfare state would later emerge. To perform the opening ceremony, they invited the Labour MP Arthur Greenwood, former Minister of Health and instigator of the 1930 Housing Act. The Mayor, W. S. Mycock, explained:

> Amongst the things the Council had done, [...] no work was more important and had taken up more time than was that in connexion with slum clearance and the rehousing of the people from the slums, from the houses which were very bad. Because Mr. Greenwood, during the time he was in office, was the author of the Act which enabled the Council to do those things it was thought most proper to ask him to perform the ceremony.[30]

---

[25]Colin Cunningham, *Victorian and Edwardian Town Halls* (London: Routledge & Kegan Paul, 1981): 219; also 60–5, 89.

[26]'Swinton Charter', *Eccles and Patricroft Journal* (3 August 1934): 4, in Salford Local History Library (SLHL).

[27]'Municipal Buildings, Swinton and Pendlebury', *Architects' Journal* (30 March 1939): 526–9.

[28]E. & O. E., 'Competition for Municipal Offices for Swinton and Pendlebury U.D.C.', *Architect & Building News* (1 June 1934): 246–7.

[29]'Swinton Town Hall', *National Builder* (November 1938): 126.

[30]'New Swinton Town Hall', *Eccles and Patricroft Journal* (22 September 1938): 10SLHL.

Figure 11.5 Percy Thomas & Ernest Prestwich, Swinton and Pendlebury Town Hall, Salford, 1934–1938. Photo: Stewart Bale, *c.* 1938; Architectural Press Archive/RIBA Collections, RIBA73823

Mycock emphasized the council's work to rehouse four thousand people, and in the last meeting at the old town hall celebrated the near-halving of the annual mortality figures since his arrival.[31] The Mayor's attitude was summarized by the council's motto, placed over his chair in the new council chamber, the familiar phrase from Cicero, 'Salus Populi Suprema Lex', translated with a political intention by the local newspaper as 'the welfare of the people is the highest law', a phrase that recurs in other similar contexts, such as Southwark Borough Council's Walworth Clinic, where 'Salus' is more literally converted to 'Health'.[32] The council clearly positioned its activities in relation to a national debate over welfare, their political support for which found expression in the building of the town hall.

---

[31]'Last Meeting', *Eccles and Patricroft Journal* (16 September 1938): 5, SLHL.
[32]'Swinton & Pendlebury New Town Hall', *Eccles and Patricroft Journal* (16 September 1938): 4, SLHL; [John Boughton], 'The Walworth Clinic, Southwark: "The Health of the People Is the Highest Law"', *Municipal Dreams*, 2013, https://municipaldreams.wordpress.com/2013/10/01/the-walworth-clinic-southwark-the-health-of-the-people-is-the-highest-law/ (accessed 24 March 2020).

Greenwood, speaking at the celebratory banquet, linked the importance of healthy housing to democracy and local government as the ideal democratic form: 'The greatest service local authorities could perform to civilization was by attempting to foster pride in civic institutions and democratic principles and trying to improve by all the agencies that could be commanded the stature and power of the people,' he stated.[33] Earlier he had claimed that '[o]ur citizens don't always realize what our system of local Government means to them in their lives and don't realize what a great inspiration a centre like this ought to be to them'.[34] Thomas and Prestwich's 'magnificent building', as Greenwood put it, would help to inspire pride in local government – not merely pride in the town.

As elsewhere, it was the recent vast expansion of local government responsibilities that had made this new town hall essential.[35] Moreover many of these services required public access to town halls of a degree forgotten today, with waiting rooms provided in the plan for those attending on medical, education or housing officers, while rates were paid in person underneath the council chamber. The architecture's severe plainness inside and out spoke of careful husbandry to this citizen audience, reflecting the fact that the loan granted by the Ministry of Health was so low that no increase in rates was needed.[36] Even the giant columns enriching the entrance to the council chamber were, as the architects highlighted in the souvenir opening booklet, of 'synthetic marble'.[37]

In Swansea in the 1930s the previously dominant Liberal party was on the wane, Labour taking control from 1933, and national debates over the role of the state impacted on the construction of the building.[38] The Guildhall was won by Percy Thomas and Ivor Jones in competition in 1929, and rapidly built, a lavish building inside and out, often described as a civic centre, since it included not only council suite and municipal offices, but also an assembly hall and law courts (**Figures 11.6–11.7**). Alongside a decorative programme representing Swansea's Viking founders and many Welsh national themes, 'Welfare' was celebrated in one of the sculptural discs on the building's exterior frieze depicting the activities of the Borough Council, showing what appears to be a wolf being kept at bay, and prominently illustrated in the souvenir booklet.[39]

When the building was opened in 1934, Swansea's councillors more conventionally called on royalty to preside in the form of the Duke of Kent. Significantly, as well as opening the building, the duke was shown a range of municipal services in action: first

---

[33]'New Swinton Town Hall'.

[34]Ibid.

[35]Untitled, undated document, SLHL, BSP/CL12; W. S. Mycock, 'Foreword', in *The Official Opening of the New Town Hall, Swinton by the Rt. Hon. Arthur Greenwood, M.P., September 17th, 1938* (Cheltenham: n. pub., 1938), unpaginated, SLHL, uncatalogued.

[36]Untitled, undated document, SLHL, BSP/CL12.

[37]Percy Thomas and Ernest Prestwich, 'Description of the Building by the Architects', in *Official Opening of the New Town Hall, Swinton*, unpaginated, SLHL, uncatalogued.

[38]W. C. Rogers, 'The Guildhall and Local Government in Swansea', in J. R. Alban (ed.), *The Guildhall, Swansea: Essays to Commemorate the Fiftieth Anniversary of Its Opening* (Swansea: Swansea City Council, 1984): 28.

[39]*Souvenir of the Opening of the Guildhall, Swansea by His Royal Highness the Duke of Kent on the Twenty-Third Day of October in the Year One Thousand Nine Hundred and Thirty-Four* (Swansea: Alexandra Print Co., 1934): 4, in West Glamorgan Archive Service, Swansea (WGAS), D 53/6/2.

Figure 11.6 Ivor Jones & Percy Thomas, Swansea Guildhall, 1930–1934. Photo: Stewart Bale, *c*. 1934; from the Collections of the National Monuments Record of Wales © Percy Thomas

came a visit to the Unemployment Welfare Centre installed in the YMCA building; then, after a visit to the British Legion, he was taken to inspect the housing estate at Townhill, and thence to Townhill school to meet the Council's Education and Housing Committees, a full day's work ending at the railway station at half past five.[40] Townhill, designed by Borough Architect Ernest E. Morgan with advice from Raymond Unwin, was one of the largest local authority housing estates of the period in Britain, sited to enjoy magnificent views of the town and sea, and with a modern open-air school.

Both were celebrated in articles by Morgan in the souvenir booklet accompanying the opening of the Guildhall and in the *South Wales Evening Post*'s commemorative supplement.[41] The newspaper also discussed the council's two other notable developments, a large new site for hospitals at Cefn Coed on which a 600-bed mental institution had been built, and the government-funded Tir John power station, begun in 1930, which

[40]'County Borough of Swansea. Opening of New Guildhall, Tuesday, October 23rd, 1934, by H.R.H. The Duke of Kent. Programme of Proceedings', WGAS, BA 2/15.

[41]E[rnest] E. M[organ], 'Architectural Features of Swansea', in *Souvenir of the Opening of the Guildhall*: 33, 35; Ernest E. Morgan, 'The Story of Swansea Told in Its Architecture', in *South Wales Evening Post* (23 October 1934) Guildhall Supplement: 22.

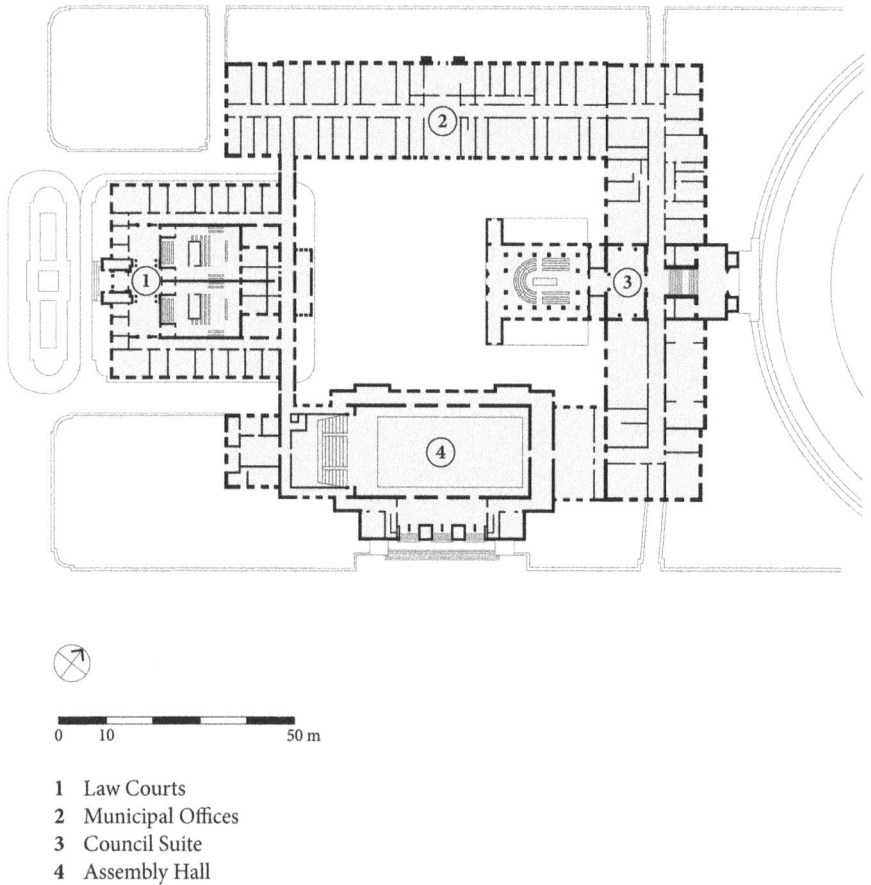

1   Law Courts
2   Municipal Offices
3   Council Suite
4   Assembly Hall

Figure 11.7 Plan of Ivor Jones & Percy Thomas, Swansea Guildhall, 1930–1934, drawn by Hannah Towler

supplied the city through the council's electricity service.[42] Both of these were built by the same contractors used for the construction of the Guildhall, E. Turner & Sons of Swansea and Cardiff, whose advertisement in the newspaper illustrated the three buildings under the heading, 'The March of Progress in Swansea'.[43] The Guildhall was thus set in context by the council and others as one element of an ambitious municipal modernization programme, raising living standards in the town, provided through state-sponsored development. Percy Thomas's municipal offices were the powerhouse of this new vision of civic life, built as a block along one side of the Guildhall to efficient modern standards. Rows of neo-Georgian windows expressed this bureaucratic function, similar to those

---

[42]H. L. Lang-Coath [town clerk since 1911], 'Swansea Municipal Government', in *South Wales Evening Post* (23 October 1934), Guildhall Supplement: 25; Morgan, 'Story of Swansea'; see also 'Swansea's New Guildhall Opened', in *The Municipal Journal* (26 October 1934): 1457–8.

[43]Advertisement, in *South Wales Evening Post* (23 October 1934), Guildhall Supplement: 19.

of the Ministry of Pensions building in Acton that, Alan Powers has argued, defined the new, classical face of modern state administration.[44]

As in many other cases, there was debate among councillors about the desirability of spending ratepayers' money on a new town hall, especially since Swansea was suffering severe unemployment in the depression, dependent as it was on the steel industry and exports of coal from its harbour.[45] Swansea Guildhall and many other municipal buildings of this period benefitted from a special grant from central government intended to relieve unemployment, something that has been noted before but the political implications of which have not been fully examined.[46] The awarding of these grants for council buildings originated with the 1929 election campaigns following the onset of the depression. Seeking to revive the Liberal party's fortunes at the general election, David Lloyd George argued that the depression created conditions similar to those of the war, implying that his successful wartime leadership was needed again for this emergency situation. He proposed a similar scale of response to the crisis from central government: 'The suffering and waste caused by unemployment are as important as was the provision of munitions during the war,' he claimed; 'South Wales and the Industrial North are our Devastated Areas.' Drawing on advice from John Maynard Keynes, he called for an enormous, comprehensive national state system of public works that would transform the nation's landscape and economy while employing those without work – especially schemes of road building, but also housing and town planning, electricity infrastructure, land reclamation and forestry.[47] Swansea's councillors later supported Oldham and Bradford in sending resolutions to the government demanding such a scheme of national works.[48]

In 1920 Lloyd George's government had already set up a modest system for this purpose, a fund administered by the Unemployment Grants Committee to which local authorities could apply for public works, and the Labour government that won the election in 1929 strengthened it in response to the depression. With the help of Swansea's Labour MP, David Williams, also an alderman, the council persuaded the committee to award a government grant for the Guildhall, arguing that the new municipal offices would create such efficiencies in administration that it counted as 'a scheme of economic development', while the building work would employ a thousand men over the three years of its construction.[49] Other councils also applied for the grant, many successfully, but the window of opportunity was narrow, as the scheme was stopped in 1931 by the Minister for Labour, Margaret Bondfield, concerned that it was being abused to subsidize

---

[44]Powers, 'Quality in Quality Street': 19.

[45]E.g. County Borough of Swansea Council Minutes, 15 April 1931, WGAS, TC 2/7.

[46]Johanna Roethe, '"A Pretty Toy" or "Purely Functional"? Town, City and County Halls in the Interwar Period', in Elain Harwood and Alan Powers (eds.), *Twentieth Century Architecture 13: The Architecture of Public Service* (London: Twentieth Century Society, 2018): 27.

[47]David Lloyd George, *We Can Conquer Unemployment* (London: Cassell & Company, 1929): 6; see also Kenneth O. Morgan, *Rebirth of a Nation: Wales 1880–1980* (Oxford: Clarendon Press, 1981): 221.

[48]County Borough of Swansea Council Minutes, 9 November 1932 and 16 November 1932, WGAS, TC 2/8.

[49]'County Borough of Swansea. Proposed New Civic Buildings. Application for Grant Towards Cost of Scheme', n.d. [c. March 1930], WGAS, D/266/1/4/4; David Williams to H. L. Lang-Coath (Town Clerk), 26 March 1930 and E. J. R. Edwards (Treasury, Whitehall) to [Lang-Coath], 9 April 1930, WGAS, TC 53/9097/3.

unnecessary buildings.[50] Percy Thomas had to calculate the cubic area of building related only to the council offices and ceremonial spaces, as the assembly hall, courts and tower were excluded from the grant. He advised the council on wording the building contract to meet the grant requirements, which stipulated that all new workers hired by the builder be sought through the local labour exchange, and that three-quarters be ex-servicemen, reward for war service remaining central to this provision over a decade after the war had ended.[51] The Guildhall received about £90,000 in funding from central government, around a fifth of its total cost. The grant was highlighted in the souvenir opening booklet, depicting the process of building itself as an act of welfare, in which central and local government collaborated.[52] The Bishop of Swansea and Brecon addressed the concern with unemployment even in the consecration prayer at the opening ceremony: 'Remember, O Lord, and bless all those who desire to labour, but lack opportunity, all who suffer thereby, and all who are tempted to lose heart,' he intoned.[53]

For Percy Thomas, the design offered an opportunity to explore ideas about the expression of civic dignity and purpose in the new democratic atmosphere of a universal franchise, within months of the extension of the vote to all adult women. The competition design of 1929 included an Ionic portico across the entrance, but in 1930 Thomas submitted a new design replacing it with a single giant arch, much the same as that he later designed for Swinton and Pendlebury town hall.[54] This alteration simplified the building's appearance, but Thomas also attributed to it a symbolic purpose: 'It was the custom some years ago to reserve the main entrance for ceremonial occasions, and provide side entrances for ordinary everyday use,' he explained in a lecture on 'The Planning of Municipal Buildings'. 'The tendency now is to use the main entrance for all purposes. I believe, from a psychological point of view, the principle is very sound. If the architecture is to have any effect upon the civic pride of the citizens, the more they use the entrance hall and grand staircase the better.'[55] The municipal offices were indeed easily accessed directly from the top of the grand staircase in Swansea (though separate entrances could be used if the main entrance was occupied for ceremonial activity). The rates office, as in other town halls, was approached by stairs to the basement either side of the grand staircase, directly after the main entrance. The short corridors of the

---

[50]Excerpt from Hansard, 22 May 1931; MGB [Margaret Bondfield] (Ministry of Labour) to Arthur Greenwood (Ministry of Health), 15 May 1931; [Margaret Bondfield], 'Unemployment Grants Committee. Grants in Aid of the Erection of Town Halls', n.d. [1931]; G. H. Ince (Ministry of Labour) to H. D. Hancock (Treasury), 6 May 1931; all in The National Archives, LAB 4/194.

[51]Percy Thomas (Ivor Jones & Percy Thomas) to Lang-Coath, 7 May 1931 and Percy Thomas to Lang-Coath, 20 March 1931, WGAS, TC 53/9097/1; the contract wording was taken from Percy Thomas's extension to the Glamorgan County Council offices in Cardiff, which also benefitted from this scheme.

[52]Edward Harris, untitled article, in *Souvenir of the Opening of the Guildhall*: 3.

[53]'County Borough of Swansea. Opening of New Guildhall, Tuesday, October 23rd, 1934, by H.R.H. The Duke of Kent. Programme of Proceedings', 8, WGAS, BA 2/15.

[54]W. S. Purchon, 'Swansea Civic Buildings Competition', *Builder*, 28 February 1930, 429–30 illustrates the original scheme; revised design dated from 'Parliamentary 16 June 1931 (unprinted)' (apparently an extract from Parliamentary Committee of County Borough of Swansea minutes of that date), WGAS, TC 53/9097/4.

[55]Percy Thomas, 'The Planning of Municipal Buildings', *Journal of the Royal Institute of British Architects* (23 February 1935): 470.

offices, designed in a compact block, further allowed 'greater accessibility to the various departments for the public', the *Builder* explained.[56] The single arch was therefore a symbol of equality between councillors and citizens and of the access of all to the services of government. So too was Thomas's landscaping, as reported at Swansea and Swinton: open lawns devoid of fussy flowers and railings ran straight up to the walls, giving the impression of complete visibility and accessibility.[57] It was a symbolic rather than literal idea, however: at Swinton two women were forced to write apologies for 'wilfully walking across the area of grass in front of the new Town Hall'.[58]

In contrast to Swinton, no expense was spared at Swansea: dramatic sculpture and fine workmanship was applied throughout; the council chamber was suffused with luxurious warmth from the panelling and gilded Bassae columns of Australian walnut and a tapestry frieze (**Figure 11.8**), and Empire timbers were liberally used throughout. Externally, the Portland stone facing in long, simple classical lines formed a striking contrast to

Figure 11.8 Ivor Jones & Percy Thomas, council chamber, Swansea Guildhall, 1930–1934. Photo: Stewart Bale, *c.* 1934; Architectural Press Archive/RIBA Collections, RIBA24585

---

[56]'Swansea Civic Centre', *Builder* (9 June 1933): 924.

[57]'Swinton & Pendlebury New Town Hall', 4; Percy Thomas and Ernest Prestwich, 'Description of the Building by the Architects', in *The Official Opening of the New Town Hall, Swinton by the Rt. Hon. Arthur Greenwood, M.P., September 17th, 1938* (Cheltenham: n. pub., 1938), unpaginated, SLHL; 'Preparing the Setting for Swansea's Civic Centre', in *South Wales Evening Post* (31 October 1933): 8.

[58]General Purposes Committee, 10 July 1939, Swinton & Pendlebury Council Minutes 1938–9, SLHL.

the surrounding clutter of Victorian terraces. Portland stone was specified in the competition conditions, which were formulated after a committee of councillors toured a selection of town halls, including recent buildings for Marylebone (Edwin Cooper, 1914–1920), Wimbledon (Bradshaw, Gass and Hope, 1928–1931) and Nottingham (Thomas Cecil Howitt, 1927–1929), all neoclassical in Portland stone, and earlier civic buildings also making significant use of the material, such as Deptford (Lanchester, Stewart & Rickards, 1905) and Lambeth (Septimus Warwick and H Austen Hall, 1905–1908).[59] The most potent model, however, was probably the great Civic Centre at Cardiff, all of whose buildings were clad in Portland stone, initially through imitation rather than compulsion.[60] This loosely planned complex of buildings of both local civic status and national (Welsh) status, including the Registry of the University of Wales and the National Museum of Wales, drew on capital city planning in the American Beaux-Arts mould, attempting to claim a status for Cardiff as an imperial capital (though it would not achieve that title for two decades).[61] Swansea thus sought to borrow such well-known associations for its own civic centre; it was, after all, a direct competitor to Cardiff as a gateway to the international market in coal.

By the 1920s, Portland stone Classicism was becoming a broadly favoured approach indicative of national and imperial institutions, adopted by organizations hoping to gain such associations themselves (banks, universities, the RIBA), and perhaps above all echoing the predominant material of war memorials, including the nearby Swansea Cenotaph, designed by Morgan along the lines of that by Edwin Lutyens in London. Thomas emulated Lutyens's Whitehall Cenotaph design method for Swansea's tower, particularly in the use of entasis, drawing its outline at full scale on the office floor.[62] Lutyens then appears to have drawn on Thomas's tower in his design for the Australian National Memorial at Villers-Bretonneux near Amiens (1935–1938). The adoption of this brand of simplified Portland stone Classicism therefore suggests that Swansea's councillors desired to represent themselves and their town as participants on equal terms within a national and imperial state, and also associates their vision of an egalitarian, welfare-focused state with the memory of war. Thomas's building provided an image of civic administration within a wider framework of British government. Welsh nationality was also emphasized – in the council chamber's tapestry depicting a druidic procession; the druid and St David sculptures over external doors; a relief panel in the Assize Hall representing the earliest records of law in Wales.[63] These elements give national inflection

---

[59]'County Borough of Swansea. Report on Visit of the Sub-Committee of the Parliamentary and General Purposes Committee to Various Civic Centres', April 1929, WGAS, BA 2/15.
[60]John B. Hilling, *The History and Architecture of Cardiff Civic Centre: Black Gold, White City* (Cardiff: University of Wales Press, 2016): 93–4.
[61]Huw Thomas, 'Spatial Restructuring in the Capital: Struggles to Shape Cardiff's Built Environment', in Ralph Fevre and Thompson (eds.), *Nation, Identity and Social Theory: Perspectives from Wales* (Cardiff: University of Wales Press, 1999): 172.
[62]Robert Dunton, interview with the author, Bath (9 March 2018).
[63]I. J. Campbell, 'An Architectural Appreciation of the Guildhall', in J. R. Alban (ed.), *The Guildhall, Swansea: Essays to Commemorate the Fiftieth Anniversary of Its Opening* (Swansea: Swansea City Council, 1984): 40, 45; Hilary Woolley, 'Art and Design in the Guildhall', in *The Guildhall, Swansea*: 85–6.

to what was otherwise a markedly British and imperial building. Imperial associations were vividly demonstrated in Frank Brangwyn's paintings in the Assembly Hall. These paintings depicted utopian scenes of luxuriant colonial vegetation harmoniously peopled with the racially diverse bodies of British subjects. They had been commissioned for the Royal Gallery at the Palace of Westminster to commemorate the empire's contributions to the war, but were then rejected and accepted instead by Swansea, and were integrated into Thomas's design.

With strong Labour and Liberal representation at Swansea and Swinton and Pendlebury, little dissension from these projects was aired in public. In other places, however, democratically enabled disputes over town hall projects articulated differing views of what the state should be and do, providing further important historical evidence about the intentions of town hall builders.

Architecture as political consensus: Tunbridge Wells

While Percy Thomas's great building at Swansea reinforced a growing consensus over a social democratic political vision, his civic centre at Tunbridge Wells became a central focus of frenetic local arguments over the role of the borough council which similarly drew on the national debate, played out through democratic processes. The council's civic centre project initiated a surge of public involvement in politics reacting against the growing dominance of the state, but Thomas's design helped to mollify and mask these anxieties by describing a modest and benevolent institutional presence for the state within the town.

Tunbridge Wells was politically very different from Swansea, represented by a Conservative Member of Parliament, Robert Gower, also an alderman and therefore active in council meetings, who was prominent in debates over the civic centre. Although most of the town's councillors were nominally independent, they tended in practice to be selected as candidates by the local Chamber of Trade and Conservative Association.[64] In 1930 the council began to advance a scheme to abandon their current town hall, a dilapidated converted Victorian market hall, by creating a swathe of new municipal buildings on a nearby site they had purchased for the purpose over the previous decade on the town's main shopping street. The functions required included staff offices and committee rooms, council chamber and associated ceremonial spaces, a police and fire station, assembly hall, a library and museum, a medical clinic and a showroom for the municipal electricity service; only the clinic and fire station were eventually omitted, largely due to site constraints. That it took over a decade to reach completion was due to vociferous public opposition, which instrumentalized local democracy to keep the scheme in doubt.

Much of this debate took place before Percy Thomas's involvement. E. Berry Webber, architect of Southampton Civic Centre, was commissioned for an initial report in

---

[64]'The New Town Hall Inquiry', *Kent & Sussex Courier* (9 January 1931): 3.

the summer of 1930, and E. Vincent Harris was then invited to design a scheme, the council spurred on by the government's Unemployment Grants Committee's support for municipal buildings. Advocating the scheme to councillors, the Mayor argued that there was 'a serious condition of unemployment in the town' and that those currently receiving 'unemployment benefits [...] would infinitely prefer to give a full day's work for the money'. His argument was that welfare payments were counterproductive, while the town's need for a 'dignified setting' for its ever-growing operations remained unmet.[65] Councillors voted unanimously to go ahead but soon faced a crisis of opposition whipped up by the town's Ratepayers' League. At a public meeting it organized, Gower spoke against the town hall project, arguing that the depression necessitated austerity for both the nation and the town; if money was to be spent, it should be on housing rather than 'lavish expenditure on town halls'. Unemployment, he argued, 'had to be considered nationally and not locally' and would not be alleviated by the building.[66]

Meanwhile the town's Chamber of Trade voted to proceed with a cheaper scheme. Keynesian principles were cited in its favour: 'in times of national depression of trade', L. W. Passmore argued,

> national credit should be used for the purpose of expenditure of the useful and improving nature. That was a fundamental fact of economics. [...] Now, therefore, was the proper time in which to proceed with a reasonable, economical, efficient and suitable scheme for a new Town Hall. Now was the time, if they wanted to do the best for themselves, and the best by the nation.[67]

Building a town hall was apparently genuinely considered by many as an act of welfare in the national interest, the latter not therefore, as Bondfield's advisers thought, a mere pretext for subsidised excess. A council meeting responding to the public debate also echoed national political arguments. Gower now supported a modest building, urging economy in the national interest, but another councillor, Phillips, argued that any such unnecessary expenditure would only help the 'extravagant administration' of the Labour government to 'ameliorate the figures'.[68] All these arguments clearly revolved around political rather than pragmatic considerations, namely whether state expenditure was desirable and whether taxation should be raised for the purpose of increased state administration. Both were features of the general election campaign of 1931 that brought down the Labour government. This local decision about a town hall was therefore conflated with national political rhetoric over the nature of the state.

The same arguments were rehearsed in Tunbridge Wells for months, as opponents to the civic centre became more organized by adopting democratic methods. A splinter

---

[65]'New Municipal Buildings', *Kent & Sussex Courier* (1 August 1930): 8.

[66]'Tunbridge Wells Ratepayers Protest', *The Argus*, 13 September 1930, unpaginated cutting, in Tunbridge Wells Borough Archives (TWBA), 549, Chamber of Trade Cuttings Book, 1930–31.

[67]'Chamber of Trade', *Tunbridge Wells Advertiser* (19 September 1930) unpaginated cutting, TWBA, 549.

[68]'No Decision Yet', *Tunbridge Wells Advertiser* (19 September 1930) unpaginated cutting, TWBA, 549.

group from the Ratepayers' League organized an unofficial referendum, receiving an overwhelming response against new buildings, leading to further arguments about the legitimacy of local democracy.[69] When the council applied for Ministry of Health sanction for a loan, the required public inquiry – usually a formality – became another forum for objection, many members of the public noisily applauding council opponents. Vincent Harris was forced to denounce a surprise alternative scheme by another architect for the Ratepayers' League, and to defend his design from accusations of excess, the phrase 'Corinthian porticos and cornices' deployed as a term of abuse.[70] Urged by the League's lawyer to consider 'whether [...] the Corporation were voicing the true opinion of the ratepayers', the inspector recommended refusal, preventing the council obtaining the funds to proceed and demanding 'a scheme on less expensive lines'.[71]

In the autumn of 1931, the civic centre's opponents stood candidates in council elections, stating that 'we all readily and wholeheartedly supported the appeal of His Majesty's [Conservative] Government to review the whole field of expenditure'.[72] They took all seven wards contested that year, a 'Municipal Bombshell', as one local paper called it.[73] But as the urgency of debates over the depression subsided in the following years, opinion in the town began to change, the Chamber of Trade urging the council to house itself in more fitting surroundings, and while presence on the council gave an official sanction to opponents' voices, they were easily outvoted.

In 1934 a competition was held, Berry Webber acting as assessor, and the material, brick, and the style, 'typical English building suitable to the neighbourhood and character of Tunbridge Wells', were determined in advance.[74] Percy Thomas and Ernest Prestwich won, no doubt largely because of the sophistication of their planning, but probably also because they placed the main axis of the council suite and arched entrance on the corner of the site facing the road junction where it would have a more convincing monumental prominence than those of competitors aligned on the street frontages. The classical orders of Harris's more Baroque conception were conspicuously absent.[75] The council only applied to the Ministry of Health for loan sanction three years later when the existing town hall threatened to collapse, and this time no opposition was voiced.[76] When

---

[69]E.g. 'The New Municipal Buildings', *Kent & Sussex Courier* (5 December 1930): 8.

[70]'The New Town Hall Inquiry': 2.

[71]'The New Town Hall Scheme', *Kent & Sussex Courier* (2 January 1931): 6; 'The New Town Hall Inquiry', *Kent & Sussex Courier* (9 January 1931): 2–3, 9; 'Town Hall Inquiry Concludes', *Kent & Sussex Courier* (23 January 1931): 2–3, 9; Borough of Royal Tunbridge Wells Council Minutes, 4 March 1931, TWBA, 417.

[72]Advertisement, 'Municipal Elections, 1931', *Tunbridge Wells Advertiser* (16 October 1931) unpaginated cutting, Royal Tunbridge Wells Chamber of Trade Newspaper Cuttings, TWBA, 800.

[73]'Municipal Bombshell', *Kent & Sussex Courier* (6 November 1931) unpaginated cutting, TWBA, 800; also 'The New Councillors' and 'Swept by the Board', *Tunbridge Wells Advertiser* (6 November 1931) unpaginated cuttings, TWBA, 800.

[74]Special (Calverley Parade Property) Committee, 26 March 1934 and 24 April 1934, Borough of Royal Tunbridge Wells, Civic Centre Committee Minutes, 1932–43, TWBA, 923.

[75]'Tunbridge Wells Civic Centre', *Builder* (16 November 1934): 839–40; 'Tunbridge Wells Civic Centre Competition: The Winners' Report', *Architect & Building News* (16 November 1934): 199–218.

[76]'No Opposition to Civic Centre Application', *Tunbridge Wells Advertiser* (12 February 1937) unpaginated cutting, in album of 'Newspaper Cuttings' 1935–42, TWBA, 801.

the council chamber was finally inaugurated in 1941, much of its interior decoration truncated due to war conditions; it was without any fanfare or special guests, and not even the architects seem to have attended.[77]

Thomas and Prestwich thus satisfied the council's need for new buildings in a fitting classical style, monumental in symmetry and simplicity, but the brick neo-Georgian version of Classicism achieved these effects with a conspicuous minimum of ornament and expense. The debates that led to the competition and the selection of this design show that, as at Swansea, the civic centre was conceived of by both sides as a manifestation of the state. In Tunbridge Wells, however, any proposal for buildings beyond the modest limits of necessity symbolized an overbearing state, a state that extended its role in society too far, demanding too much of its citizens, and acting against their will. The expressive character and form of the civic centre would shape conceptions of the state that it housed, and both were open to be forged through democratic means. Percy Thomas's architecture papered over such political tensions, expressing a consensus that did not exist. Moreover, Thomas's civic buildings shared a distinct family resemblance with those of other towns across Britain. Emulation between towns, government support and architectural convention promoted this kindred appearance. Elements expressing local identity, such as materials and sculptural ornaments, were relatively minor inflections within a consistent national building type.

A welfare ideal: The Temple of Peace and Health at Cardiff

Meanwhile, Percy Thomas's Temple of Peace at Cardiff did not have to mollify tensions but did have to represent a simple idea about welfare and the state through a utopian image concealing a more complex reality. Though much of its funding from David Davies was philanthropic, the building's aim was to demonstrate a new social vision of national and global citizenship, in which the state had an active role. The Welsh League of Nations Union disseminated support for international peace and awareness of citizenship and democracy throughout Wales, through advocacy of the League of Nations, especially through chapels and schools. Davies was a vocal supporter of the League of Nations, speaking and writing widely on world peace. The Temple of Peace's simplicity, Portland stone facing and astylar Classicism, a design change from the Ionic portico of the original design of 1931, followed from Percy Thomas's deliberate emulation of the League of Nations building in Geneva in an attempt to find an international form of architecture.[78] So too did the wide range of marbles from many countries used inside.[79] The Union's

---

[77]'Opening of the New Town Hall', *Kent & Sussex Courier* (28 March 1941): 2.
[78]'Proposed Welsh National Memorial Buildings, Cardiff', *Builder* (9 January 1931): 118; David Davies, 'Temple an Expression of Two Ideals', *Western Mail & South Wales News* (23 November 1938), Temple of Peace and Health Supplement, 2, CUASC, Temple of Peace Box.
[79]'"House Warming" at the Hall of Justice', *Western Mail & South Wales News* (4 November 1938): 7, CUASC, Temple of Peace Box.

activities included publishing curricula for schoolteachers in the subject of 'Civics', introducing pupils to concepts of community and democratic government, including local and global interdependence and dialogue.[80] Civics invited students to imagine their position as embedded within concentric rings of community networks – in which the city, the country and the nation state had equal validity within a global context. Similarly, Welsh and British (national and imperial) identities could be celebrated together without apparent conflict in an architecture that could nod to multiple identities through modest symbolic decorative elements inscribed upon a harmonious neoclassical framework: the frieze over the astylar portico of the Temple of Peace included discs with the symbols of the four British nations, for example.[81]

The Edward VII Welsh National Memorial Association occupying the second wing was an organization founded by Davies and others in 1910–1912 with the aim of eradicating tuberculosis in Wales. With the Public Health (Tuberculosis) Act of 1921, the association became a statutory organization, funded by the Welsh local authorities to discharge their duties according to the act.[82] It became effectively, therefore, a local and limited precursor of the National Health Service, in its own words, 'a rate-aided and State-aided concern'.[83] The association contributed to the cost of the Temple of Peace building, for which it was permitted a government loan by the Ministry of Health, though most of the building's funding came directly from Davies.[84] The pairing of the two organizations, the Welsh League of Nations Union and the Memorial Association, represented for Davies an intrinsic link between peace, justice and health, symbolized in three sculptures over the entrance.[85]

Just as the Temple of Peace was being built in 1937, the Memorial Association opened a tuberculosis hospital at Sully, near Cardiff, a modernist building won in competition by W. A. Pite, Son & Fairweather.[86] While the functionalism of the tuberculosis hospital

---

[80] *Teachers and World Peace* (Cardiff: League of Nations Union, Welsh National Council, 1928): 25–6, Cardiff University Archives and Special Collections, Temple of Peace Box; for more on civics, see Tom Hulme, *After the Shock City: Urban Culture and the Making of Modern Citizenship* (Woodbridge: Royal Historical Society and The Boydell Press, 2019): 47–69.

[81] 'Temple of Peace and Health, Cardiff', *Builder* (4 November 1938): 882.

[82] Linda Bryder, 'The King Edward VII Welsh National Memorial Association and Its Policy towards Tuberculosis, 1910–1948', *Welsh History Review* 13 (1986): 194–216.

[83] 'Press Notes. Hall of Nations', n. d. [1938], National Library of Wales, Aberystwyth (NLW), Welsh National Memorial Association Records (WNMAR), Box 33, folder: 'Hall of Nations and W.N.M.A. Offices. Opening Ceremony. Nov. 23rd 1938'.

[84] S. H. G. Hughes (Principal Assistant Secretary for Finance and Accountant-General, Ministry of Health, London) to [F. J. Alban] (General Secretary of the Welsh National Memorial Association), 31 December 1936, NLW, WNMAR, Box 32, 'New Offices and Temple of Peace, etc. Public Inquiry by the Ministry of Health. 3rd December 1936'; G. G. Russell (Capron & Co. [solicitors to Davies] to [F. J.] Alban, 10 March 1933, NLW, WNMAR, Box 32, folder: 'WNMA – New Offices and Hall of Nations'.

[85] 'Notes re. "The Lord Mayor and Corporation of the City of Cardiff"', November 1938, NLW, WNMAR, Box 33, folder: 'Hall of Nations and W.N.M.A. Offices. Opening Ceremony. Nov. 23rd 1938'.

[86] Monica Cherry, *Building Wales* (Cardiff: Arts Council of Wales, 2005): 12; *The King Edward VII Welsh National Memorial Association. The Sully Hospital, Sully, Glamorgan* (Cardiff: Welsh National Memorial Association, 1937), NLW, WNMAR, Box 33, folder: 'Hall of Nations and W.N.M.A. Offices. Opening Ceremony. Nov. 23rd 1938'.

showed the work of welfare in action, the Classicism of Percy Thomas's architecture gave the Temple of Peace a civic and institutional character, as 'a symbol of the struggle for national health and international peace', according to the Union's president, Dudley Howe.[87] The site was a gift from the Cardiff corporation, whose councillors welcomed the idea of such a national institution taking a prominent position within the civic centre at Cathays Park, also by now home to Dunbar Smith and Cecil Brewer's National Museum of Wales, the Registry office of the University of Wales and J. Ninian Comper's Welsh National War Memorial, besides the buildings of municipal government and higher education. Not yet officially a capital city, Cardiff was nevertheless seeking to claim such a position. The architecture of the Temple of Peace followed the civic centre's Portland stone Classicism but was the most severe of all its buildings in approach until then, the absence of mouldings seen as indicative of twentieth-century modernity, a 'modern adaptation of the classic', while the adherence to classical compositional and spatial principles and application of decorative sculpture retained the required ceremonial 'dignity'.[88]

The 'Hall of Nations' in the centre of the building was a secular ceremonial space lined with fluted marble piers, a kind of public assembly hall (**Figure 11.9**). There was no predetermined demand for such a space, however, other than the fact that the League of Nations Union held an annual conference, hitherto hiring public halls around Wales. Rather, this room had the symbolic purpose of welcoming visitors and forming their identity as citizens of this idealized world of peace and welfare. Speaking at the banquet after the opening ceremony, Davies asked, 'Is it too much to hope that every man, woman and child, from one end of our beloved country to the other [...] shall participate in this act of self-dedication of the people, by the people, for the people, by making a pilgrimage to this shrine?'[89] Always underlying these concerns of peace and health remained the memory of war, preserved through the sombre chapel-like crypt and the Book of Remembrance.[90]

The Temple of Peace perhaps came closer than any other civic building in Britain before then to embodying a visionary ideal of the social democratic state that would soon become the consensus for reconstruction after a second devastating war. Its architectural approach may not have been that which would eventually come to denote the ethos of the welfare state, but its spartan, stripped classical architecture allowed the building's creators to ascribe to it a rich political meaningfulness.

---

[87]'"House Warming" at the Hall of Justice': 7.
[88]'The Architect's Modern Adaptation of the Classic', *Western Mail & South Wales News* (23 November 1938), section Temple of Peace and Health Supplement, 3, CUASC, Temple of Peace Box. The article seems to have been written by Thomas himself, though its authorship is not credited.
[89]Davies; also NLW, WNMAR, Box 33, folder: 'Box 922. File 976/A/4'.
[90]E. R. Eaton, 'Thoughts in the Crypt and Hall of Justice', *Western Mail & South Wales News*, 23 November 1938, Temple of Peace and Health Supplement, 8, CUASC, Temple of Peace Box.

Figure 11.9 Ivor Jones & Percy Thomas, 'Hall of Nations', Welsh National Temple of Peace and Health, Cardiff, 1931–1938. Photo: Stewart Bale, *c.* 1938; Architectural Press Archive/RIBA Collections, RIBA73675

Conclusion

Percy Thomas's architecture of the 1920s and 1930s participated in a national British argument for the expansion of state welfare for the benefit of its citizens, enacted primarily at local level through councils, though embracing other institutions too – universities and charities, among many others not mentioned here, some also represented elsewhere in Thomas's work. The organizations and funding streams behind Thomas's buildings show that they were part of the state, broadly conceived, and the political discourses surrounding their creation and use set them within a culture that equated a new war-born democracy with the duty of citizens to serve each other through the administration of government. These discourses – and even some of Thomas's own architectural statements – hint at the prevailing Idealist philosophy of the state shared by many in local government, in which citizens were active participants in government and welfare was perceived as a means to promote the inclusion and participation of all people in society.[91] Architects provided the spaces for such a society to function, perhaps predominantly through housing – though this was barely represented in Percy Thomas's work as this branch of building was mainly undertaken by councils themselves. But such a growing political vision also necessitated a symbolic framework that was supposed to encourage people to see, access and identify with the work of the state and allied institutions of public service, stirring emotions of civic and national pride, while also organizing the bodies of citizens in relation to each other, and including collective spaces in which the civic body could assemble under the aegis of the state. War, its aftermath and memory may not have been necessary for this vision to emerge, but it provided an urgency and a unifying rationale for the arguments – and the architecture – that tied its bloodshed and patriotism to democracy and welfare.

Acknowledgements

Research for this chapter was funded by the Paul Mellon Centre for Studies in British Art through a Research Support Grant and a Mid-Career Fellowship, and by a Small Research Grant from the British Academy and Leverhulme Trust.

Select bibliography

Primary

Archival sources
Accrington Community Library
Bristol Archives
Cardiff University Archives and Special Collections
The National Archives
National Library of Wales, Aberystwyth
Salford Local History Library
Tunbridge Wells Borough Archives
West Glamorgan Archive Service, Swansea

Grey literature
Lloyd George, David. *We Can Conquer Unemployment.* London: Cassell & Company, 1929.

---

[91]Harris, 'Political Thought and the Welfare State'.

Souvenir of the Opening of the Guildhall, Swansea by His Royal Highness the Duke of Kent on the Twenty-Third Day of October in the Year One Thousand Nine Hundred and Thirty-Four. Swansea: Alexandra Print Co., 1934.
Teachers and World Peace. Cardiff: League of Nations Union, Welsh National Council, 1928.

Newspapers and periodicals
Accrington Observer
Architect & Building News
Architects' Journal
Builder
Eccles and Patricroft Journal
Journal of the Royal Institute of British Architects
Kent & Sussex Courier
Western Mail & South Wales News

Secondary

Articles
Powers, Alan. 'The Architecture of Public Service'. *Twentieth Century Architecture*, 13, 'The Architecture of Public Service' (2018): 7–23.
Roethe, Johanna. '"A Pretty Toy" or "Purely Functional"? Town, City and County Halls in the Interwar Period'. *Twentieth Century Architecture* 13, 'The Architecture of Public Service' (2018): 25–39.
Shasore, N. E. 'Southampton Civic Centre: Patronage and Place in the Interwar Architecture of Public Service'. *Twentieth Century Architecture* 13 'The Architecture of Public Service' (2018): 41–61.

Chapters (in edited volumes/collections)
Harris, Jose. 'Political Thought and the Welfare State 1870–1940: An Intellectual Framework for British Social Policy'. In *Before Beveridge: Welfare before the Welfare State*, edited by David Gladstone, 43–63. London: Institute of Economic Affairs, 1999.
Holder, Julian. 'A State of Approval: Neo-Georgian Architecture and His Majesty's Office of Works, 1914–1939'. In *Neo-Georgian Architecture 1880–1970: A Reappraisal*, edited by Julian Holder and Elizabeth McKellar, 122–35. Swindon: Historic England, 2016.
Powers, Alan. 'Quality in Quality Street: Neo-Georgian and Its Place in Architectural History'. In *Neo-Georgian Architecture 1880–1970: A Reappraisal*, edited by Julian Holder and Elizabeth McKellar, 13–24. Swindon: Historic England, 2016.
Rogers, W. C. 'The Guildhall and Local Government in Swansea'. In *The Guildhall, Swansea: Essays to Commemorate the Fiftieth Anniversary of Its Opening*, edited by J. R. Alban, 13–32. Swansea: Swansea City Council, 1984.

Books
Alban, J. R. (ed.). *The Guildhall, Swansea: Essays to Commemorate the Fiftieth Anniversary of Its Opening.* Swansea: Swansea City Council, 1984.
Cotton, A. Calveley. *Town Halls.* London: Architectural Press, 1936.
Cronin, James E. *The Politics of State Expansion: War, State and Society in Twentieth-Century Britain.* London: Routledge, 1991.

Cunningham, Colin. *Victorian and Edwardian Town Halls*. London: Routledge & Kegan Paul, 1981.

Darling, Elizabeth. *Re-forming Britain: Narratives of Modernity before Reconstruction*. London: Routledge, 2007.

Gladstone, David (ed.). *Before Beveridge: Welfare before the Welfare State*. London: Institute of Economic Affairs, 1999.

Harris, Bernard. *The Origins of the British Welfare State: Society, State and Social Welfare*. Basingstoke: Palgrave Macmillan, 2004.

Hilling, John B. *The History and Architecture of Cardiff Civic Centre: Black Gold, White City*. Cardiff: University of Wales Press, 2016.

Holder, Julian and Elizabeth McKellar (ed.). *Neo-Georgian Architecture 1880–1970: A Reappraisal*. Swindon: Historic England, 2016.

Hulme, Tom. *After the Shock City: Urban Culture and the Making of Modern Citizenship*. Woodbridge: Royal Historical Society and The Boydell Press, 2019.

Marwick, Arthur. *The Deluge: British Society and the First World War*. London: Macmillan, 1973.

Thomas, Percy Edward. *Pupil to President: Memoirs of an Architect*. Leigh-on-Sea: F. Lewis, 1963.

CHAPTER 12
SIR HERBERT BAKER, RHODES HOUSE AND THE ARCHITECTURE OF MEMORY
Geoffrey Tyack

Until quite recently the standard narrative of architecture in Britain after the First World War emphasized the rise of modernism to the detriment of what Nikolaus Pevsner called 'retardaire' styles. Ranging from the neo-Tudor found in countless private houses and pubs to the monumental Classicism seen in many public and commercial buildings, these styles drew upon collective memory. For John Ruskin memory was one of the seven 'lamps' of architecture, and several British architects would have echoed his assertion that it was 'in becoming memorial or monumental that a true perfection is attained by civil and domestic buildings'.[1] But what precisely should we now remember when we look at buildings put up after 1918, and how should we interpret their meaning, especially when they proclaim a message that we find uncomfortable, or even reprehensible? These questions are acutely posed by Rhodes House, the Oxford headquarters of the Rhodes Trust, established in 1903 after the death of Cecil Rhodes (1853–1902) in order to fund scholarships to Oxford University for selected male students from the British Empire and from Germany and the United States.[2] Built in 1926–1929, it throws a revealing light both on the career and reputation of one of the most successful and prolific architects operating in the British Empire of the early twentieth century, Sir Herbert Baker (1862–1946),[3] and on the public architecture of the 1920s and 1930s.

Thomas Carlyle wrote in 1841 that '[t]he history of the world is but the biography of great men'.[4] These are words that cannot have been lost on Rhodes, a clergyman's son from Bishops Stortford (Hertfordshire) who went to South Africa at the age of sixteen in 1869 and intermittently attended Oriel College, Oxford, as an undergraduate between 1873 and 1881, in the intervals of making a fortune as a diamond prospector

---

[1] John Ruskin, 'The Lamp of Memory', in *The Seven Lamps of Architecture* (1849: London, Everyman ed., 1907): 18.

[2] The scholarships were subsequently opened to non-white applicants, and in 1977 to women: see http://www.rhodeshouse.ox.ac.uk (accessed 18 April 2022).

[3] For Baker's career, see his autobiography, *Architecture and Personalities* (London: Country Life, 1944); Daniel M. Abramson, 'Baker, Sir Herbert', *Oxford Dictionary of National Biography*; A. Stuart Gray, *Edwardian Architecture: A Biographical Dictionary* (London: Duckworth, 1985): 97–9. For his South African work, see also Doreen E. Greig, *Baker in South Africa* (Cape Town and New York: Purnell, 1970); 'Baker, Sir Herbert', http://www.artefacts.co.za/main/Buildings/archframes.php?archid=60, and 'Sir Herbert Baker – in Memoriam', *South African Architectural Record* (July 1946).

[4] *Heroes and Hero-Worship*, vol. 1.

in southern Africa.[5] He later became a politician and promoter of what has been called a 'sub-empire' encompassing the modern nations of South Africa, Zimbabwe and Zambia.[6] He established the British South Africa Company in 1889, leading to the conquest of what became southern Rhodesia (now Zimbabwe), and in 1890 he became prime minister of Cape Colony. The 29-year-old Baker met him in 1892, soon after going out from England to the Cape in order to help his younger brother establish a fruit farm with funds contributed by their father. Writing in 1934, more than 30 years after Rhodes's death, Baker described the older man in Carlylean terms as 'pre-eminently a personality inspiring the highest service and hero-worship [*sic*]. He carried you with him above the material and the critical into the higher sphere of his own practical idealism'.[7]

Rhodes was always a controversial figure. His admirers hailed him as a visionary champion of Britain's imperial mission. But for one at least of his obituarists his Imperialist ideal was 'subordinated to that of keeping up dividends'.[8] And, as prime minister of Cape Colony, he was responsible for raising the property requirement for the franchise, claiming in 1894 that the Black Africans were 'children … just emerging from barbarism', that they could not be trusted with the vote, and, anticipating later Apartheid legislation, that they should be 'kept in … native reserves and not be mixed with the white men at all'.[9] This chapter, written at a time when statues and memorials to Rhodes, have been threatened or even taken down, focuses on what precisely Baker was commemorating at Rhodes House. It discusses the building's meaning within the context of Baker's other commissions for Rhodes and of post-1918 preoccupations with memory and memorials. And it emphasizes the ways in which, in Baker's hands, the architecture of the Arts and Crafts movement took on an explicitly imperial character.

Baker came from a family of gentleman farmers in Kent and grew up at Owletts, a neat, compact, brick-built house of 1683–1684 with a large garden, just outside the village of Cobham, less than 30 miles south-east of London.[10] He attended Tonbridge, a minor public school only a few miles away, and there, in the words of one of his biographers, he 'absorbed all the typically English attitudes which such a typically English institution could offer':[11] ideals of patriotism, manly self-reliance, dedication to duty and 'playing

[5]Richard Symonds, *Oxford and Empire: The Last Lost Cause?* (Oxford: Oxford University Press, 1992): 161–2; Leonard Thompson, *A History of South Africa* (New Haven and London: Yale University Press, 1996): 116–17.

[6]John Darwin, *The Empire Project: The Rise and Fall of the British World-System, 1830–1970* (Cambridge: Cambridge University Press, 2009): 229–31.

[7]Herbert Baker, *Cecil Rhodes by His Architect* (Oxford: Oxford University Press, 1934): 175.

[8]*Manchester Guardian* (27 March 1902).

[9]https://www.sahistory.org.za/sites/default/files/glen_grey_speech.pdf (accessed 18 April 2022). See also F. Verschoyle (ed.), *Cecil Rhodes: His Political Life and Speeches, 1881–1900* (London: Chapman and Hall, 1900): 371–90. The speech was delivered in the Cape Parliament on 30 July 1894.

[10]The interior was sensitively altered by Baker after the First World War: Clive Aslet, 'A Pleasure for the Birds', *Country Life* (25 March 2020): 116–21. I am grateful to James Offen for information about Baker's family and early career.

[11]Greig, *Baker in South Africa*: 11.

the game'.[12] Articled first to his uncle Arthur Baker, a pupil of George Gilbert Scott, he later entered the office of Ernest George, one of the most successful British domestic architects of the time. Here he met the young Edwin Lutyens (1869–1944), who shared his interest in local vernacular buildings. Baker joined the Art Workers' Guild in 1884, and, like Lutyens, was deeply influenced by the burgeoning Arts and Crafts movement, itself inspired by the ideal of an 'organic' rural society with its associated craft traditions, threatened at the time by agricultural depression and rapid urbanization.[13] He established an independent practice in 1890, devoted mainly to the restoration of old Kentish houses; they included the so-called Yeoman's House at Sole Street, a mile or so from Cobham, with its open hall of a type he was later to imitate in 1902–1906 in his Government House in Pretoria in South Africa, and still later at Rhodes House in Oxford.[14]

Baker's first important South African building was Groote Schuur, Rhodes's weekend residence in the shadow of Table Mountain just outside Cape Town. Originally a granary built by Dutch settlers in 1657, the house was chosen by Rhodes as a country gentleman's residence in which he could entertain guests, with an open-air stoep outside. Having leased, and later bought, the existing, much-altered, house, he employed Baker in 1892 to rebuild and extend it 'with some degree of faithfulness to the original form and type'.[15] This was the local 'Cape Dutch' vernacular, its choice celebrating the Dutch settlement of the southern tip of Africa at a time when tension was rising between Afrikaaners and the more recent Anglophone immigrants, tensions that led in 1899 to the outbreak of the Boer War. Baker admired 'Cape Dutch' architecture for its historical associations and its 'beautiful simplicity', the main external flourish taking the form of curvaceous gables, and he contributed a chapter to Alys Fane Trotter's attractively illustrated *Old Colonial Houses of the Cape of Good Hope* (London: Batsford, 1900).[16] Shaped gables were also a feature of some of Ernest George's buildings, but not of the original Groote Schuur farmhouse, which was thatched.

The interiors of the new Groote Schuur are heavy, solid and intentionally masculine in effect. In a letter to C. R. Ashbee, founder of the Guild of Handicrafts, Baker revealingly criticized the 'affectation and effeminacy' of much recent interior decoration in England, preferring 'a more sturdy and virile expression in Art … of a simple and primitive character'.[17] Rhodes, who never married, thought similarly, admiring dark teak

[12]The latter ideal was celebrated in poems such as Henry Newbolt's 'Vitaï Lampada', written in 1897: Newbolt, *Collected Poems 1897–1907* (London: Thomas Nelson, n.d.): 131–3.

[13]See, for instance, George Bourne (George Sturt), *Change in the Village* (London: Duckworth & Co., 1912), about a hamlet close to Farnham (Surrey).

[14]Arthur Oswald, *Country Houses of Kent* (London: Country Life, 1933): 26 and p. 86. His wife, whom he married in 1904, grew up at Nurstead Court, not far from Owletts, which retained substantial remnants of a fourteenth-century timber-framed aisled hall. Baker made a reconstruction drawing of it in its original form: Oswald, *Country Houses of Kent*: 14–15 and pl 43.

[15]Phillida B. Simons, *Groote Schuur* (Vlaeberg, South Africa: Fernwood Press, 1996): 9–21. I am grateful to Christopher Paterson for the loan of this book. See also Roderick Gradidge, *Dream Houses* (London: Constable, 1980): 131–8.

[16]The book was reviewed in *Architectural Review* (1 March 1900): 142–3. I am grateful to Neal Shasore for this reference.

[17]Quoted in Graham Viney, *Colonial Houses of South Africa* (Cape Town: Sruik-Winchester, 1987): 219.

panelling and ironmongery made 'as in the days of the crafts before the hostile influences of machinery'.[18] Baker was responsible for the interior decoration, introducing furniture bought in England or copied from seventeenth-century originals;[19] he later went on to choose similar furniture for Owletts, his home at Cobham, and for Rhodes House, at both of which it can still be seen.[20] For anyone visiting Groote Schuur with knowledge of either of these buildings, the sense of déja vu is inescapable.

In 1900 Rhodes paid for Baker to make a Mediterranean tour, which took him to the Greek temples at Paestum in south Italy and at Segesta and Agrigento in Sicily: a significant choice of buildings for a man who, according to Baker, believed that 'through art Pericles taught the lazy Athenians to believe in Empire'.[21] Both men admired Ruskin, whose reputation reached its peak in the years before he died in 1900; in his inaugural Slade Lecture at Oxford in 1870, given to a packed audience, he had urged Britain to 'found colonies as fast and as far as she is able, formed of her most energetic and worthiest men'.[22] Baker's architecture was rooted in these principles. His grandiloquent Rhodes Memorial of 1908–1912 (**Figure 12.1**) – a Doric peristyle reached by a flight of steps, high up on Table Mountain close to Groote Schuur – confirmed a shift to Classicism in his work; the inscription, referring to Rhodes's 'immense and Brooding Spirit', was written by Rudyard Kipling (1865–1936), who admired the 'savage and uncompromising grandeur' of ancient Greek architecture.[23] Baker had already drawn upon Hellenistic sources for two earlier memorials, put up in 1904. The first, in the Matopo Hills of Rhodesia (modern Zimbabwe), was a stone plinth, inspired by the Pedestal of Agrippa (178 BCE) on the Acropolis in Athens and commemorating the thirty-four white soldiers of the Shangani patrol who had been killed in the first Ndebele (Matabele) War of 1893, part of the Rhodes-inspired project of extending British rule north of the Limpopo River.[24] The other monument, at a crossroads in Kimberley in the Northern

---

[18]Baker, *Cecil Rhodes by His Architect*: 22; Michael Keath, *Herbert Baker: Architecture and Invention, 1892–1913* (Gibraltar: Ashanti Publications, n.d.): 29–30.

[19]Andre van Graan, 'Herbert Baker's South African Furniture', *Decorative Arts Society Journal* 37 (2013): 142. The main suppliers were Arthur Collie of Old Bond Street and Mrs Stafford Keithley of Kensington, who was later consulted about the interiors at Rhodes House. The house was refurnished in a similar fashion after a fire in 1896.

[20]Baker gave Owletts and much of its contents in 1938 to the National Trust, of which he was an enthusiastic supporter. For the Trust's historic buildings secretary the house was 'as much a memorial to him as it is of its seventeenth-century builders': James Lees-Milne, *Ancestral Voices* (London: Chatto & Windus, 1975): 130. It has been very little changed since Baker's time and is regularly opened to visitors in the summer.

[21]Baker, *Cecil Rhodes by His Architect*: 10.

[22]E. T. Cook and A. Wedderburn (eds.), *Library Edition of the Works of John Ruskin* (London: Allen, 1903–1912) 20 no. 42; F. O'Gorman (ed.), *Cambridge Companion to John Ruskin* (Cambridge: Cambridge University Press, 2015): 24–5.

[23]Baker, *Architecture and Personalities*: 9; Donal Lowry, '"The Granite of the Ancient North": Race, Nation and Memory at Cecil Rhodes's Mountain Mausoleum and Rhodes House, Oxford', in Richard Wrigley and Matthew Craske (eds.), *Pantheons: Transformations of a Monumental Idea* (Aldershot: Ashgate, 2014): 207. I am grateful to Dr Lowry for referring me to his article.

[24]Brian Roberts, *Cecil Rhodes: Flawed Colossus* (London: Hamish Hamilton, 1987): 187–8. The bronze reliefs were by the sculptor John Tweed (1869–1933), who had designed a bronze bas-relief over the entrance to Groote Schuur. Information from the late Ann Spokes Symonds.

Figure 12.1 The opening ceremony of Cecil Rhodes's Monument on Table Mountain in South Africa, by Herbert Baker, 1908. The central statue of 'Physical Energy', by George Frederick Watts, was cast in 1902, photographer unknown, RIBA Collections, RIBA60168

Cape, was inspired by the Hellenistic 'Tomb of Theron' at Agrigento;[25] it was a tribute to the twenty-seven 'Honoured Dead' from the Afrikaaner siege of the diamond-mining town at the beginning of the Boer War. Later, in 1910, Baker expressed his admiration for the 'simplicity and the grandeur of the treatment of mass, combined with the beauty of the detail and sculpture' that he had found in ancient Greek buildings. He went on to point out 'how much in architecture depends on the quality and texture of the material':[26] important considerations in all of his own buildings.

Baker stayed on in South Africa after 1902, a year which saw both Rhodes's death and the end of the Boer War. He opened an office in the same year in the boom city of Johannesburg, the financial headquarters of the Witwatersrand goldfields which transformed the economy of the former Afrikaaner republic of the Transvaal. Here he

---

[25]https://www.thesolomon.co.za/honoured-dead-memorial.html (accessed 18 April 2022). It has also been compared, less convincingly, to the Nereid Monument of *c.* 390 BCE at Xanthus in modern Turkey, partially reconstructed in the British Museum.

[26]Baker, 'Styles in Architecture in Relation to Building Problems in South Africa', *South African Journal of Science* (August 1910): 393, quoted in Nicholas Temple, Andrzej Piotrowski, and Juan Manuel Heredia (eds.), *The Routledge Handbook on the Reception of Classical Architecture* (Abingdon, 2020): 256.

became closely associated with the so-called Kindergarten:[27] a group of young, male, idealistic and predominantly Oxford-educated administrators brought together by Alfred Milner (1854–1925), the recently appointed British High Commissioner for Southern Africa.[28] A near-contemporary of Rhodes, Milner had participated in 1874, while still an undergraduate, in Ruskin's quixotic project of building a road at North Hinksey, just outside Oxford.[29] He enthusiastically endorsed Ruskin's – and Rhodes's – beliefs about Britain's Imperial mission, and Baker shared their worldview. He built up a large domestic practice in Johannesburg, designing rugged Arts and Crafts–influenced houses built of local materials for businessmen and for members of the 'Kindergarten'; they included Stonehouse (1902), at Parklands in the city's suburbs, which he shared with Lionel Curtis (1872–1955), Assistant Secretary of the Transvaal and, following the creation of the Union of South Africa in 1910, one of the founders of the 'Round Table' group, which lobbied unsuccessfully for Imperial federation.[30] And it was Baker, another 'Round Table' member, who designed the Union Building at Pretoria (1910–1913), today the seat of the South African government. Here he adopted a monumental classical/ Baroque style, which he continued to employ in his post-1918 public architecture.[31]

Lutyens was another Arts and Crafts–trained architect who experienced a classical epiphany in the early years of the twentieth century, exclaiming in a letter to Baker in 1903: 'In architecture Palladio is the game!! It is so big – few appreciate it now, and it requires training to value and realise it ... I feel sure that if Ruskin had seen that point of view he would have raved as beautifully as he did for the Gothic.'[32] In 1912 Lutyens – who had remained in Britain – was chosen as architect for the legislative and administrative buildings in New Delhi, recently designated by the British as India's capital city, and he recommended Baker as his co-architect. Planning began immediately, but the two architects fell out over the siting of Baker's administrative (Secretariat) buildings and their relationship to the Viceroy's House, designed by Lutyens on a virgin hilltop site: Lutyens famously described the outcome of the argument, in which Baker's views prevailed, as his 'Bakerloo'. Baker then left South Africa and settled in London in 1913, visiting New Delhi periodically as his buildings – which included the huge, circular Legislative Building (now the Indian Parliament) – went up in 1915–1927.[33]

Then came the war. Baker, along with Lutyens and Reginald Blomfield (1856–1942), was one of the architects charged by the Imperial War Graves Commission (IWGC) with

---

[27]Symonds, *Oxford and Empire*: 63–6.

[28]Thompson, *A History of South Africa*: 143–4.

[29]Tim Hilton, *John Ruskin: The Later Years* (New Haven and London: Yale University Press, 2000): 291, 294–5. Oscar Wilde was another participant.

[30]Keath, *Herbert Baker*: 74; Symonds, *Oxford and Empire*: 67–71. See also Herbert Baker, 'The Architectural Needs of South Africa', *The State* (May 1909): 522, cited in Saul Dubow, 'Colonial Nationalism, the Milner Kindergarten and the Rise of 'South Africanism', *History Workshop Journal* 43 (Spring 1997): 71–2.

[31]For classical architecture in early twentieth-century Britain, see Alastair Service, *Edwardian Architecture* (London: Thames and Hudson, 1977): 140–87.

[32]See Christopher Hussey, *The Life of Sir Edwin Lutyens* (London: Country Life, 1950): 121–2 (letter of 15 February 1903).

[33]See Robert Grant Irving, *Indian Summer: Lutyens, Baker and Imperial Delhi* (New Haven and London: Yale University Press, 1981): 142–63.

the design of the cemeteries and memorials for the victims of the mass slaughter on the Western Front, many of whom came from the British colonies and dominions, playing a crucial part in the allied victory.[34] Here was an opportunity to monumentalize 'sites of memory',[35] some of them on a vast scale.[36] Baker's memorial at Neuve Chapelle (finished in 1927), one of thirty-five commissions he carried out for the IWGC, commemorated the Indian troops who had died in the second Ypres offensive of 1915. Designed as a *temenos* or sacred precinct, it is enclosed within a circular wall interrupted by domed pavilions of an 'Indo-Saracenic' character and a tall column with an inscription in four languages. Baker also designed the cemeteries at Delville Wood (completed 1926), where mainly Anglophone South African soldiers bore the brunt of one of the bloodiest battles of the 1916 Somme offensive, and at Tyne Cot (1925–1927), the final resting place of 34,888 victims from across the Empire of the 1917 Passchendaele debacle.[37] With their ranks of identical, neatly aligned, headstones, these cemeteries were, and still remain, deeply moving 'sites of mourning'. But at Delville Wood the architecture and iconography were also intended to express a sense of an incipient white South African national identity within the protective embrace of the British Empire[38]; Baker told Jan Christian Smuts, later Prime Minister of the Union of South Africa, that he saw the domed pavilion overlooking the site as a 'little Rhodes memorial temple', and the figures of warriors surmounting the dome as 'a great symbol of final union'.[39]

Baker also designed several war memorials in England. In 1920 he put up a three-sided timber-framed cloister to soldiers from the village of Blackmoor (Hampshire), drawing upon local vernacular tradition but enfolding a stone pillar. He was also responsible for the memorials at Harrow School (1921–1923) and Winchester College (1922–1924), two of the public schools in which many of the members of the wartime officer corps had been educated. The Winchester memorial takes the form of a cloister with arcades of paired Tuscan columns enclosing an open, quasi-monastic central space (**Figure 12.2**). Three of the corners were dedicated to the British Dominions (Australia, Canada and South Africa), the fourth to India. Each contains a floor slab of indigenous

---

[34]For the until recently largely unrecognized contribution of black and Asian soldiers, see https://www.cwgc.org/media/noantj4i/report-of-the-special-committee-to-review-historical-inequalities-in-commemoration.pdf, and htpps://www.theguardian.com/uk-news/2021/apr/22/scandal-of-unequal-commemoration-of-uks-ww1-dead-known-about-for-years (accessed 18 April 2022).

[35]The phrase was coined by the French historian Pierre Nora in his *Les Lieux de Mémoire*, translated into English in 1998 as *Realms of Memory*. For First World War memorials, see Jay Winter, *Sites of Memory* (Cambridge: Cambridge University Press, 1995) and *Remembering War* (New Haven and London: Yale University Press, 2006).

[36]E.g. Lutyens's awe-inspiring memorial arch at Thiepval, finally unveiled in 1932: see Gavin Stamp, *The Memorial to the Missing of the Somme* (London: Profile Books, 2006).

[37]David Stevenson, *1914–1917: The History of the First World War* (London: Penguin Books, 2005): 546.

[38]A sensitive and scholarly analysis of the cemeteries of Imperial troops on the Western Front battlefields can be found in Hanna Smyth, 'The Material Culture of Remembrance and Identity' (Oxford University DPhil thesis, 2019). I am grateful to Hanna Smyth for sending me a link to her thesis and for information about some of the cemeteries.

[39]For a critical analysis of this memorial, and of Baker's buildings there, see Bill Nasson, 'Delville Wood and South African Great War Commemoration', *English Historical Review* 199, no. 480 (February 2004), especially 58–74.

Figure 12.2 The War Memorial cloister at Winchester College (1922–1924), courtesy of The Warden and Scholars of Winchester College

stone with the national symbol in brass; stone from Ypres is also incorporated into one of the walkways.[40] The outer walls are of flint, a material much used in the vernacular architecture of the surrounding chalk downland, and in Baker's own native Kent; he called the Cloister 'a work after my own heart – building in a manner which I loved in the architecture of my native country ... all made living in expression with symbols, heraldry and sculpture'.[41] These are words that can be applied to many of Baker's buildings, including Rhodes House, with its omnipresent symbolism.

Rhodes House went up while Baker's Great War cemeteries were nearing completion, and while he was involved in plans for rebuilding the Bank of England (1925–1942), the first and largest of the public commissions in London that dominated much of his post-war career.[42] The Rhodes Trust was an educational adjunct to the Imperial project to which Milner and his 'Kindergarten' had devoted much of their lives. Far

[40]https://historicengland.org.uk/listing/the-list/list-entry/1095486 (accessed 18 April 2022).
[41]Baker, *Architecture and Personalities*: 97.
[42]Daniel M. Abramson, *Building the Bank of England* (New Haven and London: Yale University Press, 2005): 205–38. Other important commissions included India House (1928–1930) in Aldwych; South Africa House (1930–1933), at the eastern end of the Strand, facing Trafalgar Square; and Church House for the Church of England (1936–1940), close to Westminster Abbey.

from contracting, the British Empire in Africa expanded after the First World War as it absorbed the former German colonies mandated by the newly established League of Nations. The trust, as described in Rhodes's will, was intended for 'young Colonists, to give breadth to their views for their instruction in life and manners, and for instilling in their minds the advantages to the Colonies as well as to the United Kingdom of the retention of the unity of the Empire'.[43] The trustees had little difficulty in choosing Baker as their architect (no competition was held); they particularly admired his Winchester cloister which, they believed, possessed 'the very rare capacity of giving character, date and quiet beauty to a modern building in unobtrusive harmony with old surroundings'.[44]

Rhodes House had three main functions: academic, administrative and commemorative. It included a library of books on Imperial history, a residence for the Trust's Oxford Secretary (Warden), and a Hall in which an annual commemorative dinner for the Rhodes Scholars could take place. Yet in many ways it was a building searching for a purpose, as Baker himself recognized. It did not house the Rhodes Scholars, who lived, as their successors still do, in accommodation supplied by the colleges of which they are members. Plans to turn it into an institute for training colonial civil servants, or a post-graduate school of government, never got off the ground.[45] By the time it was finished, in 1929, the British Empire had reached its apogee, and, with the subsequent onset of economic depression and the rise of Indian nationalism, it was already beginning to show signs of incipient decline. Milner, who 'spent his last years trying to mend the bridges that Rhodes had broken',[46] was suspicious of Baker, and had tried to prevent him from designing a building that he feared – perhaps rightly – might attract ridicule from a cynical post-war generation increasingly inspired by the modernist *Zeitgeist* and sceptical of Britain's imperial mission. So, as the project developed, the building increasingly took on the character of a memorial: to Rhodes, to Milner, who died in 1925 while the plans were taking shape, and to the Rhodes Scholars who had died in the war.

Baker claimed that Rhodes House gave him more pleasure than any of his many other commissions **(Figure 12.3)**.[47] The rectangular, one-and-a-half acre, site, just to the south of the University Museum – one of the outstanding monuments of 'Ruskinian' Gothic architecture, built in 1855–1859 – was purchased from Wadham College and was large enough to allow for the creation of a spacious garden with lawns and flower beds. Rhodes had cherished his youthful memories of 'the stately buildings and the old gardens [of Oxford], their dignity derived from their long history of high aim and noble

---

[43][Anon] *Cecil Rhodes and Rhodes House* (Oxford: Oxford University Press, 1929): 8; Symonds, *Oxford and Empire*: 164. Rhodes's views on race and empire are discussed in Duncan Bell, *Dreamworlds of Race* (Princeton, New Jersey: Princeton University Press, 2020): 129–41.

[44]Rhodes House, Oxford, Rhodes Trust papers (hereafter RT), D1a/1 RT/2637/1, 5 December 1924.

[45]Symonds, *Oxford and Empire*: 173–4.

[46]D. Howarth, '"A Home for the Spirit": The 80th Anniversary of the Rhodes Scholarships', *Country Life* (23 June 1983): 1741.

[47]Baker, *Architecture and Personalities*: 136. See also Geoffrey Tyack, 'Baker and Lutyens in Oxford', *Oxoniensia* 62 (1997): 287–97.

Figure 12.3 Rhodes House from the north, photographed soon after completion in 1928, photograph by Sydney Newberry, RIBA Collections, RIBA135620

endeavor'.[48] In a memorandum of a meeting with Milner written in 1924, shortly before the statesman's death, Baker expressed a preference for 'something very simple and elemental such as Rhodes would like'.[49] He first envisaged a building laid out on an H plan, like many Elizabethan country houses, with a south-facing central Hall flanked by two long wings, one containing the Warden's lodgings, the other with common rooms, a first-floor library and a main entrance leading from the west in Parks Road.[50] But this scheme was modified after Milner's death in 1925 to incorporate a 'Chapter House' to the north of the Hall, which could serve as a memorial to Milner and, by extension, to Rhodes. For Baker, this change of plan demanded the adoption of a more monumental style of architecture that made a sharp contrast to the cosy Cotswold-inspired vernacular favoured by Milner,[51] and thought suitable for the rest of the building. Writing to Edward Grigg (1879–1955), Secretary to the Rhodes Trust, Baker envisaged:

> a vaulted space in the vacant ground behind the hall. You know the Medici Chapel at Florence with the statues of the princes and Michael [*sic*] Angelo's symbolical

---

[48]Greig, *Herbert Baker in South Africa*: 44.
[49]RT, D1a/3 RT/2637B/1, 29 October 1924.
[50]RT, D1a/1 RT/2637/1, traced plan (undated).
[51]Gavin Stamp, 'The Don's Joke', *Country Life* (24 July 2013): 47.

figures. We have the subject I think in Milton's *Areopagitica*, 'Methinks I see in my mind a noble and puissant nation rousing herself like a strong man after sleep' … personally I should like it to be a sort of shrine for memorials of statesmen who have had the great vision of a Commonwealth of Nations.[52]

And, alluding to abortive plans of his own for a memorial cloister next to Westminster Abbey, he went on to express the hope that 'if London won't do it why should not Oxford!' By the later summer 1925 Baker's proposed octagonal 'Chapter House' had been transformed into a virtually free-standing domed rotunda, approached through an ionic portico facing South Parks Road, on the northern side of the site **(Figure 12.4)**.[53]

SOUTH PARKS ROAD

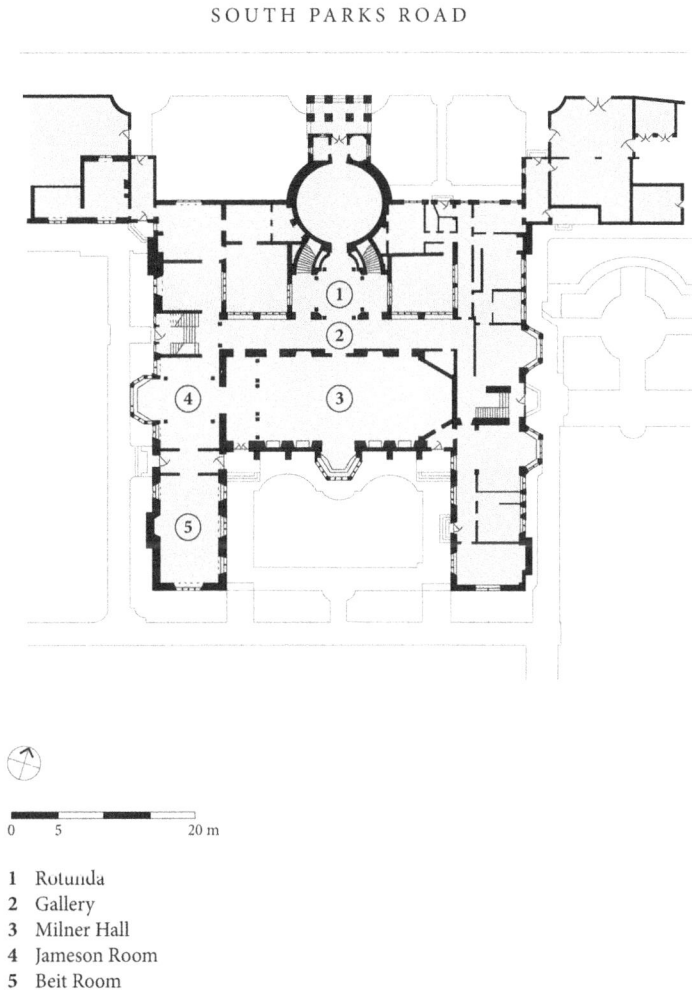

0   5   20 m

1 Rotunda
2 Gallery
3 Milner Hall
4 Jameson Room
5 Beit Room

Figure 12.4 Rhodes House, Oxford, ground plan, drawn by Hannah Towler

[52]RT, D1a/1 RT/2637/1, 2 and 7 June 1925; D1a/RT/2367K/OS4 (undated).
[53]RT, D1a/1 RT/2637/1, typed note, with plan, from Dr Randall, a Canadian Trustee, 19 October 1925.

This change of plan secured the approval of the trustees, and the portico became the main entrance to the building. It leads through the rotunda to an inner hall or vestibule, roofed with a Soaneian pendentive dome; beyond is the main Hall, looking out onto a garden. This north-south axis is bisected by a broad corridor or gallery linking the two long wings, the west wing containing the first-floor library, its eastern counterpart a warden's residence of almost vice-regal dimensions; eight servants were employed there at first, and there were seven bathrooms for residents and guests.[54]

The bulk of the building, with its steep-pitched roofs and mullioned windows, drew stylistically upon the hybrid architecture of Elizabethan and Jacobean England, as filtered through the lens of the Arts and Crafts movement (Figure 12.5). When viewed from the garden, it intentionally conjured up images of late-sixteenth- and early-seventeenth-century Cotswold manor houses, many of which had been expensively fitted up by new, moneyed owners during Baker's formative years: a process that lasted well into the twentieth century. The comfortingly homespun external effect owes much to Baker's choice of materials. His original intention was to use flint walling, as he had in the Winchester War Memorial Cloister. But Oxford owed much of its architectural

Figure 12.5 The south (garden) front of Rhodes House, photograph by Sydney Newberry, RIBA Collections, RIBA135623

---

[54]Godfrey Elton (ed.), *The First Fifty Years of the Rhodes Trust and the Rhodes Scholarships* (Oxford: Blackwell, 1953): 27, 118.

character to its easy access to limestone, and Baker finally opted for what he called 'rough walling'[55] – coursed rubble from the quarries at Bladon, a few miles away from Oxford – with ashlar from Clipsham (Rutland) for the dressings and Cotswold stone slates (since replaced) for the roofs.[56] By conforming in this way to the genius loci, as he saw it, he inaugurated a fashion that lasted in Oxford for the rest of the period: at Sir Giles Gilbert Scott's New Bodleian (now renamed the Weston) Library, completed in 1939, and in the numerous university and college buildings designed by Hubert Worthington (1866–1963), one of which, the Radcliffe Science Library extension of 1933–1934, faces Rhodes House across South Parks Road.[57]

Arts and Crafts–inspired buildings could evoke a deep-rooted nostalgia for the English rural past, comparable to A. E. Housman's elegiac 'Shropshire Lad' poems, published in 1896 and widely read during the Great War, and Ralph Vaughan Williams's beautiful tone poem 'The Lark Ascending', first performed in 1920. A similar sensibility informs the main interiors of Rhodes House, with their hand-made decoration and furniture, designed by Baker and celebrating the craft traditions of the English countryside that he had admired ever since his youth. The south-facing hall in the central block, with its open timber roof and its tall mullioned and transomed bay window, draws upon memories of the Kentish manor houses and yeomen's farmhouses that he had studied as a young man; so too does the Library, with its roof of rough beams pegged together (**Figure 12.6**). But the meeting rooms beneath – one of them named after Sir Leander Starr Jameson, best known for his part in the notorious (and unsuccessful) raid of 1895–1896, intended to trigger an uprising in the Afrikaaner Transvaal republic, the other after Alfred Beit, co-owner with Rhodes of the De Beers diamond company – recall, with their heavily beamed ceilings, the interiors at Groote Schuur and other houses designed by Baker in South Africa.

The Imperial ideal was most overtly expressed at Rhodes House through symbolism. This drew upon several distinct strands of memory.[58] One was of the ruins of Great Zimbabwe, a complex now thought to have been begun in the eleventh century CE, and unknown to Europeans until the late nineteenth century. For Baker they represented 'the link between the older civilization derived from the North or the East, and the savage barbarism of Southern and central Africa before the advent of the European';[59] their stone carvings inspired the stylised 'Zimbabwe bird' perching on the dome at Rhodes House, and carved on the newel posts of the Library staircase. The Portuguese and Dutch seaborne empires are commemorated in a relief carving of a ship over the wooden doorway into the Hall, symbolizing Henry the Navigator rounding the Cape of

---

[55]RT, D1a/1 RT/2637/2, 15 July 1925.

[56]W. J. Arkell, *Oxford Stone* (London: Faber & Faber, 1947): 27, 117–18, 142. The limestone ashlar from Headington, just outside Oxford, previously used for many of the city's most important buildings, had failed to withstand decay and smoke pollution, and the quarries had ceased to operate.

[57]Another of Worthington's buildings, further east, now the University's Department of Plant Sciences, was built in 1947–50 to house the Commonwealth (formerly Imperial) Forestry Institute.

[58]For Baker's views on architectural symbolism, see his *Architecture and Personalities*: 177–81.

[59]*Cecil Rhodes and Rhodes House* (1929): 16. The description of the building was written by Baker himself. A copy of the 'Zimbabwe bird' is still preserved in Rhodes's bedroom at Groote Schuur.

Figure 12.6 The library at Rhodes House, photograph by Sydney Newberry, RIBA Collections, RIBA135633

Good Hope; there is a similar relief over the main entrance to the building from South Parks Road. And the British Empire is celebrated in the carvings of the coats of arms of colonies and dominions that, together with the arms of Spain, Portugal and the United States, liberally adorn the building's garden front. Here and elsewhere Baker drew upon the skills of two of his most frequent collaborators: the carver Lawrence Turner (1864–1957), a former Master of the Art Workers' Guild, and the sculptor Charles Wheeler (1892–1974), who had worked on the Winchester War Memorial Cloister, and was employed later on Baker's London buildings.[60]

The rotunda, a miniature Roman Pantheon, was also intended to evoke memories of Empire, and through them to inspire Imperial commitment. Domed, centrally planned buildings had been used for commemorative purposes ever since Roman antiquity. Oxford's finest classical building, the library now known as the Radcliffe Camera (1737–1748),[61] was intended to perpetuate the memory of its donor, the wealthy physician John Radcliffe, and more recently, Birmingham's civic war memorial – the Hall

[60]For Turner, see Gray, *Edwardian Architecture*: 357 and https://sculpture.gla.ac.uk/view/person.php?id=msib2_1208266553; for Sarah Crellin, 'Wheeler, Sir Charles Thomas', *Oxford Dictionary of National Biography*. Wheeler designed the fountain and memorial plates at the Blackmoor war memorial cloister.
[61]Thomas Salmon, *The Present State of the Universities* (1744): 42–3; Stephen Hebron, *Dr Radcliffe's Library* (Oxford: Bodleian Library, 2014): 11–19.

of Memory (1922–1925) – had been built in the form of a classical domed octagon.[62] Baker believed that his rotunda at Rhodes House could impart 'some magic influence' on those who saw it.[63] Versed in the classics from his boyhood, he saw it at first as a 'heroön' or hall of fame **(Figure 12.7)**: a Valhalla through which it was essential to pass before entering the inner vestibule – named after Sir George Parkin, first organizer of the

Figure 12.7 The interior of the rotunda at Rhodes House, photograph by Sydney Newberry, RIBA135644

---

[62] Alan Borg, *War Memorials: From Antiquity to the Present* (London: Leo Cooper, 1991): 134. The architects were S. N. Cooke and W. N. Twist.
[63] Baker, *Architecture and Personalities*: 136.

Rhodes Scholarships – and the rest of the building. The names of the war dead, grouped by country of origin, are carved onto the polished stone walls of the Rotunda, and there is a quotation from Aristotle on the dome;[64] a granite slab from the Matopo hills in Zimbabwe, Rhodes's own final resting-place,[65] was placed at the centre of the floor. So a building that had been first conceived as a memorial to Rhodes and Milner acquired a wider relevance as a monument to the fallen Rhodes Scholars, and ultimately to an Empire that was to experience its own demise after the world war of 1939–1945.

Rhodes House can be seen nowadays as an expression of a vanished Imperial ideal, but it is an ideal that still has the power to arouse passions. Similar in intention to recent campaigns to topple the statues of Confederate politicians and generals in the United States, a 'Rhodes Must Fall' campaign, demanding the removal of Cecil Rhodes's statue at the University of Cape Town, began in March 2015. It spread to Oxford just two months later in May, when a much-publicized demonstration clamoured for the removal of a statue of a besuited Rhodes gazing down from a niche high on the ponderous High Street façade of Oriel College's Rhodes Building, built in 1909–1911 to the designs of Basil Champneys and funded by a legacy of £100,000 from Rhodes himself.[66] A smaller demonstration took place at Rhodes House, and a campaign was also launched to remove a plaque to Rhodes from the house in King Edward Street, close to the college, in which he had taken lodgings while studying for his degree. More demonstrations took place outside the Rhodes Building in June 2020, but at the time of writing (early 2021) the college's governing body had still not reached a final decision about the removal either of the statue or of the plaque. Rhodes House meanwhile is being remodelled as an international conference centre.

Baker's reputation sharply declined after his death in 1946. His close association with Rhodes, and his overt support for British imperialism, made him deeply suspect as decolonization gathered momentum. His reputation as an architect also suffered, initially because he was blamed, perhaps unfairly, for the removal of most of Sir John Soane's interiors at the Bank of England.[67] His buildings have often been compared unfavourably with those of Lutyens, like Soane a much-admired hero of recent British architectural history. Kenneth Clark dismissed Baker as 'a polite and thoughtful man with a positive genius for errors of design'.[68] Lutyens observed, more perceptively: 'I don't think [Baker] treats architecture as seriously as I do. He makes her the handmaiden of sentiment',[69] something that Baker

[64]Translated as 'Man's highest good proves to be activity of the soul in accordance with virtue'.
[65]He is buried under a simple stone slab close to the Shangani Patrol monument at what he called 'World's View': Lowry, in Wrigley and Craske, *Pantheons*: 194–9.
[66]See, for instance, Amit Chaudhuri, 'The Real Meaning of Rhodes Must Fall', *Guardian* (16 March 2016). For the statue, by Henry Alfred Pegram, see Edward Impey, 'The Rhodes Building at Oriel, 1904–2011: Dynamite or Designate', *Oxoniensia* 76 (2011): 100–1. For Rhodes's views on race, Roberts, *Cecil Rhodes*: 195, and Bell, *Dreamworlds of Race*: 130, 133–4.
[67]See his *apologia* in Abramson, *Bank of England*: 226–7. He argued that the Bank's original rebuilding plans were far more destructive than his own.
[68]Kenneth Clark, *Another Part of the Wood* (London: HarperCollins, 1975): 221.
[69]Christopher Hussey, *Life of Lutyens*: 285; Mary Lutyens, *Edwin Lutyens* (London: John Murray, 1980): 194.

himself went some way towards admitting.[70] When Baker went on a walking holiday with Lutyens in 1888 he took a volume of Wordsworth's poetry in his pocket; many years later Lutyens cruelly commented, after seeing Baker's 'distressing' work in New Delhi, that 'no designer should ever read poetry … If not read you have to get your eventual quota of it through and in your work and not be duped with other peoples' adjectives'.[71] Lutyens was intensely suspicious of Baker's 'literary' and associational approach to architecture, which he blamed in large part upon Ruskin, whose writings had, he believed, done 'incalculable harm' to English architecture: 'God', he wrote, 'asked Adam to name the animals after he had created them. Baker names his animals first and then starts creating around names and words'. Yet we all have to use words when we speak to each other, and for many people symbols and literary allusions are the most effective ways in which buildings can convey meaning: something that Baker recognized, nowhere more than at Rhodes House.[72]

Whether or not you agree with Lutyens or Baker depends on your view of what architecture is about, and what it is for. By the outbreak of war in 1914 Lutyens had come to believe that architecture was a self-sufficient and self-referential language, depending for its effect on the architect's understanding of the universal truths of geometry and proportion embodied within the classical orders. For Baker it was a useful art, subject to changing cultural influences and capable of transmitting meaning through craftsmanship and allusion. John Summerson recognized this distinction when he wrote that Lutyens was the 'fluke genius' of early twentieth-century British architecture, but that Baker 'may be the more representative figure of his time'.[73] The nostalgia and imperial symbolism embedded in Rhodes House reveals something of the values and preoccupations in Britain in the years after the war, when Empire was still being actively promoted and that is why we need to take it seriously now.

Select bibliography

Primary

Rhodes House, Oxford, Rhodes House papers, D1a/1 RT/2637

Secondary

Baker, H. *Architecture and Personalities*. London: Country Life, 1944.
Cecil Rhodes and Rhodes House. Oxford: Oxford University Press, 1929.
Cecil Rhodes by His Architect. Oxford: Oxford University Press, 1934.

---

[70]*Architecture and Personalities*: 88. Baker thought that Lutyens, by contrast, was 'propelled towards abstract monumental design'.
[71]Mary Lutyens, *Edwin Lutyens*: 19, 235.
[72]cf. T. S. Eliot: 'I've gotta use words when I talk to you' ('Fragment of an Agon', 1927). See also John Onians, *Bearers of Meaning: the Classical Orders in Antiquity, the Middle Ages and the Renaissance* (Princeton, New Jersey: Princeton University Press, 1990).
[73]Quoted in Keath, *Herbert Baker in South Africa*: 221.

Reconstruction

Bell, D. *Dreamworlds of Race.* Princeton, New Jersey: Princeton University Press, 2020: 129–41.

Elton, G. (ed.). *The First Fifty Years of the Rhodes Trust and the Rhodes Scholarships.* Oxford: Blackwell, 1953.

Gray, A. Stuart *Edwardian Architecture: A Biographical Dictionary.* London: Duckworth, 1985: 97–9.

Greig, D. E. *Herbert Baker in South Africa.* Cape Town and New York: Purnell, 1970.

Howarth, D. '"A Home for the Spirit": The 80th Anniversary of the Rhodes Scholarships'. *Country Life* 23 June 1983.

Keath, M. *Herbert Baker: Architecture and Invention, 1892–1913.* Gibraltar: Ashanti Publications, n.d.

Lowry, D. '"The Granite of the Ancient North": Race, Nation and Memory at Cecil Rhodes's Mountain Mausoleum and Rhodes House, Oxford'. In *Pantheons: Transformations of a Monumental Idea,* edited by R. Wrigley and M. Craske. Aldershot: Ashgate, 2014.

Nasson, Bill. 'Delville Wood and South African Great War Commemoration'. *English Historical Review* 199, no. 480 (February 2004): 58–74.

Roberts, B. *Cecil Rhodes: Flawed Colossus.* London: Hamish Hamilton, 1987.

Simons, P. B. *Groote Schuur.* Vlaeberg, South Africa: Fernwood Press, 1996.

Stewart, J. *Sir Herbert Baker: Architect to the British Empire*, (Jefferson, North Carolina: McFarland & Co., 2021).

Stamp, G. 'The Don's Joke'. *Country Life*, 24 July 2013.

Symonds, R. *Oxford and Empire.* Oxford: Oxford University Press, 1992.

Thompson, L. *A History of South Africa.* New Haven and London: Yale University Press, 1996.

Viney, G. *Colonial Houses of South Africa.* Cape Town: Sruik-Winchester, 1987.

CHAPTER 13
DIOCESE: CAIRO CATHEDRAL AND THE POLITICS OF LIBERAL ANGLICAN CHURCH DESIGN

David Lewis

The Anglican cathedral of All Saints in Cairo is an interesting case study of the design of a major British colonial building being influenced by politics in the aftermath of the war **(Figures 13.1–13.3)**. The connection between architecture and politics has been studied at sites such as New Delhi and Jerusalem, but what makes the case of Cairo Cathedral unique is that repeated changes in the design over a prolonged planning period were explicitly linked to political developments and that the building thus affected was a place of worship.

Egypt had been home to Christian communities since ancient times, and Cairo already had Armenian, Roman Catholic, German protestant and Coptic cathedrals. However, in July 1916, the Anglican Bishop of Jerusalem, Rennie MacInnes, had invited the architect Adrian Gilbert Scott to meet with him about the idea of building another cathedral in Cairo. MacInnes's own cathedral of St George, Jerusalem, had been completed less than ten years before, but the British presence in the Middle East was growing quickly, and the bishop felt Egypt was ready for its own Anglophone diocese.[1] The need was for a design that would feel comfortable to the local community yet facilitate direct participation in a larger global community of Christians.

This brief, however, was not as straightforward as it might seem. One issue that would prove a destabilizing factor in the design was that its 'local' communities were not as clearly defined as might be imagined. The congregation of largely British expats, with some other English speakers and locals mixed in, wanted to express British cultural identity as well as Egyptian. Thus, there were two cultural touchstones for the architect to express alongside the desire for an expression of international modernity. The expression of both British and Egyptian identity in a single building had political implications, and regardless of the church's intent to be politically neutral, the building committee constantly shifted its ground in an attempt to promote various political and cultural messages – asking the architect to completely redesign the cathedral at least four times on stylistic rather than functional grounds over the course of twenty years. The first design was 'Byzantine', partly inspired by local mosques; the second and third, intended to serve as memorials to the war, were Crusader Gothic. The fourth and final design was a fusion of local and international motifs, intended to demonstrate technological

---

[1]David Kroyanker, *Jerusalem Architecture* (New York: Vendome, 2002): 136.

Figure 13.1 Rendering of the exterior of Cairo Cathedral as built, 1938, courtesy of the Powell Family

Figure 13.2 Interior of Cairo Cathedral, *c*.1938, courtesy of the A. Gilbert Scott family

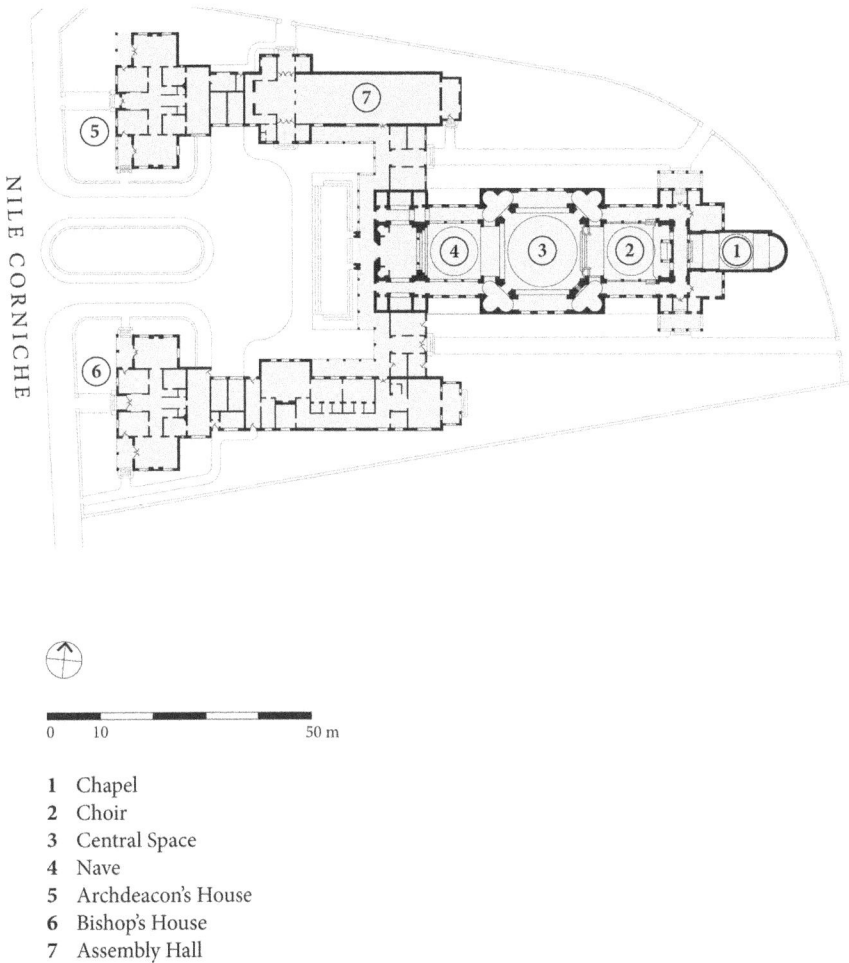

NILE CORNICHE

0   10   50 m

1 Chapel
2 Choir
3 Central Space
4 Nave
5 Archdeacon's House
6 Bishop's House
7 Assembly Hall

Figure 13.3 Plan of Cairo Cathedral as built, drawn by Hannah Towler

modernity. The building committee wanted to ensure that the cathedral, and thereby the development of the new diocese, aligned with the colonial politics of the moment.

Much can be learned about the ideology behind Cairo Cathedral by examining its consecration ceremony programme. The 1938 consecration service was choreographed by Liverpool Cathedral's Dean, Frederick William Dwelly, known for his modern, participatory liturgies especially suited to radio broadcast. William Temple, then Archbishop of York, presided and gave a sermon on Christian Unity. The service included a special greeting by the Archbishop of Canterbury, broadcast directly from Canterbury Cathedral by radio. Cairo Cathedral could both receive and transmit radio broadcasts; it became a seat of performance and ritual that could be beamed to the surrounding desert or back to Canterbury itself. The tower had a cross on top that was illuminated at night, evoking the imagery of the radio tower to mark a site from which

Anglican ideas were broadcast.[2] Whereas the other churches of Cairo inflected towards the ancient, the Anglican Church, like the British state in Egypt, declared itself to be global and technological. The missionary aspect of the church was technologized, and it advertised its presence on the modern skyline.

Cairo Cathedral was located at the intersection of architecture and William Temple's Christian Ecumenical movement. Temple, soon to be made Archbishop of Canterbury, was the leading light in a movement calling for Christians of all denominations to join together to oppose materialism and class division, lending their talents to support an active, spiritualized state. In the context of Cairo, this meant seeking to counter commercialism, and as such to act as a tempering force both on the values of officials and traders working in the imperial milieu. The historian Matthew Grimley has called this movement 'Liberal Anglicanism'.[3] An informal alliance of leading clergymen, the movement sought a strong bond between church and state, giving Christian leaders a voice in political discourse that could be used to address social concerns. The movement's underlying drive to strengthen the sense of community was physically manifested in church buildings. Liturgists, chief among them Dwelly, sought to develop pageantry and participatory ritual that made congregations feel part of a lived and shared Christian experience. This included using radio technologies to broadcast this activity to a wider segment of the population, who for reasons of infirmity, work commitments or physical proximity, could not be present in the building. Thus a new technologized Christianity could theoretically reach the entire population of a metropolis or region, drawing them together in shared experience and healing the fragmentation of the war.[4] Such vast radio audiences were not merely pipe dreams of the clergy: in the year of Cairo Cathedral's consecration, Father Charles Coughlin's radio hour in the United States, broadcast from a recording studio inside a giant stone crucifix at suburban Detroit's Shrine of the Little Flower, could boast a weekly audience estimated at two to three million.

Liberal Anglican reforms were made possible by a new architecture that embodied these community values and was suited to broadcast. The architectural language of Liberal Anglicanism was largely developed and promulgated by the firm with which Adrian was loosely affiliated, that of his brother Giles Gilbert Scott. Giles Gilbert Scott's Liverpool Cathedral, its space developed in close consultation with Dwelly, was the architectural laboratory of the movement. At Liverpool, the close collaboration between architect and dean ensured that there was sufficient and suitable space for wider participation, including experiments with dance and broadcast, as well as an aesthetic unity between the physical space and the vestments, banners and other artefacts of the liturgy. The stalls even featured matching oak stands for radio microphones. At the same

---

[2]Arthur Burrell, *Cathedral on the Nile* (Oxford: Amate, 1984): 75.

[3]Matthew Grimley, *Citizenship, Community, and the Church of England: Liberal Anglican Theories of the State between the Wars* (Oxford: Oxford University Press, 2004): 6–7.

[4]Shundana Yusaf's *Broadcast Buildings* (Boston: MIT, 2014) has explored how the discussion of architecture on radio programmes shaped architectural thinking in the 1920s and 1930s, but more remains to be done on the way religious groups closely identified with an architectural space such as a cathedral, addressed the notion of a physical architectural reality in their disembodied radio presence.

time the cathedral attempted to serve a modern metropolitan population while also acting as a spiritual welcome station for visitors from North America. As the signature structure of one of the world's best-known ecclesiastical firms, Liverpool Cathedral garnered considerable attention in the worldwide architectural press. As the first protestant cathedral built on a new site in England since the Reformation, the cathedral also garnered broad attention as a testing ground for ideas about modern Anglicanism. Liverpool's design was revered by architects and clergy particularly across the British territories and in the United States. Many major churches of the twentieth century carry its DNA from the West Point chapel in New York state to the Anglican Cathedral of Auckland, New Zealand.

It was Cairo Cathedral, however, that attempted to demonstrate the way these principles could be used to develop Christian community in places with minority Christian populations. Cairo Cathedral was an opportunity to translate the internationalist design strategy first articulated at Liverpool, carrying ideas about universalism and shared values into an international setting. Like so much architecture that followed the war, it was truly experimental, a built test of the Liberal Anglican theory about community building through architecture.

To tell the story of the design of the cathedral, it is relevant to provide some of Adrian's biography, because in addition to political concerns, the personal experience of the architect also influenced the design. In 1915, Adrian Gilbert Scott was scrambling over the sandy shore at Sulva Bay in Gallipoli amidst the explosions of battle. Water supplies for his company had run low, and the troops had become dehydrated. The 33-year-old architect had gone in search of water and was crossing the battlefield with dowsing rods, using a technique he had learned from a gardener amidst the herbaceous borders of his family's country house in Ninfield, Sussex.[5] The technique worked, and Adrian carried water back and forth to the troops under fire.[6] He was awarded the Military Cross (MC) for Gallantry, but he was somewhat traumatized by the event: for the rest of his life he would have a jug of water placed at his bedside before he went to sleep.[7] Water imagery would become a motif in his life and work, from the ornament on the first (unexecuted) version of the Aswan Dam, to the fishing symbolism he designed for the marble wave pavements and boat-shaped pulpit in St Leonard's Church, Hastings, to crashing waves in the paintings by his marine-painter father-in-law, Charles Napier Hemy, that filled the walls of his Hampstead home. As will be shown, it also played a significant role in the design of Cairo Cathedral.

When the attempt to take Constantinople failed in January 1916, British and French troops withdrew into Egypt, and Gilbert Scott spent much of the remainder of the war in Cairo and its environs. A cathedral had been planned for Cairo since before the war and would have presumably gone ahead if the war had never happened. However, the

---

[5] Margaret Powell et al., *Charles Napier Hemy and His Family*, privately printed: 8.
[6] To prevent confusion of the two Scott brothers, throughout this essay I refer to Adrian Gilbert Scott and Giles Gilbert Scott by their first names.
[7] Margaret Powell et al., *Charles Napier Hemy and His Family*, privately printed: 8.

presence of large numbers of British troops from all walks of life meant that there were a number of architects in Egypt who would not normally have been there. The Bishop of Jerusalem, Rennie MacInnes, went to the commanding officer in Cairo, General Archibald Murray, to ask for a recommendation for one who could design a cathedral. Adrian had recently reconfigured the plumbing of the general's house, and the general could therefore recommend him on 'sound practical grounds'.

The meeting with the bishop went well. Adrian came from an architectural dynasty, yet he was an important architect in his own right. He is perhaps best known today as a designer of Roman Catholic churches with signature concrete parabolic arches, such as those on London's Poplar Estate and Kensington High Street. He is also celebrated for planning the complex layout of the House of Commons, which the Gilbert Scott office described as 'like a battleship'.[8] But that was later in his career. During the period he was designing the cathedral, he was known for his own house in Hampstead, which had received extensive press coverage. A restrained neo-Georgian design in yellow brick, it was located on Frognal Way, not far from the house where he had been born on Church Row. The house was interesting not so much for its facade and sensible axial plan, but for its socially inclusive planning. He had asked each member of the family what she or he would like in a new home – one child had asked for a swing, another for his own bedroom.[9] Adrian had also asked the housemaids, who had requested a sitting room not restricted to a basement. He gave them a room at the front of the house, overlooking Hampstead Parish Church. In contrast with his kindly but reserved brother Giles, Adrian was known for his gregarious warmth. When the two brothers collaborated on architectural projects, which they often did, it was hard to say who contributed what to the design, but it was plain that Adrian played an important role in managing client relationships. He talked loudly, hunted and golfed, drank wine from his personal giant goblet, and, like his brother, liked fast American cars.[10]

He also had a clear understanding of the goals of Liberal Anglicanism. Although Giles and Adrian Gilbert Scott were themselves Roman Catholic, the ecumenical ideals of Liberal Anglicanism fit well with their personal beliefs. Raised with John Henry Newman's rhetoric of Christian community (Newman had personally converted their father, the architect George Gilbert Scott junior), the Gilbert Scotts were deeply involved in a circle of what might be termed 'Liberal Catholics'.[11] While they were growing up in Hampstead, the mystic Friedrich von Hugel tutored their mother and apologist Coventry Patmore was a neighbour. The Gilbert Scotts's ideal of the Catholic artist was thus tied up in the Liberal Catholic outlook: a stark contrast to the philosophy of contemporary Catholic artists such as Eric Gill and Hilary Pepler, who formed a colony at Ditchling, and sought to isolate themselves from broader English life. For the Gilbert Scotts, the

---

[8]Oscar Faber, 'The New House of Commons', *Architect & Building News*, CXCV, 18 March 1949: 254.
[9]Margaret Mary Scott Powell, typescript memoir, 1994, private collection.
[10]Interview with Nicholas Gilbert Scott, 27 March 2015, notes in author's possession.
[11]For more on the religious environment of their upbringing see Gavin Stamp, *An Architect of Promise* (Donington: Shaun Tyas, 2002).

Liberal Anglican social vision not only appealed but presented a bridge for sometimes-marginalized Catholics to have greater involvement in national life.

Giles especially was rapidly successful within the British establishment, becoming the youngest full Royal Academician since Turner and gaining a knighthood at the age of 44. His London club, the Athenaeum, was a hub of interaction between Catholic leaders and Liberal Anglicans. Roman Catholic Bishop David Matthew met regularly with Anglican Bishop of Chichester G. K. A. Bell in its dining room. [12]Cardinal Francis Bourne, Archbishop of Westminster, was also a member and cautiously encouraged Roman Catholic participation in William Temple's COPEC, an inter-denominational council founded in 1920 devoted to addressing areas of social concern.[13]

With a shared ideological foundation, the Gilbert Scott brothers were ideal architects to establish the architectural parameters of the Liberal Anglican Church. To encourage a sense of community in many of his parish church designs Giles brought the altar forward and moved the choir from their traditional location between the congregation and altar to a rear gallery, thus allowing him to reduce the space between the congregation and the altar. It was hoped this would increase the sense of participation in the Sacrament. At Liverpool, moving the majority of the seating to a large shared space under the crossing rather than leaving congregants in a long, echoing nave also achieved this purpose. The crossing centralized worship within the axial space of the traditional Latin-cross plan. The embrace of technology – climate control to make sure worshipers were comfortable, amplification of sound so that they could hear, electric light so that they could see their hymnals – also encouraged participation. Adrian would borrow all of these elements for Cairo. But Giles also sought to make the local community feel a part of the work of the cathedral by responding to the local community in the design. In keeping with the teachings of the Arts and Crafts movement, he used local stone and recognizable English Gothic forms. But he also encouraged a sense of belonging by applying symbolic decorative motifs related to the vocations of the local community. Windows were installed in the Lady Chapel porch at Liverpool, with Giles's support and urging, portraying British women from Julian of Norwich to Elizabeth Barrett Browning, who were intended to serve as role models. The hope was that women of the cathedral would see their own work reflected in the structure of the church. In the Rankin Porch were statues of the Liverpool professions, from dock worker to builder to housewife; here the people of Liverpool were shown as part of a shared community of Christian experience.

With his brother Giles generally taking the lead design role on the firm's most prominent projects, Cairo Cathedral was an unusual undertaking for Adrian and helped to establish his independent identity as a designer. When he was commissioned for the Cairo project, the building committee stressed that they wanted Adrian, not Giles, as lead architect because they valued his familiarity with the British community in Egypt and his knowledge of local conditions.

---

[12]Kester Aspden, *Fortress Church* (Leominster, Herts: Gracewing, 2002): 235.
[13]Cardinal Bourne served as archbishop from 1903 to 1935. Ibid., 127.

Although not mentioned in any of the architect's surviving correspondence, the creation of an Egyptian Diocese was clearly politically expedient. In response to the threat of Ottoman invasion at the start of the war, Britain had made Egypt a protectorate in 1914. The cathedral would provide a gathering place for the English-speaking expatriate community and would provide a stage for state ritual. It speaks to the importance that British leaders ascribed to it that the young architect was taken off military duty to begin preliminary design work. Returning to Britain early in 1918, Adrian withdrew to a seaside house at Beaumaris (Anglesey) in order to work on the cathedral design in peace. He despatched the drawings to the bishop by late July.

Upon first receiving the commission for the cathedral in 1916, Adrian had written excitedly to his brother that '[t]hey are open-minded about the style and will probably follow any design submitted – from Egyptian to Gothic!'[14] He wanted something suited to locale as well as the climate. His first design was broadly Byzantine Revival with elements derived from local buildings (**Figure 13.4**). Giles particularly admired the polychromatic stonework, but Adrian asked him not to mention it 'as there is a strong prejudice on the committee against anything redolent of the Turkish Bath!!!! or the mosque'.[15] He nevertheless immediately set about studying the mosques, which he felt were the only suitable local precedent. The giant arches and large areas of blank wall that he felt were characteristic can be found in all three iterations of the cathedral. Cairo mosques, he wrote to Giles, '[are] very ripping inside – perfectly delightful – no roofs – just a square courtyard & usually 4 <u>high</u> arches … with hundreds of chains hanging down

Figure 13.4 Perspective of the first cathedral design, exhibited at the Royal Academy in 1926. The Wolfsonian, Florida International University, Miami Beach, Florida, The Mitchell Wolfson, Jr. Collection

---

[14]Letter, Adrian to Giles *c.* July 1916, Adrian Gilbert Scott Papers, RIBA Archives, ScAG/1/4/41.
[15]Ibid.

with lamps cutting the shadow … the plain old plaster above & the patch of intense blue sky over all – & at night all dotted with stars!'[16] In order to keep the cathedral cool, he set deeply shaded openings close to the ground to allow cooling breezes to pass through. He described the building thus:

> The lower openings at the floor level for the admission of light and the north breeze are all arranged so that they look out on to the cool shade and green trees. The effect will be heightened by the rich fittings of the chancel, the simple interior making an excellent foil for these […] The outstanding features of the exterior are the triple domes covered in brown tiles (as on Brunelleschi's dome to Florence Cathedral). The main walls have large recessed arches which throw the inner walls where exposed into shadow as far as possible. A projecting eaves is carried round the whole building some 20 feet up, throwing the entrances into deep shadow and preventing the sun penetrating.[17]

The large ground floor windows would have all been covered with metal grills and would have folded back to admit the breeze. The *parti* of a shady pavilion in a cooling garden was to be the cathedral's defining concept.

The choice of the Byzantine style may have owed some debt to Westminster Cathedral, widely celebrated in the architectural press, and where the Gilbert Scott brothers sometimes worshipped. The style was enjoying something of a vogue in both English- and German-speaking churches, from the 1909 Roman Catholic cathedral of Kingston, Jamaica, to the grand mosaic-clad creations of Kaiser Wilhelm II in Berlin and Jerusalem.[18] The year before Adrian was asked to design the cathedral, the Byzantine-inflected style of the San Francisco Panama-Pacific Exhibition had inspired a flurry of press coverage in Britain, its ethereal domes marking the zenith of the 'white city' type of world's fair.

The Byzantine design did not gain traction with the Cairo building committee however. The previous English Church in Cairo, a Victorian Gothic edifice, was well loved, and the committee back-pedalled from their original generous attitude towards stylistic choice. They felt the story of the old church was an important part of British history in Egypt. Lord Kitchener of Khartoum had ridden to Sunday services in an open carriage, wearing a grey morning suit and top hat, with boys carrying staves running ahead to clear the road.[19] He had read the lessons at most services. The church was the

---

[16]Bishop Gwynne may have been more receptive to the influence of mosque architecture. He chose to have his portrait painted by Francis Hodge with medieval Egyptian architecture in the background (Frontispiece, *Pastor on the Nile*). Letter, Adrian to Giles *c*. July 1916, Adrian Gilbert Scott Papers, RIBA Archives, ScAG/1/4/41.

[17]'Architects' Report', typescript, May 1918, AG Scott Papers, RIBA Archives, ScAG/1/2/3.

[18]Robert Nelson, *Hagia Sophia, 1850–1950: Holy Wisdom Modern Monument* (Chicago: University of Chicago, 2004): 105–28, 187–214.

[19]Burrell, *Cathedral on the Nile*, 11.

site of his state funeral and that of other assassinated British officials. The architect's brief required the new cathedral to have a place for all of the existing brass memorial plaques, including Lord Kitchener's own, in order to underline a sense of continuity and history for the British community.

The cathedral was undoubtedly a cornerstone of the British community in a period of self-conscious empire. Inscriptions on the transferred monuments included the direct 'Justice is the foundation of empires' to the indirect 'God shall wipe away all tears from their eyes.' The inscription on the memorial to Generals Gott and Campbell read, 'and their story lives on, far away, without visible symbol, woven into the stuff of other men's lives' a frank engagement with the seemingly transient nature of expatriate imperial work.[20] Political institutions were often transient and indeed so were social clubs (the other pillar of Egyptian colonial life), but the cathedral would stand as the memorial to British souls who lived, worked and traded in Egypt. Giles Gilbert Scott had written, when describing the firm's standard in ecclesiastical work, 'I build to last a thousand years.' Here the community felt they could lay hold of non-political eternity – for the church always has a broader, more-inclusive outlook and mission.[21] Although state ritual and the cathedral were closely aligned, the church authorities were keen to stress that the relationship between the embassy and the cathedral 'was always purely pastoral.'[22] The influence was intended to go from church to state and not the other way around.

Politics in Egypt were shifting. In 1922, with growing popular hostility to British control, Egypt was declared independent. Britain announced that it would, however, continue to advise the Egyptian government in the name of 'development', facilitating the nation's modernization.[23] This represented a broader shift in British imperial policy. The British Empire now styled itself as linking local commerce to global markets and promoting economic development through the introduction of modern technology.

With this new arrangement, the British position felt less stable than it had in 1918. Egyptian political unrest increased over the course of the 1920s, and in 1924 the cathedral building committee suddenly felt it was important that the church 'should give a feeling of England; however, modified to suit local conditions'. By a 'feeling of England', the committee was understood to be asking for Gothic. One member of the committee explained that this was for the mental health of the British community. The church was a refuge, a bit of his own culture in an alien land. Another member of the community wrote a poem with the telling line, 'Inside the church the desert feels a thousand miles away.' Thus the cathedral would be England transplanted, complete with pointed arches, London-made stained glass, and roses rooted in the sandy soil. Why was Gothic, with its overtones of Britishness, suddenly considered necessary for the cathedral? In Palestine, the Mandate of the League of Nations allowed the British presence to be overt and celebrated. Crusader analogies were common. In nominally independent Egypt,

---

[20]Ibid., 100.

[21]Mark Crinson, *Modern Architecture and the End of Empire* (Aldershot, Hants: Ashgate, 2003): 5.

[22]Burrell, *Cathedral on the Nile*, 50.

[23]G. A. Bremner (ed.), *Architecture and Urbanism in the British Empire* (Oxford: Oxford University Press, 2016): 426. Crinson, *Modern Architecture and the End of Empire*: 16.

overt British presence was problematic. The church was one of the few places where Britishness could be expressed.

The official explanation for requesting a redesign from Adrian was that the building committee wanted something smaller in light of the expected reduction in the number of British expats in the country. Adrian duly produced a small Gothic design.[24] The new scheme was finished and presented to the building committee in mid-1924. 'The Cathedral is designed in a simple Southern Gothic, somewhat reminiscent of Crusader work in the East', Adrian explained, 'while the interior will have some of the feeling of the greater English College Chapels in its directness and simplicity'.[25] But then suddenly, in 1926, the committee reversed course and requested a more monumental Gothic design. The cathedral, they had decided, was to serve as a memorial for those who had died in the Gallipoli and Egyptian campaigns.[26] A large donation had been offered to get the project started, and it was hoped that the families of Americans who had been killed would also subscribe to the building fund.[27]

'There is hardly any Gothic to speak of that could serve as a precedent', Adrian wrote to Giles, 'only some Coptic catacombs'.[28] He chose to ignore the city's few examples of Gothic Revival, which he may have felt were too detached from local tradition. The Gothic Revival nineteenth-century Sayyidna al-Hussein Mosque, for instance, was seen as being sympathetic with Arab traditions (the pointed arches indeed are a shared feature), but in fact was largely a response to European architectural trends. Instead Adrian chose a 'Crusader Gothic' style more in keeping with the architectural traditions of Cyprus and Palestine but stylized in the Gilbert Scott office way.[29] The ideal of Crusader Gothic had always appealed to Bishop MacInness, who even after the creation of Bishop Gwynne as Bishop of Egypt and the Sudan retained supervisory powers over the Diocese of Cairo and must have been keeping an eye on the development of the new cathedral that had been his brainchild.[30] Adrian dutifully designed a large Gothic church with a monumental tower over a deeply shadowed porch. Large doors would have allowed Nile breezes to blow through the nave. The inspiration for the huge arched recess was once again the mosques. Gabled bays along the nave reflected those at the Charterhouse Chapel, which Giles was designing in a Crusader Gothic style around this same time, perhaps inspired by office conversations around the Cairo project. The adoption of inward-facing 'collegiate' pews at Charterhouse had been Giles's idea, meant as a reminder of the communal nature of their worship. Following this logic, the

---

[24]The drawings of this design are now lost.

[25]'Cairo Cathedral: Report Accompanying Sketch Plans', typescript, June 1924, Adrian Gilbert Scott Papers, RIBA Archives, ScAG/1/1/11.

[26]Letter, Arthur Booth (Building Committee Secretary) to Adrian, 9 December 1925, Adrian Gilbert Scott Papers, RIBA Archives, ScAG/1/1/15.

[27]'Cairo Memorial Church', n.d. (either c. 1919 or c. 1926), Adrian Gilbert Scott Papers, RIBA Archives, ScAG/1/2/2.

[28]Letter, Adrian to Giles c. July 1916, Adrian Gilbert Scott Papers, RIBA Archives, ScAG/1/4/41.

[29]Letter, 12 December 1923 Adrian to Gwynne, Adrian Gilbert Scott Papers, RIBA Archives, ScAG/1/3/16.

[30]Letter, Adrian to Giles c. July 1916, Adrian Gilbert Scott Papers, RIBA Archives, ScAG/1/4/41.

adoption of the form of a collegiate chapel in the monumental Gothic design for Cairo Cathedral aimed to encourage community among Englishmen abroad and to imbue their presence with a sense of sacred purpose. Crusader imagery was a common allegory for the Edwardian imperial project, though somewhat out of fashion by the late 1920s. Here Adrian was choosing detail in an almost theatrical way, calling on the associational power of certain forms to create the necessarily solemn but also military atmosphere suitable to a war memorial. On the funding brochure the church towered over a neighbouring civic building in the classical style, part of an intended new government quarter near the Museum of Antiquities. Sphinxes flanked the entrance to the cathedral's walled forecourt (**Figure 13.5**).

Subscriptions, however, were not forthcoming. The monumental Gothic design had to be shelved. Adrian proudly exhibited a perspective of the original Byzantine design for the cathedral at the Royal Academy in 1926. He labelled it, 'Cairo Cathedral: the 1920 design for the Kasr el Nil site, now superseded'.[31] He then sent the same image to be published in *The Builder*.[32] Does the fact that he never exhibited the Gothic design hint at his dissatisfaction with it? Gone were the features that had made the original design appropriate to the climate, features which Adrian had so carefully developed.

He was later, however, able to realize some of these features at the English Church of Port Sudan (**Figure 13.6**). Adrian received the commission for the Port Sudan church

Figure 13.5 Rendering of the expanded Gothic scheme, 1926, as published in the fundraising brochure, courtesy of the A. Gilbert Scott family

---

[31]Anonymous, *Royal Academy Exhibitors, 1905–1970*, vol. 5 (Wakefield: EP Publishing, 1981): 460.
[32]Letter. Adrian to *The Builder*, 11 May 1926, Adrian Gilbert Scott Papers, RIBA Archives, ScAG/1/1/57.

Figure 13.6 The English Church of Port Sudan, after 1939, private collection

from Llewellyn Gwynne, who had previously been Suffragan Bishop of Sudan. As bishop, he had commissioned a new cathedral for Khartoum from Robert Weir Schultz. The region was now part of the newly created Diocese of Egypt, and with Bishop Gwynne placed in charge of the new diocese, he once again found himself in charge of Sudan's churches.

At the Port Sudan church, the deep, tiered overhangs along the sides of the nave echoed the long verandas that were the defining feature of the town's architecture. The most striking element, however, was a Dudok-like tower, completed in 1939. It was wide and squat with a strong emphasis on projecting horizontal mouldings contrasted with deep vertical slits. Here, as at the cathedral, the tower was the most 'international' part of the church. It was one of Adrian's most striking designs, nearly expressionist in its power. This interior was a relative of Cairo, with broad slightly pointed masonry arches and a damask dossal in a gilded frame. Its intended message of cultures fused by modernity was much the same as Cairo's.

The final redesign of Cairo Cathedral was requested in July 1928, when a member of the building committee wrote to Adrian to inform him that a site beside the Nile had been purchased, so a new design would need to be prepared. The letter noted that the committee had withdrawn its suggestion that the cathedral style give a suggestion of England: 'We are at a critical juncture politically.'[33] Politics had once again shifted, and the committee wanted to bring the design into line with broader imperial policy for important colonial buildings. In Jerusalem, the British, in contrast with other European

---

[33]Letter, Booth to Adrian, 21 July 1928, Adrian Gilbert Scott Papers, RIBA Archives, ScAG/1/1/36.

powers, had pioneered the idea of adopting aspects of local architectural tradition when Lutyens's pupil Austen St Barbe Harrison had introduced the concept of architectural fusion from New Delhi.[34] The decision to mix aspects of local tradition into a modern design was an unusual choice for Cairo, however, where new buildings tended to adopt a polychromatic orientalism or an international Classicism, and, as historian Samuel Albert has pointed out, it marked something new for Egypt.[35]

The representation of local community at Cairo Cathedral through use of Middle Eastern forms – a Byzantine dome over the crossing, niches above door arches, tall blank walls with central openings, cushion capitals and timber side aisles (late-stage inspiration taken from Coptic architecture, probably at the urging of Bishop Gwynne)[36] – was thus taken from Liberal Anglican notions of the cathedral's function as a place to develop community. The method of the architectural expression of these theories was in keeping with the already developed practices of the firm of Giles Gilbert Scott. The Gilbert Scotts, like other architects of the day, might have referred to such references to the local building tradition as 'architectural good manners'. Other details of the cathedral, Adrian was keen to stress in his presentations were 'thoroughly up to date & modern' and 'Greek in character'.[37] Although these stylistic features were in line with trends in British colonial architecture, they were not exclusively derived from them. The alignment with the current architectural preferences of the government was seen as felicitous – Anglican leaders could sincerely adopt this fusion of cosmopolitanism and reference to local culture in an attempt to convey Christian respect for all people.

For Liberal Anglicans, the parish church ministered to local communities and served the individual at home, whereas the cathedral served the wider community – one might even say a global community of Christians. The cathedral was where the local participated in international dialogue, as one of a series of international relay stations, broadcasting the Christian message to the world. Since a major pillar of Liberal Anglicanism was community participation, the architecture of the building needed to convey these ideals. Another pillar was Christian ecumenicalism, the bringing together of disparate denominations in shared worship and the pursuit of common goals, so the cathedral needed plenty of space for hospitality and the ability to hold large crowds.

The difference between the role of the parish church and that of the cathedral was reflected in the choice of architectural styles. The design of the Anglican parish churches of Cairo, built early in the twentieth century at the urging of Canon T Gairdner, and particularly intended to serve the Arab population, tended to be Arts and Crafts

---

[34]Christopher Hussey elucidated the theory behind such fusion in, 'A Crusader's Castle of To-day', *Country Life* 70 no. 1815 (1931): 480–6.

[35]Samuel D. Albert, 'Egypt and Mandatory Palestine and Iraq', in G. A. Bremner (ed.), *Architecture and Urbanism in the British Empire* (Oxford: Oxford University Press, 2016): 427.

[36]Gwynne had a particular affinity for Coptic Church design. H. C. Jackson, *Pastor on the Nile* (London: SPCK, 1960) 14.

[37]Letter Adrian to Giles, 21 August 1918, Adrian Gilbert Scott Papers, RIBA Archives, ScAG/1/4/45.

inspired.[38] A typical example was the Church of Jesus Light of the World, a quiet, round-arched, cottagey building, with rough stone walls and a hipped tile roof whose eaves swept down in a rustic and home-like gesture.

By contrast, the final cathedral design declared its advanced modernity. From hydroelectric power, to telephone exchanges and transport infrastructure, British-backed modernization became the heart of political justifications for British military presence. The cathedral in its ultimate form was part of the British administration in Egypt's modernization programme, providing the facilities necessary for 'modern religion'. The cathedral provided clean, bright ritual space intended for broadcast and spectacle. It was equipped with cooling ceiling fans and forced air, irrigated gardens, bright lighting, the latest 'scientific' planning, reinforced concrete vaults, garages for clergy automobiles, and instead of the quadrangular courtyard found at St George's, Jerusalem, the Cairo Cathedral had wings embracing a forecourt with a traffic circle for automobile access – arriving congregants could be dropped off right at the door. There were purpose-built spaces for non-worship events, including a church hall large enough for dances or performances. A community programme was in-built, creating a bridge between the local residents and the wider community of international visitors to the cathedral, mostly consisting of European and American businessmen.

The cathedral also featured a lawn and rose garden. Water, so plentiful in Britain and so precious in Egypt, was a mark of home. It was a theme and an obsession of British residents of the Middle East. Across the region, they focused on water and the creation of gardens. At the desolate Anglo-Persian Oil Company processing station in Abadan, Iran, as Mark Crinson has discovered, despite the hasty prefabricated nature of the settlement, the presence of ragged rose bushes marked out the homes of the managers from those of the labourers.[39] When the British took Jerusalem in 1918, one of the first things the military government did was to bring in the architect C. R. Ashbee to plan streets lined with trees in the manner of an English Garden City and to build a network of public gardens along the ancient city wall. Ashbee's work was largely funded by the Pro-Jerusalem Society. British beautification efforts went hand in hand with the humanitarian aims of British missionary work in the region, and Pro-Jerusalem Society subscribers included Liberal Anglican and Liberal Catholic leaders such as the Bishop of Jerusalem and Cardinal Bourne.[40] The irrigated lawn, the flower garden maintained with great trouble, was a marker of technological prowess. To garden in the desert was a powerful metaphor.

Adrian's Cairo was no exception. The greatest British engineering projects in Egypt were devoted to moving water, from the Suez Canal, to the many Nile locks, to the projected dam at Aswan, which Adrian and his brother were initially asked to design. In

---

[38]Burrell, *Cathedral on the Nile*, 16.

[39]Crinson, *Modern Architecture and the End of Empire*, 52.

[40]Ashbee spent a large percentage of donations on stone garden seats. C. R. Ashbee, *Jerusalem, 1918–1920*, Record of the Pro-Jerusalem Society 1 (London: John Murray, 1921): 72.

the first sketches, the cathedral was surrounded by spurting fountains and bunches of palm trees. Adrian wrote to Giles early in the design process, asking him to hire William Walcot to do a perspective and stressing that the artist should exaggerate the lush foliage all around. He believed that portraying the cathedral as a sort of mirage would appeal to his sun-baked British clients.

The new site had required extensive preparations because the Nile-front property bridged a nineteenth-century French sluice gate. The cathedral itself stood at the back of the site, facing the river across a green lawn, with the neo-Georgian Bishop's House and Assembly Hall placed symmetrically on either side of the tall tower that announced its presence on the skyline. In the built cathedral, Adrian reverted to a variant of the original Byzantine design, but, as has been discussed above, with internationalizing features. The tower was meant to be a universally recognizable sign of the presence of a church, but to think of it as Gothic is perhaps not accurate – it was something more akin to the landmark towers that Austen St. Barbe Harrison recommended should mark an important civic building in the Middle East.[41] Cairo had a longer tradition of tower building than Jerusalem, and when Adrian arrived in the city, the skyline was still largely defined by the minarets and domes of the mosques. Adrian wrote to Giles, 'All Cairo is dead flat except the Citadel.'[42] The cathedral tower, Adrian explained to the building committee, 'should dominate Cairo.'[43] Towers were important for wayfinding, and therefore Cairo Cathedral could also serve as a landmark in the new traffic plan.

During the Second World War, an influx of soldiers meant that cathedral services were always full. The building became a true centre for the community as envisioned by its Liberal Anglican founders. After the war, however, with the rapid deterioration of British-Egyptian relations, the cathedral congregation declined. Protests against King Farouk and the sustained British presence in the country resulted in the 1952 burning of Shepheard's Hotel and the Country Club in the British-dominated Garden City district. The cathedral too was affected. King Farouk had recently donated some bronze grills to the church, sparking protests by republican students. The bishop, like the students, disapproved of King Farouk's personal life, and ironically, the king had meant the donation to garner goodwill with the bishop. A group described by the dean as a 'gang of hooligans' (presumably angry protestors) broke into the building soon afterwards, although they were driven out before they could do much damage. In analogy with the state of the diocese, the building itself deteriorated, with serious cracks appearing in the walls of the Assembly Hall in 1955. The foundations over the French irrigation channel had subsided. The dean wrote to Adrian for advice, but with the Suez Crisis, help and funds from the UK were cut off.[44]

---

[41]Harrison: 'It is tradition here to give all important buildings towers', Adina Hoffman, *Till We Have Built Jerusalem* (New York: Farrar, Straus and Giroux, 2016): 167.

[42]Letter, Adrian to Giles n.d. (1916), Adrian Gilbert Scott Papers, RIBA Archives, ScAG/1/4/41.

[43]Letter, Adrian to Arthur Booth, 27 January 1926, Adrian Gilbert Scott Papers, RIBA Archives, ScAG/1/1/18.

[44]'Report on the settlement of, and damage to, north & south wings of All Saints Cathedral Cairo – Egypt', typescript, *c*. 1955, Adrian Gilbert Scott Papers, RIBA Archives, ScAG/6/3.

With the arrival of the 1960s, while many Arab Christians worshipped in the cathedral, some other Egyptians continued to see the building as an unwelcome reminder of the British presence. The Governorate of Cairo issued a demolition order for the building on 25 April 1963, exactly 25 years after its consecration.[45] The site, they explained, was in the way of a new bridge across the Nile. It would have to be cleared.

The cathedral hung on until the late 1970s, while plans were made for a discrete new building in the suburbs. By the autumn of 1976, the building already had something of the air of a ruin. The addition of hoardings and debris from the bridge construction completed the site's isolation, a sandy desert only a few yards from the Nile. The cathedral faced the river across a parched lawn and dying garden. The walls of the Assembly Hall, although they had been summarily patched, were still cracked. Inside, the water had been cut off and the electricity was out, but a skeleton crew of cathedral staff was still based there, without electric fans or running water, overseeing the operations of the diocese and waiting in case some pilgrim or visitor found his way through the construction barriers and heavy traffic that made the site an island. The heaviness of the landmark cathedral evoked the image of the 'fortress church' and was meant to imply the permanent presence of the church in the civic landscape. Ironically for such a structure however, the cathedral survived barely as long as it had taken to design.

Cairo Cathedral tells the story of twentieth-century British colonial religious architecture like few other structures. Its architecture and intention were tied up in the religious and political currents of its time in a way that was surprisingly explicit for a work of architecture. Yet, although inflected for political purposes, the inclusion of local references and the presentation of a modern technological religion were not a uniquely colonial strategy, but simply the worldwide policy of the Anglican Church, found just as much in Liverpool as in Cairo. The spirit of reform was in the air.

In building the cathedral, the architect and officials in charge had believed they were making a statement that would survive as a memorial to the British community in Egypt. They felt that the choice of style carried a message about their identity that would be legible to the local and international community. They rejected the pure Gothic style in the end, when they decided that it was best to emphasize their contribution to an international ideal of modernization, rather than any ideal of British values. But it turned out that this stylistic language did not translate. In later years, many Egyptians only saw the cathedral as a reminder of previous British occupation.

Adrian Gilbert Scott did not live to see the demolition of the building, dying only two days before the demolition order was issued. The site would become a traffic intersection, one attempt at modernization falling victim to another. Shortly after the deconsecration ceremony on 10 February 1978, the walls of the cathedral crashed down, and clouds of dust billowed out over the Nile.

---

[45]Burrell, *Cathedral on the Nile*, 78.

Select bibliography

Primary

Adrian Gilbert Scott Papers, RIBA Archives
Architect & Building News
The Builder
Country Life

Secondary

Ashbee, C. R. *Jerusalem, 1918–1920: Record of the Pro-Jerusalem Society*, vol 1. London: John
    Murray, 1921.
Aspden, Kester. *Fortress Church*. Leominster, Herts: Gracewing, 2002.
Bremner, G. A. (ed.). *Architecture and Urbanism in the British Empire*. Oxford: Oxford University
    Press, 2016.
Burrell, Arthur. *Cathedral on the Nile*. Oxford: Amate, 1984.
Crinson, Mark. *Modern Architecture and the End of Empire*. Aldershot, Hants: Ashgate, 2003.
Grimley, Matthew. *Citizenship, Community, and the Church of England: Liberal Anglican Theories
    of the State between the Wars*. Oxford: Oxford University Press, 2004.
Hussey, Christopher. 'A Crusader's Castle of To-day'. *Country Life* 70 (1815 [1931]): 480–6.
Jackson, H. C. *Pastor on the Nile*. London: SPCK, 1960.
Kroyanker, David. *Jerusalem Architecture*. New York: Vendome, 2002.
Nelson, Robert. *Hagia Sophia, 1850–1950: Holy Wisdom Modern Monument*. Chicago: University
    of Chicago, 2004.
Stamp, Gavin. *An Architect of Promise*. Donington: Shaun Tyas, 2002.
Yusaf, Shundana. *Broadcasting Buildings: Architecture on the Wireless, 1927–1945*. Boston: MIT,
    2014.

SECTION V
WEDDING PEACE WITH WELL-BEING

Tecton's Finsbury Health Centre, opened in 1939, is one of the canonical buildings of the 1920s and 1930s. It represents the almost perfect alignment of new methods of construction for healthcare (concrete frames, glazed panels and facing materials, up-to-date and flexible services), with modernist design and planning (a striking 'H' plan designed to be adaptable for shifting programmes and uses), along with progressive politics (it expressed a socialist vision of centralized healthcare). Chunni Lal Katial, an Indian doctor active in local Labour Party politics, had been chair of the Finsbury Public Health Committee which had drawn up the famous Finsbury Plan for public health and amenity in the Borough and which then commissioned Berthold Lubetkin's practice to build the new health centre. This was, as Elizabeth Darling has suggested, healthcare provision 'centralised, bureaucratized … designed by architectural experts and run by health experts'.[1]

The intersection of progressive politics and progressive design was, however, precisely that – a tantalizing coincidence from which general conclusions can perhaps be too easily drawn. Modernist architects did not – *could* not – work solely for socialist clients; progressive clients did not always believe in the principles of the new architecture.

Just to the west of Tecton's modernist spacecraft is a seemingly inconsequential cottage-like structure, quaint by comparison, which had been opened just over a decade before the new health centre. Finsbury Borough Council's new Maternity and Child Welfare Clinic, designed by the architect Edwin Stanley Hall, represents the inverse of the Health Centre; a quaint neo-Georgian lodge, modest in the scale of its provision, matched by its diminutive architecture. The clinic and its building were representative of an English political and parochial conservatism. Indeed, the shift in Finsbury's political complexion almost perfectly explains this transition and paradigm shift – from the Borough Council's domination by the Municipal Reform Party and then the Ratepayers' Association (both aligned with the Conservative Party) to Labour Party control from 1928, just a year after the Maternity and Child Welfare Clinic was opened.

Architectural history's focus on the exceptionalism of the Finsbury Health Centre exemplifies and accounts for the omission of much serious analysis of the 'bread-and-butter' architecture produced at the same time. And yet, as all the essays in this volume have sought to show, by examining longer reformist trajectories, we can deepen our understanding of our everyday built environment. In contextualizing the modernization

---

[1] Elizabeth Darling, *Reforming Britain: Narratives of Modernity before Reconstruction* (Abingdon: Routledge, 2007): 79.

of healthcare, the development of its various guises, and the place of design and designers in making these manifest spatially, the neo-Georgian hut on Pine Street takes on a much greater significance.

To contemporaries, the new clinic represented the completion of a scheme which had been long in the mind of the Borough Council: to provide a new Centre constructed on the latest principles and adequately equipped for its purposes, namely 'to afford advice and assistance to expectant and nursing mothers and to protect and foster the child life of the Borough'.[2] Construction of Maternity and Child Welfare Clinics had been catalysed, as Barry Doyle's essay discusses, by the Maternity and Child Welfare Act of 1918, which mandated Special Committees for local authorities to deal with attendant issues, and which led to more widespread provision of antenatal care for expectant mothers, and support services for early years' healthcare, both intended to drive down high rates of infant mortality. In Clerkenwell mortality rates had reduced from 154 deaths in a thousand at the turn of the century to the relatively low number of 50.8 for every 1,000 by 1927.[3] In Finsbury Borough Council services included a weighing centre, distribution of (dried) milk, lectures and talks, sewing classes, clinics and dental services.[4] There was provision for a number of ailments, from constipation and dyspepsia through to more general debility. There was a hospital referral system in place, including an agreed number of beds for Finsbury infants at the Infants Hospital, Vincent Square.[5]

The new clinic combined two existing centres – one of which had grown out of the Invalid Kitchens of London branch sited at 162 Lever Street (which became the East Finsbury Maternity and Child Welfare Centre) and a second site originally at Newcastle Hall, Clerkenwell Close, but removed temporarily to the Old Session House on Clerkenwell Green.[6] The Marquess of Northampton, who had significant landholdings in Finsbury and Islington, donated the Pine Street site in anticipation of further development of the Northampton Road area of his estate. It was originally intended that the site would include accommodation for the Maternity Nursing Association to facilitate training there but this suggestion was later dropped.[7] Stanley Hall produced his

---

[2] Islington Local History Centre, Pamphlet entitled 'Ceremony of Laying the Foundation Stone of the New Maternity Centre, Pine Street': n.p., L3.153.

[3] A. E. Thomas, 'The Metropolitan Borough of Finsbury. Annual Report of the Public Health of Finsbury for the Year 1927' (1928): 10, https://wellcomelibrary.org/moh/report/b18209452/50#?c=0&m=0&s=0&cv=0&z=-0.3607%2C0.9838%2C1.4239%2C0.7331 (accessed 23 April 2022): 5.

[4] A. E. Thomas, 'The Metropolitan Borough of Finsbury. Annual Report of the Public Health of Finsbury for the Year 1923' (1924): 9–11, https://wellcomecollection.org/works/jas4wt5y (accessed 23 April 2022).

[5] A. E. Thomas, 'The Metropolitan Borough of Finsbury. Annual Report of the Public Health of Finsbury for the Year 1927' (1928): 10, https://wellcomelibrary.org/moh/report/b18209452/50#?c=0&m=0&s=0&cv=0&z=-0.3607%2C0.9838%2C1.4239%2C0.7331 (accessed 23 April 2022).

[6] The Survey of London's Clerkenwell volume includes a brief mention of the Pine Street clinic. See 'Exmouth Market Area', in Survey of London: Volume 47, Northern Clerkenwell and Pentonville, ed. Philip Temple (London, 2008): 52–83. British History Online, http://www.british-history.ac.uk/survey-london/vol47/pp52-83 (accessed 27 December 2021).

[7] See Islington Local Health Centre, Minutes of Finsbury Borough Council 25 (April 1924–April 1925), minutes of meeting (5 June 1924).

first designs in October 1924 incorporating a large lecture hall, kitchen facilities, private offices for medical staff, a dispensary, a nursery, a pram shelter in a deep veranda, and dedicated clinical consulting rooms at a cost of around £6,000 (in the end the building cost £7,500, with a £2,500 capital grant from the Ministry of Health). Though not as ambitious as the Finsbury Plan of the early 1930s, the Tory-led council did have plans for further provision on the Northampton Estate, namely a new public mortuary, and disinfecting plant and cleansing station.

The Pine Street Maternity and Child Welfare Centre contextualizes the social or architectural vision of Finsbury Health Centre. It reminds us that the idea of typological specialization in relation to healthcare was an established practice: Stanley Hall, for instance, had developed a line in hospitals and ancillary buildings which he brought to the significant partnership of Stanley Hall, Easton and Robertson in the mid to late 1930s: he produced the Nursing Home for Great Ormond Street Hospital, an isolation and maternity hospital for Queen Charlotte's Hospital at Goldhawk Road, parts of St Mary's Paddington, and the Portman Day Nursey for St Marylebone Health Society, including a specialist infant welfare centre named after the pioneering woman physician Christine Murrell. Though not radical in design terms, these were significant healthcare projects which required specialist knowledge.

The developments of the 1920s at Pine Street capture the tendency to centralize services but also to think of them holistically and as integrated in a wider provision. Even under Conservative municipal rule, there was significant capital expenditure to ensure modern facilities were available, and they were conceived of with a degree of imagination. The almost domestic vernacular of the neo-Georgian brick hut also has the faint colonial air of a single-storey bungalow complete with shutters and a veranda. The austere, stripped classical architrave with an inscribed stone tablet punching through the eves adds just a hint of formality. These features evoked specific imaginaries of rural (even colonial) airiness as well as approachable public amenity.

This recontextualization of the two Pine Street health centres has methodological implications that are explored in the final two chapters of this volume: first that the geographical and morphological histories of healthcare in twentieth-century Britain are complex, neither reducible to style nor indeed to individual buildings; second, that the relationship between architectural or spatial conception and modes of healthcare should be examined beyond the convenient alignment between politics and design philosophy. Moreover, the assumption that British healthcare was deliberately parochial and insular before the mid-1930s needs testing. As early as 1912, in the wake of the National Insurance Act which made funding provision for tuberculosis sanatoria, the *Architectural Review* was actively encouraging creative and critical collaboration between designers and medics. It declared that 'citizens who have the best interest of the community at heart' had two main challenges to face: 'The one is that of sanatoria, the other is that relating to the housing of the labouring classes.'[8]

---

[8]'Sanatoria for the Community: Suggested Discussion', *Architectural Review* (September 1912): 143.

Barry Doyle's chapter canters through the range of working-class hospital provision with particular reference to Leeds and Sheffield, while also touching on the growth of the Cottage Hospital movement which bridged urban and more local rural healthcare provision. In sum, Doyle helps us to see the complex geographies of health in this period, as well as the transformation of specific buildings and spaces within them, and this hints clearly at possible future areas of research. Harriet Richardson's piece focuses on architectural responses to new ideas in healthcare – of centralization, light and air and indeed obsolescence. She also nuances our understanding of nomenclature and style – there was a marketplace for services in mixed provision, and architecture was part of selling those services.

This volume was conceived before – and indeed was nearly complete by – the arrival of the COVID-19 coronavirus pandemic in Europe in March 2020. We added this final section to the volume because as editors we felt the need to reflect on the implications of subsequent events in this context for two main reasons. One was because comparisons were frequently drawn with the H1N1 virus – better known as the Spanish Influenza – that had ripped through populations a century before in the wake of the First World War. A volume that sought to discuss the aftermath of war would be incomplete without addressing this and challenging those comparisons. The second was because reflection about ambitious social and economic reconstruction now had a real immediacy as political commentators and designers inter alia began to do the same as their forebears in the 1920s.

In fact, as both contributors point out, there was little fundamental rethinking prompted by the Spanish Flu in architectural terms. There had been a long process of modernization and sanitization in building design and town planning, championed by reformists since the nineteenth century, in particular in relation to working-class communities. There was, therefore, an accelerated need to continue to improve the physical health of the population and to move beyond treatment to disease prevention. Moreover, conceptions of salutogenesis were fundamentally related to new forms of architectural practice and town planning – the Housing Acts of the post-war years, for instance, were delivered under the aegis of the Ministry of Health and its Housing Division led by Raymond Unwin. Richardson and Doyle's pieces encourage us to reflect on the legibility of healthcare and how architects moved beyond merely functional spaces for treatment, to try to articulate the variety of its institutions and services and their civic role, and how this was visible and legible at urban scale in a pre-NHS world. As we continue to reflect on how to accommodate this new virus – and indeed future epidemiological events – these are salutary reminders.

CHAPTER 14
SICKNESS: ADVANCES IN BRITISH HOSPITAL DESIGN AFTER THE FIRST WORLD WAR
Harriet Richardson Blakeman

Introduction

Ideas about sickness, about where responsibility lay for caring for the sick and about the locus of that care had been changing from the late nineteenth century. After the war, Lloyd George equated the health of the people with national efficiency and recuperation.[1] Health could be achieved both through preventive measures, and by healing the sick but in the immediate aftermath of the war, the latter posed a challenge. The existing hospital system was struggling with rising costs and more complex and expensive therapies and equipment. To find a solution to the problem, enquiries were set in motion that led to proposals for improving services and legislation to reform the hospital system.

At the same time, there was a steadily increasing demand for health services. A number of factors drove up demand: the growth of medical knowledge, which saw greater specialisation and thereby more demand for outpatient consultations; increasingly sophisticated surgery with better success rates that meant hospitals became the accepted proper setting for operations rather than a domestic environment; access to expensive diagnostic equipment and therapies; and a rise in accident cases needing treatment in casualty departments. Wealthier patients, formerly cared for at home, were now more inclined to be treated in a hospital, and the diminished coffers of many of the long-established charitable, voluntary hospitals were eventually replenished through the admission of paying patients. To meet the demand, existing hospitals expanded and many new ones were built. The expectations of the new clientele were reflected in the developments of hospital design.

Hospital architecture can therefore tell us more about sickness and social and political contexts, than just the ways in which design can mitigate cross-infection, or facilitate the complex requirements of the nursing and medical staff, or even act as a therapeutic device in itself, promoting cure. This chapter considers some of the chief characteristics of the hospital system as it developed after the war. It will start by looking at how hospital design had begun to evolve before the war, then go on to take a wider view, questioning how the war impacted on public health policy, considering some of the ideas that emerged about how health care should be organized and provided, and how those ideas were circulated and disseminated. It highlights the importance of the Dawson Report of 1920, examines the ways in which hospital provision diversified and

---

[1]Quoted in *Illustrated London News* (5 October 1918): 390.

expanded, and the factors driving that expansion. It focuses on the changing socio-political ideas about health and medical treatment, and the dichotomy between public and private provision. This manifested itself in contrasting responses in the design of hospitals to meet the expectations of different social classes, from the wealthy to the newly enfranchised working classes, as well as different medical needs. Often these were expressed subtly in the choice of name: nursing home rather than hospital, hospital rather than sanatorium or asylum. Finally, the paper considers how the pace of change in medical science supported prevailing ideas about architectural obsolescence.

By considering the hospital building as an artefact of its social and political context, the challenges and problems of caring for the sick or treating disease can be viewed through the lens of hospital design.[2] The large open ward, synonymous with Florence Nightingale, for example, elucidates the role of the nurse and social standing of the patients, while construction details and engineering systems illuminate ideas about cross infection and germ theory.

But we must be cautious when looking to find answers in the past to questions in the present. In the case of the COVID-19 coronavirus pandemic, there has been much attention paid to the influenza pandemic of 1919–1920. The measures that were taken then to contain the spread of the infection were reflected in the actions taken a century later, and some comfort could be taken from looking back at how society recovered when the pandemic receded. But the influenza pandemic differed in two vital respects from the coronavirus pandemic: it came and went in two relatively brief, though devastating, waves, and its effects were worse in young people than the elderly. It also struck a population already greatly weakened by the long years of the war. Influenza was not the only killer infectious disease. The pandemic occurred at a time when there was an ongoing fight against tuberculosis, while the war had also brought the ravages of venereal diseases and infant mortality to the top of the public health agenda.

As far as hospital design is concerned, it is hard to find any evidence that the influenza pandemic made an impact. Searches through contemporary literature for such a cause and effect draw a blank. While there was much discussion then as now of ventilation in crowded spaces such as public theatres or schools, and buildings were appropriated to serve as emergency hospitals, hospital buildings themselves were already designed to combat cross-infection through effective ventilation, natural or artificial, together with aseptic practices. There was as yet no consensus on the dangers from air-borne infection, but most theories agreed that isolation played an important role in minimizing the spread of disease.

During the coronavirus pandemic we learnt that space was not the only issue: the conversions of exhibition centres to emergency hospitals demonstrated that point. We

---

[2]For ways in which the architectural history of hospitals can be understood in terms of material culture see, for example: Annmarie Adams, 'Modernism and Medicine: The Hospitals of Stevens and Lee, 1916–1932', *Journal of the Society of Architectural Historians* 58 no. 1 (1999): 42–61; David Theodore, '"The Fattest Possible Nurse", Architecture, Computers, and Post-war Nursing', in Laura Abreu and Sally Sheard (eds.), *Hospital Life: Theory and Practice from the Medieval to the Modern* (Bern: Peter Lang, 2013): 273–98.

could provide the space, but what was lacking was sufficient equipment and trained staff. Those were problems that also arose after the war. Improvements to the working conditions of staff, with higher pay and training, along with better accommodation in new, well-appointed nurses' homes, did much to remedy those problems.

Pre-war changes in hospital design

At first glance, most hospitals built in Britain after the war seemed to have changed little from the standard pavilion plans of the later nineteenth century. This implies a huge gulf between the hospitals of that era and those built after the Second World War. However, closer inspection reveals subtle differences. The pavilion plan was already being tweaked before 1914, particularly in urban settings where the challenges of adapting to a restricted site or tackling polluted air produced variations. This was seen in major projects such as Alfred Waterhouse's towering saltire plan for the rebuilding of University College Hospital, London (1897–1906), where not only was the whole building constructed on a cruciform plan but the wards, too, were cruciform ensuring that every ward on every floor was both well-lit and well-ventilated despite being sited in a densely built-up part of London. At Belfast's Royal Victoria Hospital (designed 1899, completed 1906), William Henman strung out the wards side by side in a low horizontal range, cross ventilation being replaced by mechanical ventilation on the plenum system, cleaning the air mechanically drawn into the wards.[3] In Belfast it was urban pollution that dictated the design. Conversely, for rural sites where uncontaminated fresh air was abundant, the basic pavilion plan remained the go-to plan, as its basis on natural ventilation remained relevant in terms of treatment, and economical in terms of construction, nursing and administration. A late example is the RAF General Hospital at Ely in Cambridgeshire, built in 1939–1940.[4] The most obvious continuity can be seen in the emergency hospitals constructed at the outset of the Second World War which varied little from the hutted hospitals erected during the earlier conflict.

Lighting and ventilation were key areas of interest given the crucial role both were thought to have on health. New technologies and methods of construction were introduced to improve these aspects of the traditional pavilion plan. The metal windows made by Crittal allowed the hospital architect Charles Ernest Elcock to devise a type of bi-fold window for wards to allow a large expanse of the ward wall to be opened up. Although his firm of Elcock and Sutcliffe is best remembered today in connection with

---

[3] The architectural development of UCH has been comprehensively researched by Amy Spencer as part of her doctoral study of the architectural history of University College London. For the Royal Victoria see Jeremy Taylor, *The Architect and the Pavilion Hospital. Dialogue and Design Creativity in England 1850–1914* (London and New York: Leicester University Press, 1997): 187–202.

[4] H. Richardson (ed.), *English Hospitals 1660–1948* (Swindon: Royal Commission on the Historical Monuments of England, 1998): 101–2.

the Daily Telegraph building in London,[5] it made its mark with a competition-winning design for Davyhulme Hospital, near Manchester, designed in 1924 and opened in 1929, after which a steady stream of hospital commissions came their way. Elcock joined the International Hospital Association, established in 1929, attending their conferences in Vienna, New York and Brussels, and contributed to *Nosokomeion*, the association's influential journal.[6]

Elcock called his bi-folds 'sliding-folding' windows[7] and first used them at Warminster Cottage Hospital, Wiltshire, begun in 1928, where the windows occupied most of the exterior walls. Hopper windows ran above and below a section of bi-folds, all steel framed and made by Crittall. In the 1920s these were state-of-the-art and made open-air treatment considerably more comfortable than the practice of wheeling beds out of doors, or on to a veranda with a simple iron-framed glazed roof. 'Veranda wards' designed by Elcock at Hertford County Hospital (1932–1933) not only used bi-fold windows but also picked up on a European trend to compartmentalize large wards using glazed screens, with the beds turned parallel to the window wall instead of facing the window, and therefore the glare of the sun (**Figure 14.1**).[8] This design was seen at the influential Rigs Hospital in Copenhagen. The leading American hospital architect Edward F. Stevens considered the Rigs ward worthy of study, hailing it as one of the best developed in Europe. Its twenty-six-bed units were divided into eight sections, each with three or four beds, separated by screens that were raised a foot off the ground and stood at six feet high. This afforded some privacy without impeding access or air circulation.[9] It was an arrangement that responded to the re-orientation of ward blocks to an east-west alignment (rather than north-south), which allowed for long south-facing verandas and balconies to be created – maximizing the amount of sunshine and light in the ward. In Britain the change was supported by an RIBA *Report on the Orientation of Buildings*, published in 1933, which included a chapter on hospitals.[10] Some hospital wards that adopted parallel bed layouts looked very much like a traditional ward pavilion on the outside,

---

[5]In 1934 the firm designed the Arcadium Amusement Centre, unbuilt, that comprised shops, restaurants, dance halls and a swimming pool, as well as a health centre and gymnasium., for which see James Nott, 'Dance Halls: Towards an Architectural and Spatial History, *c*.1918–65', *Architectural History* 61 (2018): 220. For an account of Elcock see H. Richardson 'Charles Ernest Elcock (1878–1944)', in David Jones and Sam McKinstry (eds.), *Essays in Scots and English Architectural History A Festschrift in honour of John Frew* (Donington: Shaun Tyas, 2009): 120–30.

[6]The influential role of the journal to the development of hospital planning and design, and in the dissemination of ideas internationally has been highlighted in Julie Willis, Philip Goad, and Cameron Logan, *Architecture and the Modern Hospital: Nosokomeion to Hygeia* (Abingdon, Oxon: Routledge, 2019).

[7]*The Builder* (18 March 1932): 511.

[8]*Architects' Journal*, 76 (16 November 1932): 636, 613.

[9]E. F. Stevens, *The American Hospital of the Twentieth Century* (New York: The Architectural Record Company, revised edn., 1921): 29, 37, 40; Annmarie Adams, *Medicine by Design: The Architect and the Modern Hospital 1893–1943* (Minneapolis London: University of Minnesota Press, 2008): 95–6.

[10]*The Orientation of Buildings; Being the Report with Appendices, of the RIBA Joint Committee on the Orientation of Buildings* (London: RIBA, 1933).

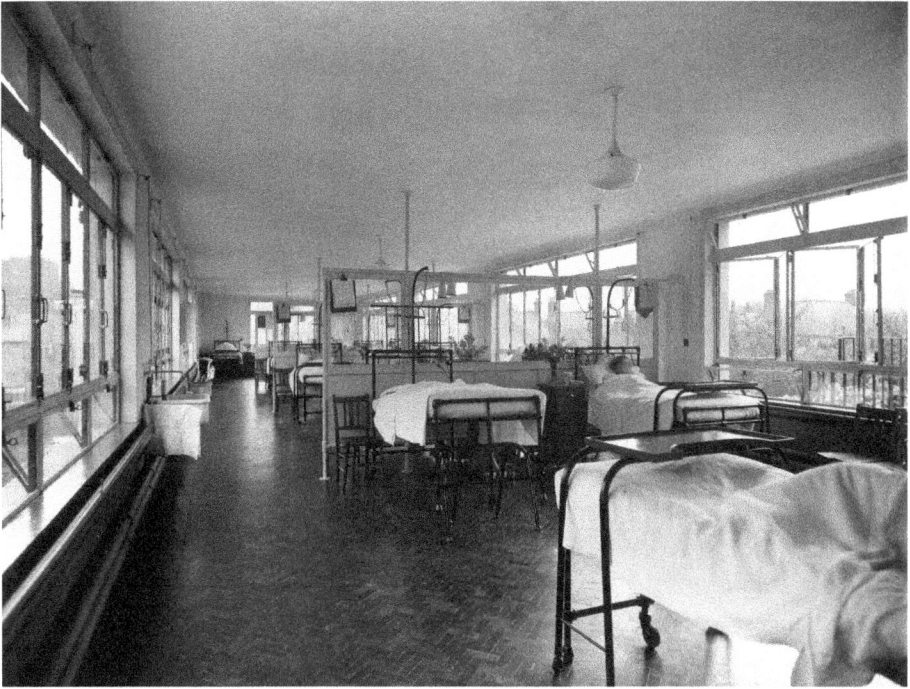

Figure 14.1 Hertford County Hospital Extension, the women's ward, Elcock & Sutcliffe (1932), photograph by Sydney Newberry, Architectural Press Archive/RIBA Collections, RIBA72304

with tall sash-and-hopper windows, such as Adams, Holden & Pearson's Southend-on-Sea General Hospital built in 1929–1932.[11]

Expansion and diversity

The war had revealed the poor health of many recruits but the lack of coordination in the existing hospital service made it ill-equipped to tackle the problem at a national level. There arose a conviction that all citizens should have access to the best means of curing disease, but there was no consensus about the exact manner of achieving this, or whether access to health care should be provided free to all. The majority thought a state-funded service not economically viable. These views were encapsulated in the Dawson Report published in 1920 on the future provision of medical and allied services.

Bertrand Dawson (later Lord Dawson of Penn) produced a vision for the future of public health care in Britain. In 1918 he had proposed a type of model health centre

---

[11]*Architects' Journal,* 76 (20 July 1932): 65–71, 97–9. It is worth noting that for the children's block wide French windows with access to a veranda on the ground floor and shallow balconies above were adopted, but in these wards the beds were placed facing the windows.

Figure 14.2 'National Welfare: A Model Health Centre of the Future', *Illustrated London News* (5 October1918): 403 © Illustrated London News Ltd./Mary Evans, 13542056/ILN

(**Figure 14.2**), and he expanded on this idea in the report of 1920. He proposed that urban centres should be served by a mix of in- and outpatient care with both preventative and curative facilities grouped together in one location. These would comprise a hospital and clinics equipped with an operating theatre, a radiographic institute, laboratory and dispensary, services for maternity, infant welfare, school hygiene and dentistry. There was also to be provision for rehabilitation – a relatively new concept – with a hydrotherapy unit, a gymnasium for physiotherapy, and playing grounds for exercises and games led by skilled instructors 'designed to secure physical fitness and beauty'.[12]

Dawson's model health centre calls to mind the civic centre as a rational grouping of allied services. In its vision of concentrating specialist services it also reflected the development of group medicine in America. The best-known exemplar was the Mayo Clinic, for which new premises had opened in 1914, but the institution was already highly regarded for its medical and surgical excellence, scientific investigation and dissemination of medical knowledge.[13] Dawson, whose own consulting rooms were in Wimpole Street, Marylebone, placed great emphasis on the importance of the profession being able to meet and discuss cases and new ideas: the very essence of the Harley Street consultant culture. An experimental clinic along these lines was established in 1922 in Brook Street, Mayfair. This private clinic provided patients with access to a range of specialists in one spot. A large house was remodelled for the purpose by the architect Charles H. Biddulph-Pinchard, who had provided Dawson with the plans to illustrate his report. Biddulph-Pinchard was not a hospital specialist; his practice had been largely built on minor country houses and churches, but that gave him a good understanding of the style and standard of internal finishes that the wealthy clientele of the clinic would expect.[14]

The Dawson Report was enormously influential; its ideas are reflected in diverse ways: in the different ideals behind the Finsbury and Peckham Health Centres; in the foundation in 1930 of the Women's League of Health and Beauty; and in the establishment of 'hospital centres' at Birmingham and Aberdeen where teaching, general and specialist hospitals were brought together on a single site.[15] Although Dawson's vision of a national network of health centres did not materialize, the 1920s and 1930s did see a boom in the construction of hospitals and allied buildings. What emerged was a mix of initiatives, that saw both continuity and innovation, with an expansion in new specialist services, municipal hospitals, and provision for the middle and upper classes. This building boom and diversity is evident in Scotland where around 225 new public hospitals, extensions or

---

[12] *The Lancet* (5 October 1918): 463; Great Britain, Ministry of Health, *Interim Report on the Future Provision of Medical and Allied Services* (London: HMSO, 1920). For a discussion of Dawson's model health centre, see David Brady 'Public or Private? London Medical Buildings of the Interwar Years', in Elain Harwood and Alan Powers (eds.), *Twentieth Century Architecture 13: The Architecture of Public Service* (London: Twentieth Century Society, 2017): 63–79.

[13] Jeanne Kisacky, *Rise of the Modern Hospital* (Pittsburgh: University of Pittsburgh Press, 2017): 198–201; *Lancet* (21 July 1923): 130–1 refers to the renown of the clinic and its founders; *Lancet* (10 July 1920): 84 discusses proposed foundation of an American Hospital in London.

[14] *The Builder* (19 May 1944), 406; *Survey of London: Vol. 40, The Grosvenor Estate in Mayfair. Part 2* (London, 1980): 18.

[15] Elizabeth Darling, *Re-forming Britain: Narratives of Modernity before Reconstruction* (Abingdon: Routledge, 2007): 51–81; Jill Julius Matthews, 'They Had Such a Lot of Fun: The Women's League of Health and Beauty between the Wars', *History Workshop* 30 (Autumn, 1990): 22–54; Martin Gorsky, '"Threshold of a new Era": The Development of an Integrated hospital System in Northeast Scotland, 1900–39', *Social History of Medicine* 17 no. 2 (2004): 247–67; J. E. Stone, 'The Birmingham Hospitals Centre', *Supplement to the British Medical Journal* 2 no. 4001 (11 September 1937): 178–80.

additions to existing establishments, were built between 1919 and 1939. More than half of these might be described as specialist institutions or services. They included thirty-six maternity hospitals or units, twenty-four nurses' homes, fifty hospitals for tuberculosis and infectious diseases, ten convalescent homes, and twenty-nine for patients with mental illness or disabilities.[16]

Some building was prompted by legislation, such as the Public Health (Prevention and Treatment of Disease) Act of 1913 which granted new powers to local authorities to treat tuberculosis. Though enacted before the war, its effect mostly came afterwards, when many county sanatoria were built, and TB wards were often part of the new, centralized county infectious diseases hospitals. Similarly, maternity provision was transformed by the Maternity and Child Welfare Act of 1918. This not only produced a new kind of health centre for women and their infants, but saw a rapid growth in the construction of maternity units at existing hospitals. As the trend for hospital confinements was encouraged and demand for accommodation rose, new hospitals were established. There was a considerable range available, from private nursing homes in converted houses, and modest wings added to cottage hospitals, to municipal maternity hospitals of up-to-date design.

Hospitals and social class

Hospital accommodation differed not only according to function but also social class. Cottage hospitals offered care for the poor above the class of paupers. First appearing in the 1860s, they continued to flourish after the war. They were usually run by local general practitioners, and it was expected that those who could afford to do so would contribute towards the cost of their stay. Cottage hospitals were often well supported by local dignitaries and tended to adapt the key elements of pavilion planning to produce architecturally attractive buildings that carefully avoided an institutional appearance. St Margaret's Hospital, Auchterarder, Perthshire (1926), just one example, was designed in a Scottish vernacular idiom by the Glasgow architects Stewart & Paterson. Many cottage hospitals established after the war were done so as war memorials, rooting them even more firmly within their communities.

Hospital design evolved to reflect the social status of these new wealthier patients, offering greater privacy without impacting on the ability of the nursing staff to supervise their charges. As demand for these new establishments gained strength, provision diversified; the usual philanthropists and medical professionals were now joined by

---

[16]These figures are based on an analysis of the Scottish Hospitals Gazetteer that I originally compiled in the early 1990s and have since been updating and revising. They are not comprehensive or definitive but give a fair indication of the range of hospital building activity in the period. Of the 225 hospital buildings established, 49 were entirely new purpose-built hospitals, 138 additions to existing hospitals, the remainder new hospitals in converted buildings. Historic Hospitals, online at https://historic-hospitals.com/gazetteer/ (accessed 10 June 2021).

business entrepreneurs.[17] The type and standard of hospitals for paying patients varied considerably. For the wealthier clientele, the name 'nursing home' was usually adopted rather than 'hospital' in order to confer social respectability and set them apart from charity or poor-law establishments. The choice of name created quite specific associations: 'nursing home' had domestic associations while 'clinic' might suggest medical excellence or innovation.

Such niceties of terminology mattered, particularly for attracting paying patients. Sully Hospital, near Cardiff, was designed for patients with tuberculosis. Usually such hospitals were called sanatoria. Perhaps here the name 'hospital' implies treatment and cure, rather than palliative care. The competition brief for Sully asked for a building that combined hygiene with comfort. W. A. Pite, Son & Fairbrother's 1931 winning design produced a stylish outward appearance along with some advanced planning. The style and coastal location gave it the air of a fashionable seaside hotel, while inside some of the wards were compartmentalized with screens and had beds parallel to the windows on the Rigs model.[18]

In the mid-1920s, a House of Commons Select Committee was appointed to consider how nursing homes might be regulated. They identified five main types: those catering for medical and/or surgical cases, maternity, cases requiring special observation and treatment, those for senile and other chronic cases, and convalescent homes. At best they might be in a purpose built and properly equipped hospital building, at worst an ill-adapted dwelling-house. The Ministry of Health and the British Medical Association were undecided as to the level of inspection or control that should be introduced. Pressure for regulation came from elsewhere. The College of Nursing presented a petition in support of registration and a requirement that at least a proportion of those in charge of the nursing should be state registered. They were backed up by the Society of Medical Officers of Health, who seem to have been on the receiving end of most of the complaints from nurses and patients. The more scientific that medical treatment and diagnosis became, the less satisfactory were unorthodox alternatives. The public were aware that it was no longer appropriate, for example, to carry out surgery in a patient's bedroom without the type of lighting, heating, ventilation and equipment for disinfection that would be found in a hospital operating theatre.[19]

In response to this growing market of patients seeking private medical treatment outside of the home, surgeons and physicians (particularly around Harley Street in London) began to offer more sophisticated treatment. This required more sophisticated

---

[17]Adrian Forty, 'The Modern Hospital in France and England', in Anthony King (ed.), *Buildings and Society: Essays on the Social Development of the Built Environment* (London, Boston, Melbourne and Henley: Routledge & Kegan Paul, 1980): 45.

[18]*Architects' Journal* (25 November 1931): 712–13, 85; *Architects' Journal* (24 June 1937): 1132–4; *Builder* (6 November 1931): 740, 744–5; *Builder* (29 July 1932): 164. Sully Hospital was built by the King Edward VII Welsh National Memorial Association for the Prevention of Tuberculosis.

[19]*Report from the Select Committee on Nursing Homes (Registration) Together with the Proceedings of the Committee, Minutes of Evidence, Appendices and Index* (London: HMSO, 1926).

private hospitals. One of the largest was the London Clinic in Marylebone constructed in 1929–1932 (**Figures 14.3 and 14.4**). The architect appointed for the scheme was Charles H. Biddulph-Pinchard, probably on the strength of his Brook Street Clinic commission. The London Clinic was radically different from a typical pavilion-plan voluntary hospital, offering accommodation for 214 patients in private rooms. The largest rooms were arranged on either side of a shared bathroom and commanded the highest rates,

Figure 14.3 London Clinic and Nursing Home, Marylebone Road, London: the entrance from Harley Street, Charles Henry Biddulph-Pinchard (1932), photograph by Sydney Newberry, Architectural Press Archive/RIBA Collections, RIBA72321

Figure 14.4 London Clinic and Nursing Home, Marylebone road: the Harley Street entrance hall, Charles Henry Biddulph-Pinchard (1932), photograph by Sydney Newberry, Architectural Press Archive/RIBA Collections, RIBA72323

while the smaller rooms were arranged in groups of six or so with shared facilities.[20] An entire wing housed suites of consulting rooms, while the main hospital was well provided with all the paraphernalia of the modern hospital.

The ethical issue of private medical provision, in which medical specialists could potentially profit from health care, led to management and financing companies being set

---

[20] *Architect's Journal* (13 January 1932): 83–8; Philip Temple and Colin Thom (eds.), *Survey of London*, vol. 51, *South East Marylebone, Part 1* (New Haven and London: Yale University Press, 2017): 385–9.

up headed by people from the business community. For the London Clinic the company was chaired by the Duke of Atholl (politician and vice-chairman of Bovril), with Allan Hepworth as managing director (Hepworth was a Director of Harrods). Hepworth and Biddulph-Pinchard, together with the surgeon Henry Sessions Souttar and the Clinic's domestic bursar Miss Bradbury, had visited clinics, nursing homes and hospitals on the Continent as part of a fact-finding mission in 1929. By the time they left, sketch plans for the hospital had already been drawn up, so the mission was primarily to gather information on how the new clinic would be equipped 'on the most modern lines'.[21]

Though modern and innovative in many ways from its overall concept to its incorporation of up-to-date technology in fixtures and fittings, the London Clinic was conservative in outward appearance and interior decoration. Both in its architectural style and in its decor, the Clinic evoked the stereotypical Harley Street consulting room, where those at the top of their profession dispensed advice in the opulent surroundings of the Georgian London town house. The *Architects' Journal* recognized its material difference from any other nursing home in the country, finding it 'really a specially planned hotel for the sick'.[22]

Mental illness and disabilities

Changes in the demand for and attitudes towards hospital treatment for mental illness are also evident after the war. 'Hospital' began to replace 'asylum' in the names of some of the new and more advanced institutions, signifying treatment and the possibility of cure, in contrast to the carceral asylum system. Those returning from the front with shell shock and other mental scars from the horrors they witnessed may have fuelled changing attitudes, but those attitudes had already been altering towards people with curable mental illnesses. There was a move towards enabling patients to be admitted to mental hospitals on a voluntary basis rather than having to go through the process of committal. Apart from the legal implications, there was the potential avoidance of social stigma and a recognition that earlier treatment was more likely to prove successful. Henry Maudsley offered the London County Council a substantial sum to establish a hospital for the early treatment of cases of acute mental disorder in 1907. Although a site had been selected in 1911, the buildings on completion were immediately handed over to the military and the Maudsley Hospital only opened in 1923.

Providing early treatment and access to treatment as a voluntary patient, without resorting to certification, were the aims of the Mental Treatment Act of 1930. The rebuilt Bethlem Royal Hospital, at Monks Orchard, Croydon, and Runwell Hospital in Essex

---

[21]H. S. Souttar, 'Modern Hospitals in Sweden and Denmark', *The Lancet* (3 August 1929): 242–4. Morland McCrae, one of the chief promoters of the London Clinic, had consulting rooms in Devonshire Place, but H. S. Souttar lived in a flat in Manchester Street.
[22]*Architects' Journal* (13 January 1932): 83.

can be seen as embodiments of this new type of mental hospital, shifting the emphasis from custodial care to remedial treatment. For both hospitals the architectural style, even something as modest as a flat roof, as well as opting for the name 'hospital' over 'asylum', identified with the more modern approach to mental health care.[23]

Attitudes to congenital forms of disability, however, seem to have become more entrenched. The removal of disabled persons from their families to purpose-built institutions where training as well as care were available stretched back to the mid-nineteenth. Increasing urbanization saw pauper institutions swelling with large numbers of people with a range of chronic mental illnesses and disabilities, housed in wholly unsuitable accommodation. The Mental Deficiency Act of 1913 had aimed to improve standards, but it was also the driver for a proliferation of 'mental deficiency institutions' established in the 1920s and 1930s. When Gogarburn Colony for Mental Defectives was being built near Edinburgh, its architect, Stewart Kaye, described the prospective inmates as 'these unfortunate people'.[24] This was a period when the theories of social Darwinism and eugenics were broadly legitimized. These institutions adopted the recommendations of the Board of Control, which replaced the Commissioners in Lunacy as the governing body in 1914. The board favoured the 'colony plan', where the patients' accommodation was provided in detached 'villas'. Combined with the advantages of a countryside location, these colonies were intended to create a happier atmosphere for the residents. The new institutions may have been an improvement, but the buildings themselves were mostly on the dreary side of utilitarian.

Although the colony or village asylum was advocated as a more benign way to accommodate long-stay patients, the associations of the term 'colony' with colonialism speaks of the paternalistic attitude of the care providers and of attitudes to all kinds of disability. It is a reminder of how pervasive coloniality was as a mindset, and its wide-reaching impact on social-political relations. It is also reminiscent of the rhetoric surrounding the suburban housing estate as 'new colonies' beyond the unhealthy city centre (see Alistair Fair's chapter on the Community Centre).

Municipal hospitals

There were some efforts to meet the expectations of the newly enfranchised in matters of hospital provision, particularly in areas where the local economy was dependent on large workforces of manual labourers, skilled or unskilled. In Scotland, Burnet, Tait and Lorne were commissioned to design Paisley's municipal infectious diseases hospital (later Hawkhead Hospital).[25] Both the choice of architects and the striking style of these

---

[23]Jonathan Andrews, Asa Briggs, Roy Porter, Penny Tucker and Keir Waddington, *The History of Bethlem* (London: Routledge, 1997): 535–66; Richardson 'Charles Ernest Elcock', 125–9; *Hansard,* HC Deb 18 June 1937, vol. 325 c 750.

[24]*Scotsman* (21 May 1929).

[25]see Alistair Fair's chapter and discussion of Tait's housing in nearby Johnston. A 'modern' image of the public sector was emerging across a range of building types.

buildings could be read as a demonstration of municipal pride and an expression of Paisley's progressive commitment to public health. Style here was more progressive than the planning, as the detached pavilions and predominantly open wards were comparatively orthodox.[26] That the local authority should have felt the need to make such a visible demonstration is suggestive of changing views about the working-class patients who might find themselves a patient in the hospital and a change in the views of the patients themselves.

There was a shift from a belief in self-help to an expectation that the state should provide medical care. It was a shift that had begun before the war, as attitudes changed towards unemployment and the provision of outdoor relief rather than admittance to a poorhouse (in Scotland) or workhouse (for the rest of Britain). The Workhouse Test was increasingly seen as unfair, and unemployment recognized as not necessarily the result of idleness.[27] Paisley was in the heart of the industrial central belt of Scotland, an area where the population increased after the war as families and young men migrated away from the poor agricultural lands of the rural north and south west. Attracted by prospects of security and affluence, the reality bred insecurity and resentment amongst the skilled workforce, and an inclination for radical politics.[28] A conspicuous municipal hospital might diffuse some of that tension and dissatisfaction.

Flamboyant architecture for a municipal hospital was relatively unusual. Elcock for one advocated the importance of planning over aesthetics. He advised the architect to 'try and forget his little architectural tricks and details, and think more on the lines of a scientific "factory for Health" rather than an imposing expanse of architectural display'.[29] His innovations in the use of bi-fold windows and the re-orientation of beds have been noted above, and it was in that kind of detail that Elcock excelled, rather than in artistic flair. The large general hospital he designed at Davyhulme, Lancashire, was one of the first entirely new hospitals built for a Poor Law Union (in this case Barton upon Irwel, Salford) under the powers of the Ministry of Health which had taken over the role of the Local Government Board on the Ministry's formation in 1919.

Although Davyhulme did not move far from the traditional pavilion-plan hospital, it reflected some recent developments. The Nightingale-style open wards were prefaced by an increased number of ancillary rooms and smaller wards, and the WCs and bathrooms were no longer housed in towers at the far end of the wards. The architect Keith D. Young, one of the best-known hospital specialists of the pre-war decades, had been one of the first to grasp the possibilities of modern plumbing to move the sanitary facilities further into the building, freeing up the ends of ward pavilions for balconies or

[26] *Architectural Review* (1 September 1936): 104–8; *Architects' Journal* (24 June 1937): 1127–8.

[27] Minority Report of the Royal Commission to Investigate the Poor Laws and the Relief of Distress, PP, 1909 (Cd. 4499), XXXVII, 719–1238; K. Morrison, *The Workhouse* (Swindon: English Heritage, 1999): 123.

[28] T. C. Smout, 'Scotland 1850–1950' in F. M. L. Thompson (ed.), *Cambridge Social History of Britain*, i (Cambridge: Cambridge University Press, 1953): 221, 235–41: Morrice McCrae, *The National Health Service in Scotland: Origins and Ideals, 1900–1950* (East Linton: Tuckwell Press, 2003): 70.

[29] C. E. Elcock, 'Hospital Building – Past, Present and Future', *Proceedings of the Royal Society of Medicine* 35 (March 1942): 361. Elcock was one of the assessors for the Sully hospital competition.

sun rooms.[30] Another innovation at Davyhulme was the division of the children's wards into six-bed bays by glazed partitions. Children were particularly vulnerable to cross-infection, and the partitions were intended to provide a barrier to infection without restricting nursing supervision.

Davyhulme hospital foreshadowed the conversion of poor-law infirmaries into municipal general hospitals enabled by the 1929 Local Government Act. This was a pivotal moment in advancing municipal health care. County and county borough councils were given control of the administration of poor law institutions, both workhouses and infirmaries, alongside their responsibilities for maternity care, infant welfare and the control of infectious diseases.[31]

Obsolescence

The levels of investment seen at Paisley and Davyhulme can be contrasted with some of the more economical measures that were taken. Temporary buildings were seen by many not just as an affordable option but one that could be justified on the grounds of hygiene: infectious diseases hospitals could be razed to the ground after a period of time, destroying any lingering germs in the fabric. They might also mitigate obsolescence.

In 1918 Bertrand Dawson had suggested that the model health centres he proposed could be temporary huts, although in the illustration commissioned by the *Illustrated London News* the buildings appear rather more substantial (see **Figure 14.2**). Hutted hospitals were mostly associated with military field hospitals, but 'temporary' hospital buildings had been widely put up by cash-strapped local authorities obliged to provide for infectious diseases.[32] By the time that Dawson's ideas had been refined and revised for the 1920 Report, the accompanying plans and elevations drawn by Biddulph-Pinchard were for permanent buildings, no longer entirely single-storeyed, although the centres were still intended to be economically constructed.[33]

---

[30]Young wrote about the desirability of getting rid of the projecting towers for sanitary facilities in 1913, and put that into practice at the women's hospital at Chelsea of 1914–16. W. Milburn, 'A Comparative Study of Modern English, Continental and American Hospital Construction'. *Journal of the Royal Institute of British Architects* 20 (8 March 1913): 300; *The Hospital* (10 July 1915): 317–20.

[31]K. Morrison, *The Workhouse* (Swindon: English Heritage, 1999): 176–7. Scotland, as ever, is similar but not quite the same as England and Wales. Much of Scotland's public health legislation came later than the equivalent acts south of the border. Instead of workhouses, Scotland had poor houses, and instead of county asylums, district asylums. The Department of Health for Scotland was created later than the Ministry in England and Wales. The Local Government Act, however, applied to Scotland as well as England and Wales, but the poor laws in Scotland had been administered by parish authorities rather than boards of guardians. Martin Gorsky's article on the development of the medical services in Aberdeen in the early twentieth century is particularly helpful in explaining some of these differences. Gorsky, 'Threshold of a New Era', 247–67.

[32]Kathryn A. Morrison 'Back to Blighty: British war hospitals, 1914–18', in Wayne Cocroft and Paul Stamper (eds.), *Legacies of the First World War* (Swindon: Historic England, 2018).

[33]'A Model Health Centre', *The Lancet* (5 October 1918): 463; Bertrand Dawson, *The Nation's Welfare: The Future of the Medical Profession* (London: Cassell & Co., 1918); Great Britain, Ministry of Health, *Interim Report on the Future Provision of Medical and Allied Services* (London: HMSO, 1920); Brady, 'Public or Private?', 64–6: for the pioneer health centre in Peckham and Finsbury Health Centre see Darling, *Re-forming Britain*, 51–80.

Reconstruction

For Dawson, a preference for hutted hospital buildings reflected the view that permanent buildings would become outdated. The idea of temporary, expendable buildings that could be replaced to meet new medical requirements was not just voiced by medical experts. Architects, too, were becoming alert to the problem of obsolescence, and hospitals seemed to be a type increasingly liable to change. In 1932 Elcock noted that medical ideas and methods of treatment were changing so rapidly that even a hospital built 15 years earlier 'could be considered obsolescent'.[34] The truth of his observation is borne out by the redundancy of once common hospital types. Specialist hospitals for tuberculosis and infectious diseases were eventually made redundant through vaccination and the development of antibiotics after the Second World War. However, the buildings themselves were adapted to meet the needs of the chronic sick, geriatrics or for people with disabilities. What made them readily adaptable was that they tended to be single storey and designed with easy access to the grounds. Despite the economic and hygienic potential of temporary buildings for hospitals, few, if any, were actually built after the war. Permanent but inexpensive hospitals were the more usual choice.

Conclusion

The main theme that emerges from an appraisal of the hospitals built in Britain during the 1920s and 1930s is a shift in focus from care of the sick poor to the treatment of a broad spectrum of society, with important architectural consequences which affected the conception and design of buildings for health. While we can see many forerunners of the National Health Service in some of the initiatives of the early twentieth century, we should not see them as having been the model or provided the blueprint for the NHS. Often they came about in response to a crisis, as much as out of changing policy or ideology. Problems were tackled locally and opportunistically, as well as through national health policies, and the different solutions adopted were seldom uncontested. An understanding of how these initiatives came about sheds light on the deep divisions that Aneurin Bevin later faced in pushing through a state-run health service, aimed at uniting the existing fragmented service, and also demonstrates decisively that the idea of medical care as a 'right of citizenship' was as much an outcome of 1918 as of 1945.[35] It dispels the idea that the years after the First World War were a proto-NHS by showing the different approaches to health care, with no inevitability of public provision for all. Hospital buildings themselves offer important sources for the study of changing conceptions of health and state responsibility. They reveal the complex intersections of medical, social, scientific and political perspectives at play in providing for individual and community health and well-being.

---

[34]*Architect & Building News* (1 April 1932): 12–13.
[35]Gorsky, 'Threshold of a new Era', 250. I would also like to thank and acknowledge the contribution of Alistair Fair whose insightful comments on the text helped to sharpen its focus. Equally, the editors of this volume gave their time generously with constructive criticism and encouragement.

Select bibliography

Primary

Periodicals
Architect's Journal
Architectural Review
British Medical Journal
Fortnightly Review
Journal of the RIBA
The Lancet
The Milbank Memorial Fund Quarterly Bulletin
Proceedings of the Royal Society of Medicine

Grey literature

Dawson, Bertrand. *The Nation's Welfare: The Future of the Medical Profession Being the Cavendish Lectures Delivered before the West London Medico-Chirurgical Society… With Introduction and Folding Plan of Model Health Centre*. London: Cassell & Co., 1918.

Ministry of Health. *Interim Report on the Future Provision of Medical and Allied Services*. London: HMSO, 1920.

Royal Institute of British Architects. *The Orientation of Buildings; Being the Report with Appendices, of the RIBA Joint Committee on the Orientation of Buildings*. London: RIBA, 1933.

Books

Stevens, E. F. *The American Hospital of the Twentieth Century*. New York: The Architectural Record Company, Revised edn. 1921.

Secondary

Adams, Annmarie. 'Modernism and Medicine: The Hospitals of Stevens and Lee, 1916–1932'. *Journal of the Society of Architectural Historians* 58, no. 1 (1999): 42–61.

Adams, Annmarie. *Medicine by Design: The Architect and the Modern Hospital 1893–1943*. Minneapolis London: University of Minnesota Press, 2008.

Brady, David. 'Public or Private? London Medical Buildings of the Interwar Years'. In *The Architecture of Public Service: Twentieth Century Architecture 13*, edited by Elain Harwood and Alan Powers, 63–79. London: C20 Society, 2017.

Campbell, Margaret. 'What Tuberculosis Did for Modernism: The Influence of a Curative Environment on Modernist Design and Architecture'. *Medical History* 49 (2005): 463–88.

Darling, Elizabeth. *Re-forming Britain: Narratives of Modernity before Reconstruction*. Abingdon: Routledge, 2007.

Forty, Adrian. 'The Modern Hospital in France and England'. In *Buildings and Society: Essays on the Social Development of the Built Environment*, edited by Anthony King, 61–93. London: Routledge & Kegan Paul, 1980.

Gorsky, Martin. '"Threshold of a New Era": The Development of an Integrated Hospital System in Northeast Scotland, 1900–39'. *Social History of Medicine* 17, no. 2 (2004): 247–67.

Kisacky, Jeanne. *Rise of the Modern Hospital*. Pittsburgh: University of Pittsburgh Press, 2017.

Matthews, Jill Julius. 'They Had Such a Lot of Fun: The Women's League of Health and Beauty between the Wars'. *History Workshop* 30 (Autumn 1990): 22–54.

McCrae, Morrice. *The National Health Service in Scotland: Origins and Ideals, 1900–1950*. East Linton: Tuckwell Press, 2003.

Morrison, Kathryn A. *The Workhouse. A Study of Poor Law Buildings in England*. Swindon: English Heritage, 1999.

Morrison, Kathryn A. 'Back to Blighty: British War Hospitals, 1914–18'. In *Legacies of the First World War,* edited by Wayne Cocroft and Paul Stamper, 180–98. Swindon: Historic England, 2018.

Nott, James. 'Dance Halls: Towards an Architectural and Spatial History, *c.*1918–65', *Architectural History* 61 (2018): 220.

Richardson, H. (ed.). *English Hospitals 1660–1948. A Survey of Their Architecture and Design*. Swindon: Royal Commission on the Historical Monuments of England, 1998.

Richardson, H. 'Charles Ernest Elcock (1878–1944)'. In *Essays in Scots and English Architectural History: A Festschrift in Honour of John Frew*, edited by David Jones and Sam McKinstry, 120–30. Donington: Shaun Tyas, 2009.

Sheppard, F. H. W. *Survey of London. Vol. 40, The Grosvenor Estate in Mayfair. Pt.2, The Buildings*. London: Athlone Press for the Greater London Council, 1980.

Smout, T. C. 'Scotland 1850–1950'. In *The Cambridge Social History of Britain, 1750–1950*, edited by F. M. L. Thompson, 209–80. Cambridge: Cambridge University Press, 1990.

Spencer, Amy Louise. *University College London: An Architectural History, 1825–1939* (2021): Doctoral Thesis, UCL (University College London).

Stevens, Rosemary. *In Sickness and in Wealth: American Hospitals in the Twentieth Century*. New York: Basic Books, 1989.

Stewart, John. 'Sickness and Health'. In *History of Everyday Life in Twentieth Century Scotland*, edited by Lyn Abrams and Callum G. Brown, 228–53. Edinburgh: Edinburgh University Press, 2010.

Taylor, Jeremy. *The Architect and the Pavilion Hospital. Dialogue and Design Creativity in England 1850–1914*. London and New York: Leicester University Press, 1997.

Theodore, David. '"The Fattest Possible Nurse", Architecture, Computers, and Post-war Nursing'. In *Hospital Life: Theory and Practice from the Medieval to the Modern*, edited by Laura Abreu and Sally Sheard, 273–98. Bern: Peter Lang, 2013.

Willis, Julie, Philip Goad and Cameron Logan. *Architecture and the Modern Hospital: Nosokomeion to Hygeia*. Abingdon, Oxon: Routledge, 2019.

CHAPTER 15
HEALTH: DEMOCRACY, DIVERSITY, DISPERSAL
Barry Doyle

Introduction

In the years that followed the war, the hospital environment of Great Britain was transformed quantitatively, socially and spatially as more and a greater range of people were able to secure treatment in increasingly diverse clinical and institutional settings. This claim contrasts with the common public perception, perpetuated after the Second World War, of pre-National Health Service health care being dominated by charity, the poor law, patient payment and limited access.[1] Though each of these elements certainly existed and affected different groups at different times,[2] nevertheless by 1938 Britain had one of the broadest and deepest health systems in the world and probably the best and most extensive hospital service. Although historians have taken a keen interest in this hospital system, especially issues of finance, management and control,[3] spatial[4] and architectural histories have drawn less attention[5] while the growth of outpatient departments, dispensaries, cottage hospitals and the municipal sector have all lagged behind assessment of urban general institutions.

[1] See: Richard Titmuss, *Problems of Social Policy* (London: HMSO, 1950). Charles Webster, *The Health Services since the War: Problems of Health Care. The National Health Service before 1957* (London: HMSO, 1988); Charles Webster, *The National Health Service: A Political History* (2nd ed. Oxford: Oxford University Press, 2002); Nicholas Timmins, *The Five Giants: A Biography of the Welfare State* (London: Fontana, 1995).

[2] Anne Hardy, *Health and Medicine in Britain since 1860* (Basingstoke: Palgrave, 2001).

[3] Martin Gorsky, John Mohan and Martin Powell, 'The Financial Health of Voluntary Hospitals in Interwar Britain', *Economic History Review* 55 no. 3 (2002): 533–57; S. Cherry, 'Accountability, Entitlement and Control Issues and Voluntary Hospital Funding, C1860–1939', *Social History of Medicine* 9 no. 2 (1996): 215–33; B. M. Doyle, *The Politics of Hospital Provision in Early Twentieth Century Britain* (London: Pickering and Chatto, 2014).

[4] See, for example, J. Mohan, '"The Caprice of Charity". Geographical Variations in the Finances of British Voluntary Hospitals before the NHS', in M. Gorsky and S. Sheard (eds.), *Financing Medicine: The British Experience since 1750* (London: Routledge, 2006): 77–92; M. Powell, 'Coasts and Coalfields: The Geographical Distribution of Doctors in England and Wales in the 1930s', *Social History of Medicine* 18 no. 2 (August 2005): 245–63.

[5] H. Richardson (ed.), *English Hospitals 1660–1948* (Swindon: Royal Commission on the Historical Monuments of England, 1998); and for international perspectives, Annmarie Adams, *Medicine by Design: The Architect and the Modern Hospital, 1893–1943* (Minneapolis: University of Minnesota Press, 2008); Jeanne Kisacky, *Rise of the Modern Hospital. An Architectural History of Health and Healing, 1870–1940* (University of Pittsburgh Press, 2017); Julie Willis, Philip Goad and Cameron Logan, *Architecture and the Modern Hospital: Nosokomeion to Hygeia* (Abingdon, Oxon: Routledge, 2019).

The war prompted extensive discussion of health – the health of the nation, how health should be organized and how health should be delivered. Improved public and personal health became political issues for the first time as society at large became interested in securing better health services. Across Europe, especially in the new nations of central Europe, but also for the older democracies, health was deployed as a symbol of national unity and identity.[6] A central feature was the establishment of Ministries of Health, including in Britain, backed up by debates about opening up and destigmatizing services.[7] Health was increasingly seen, or presented, as a right of citizenship and extended services were focused on previously under-provisioned groups like women – especially maternity services – children and the elderly, while the lower middle class and those in rural areas gained access to low-cost facilities for the first time.

This increased demand – and in particular the acquiring of the 'hospital habit' – put considerable pressure on traditional institutional provision. Urban hospitals in Britain, in the major cities of Europe and even in the white enclaves of the British Empire, had expanded hugely in the 50 years before the war.[8] But many had reached capacity and despite the promises of the Dawson Report and Onslow Commission, the financial crises of the 1920s and 1930s restricted opportunities for further physical expansion. The health centre model advocated by Dawson was rarely attempted in England – though the Gloucestershire Extension Scheme was a partial exception,[9] while the funding secured in 1921 was used for debt clearance and Onslow's request for support for thousands of new beds was rejected.[10] Reconstruction in the case of voluntary hospitals came to mean building on rather than building anew – though in the state sector there were more and more exciting projects developed.[11]

Moreover, the new demand was often away from the city centre and among those who did not always need acute treatment. Thus, the challenge became spatial rather than purely architectural. It was to extend the reach, the capacity and the demography of the institutions and their patients and to ensure more patients could be treated in a more convenient and democratic manner. Many urban hospitals were on cramped sites that

---

[6]Barry Doyle, Frank Grombir, Melissa Hibbard and Balazs Szelinger, 'The Development of Hospital Systems in New Nations: Central Europe between the Two World Wars', in Martin Gorsky, Margarita Vilar-Rodríguez and Jerònia Pons-Pons (eds.), *The Political Economy of the Hospital in History: The Construction, Funding and Management of Public and Private Hospital Systems* (Huddersfield: University of Huddersfield Press, 2020): 137–80; and the articles in the Special Issue 'Imperial and Post-Imperial Healthcare before Welfare States', *European Review of History* 28 no. 5–6 (2021): 617–834 edited by Hannah-Louise Clark and Barry Doyle.

[7]Donnacha Séan Lucey, *The End of the Irish Poor Law: Welfare and Healthcare Reform in Revolutionary and In-dependent Ireland* (Manchester: Manchester University Press, 2015).

[8]Martin Gorsky, Margarita Vilar-Rodríguez and Jerònia Pons-Pons (eds.), *The Political Economy of the Hospital in History: The Construction, Funding and Management of Public and Private Hospital Systems* (Huddersfield: University of Huddersfield Press, 2020); M. Harrison, M. Jones, and H. M. Sweet (eds.), *From Western Medicine to Global Medicine: The Hospital beyond the West* (New Delhi, Orient BlackSwan: Orient New Swan, 2009).

[9]Martin Gorsky, 'The Gloucestershire Extension of Medical Services Scheme: An Experiment in the Integration of Health Services in Britain before the NHS', *Medical History* 50 no. 4 (2006): 491–512.

[10]B. Abel-Smith, *The Hospitals, 1800–1948: A Study in Social Administration in England and Wales* (London: Heineman, 1964): 323–4; The National Archives (TNA) Ministry of Health (MH) 58.

[11]See Harriet Richardson in this volume.

limited further development, but greenfield new builds were rarely possible before the later 1930s. Thus reorganization and architectural innovation were required. Yet much hospital history has focused on the physical growth of city hospitals and the expansion of patient throughput, and in particular the financial pressures this generated, while little attention has been paid to the spatial and architectural developments that allowed for the expansion of beds and patients treated. But thinking about transformations in the layout of institutions and changes in their wider geographical spread is essential to understanding how it was possible to deliver this growth without a commensurate increase in the number of new urban hospitals.

This growth was achieved in two ways. First, spatial change which saw the space within existing institutions reformed and additional provision distributed or unlocked with a focus on efficient treatment options like expanding outpatients and better record-keeping along with relocating staff and services. Increasingly hospitals sought to build upwards and create or reorder spaces to include novel activities like laboratories and trauma services. Secondly, growth was achieved through the reorientation of treatments provided – in particular the move to incorporate life-enhancing as well as life-saving services. In this process many buildings were transformed, some were relocated and a number were built, mainly to serve populations distant from urban centres. This chapter will consider these two approaches but in order to understand how this reconstruction occurred, it will first be necessary to explain the organizational and financial changes in the hospital system by considering how ownership and funding were transformed and how this helped to increase capacity and alter the spatial configuration and distribution of hospitals

Financial and organizational change

Reconstruction and democratization required money which was something the hospital sector lacked, prompting innovations in finance and organization. A revolution took place in the mixed economy of provision which saw all providers improve their services and increase access, with an emphasis on voluntary/state partnerships funded increasingly through mutual insurance. Social and spatial transformation occurred as hospitals opened up to almost all social groups on the basis of need, not charity, while the local state expanded the quality and range of its offer, moving away from a residual service to a focus on chronic care, infectious disease and maternity. This survey will focus on the institutions established for, and largely confined to, the working class.

What was the mixed economy of hospital provision and how did it change? During the nineteenth century three types of providers emerged to meet the needs of poor patients, collectively managing 170,000 beds on the eve of the war. Acute and general treatment was provided by the voluntary hospitals, philanthropic organizations set up from the eighteenth century by local committees in the towns and cities of Britain to provide care for the 'sick poor'. These organizations received no state funding before the First World War and retained full control over whom and how they admitted patients.

The medical staff were honorary – they received no payment for their work for the hospital but used their positions to build specialist knowledge and expertise and attract private patients to their practices[12] – and most of the management was conducted by committees of volunteers elected by subscribers.[13] The hospitals employed a very small administrative staff, a growing number of paid, trained nurses and a large body of domestics who cooked, cleaned and cared for the staff and patients. Most institutions had a few resident house doctors employed on a small salary for six months to oversee the admission and day-to-day treatment of the patients. By the eve of the war there were around 800 voluntary hospitals providing just over 50,000 beds for general and specialist treatment.[14] These were mainly urban but included around 300 small 'cottage' hospitals, many with fewer than ten beds, providing care and simple treatment delivered mainly by general practitioners.[15]

The second main providers were the borough and county councils. By 1911 they had a stock of almost 40,000 beds in around 800, mostly infectious disease, institutions.[16] Municipal hospitals met a statutory obligation to protect local populations from infectious diseases, like smallpox, typhus and typhoid, scarlet fever, measles and diphtheria.[17] Increasingly, local authorities provided institutions for tuberculosis treatment and the National Insurance (NI) Act of 1911 offered funding for sanatorium treatment. Some local authorities opened maternity accommodation (another beneficiary of NI), though numbers are unclear.[18] The day-to-day costs of running municipal hospitals were met from the rates (local taxes) with capital projects funded by government loans while most authorities offered isolation hospital treatment for free to ensure compliance.[19]

The largest, though least specialized, provider was the workhouses and infirmaries of the poor law. From the 1870s workhouses began to house their sick in defined Poor

---

[12]Anne Digby, *Making a Medical Living: Doctors and Patients in the English Market for Medicine, 1720–1911* (Cambridge: Cambridge University Press, 1994).

[13]B. M. Doyle, 'Contrasting Accounting Practices in the Urban Hospitals of England and France, 1890s to 1930s', in O. Falk and A. C. Hüntelmann (eds.), *Accounting for Health. Calculation, paperwork and medicine, 1500–2000* (Manchester: Manchester University Press, 2021): 143–65.

[14]Abel-Smith, *The Hospitals*; L. Granshaw and R. Porter (eds.), *The Hospital in History* (Routledge, 1989); S. Cherry, *Medical Services and the Hospitals in Britain, 1860–1939* (Cambridge University Press, 1996): 46–8. Case studies include Doyle, *Politics of Hospital Provision*; M. Gorsky, '"For the Treatment of Sick Persons of All Classes": The Transformation of Bristol's Hospital Service, 1918–39', in P. Wardley (ed.), *Bristol Historical Resource CD-ROM* (Bristol: Bristol, University of West of England, 2000); J. V. Pickstone, *Medicine and Industrial Society: A History of Hospital Development in Manchester and Its Region* (Manchester University Press, 1985); and J. Reinarz, *Healthcare in Birmingham: A History of the Birmingham Teaching Hospitals, 1779–1939* (Boydell and Brewer, 2009).

[15]M. Emrys-Roberts, *The Cottage Hospitals, 1859–1990* (Tern Publications, 1991).

[16]R. Pinker, *English Hospital Statistics, 1861–1938* (Heineman, 1966): 61.

[17]T. Crook, *Governing Systems: Modernity and the Making of Public Health in England, 1830–1910* (University of California Press, 2016); M. Newsom Kerr, *Contagion, Isolation, and Biopolitics in Victorian London* (Palgrave Macmillan, 2018): 129; J. Steere-Williams, *The Filth Disease: Typhoid Fever and the Practices of Epidemiology in Victorian England* (Boydell and Brewer, 2020).

[18]Pinker, *English Hospital Statistics*, 56–9.

[19]Newsom Kerr, *Contagion, Isolation, and Biopolitics*, 129; A. Levene, M. Powell, J. Stewart, and B. Taylor, *Cradle to Grave: Municipal Medicine in Interwar England and Wales* (Peter Lang, 2011).

Law Infirmaries (PLIs) focused on the aged and infirm and the chronically ill and by the eve of the war approximately half of the 80,000 poor law sick beds were in PLIs.[20] In general, PLIs were large; the average number of beds in 1911 was 540, significantly bigger than the large teaching hospitals, with some, like St James' in Leeds, housing over 1000 beds for tuberculosis, mentally ill and maternity cases as well as the aged, infirm and chronically sick. Poor law medical facilities were funded from local taxes and capital by government loans.

The war left the voluntary hospitals in a critical situation. There was a crisis in medical staffing with some doctors killed in the war, others retiring while many fewer men trained as doctors, leaving a space for women to enter the hospitals.[21] Nursing staff were also in short supply, a number also killed in the war and influenza pandemic while contract changes and qualification requirements saw the cost of employing nursing staff rocket between 1918 and 1922.[22] But four years of war and nine months of pandemic influenza also created other problems for the hospital system. Many hospitals contributed to the war effort by treating wounded servicemen and sick cases from the military, putting considerable pressure on the physical resources of institutions as linen and bedding were washed more frequently and other equipment was worn out and not replaced. Lack of materials and limited funding meant routine repairs to the fabric of the hospital and medical and domestic equipment were not completed.[23]

The municipal and poor law sectors also contributed to the war effort, with most of the major military hospitals housed in infectious disease or poor law accommodation. The immediate post-war crisis was amplified by the influenza pandemic which saw staff laid low by the disease. England had an extensive infectious disease infrastructure. Investigation and control techniques had solidified in the last third of the nineteenth century to include and a large number of isolation beds and 'track and trace' systems focused on identifying the index case and then tracing all the contacts. This system spread from typhoid and cholera to person-to-person infections like smallpox, tuberculosis and venereal disease, with Medical Officers of Health providing detailed descriptions of the social, economic and demographic characteristics of patients traced during outbreaks.[24] But both institutions and tracing were ill-suited to fighting the rapid spread and fatality of influenza while the scale swamped hospital staff.[25] As the second wave peaked, the Medical Officer of Health for Leeds made arrangements to open wards at Seacroft,

---

[20]Cherry, *Medical Services*, 46; Pinker, *English Hospital Statistics*, 57–8.

[21]A. Digby, *The Evolution of British General Practice, 1850–1948* (Oxford: Oxford University Press, 1999): 154–85.

[22]C. E. Hallett, and A. S. Fell, 'Introduction: New Perspectives on First World War Nursing', in *First World War Nursing: New Perspectives* (London: Routledge, 2013): 1–14.

[23]B. M. Doyle, 'Healthcare before Welfare States: Hospitals in Early Twentieth Century England and France', *Canadian Bulletin of Medical History* 33: 1 no. 33 (2016): 174–204.

[24]R. Davidson, '"Searching for Mary Glasgow": Contact Tracing for Sexually Transmitted Diseases in Twentieth-Century Scotland', *Social History of Medicine* 9 (1996): 195–214.

[25]Barry Doyle, 'Snuffing Potash to Ward Off Flu', https://wayback.archive-it.org/16107/20210313082221/ and http://blog.wellcomelibrary.org/2014/11/snuffing-potash-to-ward-off-flu/

the city's isolation hospital, and these were 'all but completed' when nursing staff of the hospital were affected to such an extent that it was not possible to move patients in. Although other hospitals were also approached, they could not lend assistance as their staff were also similarly depleted. An emergency hospital of forty beds was opened and the new infant hospital was used for infected children.[26] In Sheffield, beds quickly ran out in both voluntary and poor law hospitals, and the infectious disease institution was used for 'badly housed' cases with additional wards opened.[27]

Resource issues were compounded by unprecedented inflation over the course of the conflict and into the early years of peace, as prices rose while shortages of materials and staff pushed up costs and wages. This had a major effect on hospital budgets because the vast majority of expenditure was on food, heating, lighting, linen and domestic staff. In 1920 the cost of coal, a huge slice of annual expenditure, doubled in Yorkshire.[28] At the same time voluntary hospital income was struggling to keep pace with rising costs. Many subscribers to the hospitals gave a fixed annual sum and rarely increased this, so its value declined sharply in the face of rapid inflation. The failure of subscribers to increase their contributions was compounded by a decline in the overall number of subscribers and by a fall in contributions from legacies and donations as tax increases ate into the amount available to gift from estates.[29] By 1920 it was clear that traditional philanthropy would not be sufficient on its own to sustain the voluntary hospitals, prompting two government enquiries – the Cave and Onslow Commissions – to consider the financial future of the hospital system.[30] The Cave enquiry provided some funding for voluntary hospitals, while Onslow concluded the state could not provide ongoing support to the voluntaries.

The response taken by the voluntary hospitals to the financial crisis laid the basis for important changes in the social and spatial distribution of patients in the coming years. The early 1920s saw an increasing number of institutions introduce patient charges, while more hospitals and groups of hospitals established contributory schemes to cover the costs for working class patients.[31] At their most basic contributory schemes offered free treatment if admitted to a scheme hospital but could include ambulance services, surgical appliances, dental treatment and convalescence.[32] Most were wholly or partly run by workers representatives – although some like Sheffield and Liverpool emerged

[26]Medical Officer of Health City of Leeds, *Report on the Health and Sanitary Administration of the City* (Leeds Corporation, 1920).

[27]Medical Officer of Health City of Sheffield, *Report on the Health and Sanitary Administration of the City* (Sheffield Corporation, 1920).

[28]Leeds General Infirmary, *Annual Report, 1919*, 10.

[29]Gorsky, Mohan and Powell, 'Financial Health'; S. Cherry, 'Before the National Health Service: Financing the Voluntary Hospitals, 1900–1939', *Economic History Review* 55: 3 (1997): 309–27.

[30]For the Cave and Onslow Commissions see National Archives, MH58; Abel-Smith, *Hospitals*, 323–4.

[31]M. Gorsky, J. Mohan with T. Willis, *Mutualism and Health Care: British Hospital Contributory Schemes in the Twentieth Century* (Manchester: Manchester University Press, 2006).

[32]B. M. Doyle, 'The Economics, Culture and Politics of Hospital Contributory Schemes: The Case of Inter War Leeds', *Labour History Review* 77 no. 3 (2012): 289–315.

out of local hospital committees.[33] Notionally limited to working men earning up to £250 in the early 1920s and £450 by the Second World War, they usually included dependents. These schemes provided a substantial injection of new cash to the hospitals and as a result by the later 1930s most institutions were operating within their means.

The post-war period also saw significant changes in the municipal and poor law sectors. In the municipal sector, cash was tight in the 1920s, especially in the north of England as local authorities took political decisions to develop specific parts of their health services with many spending little on their institutional provision in favour of Maternity and Child Welfare (MCW), tuberculosis or mental health services.[34] Moreover, the nature of infectious diseases changed, with many more cases being among children while the focus for adults switched to tuberculosis with the rise of sanatorium treatment. But it was in maternity provision that the local authorities made a significant change, setting up or expanding maternity hospitals – like that in Middlesbrough, opened in 1920 in a suburban villa – and after 1929 making use of the institutions acquired from the poor law to greatly expand facilities for institutional births.[35] This was possible because the 1929 Local Government Act broke up the poor law and transferred its services to the county and borough councils. By the Second World War over forty councils were running general hospitals with a shift of focus from the aged and infirm to surgical and medical wards and new specialisms.[36]

The most important feature of the contributory schemes for spatial change was the role they played in encouraging greater integration within the voluntary sector and between voluntary and municipal provision. Most large urban areas had at least two voluntary hospitals by the eve of the First World War; other towns normally had at least one while counties had a significant number of small cottage hospitals. Although these institutions did not necessarily compete for patients, they did compete for funds and in many cases offered duplicate services. In 1921 the Cave Commission recommended grants for the voluntary hospitals on the condition they set up local committees to coordinate and make better use of local resources. While it has been suggested these local committees only lasted long enough to claim the grant, evidence from a number of towns and cities suggests they laid the basis for future cooperation, and in some cases greater physical transformations.[37]

Joint working was most effective in areas where mutual contributory schemes developed separately from specific hospitals. In Leeds the Workpeople's Hospital Fund

---

[33]Gorsky, Mohan with Willis, *Mutualism and Health*.

[34]Levene et al., *Cradle to Grave*; J. Welshman, *Municipal Medicine: Public Health in Twentieth-Century Britain* (Oxford: Peter Lang, 2000).

[35]B. M. Doyle, 'Competition and Cooperation in Hospital Provision in Middlesbrough, 1918–48', *Medical History* 51 no. 3 (2007): 337–56; Doyle, *Politics of Hospital Provision*.

[36]J. Stewart, '"The Finest Municipal Hospital Service in the World"?: Contemporary Perceptions of the London County Council's Hospital Provision, 1929–1939', *Urban History* 32 no. 2 (2005): 327–44; A. Levene, 'Between Less Eligibility and the NHS: The Changing Place of Poor Law Hospitals in England and Wales, 1929–1939', *Twentieth Century British History* 20 no. 3 (2009): 322–45.

[37]Doyle, 'Competition and Cooperation'; Doyle, *Politics of Hospital Provision*.

(LWHF) allocated funds to the city's medical institutions on the basis of the year's work and they aimed to ensure the hospitals were able to provide treatment for its members in the quickest and most efficient manner.[38] The Sheffield Hospital Committee combined local hospital oversight with the operation of the city's successful 'Penny in the Pound' scheme which brought the voluntary hospitals closer together leading, in 1938, to the two main general hospitals merging.[39] The multi-hospital contributory schemes operating in East Anglia promoted closer working among the region's institutions, especially patient transfers for complex procedures and even to relieve waiting lists.[40] But where schemes were focused on individual hospitals, joint working was slower. In Middlesbrough the joint committee was fairly effective in identifying and discussing common problems, but the financial independence of the two main institutions led to the collapse of a merger scheme in 1938 as the medical staff opposed abandoning recently developed facilities on the two sites.[41] As this suggests, the piecemeal development of institutions in the post-war period could put a brake on more radical redevelopment in less wealthy areas.

After 1929 arrangements for patients on the voluntary hospital waiting list to receive treatment in local authority hospitals, funded by contributory schemes, expanded significantly.[42] Although relations between the two sectors could be tense, as in Middlesbrough, in Leeds the municipal institutions took increasing numbers of voluntary hospital patients and also began to develop their own acute and specialist services with the support of the medical school.[43]

Spatial change

The number of inpatient admissions to voluntary hospitals more than doubled between 1921 and 1938. This expansion was all the more impressive given the slowdown in the growth in hospital beds, the number of which rose by around two-thirds in the same period, from 67,000 to 101,000.[44] This magnitude of change was mirrored in the big cities of northern England where the number of beds in the general and specialist hospitals of both Sheffield and Leeds increased by around 50 per cent with particular growth in provision for women and maternity services.[45] On the other hand, local

---

[38]Doyle, 'Economics, Culture and Politics'.

[39]T. J. Willis, 'The Politics and Ideology of Local Authority Health Care in Sheffield, 1918–1948' (PhD thesis, Sheffield Hallam University, 2009); *The Shape of Things to Come: The Sheffield Voluntary Hospitals' Million Pound Appeal* (Sheffield: Appeal Committee, 1938).

[40]S. Cherry, 'Beyond National Health Insurance. The Voluntary Hospitals and Hospital Contributory Schemes: A Regional Study', *Social History of Medicine* 5 no. 3 (1992): 455–82; Cherry, 'Before the National Health Service'.

[41]Doyle, 'Competition and Cooperation'.

[42]Doyle, *Politics of Hospital Provision*; Cherry, 'Beyond National Health Insurance'.

[43]Doyle, 'Competition and Cooperation'; Leeds Medical Officer of Health Report, 1939; 'Sheffield Municipal and Voluntary Hospitals Joint Advisory Committee' Minutes, Sheffield City Archives NHS28/10/1: Gorsky, '"For the Treatment of Sick Persons"'. It was less the case in Norfolk, Cherry, 'Beyond National Health Insurance'.

[44]Cherry, *Medical Services* based on Pinker, *English Hospital Statistics*.

[45]Doyle, *Politics of Hospital Provision*, chs. 3 and 4.

authority hospital services did not grow significantly, remaining static between 1911 and 1938, though this masked substantial changes in bed use with a notable rise in the number allocated to maternity and the treatment of children. The nature of the patients treated by local authorities and the poor law meant the numbers admitted changed little before the late 1930s while those in infectious disease institutions were on the decline.[46]

Ongoing financial crises during the 1920s, especially in the north of England, meant building new hospitals was impossible and even erecting new blocks was challenging. A small number of new urban general hospitals were built in the 1930s, notably the private Royal Masonic Hospital in Hammersmith and the new Queen Elizabeth Hospital in suburban Birmingham. The latter was an impressive achievement with around £600,000 raised privately, much of it coming from the region's buoyant motor manufacturing industry.[47] This strategy set the pattern for ambitious new build projects in Sheffield, Bristol and Middlesbrough merging and rationalizing disparate and elderly provision.[48] But these initiatives were rare and most expansion was the result of piecemeal extension or small specialist units.

The immediate post-war period did see a flurry of extensions, some funded by war memorial collections – though many hospitals preferred the long-term income they received from bed endowment schemes set up in memory of the fallen rather than additional accommodation that just resulted in extra cost but no cash.[49] Taking some examples from Yorkshire[50] much of the new build capacity benefitted three demographics: women, children and private patients. In Leeds, for example, a new block for children – a poorly served group in the city – was opened in 1923, partly to commemorate the marriage of the Princess Royal rather than the war.[51] But there were no further additions to Leeds General until the later 1930s. Sheffield Royal Infirmary saw a large extension in 1925 of around 100 beds while Sheffield Royal Hospital saw additions in 1923 and 1925.[52] Hospitals for women and children in the two cities saw incremental additions and reorganization at the Jessop Hospital for Women (**Figure 15.1**) and a new ward at the Sheffield Children's Hospital, but no real development at the specialist hospitals of Leeds in the 1920s. Sheffield's capacity was further increased by the addition of an auxiliary hospital attached to the Jessop and a small convalescent institution for the children's hospital.[53] The greater financial stability brought by the contributory schemes allowed for a flurry of building across the two cities in the 1930s.

---

[46]Pinker, *English Hospital Statistics*.

[47]Reinarz, *Healthcare in Birmingham*.

[48]'Sheffield: Policy and Growth, 1938', TNA MH58/319; Gorsky, '"For the Treatment of Sick Persons"'; B. Doyle, *A History of Hospitals in Middlesbrough* (Middlesbrough: South Tees Hospitals NHS Trust, 2002).

[49]Alex King, *Memorials of the Great War in Britain: The Symbolism and Politics of Remembrance* (Berg, 1998): 68.

[50]For Nottingham see N. Hayes, '"Our Hospitals"? Voluntary Provision, Community and Civic Consciousness in Nottingham before the NHS', *Midland History* xxxvii (2012): 84–105.

[51]Leeds General Infirmary, *Annual Report, 1923*.

[52]Doyle, *Politics of Hospital Provision*, 47.

[53]Doyle, *Politics of Hospital Provision*, 47.

Figure 15.1 Jessop Hospital for Women, St George's Terrace, photograph by Stewart Bale Ltd (1942) © PictureSheffield.com, s07382

These developments saw some architectural innovation. At Leeds General Infirmary, the new Brotherton Wing (**Figure 15.2**) combined pay beds and outpatient units in a modernist style as did the maternity and pay block at Sheffield's Jessop Hospital. The Miners' Welfare Block at Sheffield Royal Hospital was seven storeys high and accommodated a specialist orthopaedic unit and pay beds. This novel form was partly the result of limited space in a cramped urban site, but also reflected new thinking about hospital architecture, the hospital claiming a block of 'seven floors is more conveniently worked than one of three or four floors' as it saved time and supervision was easier. Moreover, 'the higher wards are quieter and the air is better'.[54]

In addition to these developments, the significant rise in demand for voluntary hospital treatment was accommodated by a focus on speeding up patient throughput by increasing efficiency and maximizing existing space. The number of days the average patient spent in hospital fell from around 24 before the war to 18 by the 1930s.[55] This was partly achieved by more rigorous admissions policies that saw the power to decide admission shift from the philanthropists who funded the hospital to the medical staff who treated the patients, reducing the number of long-stay patients.[56] There was also

---

[54]Sheffield Royal Hospital, *Annual Report*, 1937, 16.
[55]Cherry, 'Before the National Health Service', 308.
[56]G. C. Gosling, *Payment and Philanthropy in British Healthcare, 1918–48* (Manchester: Manchester University Press, 2017).

Figure 15.2 Leeds General Infirmary, Brotherton Wing & Out-Patients Department, Kitson Parish Ledgard & Pyman, Architects, West Yorkshire Archive Service, Leeds, WYL1710/44/4

a marked reorientation of patient cases from medical to surgical where a quick and decisive cure could be assured. Reorganization of casualty departments provided greater gatekeeping, as did the arrival of NI in 1911 which shifted many patients from the hospital emergency room to the panel doctor as it allowed working men access to a general practitioner – although it still excluded women from GPs and did not include hospital treatment.[57] But it was the major reorganization of hospital space, physically and clinically, that allowed many institutions to grow bed numbers without increasing the hospital footprint.

Across the 1920s and into the 1930s staff and services were eased out so patients could move in. Most obvious was the relocation of nurses and medical staff from within the hospital to new, purpose-built accommodation, like Tapton Court for the Sheffield Royal Hospital's nurses, various developments in Leeds, including a new fifty bed home for the Leeds General nurses and the impressive St George's nurses home built in Sheffield at the end of the 1930s for Jessops.[58] Space was also made by modernizing, and often removing, kitchens and laundries from the main buildings, as happened at Leeds

---

[57]Cherry, *Medical Services*.
[58]Leeds General Infirmary, *Annual Report 1936*, 18; Jessop Hospital for Women, *Annual Report 1937*, supplement, 6.

Figure 15.3 Zachary Merton Convalescent Home, Royal Hospital, Sheffield, Tim Hale Photographic Collection © PictureSheffield.com, p00871

Maternity Hospital in the early 1930s, while efficiency and patient accommodation was secured by new admissions halls. Thus, at the Sheffield Royal Infirmary, a new registration and admissions area was central to their last major redevelopment of the period. As they noted:

> The Registration Department is an entirely new building adjacent to the Out-patient Department and consists of a commodious Waiting Hall and Registration Office for Out-patients, together with a suite of offices, modern in every respect, which accommodate the Almoner's Department ... each of the Departments ... (Surgical, Medical, Ophthalmic and Venereal Diseases) has been greatly enlarged, modernised and re-equipped. While in undertaking this reconstruction, the principal idea in the minds of the Board was to produce an Out-Patient Department of the greatest possible efficiency, another important object was to secure conditions for patients similar to those obtaining in the Surgery of the General Practitioner.[59]

This latter development was linked to the huge growth in outpatient activity that underpinned more effective utilization of resources and permitted an impressive increase

---

[59]Sheffield Royal Infirmary, *Annual Report, 1935*, 8.

in hospital work. As a result, the period saw an enormous increase in the number of outpatients and an even bigger increase in the number of outpatient visits.[60]

Much of Britain's hospital infrastructure was concentrated in urban areas as the establishment of a voluntary institution usually relied on the presence of an established urban elite and a growing number of medical professionals. As Brian Abel-Smith famously noted, the 'pattern of provision depended on the donations of the living and the legacies of the dead'.[61] As a result, rural and suburban areas were often poorly served prompting the development of small institutions known as Cottage Hospitals. Usually promoted by a local committee, individual or association, staffed by local GPs and often consisting of fewer than ten beds, they provided care, accident services and minor operations. By the outbreak of the war there were approximately 300 operating with around 5,000 beds.[62] In the years after the war the number doubled to around 600 while beds reached 10,000, driven by the changing social geography of Britain as counter-urbanization set in and coastal retirement became established.[63]

Yorkshire saw a number of new or rebuilt cottage hospitals in the 1920s and 1930s. The one in Malton, North Riding, is a good example of the developments in this period. Established in 1904 in a large villa in the centre of the town, it initially had just four beds overseen by a matron and a visiting general practitioner. Increased demand during and immediately after the war and the inappropriate nature of the existing site for expansion meant the committee decided to build a new hospital.[64] A building committee composed mainly of local dignitaries oversaw the process of commissioning an architect and raising the funds. Initial plans for a large surgical and medical hospital were dropped due to cost. Instead, a surgery focused institution was planned at the cost of approximately £18,000. Most of the funds had been raised by the time the building opened, raised by a combination of elite donation, normal fundraising and the targeting of local communities in the surrounding villages where subscriber committees were set up.

The new Malton, Norton and District Hospital opened in May 1927 on a greenfield site on the edge of the town on a slight rise commanding excellent views and exposing it to 'the freshest of breezes'.[65] Designed in a regular neo-Georgian style it had a ten bed male ward, a ten bed female ward, three cots for babies and three beds for private patients. Seen as 'up-to-date' the local press assured its readers that

[a]ll who have seen it have been warm in their praise and declare the building to be one of the best of its size in the country … it is replete with every modern equipment and eminently suitable for the needs of the district.[66]

---

[60]J. Mohan, *Planning, Markets and Hospitals* (London: Routledge, 2002); Doyle, *Politics of Hospital Provision*.

[61]Abel-Smith, *Hospitals*, 405.

[62]Emrys-Roberts, *The Cottage Hospitals*; Cherry, 'Beyond National Health Insurance'; J. Neville, 'Cottage hospitals and communities in rural East Devon, 1919–39', *in* D. S. Lucey and V. Crossman (eds.), *Healthcare in Ireland and Britain, 1850–1970: Voluntary, Regional and Comparative Perspectives* (IHR, 2015).

[63]Cherry, 'Beyond National Health Insurance', 273.

[64]*Yorkshire Gazette*, 19 September 1925.

[65]*Yorkshire Gazette*, 19 September 1925.

[66]*Yorkshire Gazette*, 21 May 1927.

Its first full year of service saw 442 patients treated paid for largely by a broad base of local five shilling subscribers drawn equally from the main towns and the villages. This figure had risen to 634 by 1938 while income had increased sharply in the preceding three years following an increase in the subscription rate while services had been improved by the addition of a new X-ray apparatus among other equipment.[67]

Medical opinion came to view the cottage hospital as badly equipped, under-resourced with inadequate nursing and staffed by general practitioners who enthusiastically attempted surgery beyond their competence. However, if we see these institutions as part of an increasingly integrated and spatially diverse hospital network, they provide the first signs of hierarchical regionalism where urban general and specialist hospitals delivered expensive, up-to-date specialties, for example, cancer treatment and radium therapy, while cottage and district hospitals met local demand for less complex procedures.[68] Although significant regional disparities in the organization and integration of healthcare provision remained, the cottage hospital tapped into a growing demand from middle class people, especially the retired, who could afford to pay a small fee and wanted a better treatment than the traditional nursing home offered. Cottage hospitals contributed to the spatial diversification of hospital services in an age where transport networks in rural areas were still developing. They took pressure off the large urban institutions by providing minor surgery, local care and first-line emergency services, a particular boon in the seaside towns and arterial routes that bulged with tourists and motorists in the summer months.[69]

The municipalization of the PLIs contributed to the social and spatial democratization of hospital care by separating the sick from the taint of pauperism and by promoting the development of new specialties, like gerontology and dermatology.[70] But these institutions varied in quality and purpose, with those in the larger cities providing increasingly modern facilities and levels of treatment to their core patient groups of the elderly, infirm and chronically ill. Part of the process of destigmatization was reconstruction and refurbishment. There were new areas for admission and new services like laundry, kitchen and heat, along with improved medical facilities. Some municipal hospitals were integrated into a recognizable system in which patients were consciously allocated to different institutions for medical not social or political reasons. But many in rural areas and poorer towns remained residual places of last resort where minimal care was provided by poorly trained staff in inadequate conditions.[71]

The main contribution of the municipal sector was in facilitating the substantial growth in institutional maternity provision that boosted hospital births and led to a significant

---

[67]*Malton and Yorkshire Gazette*, 17 March 1939.
[68]Cherry, 'Beyond National Health Insurance'; S. Cherry, 'Regional Comparators in the Funding and Organisation of the Voluntary Hospital System, *c.*1860–1939', in Gorsky and Sheard (eds.), *Financing Medicine*.
[69]R. Cresswell and B. Doyle, 'A Trip to the Coast: Interwar First Aid on the Roads and the Beach', unpublished paper delivered to the St John's History Society, 19 September 2019.
[70]Levene et al., *Cradle to Grave*.
[71]M. Powell, 'An Expanding Service: Municipal Acute Medicine in the 1930s', *Twentieth Century British History*, 8 (1997): 334–57.

Figure 15.4 Killingbeck Sanatorium, New Block from the South West, West Yorkshire Archive Service, Leeds, LLD1/3/39

decline in maternal mortality. Supported by a network of child welfare clinics, many managed by partnerships between the public and charitable sector, expectant mothers received improved antenatal care that ensured a safer confinement often funded by NI payments.[72] NI also helped fund an expansion of TB sanatoria with health departments trying to encourage more women to make use of the services. In Leeds this led to the building of an impressive women's wing at their Killingbeck Sanatorium designed in a modernist style (**Figure 15.4**).[73]

New hospital capacity in cottage hospitals and municipal institutions was supported by the development of a more integrated GP and inter-hospital referral system based on NI doctors and free contributory scheme treatment. Although some consultants criticized the ready resort to hospital referral used by NI panel doctors, in reality the growth in demand for hospital services came from sections of society who would never be able to meet consultant fees. Referral also made hospitals more efficient, promoting the growth of outpatient clinics that could be managed by assistants, nurses

---

[72]T. McIntosh, *A Social History of Maternity and Childbirth: Key Themes in Maternity Care* (Routledge, 2012).
[73]https://bmdoyleblog.wordpress.com/2015/06/03/municipal-modernism-in-the-international-style-killingbeck-sanatorium-extension-1936/

and technicians.[74] The huge growth in outpatient attendance could even influence the location of new hospital developments, with the medics in Sheffield arguing that a suburban setting would be less convenient for outpatient attendees than a new city centre location.[75]

The final pillar in the spatial transformation of hospital care was the emergence of a post-treatment network based on convalescent homes and aftercare institutions. The popularity of convalescent homes peaked in this period, and by 1937 there were almost 500 homes in operation, most provided by philanthropic agencies, around 50 by mutual groups like the Leeds Workpeople's Hospital Fund, 40 by local authorities and 12 or so by industrial concerns. Together they managed around 24,000 beds with over quarter of a million admissions annually.[76] Although many patients were admitted for a range of rest cures, a significant number were hospital discharges for patients who required care but not specialist attention.[77] Referrals often came from the hospital almoner, especially where home conditions were not conducive to effective recovery.[78] Leeds Workpeople's Hospital Fund owned three convalescent homes which they regarded as of equal importance to their funding of hospital treatment.[79] Some hospitals had access to their own convalescent homes, such as the Leeds General Infirmary's Ida and Robert Arthington convalescent hospital. Funded largely by bequests, subscribers and patient payments, the one hundred beds were designed to ease waiting lists by taking patients 'on the road to recovery'.[80] In a similar vein, Sheffield's hospitals benefitted from the Zachary Merton Trust Convalescent Home built in Fulwood in 1938 with accommodation for men, women and children (**Figure 15.3**).[81]

Reorientation of services

Much of the work of the hospital remained focused on the lifesaving activities of surgeons and physicians, but new technologies and specialisms, the expansion of out-patient treatment and the emergence of new funding mechanisms allowed for more emphasis on health and well-being as the big killer diseases of the nineteenth century receded. Hospitals began to offer life-enhancing treatments from correcting squints to removing in-growing toe nails or alleviating arthritis and rheumatism. As we have

---

[74]S. Sturdy and R. Cooter, 'Science, Scientific Management, and the Transformation of Medicine in Britain, c.1870–1950', History of Science 36 (1998): 1–47.

[75]Sheffield Staff Club Report on New Hospital, 1937, 'Sheffield Municipal and Voluntary Hospitals Joint Advisory Committee' Minutes, SCA/NHS28/10/1

[76]S. Sheard, 'Getting Better Faster: Convalescence and Length of Stay in British and US Hospitals', in L. Abreu and S. Sheard (eds.), Hospital Life, Theory and Practice from the Medieval to the Modern (Peter Lang: Oxford, 2013): 299–329.

[77]PEP, Report on the British Health Services, 266–9.

[78]Leeds Hospital for Women and Children, Annual Report, 1936, 17.

[79]Leeds Workpeople's Hospital Fund, Annual Report, 1920, 25.

[80]A. J. Ward and T. Ashton (eds.), Cookridge Hospital, 1867–1972 (Leeds, 1997): 10–14.

[81]Sheffield Telegraph 14 May 1935.

seen, services were also expanded to new social groups largely absent from the pre-war hospital, including a huge expansion of maternity and child health and welfare, a growth in services for the elderly especially in areas like orthopaedics and cancer treatment and the opening of the wards to the lower middle class.[82]

The democratization of hospital treatment brought a shift to treatments that improved the quality of life rather than curing a disease or condition. Orthoptic clinics were opened, aiming at correcting eye defects in children, especially squints. Orthopaedic departments were opened, acknowledging the emerging problems of an aging population, as well as trying to fix the poor quality musculoskeletal treatments many industrial workers had received earlier in the century. Podiatry clinics were developed as 'nobody really realised the large proportion of suffering represented by foot troubles'[83] with one Sheffield clinic running services in the afternoon with the result 'working-class women living in the surrounding districts now attend in considerable numbers in the afternoon' leaving them free in the morning, it was noted, to 'devote themselves to their domestic duties ... a very real contribution to the social economy of the neighbourhood'.[84]

The focus on older patients and women found in areas like podiatry was part of a much wider attention on new social groups. Across England three linked strategies were developed to tackle infant and maternal mortality – Mother and Child Clinics, a substantial increase in institutional confinement and more effective management of puerperal sepsis.[85] Mandated by legislation in 1918, MCW clinics developed across the country with councils either working in partnership with charities or delivering their own clinics. The clinics combined ante-natal checks by local authority doctors with delivery booking for either a maternity hospital or a midwife, and post-natal and infant check-ups for babies and small children. The close contact with expectant mothers underpinned the growth of hospital births, especially in Leeds where more than half of all babies were born in an institution by the outbreak of the Second World War. Moreover, while the number of babies born at the voluntary maternity hospital almost doubled from 15 per cent in 1923 to 29 per cent in 1938 the growth in births at the municipal institutions was spectacular, rising from 1 per cent in 1923 to 21 per cent at the end of the 1930s.[86] As this suggests, state interest, a drive to democratize services and pressure from mothers led to a significant diversification of hospital services and patients.

The improvement in services for women and children was felt beyond MCW. Many contributory schemes covered family members as well allowing women to access hospital treatment.[87] Moreover, hospitals for women increased in number and expanded

[82]Doyle, *Politics of Hospital Provision*.
[83]Vice Chair of Sheffield Royal Infirmary quoted in Doyle, *Politics of Hospital Provision*, 100.
[84]Edgar Allen Annual Report quoted in Doyle, *Politics of Hospital Provision*, 100.
[85]J. Lewis, *The Politics of Motherhood: Maternity and Child Welfare in England 1900–1939* (London: Croom Helm, 1980); McIntosh, *Social History of Maternity*.
[86]Doyle, *Politics of Hospital Provision*, 102.
[87]Gorsky, Mohan and Willis, *Mutualism and Health Care*.

their capacity.[88] The number of children treated in hospital also grew hugely on the back of school medical inspections, introduced in 1908. Engagement with the School Medical Officer often meant some kind of procedure followed, with dentistry and ophthalmology most common, while surgical procedures boomed as children were brought in batches for the removal of tonsils, adenoids and foreskins.[89]

Though less so than other groups, both the elderly and the lower middle class did see their experience of hospital services improve. In the first instance care for the aged and infirm were enhanced as wards were refurbished and staff and equipment were upgraded with more trained nurses and increased technology.[90] From the early 1920s chronic conditions like diabetes were treated through outpatient clinics.[91] The improvements in orthopaedic services described above were also beneficial to older members of the community – especially research into arthritis. The lower middle class benefitted initially from the growth of pay beds in voluntary hospitals, especially in shared wards, but also from the raising of the upper salary threshold for contributory schemes so that groups such as teachers, police officers and senior clerks were able to make use of the free wards at the country's best hospitals.[92] By the 1930s the traditional private medical sector was in severe decline as both private maternity homes and then 'nursing homes' contracted, unable to compete with the advances in medical technology and professional staff available in the voluntary hospitals. Voluntary hospitals saw this as a useful route to additional income and set about offering pay wards – the bulk specially constructed, often on the top floor. It is notable that women, excluded from the GP services of the NI system or if unmarried or non-working, made more use of private beds than men.[93]

Conclusion

Overall, the hospital system expanded such that it was able to provide care and treatment to a much wider range of people and conditions across a broader geographical area and often at little or no extra cost. The scale and quality of provision expanded while the extension of outpatient clinics and the slow integration of municipal services and rural

---

[88]Contrast the growth of institutional provision for women and children in Leeds and Sheffield. Doyle, *Politics of Hospital Provision*; E. Lomax, 'Small and Special: The Development of Hospitals for Children in Victorian Britain', *Medical History Supplement* no. 16 (1996): 50–2. Historiography on women's hospitals remains very limited.

[89]B. Harris, *Health of the Schoolchild: A History of the School Medical Service in England and Wales, 1908–74* (Buckingham: Open University Press, 1995); B. M. Doyle, 'Power and Accountability in the Voluntary Hospitals of Middlesbrough, 1900–1948', in A. Borsay and P. Shapley (eds.), *Medicine, Charity and Mutual Aid: The Consumption of Health and Welfare, c.1550–1950* (Aldershot: Ashgate, 2007): 207–24.

[90]Doyle, 'Competition and Cooperation'.

[91]Doyle, *Politics of Hospital Provision*.

[92]Gorsky, Mohan and Willis, *Mutualism and Health Care*; Gosling, *Payment and Philanthropy*; Doyle, 'Les soins hospitaliers'.

[93]R. Lewis, R. Nixon and B. Doyle, 'Health Services in Middlesbrough: North Ormesby Hospital, 1900–1948' Interim report to AHRB 1999; Leeds Hospital for Women, *Annual Report*, 1932.

cottage hospitals meant more and better treatment for a wider range of people. A service that in 1900 was still largely focused on city centre hospitals aimed on fixing adult male workers had expanded spatially to join the city to the countryside and socially to remove the stigma of poverty and open the door to the lower middle class while breaking down the barriers of gender and age that had typified the system on the eve of war. The period saw Britain's hospital system develop into the envy of the world, with more beds providing better access for a wider population free at the point of use. Yet this achievement has been largely written out of the history of the NHS and its development.[94]

The experience of 1945 and the success of the state-run, tax-funded NHS, has blinded us to the vital role played by non-state actors in building a modern, democratic and effective hospital service that was the envy of the world by 1938. To a great extent this growth took place away from the big urban general hospitals, the focus of much historiography from Abel-Smith onwards, in rural and suburban areas and through the expansion of outpatients and dispersed institutions that increased hugely the number of people able to access treatment. Moreover, it was achieved by careful and innovative use of existing spaces through reconfiguring the interior and building upwards rather than outwards to maximize the capacity. These developments, along with an understanding of the role played by cottage hospitals, convalescent homes and poor law institutions, reflect an awareness by architectural historians that the focus on the small number of cutting edge model institutions (some never built) detracts from the reality of post-war hospital provision.[95] In a similar vein, the interest of urban historians in suburbs and small towns allows us to appreciate the significance of the smaller ancillary institutions that grew outside the city and facilitated the development of hierarchical regionalism.[96] In addressing the challenges posed by the First World War, the English hospital system does offer some ideas for the NHS in its response to the experience of COVID-19. In particular, the focus on creating flexible spaces within hospitals and utilising external aftercare facilities to increase the number of patients that can be cared for could help to increase capacity in a system that often appears too lean for its own good.

Select bibliography

Primary

Archival sources
The National Archives (TNA) Ministry of Health (MH) 58.
'Sheffield Municipal and Voluntary Hospitals Joint Advisory Committee' Minutes, Sheffield City
    Archives NHS28/10/1

---

[94]Webster, *Health Services since the War*.
[95]For evidence of this approach see Willis, Goad and Logan, *Architecture and the Modern Hospital* – though even they revert to an extended discussion of the model design by Paul Nelson for Lille which was not built.
[96]R. McManus and P. Ethington, 'Suburbs in Transition: New Approaches to Suburban History', *Urban History* 34 no. 2 (2007): 317–37.

Reconstruction

Grey literature

Medical Officer of Health City of Leeds, *Report on the Health and Sanitary Administration of the City*, Leeds Corporation, 1918–38.

Medical Officer of Health City of Sheffield, *Report on the Health and Sanitary Administration of the City*, Sheffield Corporation, 1918–38.

The Shape of Things to Come: The Sheffield Voluntary Hospitals' Million Pound Appeal (Sheffield: Appeal Committee, 1938).

Newspapers and periodicals

Malton and Yorkshire Gazette

Secondary

Websites/digital resources/databases

https://bmdoyleblog.wordpress.com/2015/06/03/municipal-modernism-in-the-international-style-killingbeck-sanatorium-extension-1936/

Articles

Cherry, S., 'Beyond National Health Insurance. The Voluntary Hospitals and Hospital Contributory Schemes: A Regional Study'. *Social History of Medicine* 5, no. 3 (1992): 455–82;

Doyle, B. M., 'Competition and Cooperation in Hospital Provision in Middlesbrough, 1918–48'. *Medical History* 51, no. 3 (2007): 337–56.

Doyle, B. M., 'Healthcare before Welfare States: Hospitals in Early Twentieth Century England and France', *Canadian Bulletin of Medical History* 33.1, no 33 (2016): 174–204.

Gorsky, M., 'The Gloucestershire Extension of Medical Services Scheme: An Experiment in the Integration of Health Services in Britain before the NHS', *Medical History* 50, no. 4 (2006): 491–512.

Gorsky, M., J. Mohan, and M. Powell, 'The Financial Health of Voluntary Hospitals in Interwar Britain', *Economic History Review* 55, no. 3 (2002): 533–57.

Hayes, N., '"Our Hospitals"? Voluntary Provision, Community and Civic Consciousness in Nottingham before the NHS', *Midland History* xxxvii (2012): 84–105.

Chapters (in edited volumes/collections)

Neville, J. 'Cottage Hospitals and Communities in Rural East Devon, 1919–39'. *In Healthcare in Ireland and Britain, 1850–1970: Voluntary, Regional and Comparative Perspectives,* edited by, D. S. Lucey and V. Crossman, 117–40. University of London Institute of Historical Research, 2015.

Sheard, S. 'Getting Better Faster: Convalescence and Length of Stay in British and US Hospitals'. In *Hospital Life, Theory and Practice from the Medieval to the Modern,* edited by L. Abreu and S. Sheard, 299–329. Oxford: Peter Lang, 2013.

Books

Abel-Smith, B. *The Hospitals, 1800–1948: A Study in Social Administration in England and Wales.* London: Heineman, 1964.

Doyle, B. *A History of Hospitals in Middlesbrough.* Middlesbrough: South Tees Hospitals NHS Trust, 2002.

Doyle, B. M. *The Politics of Hospital Provision in Early Twentieth Century Britain.* London: Pickering and Chatto, 2014.

Emrys-Roberts, M. *The Cottage Hospitals, 1859–1990*. Motcombe, Dorset: Tern Publications, 1991.

Digby, A. *The Evolution of British General Practice, 1850–1948*. Oxford: Oxford University Press, 1999.

Gorsky, M., J. Mohan with T. Willis. *Mutualism and Health Care: British Hospital Contributory Schemes in the Twentieth Century*. Manchester: Manchester University Press, 2006.

Gosling, G. C. *Payment and Philanthropy in British Healthcare, 1918–48*. Manchester: Manchester University Press, 2017.

Granshaw, L. and R. Porter (eds). *The Hospital in History*. London: Routledge, 1989.

Hardy, A. *Health and Medicine in Britain since 1860*. Basingstoke: Palgrave, 2001.

King, A. *Memorials of the Great War in Britain: The Symbolism and Politics of Remembrance*. Oxford: Berg, 1998.

Levene, A., M. Powell, J. Stewart and B. Taylor. *Cradle to Grave: Municipal Medicine in Interwar England and Wales*. Oxford: Peter Lang, 2011.

Pickstone, J. V. *Medicine and Industrial Society: A History of Hospital Development in Manchester and Its Region*. Manchester: Manchester University Press, 1985.

Reinarz, J. *Healthcare in Birmingham: A History of the Birmingham Teaching Hospitals, 1779–1939*. Woodbridge, Suffolk: Boydell and Brewer, 2009.

Richardson, H. (ed.). *English Hospitals 1660–1948*. Swindon: Royal Commission on the Historical Monuments of England, 1998.

Willis, Julie, Philip Goad, and Cameron Logan. *Architecture and the Modern Hospital: Nosokomeion to Hygeia*. Abingdon, Oxon: Routledge, 2019.

INDEX

Index

Index

Index